The Routledge Handbook of Language in the Workplace

The Routledge Handbook of Language in the Workplace provides a comprehensive survey of linguistic research on language in the workplace written by top scholars in the field from around the world. The *Handbook* covers theoretical and methodological approaches, explores research in different types of workplace settings, and examines some key areas of workplace talk that have been investigated by workplace researchers. Issues of identity have become a major focus in recent workplace research and the *Handbook* highlights some core issues of relevance in this area, such as gender, leadership, and intercultural communication. As the field has developed, applications of workplace research for both native and non-native speakers have emerged. Insights can inform and improve input from practitioners training workers in a range of fields and across a variety of contexts, and the *Handbook* foregrounds some of the ways workplace research can do this. This is an invaluable resource for researchers and graduate students interested in learning more about workplace discourse.

Bernadette Vine is Research Fellow on the Wellington Language in the Workplace Project (www.victoria.ac.nz/lwp/) and Corpus Manager for the Archive of New Zealand English, both based at the School of Linguistics and Applied Language Studies in Victoria University of Wellington, New Zealand. Bernadette's research interests include workplace communication, leadership, and New Zealand English.

Routledge Handbooks in Applied Linguistics

Routledge Handbooks in Applied Linguistics provide comprehensive overviews of the key topics in applied linguistics. All entries for the handbooks are specially commissioned and written by leading scholars in the field. Clear, accessible and carefully edited, *Routledge Handbooks in Applied Linguistics* are the ideal resource for both advanced undergraduates and postgraduate students.

For a full list of titles in this series, please visit www.routledge.com/Routledge-Handbooks-in-Applied-Linguistics/book-series/RHAL

The Routledge Handbook of Language in the Workplace
Edited by Bernadette Vine

The Routledge Handbook of English as a Lingua Franca
Edited by Jennifer Jenkins, Will Baker and Martin Dewey

The Routledge Handbook of Critical Discourse Studies
Edited by John Flowerdew and John E. Richardson

The Routledge Handbook of Instructed Second Language Acquisition
Edited by Shawn Loewen and Masatoshi Sato

The Routledge Handbook of Migration and Language
Edited by Suresh Canagarajah

The Routledge Handbook of Pragmatics
Edited by Anne Barron, Yueguo Gu and Gerard Steen

The Routledge Handbook of English Language Teaching
Edited by Graham Hall

The Routledge Handbook of Language Learning and Technology
Edited by Fiona Farr and Liam Murray

The Routledge Handbook of Language and Identity
Edited by Siân Preece

The Routledge Handbook of English for Academic Purposes
Edited by Ken Hyland and Philip Shaw

The Routledge Handbook of Language and Digital Communication
Edited by Alexandra Georgakopoulou and Tereza Spilioti

The Routledge Handbook of Literacy Studies
Edited by Jennifer Rowsell and Kate Pahl

The Routledge Handbook of Interpreting
Edited by Holly Mikkelson and Renée Jourdenais

The Routledge Handbook of Hispanic Applied Linguistics
Edited by Manel Lacorte

The Routledge Handbook of Educational Linguistics
Edited by Martha Bigelow and Johanna Ennser-Kananen

The Routledge Handbook of Forensic Linguistics
Edited by Malcolm Coulthard and Alison Johnson

The Routledge Handbook of Language in the Workplace

Edited by
Bernadette Vine

NEW YORK AND LONDON

First published 2018
by Routledge
711 Third Avenue, New York, NY 10017

and by Routledge
2 Park Square, Milton Park, Abingdon, Oxon, OX14 4RN

Routledge is an imprint of the Taylor & Francis Group, an informa business

© 2018 Taylor & Francis

The right of Bernadette Vine to be identified as the author of the editorial material, and of the authors for their individual chapters, has been asserted by her in accordance with sections 77 and 78 of the Copyright, Designs and Patents Act 1988.

All rights reserved. No part of this book may be reprinted or reproduced or utilised in any form or by any electronic, mechanical, or other means, now known or hereafter invented, including photocopying and recording, or in any information storage or retrieval system, without permission in writing from the publishers.

Trademark notice: Product or corporate names may be trademarks or registered trademarks, and are used only for identification and explanation without intent to infringe.

Every effort has been made to contact copyright-holders. Please advise the publisher of any errors or omissions, and these will be corrected in subsequent editions.

Library of Congress Cataloging-in-Publication Data
Names: Vine, Bernadette, editor.
Title: The Routledge handbook of language in the workplace / edited by Bernadette Vine.
Description: New York, NY : Routledge, [2017] | Series: Routledge Handbooks in Applied Linguistics | Includes bibliographical references and index.
Identifiers: LCCN 2017007036| ISBN 9781138915855 (hardback) | ISBN 9781317425816 (web pdf) | ISBN 9781317425809 (epub) | ISBN 9781317425793 (mobipocket/kindle)
Subjects: LCSH: English language—Discourse analysis—Handbooks, manuals, etc. | English language—Business English—Handbooks, manuals, etc. | English language—Technical English—Handbooks, manuals, etc. | Business communication—Handbooks, manuals, etc. | Communication in organizations—Handbooks, manuals, etc.
Classification: LCC PE1422 .R69 2017 | DDC 420.1/41—dc23
LC record available at https://lccn.loc.gov/2017007036

ISBN: 978-1-138-91585-5 (hbk)
ISBN: 978-1-315-69000-1 (ebk)

Typeset in Times New Roman and Stone Sans
by Florence Production Ltd, Stoodleigh, Devon, UK

Printed in the United Kingdom
by Henry Ling Limited

To May and Harry

Contents

List of Illustrations — xi
List of Contributors — xiii
Preface, Meredith Marra and Jo Angouri — xix
Acknowledgements — xxiii

Introduction — xxv
Bernadette Vine

PART I
Theoretical and Methodological Approaches — 1

1 Interactional Sociolinguistics — 3
   Cynthia Gordon and Joshua Kraut

2 Conversation Analysis — 15
   Merran Toerien

3 Critical Discourse Studies — 27
   Veronika Koller

4 Linguistic Ethnography — 40
   Nick Wilson

5 Corpus Linguistics — 51
   Michael Handford

6 (Im)politeness Theory — 65
   Michael Haugh and Yasuhisa Watanabe

7 Rapport Management — 77
   Jeannie Fletcher

8 Social Constructionism — 89
   Mariana Lazzaro-Salazar

9	Communities of Practice *Brian W. King*	101
10	Genre Theory *Kieran A. File*	112

PART II
Different Workplace Settings — **125**

11	Corporate Settings *Dorien Van De Mieroop and Jonathan Clifton*	127
12	Language in Blue-Collar Workplaces *Dorte Lønsmann and Kamilla Kraft*	138
13	Language in Legal Settings *Bronwen Innes*	150
14	Service Encounters *J. César Félix-Brasdefer*	162
15	Call Centre Discourse *Jon S. Y. Hui*	175
16	Genetic Counselling *Olga Zayts*	187

PART III
Key Areas of Workplace Talk — **201**

17	Directives in Workplace Discourse *Junko Saito and Haruko Minegishi Cook*	203
18	Relational Talk at Work *Julien C. Mirivel and Ryan Fuller*	216
19	Humour in the Workplace *Bernie Chun Nam Mak*	228
20	Workplace Narratives *Hans J. Ladegaard*	242
21	Miscommunication at Work *Maria Stubbe*	258
22	Conflict Talk *Almut Koester*	272

23	Argumentation in the Workplace *Jérôme Jacquin*	284
24	Interpreting in the Workplace *Chase Wesley Raymond*	295

PART IV
Identity and the Workplace — 309

25	Gender and the Workplace *Louise Mullany and Melissa Yoong*	311
26	Leadership *Stephanie Schnurr*	323
27	Intercultural Communication in the Workplace *Janet Holmes*	335
28	Identity in the Workplace in a Context of Increasing Multilingualism *Georges Lüdi*	348
29	Men's Talk in Women's Work: Doing Being a Nurse *Joanne McDowell*	361
30	Professional Identity Construction: Cabin Crew Discourse *Barbara Clark*	373

PART V
Applications — 387

31	Vocational Education *Stefano A. Losa*	389
32	Gender, Language, and Leadership: Enabling Women Leaders *Judith Baxter*	401
33	Language Preparation for Internationally Educated Professionals *Julie Kerekes*	413
34	Language Learning On-the-Job *Lynda Yates*	425

Index — *437*

Illustrations

Figures

3.1	A three-level model for analysing discourse	28
5.1	Engineer explaining procedure to foreman	54
10.1	Analytical levels for genre researchers	116
10.2	Schematic structure of the handover meeting	119
16.1	Multiple dimensions of decision-making in genetic counselling and prenatal screening contexts	191
18.1	Mirivel's (2014) *model of positive communication*	217
19.1	Sample of a Facebook status update	238
21.1	Multi-dimensional analytic framework	265

Tables

3.1	A four-level model for analysing discourse	29
5.1	The most frequent 20 single-word items in CANBEC	55
5.2	The most frequent three-word MWUs	56
5.3	Keywords from CANBEC	58
5.4	Concordances of "if"	59
5.5	Concordances of "you have to" in external meetings	60
5.6	Interpersonal language from Example 5.3	61
10.1	Definitions of genre in the three traditions	114
17.1	Factors differentiating directives, requests, and advice	204
17.2	Distribution of directive forms	206

Contributors

Jo Angouri is Reader and Director of Undergraduate Studies in Applied Linguistics at the University of Warwick. Her research expertise is in sociolinguistics, pragmatics and discourse analysis. She has carried out research in a range of corporate and institutional contexts and has published work on language and identity, teamwork and leadership.

Judith Baxter is Emeritus Professor of Applied Linguistics at Aston University. Her areas of research specialism include gender and language, discourses of leadership, and feminist poststructuralist discourse analysis. She has written numerous journal articles on these topics as well as four acclaimed monographs.

Barbara Clark is an academic and consultant, and founder of *You Say Tomato*, a consultancy specialising in culture, communication, and safety. Barbara's research interests include safety-critical communication, cross-cultural communication, and contextual influences on miscommunication.

Jonathan Clifton has a PhD in Applied Linguistics from the University of Antwerp. He is currently working at the University of Valenciennes, France. His research interests are focused on the analysis of naturally-occurring talk to study workplace identities.

Haruko Minegishi Cook is a Professor in the Department of East Asian Languages and Literatures at the University of Hawai'i at Manoa. Her main research interests include language socialization, discourse analysis, and pragmatics. Currently, she is working on Japanese workplace discourse with a focus on adult language socialization in Japanese.

J. César Félix-Brasdefer is Professor at Indiana University. His research interests include pragmatics, discourse analysis, cross-cultural and interlanguage pragmatics, and (im)politeness theory. He has published numerous research articles in a variety of scholarly journals. His most recent book is entitled *The Language of Service Encounters: A Pragmatic-Discursive Approach* (2015).

Kieran A. File is Assistant Professor in the Centre for Applied Linguistics at the University of Warwick. His research explores issues related to language use in professional contexts including healthcare and professional sport, and draws on a range of approaches to discourse analysis including genre theory.

Contributors

Jeannie Fletcher teaches interpersonal communication and management communication at Massey University. Jeannie's research interests include: organizational contexts that foster long term capabilities underpinning creativity adaptability and innovation; the discourse of public diplomacy; and discourses of absence and silence.

Ryan Fuller (PhD, University of California, Santa Barbara) is an Assistant Professor of Management in the College of Business Administration at California State University. His research interests include business communication, conflict management, crisis communication, and positive organizational scholarship.

Cynthia Gordon is Associate Professor of Linguistics at Georgetown University and author of *Making Meanings, Creating Family: Intertextuality and Framing in Family Interaction* (2009). Her current research focuses on intertextuality and metadiscourse in online discussions.

Michael Handford is Chair of Applied Linguistics at Cardiff University. He has published on discourse in professional settings, cultural identities at work, the application of corpus tools in discourse analysis and intercultural communication, English as a Lingua Franca, and language learning.

Michael Haugh is Professor of Linguistics in the School of Languages and Cultures, The University of Queensland. He has published widely on the topics of (im)politeness, face, humour and indirectness in everyday interaction.

Janet Holmes is Emeritus Professor of Linguistics and Associate Director of the Wellington Language in the Workplace Project at Victoria University of Wellington (www.victoria.ac.nz/lwp/). She has published on many aspects of workplace discourse and language and gender.

Jon S. Y. Hui coordinates and teaches English for Specific Purposes courses at the Centre for Applied English Studies, The University of Hong Kong. His research interests include sociolinguistics, workplace English, and professional communication.

Bronwen Innes currently practises as a forensic linguist and is an Honorary Research Fellow at the University of Auckland. Her current research interests are the language of judges' summings-up to juries and the comprehensibility of legal rights information given by police to detainees.

Jérôme Jacquin is Lecturer in Linguistics at the University of Lausanne. He is also Research Associate on the Wellington Language in the Workplace Project. His research draws on insights and methods from Interactional Linguistics and Multimodal Conversation Analysis to investigate argumentation and stancetaking in ordinary, professional, and institutional settings.

Julie Kerekes is an Associate Professor in Language and Literacies Education at the Ontario Institute for Studies in Education, University of Toronto. Her research and teaching focus on language and power in conversational and intercultural institutional settings, particularly workplace ESL.

Brian W. King is Assistant Professor at City University of Hong Kong. His primary research interest is language use in communities, in particular discursive performances of gender and sexuality, computer-mediated communication, and the social construction of space/place.

Almut Koester is Professor of English Business Communication at Vienna University of Economics and Business. With a research focus on spoken workplace discourse, she is author of *The Language of Work* (2004), *Investigating Workplace Discourse* (2006), and *Workplace Discourse* (2010).

Veronika Koller is Reader in Discourse Studies at Lancaster University. Her research interests centre on corporate and health communication, and she publishes and supervizes a number of PhD students in these areas. Outside academia, Veronika is Senior Associate Analyst with consultant company Linguistic Landscapes.

Kamilla Kraft is PhD Candidate at the MultiLing centre, University of Oslo. Her research focuses on processes of labour migration and multilingualism, especially in the manufacturing economy. Kraft studies how linguistic practices and ideologies impact and often lead to stratification in a globalizing labour market.

Joshua Kraut is a doctoral candidate at Georgetown University and Assistant Professor of French and Applied Linguistics at Hope College. His research explores interactional sociolinguistics in language learning contexts as well as in religious discourse, with a particular focus on the intersection of epistemics in discourse and intertextuality.

Hans J. Ladegaard is Professor and Head of the Department of English at the Hong Kong Polytechnic University. His research interests include language attitudes and stereotypes, intercultural communication, language and gender, narratives of migration, and pragmatics and discourse analysis.

Mariana Lazzaro-Salazar is a Research Associate of the Wellington Language in the Workplace Project. She is also a Postdoctoral Fellow at Universidad Católica del Maule. Her current research focuses on intercultural communication in the Chilean healthcare system. Mariana is supported by CONICYT/FONDECYT # 3160104.

Dorte Lønsmann is Associate Professor at the Department of International Business Communication at Copenhagen Business School. The focus of her current research is multilingualism in the workplace, including language practices among blue-collar workers, language socialization, and the implementation of corporate language policies.

Stefano A. Losa holds a PhD in Sociology from the University of Geneva. Within the Faculty of Psychology and Educational Sciences at the University of Geneva, his teaching and research interests are the interactional dynamics of learning in workplace and vocational training contexts.

Georges Lüdi is Professor Emeritus at Basel University. He worked on migrant languages, multilingualism, and workplace communication, acted as deputy coordinator of the European DYLAN project, served in the Executive Board of AILA, and is Officer in the French Ordre national du mérite and Doctor h.c. (University of Neuchâtel).

Joanne McDowell is a Principal Lecturer in the School of English Language & Communication, Department of Humanities, in the University of Hertfordshire. She specializes in the area of workplace discourse, gender studies, identity construction, classroom discourse, and interactional sociolinguistics.

Contributors

Bernie Chun Nam Mak (PhD) has lectured in English language and linguistics at The Open University of Hong Kong, and now at Hong Kong Baptist University, with research interests in the symbolic performance of jargon, humour, small talk, code-switching, and swearing in the workplace in the Digital Age.

Meredith Marra is a core member of the Wellington Language in the Workplace Project at Victoria University of Wellington. She has been researching workplace discourse for 20 years, analysing the language of business meetings, (im)politeness, humour, and various aspects of identity.

Julien C. Mirivel (PhD, University of Colorado) is Interim Associate Dean for the College of Social Sciences and Communication and an Associate Professor in the Department of Applied Communication at the University of Arkansas Little Rock. His research interests include positive communication practices in interpersonal and organizational settings and communication across the lifespan.

Louise Mullany is Professor of Sociolinguistics in the School of English at the University of Nottingham. She has published widely in the area of language, gender, and workplace discourse. She is founder and director of Linguistic Profiling for Professionals, a global research-based consultancy.

Chase Wesley Raymond (PhDs 2014, 2016, UCLA) is Assistant Professor in the Departments of Linguistics and Spanish & Portuguese at the University of Colorado. His research interests center around language use in everyday life, in both ordinary and institutional contexts.

Junko Saito is Assistant Professor in the Japanese Program at Temple University, Japan Campus. Her research interests include sociolinguistics, pragmatics, and discourse analysis. Particularly, she focuses on identity construction, politeness, and speech acts in workplace discourse. She is currently working on the construction of heterosexual/masculine identities in Japanese business meetings.

Stephanie Schnurr is Associate Professor at the University of Warwick. Her main research interests are professional and medical communication with a particular focus on leadership discourse. She is the author of *Leadership Discourse at Work* (2009), *Exploring Professional Communication* (2013), and *Language and Culture at Work* (with Olga Zayts, 2017).

Maria Stubbe co-directs the Applied Research on Communication in Health (ARCH) Group at the University of Otago, and was a founding member of the Wellington Language in the Workplace Project. She has published widely in the fields of pragmatics, workplace language, and health communication.

Merran Toerien is a Senior Lecturer in Sociology at the University of York. She uses conversation analysis to study talk (mainly in institutional settings), teaches CA at undergraduate and postgraduate level, and has delivered CA short courses in the UK, China, South Africa, and the Netherlands.

Dorien Van De Mieroop is Associate Professor at the Linguistics Department of KU Leuven. Her research interests include the discursive analysis of institutional interactions and narrative analysis. She is associate editor of *Narrative Inquiry* (John Benjamins).

Bernadette Vine is Research Fellow with the Wellington Language in the Workplace Project (www.victoria.ac.nz/lwp/) and Corpus Manager for the Archive of New Zealand English. Her research interests include workplace communication, leadership, and New Zealand English.

Yasuhisa Watanabe is Lecturer in Japanese at the Asia Institute, University of Melbourne. His research pivots around the concept of face and politeness in business, journalism, and politics.

Nick Wilson is a Lecturer in Linguistics at Macquarie University, where he teaches courses on sociolinguistics and multilingualism. His research focuses on leadership in team sports and the linguistic construction of identity.

Lynda Yates is Professor of Linguistics at Macquarie University. Her research interests include adult language learning and teaching, spoken discourse, and workplace communication, particularly as they relate to transnational professionals. She has a strong commitment to the translation of research findings into practice.

Melissa Yoong is Assistant Professor in the School of English at the University of Nottingham's Malaysia Campus. Her research focuses on sexist, postfeminist, and neoliberal discourses in the mass media, in particular how these reinforce gender inequality in society.

Olga Zayts is an Assistant Professor at the Department of Linguistics, University of Hong Kong. She also leads the Health Communication Research Cluster at the Center for the Humanities and Medicine. Her research interests include interdisciplinary approaches to professional communication, particularly in medical contexts.

Preface

The field of workplace discourse research began as a collection of individuals working with small data sets and addressing local issues. Just two decades later we can now claim our place within mainstream (socio)linguistics.

It seems somewhat surprising that language in the workplace was not always a central part of the discipline; we spend a considerable proportion of our lives at work, interacting with a range of people and using an increasingly diverse range of technologies. Exploring workplace practices is an important part of understanding the human experience. The *Routledge Handbook of Language in the Workplace* offers a welcome opportunity to bring together key scholars in the field, to foreground core topics of interest and to outline dominant methodologies, thereby creating a "go to" resource for new and established researchers alike. As an overview of the field, the *Handbook* provides more than 30 chapters to complement and capture the rich activity currently underway across the globe, while simultaneously opening avenues for further research. There is—or should be—no orthodoxy for researching workplace talk. The contributors demonstrate the affordances and limitations of theoretical and methodological tools that have been widely used in the field over the years.

The pioneers of workplace discourse research eked out space for themselves in an area where other disciplines had already staked a claim. Professional communication had long been the realm of those in business studies where the organization's commercial goals were typically prioritized over communication. While there was an understanding that talk was how business was achieved and that different strategies resulted in different outcomes, systematic methods for investigating talk were not part of the standard business studies toolkit. Instead scholars relied on self-reports from experienced managers based on intuitions and personal observations. Sociolinguists have long recognized the difference between what people do and what they say they do. Linguistic and discursive approaches had something special to offer. The micro level attention to language which is the strength of workplace discourse research has provided many insights into how people interact at work, offering new understandings about the relevance of context, group norms and interactional negotiation. These core ideals are still visible in the field and underpin the methodological approaches shared by a number of the contributors to this *Handbook*.

A core aspect of the field has always been the corporate workplace and business meetings, contexts in which we see emphasis on how we get things done (directives and decision making) and how we manage relationships (small talk and humour). While this context might epitomize the stereotypical conceptualization of "business" talk, corporate organizations represent only one kind of workplace. We have thus seen steady expansion into other contexts, including healthcare, call centres and the blue-collar workplace. As a field undergoing growth there has been plenty of scope for researchers to find their own niche and to delve into new and unexplored contexts. Given the unique features of each workplace and the pace of change of organisational activity, our field is still in need of empirical studies that will bring further understandings of the complexity inherent in "doing" work through talk.

While the earliest focus was discrete communicative activities and specific organizational contexts, analysts soon began exploring how we negotiate our professional lives at work in line with the "identity turn" in the wider social sciences. This interest pushed *people* to the front of the research agenda, emphasizing the relevance of features which symbolize our membership of groups and signal our place within our communities. Gender, ethnic or age identities as well as professional and leadership identities have all found favour with scholars who pay close attention to the nuances of indexicality and stance in discourse. Drawing on theories developed in other disciplines in social sciences and acknowledging that we co-construct identity with others and in the here-and-now of our immediate context, constructionism has provided a fruitful analytic approach for processing in situ, context-sensitive discursive choices.

With maturity comes reflection and development. The areas where we have seen the most significant change are our theoretical approaches and the kinds of data we are using to address our research questions. However, the field remains dominated by the traditions of Interactional Sociolinguistics; this method underpins many of the discourse analytic approaches used to interpret workplace talk, including the application of the social constructionist lens in identity research. The tenets encourage us to analyse discourse in its wider socio-cultural context by drawing on our knowledge of the community and its norms. Understanding the context affords us access to the contextual presuppositions that the participants use when creating meaning. As a result, much of the field is qualitative and interpretive, making use of ethnographic methods to gain insights into the emic understandings of workplace talk. That is not to say that there is one single approach within the field. In fact, it remains diverse. The inherently hierarchical nature of many workplaces offers opportunities for critical scholars to challenge and bring to light hegemonic practices. And corpus approaches, especially those which make use of emerging, contextualized corpora, offer enormous potential for identifying trends for further investigation. With ever-increasingly globalized economic activity, research into multinational workplaces has raised issues around culture and meaning which are still present in current agendas. Moving from a focus on "problems" and "miscommunication" to the situated understanding of interaction, the field has expanded its interest in the politics of language. Studies on language ideology, social justice, and new racism are growing. These trends and the wide range of workplace activity described in the chapters of this Handbook highlight the diverse nature of the questions we are now addressing as researchers.

From early investigations which described the asymmetric and sequential ordering of institutional talk-at-work to the dominant focus on identity construction in more recent years, scholars have continued to explore how talk impacts upon and constitutes our working lives. An important part of the field has been to see the implications of these insights, whether making contributions to communication preparation for newcomers, for vocational education or to redress power imbalances arising out of gender and ethnic identification. The development of the field has created possibilities for using our knowledge to improve workplace communication. This has often gone hand in hand with participatory research, especially collaborations with professionals who bring their own questions and interests to the mix.

So what does the future hold for workplace discourse research?

As scholars who have worked in the field for much of its existence, our educated predictions are all about expansion. We have already seen movement in the definitions of what counts as a "workplace" setting, from call centres to factories to building sites and aeroplanes. These are all places where work occurs and where people interact. So too are homes and streets and anywhere else our phones and mobile devices can be used to interact with colleagues and clients. The use of technology and the amount of time we spend "online" changes everyday practice as well as research foci and research tools. The pace of activity is fast and goes faster than our usual academic timelines. As the way we "do work" changes, the field is also constantly repositioning and changing. The boundaries of the field are likely to stretch and possibly push back. We anticipate reflection on the scope of what counts as language in the workplace research as this occurs and look forward to more academic debate about the heart of the field and its goals.

As our own contribution to this debate we have been encouraging a focus beyond the discrete activities and contexts which dominated the early years of the field toward transition talk, that is, the negotiation of boundary crossing through talk. We are constantly moving between activities at a micro discursive level, but also between teams, countries, languages, and even occupational identities. Overlooking these transitions means having only half the picture if our shared goal is an understanding of workplace talk. As well as moving between activities and communities, we must also recognize the multiplicity of our working environments. It is encouraging to see more workplace research which moves beyond single languages to begin to echo the multilingual norm of so many societies. Similarly, we herald the inclusion of multimodal approaches to analysis: while audio recordings were once ground-breaking, capturing action through video recording is now commonplace. The affordances of technology, and our participants' familiarity with these technologies, means we have access to increasingly rich data and our analytic techniques will need to develop to make use of the richness we have available to us.

As early as the 1990s, pioneers Janet Holmes and Maria Stubbe were arguing that there is no one size fits all answer. Our ongoing challenge is to continue to heed these words and work towards nuanced, sophisticated, and contextually-sensitive interpretations. Language in the workplace is complex and our understandings and approaches must necessarily address this complexity. The field of workplace discourse has come of age. The time is ripe for a handbook to outline the progress and key concerns for the field. We trust you will enjoy reading the chapters and learning about the remarkably varied and thought-provoking ideas that our colleagues have to offer. We congratulate the editor, Bernadette Vine, and the many contributors who represent the breadth and the depth of a vibrant international field.

Meredith Marra and Jo Angouri
December 2016

Acknowledgements

My sincere thanks to the many, many people who have been involved in one way or another with the production of this book. From the team at Routledge who recruited and supported me throughout the process, to the authors who contributed such great chapters, to the reviewers who so generously gave their time and insightful feedback: it has been a privilege and inspiration to work with you all. I would also like to express my gratitude to my colleagues from the Wellington Language in the Workplace Project, Janet Holmes, and Meredith Marra, especially Janet who patiently provided valuable advice and support at all stages. Last and of course not least, I thank my neglected family and friends who have me back now—until the next time!

Introduction
Bernadette Vine

This Handbook provides a comprehensive survey of linguistic research on language in the workplace written by both established and emerging scholars from around the world. In the past 20 years an increasing number of researchers have investigated spoken and written data from workplace settings, and workplace discourse research is now a well-established field within its own right. A *Handbook on Language in the Workplace* within Routledge's *Handbooks of Linguistics* series acknowledges this and provides both current researchers and students with an invaluable resource.

This Handbook introduces core issues and topics and the 34 chapters are organized into five main parts. In Part 1, the chapters present a number of key approaches, theories, and methodologies that have been used to examine language in the workplace, from dominant approaches such as interactional sociolinguistics (Gordon and Kraut) and conversation analysis (Toerien), to approaches which have been less prevalent in this research area to date, such as critical discourse studies (Koller) and corpus linguistics (Handford). In his chapter, Wilson considers the defining characteristics of a linguistic ethnographic methodology, highlighting some important factors when undertaking workplace research. Theoretical approaches to (im)politeness are the focus of Haugh and Watanabe's chapter, while Fletcher examines rapport management. Social constructionism as a framework for theorizing workplace communication is explored by Lazzaro-Salazar, while King examines the deployment of the communities of practice framework in language in the workplace research. The final chapter in this part, by File, reviews genre theory and illustrates its analytical aims.

Part 2 outlines some key workplace settings that have been investigated in language in the workplace research. People often think of corporate workplaces when they think of workplace research, but there are many other types of workplaces. In fact, this Handbook could have been filled with 34 chapters simply focusing on different settings in which language in the workplace research has been conducted, and many different types of settings are foregrounded throughout the book. The six chapters in Part 2 just highlight some of the wide range of workplaces: from corporate (Van De Mieroop and Clifton) and blue-collar workplaces (Lønsmann and Kraft), where much of the interaction or communication takes place between colleagues, to settings where workers are often dealing with the public—in legal (Innes) and service encounter settings (Félix-Brasdefer), and call centres (Hui). Healthcare/medical settings is another area which has received a great deal of research attention over the years and one particular medical setting is covered in Zayts' chapter, although healthcare and medical settings also provide data for chapters in other parts of the book (see Lazzaro-Salazar, File, Raymond, McDowell). Zayts' chapter examines a situation where family members interact with each other, as well as a counsellor in an institutional setting, so highlights another different and interesting context of communication within a workplace setting.

In Part 3 some key topics that have been investigated in research on language in the workplace are explored. In Chapter 17, Saito and Cook present an overview of studies on workplace directives, a crucial function of talk in many workplace settings. Mirivel and Fuller explore relational talk at work, and the building of positive workplace relationships and rapport through a number of strategies. Both Mak and Ladegaard explore two other potentially relational strategies in their chapters—the use of humour and narratives respectively—although both also show how the use of these can achieve a range of other functions. Stubbe's chapter focuses on miscommunication and problematic talk at work, while Koester considers a related aspect with her exploration of conflict talk, disagreement, and impoliteness. Taking disagreement as a starting point, argumentation theory considers how people justify and argue points of view, and in his chapter Jacquin explores the importance of this approach to reasoning and decision-making in workplace contexts. In the final chapter in this part, Raymond provides an overview of research on workplace interpreting, particularly in medical and legal settings.

Another key topic which has become a strong focus more recently in language in the workplace research is identity. Part 4 covers the main areas of interest here, including chapters on gender (Mullany and Yoong), leadership (Schnurr), intercultural communication (Holmes), and multilingualism (Lüdi). Two further chapters in this part take a case study approach to issues of professional identity: McDowell explores the way male nurses talk with other nurses, while Clark examines how flight attendants construct their professional identity in incident reports and internet discussion forums.

As the field has developed, applications of workplace research for both native and non-native speakers have emerged, and the final part of the book explores a few of these. Insights can inform and improve input from practitioners training workers in a range of fields and across a variety of contexts. In the first chapter in this part, Losa shows how language is a central mediating tool in the area of vocational education. Baxter reviews theories explaining the role of language in constructing barriers for women who aspire to leadership positions in the workplace arguing that women can use language to overcome these barriers. The final two chapters in the Handbook consider issues of relevance for migrants. Kerekes addresses how workplace communication skills can be taught, as well as examining existing societal, ideological barriers that challenge migrant professionals. Yates explores language learning on-the-job, highlighting strategies for coping with the challenges of language learning in this context, as well as highlighting the potentially vital role of employers and colleagues.

All the chapters in this Handbook provide accessible summaries of the topics outlined, with many presenting examples of authentic workplace data to illustrate key issues or to demonstrate how an approach can be applied. Historical perspectives are explored, along with the contributions of current research to our understanding of workplace communication and considerations of avenues for further research. So my goal is that this Handbook provides a comprehensive introduction for anyone interested in language in the workplace. It highlights what a varied and dynamic field language in the workplace research is, and I trust it will become an essential reference guide for students and researchers around the world.

Part I
Theoretical and Methodological Approaches

Part I

1
Interactional Sociolinguistics
Cynthia Gordon and Joshua Kraut

Introduction

Interactional sociolinguistics (IS) is a primarily qualitative, interpretive approach to the analysis of discourse. Pioneered by Gumperz (1982a, 1982b) to investigate linguistic and cultural diversity and to address unequal access to economic, political, and other opportunities, IS has been applied and developed by scholars worldwide and across disciplines to provide important insights into workplace communication. IS studies of workplace interaction explain not only how and why instances of cross-cultural miscommunication occur and how communicative differences contribute to the creation of social inequalities, but also yield myriad other insights. Among them are how culture affects workplace discourse; how gender and language shape workplaces (including how language impacts women's advancement); how professional identities and relationships are discursively created; how leadership is enacted and power is negotiated; how routine encounters such as meetings (and those that are especially high-stakes, such as interviews) are constructed; and how various discursive strategies are used at work (including code-switching, humour, personal narratives and other aspects of "small talk", forms of address, and [in]directness). In short, the theories and methods of IS facilitate exploration of the conversational features and strategies through which essential workplace activities are accomplished.

In this chapter, after introducing fundamental methods and concepts of IS, we give an overview of four groups of key studies, each of which centralizes different scholars and geographical and cultural contexts: Gumperz and his colleagues (mostly in the United Kingdom); Tannen and her students (largely in the United States); Holmes and her team (in New Zealand); and the work of various scholars who have adopted IS to examine workplace talk elsewhere around the world (such as in Brazil and Hong Kong). In the conclusion, we recap contributions IS makes to our understanding of workplace communication, and suggest future research directions.

Methods and Key Concepts of Interactional Sociolinguistics

The methods and key concepts of IS were developed by anthropological linguist John Gumperz. Conducting fieldwork in the 1960s and 1970s, Gumperz observed vast linguistic and cultural diversity, especially in modern urban areas, in "gatekeeping encounters" (a term borrowed from Erickson 1975) both everyday (such as service encounters) and high-stakes (such as employment interviews). He approached these interactions with a linguist's ear and an interest in social justice; specifically he wanted to understand why members of minority and immigrant communities struggled to access needed resources (such as job training and employment), and the role of language in this struggle. Gumperz thus sought to uncover how and why miscommunication occurs in intercultural encounters by illuminating inferential processes and how the linguistic and social are reflexively related; in so doing, he also sought to ameliorate intergroup relations, and ultimately promote social justice.

To achieve these goals, Gumperz developed the multifaceted data collection and analysis processes of IS; these capture and explicate the complexity of communication as a cultural phenomenon. The foci of analysis are naturally-occurring conversations that are audio- (and sometimes also video-) recorded and systematically transcribed. Ethnographic observations contextualize recorded data; they provide interpretive touchstones for analysis of conversational features and interactional patterns by illuminating typical practices and recurrent difficulties, and by providing a deeper understanding of the particular social context in which language is used. Analysis is also shaped by a kind of post-recording interview that involves playing the recording for one or more of the participants, or for others from the cultural group of one or more of the participants, to gain their insights into what transpired. This uncovers different participant and cultural perspectives that enrich analysis.

In order to be analysed, recordings must be transcribed in detail. Ochs (1979) and others have observed that transcription is not simply methodological, but also analytic. It entails selective decision-making regarding how fine-grained a transcript should be: whether or how it should represent phenomena such as simultaneous talk, pauses, and paralinguistic features such as laughter and intonation; how to integrate (if at all) gestural and other visual elements of interaction; how to arrange participants' utterances on the page (or now screen); and how to make interpretations such as what counts as a conversational turn. These choices shape the object of analysis, highlighting some features and obscuring others. Due to the impossibility of any transcript (no matter how detailed) to capture the full richness of social interaction, scholars who use IS typically repeatedly re-listen to their recordings throughout analysis. This facilitates attention to conversational elements that are especially difficult to transcribe, yet are central to Gumperz's theorizing.

Gumperz (1982a) maintains that pitch, tone of voice, and other paralinguistic features (such as tempo, pausing, and intonation), along with linguistic features (such as lexical choice and code-switching), function as signalling mechanisms in interaction; these "contextualization cues" indicate how speakers intend their utterances to be interpreted. "Conversational inference" is Gumperz's term for the intricate (yet seemingly automatic), context-bound process of interpretation that listeners use to assess how speakers mean what they say. That each participant draws upon a set of culturally-shaped "contextualization conventions" to signal and interpret meanings explains why and how many instances of intercultural miscommunication occur. In other words, cultural knowledge and expectations profoundly shape interaction.

Gumperz's (1982a) now classic example of one such instance is drawn from a service encounter in a workplace context: the cafeteria line of a major British airport, where Indian and Pakistani cafeteria workers served meals to native Anglo-British baggage handlers. The cafeteria servers felt they were being discriminated against; the baggage handlers perceived them as uncooperative and discourteous. Gumperz demonstrates how members of the two cultural groups differently used and interpreted intonation. When the Indian and Pakistani servers offered a serving of gravy, for instance, they used a flat intonation: "Gravy". However, the native British conventions for making a polite offer involve rising intonation: "Gravy?" The servers were thus perceived to be rude by the baggage handlers, though this was not their intention. Remarking this seemingly trivial difference in use and interpretation of intonation and explaining it to members of both groups of workers actually helped improve inter-group perceptions and relationships.

Also integral to IS is the notion of "frame", as discussed by anthropologist Gregory Bateson (1972) and sociologist Erving Goffman (1974, 1981), and linked into IS by Deborah Tannen ([1984] 2005) and Gumperz (e.g., 1999). Tannen and Wallat (1993, 59–60) define a frame, or what they call an "interactive frame", as "a definition of what is going on in interaction, without which no utterance (or movement or gesture) could be interpreted." Returning to the gravy example, the baggage handlers expected rising intonation from the servers, which for them would construct a "polite service" frame wherein an offer was extended (e.g., "Would you like gravy?"), but the servers' flat intonation (polite in the context of Indian and Pakistani contextualization conventions) was interpreted as a declaration, and consequently as rude.

Tannen and Wallat (1993) identify "frame" as a key concept for understanding the challenges a paediatrician faces in a particular kind of workplace talk: a video-recorded examination of a cerebral palsied child where the child's mother was also present. Tannen and Wallat demonstrate how the physician uses what Gumperz (1982a) calls contextualization cues to indicate which frame she is interacting in at any given time, or who she is talking to and how her utterances should be interpreted, as well as to construct alignments among participants (or what Goffman [1981] calls "footing"). For instance, she uses a high-pitched teasing voice in the "social encounter frame" with the child (and the child responds with giggles); she uses a flat tone of voice and medical terminology in the "examination frame" when reporting her findings to medical residents who will later view the recording for educational purposes (which the mother and child ignore); and she speaks conversationally in the "consultation frame" with the mother (and the mother demonstrates her understanding or lack thereof). Through how the physician speaks and how she behaves nonverbally, such as keeping a hand on the child while reporting her findings, she indicates what she is doing at that moment, such as teasing the child, reporting technical information for an absent audience for whom she is a teacher/mentor, or explaining a symptom to the mother. In doing her work, the physician thus continually adjusts not only her "register" (i.e., by using lexical items, syntactic structures, and so on in audience-appropriate ways), but also the framing of the encounter, including participant alignments.

Tannen and Wallat (1993, 60) also demonstrate how frame shifts frequently resulted from mismatches in the physician's and mother's "knowledge schemas", or their "expectations about people, objects, events and settings in the world." For instance, when the mother interprets her child's "noisy breathing" as "wheezing", a sign of ill-health, the paediatrician puts the examination of the child on hold, and consults with the mother to explain that noisy breathing is normal for a cerebral palsied child. This is an important way participant expectations shape the framing of interaction.

Tannen and Wallat's analysis not only illuminates the complexity of a physician's workplace discourse as she interacts with a patient, family member, and absent medical students, but also lays the groundwork for future studies in IS by integrating the concepts of frames, schemas, and participant alignments into Gumperz's theory of conversational inference. Key studies have utilized these concepts (and others from IS and discourse analysis more broadly, as we will discuss) to investigate how workplace situations, relationships, and identities are constructed and negotiated in interaction, particularly "behind the scenes" as co-workers communicate with one another.

Key Studies

Foundational Studies by Gumperz and Colleagues (the United Kingdom)

Workplace discourse has constituted a privileged analytic site since the genesis of IS, as it involves numerous gatekeeping encounters, such as interviews and intake sessions, where speakers from ethnic and linguistic minority groups may face difficulties and experience restricted access to services and resources. Gumperz (1982a) examines an interview-counselling session involving a Pakistani mathematics instructor who had been unable to secure employment, and an Anglo-British staff member at a centre funded by the Department of Employment to address interethnic communication problems in British businesses. Both participants are proficient English speakers, yet they fail to achieve mutual understanding due to differences in cultural expectations and uses of English.

Two primary problems shape this encounter. First, participants lack a shared understanding of its purpose (in Tannen and Wallat's terms, they had different knowledge schemas). The instructor understands the scenario as a hierarchical meeting wherein the staff member may choose to grant him an additional certification he believes necessary to secure employment; thus he struggles to establish her exact status in the department, in other words if she has the authority to do so. The staff member, whose goals for the interview are to discuss the instructor's skills, classroom experiences, and training, futilely tries to redirect the conversation to those topics. Second, the participants have differing contextualization conventions. For example, the staff member mentions that the lecturer running a course (to whom the mathematics instructor had spoken) "hasn't said anything" to her about him; this is intended as an indirect request for him to provide more information about himself and his situation. Instead, there is a two second pause, and the instructor, not picking up on the indirectness, responds with a formulaic apology using emphatic, slower prosody that, in his own contextualization conventions, indicates how seriously he sees the matter. However, the staff member misses this and responds literally to the apology, and in an interruptive manner ("doesn't matter"). This is but one of many examples where conversational flow is broken, and participants are not on the same wavelength, potentially serving to "reinforce distance and maintain separateness" between them (Gumperz 1982a, 152). This, in turn, may affect whether or not the gatekeeper grants access to needed resources and support.

Gumperz and Cook-Gumperz (1982) examine how cultural differences in rhetorical strategies shape committee negotiations at a bureaucratic meeting in London. The meeting involves staff members of a West Indian youth club and native English-speaking officers of the governmental organization overseeing and funding the club's activities. The club's sole full-time employee, a social worker, feels the club is understaffed, and argues for additional full-time positions by outlining the many functions he serves, including doing housekeeping and building-maintenance tasks. His request, however, is initially seen as illegitimate in the British committee meeting context; it is treated as a personal complaint. Indeed, when the recording was played for other native English speakers familiar with meeting talk, they evaluated the social worker's discourse as impulsive and possibly somewhat rude; however, West Indian audiences did not, finding it to be direct and clear. Fortunately, in the meeting, other West Indian staff members justify the social worker's position using rhetorical strategies more familiar to British committee meetings. For instance, by referencing the important day-to-day tasks required of the social worker to adequately serve the community's youth, rather than focusing on the challenges of the lone full-time employee, they construct what is viewed as a reasoned argument (and permission to hire another full-time employee is granted).

In addition to studying how culture affects communication and access to resources, Gumperz brought IS insights to public audiences. He served as a consultant for an educational BBC television programme called *Crosstalk* (Twitchin 1979) which addressed the subtleties of intercultural communication in multicultural workplaces in London; he also prepared related written materials (Gumperz, Jupp, and Roberts 1979, 1980). Celia Roberts (e.g., 2011) has continued to investigate cross-cultural communication challenges in institutional encounters in the United Kingdom, including in employment interviews.

In summary, Gumperz's publications and collaborations established IS as an approach to cross-cultural communication that illuminates how social injustices are exacerbated when contextualization conventions and cultural assumptions differ. They also demonstrated the relevance of IS for encounters between institutional representatives and in familiar workplace contexts such as interviews and meetings. Additionally, Gumperz reached out to non-academic audiences. The work of Tannen, discussed next, continues and amplifies these trends.

Deborah Tannen and Students (the United States)

Deborah Tannen, who studied with Gumperz and Robin Lakoff, significantly developed IS. In the 1980s Tannen developed the notion of *conversational style*, which she would later bring to workplace and other public discourse contexts; this concept extends Gumperz's notion of contextualization cues to refer to all the ways speakers indicate what they mean, including features of talk such as pausing, humour, and storytelling (Tannen [1984] 2005). In *That's Not What I Meant!*, Tannen (1986) demonstrates how myriad cultural and social factors affect conversational style, including race/ethnicity, gender, socioeconomic status, and age. In *You Just Don't Understand* (Tannen 1990), Tannen focuses on gender. Following this book's publication, Tannen was approached by people in various corporations who wondered if the gendered style differences described in it were contributing to women's failure to advance at work. To explore this, she used IS methods, observing individuals in multiple organizations in the United States as they went about their workdays; asking employees to audio-record their conversations, which were then transcribed; and recording conversational interviews with individuals, their subordinates, and superiors. This study resulted in *Talking from 9 to 5* (1994b) and several scholarly publications (e.g., Tannen 1994a).

Tannen explains how gendered styles interact at work and may manifest in (often seemingly minor) misunderstandings that in turn may have serious implications for women's professional advancement. For instance, humour, frequently used to establish positive relationships, can be a point of difficulty: whereas many men tend to favour mock-hostile attacks or teasing of others (which women may misinterpret as "genuinely hostile and personal"), many women tend to use self-deprecating humour (which men may mistake as women "truly putting themselves down") (Tannen 1990, 73). Other differences include uses of directness (with women tending to be more indirect in issuing requests, for instance, as a means of saving the addressee's face) and apologies (with women's utterings of "I'm sorry" often being interpreted literally by men as accepting fault). Style differences like these may affect how work-related tasks are accomplished, whose contributions are recognized and valued, and who gets promoted.

Among Tannen's most important contributions is the demonstration of the complex interactional tightrope women walk at work: middle-class American workplaces (like many others) are largely structured around masculine conversational norms, so women are captured in what Lakoff (1975) first identified as a double bind. If they talk in ways expected of the "unmarked" male worker—such as asking someone to do something in a relatively direct, unmitigated way, or explicitly taking credit for their own contributions—they are seen as too aggressive. If, however, women abide by conversational norms traditionally associated with women, including hedging, downplaying one's superior status, and minimizing one's contribution (however important), they are viewed as ineffectual, and are passed over for promotions; in either case, they hit "the glass ceiling" (see Mullany and Yoong this volume).

Tannen (1994b) further illuminates the complexity of workplace talk through the lens of framing and by drawing on her conceptualization of linguistic strategies as ambiguous and polysemous in terms of power (or hierarchy) and solidarity (or connection). This framework (described in Tannen 1993 and elsewhere) captures the inherent interconnectedness of these relational dimensions and demonstrates how the same linguistic strategy can be a move for power or for solidarity (and is thus ambiguous), or both at once (polysemous). Analysing two recorded extracts of workplace small talk, one involving male and the other involving female colleagues, Tannen (1994b) adopts Goffman's (1967) concept of "sex-class-linked", arguing that linguistic strategies are associated with the class of women or men, rather than individuals. For example, vulgar terms are sex-class-linked with men, whereas compliments are sex-class linked with women. Further, sex-class-linked strategies such as these do not "mean" any one thing, but enable both women and men to balance status and connection moment-by-moment in conversation. Tannen also demonstrates how participants' relative status differences affect strategies' uses and interpretations. For instance, a male writer's casual complaint about his computer is interpreted by his male superior (his editor) not as sociable talk, but through a hierarchical lens, as a legitimate complaint that requires remedy; the complimenting of a female mail clerk's hair and clothing by higher-ranking female colleagues enacts both solidarity (by demonstrating appreciation) and power (by putting the lower-ranked woman on display). Tannen (1994b, 199) thus also illuminates how framing, which she glosses as "displaying our alignments", provides a productive approach for exploring language and gender.

Haru Yamada (1992, 1993), a student of Tannen, compares Japanese and American business meeting talk. She focuses on topic management, linking differences to cultural expectations regarding interaction and interpersonal relationships. As Yamada explains, the American emphasis on individuality manifests in how topics are structured in the US bank officer meetings she examines: each officer has her or his own "deals", and each opens up talk, and speaks about her or his own deal, in turn. Within the talk, topics generally flow linearly; then the officer closes her or his own deal using a formula like "that's it". In contrast, Japanese bank meeting talk is shaped by the Japanese emphasis on interdependence, especially the culture-specific concept "amae", which stresses "the reciprocal feeling of nurturing concern for and dependence on another" (Yamada 1992, 32; based on Doi 1973). Deals are not assigned to individuals; meetings do not unfold as deal-by-deal reports, anyone can open a topic, and topical boundaries are much more fluid and frequently marked by metacommunication and silence. Further, Japanese participants commonly use a circular topic organization (see Yamada 1992, 74), and avoid confrontation by dropping a topic (or they settle potential conflicts in informal conversations held before scheduled meetings).

When members of these groups come together, Americans may perceive Japanese meetings as disorganized (with "hanging" topics) and featuring uncomfortable silences, and Japanese business people as too conflict-avoidant. Japanese may perceive American meetings as overly rigid and confrontational, and American business people as insensitive and dominating. In other words, Yamada explores and explains how interactional differences contribute to cultural stereotyping. Similar to how Gumperz and Cook-Gumperz (1982) described British bureaucrats' standards for committee talk, Yamada (1992) suggests that culture-specific expectations about meeting structure and participation shape the talk.

Shari Kendall (2003, 2004, 2006), also Tannen's student, extends Tannen's exploration of why women's workplace accomplishments may go unrecognized. Using a framing approach, she examines workplace identity construction, especially regarding authority. Kendall (2004) examines the discourse of a female technical director of a radio news programme, Carol. Examining two recorded interactions Carol had with colleagues, Kendall shows how she saves face for them by framing interactions as more equality- as opposed to hierarchy-oriented. For example, in talk with a subordinate, Harold, as he gets ready to serve as a substitute operator for the soundboard, Carol describes how the soundboard works in the context of the specific show and identifies past troubles that "people" have had, rather than issuing Harold explicit directives or warnings. Further, Carol engages him in pre-show small talk that invites him to display his computer expertise; this allows him to highlight his competence. In the end, he makes no mistakes. Among directors, Carol had the fewest technical errors, yet she did not get credit for her accomplishments; Kendall suggests her way of enacting authority was not recognized as valuable. This traces back to Tannen's (1993, 1994b) framework and the double bind: Carol, in her use of sex-class-linked linguistic behaviours such as avoiding explicit directives, could be interpreted as a weak leader (if a good leader is seen to emphasize status differences, rather than solidarity).

In a related study, Kendall (2003) examines how another woman, Elaine, displays authority in workplace interactions with her two female subordinates, and at home in conversations with her 10-year-old daughter. She finds that Elaine's directives differ in these contexts: when Elaine directs her subordinates' actions, "she draws on mitigating strategies that evoke the qualities associated with sociocultural conceptions of 'mother'" (601), for instance by using inclusive "let's"; she generally does not do this at home. Elaine's workplace linguistic choices, Kendall argues, facilitate "a gendered mode of enacting authority that is recognized and appreciated by her subordinates" (618). Kendall (2006) examines a workplace conversation about family that Elaine had with an equal-ranking male colleague who is also a parent, Richard. She finds that Elaine displays a traditional caregiver identity (which is not valued in the workplace), while Richard avoids doing so. Kendall suggests that such workplace small talk may have larger repercussions in terms of advancement. Thus gendered styles of interaction may positively and negatively affect how women are perceived at work.

In summary, the scholarship of Tannen and her students Yamada and Kendall develops and extends IS as formulated by Gumperz. It demonstrates how cultural and subcultural (especially gender) conversational style differences play out at work, particularly how style differences may affect how conversation unfolds, how individuals and groups are perceived, and whether or not individuals advance.

Janet Holmes and Colleagues (New Zealand)

The Wellington Language in the Workplace Project (LWP)—which involves a team of students and scholars led by Janet Holmes, and includes core members Bernadette Vine and Meredith Marra—uses methods and theories of IS to investigate language in New Zealand workplaces. LWP data include audio- and video-recording of a range of workplace interactions, ethnographic observations by researchers, interviews with participants, focus group discussions about particular issues, and workplace documents. Like the scholarship of Gumperz and Yamada, LWP research highlights how culture shapes (and is created in) workplace discourse; like the work of Tannen and Kendall, it explores gender at work, especially as related to leadership and advancement. In addition to employing IS, some LWP research integrates other concepts—notably "community of practice" (Wenger 1998; see King this volume) which emphasizes how groups are (re)constituted in interaction. Some LWP publications also draw on critical approaches to address institutional power structures. While numerous publications have resulted from the LWP, here we focus on two book-length investigations.

In *Leadership, Discourse, and Ethnicity*, Holmes, Marra, and Vine (2011) examine discourse at four New Zealand companies, two of which can be described as culturally Pākehā (oriented to New Zealand's majority group, descended from European colonists) and two as "ethnicized" organizations that self-identify as culturally Māori (oriented to the minority indigenous group). Their findings indicate that Pākehā and Māori workplaces manifest different discourse practices. For instance, the authors uncovered different turn-taking patterns in meetings: Pākehā meetings typically involve a one-speaker-at-a-time structure, and Māori meetings, much more overlapping talk and active verbal feedback, a finding that recalls Tannen's (e.g., 1986) work on style differences, and analyses of meetings by Gumperz and Cook-Gumperz (1982) and Yamada (1992, 1993). Leadership also plays out differently. For example, in Pākehā workplaces, leaders' personal narratives may display authoritative leadership and highlight company success; in contrast, in Māori workplaces, both self-promotion and company achievements are underplayed (owing to a cultural valuing of modesty). Critical feedback to employees is generally more direct in Pākehā as compared to Māori workplaces, which feature more indirectness and humour to give this type of feedback. Such findings illuminate how enacting leadership varies across cultural groups.

Holmes' (2006) *Gendered Talk at Work* examines women's and men's discourse in professional New Zealand organizations, including leadership talk. Like Tannen (1994b) and Kendall (2004), she observes that gender expectations, along with leadership ideals that make "good woman" and "good leader" incompatible, shape workplace talk, and how women are perceived. For instance, women do not easily tell the "hero stories" that Holmes et al. (2011, 44) found Pākehā men telling; instead (and reinforcing previous findings), women's stories are generally self-deprecating. Holmes' analysis also illuminates individuals' style flexibility; she observes that "effective communicators, both female and male, typically draw from a very wide and varied discursive repertoire" (Holmes 2006, 1). IS facilitates the context-sensitive, micro-linguistic analysis required to elucidate how gender and leadership intersect in talk.

Other LWP publications include Holmes and Stubbe's (2015) investigation of how small talk, humour, advice-giving, and other features accomplish power and politeness at work, and Murata's (2014) analysis of humour in business meetings in New Zealand and Japan. Collectively, these advance our understanding of gender and culture in workplace talk, and the various linguistic strategies that constitute it.

Other Studies

Numerous other scholars use IS to investigate workplace interaction, often integrating concepts from other approaches to discourse. For example, Ostermann (2003) examines talk at an all-female police station and a feminist crisis intervention centre in Brazil. She shows how professionals' alternations between forms of the Brazilian Portuguese second person pronoun when addressing victims serve as a contextualization cue that influences relationships; for instance, a police officer's switch to "informal you" creates a more intimate footing. In another women-only study, Baxter (2014) combines IS and a critical/feminist perspective to examine how six middle-ranking managers collaborate on a project for a Master of Business Administration course. She finds that the women use various strategies—including nonverbal cues, pronoun shifts, and questions—to accomplish the team's task (building an attractive paper tower strong enough to support a glass tumbler), while simultaneously constructing different types of leadership identities, such as more hierarchical versus egalitarian.

Prego-Vázquez (2007), in a study that recalls the service/gatekeeping encounters at the foundation of IS, analyses employee/customer interactions at a workplace in Spain that supplies water, treats waste, and collects refuse. She demonstrates how frame conflicts and communicative difficulties arise when customers' discourse, such as talk introducing personal topics, clashes with expectations of the institutional context. Like Baxter, Prego-Vázquez supplements IS with a critical perspective to highlight participants' differential access to bureaucratic language and practices. Also addressing language competence, Moody (2014) analyses an American intern's interactions with colleagues at a Japanese technology firm, demonstrating how the intern effectively constructs a "foreigner" (*gaijin*) identity to lubricate interaction, especially to create a playful tone and mitigate instances of intercultural miscommunication.

Other recent studies consider workplace interaction in digital contexts. Schnurr (an LWP member) and Rowe (2008) integrate Critical Discourse Analysis and IS to investigate subversive humour in workplace emails in Hong Kong, finding that relatively powerful people use it to give unpleasant messages to their subordinates while simultaneously conveying frustration with the organization. In another email study, Gordon (a student of Tannen) and Luke (2012) use IS to examine professional identity socialization in supervisory email exchanges between counsellors-in-training and their internship supervisor in an American university context. They show how the supervisor's use of multiple linguistic strategies, including pronouns and lexical repetition, creates supervisor-supervisee solidarity and invites supervisees into the professional community of practice, both part of the everyday work of supervision.

In summary, scholars around the world productively use IS to study various aspects of workplace communication, often also integrating other concepts.

Conclusion and Future Directions

This chapter, in giving an overview of how theories and methods of IS contribute to illuminating workplace discourse, has highlighted key concepts—including contextualization cues, conversational inference, conversational style, and framing—and key scholars' work. In keeping with the interests of IS in diversity, this scholarship—from Gumperz's early work to the present—has identified how culture, race/ethnicity, gender, and other aspects of identity and experience shape individuals' discourse and how discourse accomplishes a multitude of everyday work activities. It also reveals insights into problematic and frustrating aspects of contemporary workplaces, including miscommunication, failure to achieve goals in gatekeeping encounters, and the glass ceiling. IS scholarship thus has theoretical and practical value.

An emerging research area includes how the increasingly complex work-family interface is discursively managed. A project co-directed by Tannen and Kendall (The Work and Family Project at Georgetown University, see Tannen, Kendall, and Gordon 2007) for which parents self-recorded at work and at home, addresses this interface. How workplace communication occurs via (now seemingly omnipresent) digital communication media, including and beyond email, is also an important future research direction. The struggles many women continue to face in male-dominated fields, and how changing policies (such as regarding family leave) influence workplace communication, also merit further exploration. In addition, while workplace discourse has been studied in many countries, much remains to be learned about it in African, Middle Eastern, and other contexts. Future research avenues for IS thus include not only investigating work-family interconnections and workplace communication in digital contexts, but also continuing to examine and disseminate findings about diversity and intercultural communication in workplace settings around the world.

Further Reading

For more on IS, see Gordon (2011) and Bailey (2015); the latter includes discussion of a workplace exchange from *Crosstalk* (Twitchin 1979). Gumperz (2015) provides a "personal perspective" on IS and presents several examples of talk at work. A special issue of *Text & Talk* (Auer and Roberts 2011) illuminates the impact of Gumperz and IS on understanding language use, including in workplace contexts.

Related Topics

Directives; Relational talk; Humour; Narratives; Miscommunication; Gender; Intercultural communication

Acknowledgement

The authors would like to thank Deborah Tannen for her comments on an earlier draft of this chapter.

References

Auer, Peter, and Celia Roberts, Eds. 2011. "In Honor of John Gumperz." Special issue, *Text & Talk* 31 (4).
Bailey, Benjamin. 2015. "Interactional Sociolinguistics." In *The International Encyclopedia of Language and Social Interaction*, edited by Karen Tracy, Cornelia Ilie, and Todd Sandel, 826–840. UK: John Wiley & Sons.
Bateson, Gregory. 1972. *Steps to an Ecology of Mind*. New York: Ballantine.
Baxter, Judith. 2014. "'If You Had Only Listened Carefully . . .': The Discursive Construction of Emerging Leadership in a UK All-Women Management Team." *Discourse & Communication* 8: 23–39.
Doi, Takeo. 1973. *The Anatomy of Dependence*. Translated by John Bester. Tokyo: Kodansha.
Erickson, Frederick. 1975. "Gatekeeping and the Melting Pot: Interaction in Counseling Encounters." *Harvard Educational Review* 45: 44–70.
Goffman, Erving. 1967. *Interaction Ritual: Essays on Face-to-Face Behavior*. New York: Anchor Books.
Goffman, Erving. 1974. *Frame Analysis*. New York: Harper and Row.
Goffman, Erving. 1981. "Footing." Chap. 3 in *Forms of Talk*. Philadelphia, PA: University of Pennsylvania Press.
Gordon, Cynthia. 2011. "Gumperz and Interactional Sociolinguistics." In *Sage Handbook of Sociolinguistics*, edited by Ruth Wodak, Barbara Johnstone, and Paul Kerswill, 67–84. London: Sage.
Gordon, Cynthia, and Melissa Luke. 2012. "Discursive Negotiation of Face via Email: Professional Identity Development in School Counseling Supervision." *Linguistics and Education* 23: 112–122.
Gumperz, John J. 1982a. *Discourse Strategies*. Cambridge: Cambridge University Press.
Gumperz, John J., Ed. 1982b. *Language and Social Identity*. Cambridge: Cambridge University Press.
Gumperz, John J. 1999. "On Interactional Sociolinguistic Method." In *Talk, Work and Institutional Order: Discourse in Medical, Mediation, and Management Settings*, edited by Srikant Sarangi, and Celia Roberts, 453–471. Berlin: Mouton de Gruyter.

Gumperz, John J. 2015. "Interactional Sociolinguistics: A Personal Perspective." In *The Handbook of Discourse Analysis*. 2nd ed., edited by Deborah Tannen, Heidi E. Hamilton, and Deborah Schiffrin, 309–323. Chichester: John Wiley & Sons.

Gumperz, John J., and Jenny Cook-Gumperz. 1982. "Interethnic Communication in Committee Negotiations." In *Language and Social Identity*, edited by John J. Gumperz, 145–162. Cambridge: Cambridge University Press.

Gumperz, John J., Thomas Cyprian Jupp, and Celia Roberts. 1979. *Crosstalk: A Study of Cross-Cultural Communication: Background Material and Notes to Accompany the BBC Film*. Southall: National Centre for Industrial Language Training.

Gumperz, John J., Thomas Cyprian Jupp, and Celia Roberts. 1980. *Crosstalk: The Wider Perspective*. Southall: National Centre for Industrial Language Training.

Holmes, Janet. 2006. *Gendered Talk at Work*. Malden: Blackwell.

Holmes, Janet, Meredith Marra, and Bernadette Vine. 2011. *Leadership, Discourse, and Ethnicity*. Oxford: Oxford University Press.

Holmes, Janet, and Maria Stubbe. 2015. *Power and Politeness in the Workplace: A Sociolinguistic Analysis of Talk at Work*. 2nd ed. London: Routledge.

Kendall, Shari. 2003. "Creating Gendered Demeanors of Authority at Work and at Home." In *Handbook of Language and Gender*, edited by Janet Holmes, and Miriam Meyerhoff, 600–623. Malden: Blackwell.

Kendall, Shari. 2004. "Framing Authority: Gender, Face, and Mitigation at a Radio Network." *Discourse & Society* 15: 55–79.

Kendall, Shari. 2006. "Positioning the Female Voice within Work and Family." In *Speaking Out: The Female Voice in Public Contexts*, edited by Judith Baxter, 179–197. Basingstoke: Palgrave Macmillan.

Lakoff, Robin. 1975. *Language and Woman's Place*. New York: Harper & Row.

Moody, Stephen. 2014. "'Well, I'm a Gaijin': Constructing Identity through English and Humor in the International Workplace." *Journal of Pragmatics* 60: 75–88.

Murata, Kazuyo. 2014. "An Empirical Cross-Cultural Study of Humour in Business Meetings in New Zealand and Japan." *Journal of Pragmatics* 60: 251–265.

Ochs, Elinor. 1979. "Transcription as Theory." In *Developmental Pragmatics*, edited by Elinor Ochs, and Bambi Schieffelin, 43–72. New York: Academic Press.

Ostermann, Ana Cristina. 2003. "Localizing Power and Solidarity: Pronoun Alternation at an All-Female Police Station and a Feminist Crisis Intervention Center in Brazil." *Language in Society* 32: 351–381.

Prego-Vázquez, Gabriela. 2007. "Frame Conflict and Social Inequality in the Workplace: Professional and Local Discourse Struggles in Employee/Customer Interactions." *Discourse & Society* 18: 295–335.

Roberts, Celia. 2011. "Gatekeeping Discourse in Employment Interviews." In *Handbook of Communication in Organisations and Professions*, edited by Srikant Sarangi, and Christopher Candlin, 407–432. Berlin: De Gruyter.

Schnurr, Stephanie, and Charley Rowe. 2008. "The 'Dark Side' of Humour: An Analysis of Subversive Humour in Workplace Emails." *Lodz Papers in Pragmatics* 4: 109–130.

Tannen, Deborah. 1986. *That's Not What I Meant!: How Conversational Style Makes or Breaks Relationships*. New York: Ballantine Books.

Tannen, Deborah. 1990. *You Just Don't Understand: Women and Men in Conversation*. New York: Ballantine Books.

Tannen, Deborah. 1993. "The Relativity of Linguistic Strategies." In *Gender and Conversational Interaction*, edited by Deborah Tannen, 165–188. New York: Oxford University Press.

Tannen, Deborah. 1994a. "The Sex-Class Linked Framing of Talk at Work." Chap. 6 in *Gender and Discourse*. New York: Oxford University Press.

Tannen, Deborah. 1994b. *Talking from 9 to 5: Women and Men at Work*. New York: William Morrow.

Tannen, Deborah. (1984) 2005. *Conversational Style: Analyzing Talk among Friends*. New York: Oxford University Press.

Tannen, Deborah, Shari Kendall, and Cynthia Gordon. 2007. *Family Talk: Discourse and Identity in Four American Families*. Oxford: Oxford University Press.

Tannen, Deborah, and Cynthia Wallat. 1993. "Interactive Frames and Knowledge Schemas in Interaction: Examples from a Medical Examination/Interview." In *Framing in Discourse*, edited by Deborah Tannen, 57–76. New York: Oxford University Press.

Twitchin, John, dir. 1979. *Crosstalk*. BBC.
Wenger, Etienne. 1998. *Communities of Practice: Learning, Meaning, and Identity*. Cambridge: Cambridge University Press.
Yamada, Haru. 1992. *American and Japanese Business Discourse: A Comparison of Interactional Styles*. Norwood, NJ: Ablex.
Yamada, Haru. 1993. *Different Games, Different Rules: Why Americans and Japanese Misunderstand Each Other*. Oxford: Oxford University Press.

2
Conversation Analysis
Merran Toerien

Introduction

> it is through interaction that institutions are brought to life and made actionable in the everyday world.
>
> (Heritage and Clayman 2010, 7)

From a conversation analytic perspective, talk is not best understood as the transfer of information, but rather as the primary way in which we produce social actions—like greeting, questioning, apologizing, negotiating, or agreeing—*in interaction* with our fellow humans (Drew 2003). It is through talk (together with non-vocal forms of interaction) that we build and manage our relationships, establish who we are in the world, and conduct a large swathe of our "business" (Drew 2003), be that in our social lives or the more specialized institutions that we inhabit as employees or clients/customers of some kind.

Certainly there are important features of any workplace that are not "talked into being" (Heritage 2004; Heritage and Clayman 2010). Institutions may rely on physical structures (a courthouse or doctor's surgery), apparatus (a gavel or stethoscope), and forms of action that cannot be accomplished through talk. Yet, while no amount of talk will x-ray a patient's chest, talk will play a crucial role in getting the job done—establishing the patient's consent, facilitating their compliance with the process, and subsequently delivering a diagnosis. As one of the founders of conversation analysis (CA) put it:

> Conversational interaction may then be thought of as a form of social
> organization through which the work of the constitutive institutions of societies gets done—institutions such as the economy, the polity, the family, socialization, etc. It is, so to speak, sociological bedrock.
>
> (Schegloff 1996, 4)

CA has thus developed as an attempt to understand talk *in its own right*, rather than seeing it as a proxy for, or conduit to, something described in, or lying behind, the talk (Drew 2003). It rests on the understanding that talk-in-interaction—a term denoting both verbal and other forms of interaction—is organized and orderly; if it were not, meaningful interaction would not be possible (Pomerantz and Fehr 1997). CA provides systematic ways of identifying and explicating the patterns, structures and practices that "make coherent, mutually comprehensible communication and action possible in interaction" (Drew 2005, 79). This has necessitated the use of recorded interactions as primary data, with detailed transcripts to facilitate analysis. These follow a set of conventions developed by another of CA's founders—Gail Jefferson—that capture not only *what* was said, but also features of *how* the talk was produced (see Jefferson 2004 for an explanation of this system). The increasing focus on non-vocal features of interaction has also led to the development of systems for transcribing some of these (e.g., Mondada 2014)—particularly gaze (e.g., Goodwin 1981; Kendon 1990; Rossano 2012)—although there no single agreed system.

The CA enterprise is far more than a set of analytic tools. It has become a paradigm in its own right, spanning multiple disciplines, including sociology, psychology, linguistics, and communication (Drew 2003; Heritage 1999, 2009). Moreover, from its inception in the early 1960s, CA has been concerned both with how language works in the workplace and with the work that language is used to do there.

"Basic" and "Institutional" CA: A Brief History

The story of CA's origins rests on the coincidence that one of its founders—Harvey Sacks—wanted to find a way to study "how ordinary activities get done", and had access to recorded calls to a Suicide Prevention Centre (Sacks 1995, xvii). Working at a time when tape recordings were a novelty, Sacks saw their enormous advantage: "I could study [them] again and again. And also, consequentially, others could look at what I had studied, and make of it what they could, if they wanted to be able to disagree with me" (622). Subsequently, the developing field of CA focused on "ordinary conversation" since this is understood to be "the most fundamental form of talk-in-interaction, the form from which all others derive" (Drew 2005, 74). Over several decades, the cumulative study of ordinary conversation has led to an impressive array of findings and a clear methodology for further work in this vein—often referred to as "basic" CA.

Conversation analysts have, likewise, built up extensive findings across a range of institutional settings, a highly selective list of which includes: counselling (e.g., Peräkylä 1995; Silverman 1997), calls for emergency assistance (e.g., Zimmerman 1992), radio phone-ins (e.g., Hutchby 1996), presidential press conferences (e.g., Clayman and Heritage 2002), news interviews (e.g., Greatbatch 1992), consultations with psychic practitioners (e.g., Wooffitt 2006), courtroom proceedings (e.g., Atkinson and Drew 1979), teaching (e.g., Gumperz and Herasimchuk 1975; Margutti 2004), police interviews (e.g., Benneworth-Gray 2014; Stokoe, Edwards, and Edwards 2016), doctor–patient consultations (e.g., Heritage and Maynard 2006), auctions (Heath 2012—winner of the International Society for Conversation Analysis best book award), meetings (e.g., Asmuß and Svennevig 2009; Svennevig 2012), telephone helplines (e.g., Hepburn, Wilkinson, and Butler 2014) and many more. All such interactions "involve at least one participant who represents a formal organization of some kind" (Drew and Heritage 1992, 3) and an orientation to a (set of) task(s), the completion of which is the institutionally defined goal of the interaction.

The first edited collection of such studies, *Talk at Work* (Drew and Heritage 1992), was a landmark in the development of CA as applied to the workplace, and remains a core text. Since then, several collections have appeared (e.g., Antaki 2011; Heritage and Clayman 2010; Llewellyn and Hindmarsh 2010), and CA has been described as "the dominant approach to the study of human social interaction across the disciplines of Sociology, Linguistics and Communication" (Stivers and Sidnell 2012, 1) and even "the method *par excellence*" for studying interaction (Ostermann and Kitzinger 2012, 240). Although verbal interaction has received the most attention, there has been an increasing focus on the "multimodal", "non-vocal" or "embodied" features of interaction, such as gesture and gaze (e.g., Ford and Stickle 2012; Mondada 2013). This rapidly developing area of research has begun to shed light on the complex ways in which talk and bodily conduct combine to produce meaningful social action, as well as the use of material and digital resources to accomplish activities in and outside of the workplace (Heath and Luff 2012).

Doing CA: Four Key Stages

CA is best learnt through a recursive process of reading the literature and doing analysis, ideally with face-to-face guidance from an experienced analyst and/or participation in "data sessions" (where analysts work collaboratively on data). This section cannot teach you to do CA, but it offers a basis for deciding whether to explore the approach further. I will focus on the analytic process. For a useful introduction to data collection, see Mondada (2012). Analytically, we can "distil what is a messier, iterative process into four broad stages" (Toerien 2013a, 330), namely:

1 Collection-building;
2 Individual case analysis;
3 Pattern-identification;
4 Accounting for or evaluating your patterns.

I will illustrate these through an example from research on doctor–patient interaction, which has become a substantive sub-field in "applied" CA. Stivers (2005) undertook a now classic study of nearly 600 acute paediatric consultations in the US, focusing on how physicians handled parental pressure for antibiotic prescriptions. She built several analytic collections from her recordings, including all cases in which physicians recommended non-antibiotic treatment. The following extracts provide examples.

Example 2.1 (from Stivers 2005, 952. Reproduced with permission from Elsevier)

```
 1 Doc:   uhm what I'm gonna ( ) tuh
 2        give 'im some cough
 3        medicines,
 4        (0.2)
 5 Doc:   .h and also h uh little:
 6        h medication's called .h
 7        =Albuterol?
 8        (.)
 9 Doc:   which—open up thee airway
10        uh little bit tuh help
11        him breathe uh little bit bet[ter?,
12 Mom:                                [Okay.
```

> **Example 2.2** (from Stivers 2005, 954. Reproduced with permission from Elsevier)
>
> ```
> 1 Doc:    I th:ink from what you've
> 2         told me (0.2) that this is
> 3         pro:bably .h uh kind of
> 4         (0.2) virus infec[tion,
> 5 Dad:                     [Uh huh,
> 6         (0.4) th:at I don't think
> 7         antibiotics will ki:ll,
> 8         (0.2)
> 9 Dad:    Well- [( )
> ```
>
> Dad goes on to produce an extended turn in which he explains that he recently had the same symptoms as his child. These, he reports, failed to respond to over-the-counter medication but were "taken care of" by antibiotics.

Collection-building involves *systematically* identifying all possible cases of the interactional phenomenon of interest that are evident within your dataset. This may be a social action (e.g., recommending, as in Stivers' study), a specialized activity (e.g., performing a physical examination), or a technical feature (e.g., how speakers initiate "repair" of a misunderstanding). This is not just a preliminary step. In building a collection, one makes analytic decisions about what counts as an instance of the phenomenon. Although this will be informed by the literature, CA is fundamentally *inductive*; the decision about what goes into a collection is based on what is demonstrably evident in the dataset. Thus, iterative analysis of individual cases is both a stage in its own right and a vital part of doing stages one and three.

Individual case analysis depends, among other things, on two fundamental CA concepts: "turn design" and "sequence organization". As Drew (2012, 132) puts it:

> Turn design refers to how a speaker constructs a turn at talk—what is selected or what goes into 'building' a turn to do the action it is designed to do, in such a way as to be understood as doing that action.

Sequence organization focuses on how turns relate to one another in an organized, socially meaningful way (Schegloff 2007). For example, Stivers (2005) identified two contrastive turn designs in her collection of non-antibiotic treatment recommendations: those formatted *in favour* of another treatment (boldface lines, Example 2.1), and those formatted *against* antibiotics (boldface lines, Example 2.2). She also found that parents were more likely to resist the negatively formatted turns. Thus, she identified a clear pattern in her collection: the recommendation *sequences* tended to unfold differently, depending on the *design* of the physician's initiating turn.

The final analytic stage involves trying to make sense of the pattern(s) identified. Drew (2003, 153) suggests that "very often, this will involve . . . consider[ing] *where and how* the object or pattern in question arose" and may depend on identifying "the contingency which the pattern systematically handles, or to which it offers a solution". As I discuss below, this final stage can involve understanding your findings in light of a particular theoretical construct, an institutional policy or with reference to the institution's goals. Stivers (2005) was able to provide *effective practice* recommendations on the basis of her findings, showing that a two-part recommendation—first affirmatively recommending a specific treatment and then recommending against antibiotics—addressed the dual need for physicians to secure acceptance of a non-antibiotic solution and to educate parents in why this was appropriate. In short, the final stage addresses the "so what?" question that any good research project must handle.

Broadly, these four stages hold for "basic" and "institutional" research. It is also common in CA studies of the workplace to map out the overall structural organisation of the interactions. For example, Robinson (2003) showed that four key activities typically constitute primary care consultations in the US. The fact that doctors and patients demonstrably orient to these produces a distinctive overall structure to the consultation. Heritage (2004) identifies this structure as one of the features that contributes to the "unique fingerprint" of any particular form of institutional interaction. Other features include the "specific tasks, identities, constraints on conduct and relevant inferential procedures that the participants deploy and are oriented to in their interactions with one another" (225).

What CA Brings to the Study of Language in the Workplace

CA's contributions to the study of workplace interaction are multi-faceted and nuanced. Rather than trying to summarize diverse findings—which requires more space than available—I will draw on my research experience to illustrate how CA can make three kinds of contribution, each of which rests on a detailed analysis of *how* language works *in real interactional practice*. Two or more of these contributions (among others) will often come together in a single study (Antaki 2011). For clarity, however, I will describe three distinct studies, conducted in different settings.

Doing Emotional Labour: Seeing How a Theoretical Construct Works in Practice

I started using CA during my PhD, for which I recorded a small dataset of professional hair removal sessions. Almost all previous research in beauty salons had relied on self-reports or observations without video recordings (e.g., Black 2004). I described the structural organization of the interactions and unpacked three key components: physical action (e.g., plucking or waxing), task-directed talk (e.g., asking the client to assist with the procedure), and topic talk (e.g., talking about the client's life) (Toerien and Kitzinger 2007a).

It became apparent that these could come into conflict. For instance, working with my supervisor, I observed a beauty therapist holding back from progressing the hair removal in favour of responding to the client's ongoing topic talk (Toerien and Kitzinger 2007a). This interactional moment—which almost certainly would have been missed without the recording—enabled us to see how our analysis could contribute to the sociological concept of emotional labour. Originating in Hochschild's (1983) path-breaking work, this concept has been used across a range of workplace settings to foreground the (often invisible) relational work that constitutes part of many paid jobs. Previous studies understood emotional labour to be central to beauty therapy, but did not show how it works in practice.

We were able to do so because video recordings afford a nuanced analysis of routine practices. While therapists might describe, in interviews, some of the more "spectacular" examples of emotional labour, it is not possible to recall *exactly* how one handles everyday workplace tasks. Likewise, it is impossible to record every detail in fieldnotes. Yet, as my recordings revealed, it is in the detail of how therapists navigate their "multiple involvements" that we see the extent to which emotional labour is embedded within the routines of beauty therapy (Toerien and Kitzinger 2007a, 2007b). CA provides the tools to see—and explicate—how concepts like emotional labour operate in real-time practice.

Doing Patient Choice: Seeing How Policy Works in Practice

I did not set out to use CA to investigate emotional labour—but one could. My more recent collaborative study of UK neurology consultations began with such a higher order question: how does "patient choice" work in practice? The driver was UK National Health Service (NHS) policy, which advocates increasing patients' ability to make choices about their healthcare (NHS England 2014). Yet there is little guidance on how clinicians might facilitate this and little previous research on how choice functions in real interactions (Antaki *et al.* 2008; Pilnick 2008).

Our study demonstrated that neurologists are indeed offering patients choice, and *how* they do so (Reuber *et al.* 2015). One approach was to use "option-listing" to give patients the opportunity to select from among alternative treatments (Toerien, Shaw *et al.* 2011; Toerien, Shaw, and Reuber 2013). When option-listing was used, patients and doctors almost always agreed—in separate self-reports provided just after the consultation—that the patient had been offered a choice. However, we demonstrated that even this mundane method for offering choice—akin to giving the patient a menu—was not always what it seemed. For example, we showed how the interactional "machinery" of option-listing could be used to pressure the patient into choosing the neurologist's favoured option—and yet both neurologist and patient still reported (independently) that a choice had been offered. There can be clinically sound reasons for exerting this kind of pressure. We are not, therefore, critiquing this approach *per se*. With respect to understanding how choice works, however, our analysis showed that: i) perceptions of choice may not map directly onto what can be seen in the interaction; ii) the same practices can be used to achieve very different interactional ends.

This has significant policy implications. We argue that NHS policy documents offer an oversimplified conceptualization of choice, treating its performance as self-evident. Yet the CA findings suggest otherwise. As Pilnick (2008, 527) argues with respect to guidelines on choice about antenatal testing, a major difficulty is how to move beyond simply informing women of their *right to choose*, "to creating an interactional environment in which that choice can actually be exercised". It is not enough to tell healthcare professionals to give patients choice. Even if they act on this guidance, they may do so in ways that are ineffective or counterproductive (Antaki *et al.* 2008). CA provides the tools to see—and explicate—how policies are functioning on the frontline.

Doing Back-to-Work Support: Seeing "Effective Practice" in Practice

One output of the patient choice study was to offer "effective practice" workshops for clinicians. In this final example, I will focus on a study where identifying effective practice was the central driver. Commissioned by the UK's Department for Work and Pensions (DWP), the study was the first to investigate video recordings of interviews between advisers and benefits claimants in Jobcentre Plus offices. These interactions formed part of a programme to help benefits claimants get (back) into work. Although the wider programme had been subject to evaluation, the interviews themselves had not previously been investigated in any detail (Drew *et al.* 2010). Moreover, most of the research had focused on outcomes that were *external* to the interactions, such as how many claimants secured a job. While such measures are important, they cannot tell us which practices *within* the interview are most effective. Yet these are the only factors over which advisers have direct control. Thus, we focused on *internal* measures of effectiveness, such as whether certain interactional practices evidently led to greater claimant engagement in the interview (Drew *et al.* 2010).

Again, the study showed that the details of talk really do matter. It is not enough to note on a checklist (as workplace appraisals often do) whether or not a particular activity has been conducted. *How* it is conducted can make all the difference. For example, when working with single parents claiming Income Support, advisers were expected to consider "steps towards work" for the future. At the time of recording, claimants were not required to be looking for work until their youngest child was 16. Thus, when asked if they were looking for work "at the moment", they could legitimately say "no"—and routinely did. Thus, the question format—"are you looking for work *at the moment*"—was demonstrably ineffective at opening up talk about work plans, because claimants' responses blocked further discussion. In a handful of cases, the adviser addressed the same activity in a different way, asking if the claimant was "thinking of going back to work *in the future*". This always elicited a positive response, thereby effectively opening up the discussion, allowing consideration of how the claimant might become work ready (Drew *et al.* 2014).

CA's fine-grained approach allowed us to go well beyond the usual guidance given on how to communicate well. For example, it is typical for frontline workers to be told to "ask open questions" when seeking information from clients. While of course open questions can be useful, the example above showed that the real difference can lie in a finer-grained detail. CA provides the tools to see—and explicate—such details, and to use these to provide evidence-based training in "effective practice".

To Sum Up

The common thread running through the above examples is the *detailed* focus on the phenomenon of interest *in practice*. Why this insistence on the details of interaction? There are numerous answers to this—some of which are implicit in the above discussion. Most importantly, the details matter for conversation analysts because they matter for the participants themselves. CA is founded on an ethnomethodological approach (Heritage 2009), meaning that the analyst's task is to explicate the methods the people under study are using to make sense to, and of, one another. The evidence strongly indicates that small details matter to interactants, including the selection of one word over another (e.g., Heritage *et al.* 2007), a fraction of a second's silence (e.g., Pomerantz 1984), a few laughter particles (e.g., Glenn 2003), and different intonation on the same word (Kendrick 2015). Analysing such details can be key to understanding how to introduce changes in the workplace that will be "workable" for those who must implement them.

Reflecting Critically on What CA Has to Offer

I have emphasized what CA can contribute to the study of interaction in the workplace. In this section I outline a key critique: that CA's focus on the "technical" details of interaction comes at the expense of understanding the bigger picture. This was the crux of an extensive debate (van Dijk 1999) between Billig and Schegloff (1999), sparked by an earlier paper (Schegloff 1997). There were also responses by Wetherell (1998) and Kitzinger (2000). On the critical side, some argue that CA renders analysts fatally blinkered to the big issues that ought to drive an adequate social science—questions of social identity, wider organizational structure, political context, social theory, structural inequalities, and so forth. Those who would defend CA argue that, on the contrary, it is well suited to understanding such matters, given that social life is (re)produced, in (massively) significant part, through the details of interaction (see Kitzinger 2000). It should be clear from the rest of this chapter that I favour the view that CA can speak to the "big issues". However, the thorny question of how to achieve this is by no means resolved.

This debate extends to the issue of whether CA adequately offers a critical voice on institutional practices. In part, this has to do with sources of funding. If the funder also has a stake in the institution under study, the objectives are likely to be designed to suit the institution. Whether this simultaneously meets the needs of those who access it is open to debate. As I have argued elsewhere:

> Most applied CA work to date has focused on institutions where the goals are directed towards an intuitively obvious social good, such as delivering emergency services, education, counselling or health care ... Nevertheless, in making recommendations on how to do these things, the authors are unavoidably taking a position on legitimate institutional goals.
>
> (Toerien, Irvine *et al.* 2011, 159)

Where the ethics of the institutional goals become more debatable, we have to grapple more explicitly with what sort of impact our research might have. Are we, in effect, teaching institutional representatives how to more effectively manipulate clients? Or can we remain "critical", offering evidence-based guidance that might challenge practices we consider harmful? CA itself cannot answer such questions. However, I argue that conversation analysts should engage with the wider political and ethical questions surrounding whether the institutional goals we investigate are worthy of our support (Toerien, Irvine *et al.* 2011).

Future Directions

In his reflection on "conversation analysis at Century's end", Heritage (1999) suggested that CA was likely to be combined increasingly with quantitative methods, due to its growing application to questions underpinned by a distributional logic. This has proved to be so. Examples from the illustrative domain of primary care include whether certain practices can help doctors increase patient satisfaction (Robinson and Heritage 2006) and reduce the number of concerns that patients fail to reveal (Heritage *et al.* 2007). Such questions are concerned with an association between interactional practices and their outcomes, which may be evident within the interaction or may require the collection of extra-interactional data.

For their success, such studies depend on fine-grained CA work; without this, coding of interaction for statistical analysis is unlikely to be meaningful (Heritage 1999). By demonstrating statistically significant differences in outcomes associated with differences in interactional practice, CA should be able to make convincing and useful recommendations for practitioners and policymakers. At the same time, however, there is a need for more well-trained researchers to do both "applied" and "basic" CA research. Without the latter, our understanding of language in the workplace—which is a specialized form of ordinary interaction (Heritage 1984)—will also be limited.

Finally, based on my experience of supervizing students, I believe there is growing interest in developing CA's approach to understanding identity. CA rejects treating identities as offering a ready-made explanation for what occurs in interactions (Heath 1992; Schegloff 1997); the fact of being a doctor and patient, a man and woman, a person of colour and a white person should not be *assumed* to be significant. Any interactant can be classified into multiple categories, so the question arises: what makes one particular identity *relevant* to the analysis? (Toerien 2013b). It is our analytic task to show that, and how, identity categories are produced in the interaction (Schegloff 2007). This is relatively easy when participants orient explicitly to some category (see Speer and Stokoe 2011). The real challenge—which I believe the next "generation" of conversation analysts will address in earnest—lies in how far a CA approach can go in handling the subtle ways in which participants "do being" (Sacks 1985) gendered, classed, raced, a particular kind of professional or client and so forth.

Further Reading

I hope to have provided enough of a taste of CA for you to decide whether to pursue it further. Sidnell (2010), and Sidnell and Stivers (2012) offer excellent introductions to the foundational findings and methods of CA. Heritage (2004), and Heritage and Clayman (2010) do the same for the application of CA to the study of language in the workplace.

Related Topics

Interactional sociolinguistics; Critical discourse studies; (Im)politeness theory; Genetic counselling; Miscommunication; Interpreting

Acknowledgement

With many thanks to two anonymous reviewers and Bernadette Vine for a very constructive review process.

References

Antaki, Charles, Ed. 2011. *Applied Conversation Analysis: Intervention and Change in Institutional Talk.* Basingstoke: Palgrave Macmillan.
Antaki, Charles, W. Mick, L. Finlay, Chris Walton, and Louise Pate. 2008. "Offering Choices to People with Intellectual Disabilities: An Interactional Study." *Journal of Intellectual Disability Research* 52: 1165–1175.
Asmuß, Birte, and Jan Svennevig, Eds. 2009. "Meeting Talk". Special issue, *Journal of Business Communication* 46 (1).
Atkinson, J. Maxwell, and Paul Drew. 1979. *Order in Court: The Organization of Verbal Interaction in Judicial Settings.* London: Macmillan.
Benneworth-Gray, Kelly. 2014. "'Are You Going to Tell Me the Truth Today?': Invoking Obligations of Honesty in Police-Suspect Interviews." *The International Journal of Speech, Language and the Law* 21: 251–277.
Billig, Michael, and Emanuel A. Schegloff. 1999. "Debate. Critical Discourse Analysis and Conversation Analysis: An Exchange Between Michael Billig and Emanuel A. Schegloff." *Discourse & Society* 10: 543–582.
Black, Paula. 2004. *The Beauty Industry: Gender, Culture, Pleasure.* London: Routledge.
Clayman, Steven E., and John Heritage. 2002. "Questioning Presidents: Journalistic Deference and Adversarialness in the Press Conferences of Eisenhower and Reagan." *Journal of Communication* 52: 749–775.
Drew, Paul. 2003. "Conversation Analysis." In *Qualitative Psychology: A Practical Guide to Research Methods*, edited by Jonathan A. Smith, 132–158. London: Sage.
Drew, Paul. 2005. "Conversation Analysis." In *Handbook of Language and Social Interaction*, edited by Kirsten L. Fitch, and Robert E. Sanders, 71–102. Mahwah, NJ: Lawrence Erlbaum.

Drew, Paul. 2012. "Turn Design." In *Handbook of Conversation Analysis*, edited by Jack Sidnell, and Tanya Stivers, 131–149. Chichester, UK: John Wiley & Sons.

Drew, Paul, and John Heritage, Eds. 1992. *Talk at Work: Interaction in Institutional Settings*. Cambridge: Cambridge University Press.

Drew, Paul, Merran Toerien, Annie Irvine, and Roy Sainsbury. 2010. "A Study of Language and Communication between Advisers and Claimants in Work Focused Interviews." *Department for Work and Pensions Research Report 633*. Norwich, UK: HMSO.

Drew, Paul, Merran Toerien, Annie Irvine, and Roy Sainsbury. 2014. "Personal Adviser Interviews with Benefits Claimants in UK Jobcentres." *Research on Language and Social Interaction* 47: 306–316.

Ford, Cecilia E., and Trini Stickle. 2012. "Securing Recipiency in Workplace Meetings: Multimodal Practices." *Discourse Studies* 14: 11–30.

Glenn, Phillip J. 2003. *Laughter in Interaction*. Cambridge: Cambridge University Press.

Goodwin, Charles. 1981. *Conversational Organization: Interaction Between Speakers and Hearers*. New York: Academic Press.

Greatbatch, David. 1992. "On the Management of Disagreement between News Interviewees." In *Talk at Work: Interaction in Institutional Settings*, edited by Paul Drew, and John Heritage, 268–301. Cambridge: Cambridge University Press.

Gumperz, John J., and Eleanor Herasimchuk. 1975. "The Conversational Analysis of Social Meaning: A Study of Classroom Interaction." In *Sociocultural Dimensions of Language Use*, edited by Mary Sanches, and Ben G. Blount, 81–115. New York: Academic Press.

Heath, Christian. 1992. "Gesture's Discreet Tasks: Multiple Relevancies in Visual Conduct and in the Contextualisation of Language." In *The Contextualization of Language*, edited by Peter Auer, and Aldo di Luzio, 101–127. Amsterdam: John Benjamins.

Heath, Christian. 2012. *The Dynamics of Auction: Social Interaction and the Sale of Fine Art and Antiques*. Cambridge: Cambridge University Press.

Heath, Christian, and Paul Luff. 2012. "Embodied Action and Organizational Activity." In *Handbook of Conversation Analysis*, edited by Jack Sidnell, and Tanya Stivers, 283–307. Chichester, UK: John Wiley & Sons.

Hepburn, Alexa, Sue Wilkinson, and Carly W. Butler. 2014. "Intervening with Conversation Analysis in Telephone Helpline Services: Strategies to Improve Effectiveness." *Research on Language and Social Interaction* 47: 239–254.

Heritage, John. 1984. "Conversation Analysis." Chap. 8 in *Garfinkel and Ethnomethodology*. Cambridge: Polity Press.

Heritage, John. 1999. "CA at Century's End: Practices of Talk-in-Interaction, Their Distributions and Their Outcomes." *Research on Language and Social Interaction* 32: 69–76.

Heritage, John. 2004. "Conversation Analysis and Institutional Talk: Analysing Data." In *Qualitative Research: Theory, Method and Practice*, edited by David Silverman, 222–245. London: Sage.

Heritage, John. 2009. "Conversation Analysis as Social Theory." In *The New Blackwell Companion to Social Theory*, edited by Bryan S. Turner, 300–320. Oxford: Wiley-Blackwell.

Heritage, John, and Steven Clayman. 2010. *Talk in Action: Interactions, Identities and Institutions*. Chichester, UK: Wiley-Blackwell.

Heritage, John, and Douglas W. Maynard, Eds. 2006. *Communication in Medical Care: Interactions Between Primary Care Physicians and Patients*. Cambridge: Cambridge University Press.

Heritage, John, Jeffrey D. Robinson, Marc N. Elliott, Megan Beckett, and Michael Wilkes. 2007. "Reducing Patients' Unmet Concerns in Primary Care: The Difference One Word Can Make." *Journal of General Internal Medicine* 22: 1429–1433.

Hochschild, Arlie. 1983. *The Managed Heart: Commercialization of Human Feeling*. Berkeley, CA: University of California Press.

Hutchby, Ian. 1996. *Confrontation Talk: Arguments, Asymmetries and Power on Talk Radio*. Hillsdale, NJ: Lawrence Erlbaum.

Jefferson, Gail. 2004. "Glossary of Transcript Symbols with an Introduction." In *Conversation Analysis: Studies from the First Generation*, edited by Gene H. Lerner, 13–23. Philadelphia, PA: John Benjamins.

Kendon, Adam. 1990. *Conducting Interaction: Patterns of Behavior in Focused Encounters*. Cambridge: Cambridge University Press.

Kendrick, Kobin H. 2015. "Other-Initiated Repair in English." *Open Linguistics* 1: 164–190.

Kitzinger, Celia. 2000. "Doing Feminist Conversation Analysis." *Feminism & Psychology* 10: 163–193.

Llewellyn, Nick, and Jon Hindmarsh, Eds. 2010. *Organisation, Interaction and Practice: Studies of Ethnomethodology and Conversation Analysis*. Cambridge: Cambridge University Press.

Margutti, Piera. 2004. "Classroom Interaction in an Italian Primary School: Instructional Sequences in Pedagogic Settings." PhD diss., University of York.

Mondada, Lorenza. 2012. "The Conversation Analytic Approach to Data Collection." In *Handbook of Conversation Analysis*, edited by Jack Sidnell, and Tanya Stivers, 32–56. Chichester, UK: John Wiley & Sons.

Mondada, Lorenza. 2013. "Embodied and Spatial Resources for Turn-Taking in Institutional Multi-Party Interactions: Participatory Democracy Debates." *Journal of Pragmatics* 46: 39–68.

Mondada, Lorenza. 2014. "Conventions for Multimodal Transcription." Available at https://franz.unibas.ch/fileadmin/franz/user_upload/redaktion/Mondada_conv_multimodality.pdf.

NHS England. 2014. *NHS Five Year Forward View*. London: NHS England. Available at: www.england.nhs.uk/ourwork/futurenhs/.

Ostermann, Ana Cristina, and Celia Kitzinger. 2012. "Feminist Conversation Analysis and Applied Conversation Analysis." *Calidoscopio* 10: 239–244.

Peräkylä, Anssi. 1995. *AIDS Counselling: Institutional Interaction and Clinical Practice*. Cambridge: Cambridge University Press.

Pilnick, Alison. 2008. "'It's Something for You Both to Think About': Choice and Decision Making in Nuchal Translucency Screening for Down's Syndrome." *Sociology of Health & Illness* 30: 511–530.

Pomerantz, Anita. 1984. "Agreeing and Disagreeing with Assessments: Some Features of Preferred/Dispreferred Turn Shapes." In *Structures of Social Action: Studies in Conversation Analysis*, edited by J. Maxwell Atkinson, and John Heritage, 57–101. Cambridge: Cambridge University Press.

Pomerantz, Anita, and B. J. Fehr. 1997. "Conversation Analysis: An Approach to the Study of Social Action as Sense Making Practices." In *Discourse as Social Interaction. Discourse Studies: A Multidisciplinary Introduction*. Vol. 2, edited by Teun A. van Dijk, 64–91. London: Sage.

Reuber, Markus, Merran Toerien, Rebecca Shaw, and Duncan Roderick. 2015. "Delivering Patient Choice in Clinical Practice: A Conversation Analytic Study of Communication Practices Used in Neurology Clinics to Involve Patients in Decision-Making." *Health Services and Delivery Research* 3 (7). www.journalslibrary.nihr.ac.uk/hsdr/hsdr03070/#/full-report.

Robinson, Jeffrey D. 2003. "An Interactional Structure of Medical Activities during Acute Visits and its Implications for Patients' Participation." *Health Communication* 15: 27–59.

Robinson, Jeffrey D., and John Heritage. 2006. "Physicians' Opening Questions and Patients' Satisfaction." *Patient Education & Counseling* 60: 279–285.

Rossano, Federico. 2012. "Gaze in Conversation." In *Handbook of Conversation Analysis*, edited by Jack Sidnell, and Tanya Stivers, 308–329. Chichester, UK: John Wiley & Sons.

Sacks, Harvey. 1985. "On Doing 'Being Ordinary'." In *Structures of Social Action: Studies in Conversation Analysis*, edited by J. Maxwell Atkinson, and John Heritage, 413–429. Cambridge: Cambridge University Press.

Sacks, Harvey. 1995. *Lectures on Conversation*. Edited by Gail Jefferson with Introduction by Emanuel A. Schegloff. Malden: Blackwell.

Schegloff, Emanuel A. 1996. "Issues of Relevance for Discourse Analysis: Contingency in Action, Interaction and Co-Participant Context." In *Computational and Conversational Discourse: Burning Issues—An Interdisciplinary Account*, edited by Eduard H. Hovy, and Donia R. Scott, 3–38. Heidelberg: Springer Verlag.

Schegloff, Emanuel A. 1997. "Whose Text? Whose Context?" *Discourse & Society* 8: 165–187.

Schegloff, Emanuel A. 2007. *Sequence Organization in Interaction: A Primer in Conversation Analysis*. Cambridge: Cambridge University Press.

Sidnell, Jack. 2010. *Conversation Analysis: An Introduction*. Oxford: Wiley-Blackwell.

Sidnell, Jack, and Tanya Stivers, Eds. 2012. *Handbook of Conversation Analysis*. Chichester, UK: John Wiley & Sons.

Silverman, David. 1997. *Discourses of Counselling: HIV Counselling as Social Interaction*. London: Sage.

Speer, Susan A., and Elizabeth Stokoe, Eds. 2011. *Conversation and Gender*. Cambridge: Cambridge University Press.

Stivers, Tanya. 2005. "Non-Antibiotic Treatment Recommendations: Delivery Formats and Implications for Parent Resistance." *Social Science & Medicine* 60: 949–964.

Stivers, Tayna, and Jack Sidnell. 2012. "Introduction." In *Handbook of Conversation Analysis*, edited by Jack Sidnell, and Tanya Stivers, 1–8. Chichester, UK: John Wiley & Sons.

Stokoe, Elizabeth, Derek Edwards, and Helen Edwards. 2016. "'No Comment' Responses to Questions in Police Investigative Interviews." In *Discursive Constructions of Consent in the Legal Process*, edited by Susan Ehrlich, Diana Eades, and Janet Ainsworth, 289–318. Oxford: Oxford University Press.

Svennevig, Jan, Ed. 2012. "Interaction in Workplace Meetings." Special issue, *Discourse Studies* 14 (1).

Toerien, Merran. 2013a. "Conversations and Conversation Analysis." In *Sage Handbook of Qualitative Data Analysis*, edited by Uwe Flick, 327–340. London: Sage.

Toerien, Merran. 2013b. "Using Conversation Analysis to Study Gender: An Alternative to the 'Sex-Differences' Paradigm." *Journal of Foreign Languages* 36: 2–18.

Toerien, Merran, Annie Irvine, Paul Drew, and Roy Sainsbury. 2011. "Should Mandatory Jobseeker Interviews be Personalised? The Politics of Using Conversation Analysis to Make Effective Practice Recommendations." In *Applied Conversation Analysis: Intervention and Change in Institutional Talk*, edited by Charles Antaki, 140–160. Basingstoke, UK: Palgrave Macmillan.

Toerien, Merran, and Celia Kitzinger. 2007a. "Emotional Labour in Action: Navigating Multiple Involvements in the Beauty Salon." *Sociology* 41: 645–662.

Toerien, Merran, and Celia Kitzinger. 2007b. "Emotional Labour in Action: Turn Design of Task-directed Talk in the Beauty Salon." *Feminism & Psychology* 17: 162–172.

Toerien, Merran, Rebecca Shaw, Roderick Duncan, and Markus Reuber. 2011. "Offering Patients Choices: A Pilot Study of Interactions in the Seizure Clinic." *Epilepsy & Behavior* 20: 312–320.

Toerien, Merran, Rebecca Shaw, and Markus Reuber. 2013. "Initiating Decision-Making in Neurology Consultations: 'Recommending' Versus 'Option-Listing' and the Implications for Medical Authority." *Sociology of Health & Illness* 35: 873–890.

van Dijk, Teun A. 1999. "Critical Discourse Analysis and Conversation Analysis." *Discourse & Society* 10: 459–460.

Wetherell, Margaret. 1998. "Positioning and Interpretative Repertoires: Conversation Analysis and Post-Structuralism in Dialogue." *Discourse & Society* 9: 387–412.

Wooffitt, Robin. 2006. *The Language of Mediums and Psychics: The Social Organization of Everyday Miracles*. London: Routledge.

Zimmerman, Don H. 1992. "The Interactional Organization of Calls for Emergency Assistance." In *Talk at Work: Interaction in Institutional Settings*, edited by Paul Drew, and John Heritage, 418–469. Cambridge: Cambridge University Press.

3
Critical Discourse Studies
Veronika Koller

Introduction

Writing a chapter for a handbook section titled *Theoretical and Methodological Approaches* always involves an uncomfortable exercise in boundary-setting: not only does one need to define critical discourse studies (CDS), but, by the same token, it also needs to be delineated from neighbouring disciplines. This means excluding valuable work as "not CDS" and inevitably raises the question on what the writer's authority to declare something within or beyond the pale actually rests. It is with this latent discomfort that I give an overview of workplace CDS research.[1]

I do so because such an overview is useful and important. CDS research into workplace language rather pales against, say, conversation analytical or pragmatic studies, making it necessary to raise the profile of the work that *has* been done, point out how it ties in with other studies whose authors do not see themselves as working in a critical tradition, and discuss what could help or hinder an increased uptake of critical studies of workplace discourse.

CDS: Some Defining Characteristics

In a nutshell, CDS addresses social problems in their discursive aspect, using semiosis, i.e., meaning-making through signs, including linguistic signs, as an entry point. As such, CDS is premised on the belief that language and society are mutually constitutive and mediated by discourse. In simple terms, we can define discourse as language use as social practice that is determined by social structures (Fairclough 2015). In other words, discourse is the way in which people use linguistic and other signs, and the way they behave in conversations, in order to relate to others and project an identity for themselves and others. Such language use, however, is restricted by power (e.g., seniority at work), material practices (e.g., office design) and institutions (e.g., organizational structures). To further unpack the phrase "critical discourse studies", we can understand "critical" as meaning that the starting point is a social problem that needs to be described, explained and solved, or at least suggestions made as to how it could be solved. Accordingly, CDS has been defined as a

> problem-oriented interdisciplinary research movement, subsuming a variety of approaches, each with different theoretical models, research methods and agenda. What unites them

is a shared interest in the semiotic dimensions of power, injustice, abuse, and political-economic or cultural change in society.

(Fairclough, Mulderrig, and Wodak 2011, 356)

The notion of bringing about change in society raises the question if CDS is, or should be, a form of political activism itself, or whether it merely lays the groundwork for activists to draw on. Fairclough is outspoken in his belief that CDS ought to lead to actions to improve inequality and discrimination:

> the point is not just to analyze and criticize discourse . . . and perhaps suggest changes . . . It is to analyze and criticize, and ultimately to change, the existing social reality in which such discourse is related in particular ways to other social elements such as power relations, ideologies, economic and political strategies and policies. Analyzing and criticizing representations . . . and envisaging alternatives is an important thing to do, but in CD[S] it is just a part of a wider set of objectives.
>
> (Fairclough 2015, 5)

While this remains a matter of debate, we can posit that any contribution to social change requires (a) applied work, e.g., guidelines and consultancy on language use and its relation to institutional cultures, and (b) a recontextualization of research findings in non-academic discourses, making it necessary for the researcher to become conversant with non- or semi-academic genres such as blogs or conversations with, and presentations for, research partners. For studies on workplace language, this could mean identifying a social problem that has repercussions in the workplace, for example a lack of social mobility in a society that translates into corporate mono-cultures which in turn exclude employees from non-hegemonic

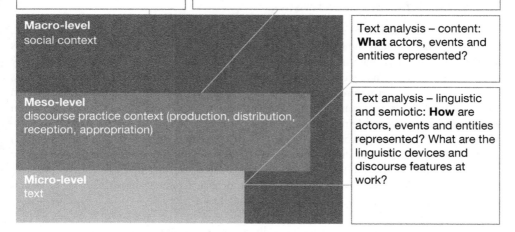

Figure 3.1 A three-level model for analysing discourse

groups from positions of power. A CDS researcher would look for a semiotic entry point into understanding how the problem is perpetuated, e.g., how the conversational norm in conference calls leads to the (self-)exclusion of less powerful participants (see Murphy 2015). Understanding the role of language in maintaining exclusion and power imbalances also requires looking at the discursive social practices between members of a community: who can engage in what sort of activity types—defined as "goal-defined, socially constituted, bounded events with constraints on participants, setting . . ., but above all on the kinds of allowable contributions" (Levinson 1979, 69)—and what can they legitimately say or write when taking part? Finally, the CDS researcher would go back to the broader social context to see how it can account for, and is reinforced by, exclusion at the micro-level.

These three levels of CDS are represented in Figure 3.1 (adapted from Fairclough 2010, 133; see also Koller 2014, 153). This model lends itself to a bottom-up analysis proceeding from the description of the text to an explanation of the textual findings by analysing the meso- and macro-level contexts. Because language and society are seen as constituting each other via discourse, a full-fledged analysis then returns to the text level to discuss how its text producers are not only influenced by contexts, but influence them in turn, constructing, reinforcing, negotiating and challenging social relations and identities through the use of language and conversational behaviour.

Before progressing to notions of critique, it seems appropriate to briefly explain the terms "linguistic devices", "discourse features", "discourse functions" and "discourse goals" from Figure 3.1. These relate to a model of discourse analysis, first introduced in Koller (2014), that can be applied both bottom-up and top-down (Table 3.1). Discourse goals at the context level—roughly equivalent to the meso-level in Figure 3.1—refer to the overall aim that the discourse producer pursues by using language as a social practice and are realized by discourse functions, which are effects of language use. For example, one way to realize the goal to persuade an audience is positive evaluation of the self. Discourse functions are in turn realized by discourse features, which take the form of particular linguistic or conversational devices. In the example, evaluation can be an effect of attribution, which can take the form of adjectives. The sample sentence at the bottom of Table 3.1 highlights the linguistic device in question.

Needless to say, language use rarely happens in individual sentences, nor is it always written. In actual texts, various linguistic devices and discourse features accumulate, meeting similar or indeed different functions. Also, spoken interaction comprises both linguistic and conversational devices; disagreeing with someone's negative assessment of what one is or does, for example, can also feed into the discourse goal of persuasion.

No matter which model is chosen for analysis, we have seen above that description and explanation alone do not make for a CDS study; for that, we need to bring in critique and

Table 3.1 A four-level model for analysing discourse

Context	Discourse goal	e.g. persuasion
Text	Discourse function	e.g. evaluation
	Discourse feature	e.g. attribution
	Linguistic device	e.g. adjectives

Example: "We aspire to become the *best* global insurer as measured by our shareholders, customers and employees" (www.zurich.co.uk/en/about-us)

arguably engage with discourse producers, distributors and receivers with a view to changing their practices. Focusing on critique, we can distinguish five forms, again moving from text to context:

1. Immanent critique, which "aims to discover inconsistencies, (self-) contradictions, paradoxes and dilemmas in text-internal . . . structures" (Reisigl and Wodak 2015, 25).
2. Socio-diagnostic critique, which "is concerned with uncovering the—particularly latent—persuasive . . . character of discursive practices. Here, we rely on our contextual knowledge and draw on social theories . . . to interpret discursive events" (Reisigl and Wodak 2015, 25).
3. Explanatory critique, which "seeks to explain why social realities are as they are, and how they are sustained or changed." This form of critique sees the meso- and macro-levels (Figure 3.1) as constituting each other, in that it "includes both explanations of particular types and forms of discourse as effects of social causes and explanations of social phenomena . . . as partly effects of discourse" (Fairclough and Fairclough 2012, 79).
4. Normative critique, which "evaluates social realities against the standard of values taken as necessary to a 'good society' [i.e.,] one which serves and facilitates human 'well-being'". This crucially "includes critique of unequal relations of power and forms of domination which are damaging to well-being and which may be manifest in discourse" (Fairclough and Fairclough 2012, 79).
5. Prospective critique, which "seeks to improve communication" (Reisigl and Wodak 2015, 25) through engaging with discourse producers and receivers, or drawing up guidelines for language use.

The third element of the phrase "critical discourse studies" also deserves a mention. Readers may be more familiar with the older term "critical discourse analysis", which was first mentioned in the title of a pamphlet: "Critical discourse moments and critical discourse analysis" (Chilton 1988). It became popular with the first edition of Fairclough's book *Critical Discourse Analysis* ([1995] 2010) and has been used in the titles of countless publications since. However, more recently a number of scholars have argued that "studies" is a more comprehensive notion than "analysis", because the latter suggests a certain method, when CDS in fact takes an eclectic approach to methods of analysis, and "also has theoretical and applied dimensions" (www.discourses.org/projects/cda/). A journal founded in 2004 is likewise called *Critical Discourse Studies*,[2] but the best indicator of the shift in terminology is perhaps that the first two editions (2001, 2009) of Ruth Wodak and Michael Meyer's widely-used edited book were titled *Methods of Critical Discourse Analysis*, while the most recent third edition (2015) is called *Methods of Critical Discourse Studies*.

Approaches to Workplace Discourse

Macro-Level Approaches: Organizational Discourse Studies

Organizational discourse studies is a well-established field whose influence on critical management and organization studies is hard to dismiss. (See Fairhurst and Putnam 2014; Grant *et al.* 2004; Mumby and Clair 1997 for overviews and edited collections.) Indeed, discourse studies of all descriptions have become so popular in organizational studies that Alvesson and Kärreman (2011, 1142) caustically observe that "[t]he only thing that unites much discourse work is the use of the term discourse". The authors go on to state that the meaning-constituting function of discourse is often assumed rather than demonstrated and demand that researchers in organizational discourse studies "cut the concept of discourse down in size, assume less, cover less, reveal more and allow a clearer space for other approaches" (1142). Their criticism is voiced against the backdrop of scholars having adopted the distinction between "small d" discourses as text-focused analysis on the one hand and "big D" Discourses on the other. However, much work in organizational discourse studies focuses on the latter, i.e., on "socially accepted associations among ways of using language, of thinking, valuing, acting, and interacting, in the 'right' places and at the 'right' times with the 'right' objects [texts]" (Gee 2011, 34). Together, these form a recognizable pattern of meaning enacted in a characteristic way of speaking, doing, and being (Robichaud 2015, 1). Discourse thus defined is seen as shaping interactions within organizational structures or, in more radically socio-constructivist versions of the approach, as constituting organizations in the first place (Brummans *et al.* 2014) rather than representing or reflecting them. However, such discourse idealist positions have been criticized for rendering the notion of "discourse" meaningless—if everything is discourse, then the term loses its explanatory power—and for neglecting material aspects of organizations, such as labour processes and space (see Fairhurst and Putnam 2014, 281–287).

Another point of critique—and the most relevant for this chapter—is that much work in organizational discourse studies restricts itself to identifying discourses, however defined, or limits textual analysis to content, "cod[ing] interactions, develop[ing] discourse themes, or draw[ing] from conceptual analyses . . . to analyze interaction processes and texts" (Fairhurst and Putnam 2014, 277).[3] As argued above, however, a full-fledged CDS study would engage in both macro-level context analysis and micro-level linguistic analysis (Fairclough 2005, 916). This point is underscored by Mautner (2016, 21), who argues that precisely because "one needs to look beyond language in a narrow sense" it is vital that language "should [be] analyze[d] with tools sharp enough to explain what role it plays in the constitution of discourse".

Micro- and Meso-Level Approaches: Conversation Analysis and Pragmatics

While some, if not most, researchers in organizational discourse studies focus on "big D" Discourses, other work addresses "small d" discourses or the minutiae of language use in text and talk. The underlying belief is that by using language in particular ways, members of an organization create, reinforce and challenge identities, roles and relations in the workplace. Conversation analysis (CA) has proved very influential in these efforts (see e.g., Drew and Heritage 1992). Many chapters in Sarangi and Roberts' (1999) anthology also use CA, but the editors devote the final part to problematizing the (over-)reliance on spoken data and CA, especially the latter's tenet that context is exclusively the accomplishment of spoken interaction, which disregards the " 'brought along' context of ideological and metapragmatic assumptions" (Roberts and Sarangi 1999, 391). Returning to the three-level framework for CDS introduced above, we can map ideology as a contextual factor onto the macro-level of context, while meta-pragmatic assumptions about what relationships and identities are at stake in the interaction are relevant at the meso-level of discourse practice, next to expectations about genre and discourse production, distribution, and reception.

Before we proceed to explicitly critical approaches, let us look at work that combines micro- and meso-level analysis of spoken interaction, using conversation analysis as a method to answer questions about pragmatic aspects of workplace talk, such as (im)politeness, humour, and the interplay of organizational and gendered and/or cultured identities. Perhaps the most wide-ranging, but certainly one of the most prolific projects to address those issues is the ongoing

Language in the Workplace project at Victoria University of Wellington, which began in 1996 (www.victoria.ac.nz/lwp). The work that draws these strands together is of particular interest here: studies on how language use that achieves politeness and/or humour is influenced by, and creates, gendered identities (Holmes and Schnurr 2005, Schnurr 2009), or how ethnicity and the performance of leadership intersect in the workplace (Holmes, Marra, and Vine 2011). Focusing on gender, Holmes (2009) uses analytical parameters from conversation analysis along with concepts from pragmatics to show how men enact different kinds of context-dependent masculine leadership identities, notably the authoritative ("hero"), paternalistic ("father") and egalitarian ("good mate") leader. The author notes that a paternalistic leadership identity is often enacted when men talk to junior female colleagues, as in this example (discussed in Holmes 2009, 198–200; transcription slightly simplified, used with permission of Springer):[4]

```
1   Len:   um + and we would need to do a verbal for this one
2   Bel:   I'm not doing it
3   All:   [laughter]
4   Sio:   [laughs] bags not //yeah\
5   Bel:   /seriously\\ //seriously\
6   Len:   /that's a\\ separate question [laughs] that's a separate question but +
           as a general principle // + last year we established\
7   Bel:   /[laughs] I don't think it'd be appropriate for me to do it\\
8   Len:   that any existing provider that we were in danger of dropping we did a verbal
           with + to ensure that they had had every opportunity
9   Aid:   mm
10  Val:   //I think Iris needs to do it\
11  Bel:   /but it wouldn't be appropriate for me to do it\\ would it
12  Len:   eh?
13  Bel:   it wouldn't be appropriate for me to do it //would it\
14  Len:   /it may\\ well be appropriate for you to do it Belinda
15         [laughter]
16  XF:    [laughs] //oh no\
17  Bel:   /I don't think it is I can't\\ I can't you know xxx I'd be biased
18  XF:    yeah
19  Len:   I think we did a verbal for them last year actually
20  Bel:   //no they weren't in anything\
21  Len:   /no they weren't in\\ the mix
22  Bel:   I'm definitely //biased Len [laughs]\
23  Len:   /alright so they need to be they need to be\\ verbalised
24  Sio:   good way of getting there [laughs]
25  Len:   we may be we may be quite keen on your bias
26  Val:   oh no
27  Bel:   use Clive [laughs] xxx no I've had enough
28  Len:   alright
```

In this interaction, Len, the team leader, is trying to find a team member to do a verbal presentation, which Belinda, a more junior employee, refuses in an unmitigated face-threatening act (turn 2). Although she had not been given the task, she is now the focus and seeks to avoid doing the presentation by bringing forth a reason why she cannot (turns 11, 13 and 17). While she initially mitigates her statements through modal verbs and tag questions ("it wouldn't be appropriate for me to do it //would it\", turn 13), she later returns to the bluntness of her initial statement ("I'm definitely //biased Len [laughs]\", turn 22) and even issues a direct command to the team leader ("use Clive [laughs]", turn 27). Although the latter two utterances are softened by a laugh, her refusal creates potential for conflict. Len does not accept her refusal until turn 28, continuing with his point despite Belinda talking over him (turns 6–7) and diffuses the potential conflict by adopting a patient, gently humorous style (e.g., "/it may\\ well be appropriate for you to do it Belinda", turn 14). According to Holmes (2009, 200), he thereby "[e]spous[es] a paternalistic or fatherly stance" which is "another way in which male leaders may appropriately do masculinity in the workplace, while also accomplishing transactional and relational objectives."

Analyses such as the above do more than describe the micro-moments of building social order through talk, in that they additionally identify and discuss meso-level factors such as institutional and interactional roles as well as acknowledge gendered and ethnicized imbalances of power, often explicitly (e.g., Holmes 2000; Holmes and Stubbe 2003; Schnurr, Marra, and Holmes 2008; Vine 2004). The scope is wide, ranging from descriptions of how humour can function to both mitigate and enact face-threatening acts, to explanations of how politeness and impoliteness maintain or challenge the power of some institutional members and the analysis of how speech acts enact control over and between team members. In an interesting experiment, Stubbe *et al.* (2003) have drawn together multiple analyses of one workplace transcript, applying lenses from conversation analysis, interactional sociolinguistics, pragmatics (especially politeness theory), discursive psychology and critical discourse analysis (367–372). This and the work mentioned above shows how power and dominance can be reproduced or challenged in workplace talk. Yet, the focus remains on the interaction itself and its situational, institutional and cultural context, with little if any discussion of macro-level ideologies that naturalize certain structures and practices while delegitimizing others. This does not detract from the value of pragmatic studies into workplace language, but it shows that they fall outside the critical framework adopted in CDS.

Integrating the Three Levels: CDS

Previous Research

CDS workplace research is dwarfed by the conversation analytical and pragmatic research referenced in the previous section.[5] This dearth of relevant research has been noted by Bargiela-Chiappini, Nickerson, and Planken (2013, 28), who observe that

> [t]ext-based or field-based research with a "critical" label remains in its infancy in business discourse . . . many linguists involved in the analysis of business language have shied away from a critical positioning that espouses a political agenda for social change and have preferred to maintain a more neutral stance.

This is further explained by Koester (2006, 20) when she states that "taking an overtly critical stance towards the more powerful members of an organization can be problematic", not least for access to data sites.

Among the notable exceptions are Wodak's (1996) early studies on workplaces such as schools, outpatient clinics, and courtrooms. More recently Wodak (2011, 113–155) conducted a detailed ethnographic study of a workday of a Member of the European Parliament (MEP) and his personal assistant, in which she describes an array of linguistic features, conversational styles, and argumentation strategies that the MEP uses when switching between frames, context and roles. Beyond description, Wodak elaborates on how discourse practices interact with shared knowledge and the materiality of buildings to provide coherence to workplace interaction. Taking things to the macro-level, she critiques how the invisibility of politicians' backstage work leads to widespread depoliticization. Iedema (2003) similarly applies a discursive lens to understand how "post-bureaucratic organizations" such as local government departments and hospitals enact and record processes of organization, thereby producing and privileging certain meanings. He analyses spoken interactions, written genres, and built materiality to show how the aim of worker self-regulation and autonomy lead to a growing variety and volume of meta-discourse about work, the production of which increasingly constitutes work itself. Iedema argues that linguistic features such as nominalization distance employees from their work and decontextualize it, even while "'localizing' is a current and persistent feature" (155) of certain genres, such as clinical records. The author pinpoints and critiques the tension and increased workload this creates for employees at the same time as worker autonomy and self-governance are upheld as positive values.

As a final example, we can note Wodak, Kwon, and Clarke's (2011) analysis of how leaders' discursive strategies help build team consensus in two extended meetings. Their work is intended to address two perceived shortcomings of work in pragmatics (see above), namely disregarding the specific contexts in which discursive functions are enacted, and failing to differentiate between discourse functions on the one hand and the linguistic and conversational devices that express them on the other. While the authors admit to "largely bracketing off interactions with the physical context" (612), their analysis of topic structure, argumentation, linguistic, and conversational devices as well as pragmatic strategies allows them to identify five discourse functions (which they call "discursive strategies")—bonding, encouraging, directing, modulating, and (re)committing—that corporate leaders employ to build consensus. The fact that the article closes on the relevance of the research for practitioners but does not engage in any explanatory, normative or prospective critique demonstrates how easily discourse studies of workplaces can become applied rather than critical.

A Case Study: Constructing Employee Identities in Mission Statements

In an illustrative case study, I analyse the mission statements of two companies to see how employees are represented from management's point of view and thereby constructed as having particular characteristics and roles (for a more detailed analysis see Koller 2011.) Taking a critical approach, the guiding question is whether this construction feeds into and expresses a social problem, e.g., exploitative practices on part of the employer. The mission statement is interesting as a genre in this regard, because one of its aims is to define ideal identities of its employees and communicate those to them. Thus, one of the overall discourse goals of mission statements is to encourage employees to identify with the ideal identity constructed for them by senior management and to promote staff loyalty, in order to increase motivation, morale and, ultimately, productivity.

The two mission statements are from food and consumer products company Nestlé and from health insurance company Aflac.[6] At the micro-level, the two texts differ notably in how they construct identities for employees. Nestlé's mission statement focuses on the company, which is not only referred to ten times compared to four mentions of employees, but is also represented as exclusively active and often acting on staff in an impersonal, nominalized way:

"guidance to staff" instead of *we guide staff, "recruitment of the right people and ongoing training and development" instead of *we recruit the right people and continuously train and develop them. Employees, by contrast, are represented as beneficiaries of the company's actions ("value that can be sustained over the long term for . . . employees") and proclaimed values ("fairness, honesty, and a general concern for people"). Employees are also indirectly assigned obligations—along with management—when the text producers state that "the success of a corporation is a reflection of the professionalism, conduct and the responsible attitude of its management and employees." In a list of stakeholders, they rank second when the writers declare that Nestlé seeks "to create value . . . for shareholders, employees, consumers, and business partners." Overall, the text is more concerned with assuring the reader that the company acts lawfully ("legislation" and "laws" are mentioned three times in the 294-word text) and with emphasizing the importance of customers and their concerns ("consumers have a sincere and legitimate interest in the behavior, beliefs and actions of the Company . . . without its consumers the Company would not exist").

By contrast, the Aflac text includes a more balanced number of mentions of staff (ten times) and company (13 times), and both are presented as predominantly active; we find the company "tap[ping] into the diverse talents . . . of our employees", just as "every employee can contribute to AFLAC's success". The Aflac text also suggests reciprocity between the two:

> If our company takes care of its employees, the employees will take care of the business . . . Engaged employees who are given what they need to grow and succeed will ensure that the business is given what it needs to grow and succeed.

When ascribed to the company, metaphoric expressions such as *"nurturing* . . . the many voices that comprise our workforce" and "*building* our valuable workforce", construct it as a benevolent parent and careful craftsperson. By the same token, employees are constructed as the beneficiaries of the company's (i.e., senior management's) actions, as in the prepositional phrases "enriching opportunities for our employees" and "good for our employees and our business". It is probably no surprise then that the Aflac text lists employees before other stakeholders ("our workforce, our communities, our customers"). Moreover, the text makes repeated mention of employees' cognitive and emotional characteristics: thus, we find nominal references to "the diverse talents, skills, backgrounds, viewpoints and perspectives of our employees" as well as adjectival attributions ("generations of passionate employees").

On the whole, Nestlé represents employees as a means to an end with little space to impact on the company other than raise its credibility with customers, whereas Aflac constructs employees as active, trustworthy, and entitled to benevolent care. In terms of immanent critique, we can therefore identify an inherent contradiction in the Nestlé text, whose producers claim that they have "a general concern for people" and seek "to create value . . . for . . . employees", but background the same employees both quantitatively, by mentioning them notably less often than the company they belong to, and qualitatively, by representing them as mostly passive. The ideal identities created for the respective companies' employees are, in the case of Nestlé, to meet "highest standards", and to show "professionalism" and a "responsible attitude", in which they need help from management in the form of "ongoing training and development". Aflac's ideal employees, on the other hand, are constructed as talented, dedicated and passionate, "grow[ing] personally and professionally" and as engaged in a mutual relationship with their employer. I have shown above how discourse features and linguistic devices are used to achieve these constructions, but what part do discursive practices play? In Goffman's (1981) terms, mission statements usually express the viewpoint of senior management, who commission it as the principal. While there are examples of more participatory forms of text production, employee participation is typically granted by management rather than being a default feature of text production. The same restrictions to access do not apply to reception, however; both texts are distributed publically online, potentially reaching a very wide audience, although Nestlé's mission statement seems mostly aimed at customers, while Aflac's appears to address employees first and foremost. Instantiating the discourse function of persuasion, the latter text is therefore better aligned with the audience to be persuaded, while the former statement appears to be aimed at persuading customers of Nestlé's value, not least by constructing an ideal employee identity.

One explanation for why Nestlé backgrounds employees in favour of consumers is that the latter have been critical of and even boycotted the company in the wake of a number of scandals faced since the late 1970s. Given the saturated and competitive markets in which the company operates, the goodwill of consumers is certainly paramount, but it is here sought at the expense of employees, who become a means to an end, further widening the institutional imbalance of power between them and management. Aflac, while not questioning power asymmetries as such, seeks a mutual relationship between employees and management, which—according to their mission statement—allows the company to thrive and, we can infer, enhance its brand image and ultimately attract customers. Indeed, Aflac has been listed among the Fortune list of 100 best companies to work for since 1998[7] and by that measure seems to foster employee wellbeing, certainly in material but also in discursive terms. Given the various potential audiences of publically available mission statements and other corporate text types, however, a focus on one particular stakeholder group may be inadvisable and text producers might do better to dedicate individual sections of a text to different groups.

Mission statements have been the butt of many jokes for their clichéd, vacuous, and pompous language.[8] My own professional experience suggests that the process of drafting them, especially if it is participatory, is more important than the final product, which has very limited uptake. This may explain why mission statements seem to be less frequent now than they were ten years ago. In any case, linguistically and discursively including and appreciating employees will only prevent covert—or even overt—exploitation if backed up by material practices.

Promoting CDS of/in the Workplace

Given that work in CDS starts from a social problem, any critical analysis is useful in places characterized by power asymmetries. It therefore seems obvious that CDS is a helpful and necessary approach to researching language and discourse in the workplace. The challenge, however, is to get access to decision-makers in workplaces who could act on the critique of internal discourse. In many cases, the potential audience that can realistically be reached by the researcher will not extend beyond future employees, i.e., students; current employees are hard to access because of possible management resistance to critical research. Senior decision-makers can be an audience if they can be persuaded that critical research furthers their strategic aims, and access to that audience is often easier for linguists working in a consulting role, which limits the research question to the brief received by the client.

So why should the management of any company be interested in critical analyses of language use and discourse practices in the workplace? Why should they want to redress power imbalances or even exploitation? While there is no doubt that some decision-makers take account of ethical concerns, the ultimate aim of any for-profit business is just that: to make a profit so that the business can continue. If more diversity, flatter hierarchies, greater employee satisfaction, and more participatory discourse practices lead to better bottom lines, the case has been made. This is not a cynical point: blaming companies for striving to make profits is like blaming schools for striving to teach pupils—it is their *raison d'être*. The question is if and how the profit motive can be reconciled with human wellbeing. Assuming that it can—and that is a rather contentious assumption—critical analysts are left with a dilemma: the ultimate argument for their critical analysis, if it is to have an impact beyond their own peer group, is that it can help to make changes within a system that is itself the object of explanatory and normative critique. Mautner (2010, 184, note 15) is optimistic, however, affirming that "[t]he dilemma can be resolved by opting for a constructively critical approach which ... shows ... how linguistic resources can be deployed to convey courtesy, empathy and professionalism". While Mautner here refers to communications training in higher education institutions, the case can also be made for talking to corporate clients: a critical analysis of workplace discourse may not change the socio-economic system in which it is embedded, but it can effect changes in discursive practice to make them less exclusionary and more balanced, and lead to more respect and participation.

From my experience as a consultant (and a parent), communicating critical research to corporate clients can be like getting a child to eat vegetables: the greens have to be smuggled in, for example by grating a courgette into a pancake. The pancake may be fatty, but at least it includes some things that are good for you. Maybe that is how to do CDS in the workplace—to sit down with discourse participants, have a close look at their diet and suggest some healthy, holistic changes.

Further Reading

For readers wanting to find out more I recommend starting with Deetz and McClellan (2009) and Mautner (2016).

Related Topics

Conversation analysis; (Im)politeness theory; Corporate settings; Humour; Gender; Enabling women leaders

Notes

1   The case can be made that the phrase "work context" is more appropriate than "workplace": not only is what counts as work a subjective perception, but work is increasingly disconnected from specific places. (Mark Read, personal communication, 11 January 2017).
2   www.tandfonline.com/toc/rcds20/current.
3   Iedema (2003, 22) distinguishes between macro-level organizational discourse studies and more linguistically oriented organizational discourse analysis. However, given the point made earlier about reductionist understandings of the word "analysis", it does not seem advisable to take up his distinction.
4   Transcription key:
[laughs] Paralinguistic features and other information
+ Pause of up to one second
... // ... \ ... Simultaneous speech
xxx Unclear utterance
? Rising or question intonation
XF unidentified female speaker
5   While it can be argued that Baxter's work on gender and leadership in corporations (see e.g., 2010; this volume) falls within the remit of CDS, she herself rejects the label CDA/CDS and positions her work in the more discourse idealist field of feminist post-structuralist discourse analysis.

6   The texts are available at www.nestle.com.eg/en/aboutus/allaboutnestle and http://hartford.jobing.com/aflac-insurance (paragraphs 2–6).
7   http://fortune.com/best-companies/aflac-50/.
8   See for example the "mission statement generator" at www.jonhaworth.com/toys/mission-statement-generator, where employees are sarcastically referred to as "peasants".

References

Alvesson, Mats, and Dan Kärreman. 2011. "Decolonializing Discourse: Critical Reflections on Organizational Discourse Analysis." *Human Relations* 64: 1121–1146.
Bargiela-Chiappini, Francesca, Catherine Nickerson, and Brigitte Planken. 2013. *Business Discourse*. 2nd ed. Basingstoke, UK: Palgrave.
Baxter, Judith. 2010. *The Language of Female Leadership*. Basingstoke, UK: Palgrave.
Brummans, Boris H.J.M., François Cooren, Daniel Robichaud, and James R. Taylor. 2014. "Approaches to the Communicative Constitution of Organizations." In *The Sage Handbook of Organizational Communication: Advances in Theory, Research, and Methods*. 3rd ed., edited by Linda Putnam, and Dennis K. Mumby, 173–194. Thousand Oaks, CA: Sage.
Chilton, Paul A. 1988. *Critical Discourse Moments and Critical Discourse Analysis: Towards A Methodology*. San Diego, CA: University of California Institute on Global Conflict and Cooperation.
Deetz, Stanley, and John G. McClellan. 2009. "Critical Studies." In *Handbook of Business Discourse*, edited by Francesca Bargiela-Chiappini, 119–131. Edinburgh: Edinburgh University Press.
Drew, Paul, and John Heritage, Eds. 1992. *Talk at Work: Interaction in Institutional Settings*. Cambridge: Cambridge University Press.
Fairclough, Norman. 2005. "Discourse Analysis in Organization Studies: The Case for Critical Realism." *Organization Studies* 26: 915–939.
Fairclough, Norman. 2010. *Critical Discourse Analysis: The Critical Study of Language*. 2nd ed. Harlow, UK: Longman.
Fairclough, Norman. 2015. *Language and Power*. 3rd ed. Abingdon, UK: Routledge.
Fairclough, Isabela, and Norman Fairclough. 2012. *Political Discourse Analysis: A Method for Advanced Students*. Abingdon, UK: Routledge.
Fairclough, Norman, Jane Mulderrig, and Ruth Wodak. 2011. "Critical Discourse Analysis." In *Discourse Studies: A Multidisciplinary Introduction*. 2nd ed., edited by Teun A. van Dijk, 357–378. London: Sage.
Fairhurst, Gail, and Linda Putnam. 2014. "Organizational discourse analysis." In *The Sage Handbook of Organizational Communication: Advances in Theory, Research, and Methods*. 3rd ed., edited by Linda Putnam, and Dennis K. Mumby, 271–295.Thousand Oaks, CA: Sage.
Gee, James P. 2011. *An Introduction to Discourse Analysis: Theory and Method*. 3rd ed. Oxford: Routledge.
Goffman, Erving. 1981. *Forms of Talk*. Philadelphia, PA: University of Pennsylvania Press.
Grant, David, Cynthia Hardy, Clive Oswick, and Linda Putnam, Eds. 2004. *The Sage Handbook of Organizational Discourse*. London: Sage.
Holmes, Janet. 2000. "Politeness, Power and Provocation: How Humour Functions in the Workplace." *Discourse Studies* 2: 159–185.
Holmes, Janet. 2009. "Men, Masculinities and Leadership: Different Discourse Styles at Work." In *Gender and Spoken Interaction*, edited by Pia Pichler, and Eva Eppler, 186–210. Basingstoke, UK: Palgrave.
Holmes, Janet, and Stephanie Schnurr. 2005. "Politeness, Humor and Gender in the Workplace: Negotiating Norms and Identifying Contestation." *Journal of Politeness Research* 1: 121–149.
Holmes, Janet and Maria Stubbe. 2003. *Power and Politeness in the Workplace: A Sociolinguistic Analysis of Talk at Work*. London: Longman.
Holmes, Janet, Meredith Marra, and Bernadette Vine. 2011. *Leadership, Discourse and Ethnicity*. Oxford: Oxford University Press.
Iedema, Rick. 2003. *Discourses of Post-Bureaucratic Organization*. Amsterdam: Benjamins.
Koester, Almut. 2006. *Investigating Workplace Discourse*. London: Routledge.
Koller, Veronika. 2011. "'Hard-working, Team-oriented Individuals': Constructing Professional Identities in Corporate Mission Statements." In *Constructing Identities at Work*, edited by Jo Angouri, and Meredith Marra, 103–126. Basingstoke, UK: Palgrave.

Koller, Veronika. 2014. "Applying Social Cognition Research to Critical Discourse Studies: The Case of Collective Identities." In *Contemporary Critical Discourse Studies*, edited by Christopher Hart, and Piotr Cap, 147–165. London: Bloomsbury.

Levinson, Stephen. 1979. "Activity Types and Language." *Linguistics* 17: 365–400.

Mautner, Gerlinde. 2010. *Language and the Market Society: Critical Reflections on Discourse and Dominance*. New York: Routledge.

Mautner, Gerlinde 2016. *Discourse and Management: Critical Perspectives Through the Language Lens*. Basingstoke, UK: Palgrave.

Mumby, Dennis K., and Robin P. Clair. 1997. "Organizational Discourse." *Discourse as Social Interaction* 2: 181–205.

Murphy, Anne. 2015. "'So Have We Heard from Everybody?' A Pragmatic Analysis of Inclusion and Exclusion in International Conference Calls." Paper presented at the regional conference of the International Communication Association, Copenhagen/Denmark, October 11–13.

Reisigl, Martin, and Ruth Wodak. 2015. "The Discourse-Historical Approach (DHA)." In *Methods of Critical Discourse Studies*. 3rd ed., edited by Ruth Wodak, and Michael Meyer, 23–61. London: Sage.

Roberts, Celia, and Srikant Sarangi. 1999. "Introduction: Revisiting Different Analytical Frameworks." In *Talk, Work, and Institutional Order*, edited by Srikant Sarangi, and Celia Roberts, 389–400. Berlin: Walter de Gruyter.

Robichaud, Daniel. 2015. "Organizational Discourse Studies." In *The International Encyclopedia of Language and Social Interaction* 107. Available at http://onlinelibrary.wiley.com/doi/10.1002/9781118611463.wbielsi162/full, accessed 20 December 2016.

Sarangi, Srikant, and Celia Roberts, Eds. 1999. *Talk, Work, and Institutional Order: Discourse in Medical, Mediation, and Management Settings*. Berlin: Walter de Gruyter.

Schnurr, Stephanie. 2009. *Leadership Discourse at Work: Interactions of Humour, Gender and Workplace Culture*. Basingstoke, UK: Palgrave.

Schnurr, Stephanie, Meredith Marra, and Janet Holmes. 2008. "Impoliteness as a Means of Contesting and Challenging Power Relations in the Workplace." In *Impoliteness in Language*, edited by Derek Bousfield, and Miriam Locher, 211–230. Berlin: Mouton de Gruyter.

Stubbe, Maria, Chris Lane, Jo Hilder, Elaine Vine, Bernadette Vine, Meredith Marra, Janet Holmes, and Ann Weatherall. 2003. "Multiple Discourse Analyses of a Workplace Interaction." *Discourse Studies* 5: 351–388.

Vine, Bernadette. 2004. *Getting Things Done at Work: The Discourse of Power in Workplace Interaction*. Amsterdam: Benjamins.

Wodak, Ruth. 1996. *Disorders of Discourse*. London: Longman.

Wodak, Ruth. 2011. *The Discourse of Politics in Action: Politics as Usual*. Basingstoke, UK: Palgrave.

Wodak, Ruth and Michael Meyer. 2015. *Methods of Critical Discourse Studies*. 3rd edn. London: Sage.

Wodak, Ruth, Winston Kwon, and Ian Clarke. 2011. "'Getting People on Board': Discursive Leadership for Consensus Building in Team Meetings." *Discourse & Society* 22: 592–644.

4
Linguistic Ethnography
Nick Wilson

Introduction

Rampton (2007a) describes linguistic ethnography (LE) as an umbrella term for a collection of approaches to the study of language that espouse an ethnographic methodology. However the scope of this is contestable and it has been the subject of much discussion as to where the lines may be drawn between LE and other similar approaches (Hammersley 2007; Blommaert 2007). This chapter discusses what might "count" as LE by examining the development of the ethnographic paradigm in linguistics, from its origins in Anthropological Linguistics, through the seminal work of Gumperz and Hymes (1972) on the Ethnography of Communication and the development of Interactional Sociolinguistics (IS), to more recent uses of LE in workplace research.

As will be seen, LE describes a wide-ranging approach to research that does not specify any one particular form of analysis and which draws heavily upon its anthropological roots. The experience of the researcher is a key part of the ontology of LE, thus according reflexive field notes a role as a data source, and encouraging researchers to examine their own journey in gaining understanding of a research site. Moreover, LE approaches view language as part of the social world; language is not a separate entity, but is closely bound up with context and identity. In essence LE provides a discovery-led framework, compatible with a grounded approach to theory building that allows a researcher to use whatever forms of linguistic analysis are pertinent to the phenomena observed in the field (Charmaz and Mitchell 2001).

Historical Perspectives

LE is recognized by most scholars as being grounded in Dell Hymes' seminal work on the Ethnography of Speaking (later Ethnography of Communication) (Hymes 1972). It was in this work that the context of a speech event was recognized as being crucial for the analysis of how interlocutors communicate and understand social meaning. However, Hymes' work was informed by his earlier research and training as a linguistic anthropologist: a discipline which could be understood as being as much, if not more, a sub-discipline of anthropology as it is of linguistics, and we can thus trace the antecedents of LE to much earlier anthropological work such as Malinowski's (1972) concept of Phatic Communion, based on his fieldwork in the Trobriand Islands (Malinowski 1922). Indeed, the term linguistic ethnography has been used by anthropologists to describe their work since the 19th century. Brinton (1898) describes his research that compares South American languages as "a linguistic ethnography of the Chaco region", demonstrating that the current meaning of the label (as used in sociolinguistics and applied linguistics) has shifted somewhat from its anthropological origin. In fact, we can see the term used as far back as 1850 to describe the process of documenting the languages of the world and their relationships (Donaldson 1850).

Moreover, anthropology espouses similar epistemological and ontological stances, and shares with LE a concern with "being there" and the process of reflexivity that is crucial to ethnographic research. Nonetheless, linguistic anthropology is primarily concerned with linguistic description and the construction of detailed accounts of languages. What distinguished Hymes' (1972, 1977) work is that he became interested not just in describing the grammar of languages, but also in how they functioned in relation to their local context. Hymes saw that understanding was conditional upon the context of an utterance, and the Ethnography of Speaking was devised in order to provide a systematic description of a speech event that would enable an analysis of language in context.

While the use of ethnographic methodology is undoubtedly rooted in anthropology, we should not overlook the other early influences on LE. In particular, the work of Erving Goffman can be considered to be highly influential in respect of his focus on ritual and the interaction order. Goffman even took an ethnographic approach to his early fieldwork which took place in a psychiatric institution and examined the social situation of the patients (Goffman 1961). In fact, Goffman was as concerned with the representation of a disempowered section of society as many present-day linguistic ethnographers are. He notes that:

> [t]o describe the patient's situation faithfully is necessarily to present a partisan view. (For this last bias I excuse myself by arguing that the imbalance is at least on the right side of the scale, since almost all professional literature on mental patients is written from the point of view of the psychiatrist and he, socially speaking, is on the other side.)
> (Goffman 1961, xviii)

Moreover, Goffman's concern with institutions and the interactions that take place therein is highly relevant to the study of Language in the Workplace and his work should be considered as foundational to not only LE, but to the study of Language in the Workplace in general.

Returning to Hymes, and the application of ethnography to the linguistic description of interaction (beyond the more broadly interactional approach of Goffman), we can see how LE and IS could be said to have developed hand in hand. This is of course very clear in the collaborative achievement of Gumperz and Hymes (1972) in effectively founding the discipline of IS, which (as discussed below and in Gordon and Kraut this volume) is an invaluable approach in the study of Language in the Workplace.

In the 21st century the term LE has come to describe an approach that started as a cluster of researchers in the UK from sociolinguistic and applied linguistic backgrounds, who valued an ethnographic approach. It has been most vociferously described by this group, identifying themselves as the UK Linguistic Ethnography Forum (Rampton *et al.* 2004), with much of the work of defining LE as a field stemming from Ben Rampton and Angela Creese. However, Rampton and Creese say that their definitions of LE are not meant to be constraining and LE is described as an "umbrella term" for a range of different types of research that share some of their aims and methods (Rampton 2007b). This could be seen in much the same way as Critical Discourse Analysis (CDA) is an umbrella term for research on discourse that is concerned with uncovering inequalities and investigating power. Unlike CDA however, under which a wide range of methodologies are employed, LE is somewhat more focused in that it always involves ethnography. Since its redefinition as a label for a specific form of linguistic research, LE has rapidly developed in terms of popularity. For example, there were 52 peer reviewed journal articles published in 2015 with LE in the title or abstract, not to mention a forthcoming handbook of LE (Tusting forthcoming) and numerous chapters appearing in a range of handbooks and textbooks on a variety of applications. There have been special issues on LE by the *Journal of Sociolinguistics* (2007) and *Text & Talk* (2010), all of which has served to establish LE as a way of carrying out research that has a shared set of values and a flexible methodological toolkit. Many of the existing works from the past 10 years that discuss LE describe it as being in its "infancy", however, given the burgeoning interest shown and the growing amount of research that claims an LE identity, perhaps we should see it as a research tradition that is now coming of age.

Critical Issues and Topics

Boundaries and Overlaps with Other Frameworks

A frequently discussed issue in LE is the concern with establishing it as an area of study that is distinct from Linguistic Anthropology. This is addressed by Copland and Creese (2015, 23), who argue that LE is a description for a "British and European" forum for research that shares objectives and methodology and centres around the importance of multiple forms of data and an ethnographically acquired insight into the lives of research participants. In this regard, similar work carried out in North America tends to fall within the scope of Linguistic Anthropology. Indeed, the antecedents in terms of theory and methodology are similar (if not identical) for both. Copland and Creese (2015) refer to six key "meta-theorists" who have inspired the development of LE, namely Hymes, Gumperz, Goffman, Erickson, Agha, and Silverstein. Yet all of these scholars are just as important for Linguistic Anthropology, and most are also considered as core figures in IS. An issue here is that due to the focus on the origins of LE as a conglomeration of researchers based in the UK, much of the scholarship places a decidedly European (if not British) limit on the boundaries of LE. This raises the question of where research carried out in other parts of the world might fit. For example, there are many examples of research that are described as LE in New Zealand (Wilson 2013; King 2014), Australia (Stephens and Neill 2011), South Africa (Van Herreweghe and Vermeerbergen 2010) and China (Pérez-Milans 2011) to name but a few. While other workplace research might not always explicitly style itself as LE (e.g., Holmes, Marra, and Vine 2011), it could be considered as such given the growing use of the label to describe a specific approach to research. In other words, as researchers, we should try to get past the desire to place geographical limits on the approaches we take and look beyond borders for research that encompasses similar values.

Another issue is the relationship between LE and IS, as it can be difficult to distinguish why some research might be described as IS rather than LE (or vice versa). One way to understand it is that LE encompasses IS; indeed Rampton (2007a, 4) describes IS as a "branch of linguistic ethnography". However, this may be seen as problematic given that IS was established much earlier as a linguistic field of study that values context, yet focuses on micro-interactions. Indeed the links and influences between IS and CA, and the micro-analysis of interaction can downplay the ethnographic focus of IS in comparison to LE, yet there is undoubted crossover (Bailey 2015; Gordon 2010). Therefore, it may be better to view LE and

IS as intersecting paradigms, in much the same way as we can view sociolinguistics and pragmatics as intersecting in some areas, such as politeness (Holmes 2015). The same could be said about the relationship between LE and Applied Linguistics (although some researchers may position LE as entirely within Applied Linguistics). We therefore move away from LE being an "umbrella term" (Rampton 2007b; Rampton *et al.* 2004; Stephens and Neill 2011; Creese 2008) and closer to an interdisciplinary forum (Copland and Creese 2015, 27).

Yet much of the value of LE lies in its versatility and that it can be regarded as an eclectic toolbox of methods (Rampton 2007b). Stephens and Neill (2011, 229) make clear the utility of LE's versatility:

> The advantage of adopting the umbrella term is that one's research does not have to stumble over the boundaries erected between the component disciplines. Suddenly it becomes acceptable to build on a Hallidayan monolithic base, but to decorate with CA and practice theory. One can also work from an ethnographic or autoethnographic approach.

From what has been said in this section thus far, it may be thought that LE is rather ill-defined, despite the numerous papers that have sought to do just that. This is perhaps due to the inter-disciplinary nature of LE: this requires an overlap and makes it difficult to draw boundaries between LE and other approaches. What we can try to do is nail down a set of criteria that describe LE research. If we aim to describe a field of research rather than try to trace its theoretical development and disciplinary antecedents as has been done thus far, we can get some way towards a more definitive framework. In what follows, these criteria are described in terms of "aims", "method", and "impact".

Aims of LE Research

The central aim of research that takes an LE approach is to understand language use and social meaning in context. However, what might be said to particularly characterize LE is that it seeks to reconcile participants' *emic* understandings of their linguistic experience with analysts' *etic* understandings (Gee 2005; Tusting and Maybin 2007). It is this aim that leads to the use of ethnography, and to the centrality of the participants in the design, execution, and analysis phases of the research. This may be realized by methods such as the playback of recording to participants in order to access their understanding of interactions (Rampton 2006). In this regard it overlaps with many other paradigms (as noted above), such as sociolinguistics, discourse analysis, and applied linguistics. That the scholars who use LE also tend towards one or more of these disciplinary affiliations shows the interdisciplinary appeal of the approach.

Method in LE Research

One of the distinguishing features of LE is that it usually involves a multiplicity of data types. It is through the analysis of the connections between these data that a linguistic ethnographer attempts to uncover the meaning of contextualized discourse. The data does not have to be interactional in nature (unlike IS), it can be textual, narrative or focus on practices of discourse production, such as journalism (Macgilchrist and Van Hout 2011; Van Hout and Macgilchrist 2010). What is important is that it is contextualized through some form of ethnographic observation, either in person or online. The extent of such observation has been the focus of discussion among linguistic ethnographers, with some saying that it is enough to carry out regular participant observations in a research site, while others believe that the researcher has to acquire "lived experience" in order to fully understand language in use from a participant's-eye view. Regardless of which position is taken, reflexivity is a crucial aspect of LE: a researcher needs to document and analyse not only what they see and hear, but also what they think when in the field and these fieldnotes are considered as valuable a source of data as whatever form of linguistic data has been collected.

Impact of LE Research

Impact has been invested with a certain meaning in a UK context that it may not have elsewhere, which refers to the way in which a piece of research has "an effect on, change or benefit to the economy, society, culture, public policy or services, health, the environment or quality of life, beyond academia" (Higher Education Funding Council for England 2015). This differs somewhat from "engagement" which is concerned with the effect a piece of research has on the lives of the (non-academic) people directly involved with it. Here, *impact* is used to encompass both of these ideas, in other words, it means that a piece of research is concerned with having a (positive) real-world effect on the participants' lives and/or that it can bring about some wider benefits in societal terms.

Current Contributions and Research

In their broad description of LE, Rampton *et al.* (2004) only refer to workplace research in relation to ethnicity, language, and inequality. I would argue that the scope of LE in terms of workplace research is much wider, and refer back to the defining criteria of LE posited above. In other words, any research that uses ethnographic methodology, focuses on authentic data pertaining to language in use, and gives something back to participants, should be considered as LE, and this widens the scope to a large amount of research on language in the workplace. In particular, rather than just focusing on ethnicity, we can also examine power inequalities evident in workplace interaction more generally, whether they relate to differences in terms of cultural background, gender, age, or some more local dimension of power such as institutional status. Crucially however, much of the recent work on Language in the Workplace is concerned with the nexus of several of these (e.g., Holmes, Marra, and Vine 2011).

Due to the expansive outlook stated above and the space constraint of a single chapter, it is not possible to review all of the Linguistic Ethnographic work being carried out on Language in the Workplace here; instead I shall briefly examine two foci of workplace research and how these relate to the broad definition of LE that is presented in this chapter.

Leadership

A topic that has attracted much interest within the field of Language in the Workplace is leadership discourse. Leadership discourse can be studied from a variety of perspectives, and with a variety of methodologies, but much of the work on leadership can be described as following a LE approach, even if it might not always explicitly identify as such. One of the issues in carrying out LE research on leadership is in addressing the impact and empowerment value of the research. One way to do this is to examine leadership interculturally and cross-culturally as Holmes, Vine, and Marra (2009) do, with the aim of addressing cultural differences in leadership discourse and potentially resolving areas of miscommunication when analysis is fed back to participants. Holmes, Vine, and Marra (2009) take a comparative approach in their research, discussing several workplaces in terms of how workplace culture intersects with wider cultural and societal norms of leadership in interaction. By collecting ethnographic data about each workplace, as well as conducting interviews with participants and recording leadership events such as meetings, Holmes, Vine, and Marra (2009) have developed a methodology and approach to leadership research (and workplace research more generally) that certainly embodies the principles of LE, even if they do not explicitly identify it as such. The analysis of leadership discourse and the approach taken by researchers in this area of workplace study are explored in depth in Schnurr (this volume).

Spaces for Learning

Similar to the development of individual leadership practices is the transmission of workplace practices from colleague to colleague in the course of everyday workplace interaction. An example of such research is that carried out by Rock (2005), who analysed the way in which police officers talked to each other about the discursive practices they used in interviews with witnesses and suspects. She found, through an ethnographic approach, that these informal conversations between officers were a key zone of interaction for the transmission of knowledge and the negotiation of local practices. Rock's work in this area can also be seen from a frontstage/backstage perspective (Goffman 1959) with much of the negotiation of practice being carried out in the informal discursive space of the workplace before an actual core activity takes place, in this case interaction with suspects. Only an ethnographic approach to research can fully capture these frontstage/backstage distinctions and identify the local realization of them in terms of the discursive spaces that are constructed (Wilson 2013).

Although such learning often takes place in the backstage, it is not always as explicit as a focus on what colleagues are doing or intend to do (Wilson 2013; Rock 2005). Often the learning that takes place in the backstage is about where a person fits within an organization, and it is also here that they can negotiate their role through a range of relational interactions. Richards (2010) has researched the use of humour among teaching colleagues in staff room situations, showing how this enables the development of collegial practices and shared identity. This finding is mirrored in research carried out by Vaughan (2007), who discusses how teachers bond over shared complaints and humour.

Main Research Methods

Fieldnotes

Essentially, the central methodology of LE is to be methodologically flexible: to collect as many forms of data as possible in order to understand the rich complexity of institutional/workplace language and how it relates to identity, power, and linguistic/discursive practices. This means that a linguistic ethnographer needs to be open to trying out new methodologies as the need arises. They may need to conduct interviews, run focus groups, collect texts, or record conversations. What all linguistic ethnographers do, however, is take field notes. Copland and Creese (2015) stress the importance of this, while pointing out that the work carried out by the researcher in taking detailed fieldnotes rarely appears in the presentation of research. Yet taking fieldnotes remains a key practice in carrying out LE, not just to document the phenomena observed by a workplace researcher, but also to record the researcher's own thoughts and experiences throughout the research process. This is a key tool when conducting later analysis as the change in understanding over the course of an ethnography can be a useful tool for understanding the perspective of a member of the workplace that one is researching. This is highly compatible with the concept of Communities of Practice, as discussed in King (this volume). This is because a key component of the communities of practice model, as it was formulated in respect to a social system of learning, focuses on the trajectory a new member of a community takes as they are socialized into the repertoire of practices that a community uses to perform its core function. Ethnography, and the development of understanding through extended participation, mirrors (or in fact *is*) this process.

Recording "Real" Interaction

In researching how people use language in the workplace, we often have to overcome the problem of how to record interactional data without compromising ecological validity. With the use of ethnographic methods by sociolinguists this can be seen as less of a problem, however the question of the influence of the presence of a recording device on participants is still important (Gordon 2013). It is important too to recognise that the very act of being involved in research changes what is observed, no matter how much we might try to minimise this (Griffin 2007). In other words, unless we are to engage in surreptitious recording (which is unethical, and in many places illegal), the only way to gain truly authentic interactional data is to either be a "native" to begin with, or to be so deeply embedded in an organization through sustained ethnographic fieldwork that one has been accepted as a part of the organization.

There are two main ways in which this can be achieved:

1   Interactional recording with ethnographer present as participant observer
2   Interactional recording by a participant with post-recording de-briefing

The first of these is where the ethnographer plays a direct role in the process of gathering data. As with other forms of ethnography, the participant observer may start out as either participant or observer (Agar 1996). This strategy accounts for the proliferation of studies of academic/educational contexts in LE (e.g., Péres-Milans 2011; Vaughan 2007; Richards 2006). One can easily apply one's ethnographic perspective to one's own workplace. Indeed, this is useful in itself in terms of reflective practice, but may also be used alongside recording to examine routine workplace interactions and critique existing practices for the benefit of some or all of the members of a workplace.

An example of this can be found in Dickinson's (2010a, 2010b) research on sign language interpreters (SLIs) which aimed to investigate the influence of an SLI on the interaction between an employer and a deaf employee. Her research involved collecting four main types of data: a questionnaire-based survey of SLIs' experiences of workplace interpreting along with practitioner journals, video recordings of interpreted workplace interactions, and video playback interviews with the main participants (Dickinson 2010a, 107). Dickinson used her experience and status as an SLI to gain access to the organization in which she carried out the research, and to the professional community of SLIs that were both participants in the research and key stakeholders in the findings. Dickinson's research could be considered an archetypal example of workplace LE, since it clearly employs multiple data sources, centralizes the importance of linguistic data, and contributes to the research that informs the professional development of SLIs and the way in which deaf people experience workplaces.

In contrast to this is a participant-based approach: where a member of an organization records their daily interactions and passes these on to the researcher. One advantage of this is that it provides the most authentic data possible (setting aside the potential influence of the known presence of a recording device). The main disadvantage is that the researcher does not "live" the experience and so the reflexive process fundamental to ethnography is missing. However, this approach is usually supplemented by interviews with the participant who recorded the data, and it could be argued that these are ethnographic interviews. Additionally, researchers undertaking this approach will often carry out ethnographic observation of a workplace prior to any recording taking place (Holmes, Marra, and Vine 2011). This is done in part to gain knowledge of the workplace norms, but also to recruit informants and to liaise with the organization so that the aims of the research are supportive of the needs of the organization. This approach has been used extensively by the Language in the Workplace Project (Holmes 2000) and although this research has not been labelled as LE, it certainly could be, based on the criteria of aims, methods and impact outlined above. Indeed, this approach is very similar to that of Rampton (2006), who recorded adolescents during their everyday interactions at school, often when he was not present. He then conducted debriefing sessions where he would listen to the recording with the students and ask them to give their views on what the recorded interaction meant to them. In this way, the students were a part of the data collection and analysis, and were able to shape the direction of the research through their input.

Ethnography of Textual Creation

The above discussion has focused on spoken interactional data, and this is one significant way in which LE can be used in the workplace. However, there are a vast number and variety of texts created in the daily activity of any organization, and these are also an important source of data for Linguistic Ethnographers. Texts might include posters and other institutional signage. For example, Milani (2013) discusses the role played by such texts in constructing a university campus as an anti-homophobic space, and discusses how the use of such texts could be used as a strategy for effecting change in an institution's spatial identity.

Within many workplaces email is a vital source of communication and may be one of the most important ways in which language is used for many employees. Research on workplace email communication is scarce, particularly that which takes an ethnographic approach in order to understand the workplace norms behind the creation of emails. One example is Yeoh (2014), who analysed the speech acts used in emails between colleagues in workplaces in New Zealand and Malaysia. She employed participant observation of these workplaces, alongside questionnaires and interviews in order to understand the local meaning behind the email practices. This mixture of methods is exactly the sort of approach taken in LE and although Yeoh does not refer to her work as LE, it could easily be described as such.

Another way in which text might be the focus of a workplace is in journalistic workplaces. Van Hout and Macgilchrist (2010) use LE as a way of uncovering and analysing the discursive construction of the process of writing an article from the perspective of a journalist, conducting their ethnography in the newsroom. They make the point that since newspaper articles are often the subject of CDA on the basis of the power they wield in shaping ideology, it is useful to examine the processes behind the production of the article, and by using LE they are able to examine the relationship between the texts and interactions that a reporter engages in in the process of producing a finished article. With this knowledge, we can gain a very different perspective than simply from analysing the finished product.

A further way in which workplace texts can be researched using LE highlights the wide range of data that can be used and how a wide-ranging and dynamic approach can be useful in uncovering local practices and challenging assumptions about texts produced in and by organizations. Woydack and Rampton (2015) use LE as a way of investigating how scripts used by operatives in call-centres are created. They compare the "master script" that workers are given with their actual calls, and analyse the differences. This is then cross-analysed with interviews with the workers and fieldnotes, building a rich picture of the workplace. They state that "call centre research has substantially over-simplified the relationship between workers and scripts" (Woydack and Rampton 2015, 4), and challenge the assumption that in this context a large amount of work-based discourse is completely constrained by organizations.

Conclusion

LE can be used for a wide range of applications in workplace research, including research on leadership (Holmes *et al.* 2003) and the communication of workplace practices (Rock 2005), as well as a range of sociolinguistic phenomena that are best studied through the collection of contextualized authentic interactions and written materials. What unites these applications of LE is their concern with ecological validity, their focus on authentic interactional data, and the idea that the research should be "useful" beyond its theoretical contribution to linguistics.

The Linguistic Ethnographer's toolkit is varied, dynamic, and can be constantly added to. It employs a multiplicity of data sources and can focus on a variety of linguistic phenomena. LE can therefore be used as a way to build a relationship with an organization and establish what is useful and interesting, to you the researcher, to the organization and to the employees. As stated above, it is crucial that not only are findings communicated back to the organization, but that organizations are involved with the design of the research. If this recommendation is adhered to then not only will it result in a rich source of linguistic data, but the research can have impact, a particularly important consideration in workplace research given the need to engage with the organization with which the research is conducted.

Further Reading

For an excellent guide through the myriad ways of collecting and organizing data, Copland and Creese (2015) is one of the most up-to-date introductions to the field of LE, although it understandably takes a predominantly British focus. For a more international discussion it is worth looking at the special issue of *Text & Talk* (2010) on LE, which contains a combination of research articles and more theoretical discussions of the topic.

Related Topics

Interactional sociolinguistics; Communities of practice; Leadership

Acknowledgement

In preparing this chapter I am grateful for the useful and constructive comments provided by Bernadette Vine and the two anonymous reviewers as well as discussions with Janet Holmes, Frances Rock, and the Linguistic Ethnography Discussion Group at Cardiff University.

References

Agar, Michael. 1996. *The Professional Stranger: An Informal Introduction to Ethnography*. 2nd ed. San Diego, CA: Academic Press.

Bailey, Benjamin. 2015. "Interactional Sociolinguistics." In *The International Encyclopedia of Language and Social Interaction*, edited by Karen Tracy, 826–840. New York: John Wiley & Sons.

Blommaert, Jan. 2007. "On Scope and Depth in Linguistic Ethnography." *Journal of Sociolinguistics* 11: 682–688.

Brinton, Daniel G. 1898. "The Linguistic Cartography of the Chaco Region." *Proceedings of the American Philosophical Society* 37: 178–205.

Charmaz, Kathy, and Richard G. Mitchell. 2001. "Grounded Theory in Ethnography." In *Handbook of Ethnography*, edited by Paul Atkinson, Amanda Coffey, Sara Delamont, John Lofland, and Lyn Lofland, 160–174. London: Sage.

Copland, Fiona, and Angela Creese. 2015. *Linguistic Ethnography: Collecting, Analysing and Presenting Data*. London: Sage.

Creese, Angela. 2008. "Linguistic Ethnography." In *Research Methods in Language and Education*. Vol. 10 of *Encyclopedia of Language and Education*. 2nd ed., edited by Kendall A. King, and Nancy H. Hornberger, 229–241. New York: Springer.

Dickinson, Jules. 2010a. "Access All Areas: Identity Issues and Researcher Responsibilities in Workplace Settings." *Text & Talk* 30: 105–124.

Dickinson, Jules. 2010b. "Interpreting in a Community of Practice: A Sociolinguistic Study of the Signed Language Interpreter's Role in Workplace Discourse." PhD diss., Heriot-Watt University.

Donaldson, John William. 1850. *The New Cratylus: Or, Contributions Towards a More Accurate Knowledge of the Greek Language*. London: John W. Parker.

Gee, James Paul. 2005. "Meaning Making, Communities of Practice, and Analytical Toolkits." *Journal of Sociolinguistics* 9: 590–594.

Goffman, Erving. 1959. *The Presentation of Self in Everyday Life*. Harmondsworth, UK: Penguin.

Goffman, Erving. 1961. *Asylums: Essays on the Social Situation of Mental Patients and Other Inmates*. New York: Doubleday.

Gordon, Cynthia. 2010. "Gumperz and Interactional Sociolinguistics." In *SAGE Handbook of Sociolinguistics*, edited by Ruth Wodak, Barbara Johnstone, and Paul Kerswill, 67–84. London: Sage.

Gordon, Cynthia. 2013. "Beyond the Observer's Paradox: The Audio-Recorder as a Resource for the Display of Identity." *Qualitative Research* 13: 299–317.

Griffin, Christine. 2007. "Being Dead and Being There: Research Interviews, Sharing Hand Cream, and the Preference for Analyzing "Naturally Occurring Data'." *Discourse Studies* 9: 246–269.

Gumperz, John, and Dell Hymes. 1972. *The Ethnography of Communication*. New York: Holt.

Hammersley, Martyn. 2007. "Reflections on Linguistic Ethnography." *Journal of Sociolinguistics* 11: 689–695.

Higher Education Funding Council for England. 2015. "REF Impact." *Higher Education Funding Council for England*. Accessed 25 March 2015 www.hefce.ac.uk/rsrch/REFimpact/.

Holmes, Janet. 2000. "Victoria University of Wellington's Language in the Workplace Project: An Overview." *Language in the Workplace Occasional Papers* 1: 1–18.

Holmes, Janet. 2015. "Sociolinguistics vs Pragmatics—Where Does the Boundary Lie?" Paper presented at IPra 2015, University of Antwerp, Antwerp, Belgium.

Holmes, Janet, Meredith Marra, and Bernadette Vine. 2011. *Leadership, Discourse, and Ethnicity*. Oxford: Oxford University Press.

Holmes, Janet, Stephanie Schnurr, Angela Chan, and Tina Chiles. 2003. "The Discourse of Leadership." *Te Reo* 46: 31–46.

Holmes, Janet, Bernadette Vine, and Meredith Marra. 2009. "Maori Men at Work: Leadership, Discourse, and Ethnic Identity." *Intercultural Pragmatics* 6: 345–366.

Hymes, Dell. 1972. "Models of the Interaction of Language and Social Life." In *Directions in Sociolinguistics: The Ethnography of Communication*, edited by John Gumperz, and Dell Hymes, 35–71. New York: Holt, Rinehart & Winston.

Hymes, Dell H. 1977. *Foundations in Sociolinguistics: An Ethnographic Approach*. London: Tavistock Publications.

King, Brian W. 2014. "Tracing the Emergence of a Community of Practice: Beyond Presupposition in Sociolinguistic Research." *Language in Society* 43: 61–81.

Macgilchrist, Felicitas, and Tom Van Hout. 2011. "Ethnographic Discourse Analysis and Social Science." *Forum Qualitative Sozialforschung* 12 (1): Art. 18. www.qualitative-research.net/index.php/fqs/article/view/1600.

Malinowski, Bronislaw. 1922. *Argonauts of the Western Pacific*. London: Routledge & Kegan Paul.

Malinowski, Bronislaw. 1972. "On Phatic Communion." In *Communication in Face to Face Interaction*, edited by John Laver, and Sandy Hutcheson, 146–152. Harmondsworth, UK: Penguin.

Milani, Tommaso M. 2013. "Expanding the Queer Linguistic Scene: Multimodality, Space and Sexuality at a South African University." *Journal of Language and Sexuality* 2: 206–234.

Pérez-Milans, Miguel. 2011. "Caught in a "West/China Dichotomy': Doing Critical Sociolinguistic Ethnography in Zhejiang Schools." *Journal of Language, Identity & Education* 10: 164–185.

Rampton, Ben. 2006. *Language in Late Modernity: Interaction in an Urban School.* Cambridge: Cambridge University Press.

Rampton, Ben. 2007a. "Linguistic Ethnography, Interactional Sociolinguistics and the Study of Identities." *Working Papers in Urban Language and Literacies* 43: 1–14.

Rampton, Ben. 2007b. "Neo-Hymesian Linguistic Ethnography in the United Kingdom." *Journal of Sociolinguistics* 11: 584–607.

Rampton, Ben, Karin Tusting, Janet Maybin, Richard Barwell, Angela Creese, and Vally Lytra. 2004. "UK Linguistic Ethnography: A Discussion Paper." *UK Linguistic Ethnography Forum.* www.ling-ethnog.org.uk.

Richards, Keith. 2006. *Language and Professional Identity: Aspects of Collaborative Interaction.* Basingstoke, UK: Palgrave Macmillan.

Richards, Keith. 2010. "Professional Orientation in Back Region Humor." *Text & Talk* 30: 145–167.

Rock, Frances. 2005. "'I've Picked Some up from a Colleague': Language, Sharing and Communities of Practice in an Institutional Setting." In *Beyond Communities of Practice: Language, Power, and Social Context*, edited by David Barton, and Karin Tusting, 77–104. Cambridge: Cambridge University Press.

Stephens, Mia, and Roy Neill. 2011. "'You Do Know It's Only Got One Bathroom': Biography, Wine and Small Stories." *Memory Studies* 4: 221–233.

Tusting, Karin, Ed. 2018. *Routledge Handbook of Linguistic Ethnography.* Abingdon, UK: Routledge.

Tusting, Karin, and Janet Maybin. 2007. "Linguistic Ethnography and Interdisciplinarity: Opening the Discussion." *Journal of Sociolinguistics* 11: 575–583.

Van Herreweghe, Mieke, and Myriam Vermeerbergen. 2010. "Deaf Perspectives on Communicative Practices in South Africa: Institutional Language Policies in Educational Settings." *Text & Talk* 30: 125–144.

Van Hout, Tom, and Felicitas Macgilchrist. 2010. "Framing the News: An Ethnographic View of Business Newswriting." *Text & Talk* 30: 169–191.

Vaughan, Elaine. 2007. "'I Think We Should Just Accept . . . Our Horrible Lowly Status': Analysing Teacher–Teacher Talk within the Context of Community of Practice." *Language Awareness* 16: 173–189.

Wilson, Nick. 2013. "Interaction without Walls: Analysing Leadership Discourse through Dramaturgy and Participation." *Journal of Sociolinguistics* 17: 180–199.

Woydack, Johanna, and Ben Rampton. 2015. "Text Trajectories in a Multilingual Call Centre: The Linguistic Ethnography of a Calling Script." *Tilburg Papers in Culture Studies* 124: 1–24.

Yeoh, Jackie Lay Kean. 2014. "Workplace Email Communication in New Zealand and Malaysia: Three Case Studies." PhD diss., Victoria University of Wellington.

5
Corpus Linguistics
Michael Handford

Introduction

This chapter will discuss corpus linguistics (hereafter CL) as a methodology, and its relevance to studies of workplace communication. Before moving on to the details of what the methodology involves, I will discuss a few important background issues. First, however, what is meant here by the word "corpus"? In CL, a corpus is a *principled* collection of texts, which can be analysed using computer software. These texts may be written texts, transcripts of spoken recordings, or multimodal texts, which have been carefully selected to represent the discourse in question. Crucially the texts are representative of a language or a variety of language (Sinclair 1991; Biber, Conrad, and Reppen 1998; O'Keeffe, Carter, and McCarthy 2007; Flowerdew 2012). These can then be inputted into a computer (often in the form of text files) and analysed, using both quantitative and qualitative methods. In many corpus studies, corpus analysis involves first producing quantitative results, which are then explored in more detail; in other words, the corpus tools show us potentially interesting items, which can then be analysed in longer extracts (co-text) and with reference to relevant background information (wider context).

Background

The theoretical stance assumed in CL, specifically, the question of whether CL is inherently positivistic (see Stubbs 2007) is an interesting one, given that a CL methodology shares certain features with the scientific method. For instance, it is the case that CL employs quantitative tools and statistics (along with qualitative tools); because the findings may be replicable and potentially generalizable, it can also be used for hypothesis testing; furthermore, from a theoretical perspective, CL assumes an empirical epistemology. These features of CL do not, however, entail an empirical ontology, i.e., positivism (Stubbs 2007); in other words, although CL assumes that data must be observable (for instance in the form of texts in the corpus), the texts themselves are not seen as the essence of the language, or that the only reality is that which can be observed. Therefore CL is not positivistic, but it is empirical, and allows the researcher to "demonstrate order where only randomness and idiosyncrasy were visible" (Stubbs 2007, 131). As such, it is compatible with other text-based approaches to language analysis, such as conversation analysis, pragmatics, linguistic anthropology, discursive psychology and discourse analysis (see Gee and Handford 2012), as they also may assume an empirical epistemology. Indeed, it is argued here that combining CL with such approaches leads to more insightful analyses (Baker 2006).

Although this chapter focuses on the analysis of spoken interactions in workplace settings, research has been conducted into written workplace language using corpus tools (e.g., Nelson 2000; Nickerson 2000; Koller 2004); also, Connor and Upton (2004) is a wide-ranging collection of chapters on corpus approaches to the analysis of written and spoken professional discourse. In terms of research on purely spoken workplace interactions, there is also a growing amount of corpus-informed research into internal and external spoken business communication (Nelson 2000; Koester 2006, 2010; Cheng 2007; Poncini 2004; Berber Sardinha and Barbara 2009; Handford 2010a; Handford and Koester 2010; Handford 2014a), the construction industry (Handford and Matous 2011, 2015; Tsuchiya and Handford 2014; Handford 2014b), and recently from a gender in the workplace perspective (Mullany 2016).

One of the key benefits of a corpus approach is that it allows us to unearth aspects of language that would otherwise remain hidden (Sinclair 1991; Stubbs 1996; Baker 2006). In what has become probably the most famous quote among corpus linguists, "the language looks rather different when you look at a lot of it at once" (Sinclair 1991, 100), within and across contexts, and in the language system itself (Stubbs 2007). This is why computer software plays a necessary role in CL: it allows us to see a lot of language at once, and enables the analysis of a lot of language virtually instantaneously. This perspective means that patterns and generalizations can be pinpointed that hitherto may have remained unknown or unproven. For instance, CL has allowed researchers to infer the underlying evaluative force, or connotation, a linguistic item has in context through analysing a large collection of instances of the item in question. In CL, this is termed an item's "semantic prosody" or "discourse prosody" (Louw 1993; Stubbs 1996; Hunston 2002). Understanding the underlying evaluative force is important because it demonstrates the way particular discourse communities are positioning the topic, that is their stance towards that topic.

In the definition of a corpus above, the texts which comprise the corpus represent a language or a variety of language. While this is a somewhat simplistic description and elides discussion of what "a language" or a "language variety" is, it does help us understand two general tendencies in CL (see Flowerdew 2004). Corpora increasingly tend to be very large, such as the British National Corpus, which totals around 100 million words and is meant to represent spoken and written British English as it was used in the late 20th century. In other words, it is meant to represent "a language". In contrast to such large, or "mega" corpora, some of which contain billions of words, recent research in CL has also seen the proliferation of smaller, specialized corpora which represent some variety, genre, or register of a language. It is the latter type of corpus which is more suited to workplace-based research (e.g., Connor and Upton 2004; Handford 2010b). Many of the criticisms of CL, for instance that it is a number-crunching tool or that it is inherently decontextualized, are concerned with larger corpora, and accordingly are not relevant to specialized corpora (see Baker 2006 and Handford 2010b for further discussion of criticisms).

Methodological Steps

In order to demonstrate several corpus methods, data and findings from two sources will be used in this chapter: a small amount of data collected on a construction project in Hong Kong, and from CANBEC (the Cambridge and Nottingham Business English Corpus[1]). The Hong

Kong data, which is part of a larger construction industry corpus,[2] totals around 13,000 words of interactions collected over a week (see Handford and Matous 2011). CANBEC is a one-million-word corpus of spoken business interactions, with about 900,000 words of authentic business meetings (see Handford 2010a). As such, CANBEC can be categorized as a fairly large specialized corpus of spoken language, and it is to date the largest corpus of authentic business meetings in existence. In contrast, the Hong Kong data is a very small amount of data that is not intended to be representative (i.e., it is not a corpus in itself, but part of a corpus); the intention is to show that corpus analysis of workplace discourse (CAWD) does not require large amounts of data to provide original and interesting findings.[3]

The "Understanding Context" Tool

In answer to the question of why specialized corpora are more suitable for research into workplace discourse than mega-corpora, the reason is context (Handford 2014b). According to Charles and Charles (1999), the most critical element of the analysis of professional discourse is the exploration of the relationship between text and context, because without background knowledge it is often impossible to understand what the interaction or document is about. The relationship between text and context is, of course, central in all types of discourse analysis (Gee 2005; Flowerdew 2014).[4] But it is particularly so in professional and workplace contexts because of the high degree of shared knowledge and practices in workplace communities: there is a prevalence of both jargon on the one hand and vague or explicitly deictic language on the other—both of which present challenges for the analyst.

If we consider large corpora for a moment, they enable us to see patterns at a largely decontextualized, generalized level of language (Hunston 2002). For instance, such corpora can tell us which words are the most frequent in a language, or whether a multi-word unit (e.g., "at the end of the day") is more frequent in spoken or written English. If however we want to understand how a particular group of speakers typically use a particular form of language in a particular type of speech act or genre, with what purpose and with what possible ramifications, in other words the context in which the language is used and which it reflexively reinforces (Gee 2005), then large corpora cannot help us very much. With a smaller, specialized corpus, in contrast, collecting a range of other data sources, and applying a range of qualitative methods, which enable a deeper level of analysis, is far more feasible.

As way of an example, Example 5.1 highlights the importance of context in understanding professional or workplace texts.

Example 5.1 (from Handford and Matous 2011, 96)[5]

Speaker 1: and then and (I go to this here) they can connect here +
Speaker 2: hmm +
Speaker 1: with (an opposite) side +
Speaker 2: hmm +
Speaker 1: and then and then we measure there
Speaker 2: hmm
Speaker 1: and there

Without any contextual information it is impossible to make much sense of this interaction. In fact, it is taken from a large construction project in Hong Kong, and speaker one is a male Japanese engineer in his early 30s responsible for a part of the project. He is explaining a procedure that needs following to the foreman, a Hong Kongese male in his early 50s. The interaction takes place in the Portacabin on the site, and while talking, speaker 1 is drawing a picture with a pencil to demonstrate the procedure (see Figure 5.1).

Following this exchange, the foreman then communicates this information to the local contracted labourers. The instruction is in response to a problem on site that has caused delays. The interaction is interesting from a corpus perspective because it contains a high density of place deictics such as "here" and "there". Place deictics are very frequent in this construction data, but not in many other industries, and are used in conjunction with gestures and other types of non-verbal communication (Handford and Matous 2011). This finding about the surprising high frequency of words like "this" and "here" (accounting for 2.55 per cent and 1.18 per cent of all words in the data, respectively) was produced independently of the researchers using the corpus method known as keyword analysis (see below).

In terms of the collection of background data that can enable a more contextual interpretation of the (spoken or written) texts that comprise the corpus, there are several potential sources, notwithstanding the problems inherent in every data source (see Wilson this volume). Probably the most useful source is interviews with the participants themselves, which can help understanding of the participants' professed perceptions of the immediate context and the wider context in which the interactions take place. However, there are potential issues with representativeness and reliability. For instance, in terms of the former it is often practically difficult to interview all participants involved in an interaction at work, and thus achieve a fully representative collection of perspectives. In terms of reliability, there are well-documented challenges with interview data in many contexts; in work contexts, employees may be more constrained about divulging information or may be concerned about the potential ramifications of disclosing sensitive or critical information to a relatively unknown outsider. Nevertheless, interview data can still provide a very rich source of background information that can be triangulated with other sources to achieve a plausible interpretation of what is going on in the texts. Other sources include interviews with other experts in the field, field notes, questionnaires, focus group discussions, and if possible video data. It was the video data that enabled the researchers (Handford and Matous 2011) to gain a better understanding of why place deictics are statistically significant in this construction industry context, and it was through

Figure 5.1 Engineer explaining procedure to foreman

follow-up interviews with engineers that we were able to appreciate the importance of several visual and non-linguistic semiotic modes in construction projects, such as photographs, equations, designs and hand drawings. For further discussion of context in CAWD see Handford (2014b).

The "Frequency" Tool

The most straightforward type of corpus tool is the frequency list, that is a list of the most frequent items in the data. CL is based on the premise that frequently occurring items are important items. This is not to suggest that infrequent words are inconsequential, or that frequency and saliency are always equivalent, but that if a word or multi-word unit (i.e., a string of more than one word, hereafter MWU) occurs frequently, it must be doing something important in the discourse.

Single-Word Frequency Lists

The most frequent word in CANBEC is "the", accounting for 3.76 per cent of all words in the corpus. One question language learners and linguists may ask is, "How is spoken business English different from written English, or everyday spoken English?" If we compare this frequency of "the" in business meetings to written language and to everyday spoken language, "the" in business meetings (as evidenced by CANBEC) falls between both, but towards spoken (see Handford 2014b, 126). This is as we might expect: business meetings feature more "content" in terms of transferred information than everyday conversations between friends and family (Handford 2010a), but would still be less "lexically dense" than written language given the inevitable psycholinguistic constraints on processing information that are part of

Table 5.1 The most frequent 20 single-word items in CANBEC

#	item	frequency	%
1	the	32,032	3.76
2	and	19,650	2.31
3	to	18,403	2.16
4	I	16,494	1.94
5	a	16,318	1.92
6	you	15,869	1.86
7	it	15,553	1.83
8	yeah	14,927	1.75
9	that	14,290	1.68
10	we	12,078	1.42
11	of	11,479	1.35
12	in	9,011	1.06
13	is	8,660	1.02
14	er	8,059	0.95
15	so	7,983	0.94
16	it's	7,655	0.9
17	but	6,882	0.81
18	on	6,867	0.81
19	for	6,210	0.73
20	have	5,905	0.69

spoken interactions (Chafe 1994). In other words, in face-to-face interactions in real time, we cannot reread the information or read slowly; the higher proportion of nouns in written language compared to spoken language accounts for the higher frequency of the definite article. The preceding sentence exemplifies this.

Among the other most frequent items in CANBEC, there are several that are also extremely frequent in other contexts (such as everyday English and written English). In fact, in a comparison of the 50 most frequent items in CANBEC and a corpus of everyday spoken English (SOCINT, see below), 44 are the same (Handford 2010a, 101). Furthermore, most of these most frequent single words are "functional" words, such as prepositions, pronouns, and articles. This finding reflects one of the drawbacks of frequency lists of single items: they can be fairly uninformative. While the above discussion of the definite article may be interesting for linguists, it is not particularly informative for researchers, or practitioners of professional communication.

Frequent MWUs

While frequency lists of single items are a rather blunt instrument, this is arguably not the case for frequent MWUs. One of the most profound findings from CL is that so much of our language is indeed formulaic: many traditional approaches to linguistics assumed a "slot and filler" approach to grammar and vocabulary (Cook 1990), with grammar providing the slots and speakers putting single words into the slots to form sentences. Much corpus research (Sinclair 1991; Stubbs 1996; Hunston 2002) has shown that in fact, a lot of language is made up of preformed "chunks" (MWUs), many of which perform specific pragmatic functions. It is this form-function relationship that is particularly interesting, in that it concerns the communicative goals and the social actions people at work perform, and the language they typically use to do so.

When we consider that this is a list of the most frequent business MWUs, it may be surprising that there are no MWUs that are stereotypically to do with business, such as "merger and acquisition" or "profit and loss". Many of the most frequent items are interpersonal, in that they are more concerned with managing relationships and reflect a clear concern for "face" (Goffman 1967). For instance, "I don't know" is often used in CANBEC meetings to hedge suggestions or potentially face-threatening acts. Similarly, "I don't think", "I mean I", "a bit of" and "and I think" are typically used to soften the message the speaker is conveying. The modal expression "we need to" is extremely frequent in all types of meetings, and is used

Table 5.2 The most frequent three-word MWUs

#	item	frequency	%
1	I don't know	578	0.07
2	a lot of	478	0.06
3	at the moment	472	0.06
4	we need to	427	0.05
5	I don't think	349	0.04
6	the end of	341	0.04
7	I mean I	245	0.03
8	a bit of	220	0.03
9	and I think	217	0.03
10	be able to	217	0.03

typically by managers to other managers or to subordinates in internal meetings, and also from company to company in external meetings. It is multifunctional, in that it can be used, for instance, to direct others in a face-protecting way, talk about the speaker's own group's obligations, outline the desired future direction of the group, or respond to an immediate problem.

While only the top 10 most frequent three-word items from CANBEC are shown here, other lists of MWUs in the corpus exhibit a similar tendency towards the interpersonal. For instance, the most frequent two-word item is "you know" and is typically used as a hedge, and the most frequent six-word unit is "at the end of the day". This long, frequent MWU is again typically used as a way of hedging or softening face-threatening communication; in the external manufacturing meeting below between vehicle manufacturers collaborating on a project, the speaker is trying to persuade the other company of the need to focus on the production model.

Example 5.2

S1:   the production model has to take priority in my opinion because
        at the end of the day that's the thing that we're here to do you know

---

In order to appreciate the mitigating impact "at the end of the day" has, if it is removed from the turn, the message appears far more direct. It should also be noted that such hedging expressions often cluster together; in this short turn there are also "in my opinion", "the thing", and "you know".

Such frequent interpersonal prefabricated language reflects the strong tendency towards face-protecting communication that is evident in CANBEC, and in many other studies of spoken and written professional communication (e.g., Boden 1994; Holmes and Stubbe 2003; Bhatia 2004; Koester 2006, 2010). In other words, rather than the stereotyped "hard-nosed" win–lose approach to business we may see portrayed in the media, interlocutors spend a lot of time on maintaining and developing relationships in many professional interactions. As Bhatia states, business activity "always thrives in building positive relations between various participants" (2004, 15). This is not to say people do not disagree, or that interlocutors in workplaces are unerringly polite,[6] but it is telling that in CANBEC there are no instances of the direct expression "I disagree with you", but there are 232 instances of "yes/yeah, but".

This short discussion of frequency in CANBEC indicates some of the advantages of a CL approach: while not replacing the need for decision-making over which frequent items to analyse further, it does highlight interesting language independent of the researcher's bias; also, it allows us to make generalizations about findings provided the data is made up of a collection of representative texts, rather than just a small number.

The "Keyword" Tool

As with frequency lists, there are various software packages available that will run keyword searches, for instance Antconc (Anthony 2014) and Wordsmith Tools (Scott 2011). Whereas frequency lists tell us the words that are used most frequently, keyword lists show us which words typify the genre or area under examination. They do this by comparing the dataset in question with a larger reference corpus, and showing which words are statistically significant in our corpus (for example using statistical measures such as chi-squared test). Usually, this means many of the most frequent but not particularly interesting items from the corpus, such as articles and many other "functional words" do not appear as keywords because they are shared across many contexts, and instead there are items that are more specific to the genre or domain in question. Therefore keyword lists of single words tend to be much more interesting and useful than frequency lists.

Below is the list of the top 15 keywords from CANBEC, when compared to a larger reference corpus of everyday spoken English called SOCINT[7] (with percentages in parentheses). This reference corpus was chosen because it helps answer the important question, "How is business English different from everyday English?"; without a corpus approach it is very difficult to answer such a question in a non-anecdotal manner.

The list contains some potentially surprising findings. When asked to predict the top keyword in business meetings compared to everyday English, terms like "sales" or "profit" are often suggested. But the top keyword is in fact the pronoun "we". This is surprising because "we" is also used very commonly in everyday situations, but it is more than three times more frequent in CANBEC than in everyday English. "We" is a fascinating item because it can be used to signal so many different identities or roles (Poncini 2004; Handford 2014a), both in business and in other areas such as politics. For instance, "we" can be used inclusively or exclusively, and at work is typically used to signal organizational identities (e.g., the speaker's company or work-team). It can also signal professional identities (e.g., "we engineers"), strategically (for instance "we" meaning "you"), or with strategic vagueness (deliberatively obfuscating who the referents are).

Other arguably surprising items among these top keywords (it should be noted that the whole keyword list contains several hundred statistically significant items) include "if", "need" (almost always as a semi-modal verb), "will" (again as a verb), and "okay". As with "we", "if" is interesting because it is used so commonly in everyday situations. Its higher than

Table 5.3 Keywords from CANBEC

#	item	Frequency (%)
1.	we	(1.95)
2.	okay	(0.35)
3.	the	(3.76)
4.	customer	(0.06)
5.	need	(0.21)
6.	order	(0.07)
7.	meeting	(0.07)
8.	sales	(0.04)
9.	thousand	(0.09)
10.	hundred	(0.11)
11.	if	(0.63)
12.	which	(0.25)
13.	will	(0.21)
14.	customers	(0.04)
15.	per	(0.05)

expected frequency in meetings can be accounted for by two main uses. First, in problem-solving situations, especially when interlocutors are proposing possible solutions and thinking through potential courses of action (e.g., "I think if we . . ."). Second, it is used in politeness expressions such as "if you look at the screen".

The "Concordance Lines" Tool

One of the benefits of CL is that a lot of data can be analysed, but this inevitably creates challenges in itself. For instance, in the above discussion of "if", how can we know the way such an item is used without reading through each of the texts individually? One solution to this is the use of concordance lines. As way of an example, Table 5.4 shows some concordance lines of the keyword "if" from an external pharmaceutical meeting. With concordance lines, it is possible to read them "vertically" in order to see potential patterns of use at both the lexical/grammatical level, and in terms of patterns of meaning. For instance, in these lines we can see that "if" is often followed by the keyword "we", and sometimes preceded by another CANBEC keyword "so", to form a pattern "so if we"; furthermore, there are examples of "if" being used as a politeness marker (lines 1, 4, and 6), and in problem-solving exchanges (lines 2, 3, and 5).

Table 5.4 Concordances of "if"

1	Okay. Erm so I think again we i= **if** I'll add that to the minutes. We've
2	Yeah. +and then (??). I= **if** there's a brief reason why as well.
3	we're assuming everything's five days so **if** we built a ninety eight day lead time into
4	me er same sort of er agenda as normal **if** we can work through the logistics work
5	Yeah. So if we **if** we know the information in advance
6	by next month. And yeah. **If** we talk about er the summary of the list

The "Discourse Prosody" Tool

As well as examining lexicogrammatical patterns and patterns of meaning, concordance lines also allow the analyst to infer the connotational meaning a linguistic item can have across a range of texts, that is its evaluative function. In CL, this is termed "semantic prosody" or "discourse prosody" (the latter term is preferred here). While there is debate about the extent to which words have connotational versus denotational meaning, and also about the importance and level of context in understanding an item's discourse prosody (e.g., Stubbs 1996; Hunston 2002; Handford 2010a), this method has unearthed some powerful insights into the (often implicit) stance speakers and writers take towards issues and actions in society (Stubbs 1996; Baker 2006). By examining many uses across multiple texts, patterns of evaluation can be inferred.

One of the most frequent MWUs in CANBEC is "you have to", and it occurs most frequently in manager-subordinate internal meetings, with the manager directing the subordinate (e.g., "in order to do that you have to use HTTP"). In this context, the discourse prosody is unsurprisingly one of obligation placed on the listener (i.e., the subordinate). The following concordance lines (Table 5.5) are from external meetings, where there may be no binding contract between the parties. By examining this different context (that of inter-organizational meetings), we can see whether the MWU has the same connotative meaning.

Theoretical and Methodological Approaches

Table 5.5 Concordances of "you have to" in external meetings

1	We use the same plug like when **you have to** buy a special. No. It would be the
2	can't read my own sometimes. Mm. What **you have to** do is get the paper and twist it round
3	some of them. But it might be that **you have to** give them three months' notice. Or in
4	and I'm ever so sorry about this but erm **you have to** understand there's a new vehicle
5	(laughs). You're right. What **you have to** put up with George. (laughs). Okay.

Here there is far less of a sense of obligation: instead, there is evidence for a discourse prosody of suggesting procedures with no parallel sense of interpersonal obligation or potential face-threat (e.g., lines 1, 2, and 3). Line 4 is a more idiomatic usage forming part of an apology, and line 5 is a humorous aside about what the company boss has to endure. While five concordance lines are not enough data on which to draw strong conclusions, this contrast in different discourse prosodies according to the context (internal versus external meetings) is in fact borne out across CANBEC meetings (Handford 2010a, 41–42). This example highlights the importance of considering context when analysing meaning in use in workplace settings.

The "Drilling Down" Tool

CAWD involves a lot of "drilling down" into actual texts to understand how such frequent items are actually being used by interlocutors, in other words moving from quantitative to qualitative analysis, from frequency to meaning in context. Concordance lines are one way, but they only provide a small amount of co-text. It is therefore also useful to look at longer extracts, including extended concordances. The following extract is from an internal (i.e., intra-organizational) meeting in a medium-sized UK-based IT company. The meeting is between the finance director (speaker 2), the technical director (speaker 1, called Doz), and the sales director (speaker 3). The finance director is indirectly criticizing the way the technical team have been working and the fact they now need to change to a more project management based approach.

Example 5.3

S2:	I think it's also really important +
S3:	yeah that's not a bad idea +
S2:	something we need to work forward to is is- which is a bit controversial but is also the attitude as well is that it is very now if this is going to happen and it's project management driven to be honest with you Doz their +
S1:	mm +
S2:	attitude's got to be customer you know "good morning this is your salary talking" +
S1:	mm +
S2:	is very much gonna be the way it'll go forward

The extract is fairly typical of such upper management internal meetings in CANBEC: they feature a combination of, on the one hand, potentially face-threatening suggestions, recommendations and sometimes directives, and on the other language with clear interpersonal focus, such as hedges and intensifiers. Table 5.6 lists the items in this extract and the categories to which they belong.

The categories and language in Table 5.6 are very typical of the language used in CANBEC: several of the items have been discussed already, for example the keywords "we" and "if" and the frequent MWUs "we need to" and "you know"; other items such as vague metaphors and idioms are also used consistently in CANBEC. But, as with "you have to", the goals of the speakers, their relationship and other contextual factors constrain the meaning. For instance, metaphors and idioms are typically used convergently, but they can also be used to exacerbate a conflictual situation (Handford and Koester 2010). In other words, the meaning of words is found in the shared communicative practices which they invoke, rather than in the items themselves (Gee 2005).

Table 5.6 Interpersonal language from Example 5.3

Type of language	Example from extract
Hedging expressions	I think
	a bit
	to be honest with you
	you know
Vague language	something
The pronoun 'we'	we
Deontic modal forms	(we) need to
	got to be
	gonna be
Expressions with 'if'	if this is going to happen
Metaphors and idioms	work forward to
	go forward
Vocatives	Doz
Hypothetical reported speech	"Good morning this is your salary talking"
Intensifiers	really important
	very much
Back channels	Yeah
	Mm

Conclusion

This chapter has given a brief overview of some of the corpus methods that can be employed when analysing workplace encounters, such as frequency lists, keywords and discourse prosody, and has intended to demonstrate how CL can add value to research into workplace discourse. Throughout the chapter, the importance of considering context when doing corpus linguistics was emphasized. The reflexive relationship (Gee 2005) between text and context is critical for understanding what people mean when they talk at work, and for understanding the implications of such talk.

One of the defining features of workplace talk is the negotiation of obligation and responsibility for work done, work not done, and work that needs to be done; one interesting finding from studies of actual interactions (e.g., Boden 1994; Holmes and Stubbe 2003; Koester 2006; Handford 2010a) is that these negotiations are often framed in such apparently relational language. This begs the question, why do speakers spend so much time attending to the face-needs of others? While space constraints preclude a discussion here, the question itself indicates the limits of a corpus approach that does not embed context into the analysis: corpus findings can show us what people do, but they cannot in themselves tell us why people do it. Nevertheless, corpus research has allowed us to describe with far less uncertainty what people actually say at work, rather than what they, or we, think they say. In future, corpus tools can be further aligned with other methods to provide multiple perspectives on the same data, to enable better understanding of the *how* and the *why* of workplace communication.

Further Reading

Baker (2006) is a useful and highly accessible guide to combining corpus linguistics and discourse analysis.

Handford (2010a) is a book-length corpus-informed study of the language used in meetings.

Koester (2010) provides a comprehensive overview and discussion of research and issues in workplace communication.

McCarthy and O'Keeffe's (2010) handbook provides chapters on key theoretical, methodological, and practical research in corpus linguistics by the leading figures in the field.

Corpus Tools

Some of the most popular corpus tools are:

Antconc	www.laurenceanthony.net/software.html
Wordsmith Tools	www.lexically.net/wordsmith/
SketchEngine	www.sketchengine.co.uk/
Wmatrix	http://ucrel.lancs.ac.uk/wmatrix/

Online Resources

These are some freely available online resources for doing CAWD.

Hong Kong profession-specific corpora, such as financial services and engineering. Retrieved 30 November, 2015 http://rcpce.engl.polyu.edu.hk/default.htm.

VOICE (Vienna-Oxford International Corpus of English) corpus of ELF (English as a Lingua Franca). Contains some spoken business interactions which can be analysed separate from the rest of the corpus. Retrieved 30 November 2015 from http://voice.univie.ac.at.

Enron Corpus (which contains about 500,000 emails by about 150 users, mostly senior management of Enron). Retrieved November 30, 2015 from www-2.cs.cmu.edu/~enron/.

Mike Nelson's business English lexis site. Retrieved November 30, 2015 from http://users.utu.fi/micnel/business_english_lexis_site.htm.

Related Topics

Genre theory; Corporate settings; Relational talk

Notes

1. I was the researcher responsible for compiling and developing CANBEC. The Project Directors are Professor Ronald Carter and Professor Michael McCarthy. Copyright for the corpus is owned by Cambridge University Press, who have kindly given permission for the reproduction of findings in this chapter.
2. This is the CONIC (Construction Industry Corpus). Funded by a grant from the JSPS, project number 00466781. Project Director Michael Handford.
3. The evidence for this assertion is that the paper cited here (Handford and Matous 2011) won the *English for Specific Purposes* Horowitz Prize for best article of the year, and the paper was also chosen as one of the top 10 best corpus-based research articles in Flowerdew (2012).
4. Discourse analysis is used here as an umbrella term for any type of analysis that seeks to understand how people create and interpret meanings in actual situations, including CL (see Gee and Handford 2012).
5. Transcription Conventions from Holmes and Stubbe (2003, 181):
   + Pause of up to one second
   (hello) Transcriber's best guess at an unclear utterance
6. Research into construction meetings, for instance, suggests that this industry may have a different default setting in terms of face (e.g., Tsuchiya and Handford 2014).
7. SOCINT stands for the social and intimate subcorpus of CANCODE, the Cambridge and Nottingham Corpus of Discourse English. Project Directors Professor Ronald Carter and Professor Michael McCarthy. Copyright Cambridge University Press.

References

Anthony, Laurence. 2014. *AntConc. Version 3.4.3.* [Computer Software]. Tokyo, Japan: Waseda University. Available from www.laurenceanthony.net/.
Baker, Paul. 2006. *Using Corpora in Discourse Analysis*. London: Continuum.
Berber Sardinha, Tony, and Leila Barbara. 2009. "Corpus Linguistics." In *Handbook of Business Discourse*, edited by Francesca Bargiela-Chiappini, 105–118. Edinburgh: Edinburgh University Press.
Biber, Douglas, Susan Conrad, and Randi Reppen. 1998. *Corpus Linguistics: Investigating Language Structure and Use*. Cambridge: Cambridge University Press.
Bhatia, Vijay. 2004. *Worlds of Written Discourse*. London: Continuum.
Boden, Deirdre. 1994. *Talk at Work*. Cambridge: Polity Press.
Chafe, Wallace. 1994. *Discourse, Consciousness and Time*. Chicago, IL: University of Chicago Press.
Charles, Marjaliisa, and David Charles. 1999. "Sales Negotiations: Bargaining through Tactical Summaries." In *Business English: Research into Practice*, edited by Martin Hewings, and Catherine Nickerson, 71–99. London: Longman.
Cheng, Winnie. 2007. "The Use of Vague Language across Spoken Genres in an Intercultural Hong Kong Corpus." In *Vague Language Explored*, edited by Joan Cutting, 161–181. Basingstoke, UK: Palgrave Macmillan.
Connor, Ulla, and Thomas A. Upton, Eds. 2004. *Discourse in the Professions: Perspectives from Corpus Linguistics*. Amsterdam: John Benjamins.
Cook, Guy. 1990. *Discourse*. Oxford: Oxford University Press.
Flowerdew, Lynne. 2004. "The Argument for Using English Specialized Corpora to Understand Academic and Professional Settings." In *Discourse in the Professions: Perspectives from Corpus Linguistics*, edited by Ulla Connor, and Thomas A. Upton, 11–36. Amsterdam: John Benjamins.
Flowerdew, Lynne. 2012. *Corpora and Language Education*. Basingstoke, UK: Palgrave Macmillan.
Flowerdew, John, Ed. 2014. *Discourse in Context*. London: Continuum.
Gee, James Paul. 2005. *An Introduction to Discourse Analysis*. London: Routledge.
Gee, James Paul, and Michael Handford, Eds. 2012. *Routledge Handbook of Discourse Analysis*. London: Routledge.
Goffman, Erving. 1967. *Interaction Ritual: Essays on Face-to-Face Behaviour*. New York: Anchor Doubleday.
Handford, Michael. 2010a. *The Language of Business Meetings*. Cambridge: Cambridge University Press.

Handford, Michael. 2010b. "What a Corpus Can Tell Us about Specialist Genres." In *Routledge Handbook of Corpus Linguistics*, edited by Michael McCarthy, and Anne O'Keeffe, 255–269. Abingdon, UK: Routledge.

Handford, Michael. 2014a. "Cultural Identities in International, Interorganisational Meetings: A Corpus-Informed Discourse Analysis of Indexical *We*." *Language and Intercultural Communication* 14: 41–58.

Handford, Michael. 2014b. "Context in Spoken Professional Discourse: Language and Practice in an International Business Meeting". In *Discourse in Context*, edited by John Flowerdew, 113–132. London: Continuum.

Handford, Michael, and Almut Koester. 2010. "It's Not Rocket Science': Metaphors and Idioms in Conflictual Business Meetings." *Text & Talk* 30: 27–51.

Handford, Michael, and Petr Matous. 2011. "Lexicogrammar in the International Construction Industry: A Corpus-Based Case Study of Japanese-Hong-Kongese On-Site Interactions in English." *English for Specific Purposes* 30: 87–100.

Handford, Michael, and Petr Matous. 2015. "Problem-Solving Discourse on an International Construction Site: Patterns and Practices." *English for Specific Purposes* 38: 85–98.

Holmes, Janet, and Maria Stubbe. 2003. *Power and Politeness in the Workplace*. London: Longman.

Hunston, Susan. 2002. *Corpora in Applied Linguistics*. Cambridge: Cambridge University Press.

Koester, Almut. 2006. *Investigating Workplace Discourse*. Routledge: London.

Koester, Almut. 2010. *Workplace Discourse*. London: Continuum.

Koller, Veronika. 2004. "Businesswomen and War Metaphors: Possessive, Jealous and Pugnacious?" *Journal of Sociolinguistics* 8: 3–22.

Louw, Bill. 1993. "Irony in the Text or Insincerity in the Writer? The Diagnostic Potential of Semantic Prosodies." In *Text and Technology*, edited by Mona Baker, Gill Francis, and Elena Tognini-Bonelli, 157–176. Amsterdam: John Benjamins.

McCarthy, Michael, and Anne O'Keeffe, Eds. 2010. *Routledge Handbook of Corpus Linguistics*. Abingdon, UK: Routledge.

Mullany, Louise. 2016. *The Sociolinguistics of Gender in Public Life*. Basingstoke, UK: Palgrave.

Nelson, Michael. 2000. "A Corpus-Based Study of Business English and Business English Teaching Materials." PhD diss., University of Manchester.

Nickerson, Catherine. 2000. *Playing the Corporate Game: An Investigation of the Genres and Discourse Strategies in English used by Dutch Writers*. Amsterdam: Rodopi.

O'Keeffe, Anne, Ronald Carter, and Michael McCarthy. 2007. *From Corpus to Classroom*. Cambridge: Cambridge University Press.

Poncini, Gina. 2004. *Discursive Strategies in Multicultural Business Meetings*. Bern: Peter Lang.

Scott, Michael. 2011. *Wordsmith Tools. Version 5*. Oxford: Oxford University Press.

Sinclair, John. 1991. *Corpus, Concordance, Collocation*. Oxford: Oxford University Press.

Stubbs, Michael. 1996. *Text and Corpus Analysis*. Oxford: Blackwell.

Stubbs, Michael. 2007. "On Texts, Corpora and Models of Language." In *Text, Discourse and Corpora*, edited by Michael Hoey, Michaela Mahlberg, Michael Stubbs, and Wolfgang Teubert, 163–190. London: Continuum.

Tsuchiya, Keiko, and Michael Handford. 2014. "A Corpus-Driven Analysis of Repair in a Professional ELF Meeting: Not 'Letting it Pass'." *Journal of Pragmatics* 64: 117–131.

6

(Im)politeness Theory

Michael Haugh and Yasuhisa Watanabe

Introduction

The roots of (im)politeness research stretch back to the inception of the field of pragmatics in the early 1970s. However, it was not until the mid-1980s, following the publication of Leech's (1983) seminal textbook, and the republication of Brown and Levinson's (1987) politeness theory in the form of an extended book-length study, that politeness really started to become an important area of study in its own right. Indeed, since the turn of this century, in part stimulated by Eelen's (2001) seminal critique of politeness theory, and the move to study impoliteness alongside politeness, the field of (im)politeness has become an increasingly strong force in pragmatics and related disciplines. Roughly 10 per cent of papers published in the *Journal of Pragmatics* since the mid-1980s have focused on (im)politeness (Jucker and Rüegg 2017), for instance, and the frequency of the use of "politeness" as a keyword has increased exponentially since the late 1990s. In response to this growth, a journal dedicated to such research, the *Journal of Politeness Research*, was launched in 2005, and a handbook specifically focused on linguistic (im)politeness has been published (Culpeper, Haugh, and Kádár 2017).

Accompanying this steady growth in the number of studies focusing on (im)politeness, the field has also witnessed the emergence of an increasingly diverse range of theoretical approaches. While Brown and Levinson's approach dominated the field until the late 1990s, to the extent that it is sometimes even to this very day considered synonymous with politeness theory (Brown 2015; Wikipedia 2016), there is in fact now a wide range of different theoretical accounts of (im)politeness. For those new to the field, or even for established researchers, the wide range of theoretical approaches on offer can appear somewhat daunting. Indeed, while a diverse range of views is perhaps a sign that a field is dynamic and thriving, and also reflects the multifaceted nature of the object of theorization, it does pose significant challenges for those attempting to navigate this seemingly complex theoretical space.

The aim of this chapter is thus to provide a brief overview of theories of (im)politeness and highlight what different theoretical approaches offer with respect to furthering our understanding of (im)politeness as a social and pragmatic phenomenon. The chapter begins, in the following section, by tracing developments in (im)politeness theory from the early 1970s through to the diverse range of theoretical approaches on offer today. We then consider how the selection of a particular theoretical stance should be guided by the specific focus of one's research. In section four, building on the distinction between user (first order) and observer (second order) perspectives on (im)politeness, we discuss the affordances and constraints of two particular theories of (im)politeness that draw from user and observer perspectives, respectively, using some data gathered from an intercultural workplace as a touchstone. The chapter concludes with a brief discussion of some implications of the current trends in theorizing (im)politeness for research that focuses on (im)politeness in the workplace.

Developments in Politeness Theory

Like many areas in the social sciences, the academic study of politeness, and subsequently impoliteness, was inspired by an everyday notion. A lay account of a seemingly everyday phenomenon does not, however, pass muster as scientific research. The notion of *politeness* in English is also an unlikely candidate for building a theory that is applicable across languages and cultures. For that reason, early attempts to theorize politeness sought to distance themselves from these everyday notions. Politeness is defined in this "first wave" of politeness research as a set of strategies for maintaining good relations and avoiding interpersonal conflict (Brown and Levinson 1987; Lakoff 1973; Leech 1983). These first wave theories are largely rooted in Gricean pragmatics and traditional speech act theory.

However, it is now widely acknowledged that both Gricean pragmatics and speech act theory are overly centred on the analysis of utterances. They also arguably treat English as an unmarked standard for theorization (Culpeper and Haugh 2014). Thus, despite being intended as universally applicable, many scholars have argued that first wave approaches neglect politeness at the discourse level (Kasper 1996; Usami 2002), and are grounded in an Anglo-centric view of interpersonal relations (Ide 1989; Mao 1994; Matsumoto 1988). These mounting critiques spawned a realization that in positing these avowedly scientific conceptualizations of politeness, the proper object of study had been somewhat obscured. Yet as Eelen (2001, 253) argues,

> [a] situation in which the scientific account contradicts informants' claims and dismisses them as being 'wrong' does not represent a healthy situation. Such a practice immediately leads to a rupture between scientific and commonsense notions, causing the theory to lose its grasp on the object of analysis. In an investigation of everyday social reality informants can never be 'wrong', for the simple reason that it is their behaviour and notions we set out to examine in the first place.

Eelen's (2001) critique heralded a broader discursive shift in the theorization of politeness, in which the focus was shifted squarely onto participants' understandings of politeness as they arise in various forms of discourse or social interaction. This move was predicated on the distinction between "first order" and "second order" notions of politeness, which was initially proposed by Watts, Ide, and Ehlich (1992). The former is associated with the understandings of participants themselves. These first-order understandings are reflected in ordinary talk about (im)politeness, as well as the evaluations they themselves make in situated interactions. The latter is associated with the understandings of observers, specifically scientific observers, and are generally couched in terms of some form of systematic theory of the object in question.[1]

The second wave approaches to theorizing politeness, which were developed in the early 2000s, advocate a focus on first order understandings of participants themselves as the proper object of study. They also propose that the theorization of politeness be grounded in the social practice theories of Bourdieu or Foucault (Eelen 2001; Mills 2003; Watts 2003). As a consequence of this emphasis on social theorization, the very definition of politeness itself is regarded by discursive politeness researchers as open to contestation. The proper focus of politeness research is, in their view, analysing how understandings of politeness are contested, and what gives rise to its inherent contestability.

However, this shift to studying lay, common-sense understandings of politeness subsequently met with resistance from scholars who argued that it left the researcher little to do aside from documenting participants' varying accounts of politeness (Terkourafi 2005). They were also criticized for not providing an over-arching theoretical account of how politeness underpins social order both across and within different relational networks or communities. In addition, while it was acknowledged in second wave approaches that there is inevitably variability across speakers of a language with respect to how they conceptualize and enact politeness, there was no systematic attempt to theorize or empirically study this variability (Haugh 2007).

Such counter critiques thus inspired a "third wave" of theorization in politeness research from the mid-2000s onwards in which the aim among theorists has been to develop scientific accounts of politeness that are consonant with the understandings of participants, although not confined to or overly constrained by such accounts. In these third wave accounts of politeness, the focus has shifted squarely to politeness as involving "subjective judgements about the social appropriateness of verbal and non-verbal behaviour" (Spencer-Oatey 2005, 97), and (im)politeness itself is broadly conceptualized as a type of interpersonal attitude or attitudinal evaluation. The pendulum has thus swung back to sit somewhere between lay and scientific accounts of politeness, with the general consensus being that a theory of (im)politeness should offer a systematic, internally coherent account of how these subjective judgements, or (inter)subjective attitudinal evaluations arise, and what role such evaluations play in interpersonal relations.

Yet despite this apparent consensus, there is now a diverse range of theoretical accounts of (im)politeness on the market. Each of these is grounded in different sets of epistemological assumptions about the nature of (im)politeness and draw from various different methods of analysis. For instance, the discursive-materialist approach (Mills forthcoming; van der Bom and Mills 2015) is informed by a Foucauldian account of discourse and Marxist accounts of ideology, while the interactional approach (Haugh 2013, 2015) is largely informed by ethnomethodological conversation analysis. Although both favour close qualitative analyses of various forms of discourse data, the former is primarily concerned with the ways in which disputes over what counts as polite reflect broader social struggles, while the latter focuses primarily on analysing the social practices by which such evaluations arise. They can be contrasted with a second cluster of (im)politeness theories that are grounded in neo-Gricean pragmatics, such as the frame-based approach (Terkourafi 2001, 2005), or the revised maxims-based approach proposed by Leech (2014). The latter tend to favour quantitative analyses of data sourced from language corpora. A third cluster of theoretical accounts gravitate towards analysing the ways in which (im)politeness is connected with claiming, attributing or disputing identities. These include the discursive-relational approach (Locher 2006, 2008), the genre approach developed by Garcés-Conejos Blitvich (2010, 2013), and the interactional sociolinguistics approach (Holmes, Marra, and Vine 2011). The latter tend to favour qualitative discourse analytic methods, supplemented to varying degrees by observer coding of particular social variables. Finally, lying between these two clusters is the sociopragmatic approach of Culpeper (2011, 2015), which builds on the broader rapport management framework developed by Spencer-Oatey (2005).[2]

However, despite the fact that a range of different theoretical accounts of (im)politeness have emerged in the past two decades, many scholars nevertheless still continue to employ first wave theories of politeness in their research, particularly those working outside of pragmatics, with Brown and Levinson's (1987) face-saving account being by the far the most popular choice among many scholars to the present day. What we have, then, is a situation in which there are now a multitude of different theoretical accounts that are drawn on by scholars in undertaking research about (im)politeness. The challenge for researchers is that while these various different theories of (im)politeness may seem *prima facie* complementary, there is in fact no straightforward way to work across them. For some scholars this is claimed to be a function of the object of study itself, which is argued to defy any attempt to provide an overarching theory (Mills 2003; Watts 2005). Indeed, given the inherent complexity of social life, it appears that the development of a grand theory of social interaction is an increasingly remote possibility, simply because such a theory would have to be itself highly complex to the point that it would likely become untenable for researchers to put into practice. However, this leaves those studying (im)politeness in the seemingly unenviable position of having to navigate across a diverse range of theoretical approaches. This naturally raises the question of which theoretical account or accounts might be useful for those wishing to undertake research about (im)politeness in the workplace.

Politeness Theory and Studies of Language in the Workplace

In order to address the question of what different theories of (im)politeness offer to studies of language in the workplace, it is important for us to first consider the kinds of research questions that any particular theory lends itself to asking (Christie 2015; Locher 2015). Any theoretical account, whether a scientific theory developed by a professional analyst, or a folk theory shared among lay observers, both affords and constrains a range of understandings (Arundale 2013). A theory is a bit like the different sorts of magnifying instruments that are used in the physical sciences to view different aspects of the natural world. We can enlarge the physical world at varying degrees of detail through such instruments. A magnifying glass allows us to examine closely the structure of a leaf. A standard desktop microscope allows us to observe the individual cells that make up the leaf, while an electron microscope allows us to see inside cells to the components that make them up. Yet in being able to observe the inner components of cells we necessarily lose sight of the overall structure of the leaf. These different instruments thus both afford and constrain what we can observe. It's not that the viewpoint offered by the electron microscope is "correct" and that of the magnifying glass is "incorrect". Both instruments, if calibrated appropriately to the object in question, offer a means of observation that the other does not afford. However, this is not to say that one cannot compare the relative utility of each. It would be fair to say that the electron microscope has advanced our understanding of cellular structure much further than the magnifying glass.

Theories of (im)politeness are analogous in that they afford a certain view of social interaction, making certain phenomena more salient, while at the same time necessarily backgrounding other possible understandings, and so also constrain what we can legitimately observe. In order to accomplish best fit between one's research agenda and theoretical approach, then, it is important to be aware of what understandings the theory in question both affords and constrains. It is also important to be aware of the underlying epistemological and ontological commitments of that theory (Haugh 2012; Kádár and Haugh 2013). Most theorists take a social realist ontological stance in relation to (im)politeness. That is, it is assumed that while (im)politeness is itself a social construction and has no material reality in the way that a tree might be considered to have, it is nevertheless something that users treat as real, and so forms part of our social reality. However, the epistemological commitments of different theories of (im)politeness vary considerably. For Brown and Levinson (1987), for instance, politeness consists in what is coded by the professional analyst as a politeness strategy. These politeness strategies can be traced to individual utterances. For Mills (2003) and Locher (2008), in contrast, politeness consists in what is oriented to by participants themselves as a matter of (im)politeness, that is, what can be labelled as *polite, courteous, civil* and so on by lay observers. Such evaluations only become apparent through analysing the to-and-fro of discourse itself or through examining social discourses on (im)politeness. To evidence an analytical claim when drawing from Brown and Levinson's approach, a researcher may examine the degree to which independent coding of data by different researchers yields similar results. To evidence analytical claims undertaking a discursive analysis, a researcher may draw evidence from metapragmatic comments made by participants in post-event interviews (van der Bom and Mills 2015).

More broadly speaking, (im)politeness can be understood from the perspective of the users themselves, that is, the understandings of participants engaged in some form of social interaction (a first order understanding), or from the perspective of observers of such interaction (a second order understanding), which is generally held to be that of the professional analyst. The perspective of users as opposed to observers of social interaction is qualitatively different. Given each has its own limitations, more recent theories of (im)politeness have moved to explicitly draw from both. Yet due caution should be exercised in attempting to do so, in order to avoid the understandings of analysts inadvertently masquerading as those of the participants, and vice versa. Ultimately, what is most important is ensuring that there is an appropriate degree of compatibility between one's research questions, the theoretical apparatus selected to seek answers to these questions, and one's methodology (Locher 2015), including the type(s) of data selected for analysis, the methods used to collect it, and methods drawn upon in analysing that data (Culpeper, Haugh, and Terkourafi forthcoming).

In order to understand in less abstract terms what this might involve, in the following section, two distinct theoretical approaches are applied to the analysis of a workplace interaction where issues of (im)politeness appear to be salient. The aim here is not to demonstrate that one is inherently "better" than the other, but to consider both what understandings each theoretical approach affords and constrains, and what methods of analysis might be commensurate with each.

Applying Politeness Theory to Workplace Data

In this section, two quite distinct theories of (im)politeness, the classic first wave theoretical approach of Brown and Levinson (1987), and a representative third wave theory, the interactional approach postulated by Haugh (2013, 2015), are examined with respect to what light they shine on issues of (im)politeness that arose in a work meeting held in a Japanese company based in Australia. The first theoretical approach has been selected because it is one that has been frequently used in studies of politeness in the workplace. The second has been selected because it echoes many of the analytical themes attended to in Brown and Levinson's approach, including the emphasis placed on grounding one's analysis of (im)politeness in an analysis of social action (cf. "speech acts" in Brown and Levinson's approach), and the way in which potential evaluations of (im)politeness in any particular moment in time need to be positioned with respect to the ongoing relationships of those participants (cf. the notions of "power" and "distance" in Brown and Levinson's approach). There is yet another further connection between the two in that the move to draw from research and methods in ethnomethodological conversation analysis is explicitly advocated by Brown and Levinson (1987) in a reflective introduction to their theory. Indeed, Brown (2015, 329) has recently reiterated that this constitutes an important new direction for research in politeness.[3]

In order to compare and contrast what these two theoretical accounts of (im)politeness bring to an analysis of workplace interaction, the data excerpt in question needs to first be appropriately contextualized. The recording was made as part of an ethnographic study of a Japanese export company based in Sydney that was undertaken by Watanabe (2009). There are three participants involved in this interaction: Naoko, Carl, and Satomi. While Naoko is General Manager with responsibility for administration and accounts along with ordering new products, and so has a role-based entitlement to issue directives to the other two participants, she claimed in interviews with the researcher that she prefers her subordinates to "notice what is needed" (Watanabe 2009, 150). Satomi is Head of public relations and packaging, while Carl works in marketing and development under the direction of Matthew (who was not present during the meeting in question). Naoko and Satomi are Japanese females in their thirties, while Carl is an Australian male, of Indonesian descent, in his early twenties, who speaks Japanese, but is not fluent. In interaction, then, it appears that there are a range of classic sociolinguistic variables of possible relevance, including the participants' cultural background, linguistic and pragmatic competence in Japanese, gender and age. The question of whether such differences are relevant to this particular interaction, is, of course, an empirical one.

The following excerpt, which has been transcribed using conversation analysis conventions (Jefferson 2004), and is accompanied by a translation into English, begins with Naoko explaining the implications of changes to their distribution network for how food tests are conducted. After Carl joins the conversation, Naoko invites Satomi to take part as well.

Example (from Watanabe 2009, 153–154)

Office day: 11:50AM

20	N:	*soi dorinku toka mo:*
21		*nyuu purodakuto mo:*
22		*J ni kaeru mae ni:=*
		("before we change [the distribution route of] the soy drinks and others to Company J")
23	N:	*=chotto Satomi san mo kīte oite ne*
		("Satomi, can you listen to this as well")
24	S:	*n:?* ((S sits up and turns in N's direction))
		("huh?")
25	N:	*J ni kaeru mae ni:* (.) *tesuto ga*
26		*hitsuyō kamo shirenai=*
		("Before [we] change to company J, we might have to do the tests")
27	N:	*<ima sore Itami san ni kakunin*
28		*shite moratteru> kara:*
		("I have asked Mr. Itami [from company J] to check that for us")

29	C:	↑*ah*::. ("yeah")
30 31	N:	*ima made hora Y ga fūdo tesuto wo shite inpootaa mo Y datta desho*= ("until now Company Y did the food test, and the importer was also Company Y, wasn't it?")
32	C:	*n:: sō sō* ("hm:: yes yes")
33	N:	*dakedo Y no kono tesuto wo tsukatte J ga inpōtā ni narenai kamo shirenai kara: (.) pakkēji jō de?* ("but using [the result of] the test conducted by Company Y, Company J may not be able to print on the package that they are the importer")
34	S:	((turns her head to N))
35 36	N:	*dakara sore ga dō nanoka tte iu no wa ima Itami san ni kīte moratteru kara:* ("so I have asked Mr. Itami to investigate what is happening with that for us")
37	C:	*kibishii ne:* ("that's tough")
38 39	N:	*dakara N no honrai wa ima kakatteru ōdā? kyo kakeru ōdā mo*= ("so I wanted to change the label of what should be the current order [product N], the one we are going to order today as well")
40	C:	((nods numerous times))
41 42 43	N:	=*J ni raberu wo kaetakatta-n dakedo ( ) dakedo tesuto (.) ga: dame dattara: (.) sonomama* ("to Company J, but if [we can't use] the test results, [we can] leave it as Company Y")
44	C:	*Y ni sonomama* ("leave it as Company Y")
45		(4.5)
46 47 48	C:	*a sokka (2.5) moshi J ni nattara Satomi san wa* ((looks at S then back to N)) *zenbu jissai ni shinakya ikenai.* ("ah, that's right, if it changes to Company J, Satomi must actually do all [of the new labels]")
49		(1.0)
50 51	N:	<*sō sō sō*> *sore mo* ((C looks at S)) *aru kara* ("yes yes yes, that is the case as well")

Naoko offers an extended explanation about the legal obligations associated with changing the company from which they source the soy drinks they are currently exporting (lines 20–43). What is notable here is that it is Carl who provides the upshot, namely, that he will need to assist Satomi to redesign the label, as long they can get the required test results from the new company (lines 46–48).

From the perspective of Brown and Levinson (1987) this appears to constitute an example of "hinting", an off-record politeness strategy through which Naoko exhibits her concern for the "negative face" of Carl and Satomi, namely, their claim to freedom of action and freedom from imposition by, ostensibly at least, offering them options as to whether or not they comply. Given Naoko ostensibly has an institutional role that confers on her the right to issue directives more generally, it is not entirely clear why such a directive could be perceived as face threatening by Carl and Satomi to the extent that an off-record politeness strategy is warranted. Nevertheless, while her exact motivations are unclear, this analysis remains plausible, namely, that "politeness" arises here through Naoko "hinting" at what she wants the other two to do, particularly for Carl, who is a speaker of English. Specifically, politeness takes the form of a particularized conversational implicature that is generated by flouting the maxim of relation (that is, by not making explicitly relevant the upshot of what she is explaining here) (Grice 1975; Brown and Levinson 1987, 213). In order to ascertain whether the use of this particular politeness strategy is a function of the gender of the participants or other social variables, we would need to collect a number of interactions where such "hints" arise and code these variables to see whether a pattern emerges. Brown and Levinson's theory is thus not designed to tease out why on this occasion a particular strategy was employed, and what was accomplished through its implementation in this case. Instead, it is better suited to identifying trends across relatively large datasets.

Haugh's (2013, 2015) interactional approach draws from a combination of research and methods in ethnomethodological conversation analysis with ethnography. In such an approach, one of the primarily analytical questions concerns the issue of "why that now?" That is to say, an interactional analysis focuses on teasing out why a particular practice occurs and what is accomplished through it in this particular sequence. From an interactional pragmatics perspective, Naoko here displays "concern" for her ongoing relationship with Carl and Satomi. This is accomplished through attenuating the upshot of her prior explanation. Specifically, in leaving a long gap (line 45) following her extended explanation (lines 20–43), Naoko hearably withholds an upshot (Schegloff 1995, 198), thereby prompting Carl or Satomi to figure out the upshot and demonstrate their understanding of it (Haugh 2015). Following Carl's explication of the upshot, namely, that they will need to redesign the labels on the soy drink product (lines 46–48), Naoko emphatically confirms his understanding (lines 50–51).[4] In attenuating this upshot, then, Naoko avoids issuing a directive to Carl and Satomi that they change the label by proffering an opportunity for them to "notice what is needed". In so doing, Naoko indicates that she is being attentive to their respective professional faces, as prompting them in this way allows them to demonstrate their own professional competence (Watanabe 2009, 154).

From an ethnomethodological perspective then, Naoko thus appears to be orienting to the possible *meiwaku* ('trouble') involved here, not only for Carl and Satomi, but for herself as well (Gagné 2010, 132). That is, in providing Carl and Satomi with the opportunity to offer to take responsibility for this change themselves, Naoko not only construes such a change as *meiwaku* ('trouble') for them, but as something that would incur *futan* ('burden') for her if she were to directly request such a change. This is because *meiwaku* not only involves "a feeling or status of being troubled and feeling uncomfortable due to the deeds of another party

... but the term also connotes a sense of 'debt'—a reflexive force of debt that returns to oneself" (Gagné 2010, 131). In other words, "requesting" is not conceptualized so much as a possible "imposition" on the recipient's negative face so much as a source of *meiwaku* ('trouble') for both parties.

These two different theoretical approaches thus result in quite different analyses of what has transpired here. In Brown and Levinson's approach, the analyst would code this as an instance of an off-record politeness strategy, namely, "hinting". This hinting would be analysed as "polite" because it shows concern for the recipient's "negative face". In the interactional approach, close attention is paid to what Naoko is accomplishing through prompting the others to figure out the upshot for themselves, in this case, she proffers an opportunity for them "notice what is needed". In so doing, she appears to be enculturating Carl, in particular, into a company culture where they are "attentive" to the unstated needs of others (Fukushima and Haugh 2014). She also thereby avoids a sense of "indebtedness" that might otherwise arise through issuing a more straightforward directive. The latter approach thus generates an emically-grounded "thick description", but due to its orientation to the analysis of local sequential contingencies, it can be less straightforwardly applied across large tracts of data.

In sum, while the explanations generated through these two theoretical accounts are quite distinct, both are arguably plausible. The former foregrounds a largely second order, observer-based account that can be applied across multiple languages and cultures, thereby facilitating ready cross-cultural comparisons (albeit based on an account that is not necessarily consonant with the understandings of the participants themselves). The latter approach is largely a first-order, user-based account, as it ties the analysis more closely to the details of how the social action in question is interactionally accomplished, and also foregrounds how accomplishing the action in this way might be evaluated by those participants. In so doing, it provides a detailed picture of a specific interactional practice, "prompting understandings" (Haugh 2016), that enables comparisons with other practices, as well as offering insight into the cultural logic (Enfield 2000) that underpins the evaluations of this practice. Each of these two approaches is clearly suited to quite different research agendas. Ultimately, then, what should be determining one's choice of theoretical approach are the research questions one is seeking to answer.[5]

Conclusion

We have considered a wide range of different theoretical accounts of (im)politeness in this chapter. One might, of course, quite legitimately raise the question as to why so many different theories of (im)politeness have been developed by scholars in the field. In response, it could be argued that the current situation reflects the complex, multi-faceted, and multi-layered nature of social interaction. On that view, it is not in fact reasonable to expect the intricacies of social interaction to be reduced to a few simple principles of (im)politeness that are applicable across multiple languages and cultures. This is not to say, however, that all these different theoretical accounts can be considered straightforwardly complementary. What needs to be appreciated is that any particular theory of (im)politeness both affords and constrains our understanding of the phenomenon in question. In researching (im)politeness in the workplace, then, what drives one's choice of theoretical approach should ultimately be one's specific object of study and one's research questions therein, as well as one's method(s) of choice.

Finally, it is important to bear in mind that the study of (im)politeness in the workplace need not simply involve the application of existing theories of (im)politeness. Such studies potentially have much to offer to the further theorisation of (im)politeness itself. Not only is the workplace a site where many of us spend much of our lives engaged in some form of social interaction, but it is also a site which we can systematically study the competing forces of globalization and localization, and their effects on the ways in which we engage in social interaction. Studies of (im)politeness in the workplace thus have the potential to further our understanding of how the moral grounds underpinning evaluations of (im)politeness are negotiated in complex social settings. A workplace encompasses a complex confluence of norms for evaluation that are simultaneously rooted in the workplace as a community of practice, the varying cultural viewpoints that participants may bring to encounters within many workplaces, and the broader, sometimes competing societal norms that can be invoked by users in that workplace.

Further Reading

Bargiela-Chiappini and Harris (2006) provide a very useful overview of how studies of politeness in the workplace have drawn from different theoretical frameworks, as well as identifying some of the key issues for the study of (im)politeness in the workplace.

Holmes and Schnurr (2017) illustrates how (im)politeness in the workplace can vary across different countries, institutions and companies, building, in particular, on studies from the Wellington Language in the Workplace project.

Related Topics

Interactional sociolinguistics; Conversation analysis; Rapport management; Relational talk; Conflict talk; Intercultural communication

Notes

1. See Haugh (2012), and Kádár and Haugh (2013, 83–103) for a more granular account of this distinction.
2. See Fletcher (this volume) for further discussion of rapport management theory and its relevance for studies of (im)politeness, and interpersonal relations more generally, in the workplace.
3. An additional reason for making a comparison between Brown and Levinson's approach and Haugh's approach is that the latter is one with which both of us are very familiar.
4. Notably, the formulation of Naoko's response indicates that there may be some other actions required on their part (*sore mo aru*, "that as well"), but this is not explicitly discussed in subsequent talk (data not shown).
5. Other theories of (im)politeness would, of course, bring our attention to yet other dimensions of this sort of data and how they intersect with (im)politeness. These might include, for instance, issues of identity (e.g., Locher 2008), the role of the broader genre in which such interactions are enacted (e.g., Garcés-Conejos Blitvich 2010), or the sociocognitive mechanisms underpinning the inferential work accomplished by these participants (e.g., Terkourafi 2005).

References

Arundale, Robert. 2013. "Conceptualizing 'Interaction' in Interpersonal Pragmatics: Implications for Understanding and Research." *Journal of Pragmatics* 58: 12–26.
Bargiela-Chiappini, Francesca, and Sandra Harris. 2006. "Politeness at Work: Issues and Challenges." *Journal of Politeness Research* 2: 7–34.

Brown, Penelope. 2015. "Politeness and Language." In *International Encyclopedia of the Social and Behavioural Sciences*, edited by James D. Wright, 326–330. Amsterdam: Elsevier.
Brown, Penelope, and Stephen Levinson. 1987. *Politeness. Some Universals in Language Usage*. Cambridge: Cambridge University Press.
Christie, Chris. 2015. "Epilogue. Politeness Research: Sociolinguistics as Applied Pragmatics." *Journal of Politeness Research* 11: 355–364.
Culpeper, Jonathan. 2011. *Impoliteness: Using Language to Cause Offence*. Cambridge: Cambridge University Press.
Culpeper, Jonathan. 2015. "Impoliteness Strategies." In *Interdisciplinary Studies in Pragmatics, Culture and Society*, edited by Alessandro Capone, and Jacob Mey, 421–445. New York: Springer.
Culpeper, Jonathan, and Michael Haugh. 2014. *Pragmatics and the English Language*. Basingstoke, UK: Palgrave Macmillan.
Culpeper, Jonathan, Michael Haugh, and Dániel Z. Kádár, Eds. 2017. *Palgrave Handbook of Linguistic (Im)politeness*. London: Palgrave Macmillan.
Culpeper, Jonathan, Michael Haugh, and Marina Terkourafi. Forthcoming. *Pragmatics: Methods and Analysis*. Cambridge: Cambridge University Press.
Eelen, Gino. 2001. *A Critique of Politeness Theories*. Manchester: St. Jerome.
Enfield, Nick J. 2000. "The Theory of Cultural Logic." *Cultural Dynamics* 12: 35–64.
Fukushima, Saeko, and Michael Haugh. 2014. "The Role of Emic Understandings in Theorizing Im/politeness: The Metapragmatics of Attentiveness, Empathy and Anticipatory Inference in Japanese and Chinese." *Journal of Pragmatics* 74: 165–179.
Gagné, Nana Okura. 2010. "Reexamining the Notion of Negative Face in the Japanese *Socio* Linguistic Politeness of Request." *Language and Communication* 30: 123–138.
Garcés-Conejos Blitvich, Pilar. 2010. "A Genre Approach to the Study of Im-politeness." *International Review of Pragmatics* 2: 46–94.
Garcés-Conejos Blitvich, Pilar. 2013. "Introduction: Face, Identity and Politeness. Looking Backward, Moving Forward: from Goffman to Practice Theory." *Journal of Politeness Research* 9: 1–33.
Grice, H. Paul. 1975. Logic and Conversation. In *Speech Acts*. Vol. 3 of *Syntax and Semantics*, edited by Peter Cole, and Jerry Morgan, 41–58. New York: Academic Press.
Haugh, Michael. 2007. "The Discursive Challenge to Politeness Theory: An Interactional Alternative." *Journal of Politeness Research* 3: 295–317.
Haugh, Michael. 2012. "Epilogue: The First-Second Order Distinction in Face and Politeness Research." *Journal of Politeness Research* 8: 111–134.
Haugh, Michael. 2013. "Im/politeness, Social Practice and the Participation Order." *Journal of Pragmatics* 58: 52–72.
Haugh, Michael. 2015. *Im/politeness Implicatures*. Berlin: Mouton de Gruyter.
Haugh, Michael. 2016. "Prompting as a Higher-Order Pragmatic Act." In *Pragmemes and Theories of Language Use*, edited by Keith Allan, Alessandro Capone, and Istvan Kecskes, 167–190. New York: Springer.
Holmes, Janet, Meredith Marra, and Bernadette Vine. 2011. *Leadership, Discourse, and Ethnicity*. Oxford: Oxford University Press.
Holmes, Janet, and Stephanie Schnurr. 2017. "(Im)politeness in the Workplace." In *Palgrave Handbook of Linguistic (Im)politeness*, edited by Jonathan Culpeper, Michael Haugh, and Dániel Z. Kádár, 635–660. London: Palgrave Macmillan.
Ide, Sachiko. 1989. "Formal Forms and Discernment: Two Neglected Aspects of Universals of Linguistic Politeness." *Multilingua* 8: 223–248.
Jefferson, Gail. 2004. "Glossary of Transcript Symbols with an Introduction." In *Conversation Analysis: Studies from the First Generation*, edited by Gene Lerner, 13–23. Amsterdam: John Benjamins.
Jucker, Andreas, and Larssyn Rüegg. 2017. "(Im)politeness and Developments in Methodology." In *Palgrave Handbook of Linguistic (Im)politeness Research*, edited by Jonathan Culpeper, Michael Haugh, and Dániel Z. Kádár, 403–429. London: Palgrave Macmillan.
Kádár, Dániel Z., and Michael Haugh. 2013. *Understanding Politeness*. Cambridge: Cambridge University Press.
Kasper, Gabriele. 1996. "Politeness." In *Handbook of Pragmatics: 1996 Installment*, edited by Jef Verschueren, and Jan-Ola Ostman, 1–20. Amsterdam: John Benjamins.
Lakoff, Robin. 1973. "The Logic of Politeness; Or Minding Your P's and Q's." *Chicago Linguistics Society* 9: 292–305.

Leech, Geoffrey. 1983. *Principles of Pragmatics*. London: Longman.
Leech, Geoffrey. 2014. *The Pragmatics of Politeness*. Oxford: Oxford University Press.
Locher, Miriam. 2006. "Polite Behaviour within Relational Work: The Discursive Approach to Politeness." *Multilingua* 25: 249–267.
Locher, Miriam. 2008. "Relational Work, Politeness, and Identity Construction." In *Handbook of Interpersonal Communication*, edited by Gerd Antos, and Eija Ventola, 509–540. Berlin: Mouton de Gruyter.
Locher, Miriam. 2015. "Interpersonal Pragmatics and its Link to (Im)politeness Research." *Journal of Pragmatics* 86: 5–10.
Mao, LuMing. 1994. "Beyond Politeness Theory: 'Face' Revisited and Renewed." *Journal of Pragmatics* 21: 451–486.
Matsumoto, Yoshiko. 1988. "Reexamination of the Universality of Face: Politeness Phenomena in Japanese." *Journal of Pragmatics* 12: 403–426.
Mills, Sara. 2003. *Gender and Politeness*. Cambridge: Cambridge University Press.
Mills, Sara. Forthcoming. *English Politeness: A Materialist Discursive Approach*. Cambridge: Cambridge University Press.
Schegloff, Emanuel. 1995. "Discourse as Interactional Achievement III: The Omnirelevance of Action." *Research on Language and Social Interaction* 28: 185–211.
Spencer-Oatey, Helen. 2005. "(Im)Politeness, Face and Perceptions of Rapport: Unpackaging their Bases and Interrelationships." *Journal of Politeness Research* 1: 95–120.
Terkourafi, Marina. 2001. "Politeness in Cypriot Greek: A Frame-based Approach." PhD diss., Trinity Hall, Cambridge University.
Terkourafi, Marina. 2005. "Beyond the Micro-Level in Politeness Research." *Journal of Politeness Research* 1: 237–262.
Usami, Mayumi. 2002. *Discourse Politeness in Japanese Conversation: Some Implications for a Universal Theory of Politeness*. Tokyo: Hituzi Syobo.
van der Bom, Isabelle, and Sara Mills. 2015. "A Discursive Approach to the Analysis of Politeness Data." *Journal of Politeness Research* 11: 179–206.
Watanabe, Yasuhisa. 2009. "Face and Power in Intercultural Business Communication." PhD diss., Griffith University.
Watts, Richard. 2003. *Politeness*. Cambridge: Cambridge University Press.
Watts, Richard. 2005. "Linguistic Politeness Research: *Quo vadis?*" In *Politeness in Language. Studies in its History, Theory and Practice*. 2nd ed., edited by Richard Watts, Sachiko Ide, and Konrad Ehlich, xi-xlvii. Berlin: Mouton de Gruyter.
Watts, Richard, Sachiko Ide, and Konrad Ehlich. 1992. "Introduction." In *Politeness in Language. Studies in its History, Theory and Practice*, edited by Richard Watts, Sachiko Ide, and Konrad Ehlich, 1–17. Berlin: Mouton de Gruyter.
Wikipedia. 2016. "Politeness Theory." Available at https://en.wikipedia.org/wiki/Politeness_theory (accessed 29 May 2016).

7
Rapport Management
Jeannie Fletcher

Introduction

The management of interpersonal relations is one of the most important if not the most important aspect of workplace communication. It impacts not only relations between colleagues, managers, clients, and suppliers but also the transactional process and outcomes of the workplace. The Rapport Management framework focuses on the use of language to promote, maintain, neglect, or challenge harmonious social relations (Spencer-Oatey 2008b, 3). Spencer-Oatey uses the term "rapport" to refer to people's subjective perceptions of (dis)harmony or smoothness–turbulence in interpersonal relations. She identifies three key factors that influence rapport: "face sensitivities", "interactional goals" and "sociality rights and obligations" (discussed further below). The ways in which we manage these influences underpin the notion of "rapport management". Underlying assumptions of the framework are that all language use influences interpersonal rapport; that people try to manage their relations with others; and that what constitutes appropriate behaviour is governed by cultural conventions as well as contextual and individual preferences (Spencer-Oatey 2008b, 8).

While utilizing the fine-grained discourse strategies inherent in politeness theory, a point of departure from politeness theory is that with the rapport management approach no sentence is inherently polite or impolite (a point also made by Fraser and Nolan 1981). Politeness is a social judgement—the conditions under which expressions are used and the appropriateness of that use are evaluated by others. The Rapport Management framework expands on politeness theory to incorporate these notions. As well, an enhanced concept of face, a dual focus on both speaker and hearer, and the belief that *all* language use impacts the development of interpersonal rapport, combine to address various widely recognized critiques of politeness theory, e.g., Eelen (2001). These are: that politeness theory places more importance on speaker than hearer; that the concept of face is underspecified in that it fails to take account of eastern perceptions of face (Matsumoto 1988); and that certain speech acts have an inherent impact on politeness regardless of context. Although these critiques can be seen as addressed implicitly within politeness theory, the rapport management framework accounts for them explicitly, thus incorporating, even foregrounding, a comprehensive consideration of context. In utilizing the fine grained analysis of discourse strategies of politeness theory and extending this to incorporate multiple dimensions of context, Spencer-Oatey has developed a multi-level framework that enables a systematic exploration of how language is used to manage relationships.

Factors Underpinning the Management of Interpersonal Rapport

Spencer-Oatey (2008b, 8) identified three key influencing factors at the heart of rapport management: "face sensitivities", "interactional goals", and "sociality rights and obligations". Although an interaction may feature any one of these most strongly, the influence of all three is both simultaneous and interactive—drawing attention to the dynamic nature of interaction. In characterizing "face sensitivities", Spencer-Oatey (2008a, 13) cites Goffman in defining face as "the positive social value a person effectively claims for himself by the line others assume he has taken during a particular contact". People have both a fundamental desire to be evaluated positively by others and a desire to not have their negative qualities acknowledged. Face sensitivities can apply to any or all of the various aspects of a person's sense of identity: the self as an individual (individual identity); the self as a member of a group (collective identity); and the self in relation to others (social identity).

In workplace communication, as in communication generally, the second influencing factor—"interactional goals"—can be either transactional, relational or both, and the different ways in which these are approached are subject to cultural, individual, and contextual factors. Influences include the type of activity and the social/interactional roles and relations of participants. Managing interaction towards the achievement of interactional goals differs across cultures, reflecting the relative importance of for instance, role relationships, turn taking, positioning of goal oriented and social talk. When these differences go unrecognized or are poorly managed they can threaten rapport.

The third factor underpinning the management of interpersonal rapport—"sociality rights and obligations"—refers to "the fundamental social *entitlements*" [emphasis in original] (Spencer-Oatey 2008a, 13) that each person claims for themselves. When perceptions and expectations regarding what counts as normal behaviour within particular activity types and interactional contexts are not met, people may feel annoyed or offended. As well as differing between cultures, many such behavioural norms and conventions are not arbitrary but value laden and somewhat prescriptive, reflecting deeply held beliefs about for instance hierarchy and conventional behaviours. Termed "socio-pragmatic interactional principles (SIPs)" (Spencer-Oatey and Jiang 2003), they determine the appropriateness of behaviour in a given context and what Brown and Levinson (1987) and Thomas (1995) term "allowable contributions". Awareness and effective management of such conventions has a significant impact on successful cross-cultural communication.

SIPs are often based in contractual legal agreements and requirements. In the workplace they may for instance reflect conventions relating to appropriate behaviours for a particular role, or conventions regarding turn-taking—for instance in a company meeting, a job interview, a customer relations encounter or a contract negotiation. Spencer-Oatey (2008a, 16) identifies two SIPs in particular as being of fundamental importance. These are "equity"—the belief that we are entitled to personal consideration from others, that we are treated fairly and not unduly imposed upon; and "association"—the belief that we are entitled to association with others.

Although people commonly orient their interactions towards building rapport through mutual support, this is by no means always the case. People's orientation to rapport can and often does shift throughout the course of interaction and may encompass all of the four orientations identified by Spencer-Oatey (2008a, 32). A "rapport enhancement" orientation shows a desire to strengthen or enhance harmonious relations; whereas a "rapport maintenance" orientation involves the interactional work people do to protect already established relations. It is not uncommon however for people to overlook, ignore or simply be unconcerned about the quality of relations. This is termed "rapport neglect" and it can and often does threaten rapport. There are also many instances where people actively seek to challenge or impair harmonious relations through a "rapport challenge" orientation. Interactions in a range of workplace contexts may exhibit several or all of these orientations, especially where people must work together across practice boundaries to achieve a common goal or output.

Since all use of language impacts the development of rapport through people's interpretations of what is said, rapport management extends consideration beyond the illocutionary domain (which has traditionally been the main focus of politeness theory) to include the lexical, participation, discourse, and stylistic domains. Together these facilitate a richly nuanced view of the way language is used to manage social relationships.

Rapport Management in the Workplace

The emergence of the Rapport Management framework parallels a shift in both intercultural research and workplace communication, from a focus on difficulties and miscommunication, to incorporate a close examination of how people build effective collegial relations, a shift which aligns with the notion of Appreciative Enquiry (Hammond 1996). When analysis focuses only on the problematic or unsuccessful aspects of communication, many effective elements and processes can be overlooked. By focusing on what *is* effective or impacts in various ways on the development of rapport, negative aspects are thrown into contrast. It is also important to remember that effective communication does not simply involve untroubled interactions and unruffled harmony. The path to effective communication is not always smooth. The Rapport Management framework accounts for interaction holistically and includes consideration of both positive and negative impacts arising from rapport neglect and rapport challenge, and their interaction with rapport enhancement and maintenance strategies. This is especially relevant in workplace communication where various communicatively and relationally challenging interactions are part of organizational life.

In our private lives we may choose whom we interact with but this is not so in the workplace. It is important to establish and maintain effective working relationships with colleagues, clients, and suppliers. Some of these are ongoing relationships and some are short term. Together with the range of workplace contexts such as meetings, service encounters, interviews, conferences, performance evaluations, negotiations, and mediated interactions these place multiple demands on our communicative competencies. Workplace research from a linguistic perspective provides many insights into valued competencies together with how and why they work. In some contexts, people are very much aware of the need to manage rapport, while in others potential sources of miscommunication or misunderstanding often go unrecognized.

Managing Rapport at the Boundary of the Organization

At the interface between the organization and the outside, people are generally aware of the need for care in managing interaction. One context of such interaction is the employment interview. As a formal context at the boundary of the organization the employment interview is characterized by a range of social obligations and expectations on the part of both the candidate and the interviewer, and as a gatekeeping encounter which largely determines who is appointed to the position, it is important to both parties. A key aspect of positive self-presentation by candidates is their competence in developing rapport with the interviewer or interview team. Kerekes' (2007) study of intercultural pre-employment interviews conducted in English in a large north American employment agency, found that for both native speaker and non-native speaker candidates the most important factor was the ability to develop rapport with the interviewer and in particular to convey a sense of trustworthiness. Effective interviews were characterized by the co-construction of a sense of solidarity through affiliative discourse strategies, appropriate use of small talk and the candidate displaying a flexible approach to the demands of the potential position. Successful candidates were able to compensate for mistakes made and effectively answer questions about gaps or shortcomings in their CVs. Candidates evaluated as not suitable were much less effective in developing rapport. In particular, they failed to convey a sense of trustworthiness, for instance by offering inappropriate referees or asking for a salary beyond the scope of the position advertised. Often these candidates (whether native or non-native speakers of English) provided monosyllabic answers to questions and had poorly written CVs. In this sense they failed to meet both the social expectations of the interviewer and their substantive obligations as applicants for employment, resulting in an unfavourable impression and an unsuccessful application.

Creating a favourable impression through the development of positive rapport has also been identified as a characteristic of successful salespeople. Researching how rapport is established in business-to-business field sales encounters, Clark, Drew, and Pinch (2003) analysed the verbal strategies of salespeople and found that those who were most successful focused on creating a favourable impression by being friendly, using affiliative moves such as engaging in small talk about the prospect's special interests, and using humour. Engaging the prospect in this way had the effect of "selling" the prospect a likeable version of the salesperson's identity. Interestingly, the researchers found that despite both parties being aware that the identity constructed was not entirely genuine, this strategy nonetheless resulted in higher sales for those colleagues who used this approach. Also, such a strategy is not uncommon and therefore not entirely unexpected in sales encounters.

Pleasing the customer is a normal requirement of employees in both the retail and service sectors and many such interactions are mediated rather than face-to-face. Hui's (2014) study focusing on rapport management in call centres found that effective management incorporated appealing to customers' quality face and respecting association rights. Hui also identified rapport development in this context as progressing through four stages: initial establishment of rapport; co-operative meaning making; engagement; and exceeding customer expectations. The quality of these interactions influenced efficiency, customer satisfaction and company reputation.

A unique range of expectations govern interactions in each workplace. In the health sector the context of general practice interactions is strongly influenced by the social expectations and obligations associated with the roles of doctor and patient. Hernández-López (2011) explored rapport maintenance and enhancement strategies in two such contexts, focusing on negotiation strategies used in general practice in Spain and England with regard to sensitive decision-making. In both cultures commonalities were found in *initiating* decisions, with patients using (dis)agreement and/or self-diagnosis, while doctors displayed empathy, showed explicit or implicit (dis)agreement, expanded their explanations and provided options. Differences between the two cultures were however found in the *process* of negotiation. Whereas Spanish interlocutors preferred to negotiate through explicit or implicit expression of opinions and had a high tolerance of disagreement, building rapport in British interactions was characterized by the discussion of different alternatives and valuing the others' freedom to act.

Researchers focusing on rapport management sometimes focus on one specific conversational strategy. Lazzaro-Salazar's (2013) study explored the role of conversational overlaps in an education setting. They were found to be a purposeful way to display interest and involvement in a conversation, and where a second speaker was adding information relevant to the comment of a current speaker, overlaps were not perceived as disruptive or as an attempt to take over the conversation. Rather they demonstrated interest and showed support for the speaker's idea. They were also sometimes used to *rescue* a speaker who was having difficulty expressing an idea, thus achieving a kind of conversational duet as well as saving the face of a speaker who finds it difficult to express their thoughts. Furthermore, contributing new but relevant information in this way helped to express affiliation, build solidarity and support colleagues working together towards a common goal. Overlaps that were found to be disruptive were those that took the turn away from the current speaker or contradicted what they were saying.

A television show is not often thought of as a workplace. It is however a media workplace, a boundary between the organization and its public and a site of direct face-to-face interaction between the two. Such encounters provide both visual and linguistic evidence that illustrates a range of orientations to rapport as well as the ways in which they interact and can shift throughout the course of an encounter. A dramatic example of two different orientations and the shift between them is Bayrataroğlu and Sifianou's (2012) exploration of interaction in the UK quiz programme *The Weakest Link*. Here the hostess takes a rapport enhancement orientation, utilizing affiliative strategies to develop rapport to an extent where she can challenge, indeed attack, the contestant's face sensitivities to make a show for the audience of what Watts (2003, 260) terms "sanctioned aggressive facework". This exploitative approach to interaction for public amusement is mitigated only by the "speak to the camera" section, where participants can reply and comment directly to the audience. It also has to be acknowledged that participants have presumably seen the show prior to entering, must therefore know its format, and in this sense give tacit approval for these strategies to be used on them. Nonetheless it illustrates an exploitative approach to interaction in which the more powerful participant, the hostess, is licensed to attack contestants' faces for the amusement of others, and for personal recognition—albeit as "the rudest person on television" (Bayrataroğlu and Sifianou 2012, 143). Furthermore, since it attracts over four million viewers, the approach and strategies used are sanctioned by the organization (BBC Television).

Interactions such as these at the boundary of organizations are widely recognized as important. Equally important, however, are collegial relationships between the people and communities within the organization, which in a very real sense construct the organization through their day-to-day interactions and enactment of collegial relations (Gunnarsson 2005). An important consideration here is the negotiation of rapport across cultural boundaries.

Rapport and Collegial Interaction in Intercultural Workplace Contexts

Although the examples discussed above generally feature interlocutors of the same culture, in many workplaces people must interact with clients or colleagues from a wide range of other cultures. With the rapid expansion of Business English as a lingua franca (BELF), arising in part from advances in technology and the expansion of international business, it is not uncommon for international business organizations to have no native speakers of English (Pullin 2010). Although this would appear to be a significant disadvantage, Pullin notes that Firth (2008) has shown BELF to be "interactionally robust", and its speakers to be "resourceful in avoiding or overcoming misunderstandings and achieving understanding despite non-standard usage" (Pullin 2010, 457). Researching international communicative competence, Pullin's (2010) study of social talk among colleagues in a Swiss BELF context found that colleagues from different cultures chose topics of common interest to talk amongst themselves and build relationships. Music and food were frequent topics enabling everyone to participate in building common ground, thus satisfying the expectation of being included, contributing to solidarity, and supporting the development of rapport. This illustrates the fundamental importance of the SIP of "association" through participants' purposeful engagement in relational work despite language barriers, and its achievement through mutual engagement in non-transactional talk about topics common to all cultures.

There are many pitfalls in cross-cultural workplace communication and Spencer-Oatey argues that it is especially important to take account of SIPs in such contexts. The potential for misunderstanding is increased when people move between cultures and countries in the course of their work. In the education sector for instance teachers occasionally have the opportunity to extend their experience and expertise by engagement in the education systems of other countries. Crawshaw and Harrison (2007) found SIPs to be an important factor in misunderstandings between English language teaching assistants and their mentors in French primary schools. This concerned the established prerogative of the state to set the curriculum and the teachers' obligation to implement it (233). The teaching assistants were not sufficiently aware of the role played by politics in the French education system and as a result they had quite different perceptions of both power differentials and the (non-arbitrary) rights and obligations associated with their roles. All parties made incorrect assumptions and inappropriate remarks that lead to confrontation. These misunderstandings not only caused disharmony within the interactions but damaged the professional relationships between those involved. Although efforts at repair achieved "an uneasy compromise", later reflections by the parties involved suggested that the professional relationships could only be restored with further effort (253). This research exemplifies how such context variables can be specific to national cultures and illustrates the need for speakers to manage the role played by politics in communicative situations.

Achieving friendly relations can be especially challenging in cross cultural service sector workplaces. Ryoo (2005) studied the development of friendly relations between Korean immigrant shopkeepers and their African American customers in a small Midwestern town. Although this context is typically known for its tense relations, Ryoo found that Korean shopkeepers in this town were able to establish effective rapport through focusing on the relational (especially small talk and humour) rather than the transactional aspects of the interaction. Ryoo notes that this is somewhat unusual and believes the contrast with the more commonly recognized tense relationships between these two groups arises from the location of the study, a small Midwestern town with a low crime rate, rather than large cities where previous studies have typically been located.

Small talk as a strategy to bridge cultures presents its own pitfalls. What works as small talk in one culture may not work in another. Mak and Chui (2013) found that in the context of socializing an immigrant from the Philippines into a Hong Kong workplace, small talk proved to be both an instrument of socialization and a hurdle to its success, since the newcomer's small talk was associated with Filipino core values while that of her new colleagues reflected the social customs and values of Hong Kong.

Hidden Boundaries in Managing Rapport in Workplace Communication

The term "culture" is typically associated with different nationalities and/or ethnicities. However, industry sectors and organizations of all kinds develop cultures associated with their values, traditions and beliefs. Furthermore, subcultures form around the different professions and practice communities that comprise the organization and these find expression in the communicative practices of those who work there. Spencer-Oatey (2008b, 3) defines culture as follows:

> Culture is a fuzzy set of basic assumptions and values, orientations to life, beliefs, policies, procedures and behavioural conventions that are shared by a group of people, and that influence (but do not determine) each member's behaviour and his/her interpretations of the "meaning" of other people's behaviour.

The "fuzziness" of basic assumptions and values inherent in this concept of culture suggests how easy it is for communication problems to arise in managing rapport across the kinds of organizational and professional boundaries inherent in the workplace. These assumptions and values manifest for instance in distinctive perspectives, ways of setting up and solving problems, forms of humour, ways of communicating, attitudes, beliefs, behavioural conventions, and language. This enables efficient communication among members of the group through a common understanding, distinguishing them as part of that subculture and identifying them as "in-group" members. What often goes unrecognized however, is that communicating across boundaries between such sub-cultures presents the same range of challenges as communicating across ethnic and national cultures and these are at the heart of many if not most "communication problems" experienced by organizations. Small misunderstandings and incorrect assumptions can quickly escalate into larger conflicts and impede or derail important organizational goals and projects, often with far reaching consequences.

Recent research has shown that communication between people belonging to different workplace practice groups (e.g., accountants, designers, engineers, administrators) requires communicative competencies similar to those required between people of different ethnic cultures. Problems and misunderstandings can and do arise when people from the different subcultures must work together to achieve organizational goals. Workplace meetings are one such context. Holmes and Stubbe (2003, 56) note that meetings "provide sites for the manifestation of politeness, respect and disrespect, collegiality and solidarity, i.e., various aspects of rapport management".

Indeed, the transactional business of the group will often not proceed until what organizational researcher Tsoukas (2009) terms "a mode of relational engagement" is achieved. Tsoukas (2009, 941) notes that

> dialogue is productive depending on the extent to which participants engage relationally with one another. When this happens participants are more likely to actively take responsibility for both the joint tasks in which they are involved and for the relationships they have with others.

This is especially important in contexts where people from different professions and practice groups must work together to develop and produce new knowledge in the form of a new system, product, process, or way of doing things.

Exploring rapport management in a cross functional project team involving members from five different specialty areas, Fletcher (2014) found that the path to establishing rapport among participants involved both rapport neglect and rapport challenge with the potential for conflict escalation in the early stages of the initial project meeting. A peripheral member's lateness for an important meeting threatened the face sensitivities of the newly appointed project leader by failing to observe the behavioural obligations of such membership. He arrived late for the meeting and did not offer an apology. The project leader's sarcastic comment "glad you could join us" (363) constituted rapport challenge with potential for escalation to conflict. However, the experienced project members stepped in and managed the situation with humour. Knowing that the latecomer was taking time out to play a console game as he tried to work out a solution to a technical challenge, and that he had to save his character and exit from the game, they began a humorous discussion of the game, reducing tension by involving the new project leader. One of the experienced members challenged the latecomer saying "what's all this garbage about having to save?", thus drawing the latecomer's attention to the group's expectations around punctuality. The meeting then smoothly proceeded with the transactional business. In managing the situation the experienced members collaboratively and effectively re-oriented the interaction towards the enhancement of rapport. These collegial and solidary strategies contributed to the transactional goals of the meeting by fostering good relations and keeping the meeting on track.

This supports Tsoukas' findings mentioned above, since it was only once this relational engagement was achieved that the group was able to move forward with the transactional phase of the meeting. Many organizational projects are delayed or even derailed when participants lack the communicative competencies to manage interpersonal rapport effectively. The subsequent impact on both technical and professional performance as well as "the bottom line" can be substantial.

Leader–Member Relations

One of the most sensitive areas in the management of rapport in workplace communication is leader–member relations, which as well as being frequent and important can also be a leading cause of employee distress (Campbell, White, and Johnson 2007). Campbell, White, and Johnson (2007) found that leaders and members have different perceptions of the quality of their relationships and that the management of interpersonal rapport has a substantial impact on these relations. An especially challenging aspect is the management of what Campbell, White, and Johnson term "necessary evils"—when managers must reprimand, provide negative feedback or act in ways that may negatively impact employees and as a result may influence their perceptions of justice or injustice associated with these interactions. Relationship maintenance behaviours were found to be crucial since "necessary evils" have the potential to threaten rapport through their impact on both quality face and identity face sensitivities. Criticism, for instance, especially if in front of others, can threaten quality face and social identity face; ordering or requesting can threaten autonomy rights; and not listening or giving attention can threaten association rights. Interactions begun by consulting for instance were identified as much more likely to have a positive outcome than those begun by simply directing or informing. Violations of face sensitivities relating to identity, autonomy, association rights and quality were found not only to underpin feelings of injustice but also to impact negatively on a willingness to contribute.

Sometimes violations of face are intentional. Tracy (2002) proposed that people may want to make a variety of identity claims apart from the claim to be pleasant and likeable. Lauriks,

Siebörger, and De Vos (2015) found that discordant relationships were used strategically in an African small business context.

Contributions of Rapport Management

As Spencer-Oatey (2008b, 2) notes "all language use can affect people's interpretations of how appropriately face, sociality rights and interactional goals are managed." One of the most significant contributions of Rapport Management research is its highlighting of the role of small talk in workplace communication. As part of the discourse domain, encompassing topic choice and management, small talk includes off-topic social talk. In contrast to transactional talk which is "focused, context bound on-task talk with high information content" (Holmes 2000, 36–37), small talk is social, has less referential content and includes utterances such as greetings and partings (these latter are known as phatic communication). Small talk was for decades regarded as unimportant, as a distraction from transactional talk and a digression from the serious business of the workplace. However recent research demonstrates that it is anything but small. Pullin (2010) identified small talk to be a key component of "international communicative competence" enabling colleagues in an international BELF workplace to effectively build rapport despite cultural and linguistic barriers. It also served to mitigate power since managers would join in such conversations. In Clark, Drew, and Pinch's (2003) study on effective sales techniques small talk was used by the most effective sales people in developing affiliation with prospective purchasers, and Kerekes (2007) found small talk to be a distinctive feature of interactions between successful applicants and interviewers in employment interviews. This supports the findings of Holmes and Stubbe (2003) and Marra (2003) who found small talk occurred as a boundary marker at the beginning and ending of meetings as well as within transactional talk—to oil the wheels of collegiality and to both construct and mitigate power in workplace relationships. Thus small talk inherently supports the transactional processes of the workplace.

In many cultures, small talk plays an important strategic role managing interpersonal rapport in business negotiation, with significant implications for ongoing and future interactions. In Chinese culture for instance, Yang (2012) notes small talk as a core strategy whose positioning reflects participants' evaluation of the relationship. As a communicative behaviour it is also a social expectation in Chinese business negotiations where it comprises "a meaningful, politic and intentional activity" (101).

A second contribution of Rapport Management is its value as a bridge between micro and macro-levels of analysis. Although it utilises the fine grained linguistic strategies of politeness theory, it draws these together with broader level concepts—in particular the three key factors that influence rapport ("face sensitivities", "interactional goals", and "social rights and obligations"). These make the framework accessible to disciplines other than linguistics, thereby facilitating and supporting cross-disciplinary research.

As well as contributing significant insights into many aspects of workplace communication, research using the Rapport Management framework provides an interesting opportunity and an inherent responsibility for researchers to apply its concepts to planning, executing and reflecting on their research process. Researchers are reliant on the goodwill of organizations' CEOs and senior managers for access to the organization and its people. As outsiders they depend on the generosity and cooperation of these people for the provision of opportunities to observe situations, activities, resources and communicative interactions that illustrate the ways in which interpersonal rapport is managed in the workplace (Marra 2008). As insiders, research participants provide potential explanations and insights into cultural norms. Besides being an ethical requirement of research, advising participants that they may withdraw their contribution at any time supports the development of trust and gives participants confidence that their interests are being safeguarded (307–308). This in turn supports the individual and organizational identities of participants as well as demonstrating that their face sensitivities are considered along with the goals of the research. These considerations are especially important when researchers from one culture locate their study and gather data in an organisation of a different ethnicity. Development of rapport between such researchers and their participatory workplaces must be negotiated with explicit consideration of the cultural values that govern that workplace (Marra 2008).

Considerations for Further Research

An especially rich area for new research in rapport management is the field of veterinary medicine—where practitioner–client relations are the lifeblood of the profession. Although the actual patients are animals, their owners are key participants and veterinarians have the simultaneous challenges of providing clinical care for the animal and relational care for the owner (Cornell and Kopcha 2007). Such relationships are often long term and can at times involve high levels of emotion especially when the animal is ill or injured. The value of competence in managing interpersonal rapport is increasingly recognized in both veterinary practice and in veterinary education.

Research focusing on the relationship between the communicative competencies involved in rapport management and the long-term sustainability of the organization also has much to offer. For instance, since solid collegial relations and the effective management of interpersonal rapport underpin the development of trust and the social capital essential for knowledge sharing and creativity, how do these play out in mediated environments? Communication in 21st-century organizations is increasingly characterized by what is termed "virtual interaction". The multitude of technologies that are ubiquitous in today's workplaces are tools—albeit with distinct affordances, scope and reach. However, the interactions they facilitate are real. The scope and reach of these technologies mean that we are not always aware of the ethnicities of those we interact with, especially when there are multiple participants. Participants may also be in different time zones. Research is needed into how rapport and collegial relationships are managed in these contexts, as well as how to effectively negotiate the intersection of the various technologies.

Further Reading

Fletcher (1999) presents a framework for the analysis of Relational Practice—the often overlooked or downplayed "little things" people do that make a big impact on interpersonal relations in the workplace. Relational Practice has subsequently been shown to also have a direct impact on transactional workplace processes and outcomes.

Ho (2011) explores differences between core and peripheral members of a community of practice in their management of request emails, while Lam (2009) provides interesting insights into the ways in which leaders' management of interpersonal rapport impacts leader-member relations. Planken (2005) gives a comparative analysis of the ways in which professional and aspiring negotiators manage interactional "safe talk", and their relative effectiveness in maintaining professional distance.

Spencer-Oatey (2002) examines the motivational concerns that underlie the management of interpersonal relations. She presents her argument for the fundamental difference between the concepts of face and sociality rights, a key feature of the distinction between the rapport management framework and politeness theory.

Related Topics

(Im)politeness theory; Communities of practice; Service encounters; Call centre discourse; Relational talk; Conflict talk; Intercultural communication

References

Bayrataroğlu, Arin, and Maria Sifianou. 2012. "The Iron Fist in a Velvet Glove: How Politeness Can Contribute to Impoliteness." *Journal of Politeness Research* 8: 143–160.
Brown, Penelope, and Stephen Levinson. 1987. *Politeness: Some Universals in Language Usage*. Cambridge: Cambridge University Press.
Campbell, Kim Sydow, Charles D. White, and Diane E. Johnson. 2007. "Leader–Member Relations as a Function of Rapport Management." *Journal of Business Communication* 40: 170–194.
Clark, Colin, Paul Drew, and Trevor Pinch. 2003. "Managing Prospect Affiliation and Rapport in Real-Life Sales Encounters." *Discourse Studies* 5: 5–31.
Cornell, Karen K., and Michelle Kopcha. 2007. "Client–Veterinarian Communication: Skills for Client Centered Dialogue and Shared Decision Making." *Veterinary Clinics: Small Animal Practice* 37: 37–47.
Crawshaw, Robert, and Julia Harrison. 2007. "Politics and Pragmatics in the Cross-Cultural Management of "Rapport'." *Language and Intercultural Communication* 7: 217–239.
Eelen, Gino. 2001. *A Critique of Politeness Theories*. Manchester: St. Jerome.
Firth, Alan. 2008. "The Lingua Franca Factor." Paper presented at the ELF Forum: The First International Conference on English as a Lingua Franca, University of Helsinki, Finland.
Fletcher, Jeannie R. 2014. "Social Communities in a Knowledge Enabling Organizational Context: Interaction and Relational Engagement in a Community of Practice and a Micro-Community of Knowledge." *Discourse and Communication* 8: 351–369.
Fletcher, Joyce K. 1999. *Disappearing Acts: Gender, Power and Relational Practice at Work*. Cambridge, MA: MIT Press.
Fraser, Bruce, and William Nolan. 1981. "The Association of Deference with Linguistic Form." *International Journal of the Sociology of Language* 27: 93–111.
Gunnarsson, Britt-Louise. 2005. "The Verbal Construction of Organizations." In *Communication in the Workplace*, edited by Britt-Louise Gunnarsson, 78–90. Uppsala: Uppsala Universitet.
Hammond, Sue Annis. 1996. *The Thin Book of Appreciative Enquiry*. Plano: Thin Book.
Hernández-López, María de la O. 2011. "Negotiation Strategies and Patient Empowerment in Spanish and British Medical Consultations." *Communication & Medicine* 8: 169–180.
Ho, Victor C. K. 2011. "Rapport—How the Weight it Carries Affects the Way it is Managed." *Text & Talk* 31: 153–172.
Holmes, Janet. 2000. "Doing Collegiality and Keeping Control at Work: Small Talk in Government Departments." In *Small Talk*, edited by Justine Coupland, 32–61. London: Longman.
Holmes, Janet, and Maria Stubbe. 2003. *Power and Politeness in the Workplace: A Sociolinguistic Analysis of Talk at Work*. London: Pearson.
Hui, Jon S. Y. 2014. "Analysing Interpersonal Relations in Call-Centre Discourse." PhD diss., Victoria University of Wellington.
Kerekes, Julie. 2007. "The Co-Construction of a Gatekeeping Encounter: An Inventory of Verbal Actions." *Journal of Pragmatics* 39: 1942–1973.
Lam, Christopher. 2009. "The Linguistic Patterns that Lead to Rapport Management, Trust, Interactional Justice, Support, and Leader-Member Exchange." PhD diss., Illinois University of Technology.
Lauriks, Sanne, Ian Siebörger, and Mark De Vos. 2015. "'Ha! Relationships? I Only Shout at Them': Strategic Management of Discordant Rapport in an African Small Business Context." *Journal of Politeness Research* 11: 7–39.
Lazzaro-Salazar, Mariana. 2013. "Investigating Nurses" Professional Identity Construction in Two Health Settings in New Zealand." PhD diss., Victoria University of Wellington.

Mak, Bernie Chun Nam, and Hin Leung Chui. 2013. "A Cultural Approach to Small Talk: A Double-Edged Sword of Sociocultural Reality during Socialization into the Workplace." *Journal of Multicultural Discourses* 8: 118–133.

Marra, Meredith. 2003. "Decisions in New Zealand Business Meetings: A Sociolinguistic Analysis of Power at Work." PhD diss., Victoria University of Wellington.

Marra, Meredith. 2008. "Recording and Analysing Talk across Cultures." In *Culturally Speaking: Culture, Communication and Politeness Theory*, edited by Helen Spencer-Oatey, 304–321. London: Continuum.

Matsumoto, Yoshiko. 1988. "Re-Examination of the Universality of Face: Politeness Phenomena in Japanese." *Journal of Pragmatics* 12: 403–426.

Planken, Brigitte. 2005. "Managing Rapport in Lingua Franca Sales Negotiations: A Comparison of Professional and Aspiring Negotiators." *English for Specific Purposes* 24: 381–400.

Pullin, Patricia. 2010. "Small Talk Rapport and International Communicative Competence: Lessons to Learn from BELF." *International Journal of Business Communication* 47: 455–476.

Ryoo, Hye-Kyung. 2005. "Achieving Friendly Interactions: A Study of Service Encounters between Korean Shopkeepers and African-American Customers." *Discourse & Society* 16: 79–105.

Spencer-Oatey, Helen. 2002. "Managing Rapport in Talk: Using Rapport Sensitive Incidents to Explore the Motivational Concerns Underlying the Management of Relations." *Journal of Pragmatics* 34: 529–545.

Spencer-Oatey, Helen. 2008a. "Face, (Im)politeness and Rapport." In *Culturally Speaking: Culture, Communication and Politeness Theory*, edited by Helen Spencer-Oatey, 11–47. London: Continuum.

Spencer-Oatey, Helen. 2008b. "Introduction." In *Culturally Speaking: Culture, Communication and Politeness Theory*, edited by Helen Spencer-Oatey, 1–8. London: Continuum.

Spencer-Oatey, Helen, and Winying Jiang. 2003. "Explaining Cross-Cultural Pragmatic Findings: Moving from Politeness Maxims to Socio-Pragmatic Interactional Principles (SIPs)." *Journal of Pragmatics* 35: 1633–50.

Thomas, Jenny. 1995. *Meaning in Interaction: An Introduction to Pragmatics*. Harlow, UK: Pearson Education.

Tracy, Karen. 2002. *Everyday Talk: Building and Reflecting Identities*. London: Guilford Press.

Tsoukas, Haridimos. 2009. "A Dialogical Approach to the Creation of New Knowledge in Organizations." *Organization Science* 20: 941–957.

Watts, Richard. 2003. *Politeness*. Cambridge: Cambridge University Press.

Yang, Wenhui. 2012. "Small Talk: A Strategic Interaction in Chinese Interpersonal Business Negotiations." *Discourse and Communication* 6: 101–124.

8
Social Constructionism
Mariana Lazzaro-Salazar

Introduction

Social constructionism is a theoretical paradigm which initially highlighted the social nature of knowledge development and it can be traced back to German studies on the sociology of knowledge in the 19th century (see Allen 2005). In the 1960s Berger and Luckmann's (1967) seminal work *The Social Construction of Reality* was published, inspiring scholarly disciplines investigating language, discourse and culture, such as anthropology, sociology, and linguistics, to conduct constructionist work (see Foster and Bochner 2008).

One of the basic tenets of social constructionism is that humans construct the world through social practices and, thus, it favours a subjective understanding of social phenomena emphasizing the idea that realities are, to a considerable extent, constructed when social actors interact with each other (Weedon 1997). In this light, social constructionism challenges notions of objective realities, rejecting essentialist explanations about social phenomena as inevitable, uncontested and never-changing in an effort to avoid taken-for-granted assumptions of the world (Allen 2005). In this context, language is considered a fundamental aspect of constructionist processes as it is a vehicle through which social actors both represent *and* construct social realities (Foster and Bochner 2008).

The interactional and relational conception of communication that characterizes social constructionism has attracted a considerable amount of attention from sociolinguists devoted to workplace research, who found a way to investigate how language is used to create and negotiate knowledge (see, for instance, the construction of diagnosis and illness in Brown 1995), and to accept, reproduce, negotiate, reject, and align with a myriad of social stances as these are enacted in situated practices. The latter has been a major focus of workplace research as scholars have investigated the social construction of masculinities (e.g., Courtenay 2000), leadership roles (e.g., Ladegaard 2011), and interactants' ethnic orientations (e.g., Marra, King, and Holmes 2014), to give a few examples. Moreover, social constructionism has been applied to the study of discourse in workplace interaction from a number of well-known and compatible research traditions such as conversation analysis, critical discourse analysis, interactional sociolinguistics and discursive psychology (see Gunnarsson, Linell, and Nordberg 1997; and Hanson-Easey and Augoustinos 2012), and its underlying principles characterize notions such as the community of practice (see Ladegaard 2011).

With the aim of showing how social constructionism informs and enhances our understanding of communication phenomena, this chapter unpacks the main assumptions that define social constructionism as the vehicle through which to understand the dialogic nature of human relations in workplace interaction. Because the theoretical assumptions of social constructionism are better understood when discussed within the boundaries of social interaction, the chapter illustrates the main principles by drawing on data collected in a large public healthcare institution in New Zealand (Lazzaro-Salazar 2013). The examples chosen show how a group of nurses and their nurse manager dialogically construct and negotiate different aspects of their professional identity, namely, their leadership, expert stances, and cultural alignments, in semi-formal workplace meetings. The chapter finishes by offering reflections on future avenues of social constructionist inquiry focusing, in particular, on intercultural workplace research.

Main Guiding Principles of Social Constructionism in Workplace Communication

Interactional Construction of Knowledge: Language as Action in Everyday Talk

Constructionist inquiry addresses issues on the consequences of the social through the understanding of the social processes involved in interaction (see Foster and Bochner 2008). From this point of view, social constructionism supports the philosophical view that language is a social practice that constructs and contests social meanings as social actors collaboratively construct talk and, as a result, social realities, in locally situated interaction (Gunnarsson, Linell, and Nordberg 1997). This conception of language in interaction emphasizes the importance of discursive practices as a way to perform social action and transmit cultural knowledge, which has been acknowledged in the literature at both macro and micro levels of workplace inquiry.

At the macro level, organizational scholars from different fields and traditions have increasingly recognized the importance of discourse in the daily routines of an institution because "the internal structure of organizations [such as their power structures and genres] is . . . managed and displayed through talk" (Fasulo and Zucchermaglio 2002, 1121). This view of workplace communication supports the claim that institutions are constituted through language as the means through which institutional practices are reproduced, renewed and reshaped to construct workplace routines, norms and relationships, i.e., their organizational culture (Bucholtz and Hall 2010; Fairclough 2003). This approach to the study of institutional discourse has placed professional talk at the centre of much sociolinguistic inquiry, prompting scholars to study how organizational cultures provide the resources for individual and group action and how it can also provide a source of constraint to individual agency, focusing on socialization processes where narratives (Barone and Lazzaro-Salazar 2015), small talk (Coupland 2014), requests (Svennevig and Djordjilovic 2015; Vine 2004), and apologies (Basford, Offermann, and Behrend 2014), for instance, are shown to be key elements of organizational culture.

This perspective of the socially constitutive nature of language and interaction has not always dominated our understanding of communication phenomena, however, but has evolved from a more rhetorically oriented view of talk that strongly characterized communication studies until the 1970s when scholarship on the view of social interaction began to focus on its more empirical aspect of actual communication-as-practiced. In this regard, Berger and Luckmann's

(1967) work directed scholarly attention to the possibility of placing everyday interactions at the centre of inquiry so that scholarly endeavours focused on how communication processes actually occur in real interactions and how they help to generate knowledge and construct social realities. As a result of this shift from "objectivist" and "realist" to more subjective orientations to social constructions, communication researchers started focusing on the patterns of the group rather than solely on those of the individual, as meaning is conceptualized as arising from social systems rather than merely from individual members of society. By the 1980s, communication was widely acknowledged as a form of action "through which individuals create and manage their social realities", emphasizing the idea that "meaning must be negotiated and coordinated and thus that it is produced transpersonally" (Foster and Bochner 2008, 89).

As a result of this advancement in our understanding of social communication, the field of workplace research moved towards more empirical paradigms and interpretative methods as it started to focus on micro analytical structures of workplace interaction. In this light, identity studies in particular have come to heavily rely on this interactional principle of social constructionism as a core aspect of identity formation processes at both the intra and interpersonal levels. Acknowledging a certain level of inherent tension between macro and micro social structures (e.g., Lazzaro-Salazar 2013), social constructionist views on identity formation contend that the intra and the interpersonal are inextricably interrelated, that is to say, one is not believed to happen without the other. Thus, at its intrapersonal level, it is argued that for social actors to attempt to claim any given social identity, they need to perform certain acts, that is to say, a "socially recognized, goal-directed behaviour" such as asking for permission, and to display certain stances, that is to say, "a socially recognised point of view or attitude" (Ochs 1993, 288). This, following Foucault's (1988) views on identity, means that identity formation is not an external process that "happens" to the social actor but rather an internal one in which the social actor becomes the "agent" of their own identity construction (see agency as the "socioculturally mediated capacity to act" in Ahearn 2001, 112; see Skeggs 2008 for a critique of Eurocentric conceptions of identity construction; also see Martin and Nakayama 2015). Thus, a social actor's identity becomes "a product of our ongoing performances of acts" in a process through which they manage certain positionings over others as they make choices regarding their preferred orientation of the self when they interact with relevant others (Pennycook 2004, 8; also see "positionality principle" in Bucholtz and Hall 2010). This concept has been extensively developed as one of the pillars of sociolinguistic theories such as performativity theory in gender studies (see Butler 1990; see Pennycook 2004 for a comprehensive review of performativity theory), which is partly responsible for widely employed phrases such as "performing identity", "an act of identity", and "doing identity."

In order to illustrate how social actors manage social positionings to construct a preferred image of the self, Example 1 shows how the identity construction of Tina, a registered nurse, does not align with her institutionally sanctioned role but rather discursively constructs her as a leader among her peers.

In this example, Tina stands out from her group of colleagues and constructs herself as a leader by virtue of her discursive behaviour when she reflects on how handovers develop in her ward. Tina achieves this by constructing the other nurses as an outgroup ("they" in lines 1 and 6), rejecting any subjective association with the group of nurses ("people" in line 4) and constructing herself as the sole member of an ingroup ("I" in lines 2 and 5) that seems to hold the monopoly of appropriate professional practice. Tina phrases her request of not handing over information related to discharged patients in the form of an order (line 2), which is very frequently associated with leadership roles, to then outline some of the principles of

> **Example 8.1**[1]
>
> Context: Eve, the ward's manager at a hospital, asks a group of registered nurses to provide feedback regarding the way handovers develop in their ward. Tina, one of the registered nurses, replies:
>
> 1   Tina: half the time they're going OFF the topic . . .
> 2   and i don't wanna hear about
> 3   patients that are being ↑ discharged . . .
> 4   people seem to give handovers of patients that aren't there on the ↑ floor
> 5   so it's a waste of my time when i just wanna get on the floor . . .
> 6   cos they're only supposed to give the basics . . .
> 7   it's going back to basic nursing

the nursing profession (lines 6 and 7). This helps her build her professional accountability and legitimizes her claims (see Lazzaro-Salazar 2013). These discursive resources serve Tina to build herself in a more authoritative position than her fellow nurses, even if it is only for the duration of her turn. This example then shows that leadership, for instance, may not always be a reflection of institutionally assigned roles but may be a dialogically constructed orientation of the self that emerges in interaction when social actors employ certain discursive resources that help them to index such stances.

Naturally, acts of identity do not happen in a vacuum but occur, as in the case of Example 8.1, when social actors participate in everyday workplace activities where interactions with co-workers cause social actors to orient and, if need be, reorient and negotiate their identity on a moment-by-moment basis. This adds the interpersonal level of understanding of social identity construction that rests on the principle that social phenomena are relational and emerge in local interaction (Hall 2012; also see relational theory in Fletcher 1999). It is then in social interaction that social actors face the need to position themselves in regards to certain stances in order to reproduce and interpret certain identities when they interact with significant others (see Benwell and Stokoe 2006) as these are reworked to fit the interactional goals of the moment, and are, thus, interactionally accomplished (Cerulo 1997). It is then only by investigating how an interaction develops that we can begin to explore how identities are negotiated and enacted. In this light, prevailing social constructionist theories on identity formation argue that while act, stance, and agency constitute the backbones of definitions of the self-constructed aspect of identity, this intrapersonal aspect of identity formation can only be interpreted and understood when investigated in relation to its contextually mediated aspect which influences the agentive attribute of social processes (see Giddens 1999).

The Situated Nature of Social Action: The Role of the Interactional Context

This last consideration takes us to another assumption that characterizes social constructionism. According to social constructionists, the interactional context becomes paramount in guiding scholars' interpretation of social construction phenomena. When they interact, social actors have a choice of a range of, usually intersecting, identities (such as gender and professional) that are available to them at any given point in the interaction. Identities are naturally multifaceted, that is to say, there are a number of subidentities that may conflict or align with each other as they serve different purposes in an interaction (Cooper and Olson 1996). The choice of identity or identities and their interactional relevance are dynamic as they are "responsive to [also dynamic] contextual conditions" (Hall 2012, 33). As Dannels (2000) explains, the negotiation of identities within situated contexts of interaction will result in one particular identity or facet of an identity being more salient at any given moment than others (see Pennycook 2010; Renkema 2004). The choice of identity and identity orientation then will shift as these are adapted and adjusted to fit the changing conditions of the context that surrounds identity claims. No one interactional context is the same; the contextual features are dynamic and are different from interaction to interaction, and these may even change within the same interaction. Thus, each interactional event calls for a constant reconsideration of social actors' choice of identity orientation and the way of displaying it (Haddington 2006). This reflects the social constructionist assumption that there are multiple social realities, that these realities form a network or web of social realities which interact with each other and which will be made relevant and reoriented in interaction depending on the demands of its context.

In this light, social constructionism views "context" as a conjunction of interactional features such as speech situation, interactants, physical and cultural setting, discursive resources, shared background assumptions, topic of the conversation, (institutionally sanctioned) roles of the participants, and interactional activities within which an interactional event is embedded, all or some of which may, to different degrees, become relevant at different stages of an interaction in the process of identity formation (Duranti and Goodwin 1992; also see van Dijk 2006). The following example illustrates the contextual nature of identity construction by showing how the speech situation in which Susan, a registered nurse and nurse delegate, is involved seems to strongly mediate her group alignment choices. Bringing together other aspects of social constructionism discussed so far, the example also shows how stances are interactionally constructed and reoriented in conversation as their context changes.

Complaining is an inherently face-threatening act (see Lerman 2006) which has the potential to offend its recipient, causing both the speaker and the interlocutor to lose face. In order to maintain relational harmony, Susan needs to manage how she expresses the complaint so that it does not damage either her image or that of her interlocutor's, maintaining relational

---

Example 8.2

Context: Susan, a nurse delegate, is telling Nick, the charge nurse manager, that some nurses have complained about the number of night shifts they have been assigned. In the example Susan explains what she has told these nurses.

1	Susan:	yeah i told that's what i told um
2		those the girls
3		if five nights or six m- mornings comes up
4		just relook at the roster and
5		you know {increased volume}: and come and
6		see you can explain to them how that works:
7	Nick:	yeah that's right so
8		and if they ARE saying to you
9		just explain again

harmony (see comprehensive analysis in Lazzaro-Salazar 2013). Using the same discursive strategy as Tina in Example 8.1, but guided by a different relational purpose, Susan achieves this by voicing the complaint on behalf of a supposedly non-present third party, positioning herself as an outsider to this group of complaining "girls" (line 2). She later reinforces this stance through the use of "them" (line 6) to refer back to "the girls", unequivocally indexing her disaffiliative stance in regards to the complaints (see Fasulo and Zucc14 2002). In this way, Susan locally constructs an outgroup that seems to be bigger than her functional ingroup in which she is possibly the only member, and orients towards her role as the nurse delegate rather than as a fellow nurse within the team. This places her in the powerful position of being the link between the management and the nursing staff and counterbalances the effects of a complaint in an effort to avoid conflict in a potentially face-threatening situation.

It should be mentioned, however, that "the girls" seems to be an emotionally and positively loaded term (see considerations of "collectivism" in Kashima *et al.* 1995) (cf. "people" and "the nurses" in Example 8.1). Thus, although in the context of this conversation this phrase is used to display disaffiliative behaviour, she may be also indexing a certain closeness with the group by making this apparent familiarity relevant through her discursive choice. Attesting to the multifaceted aspect of social reality that characterizes social constructionism, this could suggest that Susan may not regard "the girls" as an outgroup at all times; rather she may sometimes consider herself a member of this group but given the potentially face-threatening context of the current interaction she may find it more useful to distance herself from that group momentarily.

Moreover, as part of the context in which one constructs an identity, this also involves how relevant others react to our display of group membership stances, that is to say, how they accept or reject our positioning in interaction. In the case of this example, as Nick responds to the complaint, he too runs the risk of engaging in face-threatening behaviour when communicating his decisions in relation to the complaint. Thus, Nick also orients to maintaining harmonious relations and chooses to accept Susan's self-positioning as a non-member of "the girls" group in line 8 when he uses the pronoun "they" to make reference to "the girls" and later addresses Susan by the pronoun "you", which further supports his construction of Susan's identity (line 8). Nick then aligns with Susan's identity claim as a leader within the team of nurses when he acknowledges that the other nurses approach her for consultation (line 8) and when he tells her what to explain in line 9.

As the same conversation develops, however, its context changes as Susan and Nick discuss other issues of their monthly schedule. As Example 8.3 shows, this contextual change in the conversation (from a complaint in Example 8.2 to a simple request for information in Example 8.3) prompts Susan to reorient her stance and to construct herself as a member of "the girls'" group (notice use of "we" in lines 2 and 5).

Example 8.3

1	Susan:	the one thing nick
2		are we allowed to do
3		only request night shifts for
4		a month...
5		if we request for it

A fundamental consideration that stems from this analysis is that the discursive practices involved in the enactment and negotiation of identity, such as the construction of multiple group memberships, are context-sensitive as they need to adapt in order for them to be appropriate and relevant to the interaction (see Fairclough 1995; McKenna 2004). Any social construction is then a contextually mediated process because the context of interaction plays a significant role in, for instance, how identities shift through the course of interaction, and how they are interpreted, negotiated, reworked, and reinterpreted among social actors according to their perceptions, their interactional needs and the interactional development of the conversation.

One further point to be made in regards to the situated nature of social interaction is that social actors' stances are also partly evaluated by interlocutors in relation to their interpretations of previous social experiences of social interaction (Apker and Eggly 2004) and the social expectations they hold of the identity embodied by those stances (Saito 2012), both of which inevitably become part of the social context in which an interaction is embedded. In regards to social actors' previous interactional experiences, Beijaard, Verloop, and Vermunt (2000, 750) note that the ongoing process of social construction involves "the interpretation and reinterpretation of experiences as one lives through them", which constitutes and refines social actors' conceptions of social reality and identity. Consequently, one's identity is also partly the result of negotiations of past experiences in the workplace. In regards to social actors' expectations, these are built in light of certain sociocultural aspects such as the kind of behaviour that is considered to be morally and socially appropriate or acceptable (see Cook 2011). Following this line of thought, while among the several varieties of social constructionism (see Danziger 1997) certain approaches to social processes focus on the interdependence of subjective agency and the local contextual conditions (as illustrated above), others support the claim that realities should be interpreted as sociocultural constructs deriving from social actors' experiences and expectations (Gunnarsson, Linell, and Nordberg 1997).

Historical and Cultural Perspectives of Social Constructionism

The historical approach to socio-constructionism addresses the issues of how any given genre, discourse or social routine, for instance, was constructed and sustained over time, for whom, in response to what needs and why in such particular ways and not others. In this view, social constructions "derive knowledge of the world from larger social discourses, which can vary across time and place, and which often represent and reinforce dominant belief systems" that are historically constructed and culturally specific (Allen 2005, 35).

Radical supporters of this view believe that social phenomena should be entirely interpreted through this historical constructionist perspective as social constructions are exclusively, in their view, influenced by historical and cultural factors (Gunnarsson, Linell, and Nordberg 1997). When applied to workplace research, however, such historical and cultural constructs may not always be readily available and/or accessible to social researchers. Nevertheless, it is important to reflect on the fact that analytic consideration of workplace communication that does not take historical factors into account can certainly also prove valuable to the social sciences.

Possibly in response to such constraints arising from the radical views of historical social constructionism, a growing number of scholars are in favour of a more moderate view of this aspect of social constructionism by which the local and the historical and cultural perspectives are believed to be complementary rather than exclusive. Advocates of this view insist on analysing discourse considering *both* its historical and sociocultural *and* its situational contexts in order to offer insights into how discourse reproduces and maintains social relations and activities. In other words, while on the one hand, knowledge systems and interactional routines are believed to be partly constructed *in situ*, that is to say, at the local level of interaction, it is also recognized that, on the other hand, social constructions also heavily depend on the historical factors (be they social, political and/or ideological) through which social actors create social categories and meanings at larger community levels (e.g., Lazzaro-Salazar 2016, 2013). To illustrate this, the following example shows how Mandy, a registered nurse, draws on both local and larger-community cultural resources in order to, first, support the decision of a fellow nurse regarding carrying mobile phones when with patients, and, second, construct a positive professional self-image.

Example 8.4

Context: a group of nurses and their charge nurse manager evaluate the practice of carrying the ward's portable phones while doing their medication rounds. Lisa, a nurse coordinator, has explained that in her view this practice is inappropriate and rude. Mandy supports Lisa's opinion on this matter.

```
1      Mandy:   you're right {talking to Lisa}
2               i mean i wouldn't answer the phone
3               if it was in my pocket . . .
4               i mean if you're toileting a patient
5               the last thing you do is go
6               HELLO {laughs} . . .
7               this is all about releasing time TO CARE. . .
8               so you're not going to be disturbing your care with
9               with phone calls
```

Mandy builds her support for Lisa's opinion at the local cultural level by reflecting on her team's professional practices when she puts herself in Lisa's shoes (lines 1–3) and provides a specific example of how answering the phone would jeopardize nursing practice in their ward (lines 4–6). Mandy also builds her support at the larger cultural level by drawing on discipline values and practices when she explains that it is all about "releasing time to care" (lines 7–9).

For a lay audience, the phrase "releasing time to care" is possibly self-explanatory, pointing at prioritizing caring duties over other tasks in the ward. Though this is partly true, for the expert audience the phrase embodies a trust-wide programme with the full title *Releasing Time to Care—the Productive Ward* (see Wilson 2009). This programme is part of the reform of the healthcare system undertaken in the UK in 2007 with the aim of "improving ward processes and environments to help nurses and therapists spend more time on patient care thereby improving safety and efficiency" (National Health Service 2006–2013). Mandy's contribution re-creates the value of caring by reflecting on what she believes to be good nursing practice. To achieve this, at the local level of the interaction, Mandy constructs her professionalism by drawing on conceptualizations embedded in a long-standing international scheme that aims to regulate nursing practice more widely, becoming part of the nursing culture at the discipline level (see Chitty 2011), while, at the same time, she reflects on how this programme impacts their nursing practice at the local level.

As this example illustrates, the historical and *in situ* construction processes are mutually constitutive, and workplace researchers concerned with these two perspectives of social constructionist analysis explore how these processes relate to each other. This relationship, some claim, facilitates a more critical exploration of the current professional practices of social groups and enables the researcher to connect micro-level analysis to a larger social reality (see Foster and Bochner 2008).

Future Avenues of Inquiry: Rethinking Intercultural Communication

In line with the view that language is the "site for the construction and contestation of social meanings" (Weedon 1997, 21), one further point to be made regarding social constructionist principles stems from the idea that talk is action in context. It follows that if we can do things by talking, then we can logically assume that we can encourage, and even cause, social change through talk (Eggins and Slade 1997). This stands as the critical view of social constructionism, which challenges taken-for-granted assumptions of the world (Allen 2005) and represents a relatively new movement in the field of communication studies that is targeted at social transformation (Foster and Bochner 2008).

What if, then, we challenged taken-for-granted assumptions of cultural representations in intercultural workplace interactions? Intercultural interaction has been one of the major focuses of workplace research over the last decades. However, although this research interest has hugely developed at the same time as social constructionist views of workplace interaction evolved to embrace the guiding principles outlined above, scholarly considerations of intercultural communication phenomena do not seem to have, for the most part, advanced at the same pace. As a result, traditional views of intercultural interaction are still dominant in workplace research.

Traditionally, intercultural communication studies in the workplace have been guided by the fixed notion of interactants' ethnic and/or national community membership as a baseline for the interpretation of communicational phenomena. Data analysis in this context has been related to interactants' different cultural assumptions, expectations and norms of behaviour arising from the fact that they come from different ethnic/national backgrounds. However, what happens when professionals from a myriad of ethnic, and national, backgrounds have worked together for a considerable number of years and can be claimed to be members of a well-established community that has, over time, developed its own local culture? Would it still be fair and appropriate to analyse such interactions from a national perspective, considering ethnic individualities?

As I have discussed elsewhere (Lazzaro-Salazar 2009), members of multicultural teams that have worked together for a fair number of years may converge in, for instance, the use of overlapping speech as they have developed shared institutional practices regarding their "ways of engaging in doing things together" (Wenger 1999, 125). In the case of healthcare communication in particular, I have shown how a multicultural group of nurses, who have, on average, been members of their teams for five years, have developed a shared understanding of their practices (Lazzaro-Salazar 2013), which became particularly salient in nurses' evaluations of professional practices as these reflected on the essential nursing values at both the wider (as members of the nursing profession; see imagined communities in Paltridge 2015) and the local (as members of that institution, that particular ward and team) community levels (Lazzaro-Salazar 2016). These nurses' distant (and often more stable) and local (and, thus, more dynamic) professional community alignments constitute a cultural activity in the context of a jointly negotiated enterprise that reflects their own local professional culture.

In this regard, when reflecting on the role of social constructionist views of workplace interaction, some scholars argue for the lack of balance between "the reproduction of culturally well-established patterns and the production of new social and communicative meaning in situated action" (Gunnarsson, Linell, and Nordberg 1997, 2), to the point of considering social constructionism as "problematic" for disregarding "the relative solidity and permanence of social entities" (Fairclough 2003, 209). If, however, we analysed intercultural communication in the workplace by adopting the more moderate perspective of social constructionism whereby the historical and the *in situ* constructions of social reality are mutually constitutive, then the study of culture may transcend geographical boundaries providing space for a discussion of cultural matters arising from a critical social constructionist perspective. Naturally, social change in this context rests on the fact that this view of intercultural communication would prompt scholars from various disciplines to reconsider and problematize intercultural phenomena with the aim of providing a more constructionist description of (inter)cultural representations. This may be one of the most challenging tasks that lies ahead of those advocates of social constructionism who are devoted to workplace research.

Further Reading

Burr (2015) is a clear and easy-to-read book that covers all the aspects of social constructionism that have been briefly discussed in this chapter in greater depth.

Holmes and Stubbe (2015) provides a wonderful read of a hands-on research approach to social constructionism as it shows through a wealth of examples how people communicate with each other and how meanings are negotiated and contested in naturally-occurring conversations in workplaces.

Ladegaard and Jenks (2015) discusses the issue of culture in a globalized world from a critical socio-constructionist perspective, providing further insights into what is here proposed as a future research avenue.

Related Topics

Interactional sociolinguistics; Communities of practice; Relational talk; Leadership; Intercultural communication; Men's talk in women's work; Professional identity construction

Note

1 Simplified transcripts are presented here.
   Transcription Conventions
   ME   Capital letters indicate emphatic stress
   {laughter}   Paralinguistic features and clarifications in curvy brackets
   . . .   Indicates that some lines of transcription have been deleted
   ↑   rising intonation
   me: colon indicates stretching of sound it follows
                     All names used in the examples are pseudonyms.

References

Ahearn, Laura. 2001. "Language and Agency." *Annual Review of Anthropology* 30: 109–137.
Allen, Brenda. 2005. "Social Constructionism." In *Engaging Organizational Communication Theory and Research: Multiple Perspectives*, edited by Steve May, and Dennis K. Mumby, 35–53. California: Sage.

Apker, Julie, and Susan Eggly. 2004. "Communicating Professional Identity in Medical Socialization: Considering the Ideological Discourse of Morning Report." *Qualitative Health Research* 14: 411–429.

Barone, Susan, and Mariana Lazzaro-Salazar. 2015. "'Forty Bucks is Forty Bucks': An Analysis of a Medical Doctor's Professional Identity." *Language & Communication* 43: 27–34.

Basford, Tessa E., Lynn R. Offermann, and Tara S. Behrend. 2014. "Please Accept My Sincerest Apologies: Examining Follower Reactions to Leader Apology." *Journal of Business Ethics* 119: 99–117.

Beijaard, Douwe, Nico Verloop, and Jan Vermunt. 2000. "Teachers' Perceptions of Professional Identity: An Exploratory Study from a Personal Knowledge Perspective." *Teaching and Teacher Education* 16: 749–764.

Benwell, Bethan, and Elizabeth Stokoe. 2006. *Discourse and Identity*. Edinburgh: Edinburgh University Press.

Berger, Peter, and Thomas Luckmann. 1967. *The Construction of Reality: A Treatise in the Sociology of Knowledge*. New York: Anchor Books.

Brown, Phil. 1995. "Naming and Framing: The Social Construction of Diagnosis and Illness." *Journal of Health and Social Behavior* Extra Issue: 34–52. www.jstor.org/stable/2626956.

Bucholtz, Mary, and Kira Hall. 2010. "Locating Identity in Language." In *Language and Identities*, edited by Carmen Llamas, and Dominic Watt, 18–28. Edinburgh: Edinburgh University Press.

Burr, Vivien. 2015. *Social Constructionism*. London: Routledge.

Butler, Judith. 1990. *Gender Trouble: Feminism and the Subversion of Identity*. London: Routledge.

Cerulo, Karen. 1997. "Identity Construction: New Issues, New Directions." *Annual Review of Sociology* 23: 385–409.

Chitty, Kay. 2011. "Nursing's Pathway to Professionalism." In *Professional Nursing Concepts & Challenges*, edited by Kay Chitty, and Beth Black, 60–76. Missouri, MO: Saunders Elsevier.

Cook, Haruko M. 2011. "Language Socialization and Stance-Taking Practices." In *Handbook of Language Socialization*, edited by Alessandro Duranti, Elinor Ochs, and Bambi Schieffelin, 296. Malden, MA: Wiley-Blackwell.

Cooper, Karyn, and Margaret Olson. 1996. "The Multiple 'I's' of Teacher Identity." In *Changing Research and Practice: Teachers' Professionalism, Identities and Knowledge*, edited by Michael Kompf, Richard Bond, Don Dworet, and Terrance Boak, 78–89. London: Falmer Press.

Coupland, Justine, Ed. 2014. *Small Talk*. 2nd ed. Oxon: Routledge.

Courtenay, Will. 2000. "Constructions of Masculinity and Their Influence on Men's Well-Being: A Theory of Gender and Health." *Social Science & Medicine* 50: 1385–1401.

Dannels, Deanna P. 2000. "Learning to Be Professional Technical Classroom Discourse, Practice, and Professional Identity Construction." *Journal of Business and Technical Communication* 14: 5–37.

Danziger, Kurt. 1997. "The Varieties of Social Construction." *Theory & Psychology* 7: 399–416.

Duranti, Alessandro, and Charles Goodwin, Eds. 1992. *Rethinking Context: Language as an Interactive Phenomenon*. Cambridge: Cambridge University Press.

Eggins, Suzanne, and Diana Slade. 1997. *Analysing Casual Conversation*. London: Equinox.

Fairclough, Norman. 1995. *Media Discourse*. London: Edward Arnold.

Fairclough, Norman. 2003. *Analysing Discourse: Textual Analysis for Social Research*. Oxon: Psychology Press.

Fasulo, Alessandra, and Cristina Zucchermaglio. 2002. "My Selves and I: Identity Markers in Work Meeting Talk." *Journal of Pragmatics* 34: 1119–1144.

Fletcher, Joyce. 1999. *Disappearing Acts. Gender, Power and Relational Practice at Work*. Cambridge, MA: MIT Press.

Foster, Elissa, and Arthur Bochner. 2008. "Social Constructionist Perspectives in Communication Research." In *Handbook of Constructionist Research*, edited by James Holstein, and Jaber Gubrium, 85–106. New York: Guilford Press.

Foucault, Michel. 1988. *Technologies of the Self*. Massachusetts, MA: University of Massachusetts Press.

Giddens, Anthony. 1999. *Sociology*. Cambridge: Polity Press.

Gunnarsson, Britt-Louise, Per Linell, and Bengt Nordberg, Eds. 1997. *The Construction of Professional Discourse*. London: Pearson.

Haddington, Pentti. 2006. "The Organization of Gaze and Assessments as Resources for Stance Taking." *Text & Talk* 26: 281–328.

Hall, Joan. 2012. *Teaching and Researching Language and Culture*. London: Pearson.

Hanson-Easey, Scott, and Martha Augoustinos. 2012. "Narratives from the Neighbourhood: The Discursive Construction of Integration Problems in Talkback Radio." *Journal of Sociolinguistics* 16: 28–55.

Holmes, Janet, and Maria Stubbe. 2015. *Power and Politeness in the Workplace: A Sociolinguistic Analysis of Talk at Work*. 2nd ed. London: Routledge.

Kashima, Yoshihisa; Susumu Yamaguchi, Uichol Kim, Sang-Chin Choi, Michele Gelfand, and Masaki Yuki. 1995. "Culture, Gender, and Self: A Perspective from Individualism-Collectivism Research." *Journal of Personality and Social Psychology* 69: 925–937.

Ladegaard, Hans J. 2011. "'Doing Power' at Work: Responding to Male and Female Management Styles in a Global Business Corporation." *Journal of Pragmatics* 43: 4–19.

Ladegaard, Hans J., and Christopher Jenks. 2015. "Language and Intercultural Communication in the Workplace: Critical Approaches to Theory and Practice." *Language and Intercultural Communication* 15: 1–12.

Lazzaro-Salazar, Mariana. 2009. "The Role of /Overlaps\ in Intercultural Workplace Interaction." MA diss., Victoria University of Wellington.

Lazzaro-Salazar, Mariana. 2013. "Investigating Professional Identity Construction in Intercultural Health Settings in New Zealand." PhD diss., Victoria University of Wellington.

Lazzaro-Salazar, Mariana. 2016. "Downscaling Culture in Intercultural Interaction: The Case of Nurses' Professional Values in New Zealand." In *Downscaling Culture: Revisiting Intercultural Communication*, edited by Jaspal Singh, Argyro Kantara, and Dorottya Cserz", 114–140. Newcastle, UK: Cambridge Scholars.

Lerman, Dawn. 2006. "Consumer Politeness and Complaining Behavior." *Journal of Services Marketing* 20: 92–100.

Marra, Meredith, Brian W. King, and Janet Holmes. 2014. "Trivial, Mundane or Revealing? Food as a Lens on Ethnic Norms in Workplace Talk." *Language & Communication* 34: 46–55.

Martin, Judith, and Thomas Nakayama. 2015. "Reconsidering Intercultural (Communication) Competence in the Workplace: A Dialectical Approach." *Language and Intercultural Communication* 15: 13–28.

McKenna, Sioux. 2004. "The Intersection between Academic Literacies and Student Identities." *South African Journal of Higher Education* 18: 269–280.

National Health Service, England, Institute for Innovation and Improvement (2006–2013). The productive ward: Releasing time to care. Available at: www.institute.nhs.uk/quality_and_value/productivity_series/productive_ward.html.

Ochs, Elinor. 1993. "Constructing Social Identity: A Language Socialization Perspective." *Research on Language and Social Interaction* 26: 287–306.

Paltridge, Brian. 2015. "Language, Identity, and Communities of Practice." In *Language and Identity across Modes of Communication*. Vol. 6, edited by Dwi Djenar, Ahmar Mahboob, and Ken Cruickshank, 15–26. Berlin: Walter de Gruyter.

Pennycook, Alastair. 2004. "Performativity and Language Studies." *Critical Inquiry in Language Studies* 1: 1–19.

Pennycook, Alastair. 2010. *Language as a Local Practice*. London: Routledge.

Renkema, Jan. 2004. *Introduction to Discourse Studies*. Amsterdam: John Benjamins.

Saito, Junko. 2012. "Construction of Institutional Identities by Male Individuals in Subordinate Positions in the Japanese Workplace." *Pragmatics* 22: 697–719.

Skeggs, Beverly. 2008. "The Problem with Identity." In *Problematizing Identity: Everyday Struggles in Language, Culture, and Education*, edited by Angel Lin, 11–34. London: Routledge.

Svennevig, Jan, and Olga Djordjilovic. 2015. "Accounting for the Right to Assign a Task in Meeting Interaction." *Journal of Pragmatics* 78: 98–111.

van Dijk, Teun A. 2006. "Discourse, Context and Cognition." *Discourse Studies* 8: 159–177.

Vine, Bernadette. 2004. *Getting Things Done at Work: The Discourse of Power in Workplace Interaction*. Amsterdam: John Benjamins.

Weedon, Christine. 1997. *Feminist Practice and Poststructuralist Theory*. 2nd ed. London: Blackwell.

Wenger, Etienne. 1999. *Community of Practice: Learning, Meaning, and Identity*. Cambridge: Cambridge University Press.

Wilson, Gwyneth. 2009. "Implementation of Releasing Time to Care—The Productive Ward." *Journal of Nursing Management* 17: 647–654.

9
Communities of Practice
Brian W. King

Introduction

The notion that a specific type of community—a community of practice—can emerge through sustained social interaction in a shared endeavour was first generated by Lave and Wenger (1991) and Wenger (1998) to better theorize the undeniably social nature of learning. Inevitably, part of becoming a member of a new workplace or a new team within the same workplace (indeed any co-present aggregate, or grouping, of people who interact regularly) is to learn ways of doing things with language that have arisen in that social milieu. This important role for language in communities of practice has inspired scholars working in language studies to further explore how gaining membership in a community of practice involves gaining a command of its various idiosyncratic discursive practices (Bucholtz 1999; e.g., Eckert and McConnell-Ginet 1999; Eckert and Wenger 2005; Holmes and Meyerhoff 1999).

Lave and Wenger grounded their early theorizing in workplace apprenticeship examples, looking at how "newcomers" learned from "old timers" as legitimate peripheral participants; that is, members on the edge of the community who are permitted to remain at the edges temporarily, gradually moving towards core membership as they learn the shared ways of doing in that community and develop identities as insiders or perhaps becoming marginalized if they are unsuccessful or even remaining as legitimate peripheral participants long term. Therefore, it should not be surprising that language in the workplace researchers were early adopters of communities of practice as a way to theorize group membership and identity (e.g., Holmes and Marra 2002; Holmes and Stubbe 2003; Mullany 2008; Schnurr 2009a). It has proved to be a very fruitful model for these purposes, and in the rest of this chapter I will explore how the model has developed on a mutually reformulating path with the field of language in the workplace. I will also make some suggestions for further possible applications of communities of practice as the field broadens and begins to turn its attention to an increasingly wider diversity of workplace environments and activities.

Historical Perspectives

Community of practice approaches have been deployed widely in applied language studies and sociolinguistics for the past 20 years. During the earliest applications, in language and gender research (e.g., Eckert and McConnell-Ginet 1992; Ehrlich 1999), it became obvious that this was a powerful theoretical model for examining both the actions of participants and the social structures that they reproduce and resist (Bucholtz 1999). Subsequently the concept of communities of practice has also played an important role in the examination of language in the workplace (Angouri and Marra 2011; Holmes 2006a; Holmes and Stubbe 2003; Holmes and Woodhams 2013; Marra, Schnurr, and Holmes 2006; Mullany 2006, 2007; Ostermann 2003; Schnurr 2009b) and other fields.

The earliest systematic application of the model in language in the workplace research appeared in the New Zealand case study outlined in the book *Power and Politeness in the Workplace* by Janet Holmes and Maria Stubbe (2003). In this book and in related articles that preceded it, contextual differences between workplaces and even differences between teams in the same workplace were theorized using a communities of practice approach. Their study has been highly influential and provided an excellent model for other researchers to follow while conducting research in workplaces and applying a social constructionist lens. The analyses demonstrated that, for example, very different routines for the management of meetings could develop depending upon the localized practices that had supposedly been negotiated through mutual engagement in the various communities of practice.

The model also afforded insight into how humour is used in nuanced ways in different communities of practice with implications for power relationships and performances. It is important to observe, however, that the status of these various groups as communities of practice was not treated as an empirical question by the authors, rather communities of practice remained implicit. That is, to some extent it was presupposed that the practices under observation were localized ones, negotiated as part of mutual engagement rather than via other possible modes of belonging (i.e., other than mutual engagement), and rather than comprising cultural practices that are more widely recognizable. This presupposition was reasoned from the logical idea that the participants were members of groups who had regularly engaged with one another, and from the presence of certain characteristics highlighted by Wenger (1998) such as "verbal shorthand" noticed during the ethnographic phase of their methodology. With due attention paid to such characteristics the workplace setting seems a convincing one in which to proceed with a tacit assumption that localized practices were in view. But as Holmes and Stubbe's project has inspired more and more researchers who have emulated their approach, it is important to ask whether the community of practice model has come to be taken for granted and highly implicit in language in the workplace research and thereby reified in ways that now require closer examination. This question will be revisited in subsequent sections.

Critical Issues and Topics

Despite the frequent application of community of practice in sociolinguistics and applied language studies more broadly, there has been only one volume that has examined and developed aspects of the theory as applied in language studies, namely Barton and Tusting 2005a. This volume raised a number of questions about what its editors and authors perceived to be the limitations of the communities of practice model as it had been used heuristically in applied language studies up to that time. The contributing authors make suggestions about how to elaborate communities of practice as a model by either combining it with models from other disciplines, for example "language-in-use" approaches from speech community theory (e.g., Creese 2005), or replacing it with other heuristics that overcome the identified limitations (e.g., the "semiotic social spaces" of Gee 2005b). The editors of the volume expressly set out to deconstruct the communities of practice model on the basis that Wenger's (1998) formulations of the dynamics of communities of practice do not "bring out" theoretical elements of language, literacy, discourse, and power that they asserted were "missing or underdeveloped" (Barton and Tusting 2005b, 6).

However, in the end, essentially what most of these contributions brought to light was not that the communities of practice model necessarily needs elaboration but rather that multi-perspectival research incorporating communities of practice allows a greater diversity of problems to be investigated. Thus, if one uses communities of practice in tandem with other compatible models such as those outlined in the previous paragraph, the combination can result in certain synergies in research. These outcomes could perhaps explain why none of these critiques seemed very surprising to many working in language in the workplace research at the time because it is what researchers in this field had already begun to do using interactional sociolinguistics (e.g., Holmes and Stubbe 2003). Therefore, ultimately, the communities of practice model has continued to be very useful in language in the workplace research over the past decade with little if any need for alteration or enhancement. On the other hand, what has become richer and more diverse over time is knowledge about how to best apply it, where and when.

The only contribution in Barton and Tusting (2005a) to focus on workplace settings is Myers (2005) who calls for a more complex notion of discourse to be incorporated into communities of practice theory in order to account for issues of power and legitimacy in the workplace, and how one gains legitimacy or alternatively does not have it granted to them. This critique was echoed in earlier chapters of the book and was similar at the time to that of Davies (2005) who also called for an integration of "missing concepts" into communities of practice theory such as hierarchy and acceptance. However as Eckert and Wenger indicated in their response to Davies' critique, "There is always a delicate balance in the construction of a model between the work that the model does and the work that the model demands" (Eckert and Wenger 2005, 588). In other words one must be careful about what gets built into a model because those elements cease to be empirical. That is, they cease to be elements that need to be researched and explained in relation to communities of practice. Their point is that instead of asking for elaborations of the theory or replacements of it, as all of the aforementioned critiques of communities of practice have tended to do, ethnographic empirical investigations and analysis are what is required. It is in such investigations that power, hierarchy, language-in-use, or activity can be explained rather than via further development of the model itself in order to have the model do the explaining.

Another type of critique focuses not on what should or should not be included in the model but instead queries in which research contexts the model might apply. The wide use of communities of practice has at times led to its use as a "catch phrase" as much as an actual model or framework. It has gained a strong ontological status rather than being treated itself as an empirical question. In other words, it has been reified to the point where aggregates of people in a research context are just presumed to be a community of practice whereas the alternative stance would require researchers to build the verification of a group's status as a community of practice into the investigation (King 2014). This critique is driven by an emphasis on other modes of belonging besides mutual engagement that might have had (or might be having) an effect on the status of practices under observation during research. These distinctions are significant, for in discourse analysis a great deal of interpretation can depend on the notion that people in a group somehow share localized language practices (King 2014). Community of practice can instead be framed as one way among many of viewing a group and its practices; that is, one way among many of conceiving of aggregates of people and the practices they enact during meaning making (Gee 2005a). Other frameworks include communities of the imagination (Wenger 1998), communities of alignment (Wenger 1998), nexus of practices (Scollon 2001), and publics (Warner 2002). A given aggregate of people and their practices might be better described by some of these other models, or those people might indeed form a community of practice that is also in interaction with or nested within other types of communities such as speech communities (Creese 2005), micro-communities of knowledge (Fletcher 2014) or affinity spaces (Gee 2005b; see also Mak and Chui 2013). Thus heightened vigilance is required in language in the workplace research so that application of the community of practice model becomes more consistently critical and sophisticated.

Current Contributions and Research

Communities of practice have served as a useful model for scholars studying leadership in real workplaces (e.g., Holmes 2009; Schnurr 2009b; Vine et al. 2008), and Nick Wilson (in press) has been doing innovative work on the ways in which leaders within an organization come to form a community of practice of their own but as part of a distributed leadership structure (cf. Choi and Schnurr 2014). By seeing leadership as a set of situated practices rather than as a quality or disposition of an individual, language in the workplace researchers are better able to explain how leaders emerge through the use of language and other practices and to see how the leaders of a team fit within the broader "constellation" of communities of practice in that workplace.

Using sports teams as inspiration, Wilson (2010; in press) reminds us that Wenger (1998) theorizes that multiple communities of practice can co-exist and overlap as a constellation of communities, with some members belonging to numerous communities of practice at various levels of core versus peripheral membership. A given leader in an organization might, then, have become a core member of the "leadership" community of practice while simultaneously remaining a peripheral member of a "working practice" community of practice of which they had previously been a core member prior to promotion (Wilson in press). This type of situated learning around leadership requires mutual engagement, and therefore Wilson argues that a leadership community of practice is unlikely to develop unless an organization has a distributed leadership model.

As mentioned in the section on critiques of the communities of practice model above, it has been important for those using it in language in the workplace research not to simply presume that the practices under observation have developed locally. Rather, knowing which practices are more broadly recognizable and which have taken on localized, specialized meanings is an empirical question best addressed through ethnographic research (Eckert and McConnell-Ginet 2007; Eckert and Wenger 2005; King 2014). In a similar manner, Fletcher (2014) argues that it is important to understand that workplace teams often come together in transient ways to work on projects, sent into new groupings from various other communities of practice to generate ideas or solve problems together and then disband back into their longer-term communities of practice. Fletcher uses the term micro-communities of knowledge (von Krogh, Ichijo, and Ikujiro 2000) to describe these ephemeral but useful groupings in which there are no old-timers or newcomers and there is little time for a shared repertoire to develop. Rather these groups bring together a range of knowledge and expertise at various levels, developed in their respective communities of practice, and then, while in the micro-community of knowledge, gain exposure to new insights and social norms that can then be taken back with them. It is perhaps in this way that we see how the various communities of practice in a constellation can truly imbricate in interesting ways, resulting in the introduction of innovation into longer term communities of practice whose respective shared repertoires are always developing.

An interesting recent contribution has been to ask whether communities of practice can extend outside the formal workplace and continue to develop "after hours" through the internet. Investigators in one study conclude that analysis of after-hours Status Updates in Facebook by co-workers in a catering team raises questions about the "joint enterprise" and "mutual engagement" of people whose activities include posting but also "liking" the posts of others, or even passively consuming the posted content without directly participating (Mak and Chui 2013). Evidence of Wenger's key criteria elements (e.g., jargon and shortcuts, lack of preambles, etc.) seems to be very thin in that context, and so the authors suggest that this workplace-oriented Facebook group likely does not comprise a separate community of practice on its own. Their analysis is an illuminating example of the need to critically investigate whether a group of people under observation is in fact a community of practice or alternatively some other social aggregate or, perhaps, in the midst of becoming a community of practice but one that is not yet highly developed (see Critical issues and topics above). As useful as it is to know that the Facebook users in the workplace under investigation probably do not represent a separate community of practice, this finding does not preclude the possibility that the Facebook group observed is one more "space" in a workplace community of practice that exists as an offline/online continuum. That is, the practices deployed might be part of a broader shared repertoire, aspects of which apply both in the kitchen and on Facebook. The researchers do acknowledge the possibility that certain norms of doing humour, for example, might transfer between sites but suggest that there is still a need for separate "'shared repertoires' which allow colleagues to dis/prove their membership in Facebook" (Mak and Chui 2013, 100). However this conclusion begs the question of why they would need to do this type of membership work in Facebook if they are already core members of the broader community of practice. Although the point is well taken that other models might conceptualize these Facebook interactions better than the communities of practice model does, to prematurely conclude so would be to risk reifying an offline/online separation that might not be very relevant in the end. Hopefully further ethnographic studies can delve further into this very question and expand knowledge of how to employ communities of practice during investigations of workplaces that increasingly do function in an online/offline spatial continuum.

A less commonly examined type of community of practice is the kind that forms in a blue-collar work environment where apprenticing is the normal way to induct new employees. In an interesting New Zealand case study of a construction site community of practice (Holmes and Woodhams 2013), the importance of both transactional and relational dimensions of discourse is made clear. Analysing these two dimensions separately permits insight into how newcomers gain membership in a community of practice, and the analysts are able to demonstrate that two apprentices are at different points in their "inbound trajectory" towards core membership of the community of practice. Ways of communicating are seen to be just as important as technical jargon as part of professional identity performances in the blue-collar setting, as has been demonstrated previously in white collar workplaces (Baxter 2010; Holmes and Stubbe 2003; Mullany 2007). In the building site context, micro- and meso-levels of interaction are found to blend as members become members of the work site team and the company at the same time. In these ways this study of a building site has added valuable nuances to knowledge about communities of practice in the workplace.

Another study that focuses on the induction of new employees demonstrates the importance of metaphor as part of the process of organizational socialization (Woodhams 2014). An insider in a government department in New Zealand uses a HOSPITAL metaphor (among others) to explain to a new intern how the job they are doing fits into the broader scheme of the workplace. Metaphors are seen to be pervasive as part of such talk and at times challenging for L2 English speakers to understand. This inability to understand can place limits on the likelihood of newcomers to integrate successfully. Similarly, certain ways of negotiating disagreement in New Zealand workplaces have also been found to limit situational learning of L2 interns in a community of practice (Marra 2012). When they disagree, their disagreements are not taken up but rather re-cast as misunderstandings or miscommunication. That is, instead of engaging in a conversation about what the newcomer disagrees with, their interlocutor suggests that the newcomer simply does not understand the whole situation or has misunderstood the meaning of what was said. This tendency prevents the newcomers from learning the norms for how to enact disagreement, potentially curtailing their professional identities in the New Zealand workplace context.

Workplace humour has also been found to depend very much on localized practice, with the amount, types, and construction of it helping to shape the distinctiveness of various workplaces (Holmes 2006b; Holmes and Marra 2002; Richards 2010), and so the communities of practice model has provided a useful framework for studying its effect on workplace relations (Mak, Liu, and Deneen 2012; Murata 2014; Schnurr and Mak 2009). Throughout the cited literature on humour above, effort is made to justify the application of the community of practice model by identifying that the teams of people under analysis are indeed mutually engaged and co-present as part of a joint enterprise. In terms of identifying shared repertoires that include humour, by comparing between various teams it is demonstrated that the practices differ significantly (Murata 2014), and this finding is interpreted implicitly as evidence that the practices have developed locally and emerged from "mutual engagement" as opposed to Wenger's other identified "modes of belonging" (e.g., imagination and alignment—Wenger 1998). That is, an "educated guess" drives the conclusion that these patterns of practice around humour are not more widely recognizable and therefore their use in a particular workplace might be driven by other types of alignments besides mutual engagement. To not treat the formation of localized humour practice as the focus of empirical research in no way detracts from the validity of these studies or their importance. However to focus more directly on identifying the status of practices (humorous or otherwise) and verifying how they have been localized through mutual engagement (e.g., Gardner and Miller 2013; King 2014), if indeed they have, would open new vistas of research in language in the workplace research, permitting more social nuances of workplace cultures to emerge.

Main Research Methods

Ethnographic perspectives on research have long been identified as the most appropriate way to determine the status of practices being observed (Eckert and Wenger 2005) and thereby the status of an aggregate of people as a community of practice or otherwise (Eckert and McConnell-Ginet 2007). A time-tested research design for workplace research has been developed by Janet Holmes and the New Zealand Language in the Workplace team (Holmes 2006a; Holmes et al. 2011; Holmes and Stubbe 2003). With guidance from the research team, the participants themselves collect the spoken data required for the project. The participants audio-record their interactions in the everyday workplace, a process that is entirely within their control rather than the control of the researcher, and some video recordings are also conducted by the research team, an exercise in which cameras are turned on and left running while the researchers exit the room. Based on the extensive experience of researchers in the workplace project, this approach is valuable in that it minimizes the involvement of researchers in the process of data collection thus mitigating the observer's paradox to some extent. Because of the intense nature of analysis, data recording is typically restricted to a period of several weeks. Forty to fifty hours of recording constitutes a large data set (cf. 25 hours in Holmes and Woodhams 2013). In addition to these well-tested methods, by expanding the time spent doing ethnographic observation, there is an opportunity to include as part of empirical analysis the identification *in the data* of community of practice formation and ongoing development. One way this can be done is by paying close attention to the ethnographic observer's own experiential processes of identifying and mastering aspects of a shared repertoire that at first only make sense to old-timers in the community (e.g., King 2014). By being self-reflexive in this way, much that would be implicit about the community's practices can emerge more explicitly.

Future Directions

By way of possible innovation the discussion of communities of practice at work could be expanded to include research into mobile workplaces, workplaces (stationary or mobile) with mostly transient membership, and the relationship between workplaces, community belonging, layered timescales, and spatial trajectories. As Marra (2014) has emphasized, scholarship on workplace discourse has reached a level of maturity to allow researchers to look beyond discrete activities and snapshots of activity. Rather it is beneficial also to explore the transitions between activities (cf. Holmes 2015) and to include new trajectories such as changing identities, new communities of practice, and mobility, for this is where we find the real complexities of workplace interaction (see also Filliettaz 2010b; Holmes 2015). In this way we can focus on "recent contexts developed in response to new patterns of mobility, migration and internationalization" (de Saint-Georges 2013, 5).

Empirically, studies need to examine communication strategies as members of a workplace community of practice work together to overcome the specific challenges inherent in moving between multiple worksites in addition to the general challenges of workplaces. Focusing on a mobile team of co-workers would permit the examination of workplace practices in relation to place and space in novel ways. Places (and their ongoing construction in space) are important as articulation points for communities which might form there or pass through them (King 2014). Thus there are various unaddressed questions which can be examined. If a community of practice forms in a fixed location and then becomes mobile, which aspects of its shared communicative repertoire remain behind or persist? Do the members develop strategies for dealing with mobility by interpreting their constantly changing surroundings? This research can build on insights gained in research on sports teams as communities of practice (Wilson 2010; Wilson 2013), shifting focus to professional sports teams as they perform their workplaces in shifting sites.

The international mobility of the workforce means that research in multilingual workplace communities of practice and communities using languages other than English still need to keep proliferating (Holmes and Marra 2014). The rhetoric surrounding multilingualism in corporate discourse might lead to the impression that multilingual migrants are considered assets in the workplace, but the evidence has been very mixed (Roberts 2010). Within certain workplaces, multilingualism and competent use of a lingua franca are practices that carry status among equals in communities of practice (Day and Wagner 2007) while in others being multilingual or bilingual does not afford any extra status in the workplace (Duchêne 2009) or can even result in marginalization (Lønsmann 2014). These investigations of multilingualism in workplaces could benefit from a more direct empirical focus on processes of situated learning and community membership (e.g., Filliettaz 2010a) as well as verification of the status of the practices under observation.

Research can also address unanswered questions such as how leadership, teamwork, and hierarchies are constructed in a setting that is neither a "white collar office" environment nor a "blue-collar labour" setting. Rather it is a distinctly different type of workplace community, one focused on pedagogical outcomes and challenges, a focus that has been neglected in workplace communication research (de Saint-Georges 2014). Scholars investigating language use in workplaces strongly advocate the importance of localized community practices, but there is a dearth of research that empirically examines the on-going development of such practices in school staffrooms, corridors, resource rooms, and conference rooms. Survey and interview based research in educational policy and planning has demonstrated that teaching capacities are directly linked to the stable and positive professional identities of educators, and the development of these identities is closely associated with working conditions and relationships with colleagues. As in language in the workplace research, there is a growing consensus that teacher identity is socially constructed, dynamic, fluid, complex, and multi-faceted; it is a process of becoming that mediates and impacts classroom practices (e.g., Akkerman and Meijer 2011; Hong 2010). Furthermore the professional identities of teachers are reportedly influenced by working conditions, particularly by leadership support practices (or their lack) and relations with colleagues. Crucially, a teacher's sense of these identities needs to be fairly stable and positive if their on-going teaching capacities are going to be of benefit to students (Day 2012). This leads to the question of how teacher identity can be described more fully, a question that remains largely under-explored but which language in the workplace as a field is very well positioned to investigate through its tried and tested ethnographic case study approaches, particularly via a critical application of the community of practice model. Three dimensions of teacher identity have been identified by Day (2012):

- Socio-cultural (i.e., social and policy expectations of what good teaching is)
- Workplace (i.e., workplace conditions and relationships)
- Personal (i.e., biography and experience—life outside the school)

Future research by language in the workplace scholars can focus on this identified "workplace" aspect of educator professional identity, zeroing in on the communicative practices of teams of educators mutually engaged in their joint enterprises.

In conclusion, it is clear that the Communities of Practice model has been, and continues to be, a useful and powerful tool in the investigation of language in the workplace. As the field moves forward, continually broadening in focus, it is important that scholars pay attention to the critiques reviewed here. By doing so, we can ensure that Communities of Practice and Language in the Workplace continue to evolve on a mutually reforming pathway, resulting in richer insights for the field.

Further Reading

Holmes and Meyerhoff (1999) serves as an introduction to a special issue of the journal on communities of practice. It and its accompanying articles provide a critical and thorough introduction to communities of practice as deployed in conjunction with interactional sociolinguistics.

Davies (2005) and the response articles in the "Dialogue" section of the same issue of the *Journal of Sociolinguistics* (Eckert and Wenger 2005; Gee 2005a) provide some very useful critical discussion of communities of practice as a model.

Although Jones (2014) is not focused on workplaces per se, but rather on sexual identity performances in communities of practice more generally, it provides a very lucid and up-to-date exploration of communities of practice in ethnographic research.

Related Topics

Linguistic ethnography; Corporate settings; Blue-collar workplaces; Relational talk; Humour; Gender; Leadership; Intercultural communication; Men's talk in women's work; Professional identity construction; Vocational education; Language learning on-the-job

References

Akkerman, Sanne F., and Paulien C. Meijer. 2011. "A Dialogical Approach to Conceptualizing Teacher Identity." *Teaching and Teacher Education* 27: 308–319.
Angouri, Jo, and Meredith Marra. 2011. "'OK One Last Thing for Today Then': Constructing Identities in Corporate Meeting Talk." In *Constructing Identities at Work*, edited by Jo Angouri, and Meredith Marra, 85–100. Basingstoke, UK: Palgrave Macmillan.
Barton, David, and Karin Tusting. 2005a. *Beyond Communities of Practice*. Cambridge: Cambridge University Press.
Barton, David, and Karin Tusting. 2005b. "Introduction." In *Beyond Communities of Practice*, edited by David Barton, and Karin Tusting, 1–13. Cambridge: Cambridge University Press.
Baxter, Judith. 2010. *The Language of Female Leadership*. Basingstoke, UK: Palgrave Macmillan.
Bucholtz, Mary. 1999. "'Why Be Normal?': Language and Identity Practices in a Community of Nerd Girls." *Language in Society* 28: 203–223.
Choi, Seongsook, and Stephanie Schnurr. 2014. "Exploring Distributed Leadership: Solving Disagreements and Negotiating Consensus in a 'Leaderless' Team." *Discourse Studies* 16: 3–24.
Creese, Angela. 2005. "Mediating Allegations of Racism in a Multiethnic London School: What Speech Communities and Communities of Practice Can Tell Us about Discourse and Power." In *Beyond Communities of Practice*, edited by David Barton, and Karin Tusting, 55–76. Cambridge: Cambridge University Press.
Davies, Bethan. 2005. "Communities of Practice: Legitimacy Not Choice." *Journal of Sociolinguistics* 9: 557–581.
Day, Christopher. 2012. "New Lives of Teachers." *Teacher Education Quarterly* 39: 7–26.
Day, Dennis, and Johannes Wagner. 2007. "Bilingual Professionals." In *Handbook of Multilingualism and Multilingual Communication*, edited by Peter Auer, and Li Wei, 390–404. Berlin: Mouton de Gruyter.
de Saint-Georges, Ingrid. 2013. "Multilingualism, Multimodality and the Future of Education Research." In *Multilingualism and Multimodality: Current Challenges for Educational Studies*. Vol. 2 of *Future of Education Research*, edited by Ingrid de Saint-Georges, and Jean-Jacques Weber, 1–8. Rotterdam: Sense.
de Saint-Georges, Ingrid. 2014. "Preparing Teachers for the Multilingual Classroom: Lessons from Teacher Practicum in Luxembourg." Paper presented at 4th International Conference of Applied Linguistics and Professional Practice, University of Geneva.
Duchêne, Alexandre. 2009. "Marketing Management and Performance: Multilingualism as a Commodity in a Foreign Call Centre." *Language Policy* 8: 27–50.
Eckert, Penelope, and Sally McConnell-Ginet. 1992. "Think Practically and Look Locally: Language and Gender as Community-Based Practice." *Annual Review of Anthropology* 21: 461–488.
Eckert, Penelope, and Sally McConnell-Ginet. 1999. "New Generalizations and Explanations in Language and Gender Research." *Language in Society* 28: 185–201.
Eckert, Penelope, and Sally McConnell-Ginet. 2007. "Putting Communities of Practice in Their Place." *Gender and Language* 1: 27–38.

Eckert, Penelope, and Etienne Wenger. 2005. "Communities of Practice in Sociolinguistics: What Is the Role of Power in Sociolinguistic Variation?" *Journal of Sociolinguistics* 9: 582–589.

Ehrlich, Susan. 1999. "Communities of Practice, Gender, and the Representation of Sexual Assault." *Language in Society* 28: 239–256.

Filliettaz, Laurent. 2010a. "Guidance as an Interactional Accomplishment: Practice-Based Learning within the Swiss VET System." In *Learning Through Practice: Models, Traditions, Orientations and Approaches*, edited by Stephen Billet, 156–179. London: Springer.

Filliettaz, Laurent. 2010b. "Interactions and Miscommunication in the Swiss Vocational Education Context: Researching Vocational Learning from a Linguistic Perspective." *Journal of Applied Linguistics and Professional Practice* 7: 27–50.

Fletcher, Jeannie. 2014. "Social Communities in a Knowledge Enabling Organizational Context: Interaction and Relational Engagement in a Community of Practice and a Micro-Community of Knowledge." *Discourse & Communication* 8: 351–369.

Gardner, David, and Lindsay Miller. 2013. "Self-Access Managers: An Emerging Community of Practice." *System* 41: 817–828.

Gee, James Paul. 2005a. "Meaning Making, Communities of Practice, and Analytical Toolkits." *Journal of Sociolinguistics* 9: 590–594.

Gee, James Paul. 2005b. "Semiotic Social Spaces and Affinity Spaces: From the Age of Mythology to Today's Schools." In *Beyond Communities of Practice*, edited by David Barton, and Karin Tusting, 214–232. Cambridge: Cambridge University Press.

Holmes, Janet. 2006a. *Gendered Talk at Work*. Oxford: Blackwell.

Holmes, Janet. 2006b. "Sharing a Laugh: Pragmatic Aspects of Humor and Gender in the Workplace." *Journal of Pragmatics* 38: 26–50.

Holmes, Janet. 2009. "Men, Masculinities and Leadership: Different Discourse Styles at Work." In *Gender and Spoken Interaction*, edited by Pia Pichler, and Eva Eppler, 186–210. London: Palgrave.

Holmes, Janet. 2015. "Making Transitions: The Role of Interaction in Joining a Workplace Community of Practice." *Novitas-ROYAL* 9: 77–92.

Holmes, Janet, and Meredith Marra. 2002. "Having a Laugh at Work: How Humour Contributes to Workplace Culture." *Journal of Pragmatics* 34: 1683–1710.

Holmes, Janet, and Meredith Marra. 2014. "The Complexities of Communication in Professional Workplaces." In *Routledge Handbook of Language and Professional Communication*, edited by Vijay Bhatia, and Stephen Bremner, 112–128. London: Routledge.

Holmes, Janet, and Miriam Meyerhoff. 1999. "The Community of Practice: Theories and Methodologies in Language and Gender Research." *Language in Society* 28: 173–183.

Holmes, Janet, and Maria Stubbe. 2003. *Power and Politeness in the Workplace: A Sociolinguistic Analysis of Talk at Work*. London: Longman.

Holmes, Janet, and Jay Woodhams. 2013. "Building Interaction: The Role of Talk in Joining a Community of Practice." *Discourse & Communication* 7: 275–298.

Holmes, Janet, Angela Joe, Meredith Marra, Jonathan Newton, Nicky Riddiford, and Bernadette Vine. 2011. "Applying Linguistic Research to Real World Problems: The Case of the Wellington Language in the Workplace Project." In *Handbook of Communication in Organisations and Professions*, edited by Chris Candlin, and Srikant Sarangi, 533–549. Berlin: Mouton de Gruyter.

Hong, Ji Y. 2010. "Pre-Service and Beginning Teachers' Professional Identity and Its Relation to Dropping out of the Profession." *Teaching and Teacher Education* 26: 1530–1543.

Jones, Lucy. 2014. "'Dolls or Teddies?' Constructing Lesbian Identity Through Community-Specific Practice." *Journal of Language and Sexuality* 3: 161–190.

King, Brian W. 2014. "Tracing the Emergence of a Community of Practice: Beyond Presupposition in Sociolinguistic Research." *Language in Society* 43: 61–81.

Lave, Jean, and Etienne Wenger. 1991. *Situated Learning: Legitimate Peripheral Participation*. Cambridge: Cambridge University Press.

Lønsmann, Dorte. 2014. "Linguistic Diversity in the International Workplace: Language Ideologies and Processes of Exclusion." *Multilingua* 33: 89–116.

Mak, Bernie Chun Nam, and Hin Leung Chui. 2013. "Colleagues' Talk and Power after Work Hours: A Community of Practice in Facebook Status Updates?" *Discourse, Context and Media* 2: 94–102.

Mak, Bernie Chun Nam, Yiqi Liu, and Christopher Charles Deneen. 2012. "Humor in the Workplace: A Regulating and Coping Mechanism in Socialization." *Discourse & Communication* 6: 163–179.

Marra, Meredith. 2012. "Disagreeing without Being Disagreeable: Negotiating Communities as an Outsider." *Journal of Pragmatics* 44: 1580–1590.
Marra, Meredith. 2014. "The Talk Between: Preparing for Transitions at Work." Paper presented at 4th International Conference of Applied Linguistics and Professional Practice, University of Geneva.
Marra, Meredith, Stephanie Schnurr, and Janet Holmes. 2006. "Effective Leadership in New Zealand Workplaces: Balancing Gender and Role." In *Speaking Out: The Female Voice in Public Contexts*, edited by Judith Baxter, 240–260. Basingstoke, UK: Palgrave.
Mullany, Louise. 2006. "'Girls on Tour': Politeness, Small Talk, and Gender in Managerial Business Meetings." *Journal of Politeness Research* 2: 55–77.
Mullany, Louise. 2007. *Gendered Discourse in the Professional Workplace*. Basingstoke, UK: Palgrave Macmillan.
Mullany, Louise. 2008. "'Stop Hassling Me!': Impoliteness, Power and Gender Identity in the Professional Workplace." In *Impoliteness in Language: Studies on Its Interplay with Power in Theory and Practice*, edited by Derek Bousfield, and Miriam A. Locher, 231–255. Berlin: Mouton de Gruyter.
Murata, Kazuyo. 2014. "An Empirical Cross-Cultural Study of Humour in Business Meetings in New Zealand and Japan." *Journal of Pragmatics* 60: 251–265.
Myers, Greg. 2005. "Communities of Practice, Risk and Sellafield." In *Beyond Communities of Practice*, edited by David Barton, and Karin Tusting, 198–213. Cambridge: Cambridge University Press.
Ostermann, Ana Cristina. 2003. "Communities of Practice at Work: Gender, Facework and the Power of Habitus at an All-Female Police Station and a Feminist Crisis Intervention Center in Brazil." *Discourse & Society* 14: 473–505.
Richards, Keith. 2010. "Professional Orientation in Back Region Humour." *Text & Talk* 30: 145–167.
Roberts, Celia. 2010. "Language Socialization in the Workplace." *Annual Review of Applied Linguistics* 30: 211–227.
Schnurr, Stephanie. 2009a. "Constructing Leader Identities through Teasing at Work." *Journal of Pragmatics* 41: 1125–1138.
Schnurr, Stephanie. 2009b. *Leadership Discourse at Work: Interactions of Humour, Gender and Workplace Culture*. Basingstoke, UK: Palgrave Macmillan.
Schnurr, Stephanie, and Bernie Mak. 2009. "Humor as an Indicator of Workplace Socialization." In *Language for Professional Communication: Research, Practice and Training*, edited by Vijay K. Bhatia, Winnie Cheng, Bertha Du-Babcock, and Jane Lung, 131–145. Hong Kong: Hong Kong Polytechnic University.
Scollon, Ron. 2001. *Mediated Discourse: The Nexus of Practice*. London: Routledge.
Vine, Bernadette, Janet Holmes, Meredith Marra, Dale Pfeifer, and Brad Jackson. 2008. "Exploring Co-Leadership Talk through Interactional Sociolinguistics." *Leadership* 4: 339–360.
von Krogh, Georg, Kazuo Ichijo, and Nonaka Ikujiro. 2000. *Enabling Knowledge Creation: How to Unlock the Mystery of Tacit Knowledge and Release the Power of Innovation*. New York: Oxford University Press.
Warner, Michael. 2002. *Publics and Counterpublics*. New York: Zone Books.
Wenger, Etienne. 1998. *Communities of Practice: Learning, Meaning and Identity*. Cambridge: Cambridge University Press.
Wilson, Nick. 2010. "Bros, Boys and Guys: Address Term Function and Communities of Practice in a New Zealand Rugby Team." *New Zealand English Journal* 24: 33–54.
Wilson, Nick. 2013. "Interaction without Walls: Analysing Leadership Discourse through Dramaturgy and Participation." *Journal of Sociolinguistics* 17: 180–199.
Wilson, Nick. In press. "Developing Distributed Leadership: Leadership Emergence in a Sporting Context." In *Challenging Leadership Stereotypes: Discourse and Power Management*, edited by Stephanie Schnurr, and Cornelia Ilie. New York: Springer.
Woodhams, Jay. 2014. "'We're the Nurses': Metaphor in the Discourse of Workplace Socialisation." *Language & Communication* 34: 56–68.

10
Genre Theory
Kieran A. File

What is Genre and Why is it Important for Workplace Research?

A personal genre-related experience came to mind when I began to write this chapter. It concerns my first Humanities faculty board meeting as student representative for the Postgraduate Students' Association. At the time I had very little experience with meetings in general, so a formal board meeting with over 40 academics present was quite a daunting prospect. I was not completely sure of the purpose of these meetings; were we meant to finalize faculty-related decisions, raise issues or agree on actions? I did not know how long the meetings would take (I suspected a while), nor did I know how the meeting would progress from start to finish. From my previous experience with meetings, I suspected it would be quite a linear cycling through the agenda items, but was not sure. All I knew was that it was my job to raise issues on behalf of the postgraduate student body. However, even with regards to my role, I did not know when I was supposed to raise these issues, or how or when I was supposed to indicate my desire to raise an issue. I was also not told about the voting procedures of board meetings, and was taken by surprise when I suddenly found myself in the middle of a vote.

A genre theorist reading the above might argue that the knowledge I was lacking, at least in part, was genre knowledge, or an understanding of the board meeting genre. Meetings can be considered one of a number of genres, or a "genre family" (Martin 2002), that we use in the workplace, and, like other bounded text-level phenomena, meetings have a set of culturally understood social purposes, expectations and norms that are realized through a set of recognizable linguistic actions and features.

Genres can be seen as text-level cultural resources that reflect the way particular cultural or social groups *do* things with their language. Seen from this perspective, genre theorists play an important role in helping to develop an understanding of the way our texts reveal important social and cultural information about the purposes and goals of texts and the expectations (or norms) regarding the behaviour of users of the texts. The analytical task for genre researchers is to explore the way these cultural and social norms are constructed in and realized through language, by paying close attention to macro and micro textual patterns and linguistic features evident in a set of texts representative of a genre.

For some schools of thought in genre theory, it is also part of the mission to make these insights available to new members of the culture or community, particularly (but not exclusively) those who are not from the native speaking population. This has been a relevant concern for workplace discourse researchers more generally (Angouri 2010; Riddiford and Newtown 2010), and, in an increasingly globalized world, genre research that explores workplace texts can be usefully applied to help empower non-native speakers with the linguistic knowledge they need to be successful members of their workforces.

In this chapter I will apply genre theory to explore the social purposes and linguistic features of a member of the meeting genre family—the handover meeting in a nursing context. The healthcare sector is becoming an increasingly internationalized one with doctors and nurses from a range of countries working in English speaking countries. It is also a high stakes encounter where genre knowledge may have important implications for managing the safe and ongoing care of the patients. Genre researchers can help in this endeavour by locating linguistic features of key bounded textual events, such as nurse handover meetings, that can help non-native speaking nurses understand the social and communicative goals of these textual events and the way speakers draw on macro and micro linguistic features to achieve these goals.

Genre Theory in Applied Linguistics: Social Purpose and Linguistic Profile

Before illustrating genre theory in action, some important theoretical assumptions need to be outlined. Genre theory, like other forms of discourse analysis, is broadly interested in the relationship between "language" and "society". The basic assumption of genre theory, one that informs analytical inquiry, is the idea that we draw on recurring ways (through "language") of solving a range of recurring social and/or communicative problems or purposes in our everyday and professional lives ("society"). For example, when faced with the need to run a meeting, deliver an academic presentation, or engage in a sales exchange, we draw on an (historical) understanding of how members of our society or culture typically manage these textual encounters. For the genre researcher, developing an understanding of the macro and micro linguistic patterns that have come to represent stable ways of addressing these recognizable and recurring social and/or communicative activities is a primary concern.

Genre, as a subfield of discourse analysis and applied linguistics, developed out of earlier sociolinguistic concerns with accounting for language variation in different contexts of use. Prominent sociolinguists such as Hymes (1974) considered genre a key feature in accounting for the variation exhibited by speakers in different social settings, identifying it as a component of his SPEAKING framework. Allied concepts from different fields, such as "activity types" in ethnomedothology (Levinson 1992), also assume variation and even restriction on linguistic choices based on the particular activity being engaged in. Early sociolinguistic studies of narratives were also particularly influential for genre researchers (see e.g., Labov and Waletzky 1997), as they illustrated how macro-level text analysis could be used to reveal interesting structural regularities in the way people tell stories.

From this earlier work, genre analysis has developed into a dedicated subfield of its own within applied linguistics. Three different schools of thought are often referred to as influential in exploring the issue of genre from an applied linguistics perspective. They are the Sydney School employing a Systemic Functional Linguistics (SFL) model of language, the English for Specific Purposes (ESP) approach, and the New Rhetoric approach, an approach more aligned with composition studies and rhetorical studies. Abridged versions of commonly cited definitions of genre from these three different approaches have been provided in Table 10.1.

Table 10.1 Definitions of genre in the three traditions

Systemic Functional Linguistics (SFL)	English for Specific Purposes (ESP)	The New Rhetoric approach
Genres are staged, goal-oriented social processes (Martin and Rose 2008, 8)	Genres are communicative events that have a recognizable communicative purpose and that have characteristic structures, styles, content, and intended audiences (Swales 1990, 36)	Genres are typified rhetorical actions based in recurrent situations (Miller 1984, 151)

Space does not permit a detailed comparison of these different approaches here, and there are useful comparative reviews that have already been compiled (see e.g., Hyon 1996; Muntigl and Gruber 2005). Any researcher approaching a linguistic investigation of genre will want to consider the way these different schools conceptualize genre, the methods they typically employ, and the typical analytical outcomes of studies from these different schools when making decisions about which approach or approaches to draw on. However, some researchers have noted the differences between the three approaches have become less distinct (Bazerman, Bonini, and Figueiredo 2009, 4), as the findings from these different schools begin to inform each other theoretically and methodologically.

One evident difference is the degree to which the focus of analysis is on textual and linguistic structures, with some scholars exhibiting differing degrees of interest in text or context of a particular genre (Bhatia 2006, 7). The New Rhetoric approach, for example, has typically prioritized investigation of genres in their social contexts, paying a greater attention to describing the contextual aspects of the genre and the social purpose(s) a genre performs in a given context. While all approaches to genre theory show a concern for analysing text in social context, the New Rhetoric approach prioritizes this relationship, and, through the employment of ethnographic inquiry, the analytical outcome is often a rich description of the contexts in which genres are employed and the social action these genres are employed to achieve in their contexts of use (see Hyon 1996).

The ESP and SFL schools, those schools more predominantly positioned within (Applied) Linguistics, have typically shown a greater concern with identifying linguistic realizations of genres. Researchers from these schools often look to develop a "linguistic profile" of a given genre, aiming to illustrate the functional relationship between recurring language patterns and the recurring social or communicative purpose of a genre. Perhaps unsurprisingly, it is these two schools that aim to apply their findings to help new or unfamiliar users of a given genre. Researchers drawing on an SFL approach have carried out a considerable amount of their work on genres in educational contexts, with the aim of empowering non-native speakers with the genre knowledge they need to be able to succeed at school (see Martin and Rose 2008; Rose and Martin 2012).

Analysing the Linguistic Profile of a Genre: Methodological and Analytical Considerations

For researchers interested in exploring the linguistic profile of a particular genre there are several important considerations at a methodological level and a number of options when it comes to analysing a given genre. Methodologically, primary among these considerations is the importance of collecting authentic and complete instances of the genre under analysis. To be able to make claims about a given genre, complete texts are needed if a researcher is to be able to describe the bounded nature of the genre. The number of texts can also be an important consideration. There is no magic number of texts that it is necessary to collect for a genre analysis. Instead, researcher goals and real world data collection factors and constraints will influence decisions (and realistic options) regarding the number of texts needed. For a broad analytical exploration of the features of the genre as evident across a set of texts the researcher will require a greater number of texts to support their claims, whereas a close case study may explore one or two problematic examples in depth.

Another methodological consideration concerns the employment of additional forms of data to help researchers develop a fuller picture of a genre. While close linguistic analysis of transcripts of authentic texts is of primary concern, additional forms of data can add important contextual information and can help researchers develop their "warrant" for claims (Edge and Richards 1998). Ethnographic interviews with typical users of a genre is one additional form of data that has been employed in previous genre studies. While ethnography is a primary data collection method in New Rhetoric studies of genre (Hyon 1996), the goal in more linguistically-oriented studies of genre is to use ethnographic insights to inform, validate or problematize findings from linguistic analysis. This process may prove particularly insightful when analysing genres from a community that the researcher is not a participating member of and where the users are from specialist or professional communities (Bhatia 1997, 313).

Analysing Genres: What to Look For

As mentioned above, a common analytical concern for genre theorists is explaining the relationship between the social or communicative purpose of a genre and the linguistic features constrained by, or used to help "realize" that social or communicative purpose. Halliday's concept of realization can be helpful when conceptualizing and exploring this relationship (see e.g., Eggins and Slade 1997, 51; Martin and Rose 2008, 23). Because the relationship between social or communicative purpose and language use is intertwined, analysis will often be bidirectional, involving the back-and-forth development and testing of a theory about the social purpose of a genre from detailed analysis of its recurring linguistic features. Top down ethnographic insights can also be used in this process to motivate particular linguistic analysis or to triangulate or problematize findings from the linguistic analyses.

When analysing the linguistic realization of a genre's social purpose, analysts can draw on a range of linguistic levels and linguistic phenomena at both macro and micro levels. At a macro level, abstract functional categories or patterns above the clause such as stage and move are often the target for genre researchers. Stages, for example, are functional constituents that perform a role in the overall achievement of a text's social purpose (Eggins and Slade 1997, 233). Genre researchers are particularly interested in identifying and defining the functional nature of the different stages a particular genre exhibits and how the different stages realize the social or communicative purpose of the genre.

When exploring these macro level patterns further, the way stages progress from start to finish is often a target for analysis, a feature often referred to as schematic structure. Also of interest are patterns regarding the obligatory and optional nature of the stages identified and any patterns regarding the repetition of particular stages. In some cases, a genre may have several optional stages that can be employed in particular situations. However, obligatory stages are necessary if a genre is to achieve its social purpose. Obligatory and optional stages may recur as well, and this can be important information for researchers interested in exploring the options for and constraints on speakers of a particular genre.

At the more micro level, genre researchers can explore patterns related to the discourse or meaning acts that realize the stages of a set of texts. In spoken texts, a focus on the micro can also include attention to the turn taking and interactional patterns and potentialities available to speakers. At a finer level still, more concrete linguistic patterns at a lexicogrammatical level are also invoked by speakers in the performance of a given genre, and are therefore a relevant target for analysis and description of a genre. These micro level features can be explored in relation to the way they realize higher level discourse and meaning features or higher still macro stages, or, in some cases, as linguistic markers of a genre in their own right, particularly in relation to formulaic utterances that may index a particular genre (Kuiper 2009).

Figure 10.1 highlights these different analytical levels and the potential realisational relationships between the levels that can be explored.

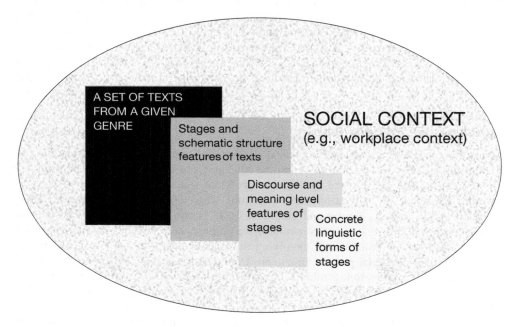

Figure 10.1 Analytical levels for genre researchers

Figure 10.1 also highlights another important factor concerning the analysis of genre texts; while separating these different analytical interests can make the process and presentation of analysis an easier prospect, it is important to realize that genre theory's power comes from its ability to demonstrate links between these different levels of analysis and to capture the complexity of language in use in society.

Applying Genre Theory: Exploring the Linguistic Profile of the Nurse Handover Meeting Genre

This section briefly demonstrates how genre theory concepts and analytical choices can be applied to develop a linguistic profile of a common workplace meeting in the health sector, the nursing handover meeting. There has been an increasing interest in the professional communication of nurses (see MacDowell this volume), and in the handover meeting as a site for nursing communication (Kerr 2002; Payne, Hardey, and Coleman 2000; Strange 1996). Nursing handover meetings are an important resource in the management of 24-hour revolving hospital care. As nurses change shifts, the incoming nurses need to be brought up to date on the patients' needs, making handover meetings a crucial encounter for safely managing these transitions. They are high stakes meetings and have been identified by those working in the health care sector as points where nursing care can fail (Behara *et al.* 2005).

To date, little genre-focused discourse analysis has been conducted on these meetings. The data and findings presented here come from a broader project exploring the nursing handover meeting as a professional genre of language use in a New Zealand nursing context (Lazzaro-Salazar 2013; Lazzaro-Salazar and File forthcoming).[1] Example 10.1 is from this project's dataset and will be used to illustrate genre concepts such as social purpose, macro level concepts stage and stage progression, and micro level linguistic realizations of the genre, including turn taking to develop a linguistic profile of these handover meetings. The extract has been presented within an overall schematic representation of a complete handover meeting. This schematic will be discussed further below.

Example 10.1 Handover meeting schematic and extract[2]

Opening
^
Patient Status Update (iterations 1–9)
^
Patient Status Update (iteration 10)

1	Chair:	Mr Richmond (4.0)
2		(unclear words) rehab
3		ah right had this discussion yesterday
4		hasn't changed

^
Patient Status Update (iteration 11)

5		Mr Grayson (1.1) stroke team?
6	Nurse1:	yeah + we um still don't know that rehab's gonna be on or not
7		he's had one stroke and was meant to rehab um had a has had a
8		major stroke um
9	Nurse2:	it does say in the EMT note he's not to go /out to rehab\
10	Nurse1:	/he's not to go\ out to
11		rehab but now we questioned it yesterday didn't they
12	Nurse2:	(unclear words)
13	Nurse1:	oh she said but I see they've questioned it yesterday because he's
14		made + he's swallowing now
15	Nurse3:	he is swallowing but I agree with Jane we were talking about either
16		palliation or placement
17	Nurse2:	mhm

117

18	Nurse1:	yeah
19	Chair:	not rehab + okay
20	Nurse2:	no
21	Nurse1:	he's quite ill really
22	Chair:	right so we've ruled one out of the three
23	Nurse2:	mhm
24	Nurse1:	but I see somebody else had brought up rehab again so + we're
25		going round a /bit but yeah\
26	Nurse2:	/I don't think so\
27	Nurse1:	no
28	Nurse2:	considering the rehab consultant said that she wouldn't /probably\
29	Nurse1:	/no that's\
30		right that's right + yes
31	Chair:	alright + so who's making that call then placement or /palliative\
32	Nurse2:	/doctor\
33	Nurse1:	the doctors
34	Chair:	alright
35	Consultant:	so when you're saying placement or palliation are you saying he
36		might not make it out of hospital /is what you're\ saying versus
37		he might stabilize to go to hospital after care
38	Nurse2:	/mm mm\
39	Nurse3:	yeah
40	Consultant:	yep okay
41	Nurse1:	he's a seventy-seven + seventy-year-old ex-diplomat with a
42		twelve-year-old son + hmm + there's all kinds of things going on
43		in the family + very stressed wife so we're supporting her well
44	Chair:	good that's good to hear +

^

Patient Status Update (iteration 12)

45	Mr Ferguson (3.0) eighty-four-year-old with lethargy and
46	decreased appetite
47	sounds like a dietician doesn't it
	[meeting continues]

^

Patient Status Update (iteration 13–20)

^

Closing

Macro Level Genre Knowledge: Stage, Stage Progression and Social Purpose of the Nursing Handover Meeting

As mentioned above, genre theorists look for evidence of macro-level stages of a particular set of texts. They try to define the functions of stages from analysis of the linguistic activity of participants in these different stages, and they try to identify the way these stages progress from start to finish as they help to realize the genre's social purpose.

The nurse handover meeting appears, in this dataset, to involve three stages: Opening (O), Patient Status Update (PSU), and Closing (C). In identifying the functions of these different stages and their progression, the Opening stage signals the beginning of the official business of the meeting, and often signals the need to put other conversations on hold in order to begin the handover meeting. This is followed by the Patient Status Update stage—the primary stage of the meeting. From a closer look at the linguistic activity in these Patient Status Update stages (discussed further below), they appear to function as a way of pooling the current knowledge and understanding about a patient's progress in order to make on-going care plans for these individual patients (one of which may be discharge). This stage is repeated as often as is needed to address all patients on the ward (in this meeting it was repeated 20 times) and until the meeting is brought to a close by a short Closing stage.

In accounting for the progression of meetings, genre theorists often develop structural diagrams and representations of the stages, drawing on symbols that help to illustrate the stages, the obligatory or optional status of the stages, and the patterns regarding the iteration and progression of these stages (see Hasan 1989 for a useful illustration). The handover meeting in Example 10.1 could be represented by Figure 10.2.

Figure 10.2 Schematic structure of the handover meeting

The stages are represented in the order in which they occur and progression through these stages is represented by the ^ symbol. The arrow ↻ represents the potential recurrence of a given stage, and the brace brackets {...} can delimit those stages that are part of the recurrence. There are other possible structural realities of a text. For example, if there were optional stages, these would be placed in rounded brackets (see Hasan 1989 for further details).

Based on this evidence of recurring macro level textual stages and patterns, the nursing handover meeting appears to achieve an important social purpose in the wider context of nursing care: the coordination of on-going patient care across nursing shifts. This is realized by the obligatory stage Patient Status Update, without which the meeting would fail to achieve its social purpose.

Micro-Level Genre Knowledge: Functional, Interactional and Lexicogrammatical Realization Patterns

To support this sort of claim, genre theorists also account for the activity of participants at more micro levels, exploring how the different stages are realized with more micro level linguistic features such as speech actions, interactional activity (in the case of dynamic, multiple party genres) and specific lexicogrammatical choices made by the speakers. From the dataset being reported on here, the Opening stage can be drawn out as participants settle into the business of doing nursing handover. This is usually realized by a discourse marker and an attempt to begin the meeting ("right, shall we get started"). The Closing stage tends to be quite short, ended by the chair, often through a token of thanks (see Lazzaro-Salazar and File forthcoming for further details).

With respect to the Patient Status Update stage, participants appeared to draw on a range of micro-level linguistic features that allowed them to realize the purpose of this stage (the pooling the current knowledge on patients). These features illustrate a need to identify a patient for discussion, negotiate, and identify their current status and care procedures, and decide on a plan of action or assign care to a particular nurse.

Readers may have noticed the use of titles and names to identify a patient and to signal the beginning of each Patient Status Update iteration (lines 1, 5, 45 and 48). This action is carried out by the chair and functions as a request to those present for any updates on the status of the identified patient. Sometimes the chair will provide a short description of the patient's health concern (see lines 45–46), perhaps as a way of further identifying the patient to those present, or in introducing a new patient to those nurses present.

After identifying a patient, the meeting participants then negotiate their current understanding of this patient's status and decide on the next steps regarding care. As iterations 10 (lines 1 to 4) and 12 (lines 45 to 47) illustrate, this can be quite a rapid process perhaps in cases where the chair possesses the information needed to provide an update or where little has happened since the previous meeting (as is the case in iteration 10). However, iterations of this stage can be more drawn out as is illustrated by iteration 11 (lines 5 to 44). These cases show that participants can also work together in these meetings to develop an understanding of the patient's care status. Elicitation and response sequences can be employed to draw out specific information or to seek clarification on matters related to the patient. In iteration 11, line 5, the chair elicits an update from a particular sub-team present at the meeting. However, participants can also negotiate entry to the interaction without being invited, so as to volunteer their own insights (see e.g., Nurse 3's entry in line 15).

In bringing a Patient Status Update stage to a close, the chair will often employ summarizing acts to summarize decisions or the current patient status (lines 3 to 4), or evaluative acts to evaluate a plan of action agreed upon by those present at the meeting (line 44). They may also direct others to the need to identify the next course of action (line 31) hence performing a key role in helping the stage and the meeting more broadly to achieve its wider social purpose.

At a lexicogrammatical level, across all of these iterations, all participants use a considerable amount of technical lexical items (e.g., palliative), acronyms (e.g., EMT) related to the field of nursing, vocabulary that has specific meanings in a medical context (e.g., consultant, placement, rehab), and vocabulary that allows participants to offer descriptions of patients' health (e.g., lethargy, stroke, stressed).

Using and Applying Genre Analysis Findings: Developing Genre Knowledge

As suggested above, findings from linguistically informed analyses of workplace genres can be applied to inform pedagogical interventions that aim to help new users of a genre develop genre knowledge. Returning briefly to the personal anecdote at the beginning of this chapter, not knowing how to behave in the faculty board meeting left me feeling uncomfortable. The stakes were quite high for me, and behaving in an inappropriate fashion may have led to face loss for myself and the students' association I was representing. However, the process of developing genre knowledge in some professions is arguably higher stakes, and the nursing context is one of these professions.

For second language nurses working in English speaking environments, the development of handover meeting genre knowledge may primarily involve the development of the linguistic knowledge they need to be able to perform their role and be interpreted appropriately by other nurses. Having this knowledge can also help non-native speakers develop and construct their professional identities (Dressen-Hammouda 2008). With this in mind, several findings could usefully be generalized from the above analysis to inform specific language training for non-English speaking nurses (in particular those arriving in a New Zealand context) regarding the linguistic norms and expectations of these important meetings. These might include:

- Help with linguistic knowledge needed to realize the primary social purpose(s) of these meetings. From a referential perspective, participants in these meetings seem to be concerned with eliciting and offering information about the ongoing care of patients on the ward. Helping non-native speakers develop linguistic awareness and strategies, such as understanding the different ways information can be requested and the way summarizing acts are constructed in ways that indicate actions for nurses, is likely to be relevant in helping non-native speaking nurses to successfully participate as both speakers and listeners in these meetings.
- Help identifying textual progression boundary markers. While the Opening and Closing stages may not be as high stakes, the main stage of these meetings (Patient Status Update) is crucial to the success of the ongoing care of patients. Understanding that meetings can progress through Patient Status Updates quite rapidly (as in iterations 10 and 12 above), and that each iteration is signalled by the use of a title and surname, will give new participants insights as to what to listen out for when they need to volunteer their own insights about a particular patient's ongoing care.
- Help developing turn-taking skills needed to perform actively in these meetings. Connected to the above point, nurses may be required to provide updates to the nursing team regarding a patient's ongoing care without being explicitly and directly invited to. Participants may therefore need to compete for the floor, and learn how to interact appropriately in this sort of multiparty interaction.
- Help interpreting the role of the chair in these meetings. Connected to the turn-taking patterns second language nurses can benefit from an understanding of the role of the chair and their role in eliciting and confirming courses of action for patients. This may involve providing help interpreting the linguistic actions of the chair, and help developing linguistic actions for responding to interaction with the chair. Also, if a senior non-native speaking nurse was asked to take this role, an understanding of the linguistic features of chairs in this genre would be particularly relevant.
- Help developing control of technical vocabulary. Not only can this be useful for describing patient status and health issues, but other speakers also assume this language is known and therefore control of technical vocabulary is crucial to participating in these meetings, and is an important way professional identity as a nurse can be indexed.

This is not an exhaustive list and readers may have identified further linguistic features of importance or relevance to these meetings. However, it does demonstrate how genre analysis can be used to develop specific insights into the social and linguistic features needed to understand and participate in a given genre. Important genres in other professions, particularly those experiencing challenges integrating an increasingly international workforce, could also be usefully explored with these goals in mind.

Looking Forward: Post-Structuralism and Genre

As has been argued in this chapter, genre theorists can contribute a deeper understanding of the way we use language in society. Genre theorists from more applied linguistic backgrounds do this by exploring the relationship between the social or communicative purposes of recurring social encounters and the language used to help realize these purposes.

However, genre theory has been criticized for being somewhat reductionist in nature, arriving at idealized structures of texts. Recent findings regarding the hybridization of genre forms have highlighted this issue (Ekström 2011; Lauerbach 2004; Thornborrow 2010). While genre theorists do not usually claim that their models are absolute and total representations of a genre, a research agenda concerned with exploring the linguistic realization of a given genre in a range of different social contexts may help genre theorists to address such weaknesses. Efforts to conduct contrastive analysis of genres in different social contexts have already provided interesting insights into genre realization in some linguistic domains (Hauser and Luginbühl 2012). The development of concepts to explore paradigmatic relations between and across genres and genre interactions has also allowed genre researchers to contribute to broader discussions of professional practice (Bhatia 2006; Swales 2004).

Such an agenda would allow genre researchers to both explore differences and account for these differences, and also identify stable features of and influences on genres across different social contexts. With respect to the extract analysed in this chapter, for example, does gender (the chair of this particular meeting is male) play a role in the macro and micro realization of the genre? Is the New Zealand setting a particular influence on the linguistic profile of this particular genre, or does the simple structure of these meetings suggest a profession, more generally, under considerable time pressure? Exploring genres in their situated contexts of use and accounting for aspects of these contexts would help develop more complex theories regarding the realization of genres, which would ultimately be of interest to those practitioners who stand to benefit from genre research findings.

Finally, with increasing internationalization of workplaces around the globe, questions are starting to emerge regarding the nature of genres and language use in multicultural contexts (Holmes and Marra 2014). Genre research has paid very little attention to cross cultural and intercultural variation (Bhatia 1997, 318–319). While researchers have identified cultural differences in the way meetings are conducted (Köhler, Cramton, and Hinds 2012), many questions remain that a genre level analysis can help answer. For example, do multicultural groups construct different normative patterns in the realization of genres? Can cultural differences at a text and social purpose level account for intercultural miscommunication? A genre analyst can provide the linguistic tools and theoretical basis for conducting such explorations.

Further Reading

Angouri and Marra (2010) provide an account of another meeting genre—business meetings. They provide evidence of some generalizable features of these meetings, and focus particularly on the chair's role in shaping activity in business meetings.

Christie and Martin (1997) provide analytical examples and discussions of a range of genres from workplace and educational contexts using an SFL approach.

Bhatia (2008) argues for a more multiperspective and multidimensional approach to the analysis of workplace genres, one that includes a focus on professional practices. Understanding these professional practices can add further depth to our understanding of the linguistic actions taken by users of a genre.

Related Topics

Service encounters; Genetic counselling; Intercultural communication; Men's talk in women's work; Language preparation

Notes

1 This data was collected thanks to a Victoria University of Wellington PhD Scholarship (Lazzaro-Salazar 2013).
2 Transcription conventions
   +   a short pause of less than a second
  (3.0)   a longer pause, given in number of seconds
  /...\   overlapping talk
  (unclear words) unclear sections of recording

References

Angouri, Jo. 2010. "Using Textbook and Real Life Data to Teach Turn Taking in Business Meetings." In *Handbook of Teaching Materials*, edited by Nigel Harwood, 373–395. New York: Cambridge University Press.
Angouri, Jo, and Meredith Marra. 2010. "Corporate Meetings as Genre: A Study of the Role of the Chair in Corporate Meeting Talk." *Text & Talk* 30: 615–636.
Bazerman, Charles, Adair Bonini, and Débora Figueiredo, Eds. 2009. *Genre in a Changing World*. Fort Collins, CO: WAC Clearinghouse.
Behara, Ravi, Robert L. Wears, Shawna J. Perry, Eric Eisenberg, Lexa Murphy, Mary Vanderhoef, Marc Shapiro, Christopher Beach, Pat Croskerry, and Karen Cosby. 2005. "A Conceptual Framework for Studying the Safety of Transitions in Emergency Care." In *Concepts and Methodology*. Vol 2. of *Advances in Patient Safety: From Research to Implementation*, edited by Kerm Henriksen, James B. Battles, Eric S. Marks, and David I. Lewin. Rockville, MD: Agency for Healthcare Research and Quality (US). Retrieved from www.ncbi.nlm.nih.gov/books/NBK20522.
Bhatia, Vijay. 1997. "Introduction: Genre Analysis and World Englishes." *World Englishes* 16: 313–319.
Bhatia, Vijay. 2006. "Discursive Practices in Disciplinary and Professional Contexts." *Linguistics and the Human Sciences* 2: 5–28.
Bhatia, Vijay. 2008. "Genre Analysis, ESP and Professional Practice." *English for Specific Purposes* 27: 161–174.
Christie, Frances, and J. R. Martin, Eds. 1997. *Genre and Institutions: Social Processes in the Workplace and School*. London: Cassell.
Dressen-Hammouda, Dacia. 2008. "From Novice to Disciplinary Expert: Disciplinary Identity and Genre Mastery." *English for Specific Purposes* 27: 233–252.
Edge, Julian, and Keith Richards. 1998. "May I See Your Warrant, Please?: Justifying Outcomes in Qualitative Research." *Applied Linguistics* 19: 334–356.
Eggins, Suzanne, and Diana Slade. 1997. *Analysing Casual Conversation*. London: Cassell.
Ekström, Mats. 2011. "Hybridity as a Resource and Challenge in a Talk Show Political Interview." In *Talking Politics in Broadcast Media: Cross-Cultural Perspectives on Political Interviewing, Journalism and Accountability*, edited by Mats Ekström, and Marianna Patrona, 135–155. Amsterdam: John Benjamins.
Hasan, Ruqaiya. 1989. "The Structure of a Text." In *Language, Context, and Text: Aspects of Language in a Social-Semiotic Perspective*. 2nd ed., edited by Michael A. K. Halliday and Ruqaiya Hasan, 52–69. Oxford: Oxford University Press.

Hauser, Stefan, and Martin Luginbühl, Eds. 2012. *Contrastive Media Analysis: Approaches to Linguistic and Cultural Aspects of Mass Media Communication*. Amsterdam: John Benjamins.

Holmes, Janet, and Meredith Marra. 2014. "The Complexities of Communication in Professional Workplaces." In *Routledge Handbook of Language and Professional Communication*, edited by Vijay Bhatia, and Stephen Bremner, 112–128. Abingdon, UK: Routledge.

Hymes, Dell. 1974. *Foundations in Sociolinguistics: An Ethnographic Approach*. Philadelphia, PA: University of Pennsylvania Press.

Hyon, Sunny. 1996. "Genre in Three Traditions: Implications for ESL." *TESOL Quarterly* 30: 693–722.

Kerr, Micky P. 2002. "A Qualitative Study of Shift Handover Practice and Function from a Socio-Technical Perspective." *Journal of Advanced Nursing* 37: 125–134.

Köhler, Tine, Catherine Durnell Cramton, and Pamela J. Hinds. 2012. "The Meeting Genre Across Cultures: Insights From Three German-American Collaborations." *Small Group Research* 43: 159–185.

Kuiper, Kon. 2009. *Formulaic Genres*. Basingstoke, UK: Palgrave Macmillan.

Labov, William, and Joshua Waletzky. 1997. "Narrative Analysis: Oral Versions of Personal Experience." *Journal of Narrative and Life History* 7: 3–38.

Lauerbach, Gerda. 2004. "Political Interviews as Hybrid Genre." *Text* 24: 353–397.

Lazzaro-Salazar, Mariana, and Kieran A. File. Forthcoming. "Nursing Handover as Genre." Target Journal: *Discourse Studies*.

Lazzaro-Salazar, Mariana. 2013. "Investigating Nurses' Professional Identity Construction in Two Health Settings in New Zealand." PhD diss., Victoria University of Wellington.

Levinson, Stephen C. 1992. "Activity Types and Language." In *Talk at Work: Interaction in Institutional Settings*, edited by Paul Drew, and John Heritage, 66–100. Cambridge: Cambridge University Press.

Martin, J. R. 2002. "A Universe of Meaning—How Many Practices?" In *Genre in the Classroom: Multiple Perspectives*, edited by Ann M. Johns, 269–278. Mahwah, NJ: Lawrence Erlbaum.

Martin, J. R., and David Rose. 2008. *Genre Relations: Mapping Culture*. London: Equinox.

Miller, Carolyn R. 1984. "Genre as Social Action." *Quarterly Journal of Speech* 70: 151–167.

Muntigl, Peter, and Helmut Gruber. 2005. "Introduction: Approaches to Genre." *Folia Linguistica* 39: 1–18.

Payne, Sheila, Michael Hardey, and Peter Coleman. 2000. "Interactions between Nurses during Handovers in Elderly Care." *Journal of Advanced Nursing* 32: 277–285.

Riddiford, Nicky, and Jonathan Newton. 2010. *Workplace Talk in Action: An ESOL Resource*. Wellington: School of Linguistics and Applied Language Studies, Victoria University of Wellington.

Rose, David, and J. R. Martin. 2012. *Learning to Write, Reading to Learn: Genre, Knowledge and Pedagogy in the Sydney School*. Sheffield, UK: Equinox.

Strange, Frank. 1996. "Handover: An Ethnographic Study of Ritual in Nursing Practice." *Intensive and Critical Care Nursing* 12: 106–112.

Swales, John. 1990. *Genre Analysis: English in Academic and Research Settings*. Cambridge: Cambridge University Press.

Swales, John. 2004. *Research Genres: Explorations and Applications*. Cambridge: Cambridge University Press.

Thornborrow, Joanna. 2010. "'Going Public': Constructing the Personal in a Television News Interview." *Discourse & Communication* 4: 105–123.

Part II
Different Workplace Settings

11
Corporate Settings
Dorien Van De Mieroop and Jonathan Clifton

Introduction

Much has been written about language in the workplace in business environments, and this body of research spans many genres, themes, and methodologies. Genres associated with corporations such as business meetings (e.g., Asmuß and Svennevig 2009), job interviews (e.g., Kerekes 2007), appraisal interviews (e.g., Clifton 2012a), and business speeches (e.g., Van De Mieroop 2005) have been the focus of extensive research. Similarly, many themes related to the corporate world such as leadership (see Schnurr this volume), intercultural communication (see Holmes this volume), storytelling (see Ladegaard this volume), decision making (e.g., Clifton 2012b), and negotiating (e.g., Francis 1986) have also been studied. Moreover, these themes and genres have been analysed from a variety of methodological angles, such as ethnomethodology, conversation analysis, sociolinguistics, and systemic functional linguistics (for an overview, see Iedema and Wodak 1999, 7–10). In this chapter, rather than trying to cover this huge variety of genres, themes, and methods, we focus on talk in corporate settings from a more general perspective.

A corporation is commonly understood to be "a large business or company" (*Collins English Dictionary*), but it is also a legally defined business structure which is considered to be a "person" and who, as a "person", may own property, sue and be sued, incur debts, and so on. Despite common usage, both legal and lay, that defines the corporation as an entity, the ontological status of a corporation is the focus of much debate, which also has a linguistic aspect. Are corporations talked into being through language? Do pre-existing structures define language use in corporate settings? Is there a delicate balance between structure and agency in which language plays a role? Before we go into this, we first sketch the significant changes that corporations have undergone over the past decades.

Historical Perspectives

From the end of World War II until the early 1970s, massive, unsaturated markets for consumer goods existed and large corporations that engaged in mass production had unprecedented success (Gee, Hull, and Lankshear 1996, 17). During this period, the vast majority of employees were industrial workers who carried out mindless and repetitive mechanical tasks which formed part of a larger task that was beyond the workers' understanding. A stereotypical example of such an "old economy" corporation is the Ford Motor company in which "assembly-line mass production ... required of workers minimal skills and decreased mechanical know-how" (Hull 2001, 17). Moreover, these "old economy" corporations were characterized by a traditional hierarchical structure in which the middle management functioned as the "brains" of the corporation that passed on information from the top to the bottom (Gee, Hull, and Lankshear 1996, 17).

Then around the 1980s, as globalization became more apparent, the markets became saturated with consumer goods, competition became fiercer, and consumers became more fickle. Furthermore, the economy became science-and-technology driven which significantly increased the pace of change, eventually leading to hypercompetition (Gee, Hull, and Lankshear 1996, 17–18). These changes marked the transition to the "New Work Order" or "New Capitalism" (Gee, Hull, and Lankshear 1996; Fairclough 2002).

In this New Capitalist world, "old economy" material products *per se* lost their importance as they were superseded by a knowledge-based economy. This was because it was through the knowledge to design and to innovate that these products were turned into "high quality" goods and symbols of identity and lifestyle. Since the 1980s, these new "knowledge endowed" goods have competed with other goods in a fully globalized and saturated market. Furthermore, this shift from material to semiotic production (Flowerdew 2002) has made language an increasingly important aspect of social practice because "goods" are often no longer material, rather they tend to "have a linguistic or partly linguistic character" (Chouliaraki and Fairclough 1999, vii). Consequently, this "historic shift" to a New Work Order coincided "with micro- and macro-level discoursal shifts" (Sarangi 2005, 163).

A further consequence of the ascendance of the New Work Order was the thinning of the ranks of middle managers, who were considered to slow the business down. Hence, as knowledge, information, and responsibility were pushed down from middle management to the lower-level workers (Gee, Hull, and Lankshear 1996, 18), old industrial jobs were largely replaced by knowledge-based jobs. Another important aspect of this new knowledge-based economy was that it entailed the abolition of explicit top-down hierarchies. These were replaced by more egalitarian systems which were characterized by new social practices and new social identities for the allegedly *empowered* employees (Gee, Hull, and Lankshear 1996, 19–21). For example, Koller argues that in "old economy" corporations the top management would typically impose a corporate text upon the employees. This top-down process of text production projected a powerless identity onto the employees and confined them to the passive reception of the text. In the flatter hierarchies typical of the new economy, such a top-down process is often considered inappropriate. Consequently, other bottom-up processes have been established so that corporate texts are now seen as being "owned" by all the employees (Koller 2008, 163).

As a consequence of this flattening of organizational hierarchies in which workers are now considered to be "partners", "fast capitalist texts" describe new core values, such as liberation, trust, and collaboration (Gee, Hull, and Lankshear 1996, 29). Yet, for this system to work, it is of course imperative that these "worker-partners" are fully committed to the corporation and that they fully embrace the vision of their employer. This requires a revision of the workers' identities so that they become congruent with "the definitions of self and worker that are being promoted [by the corporation]" (Hull 2001, 17). Hence, the workers' identities have become "a locus and target of organisational control", and so they are now *regulated* by means of "training and promotion procedures [that] are developed in ways that have implications for the shaping and direction of identity" (Alvesson and Willmott 2002, 623, 625). These—possibly *regulated*—identities are especially enacted when workers perform new and different "language and literacy tasks" while engaging in team-based "consultative and participatory processes with co-workers" (Iedema and Scheeres 2003, 318). Even though workers are rarely prepared for these new responsibilities, the ability to not only *do*, but also to *talk*, work is crucial. This is because the workers now not only have to textualize "what they do", but they also have to textualize "who they are" (Iedema and Scheeres 2003, 335). Unsurprisingly, in practice, this textualization often demonstrates that many workers have invented a myriad of ways to transform and subvert these projected identities (Hull 2001, 21). Further, as consumers and critics increasingly pressure companies to "behave according to ethical standards" (Koller 2008, 159), professional identities may become increasingly hybrid, as organizational actors struggle to "manage the tensions resulting from the concomitant search for profit and social responsibility" (Ghadiri, Gond, and Brès 2015, 594).

In sum, on the one hand, business managers and consultants tend to conclude in their "fast capitalist texts" that the New Work Order results in an overall empowerment of the workers, who are now able to challenge their superiors or the company's rules and regulations. On the other hand, from, among others, the perspective of socioculturalism and (critical) discourse analysis, researchers have questioned whether organizations are *really* more egalitarian, or whether this egalitarianism is just a form of window dressing which strategically hides more subtle forms of managerial hegemony, thus creating "new hierarchies while undermining others" (Sarangi and Roberts 1999b, 10). Of course, the latter interpretation actually makes it more difficult for workers to challenge the corporate hierarchy. This is because the exercise of managerial power becomes less tangible when it is hidden underneath the allegedly egalitarian corporate structure.

Critical Issues

The issue of how to study the relation between language and these New Work Order corporations, is a matter of debate. Using an admittedly somewhat crude taxonomy, we first discern at one end of the spectrum, a naïve realist approach. This approach considers that the pre-discursive existence of "objective" material and structural realities define the essence of the organization (Reed 2005, 1621). From this perspective, talk is a mirror which reflects the reality of the situation and the corporation *as it is* (Potter 1996, 97). Talk is thus viewed as nothing more than a by-product of corporations, because once we *know* the underlying structure of the corporation we *know* how organizational players will talk. In such a naïve realist approach, organizational players are considered to be passive recipients who merely act out scripts dictated by pre-discursive structures.

Second, in the middle of the continuum, corporate entities are considered to be the result of the interplay between structure and agency in which historical, political, and social forces interact with talk to produce the corporation. As Reed (2010, 154–155) argues "the process of local construction [of the organization] is necessarily dependent on non-local relationships, resources, and practices that make it possible in the first place". From this perspective, workplace language is important but it is not *the* quintessential element. Critical discourse analysts such as Fairclough argue that a researcher should focus on both the "social structuring of semiotic diversity (orders of discourse)" and on "the productive semiotic work which goes on in particular texts and interactions" (Fairclough 2001, 124). Consequently, the relation between the macro-structures of the organization and the micro-realizations of the organization in talk are taken into account in the analyses.

Third, social constructionist approaches to organizations (see Lazzaro-Salazar this volume) are situated at the other end of the continuum. From this perspective, structure and action are collapsed into one, and as Reed (2005, 1622) points out, organizations are conceptualized as "discursive constructions and cultural forms that have no ontological status or epistemological significance beyond their textually created and mediated existence". Thus, following Potter's (1996, 98) metaphor, this approach considers language to be a construction yard in which the world is constituted as people talk it, write it, and argue it. And more specifically, from an organizational perspective, Boden (1994, 15) claims that: "through the timing, placing, pacing, and patterning of verbal interaction, organisational members actually constitute the organisation as a real and practical place." The structure of the firm does not therefore pre-exist the firm, but action (talk) and structure are mutually constitutive: the corporation, therefore, consists of matters that are oriented to by organizational players, as evidenced in their talk, and the corporation thus reflexively becomes an essential resource for going about workplace activities. Consequently, as organizational players talk, the corporation is (re)produced as an external and constraining social fact. Moreover, through orienting to the corporation in a particular way, it is constructed in talk through elements such as: turn-taking organization; sequence organization; turn design; lexical choice; and epistemological and other forms of asymmetry (Heritage 1997, 164). Hence, the corporation becomes visible through what organizational players consider to be allowable contributions to talk (Levinson 1992) and through how they orient to the larger Discourses that instantiate talk, and which reflexively are instantiated by talk.

In other words, Gee's distinction (1999) between discourse (little-d) and Discourse (big-D) is relevant here. Applied to corporations, little-d discourse refers to the micro-practices of talk and the processes through which organizational actors construct emotions, knowledge, identities, and so on which accomplish the organization. Big-D Discourse can be defined as "the entire interlocking web of practices, structures, and ideologies: a system of understanding and exploration that prefigures which practices and interpretations are available, and how practices and structures are understood" (Kiesling 2006, 262). In the case of corporations, these refer to Discourses of, for example, management, leadership, the market and so on. Big D-discourse and little d-discourse therefore are not separate entities, rather they are reflexively linked so that one invokes the other. Therefore, through workplace talk, New Work Order Discourses of what a corporation is, or should be, are instantiated, and reflexively these Discourses set the boundaries for workplace interaction. One of the consequences of such an approach to organization in which Discourse and discourse are inseparably entwined is that a researcher has much to gain from studying the organization on the *terra firma* of social interaction as it emerges in talk, and thus language in the workplace should be of central interest to scholars in the field of organizational studies and management.

Current Contributions and Research

Taking the communicative constitution of the organization (Cooren *et al*. 2011) as our starting point, in this section we consider how the Discourse of the New Work Order is talked into being as a particular version of the corporation is invoked. In order to study this interplay between the Discourse (big-D) of the New Work Order and discourse (little-d), we focus on gatekeeping in corporate settings. Gatekeeping can be defined as a way of enforcing normative expectations of compliance with organizational premises (Baraldi 2013, 357). Gatekeeping is thus quite paradoxical within the context of the New Work Order because on the one hand the New Work Order relies on flatter hierarchies and on workers taking more responsibility, yet on the other hand it requires that these workers "fit" with the corporation's vision and its "way of being and way of doing things". This can give rise to the notion of unobtrusive control (Tompkins and Cheney 1985, cited in Yeung 2004a, 84) in which management instils organizational premises into the employees and so (paradoxically) obliges them to fit with New Work Order Discourses of autonomy, participative decision making, industrial democracy, and so on. However, as well as being a form of repressive interaction, gatekeeping can also function in a supportive or facilitative way that opens gates for those who "fit" certain requirements (Holmes 2007). Gatekeeping is therefore a prime site in which this paradox is revealed in workplace language choices.

In particular, we can discern a difference between gatekeeping at the boundary of the organization and in-company gatekeeping. The first type of gatekeeping monitors access to the organization. This can be observed in job interviews in which applicants have to convince the interviewers, as gatekeepers of the corporation, that they are good candidates for the job. As various studies have demonstrated, the success of job candidates is not only related to "their job qualifications or to their own verbal and nonverbal behavior" (Kerekes 2006, 54), it is also related to the extent to which interlocutors manage to "develop a positive rapport with one another by establishing co-membership" (Kerekes 2007, 1943; see also Erickson and Shultz 1982). Successful candidates thus talk into being identities that are coherent with those of the interviewer, who, as a representative of the company, monitors whether these identities "fit" the expectations of the company, or not.

Second, Holmes has argued that "boundary-monitoring is equally pervasive within organisations" and in-company gatekeeping allows researchers to "explore the ways in which it [i.e., gatekeeping] is interactionally achieved between people who know each other and work together" (Holmes 2007, 1995). On the one hand, researchers have looked at the various ways in which gatekeeping is performed in everyday workplace interaction. For example, Yeung (2004a; 2004b) has looked at gatekeeping in decision-making in banks and Wasson (2000) has looked at the way in which consensus is achieved in business meetings through subordinates censuring their contributions so as to align with the opinions of their superiors. On the other hand, there are, of course, intra-organizational gatekeeping encounters which are specifically designed to have significant "implications for the future career or status of one of the participants" (Holmes 2007, 1995). An example of such an encounter is the performance appraisal interview, which has often either replaced or taken up a complementary position in relation to the traditional evaluative interview. These performance appraisal interviews are typically framed as particularly participative and empowering organizational practices in which evaluation is usually presented as a bi-directional process (i.e., employees often also evaluate their employers during these interviews). Such interviews can thus be seen as a direct result of structural changes in corporations due to the New Work Order, in which it is considered problematic to evaluate employees in a top-down way (Fletcher 2001). It is thus not surprising that nowadays, employers may be found to frame the negative assessments of their employees as socially problematic actions (Asmuß 2008; Clifton 2012a) and to complement them with extensive face work (Van De Mieroop and Schnurr forthcoming). Nevertheless, performance appraisal interviews are typical media for control of "identity regulation" (Alvesson and Willmott 2002). This is because during these interactions employers often attempt to correct employees who have not adopted a professional identity that is promoted by the company.

A Brief Illustration

In order to make this more tangible, we present one short example that we analyse from a social constructionist angle. The fragment was taken from a performance appraisal interview that took place in Belgium in 2011 in a commercial laboratory that performs analyses of blood samples. Even though this is not a typical large corporation, the data collected at this research site illustrate that this lab has adopted structures and procedures that are typical of New Work Order corporations. This thus demonstrates that New Capitalist ideologies have spread far beyond the boundaries of large scale corporations.

In the extract below, the matter under discussion is a typical New Work Order practice, namely the employees actively have to demonstrate that they meet the norms of quality control. These norms have been institutionalized in the form of time-consuming paperwork that each employee has to fill out. This illustrates the shift from workers who carry out mindless, repetitive tasks to knowledge workers who also have to reflect on their work and textualize these reflections in oral or written form (cf. Iedema and Scheeres 2003).

The employee who is being interviewed has adopted a dissident professional identity regarding this shift in business practice: she explicitly states that she perceives her job as a "blood test assembly line". She thus constructs a typical "old economy" worker identity. As she also expressed her lack of interest in getting promoted, the superior has limited means to pressure the employee[1] and transform her professional identity into one that fits the ideological framework of the New Work Order. Given her lack of any interest in the "knowledge side" of her job, it is not surprising that the employee complains about the "quality control" paperwork. After a lengthy discussion with the superior about the usefulness/uselessness of this paperwork, the following fragment occurs:

Extract from a performance appraisal interview (E = employee; S = superior)[2]

```
1    E    yes but yes, it's it's all too crazy,
2         when you look what >kind of
3         >>([deficits       [         )<<
4    S                       [yes
5    S    no no but okay
6         for me it is just about
7         erm pay attention to it hey
8         you you have your opinion about this
9         everyone is also allowed to have their own opinion
10        but pay attention to it that you you give it
11        in a bit more nuanced way
12        certainly when younger colleagues are present
13   E    mmm
14   S    because they nevertheless look up to you
```

After the superior has ended an extended turn with a series of arguments in favour of the paperwork (prior to the extract), the employee answers with a pro-forma agreement ("yes but yes", line 1), delaying the upcoming dispreferred response. In this response, through using the boosted formulation "it's all too crazy" (line 1), the employee still evaluates the paperwork very negatively. She accounts for her evaluation in lines 2 and 3, and the superior overlaps this account with a few affirmative particles (line 4). In line 5, the superior takes a third turn in which the negative particles ("no no") and the contrastive conjunction ("but") preceding the topic closing particle ("okay") indicate that no agreement has been reached. So at this point, the superior gives up her attempts to "regulate" the employee's professional identity.

In the subsequent lines, the superior shifts the focus away from "identity regulation" as she now admits that the employee has a deviant opinion (line 8) which she can neither change, nor forbid ("everyone is also allowed to have their own opinion", line 9). Instead, she engages in damage control, and now tries to silence this opinion which goes against the official standpoint of the organization. In line 10, she instructs the employee to be careful regarding the way in which, and in whose presence, she voices this opinion (respectively: "a bit more nuanced", line 11; and "when younger colleagues are present", line 12). So, the superior's damage control is oriented to preventing the employee from infecting her younger colleagues' professional identities with her critical ideas. This instruction is then mitigated slightly in the closing line of the fragment, in which the superior formulates a compliment, as she says these colleagues "look up to" the employee. However, the compliment is somewhat ambiguous due to the addition of the adverb "nevertheless" (*toch* in the Dutch original), which is also pronounced emphatically. This frames the fact that the employee is respected due to her senior status as a bit undesirable, as the junior employees who admire her might also be inspired by her subversive, "old economy" identity.

This extract illustrates the paradoxical ideology of the New Work Order: on the one hand, the flatter hierarchy empowers employees who now have specific media, such as performance appraisal interviews, to formulate their criticisms of the organization and their superiors. In principle, such criticism is welcomed in New Capitalist organizations, as all workers should have the necessary knowledge to identify potential deficiencies in the organizational structure and should be able to formulate constructive criticism. On the other hand, this only works if the employees' professional identities "fit" the "managerially designed and designated identities" (Alvesson and Willmott 2002, 621). In this case, the employee is quite tenacious in resisting the propagated identity as she refuses to agree with the superior's lengthy argumentation in favour of the "quality control" paperwork. Interestingly, it is actually the more lateral hierarchical structure that makes such a persistent refusal possible. Hence, after a while, the superior resorts to damage control, which consists in silencing the employee to prevent her dissident identity from being adopted by others. This damage control is strongly interactionally negotiated. This is because, on the one hand, it is imposed through the use of imperatives ("pay attention", line 7 and 11) and, on the other hand, it is mitigated by means of hedges (e.g., "a bit", line 11) and an—albeit ambiguous—compliment (line 14).

Overall, the extract demonstrates that even though other mechanisms are at work in New Capitalist organizations, the end result often remains the same, namely that deviant opinions and criticisms are silenced. Thus, this brief illustration suggests that the ideal of egalitarianism only applies to those who "march to the beat of the New Work Order" (Hull 2001, 21) and that workers who adopt dissident identities are corrected or silenced in strategic and often subtle ways.

Recommendations for Practice

Considering the Janus-faced nature of the New Work Order which, on the one hand, promises more liberty in a knowledge intensive economy, yet on the other hand demands that employees fit with the spirit of the New Capitalism, it is important for organizational players to realize this double bind and to be aware of its potential for hegemony in which people willingly buy into a system of power which is in fact to their detriment (Gramsci 1971). From a social constructionist perspective, it is therefore important for organizational players to understand that the corporation can always be constructed differently. An awareness of the performative nature of language could have an emancipatory effect since organizational players would no longer be cast as passive recipients acting out predefined roles within a corporation. Moreover, from a practical perspective, if a worker does not want to passively accept a professional identity in somebody else's organizational landscape, then it is essential that the centrality of language and its ability to construct an alternative identity in an alternative landscape (that perhaps challenges the New Work Order) is impressed upon practitioners. However, as Potter (1996, 230) argues, raising awareness of the performative nature of language as an emancipatory act is delicate. This is because, in a corporate context, it is often only the managerial elites who have access to training that could improve their language skills and thus their abilities to author the corporate landscape.

Further, another delicate issue in applying the insights of linguistics to business practices is that, again as Potter (1996) points out, many corporate players are no doubt already highly skilled language users—whether they are aware of it or not. Therefore, perhaps the best way of introducing insights from linguistics into the corporate world is first to contest widespread lay understandings that view language as secondary, and inferior, to action (Clifton 2012b) with an understanding of the performative nature of language: language actually does things, including constituting the organization. Such an awareness of the centrality of language to business practice could perhaps best be achieved through reflective practice (Schön 1983) in which linguists encourage practitioners to reflect upon their language use. For example, Roberts and Sarangi (2003) report having used such a reflective approach to the analysis of naturally-occurring workplace interaction with success.

The advantage of using naturally-occurring data as a basis for reflection, is that it is not based on invented (and often idealized) dialogues that are usually found in the "how to books" which only provide very "thin descriptions" (Sarangi and Roberts 1999b, 2). For example, Clifton (2012a) points out that our stocks of interactional knowledge concerning workplace language (i.e., normative models and theories or quasi-theories about interaction that are found in professional texts, training manuals and so on, Peräkylä and Vehviläinen 2003, 729–730) are largely derived from simulations, questionnaires, and interviews and so little of the advice that is provided to practitioners is actually based on fine-grained analyses of naturally-occurring workplace language. The consequence of such prescriptive advice based on invented data is that it is often faulty and can lead to poorer communication (Cameron 2000). If, as outlined above, being a good communicator is about being aware of language practice, then a greater awareness of, and hence reflection on, practice is needed rather than prescriptive teaching. This is because, as Cameron (2000, 178–179) argues, prescriptive approaches to communication training neither produce "better communication" nor more "skilled" and "empowered" communicators. Instead, the true measure of a skilled communicator is the ability to reflect upon talk and to choose strategies that are likely to be appropriate and effective within a given situation.

Future Directions

Studies that aim to bridge the gap between research and practice remain rare and more research in this vein would provide greater opportunities for a wider audience of practitioners to appreciate that *talk is organizing* (Weick 2004). However, the focus of such a move would ideally not be on workplace talk alone: first, there is a growing trend within the field of language in the workplace that considers other forms of modality as well as talk. For example, researchers such as Lindström and Mondada (2009) point out that all forms of communication such as gaze, body positioning, space, artefacts, and architecture have a role to play in the constitution of the organization. Second, it is not only talk in the workplace by corporate players that talks the corporation into being, it is also the talk of outside stakeholders such as suppliers, clients, and so on (McPhee and Zaug 2000). This area also remains a relatively under-researched field. Third, texts and documents such as shareholders' statements, advertising, minutes of meetings, quality manuals, and so on are artefacts that have a crucial role to play in the constitution of an organization as well (Benoit-Barné and Cooren 2009). Examining the interaction between corporations, talk, written texts, and other artefacts is also a promising avenue of future research. Finally, researchers from linguistics and organizational studies could strive for greater synergy. Thus, while it is true that the linguistic turn in organizational studies is increasingly being accepted (Alvesson and Kärreman 2000) and that consequently the boundaries between linguistics and organization studies are becoming more porous, future research would most certainly benefit from more transdisciplinary work that could deepen our understanding of the myriad of ways in which corporations are talked into being in the era of New Capitalism.

Further Reading

Boden (1994) provides the classic ethnomethodological account of how organizations are talked into being.

Cooren (2015) is the latest offering from François Cooren, who is one of the key players in the Montreal School which has produced numerous works concerning the communicative constitution of organization (CCO).

Gee, Hull and Lankshear (1996) is the standard work about the implications and contradictions of *The New Work Order*. It discusses how the apparently less hierarchical structures of companies in the information age affect language, literacy, and learning.

Iedema and Scheeres (2003) demonstrates in practice how the textualization of work is performed and the "reflexivization" of worker identity is achieved in two very different workplace sites—a gaming machine factory and a metropolitan teaching hospital.

Sarangi and Roberts (1999a) is a collection of papers offering an interdisciplinary view on professional talk and its constitutive role in workplace practice, thereby also illustrating how professional identities are talked into being in relation to the institutional order.

Related Topics

Social constructionism; Blue-collar workpaces; Legal settings; Leadership; Enabling women leaders

Notes

1. The employee has a long-term contract and so threatening to fire her, or actually firing her, are hardly options.
2. The extract is literally translated from the Dutch original, which is not provided here for reasons of space. We are grateful to Eveline Vrolix for collecting the data. See Jefferson (2004) for transcription conventions.

References

Alvesson, Mats, and Dan Kärreman. 2000. "Taking the Linguistic Turn in Organizational Research. Challenges, Responses, Consequences." *The Journal of Applied Behavioral Science* 36: 136–158.

Alvesson, Mats, and Hugh Willmott. 2002. "Identity Regulation as Organizational Control: Producing the Appropriate Individual." *Journal of Management Studies* 39: 619–644.

Asmuß, Birte. 2008. "Performance Appraisal Interviews: Preference Organization in Assessment Sequences, *Journal of Business Communication* 45: 408–429.

Asmuß, Birte, and Jan Svennevig. 2009. "Meeting Talk. An Introduction." *Journal of Business Communication* 46: 3–22.

Baraldi, Claudio. 2013. "Forms of Decision Making Gatekeeping and Dialogic Coordination in CISV Organizational Meetings." *Journal of Business Communication* 50: 339–361.

Benoit-Barné, Chantal, and François Cooren. 2009. "The Accomplishment of Authority Through Presentification: How Authority Is Distributed Among and Negotiated by Organizational Members." *Management Communication Quarterly* 23: 5–31.

Boden, Deirdre. 1994. *The Business of Talk: Organizations in Action.* Cambridge: Polity Press.

Cameron, Deborah. 2000. *Good to Talk: Living and Working in a Communication Culture.* London: Sage.

Chouliaraki, Lilie, and Norman Fairclough. 1999. *Discourse in Late Modernity: Rethinking Critical Discourse Analysis.* Edinburgh: Edinburgh University Press.

Clifton, Jonathan. 2012a. "Conversation Analysis in Dialogue with Stocks of Interactional Knowledge: Facework and Appraisal Interviews." *Journal of Business Communication* 49: 283–311.

Clifton, Jonathan. 2012b. "A Discursive Approach to Leadership. Doing Assessments and Managing Organizational Meanings." *Journal of Business Communication* 49: 148–168.

Collins English Dictionary, online version, available at: www.collinsdictionary.com/dictionary/english/corporation.

Cooren, François. 2015. *Organizational Discourse: Communication and Constitution.* Cambridge: Polity.

Cooren, François, Timothy Kuhn, Joep P. Cornelissen, and Timothy Clark. 2011. "Communication, Organizing and Organization: An Overview and Introduction to the Special Issue." *Organization Studies* 32: 1149–1170.

Erickson, Frederick, and Jeffrey J. Shultz. 1982. *The Counselor as Gatekeeper: Social Interaction in Interviews.* New York: Academic Press.

Fairclough, Norman. 2001. "Critical Discourse Analysis as a Method in Social Scientific Research." In *Methods of Critical Discourse Analysis*, edited by Ruth Wodak and Michael Meyer, 121–138. London: Sage.

Fairclough, Norman. 2002. "Language in New Capitalism." *Discourse & Society* 13: 163–166.

Fletcher, Clive. 2001. "Performance Appraisals and Management: The Developing Research Agenda." *Journal of Occupational and Organisational Psychology* 74: 473–487.

Flowerdew, John. 2002. "Globalization Discourse: A View from the East." *Discourse & Society* 13: 209–225.

Francis, David W. 1986. "Some Structures of Negotiation Talk." *Language in Society* 15: 53–80.

Gee, James Paul. 1999. *An Introduction to Discourse Analysis: Theory and Method.* London: Routledge.

Gee, James Paul, Glynda Hull, and Colin Lankshear. 1996. *The New Work Order.* London: Saint Leonards Allen and Unwin.

Ghadiri, Djahanchah P., Jean-Pascal Gond, and Luc Brès. 2015. "Identity Work of Corporate Social Responsibility Consultants: Managing Discursively the Tensions between Profit and Social Responsibility." *Discourse & Communication* 9: 593–624.

Gramsci, Antonio. 1971. *Selections from the Prison Notebooks of Antonio Gramsci.* London: Lawrence Wishart.

Heritage, John. 1997. "Conversation Analysis and Institutional Talk: Analyzing Data." In *Qualitative Research: Theory, Method and Practice*, edited by David Silverman, 161–182. London: Sage.

Holmes, Janet. 2007. "Monitoring Organisational Boundaries: Diverse Discourse Strategies Used in Gatekeeping." *Journal of Pragmatics* 39: 1993–2016.

Hull, Glynda. 2001. "Constructing Working Selves: Silicon Valley Assemblers Meet the New Work Order." *Anthropology of Work Review* XXII: 17–22.

Iedema, Rick, and Hermine Scheeres. 2003. "From Doing Work to Talking Work: Renegotiating Knowing, Doing, and Identity." *Applied Linguistics* 24: 316–337.

Iedema, Rick, and Ruth Wodak. 1999. "Introduction: Organizational Discourses and Practices." *Discourse & Society* 10: 5–19.

Jefferson, Gail. 2004. "Glossary of transcript symbols with an introduction." In *Conversation Analysis: Studies from the First Generation*, edited by Gene H. Lerner, 13–31. Amsterdam: John Benjamins.

Kerekes, Julie A. 2006. "Winning an Interviewer's Trust in a Gatekeeping Encounter." *Language in Society* 35: 27–57.
Kerekes, Julie A. 2007. "The Co-Construction of a Gatekeeping Encounter: An Inventory of Verbal Actions." *Journal of Pragmatics* 29: 1942–1973.
Kiesling, Scott F. 2006. "Hegemonic Identity-Making in Narrative." In *Discourse and Identity*, edited by Anna De Fina, Deborah Schiffrin, and Michael Bamberg, 261–287. Cambridge: Cambridge University Press.
Koller, Veronika. 2008. "Identity, Image, Impression: Corporate Self-Promotion and Public Reactions." In *Handbook of Communication in the Public Sphere*, edited by Ruth Wodak and Veronika Koller, 155–180. Berlin: Mouton de Gruyter.
Levinson, Stephen C. 1992. "Activity Types and Language." In *Talk at Work: Interaction in Institutional Settings*, edited by Paul Drew, and John Heritage, 66–100. Cambridge: Cambridge University Press.
Lindström, Anna, and Lorenza Mondada. 2009. "Assessments in Social Interaction: Introduction to the Special Issue." *Research on Language and Social Interaction* 42: 299–308.
McPhee, Robert D., and Pamela Zaug. 2000. "The Communicative Constitution of Organizations. A Framework for Explanation." *The Electronic Journal of Communication* 10. www.cios.org/EJCPUBLIC/010/1/01017.html.
Peräkylä, Anssi, and Sanna Vehviläinen. 2003. "Conversation Analysis and the Professional Stocks of Interactional Knowledge." *Discourse & Society* 14: 727–750.
Potter, Jonathan. 1996. *Representing Reality: Discourse, Rhetoric and Social Construction*, London: Sage.
Reed, Michael. 2005. "Reflections on the 'Realist Turn' in Organization and Management Studies." *Journal of Management Studies* 42: 1621–1644.
Reed, Mike. 2010. "Is Communication Constitutive of Organization?" *Management Communication Quarterly* 24: 151–157.
Roberts, Celia, and Srikant Sarangi. 2003. "Uptake of Discourse Research in Interprofessional Settings: Reporting from Medical Consultancy." *Applied Linguistics* 24: 338–359.
Sarangi, Srikant. 2005. "Social Interaction, Social Theory and Work-related Activities." *Calidoscopio* 3: 160–169.
Sarangi, Srikant, and Celia Roberts, Eds. 1999a. *Talk, Work and Institutional Order: Discourse in Medical, Mediation and Management Settings*. Berlin: Mouton de Gruyter.
Sarangi, Srikant, and Celia Roberts. 1999b. "The Dynamics of Interactional and Institutional Orders in Work-Related Settings." In *Talk, Work and Institutional Order: Discourse in Medical, Mediation and Management Settings*, edited by Srikant Sarangi, and Celia Roberts, 1–57. Berlin: Mouton de Gruyter.
Schön, Donald A. 1983. *The Reflective Practitioner: How Professionals Think in Action*. New York: Basic Books.
Tompkins, Phillip K., and George Cheney. 1985. "Communication and Unobstrusive Control." In *Organizational Communication: Traditional Themes and New Directions*, edited by Robert D. Mcphee, and Phillip K. Tompkins, 179–210. Beverly Hills, CA: Sage.
Van De Mieroop, Dorien. 2005. "An Integrated Approach of Quantitative and Qualitative Analysis in the Study of Identity in Speeches." *Discourse & Society* 16: 107–130.
Van De Mieroop, Dorien, and Stephanie Schnurr. Forthcoming. "'Doing Evaluation' in the Modern Workplace: Negotiating the Identity of 'Model Employee' in Performance Appraisal Interviews." In *Negotiating Boundaries at Work*, edited by Jo Angouri, Meredith Marra, and Janet Holmes. Edinburgh: Edinburgh University Press.
Wasson, Christina. 2000. "Caution and consensus in American business meetings." *Pragmatics* 10: 457–481.
Weick, Karl E. 2004. "A Bias for Conversation: Acting Discursively in Organizations." In *Sage Handbook of Organizational Discourse*, edited by David Grant, Cynthia Hardy, Cliff Oswick, and Linda L. Putnam, 405–412. London: Sage.
Yeung, Lorrita. 2004a. "The Paradox of Control in Participative Decision-Making: Gatekeeping Discourse in Banks." *International Journal of the Sociology of Language* 66: 83–104.
Yeung, Lorrita. 2004b. "The Paradox of Control in Participative Decision Making: Facilitative Discourse in Banks." *Text* 24: 113–146.

12
Language in Blue-Collar Workplaces
Dorte Lønsmann and Kamilla Kraft

Introduction

Do blue-collar workplaces need their own chapter in a book on *Language in the Workplace*? While language and communication are viewed as essential parts of the work of service and administration workers, so-called white-collars, the link between language and communication and manual workers, so-called blue-collars, may seem less obvious. "Working-class speech" has received much attention as a sociolinguistic reference category, but blue-collar workspaces are underrepresented in the literature on language in the workplace. This chapter aims to show that language and communication play a significant part in the everyday work and social lives of blue-collar workers. We present an overview of research on language and blue-collar workers with a particular focus on how language competence, use, and ideologies in blue-collar workplaces are influenced by a late-capitalist labour market characterized by globalization, mobility and migration.

Defining Blue-Collar Workers

Definitions of blue-collar workers commonly refer to manual, hard physical work, and always index people on "the floor". As Gibson and Papa (2000, 68) note:

> The term "blue-collar" refers to skilled tradespeople, factory workers, farmers and other labourers, as compared to "white collar" (professional and managerial) and "pink collar" (secretarial and service) occupations (Halle, 1984). Blue-collar work generally connotes an occupation in which a person engages in some type of physical labor that is paid in an hourly, rather than fixed, wage (Lederer, 1987).

This definition proposes a clear distinction between different classes of workers in terms of occupation, but as Savage *et al.* (2013) point out, new regimes of work require class categories to be recast to focus on what characterizes these forms of work, e.g., precarity. Therefore, when we write "blue-collar" we refer to labourers in the primary or secondary sectors, whose job is often, but not always, temporary, and low-status.

Critical Issues and Topics

Language and Identity in Blue-Collar Workplaces

Stereotypes about blue-collar workers and their language use are often strong. The Danish expression *skurvognssnak* (literally "construction trailer talk") and the English expressions "swearing like a sailor/trooper/dock worker" all point to underlying stereotypes about the language of blue-collar workplaces being associated with rough and impolite styles of speaking. An article from the *Georgia State Law Review* (Brannan 2000) shows how such stereotypes about blue-collar language have impacted judgments in court cases where blue-collar workers have sued employers over a hostile work environment. Brannan finds that judges' decisions depend on the setting so that discriminatory and offensive behaviour is more tolerable in blue-collar settings. In her review Brannan points to several cases where the court voted in favour of the employer, i.e., dismissing the blue-collar employee's claim that s/he was harassed, based on the context of the blue-collar workplace where "humor and language are rough hewn and vulgar" (2000, 797). The stereotypes underlying the judges' rulings paint a picture of blue-collar workplaces and workers as people doing dirty and dangerous work in a coarse and vulgar setting where the norms for language use are different than in other types of workplaces. Yet, while stereotypes about specific work genres of talk may have consequences for workers, they do not necessarily reflect the ways blue-collar workers themselves understand their work and identity.

Studies looking at blue-collar identity have found that miners and construction workers, for example, see their workplace and its norms as different from those of white-collar workplaces. Lucas and Buzzanell's (2004) study of American miners focuses on how these blue-collar workers make sense of career and success. They find that through the concept of *sisu* (from Finnish, meaning "determination"), the miners construct an occupational culture that enables them to find dignity and meaning in work that outsiders see as dirty, dangerous, and low-paying. Lucas and Buzzanell argue that *sisu* as a philosophy or occupational ideology may be unique to blue-collar work (2004, 286). In a similar vein, Lucas (2011) finds that miners construct a positive self-identity about their occupational and social positions by arguing that all work is valuable and important, and that dignity is based on the quality of the work. In Gibson and Papa's (2000) study of an American factory, the workers' identity is based around a strong work ethic. The workers argue that to work at the company you have to be an extremely hard worker, and a very motivated and conscientious worker. Hard work becomes a display of masculinity with workers constructing their identity around the idea of body-punishing work and the ability to withstand the rigors of blue-collar life.

In blue-collar contexts gender and ethnicity are often pertinent identity categories. Baxter and Wallace (2009) show how male British construction workers construct their occupational identity in relation to threatening outgroups such as Polish immigrant workers and rival builders. By doing so, the workers construct a strong sense of solidarity and a cohesive normative identity as white, British, working-class and male. As for women, these are viewed as so unthreatening to male experiences in the building trade that they do not even qualify for a place in the "out-group". Baxter and Wallace argue that this "negative semantic space" makes it difficult for women to enter the profession. Many of the cases presented in Brannan (2000) also show how women's entry into traditionally masculine workplaces has been resisted by male workers through the use of sexually offensive language and sexual propositions. Tallichet (1995) investigates how resistance to women coal miners' integration has inhibited their job advancement. She finds that men's sexualization of women miners, i.e., their use of sexual harassment, gender-based jokes, and profanity that objectifies and diminishes women, functions to emphasize gender differences in the workplace. This contributes to maintaining the gendered relations between women and men, where women are first and foremost seen as women and only second as workers. It also defines which positions in the work hierarchy are considered appropriate for women so that stereotypes about women being unsuited for working with machinery keep them in more menial mining jobs and support roles for the men. In these studies blue-collar workplaces are constructed as places of hard work, determination, dignity, and masculinity, with little or no space for women. In contrast, a number of studies focusing on language use in blue-collar workplaces show another picture of gender relations and of the social meaning of the linguistic repertoires of joking and profanity.

Holmes and Woodhams' (2013) study of New Zealand construction workers focuses on the socialization process of becoming a legitimate member of this blue-collar community of practice. The analysis provides insights into how workers negotiate their own and others' membership of the professional community of practice through the use of technical jargon, different kinds of directives, humour, and relational talk. Holmes and Woodhams' analysis also points to the fact that both transactional and relational skills are necessary to become a fully-fledged member of this blue-collar workplace community of practice.

In another series of studies focusing on a blue-collar factory work team, Holmes and colleagues investigate the role of specific kinds of language use in creating solidarity and constructing a workplace culture. Daly *et al.* (2004) focus on the use of expletives in complaints and "whingeing" within this blue-collar team. They find that complaints and refusals are expressed in a very direct and apparently confrontational manner with frequent use of expletives (2004, 959). Interestingly, the expletive "fuck" is in this context used for a variety of purposes, including as a strategy for redressing the face threat of complaints and refusals on the factory floor. Daly *et al.* argue that in this particular blue-collar community of practice, "fuck" is in fact used to express positive politeness and solidarity. Holmes and Marra (2002) investigate how workplace humour contributes to workplace culture. They find that humour in a factory setting is characterized by one-liners and competitive sequences, and that as in the study of expletives, this apparently confrontational language use is more frequent in the blue-collar setting than in white-collar settings. Holmes and Marra argue, however, that the style of humour in the factory setting reflects the team's close working relationship, and that humour is used to cement highly solidary relationships and to make routine tasks more interesting. In the same vein, but in a Swedish setting, Nelson (2014) shows how immigrant industrial workers make use of challenging and competitive humour as well as swearing to create in-group solidarity and create social integration in the workplace.

These sociolinguistic ethnographic studies of language in blue-collar contexts thus present a complex image of language use and identity in blue-collar workplaces that challenges existing stereotypes about gender and blue-collar workplaces. The above studies emphasize the importance of understanding the meaning of particular language use as embedded in specific contexts. At the same time they also show how beliefs about language use and stereotypes may legitimize injustice in the workplace.

Multilingualism, Migration, and Labour

The inclusion of migrants into the labour market is often understood as a matter of acquiring the proper language skills. This is evident in Cohen-Goldner and Eckstein's (2008) quantitative study on male immigrants from Russia to Israel and their likelihood of being placed in blue- or white-collar jobs based on their "local accumulation of human capital and imported skill" (837). The authors conclude that both participation in training programmes and knowledge of Hebrew and English affect mean wage offers and job offer probabilities. While Cohen-Goldner and Eckstein argue for the benefits of immigrant training programmes and the usefulness of acquiring the local language, other scholars, taking an ethnographic approach, are more sceptical about these programmes and their effects. Allan (2013) shows that language programmes for immigrant workers in Canada often focus on the lacking skills of the migrant workers and hence work as an instrument for legitimizing structural systems of stratification between migrant and local workers. Other studies of migrant workers and the labour market have demonstrated how social stratification of migrants can often also be seen in the work they get in the new societies, and how such inequalities are often sought to be balanced through programmes of language teaching for migrant workers, legitimizing a logic about migrant workers' lack of access to work being caused by their lack of command of the local language (Goldstein 1997, 25–28). Lack of competence in the local language may also be used as a justification to place migrant workers in underpaid entry-level jobs until they have learnt more of the local language. Yet, as Strömmer (2015) demonstrates, these jobs provide little chance of improving language competence and instead become "dead-end" jobs (21).

The logic of skill accumulation as a need for migrant workers is challenged through a range of studies that reveal other relations at play in the access to work. Erickson and Schultz (1982) describe institutional encounters as intrinsic moments of gate-keeping, while Bremer *et al.* (1996) demonstrate a range of challenges for migrants in their social as well as professional lives. A core finding of the latter study was that in interactions migrant workers are often charged with the primary interactional responsibility to counter the linguistic asymmetries between them and their local interlocutors. Tranekjær (2015) demonstrates that migrants who go through interviews for internships in different institutions do not have problems communicating, but are often met with cultural and religious stereotypes from the interviewers. In the same vein, Roberts (2013) shows how migrant workers applying for low-status jobs in the UK often do not make it through the interviews because of their inability to produce narratives which reflect an Anglo-American style of narration and rhetoric; a so-called "linguistic penalty". Often, it is their inability to perform as an interviewee in this highly culture-specific way which means that they do not get the job.

In their study of meat workers in Australia, Piller and Lising (2014) demonstrate that language rarely matters for the worker in the workplace because of the type of work carried out: "All the participants reported that the speed and physically demanding nature of their work left virtually no scope for talk during work" (2014, 47). This also meant that the Filipino migrant workers had little opportunity to gain or improve English competences—even though this was seen by their colleagues and by themselves as important for other aspects of socialization into the new community. Contrary to these findings, Duchêne (2011) shows that linguistic resources can be very important in the work carried out by blue-collar workers. In his study of luggage handlers in Zürich Airport, he demonstrates that this low-status job is often given to immigrants not least because of their limited proficiency in the official languages, German and French. Yet, the company has implemented systems that can make use of the migrant workers' various linguistic resources so that the front-line personnel can call upon the luggage handlers should the official languages or English not suffice to serve a customer. This enables the company to profit on employees with flexible skills while the luggage handlers themselves receive little else than a chance to become visible for a brief period of time.

While migrant workers who have to settle in a country and gain access to the labour market are likely to be subjected to the conditions described above, another category of workers are the "temporary", "transnational", or "guest" workers who are faced with slightly different challenges. Most of the time, getting access to jobs is not a problem for them because they fill structural holes in the labour market of the host country. However, as pointed out by Duchêne and Heller (2012), mobile migrant workers who do not settle permanently (or are not expected to) are often not considered worth the investment of language training.

As Kraft (2017) shows in her work on construction workers in Norway, even though some temporary migrant workers are employed for several years, and serve important functions related to language work, employers will continue to attend to the logic of temporariness as a way to explain why language training is not being facilitated. At the same time, there is a strong orientation towards the importance of the local language, and policies, embedded in logics of e.g., safety, promote this language. For example, one of the construction sites' Head of Safety and Security had decided that Norwegian should be the official language of the workplace. After being asked what this language policy entailed in practice, he answered:

Example 12.1

HS: nei det, i praksis betyr det at vi godtar i utgangspunktet at vi ska ha norsktal:ende baser og øh: formenn. heller si formenn og baser og: og prosjektledere ska være norsktalende eller skandinavisktalende for å være helt korrekt da.

HS: well, in practice it means that we in principle accept that we have to have norwegian-speaking team leaders and foremen. rather say foremen and team leaders and: and project leaders have to be norwegian-speaking, or scandinavian-speaking if we are to be completely correct.

This means that professional opportunities are explicitly dependent on language resources. In addition, while this policy appears to favour Norwegian speakers, it does contain an amount of flexibility; speakers of other Scandinavian languages can also hold these positions. This reflects a common ideology of Scandinavian linguistic and cultural interconnectivity. While specific linguistic resources are officially required for all managerial positions, the internal structures of the workplace are dependent on a large body of temporary Polish workers. Unofficial team leaders are then needed for organizing these workers, a task that requires linguistic resources in both Polish and Norwegian. This means that some workers self-skill in acquiring sufficient Norwegian to take care of this task. This is rewarded in different ways, such as salary bonuses and potentially a permanent position with a contractor. In this workplace, multilingual competences of blue-collar workers are not only important to production efficiency but also in relation to upholding national regulations of safety in the sector. Talking about permanent employment of the Polish leased workers, one of the contractor's safety and quality coordinators explained how their linguistic resources in Norwegian may be a benefit in this regard:

> **Example 12.2**
>
> | | |
> |---|---|
> | Coordinator: | hvis vi har en fra [company name] som er polsk, som snakker bra norsk? (0.8) så tilfredsstiller vi et lovkrav om kommunikasjon, (0.7) så lager jeg en sikker jobbanalyse, så kan han hjelpe meg å få det på polsk. |
> | Interviewer: | mm? |
> | Coordinator: | kravet er at v- (0.2) de ska kunne få (0.5) det på sitt språk |
> | Coordinator: | *if we have someone from [company name] who is Polish, who speaks good Norwegian? (0.8) then we can satisfy a legal requirement about communication, (0.7) so if I make a safety job analysis, he can help me get it in Polish* |
> | Interviewer: | mm? |
> | Coordinator: | *the requirement is that w- (0.2) they have to get (0.5) it in their language* |

In short, a transactional language skill for the workplace, e.g., making translations, may very well be an opportunity for the migrant worker to increase professional status and decrease job precarity. This is important, Kraft argues, as the sector often is dominated by structural stratification, and migrant workers typically are imagined as less qualified workers, posing a real barrier for their opportunities of permanent employment.

This section has shown that a lack of language competences for some blue-collar work migrants is problematized to the extent that it bars them from entering the labour market, but has also demonstrated the central role of institutional gatekeepers. We have also seen how the language skills of blue-collar workers are central to organizational goals of customer service, efficiency, safety, and profit, though obtaining these competences is often left up to the workers themselves.

International Blue-Collar Workplaces: Inclusion and Exclusion

Multilingualism is not only an issue for blue-collar work migrants; some blue-collar workers meet internationalization at home. When traditionally local blue-collar workplaces become increasingly internationalized, often because the larger organization does, it has consequences for blue-collar workers who often find it difficult to meet the demands of the new international language environment. In many European companies, the solution to the increased linguistic diversity brought on by internationalization processes and strategies is to introduce English as a corporate language. The consequences of introducing English in companies based in non-English-speaking countries have been the focus of a number of studies in recent years both in sociolinguistics and in the field of language in international business. Most of these studies focus, however, on either managers or white-collar workers. While white-collar employees may experience language-based exclusion when English is introduced as a corporate language, they typically have more education and more language training than blue-collar workers. Changing from the local language to English may therefore be a particular challenge to blue-collar workers.

Lønsmann (2015) investigates the use of English as a corporate language in a pharmaceutical company in Denmark. In the blue-collar service department the workers clean the buildings, man the gate and do groundskeeping. The majority of these workers are Danish, with a small minority being immigrants. Lønsmann focuses on one team of six service assistants. When asked about language use at work, all six answer "Danish".[1] When asked about other language competences, only one claims to have some English proficiency. The ethnographic study shows, however, that the service assistants encounter English at work every day. Computer programs are in English, and on the walls are signs and posters in English. To some extent the service assistants ignore this use of English, but it can also be a source of frustration. All signs with department names and locations are in English. Furthermore, the service assistants are required to check their email every day, and while their head of department always writes to them in Danish, other emails are in English, and this poses another problem, which is often handled by simply deleting emails in English.

The participant observation revealed that not all the service assistants used the computer. Instead they relied on their co-workers to get the information they needed. For the service assistants, English is a barrier that keeps them from easy access to information provided on signs and in emails, but also from opportunities for social mobility. As one of them says:

Example 12.3

Thea: og så kunne der måske være at man kunne komme lidt længere
end bare rengøring ja at man kunne søge noget andet
hvis man kunne det engelsk også på computeren ik
og så længe du ikke kan det så må du jo så blive dernede

Thea: *then you might be able to go a little further than just cleaning*
you could look for something else
if you knew English also on the computer right
and as long as you don't know it you have to stay down there

Thea here links English skills with opportunities for a better job, going "a little further than just cleaning". In this workplace the blue-collar workers are excluded from basic information because English has been introduced as a corporate language, but their lack of English skills also affects their career prospects. Nelson (2014) found similar results in a Swedish setting. As shown in Lønsmann (2014), the language ideology that positions all Danes as competent English speakers means that the actual diversity in English competence among Danes is "erased". When the Danes are constructed as a homogeneous group of proficient English users, the Danes with no English competences become invisible and so does the exclusion they experience in the workplace.

While the above case study shows the importance of English for the blue-collar workers, another ethnographic case study by Lønsmann reveals that English is not always helpful in the internationalized blue-collar workplace. The warehouse workers in this study all speak Danish, some English and some of them also some German. They interact daily with truck drivers with different language resources. While many are Danish, some are Eastern European, typically Czech or Bulgarian drivers. A small minority of these drivers knows a little English or German, but most do not. This means that while the warehouse workers are a homogeneous Danish group, the loading docks constitute a transnational and multilingual setting. This was an issue repeatedly pointed out by warehouse staff, in interviews or informally. An example from the field notes illustrates how a Danish warehouse worker interacts with a truck driver:

Example 12.4

Sue uses Danish to the Bulgarian truck driver, e.g., "Værsgo" [*Here you go*], when she hands him back the paperwork. A little while later she says over my shoulder: "Den er klar til dig" [*It is ready for you*]. When I turn around, she is talking to the Bulgarian driver again. When he leaves, he says: "Bye bye", and Sue replies: "Bye bye". She says that he comes here often. He is one of the regulars, driving between Denmark and Sweden.

Sue and the driver here use a range of communicative strategies to complete the interaction. Sue speaks Danish, although she cannot expect the driver to understand much, if anything, and they both use the English phrase "bye bye". More implicitly, the interaction relies on routine. The warehouse workers and truck drivers operate within a specific frame of expectations: The truck driver is there to deliver or pick up goods, and the warehouse worker facilitates this process. Each step of the process within the interaction is known to both parties from the beginning.

The study shows that the warehouse workers use a wide range of strategies to communicate with the truck drivers, and often use several strategies simultaneously. The participants may choose to speak in Danish, English or less often German while at the same time using gestures to communicate their intent. This is often supported by written communication such as order numbers written on consignment notes or the driver's phone. When these strategies are not sufficient, the warehouse workers use mediators to get the message across, e.g., by asking an English- or German-speaking truck driver to pass on the message to the other driver. Most interactions proceed smoothly, however, because they rely to a large extent on shared professional knowledge. Only when unexpected events, such as delays or missing paperwork, happen, do breakdowns occur, and this is typically when the administration and/or agent is called to act as mediator. In a study of how Hungarian truck drivers manage multilingual encounters, Juhász (2013) finds that despite their limited foreign language competences (mostly in German), the truck drivers themselves report that their language competences are adequate to do their jobs. Juhász' informants report a variety of strategies used for communicating across linguistic borders, including simplifying messages (such as *Schuldi'bitt* for the German *Entschuldigung, bitte*/"Excuse me, please"), repetition, rephrasing, gesturing, miming, and drawing. Juhász also points out that because the truck drivers encounter the same situations regularly, e.g., loading goods, and only rarely face linguistically new situations, their limited linguistic competence is sufficient for their needs.

Despite the diverse practices reported above, English still holds a privileged position among the Danish warehouse workers. Several of them use the expression "*they cannot communicate*" about the Eastern European truck drivers to describe their lack of English competence. In the following excerpt Jen presents the problem:

> **Example 12.5**
>
> Jen: der kommer sommetider en chauffør eller et eller anden ud til os . . .
> og de kan jo hverken engelsk eller tysk
> eller noget som helst
> så der bliver sådan lidt øh ((tegnsprogs lidt))
> Interviewer: ja okay
> Jen: så går det jo
> *Jen: sometimes a truck driver comes in*
> *. . . and they know neither English nor German*
> *or anything at all*
> *so then it becomes kind of uh ((sign language a little))*
> *Interviewer: yes okay*
> *Jen: so we manage*

This quote illustrates the common sense understanding that the problem is that sometimes drivers come in who do not speak English or German (which are consistently referred to as the warehouse workers' preferred lingua francas). Danish is not mentioned probably because it is not expected that foreigners would know Danish. The quote also illustrates one of the solutions: the work gets done with the use of gestures. Jen here constructs the drivers' lack of competence in certain languages as problematic, while acknowledging that the work still gets done in spite of this: "we manage" as she says. This and other examples contribute to positioning English as the legitimate, or even required, lingua franca for transnational communication in blue-collar settings. This language ideology neatly places the burden of making themselves understood on the Eastern European truck drivers and position them as "the ones with the problem".

Main Research Methods for Researching Language in Blue-Collar Workplaces

Most of the studies reviewed above use ethnographic methods to investigate language in blue-collar workplaces, including participant observation, interviews, and recordings of interaction. We would like to use this section to point out two issues that may be of particular interest to researchers setting out to investigate blue-collar settings ethnographically.

The first issue that presents itself is that of gaining access. In addition to gaining access to the organization itself, the researcher also needs to gain access to the individual informants, and this may be an issue both of consent and of trust. Blue-collar informants may have less power to say "no" to participating in research projects and be less informed about the project because access to this type of informant typically goes through the manager (Lønsmann 2016). Another challenge is that it might be harder for the researcher to create rapport and gain the trust of these informants because of the greater professional distance between the typical researcher and the typical blue-collar informant. One typical fear is that the researcher is sent by management to check up on their work. In these situations it can be useful for researchers to reflect on how they position themselves in relation to informants. Positioning themselves firmly as an outsider (i.e., not paid by the organization, and not following the manager's directions) can help the researcher create trust and minimize resistance. On the other hand, Baxter and Wallace (2009) were able to use Wallace's insider position as a young male and an occasional member of the work crew to gain access to the site and to individual informants. Reflecting on other types of positionality may also be useful, as researchers can draw on various resources to help them create rapport with informants, e.g., by considering how they dress, speak or position themselves in relation to informants.

The physical circumstances surrounding fieldwork in blue-collar workplaces often present a challenge. Where the researcher often fits neatly in a corner of an office space with the computer or notebook ready for field notes, it is often more challenging to find a suitable space in a warehouse or a factory, and the researcher may end up crouching on a pallet in a corner looking and feeling out of place (Franziskus 2013). Another frequent practical challenge is the noise level. Recording good quality talk in a building site with the constant background of hammering, drilling and radio noise is difficult, as described by Holmes and Woodhams (2013). In addition there is the issue of finding a safe place to locate equipment (Holmes and Stubbe 2015). In combination with the fact that participants tend to move around, researchers are often required to use inventive solutions especially for recording interactions. One solution, described by Holmes and Woodhams, is to use armbands to position recorders on the non-hammering arms of builders; another, used by Kraft (2017), is to use helmet cameras for recording the interactions of builders and laundry workers.

Future Research Directions

Language gives unique insights into how work conditions change and remain the same. More research on the different sectors, looking at e.g., the actual communication practices and how these (dis)align with official requirements and policies, is required to give a fuller picture of the dynamics between language, work, and the economy. We believe that studies drawing on linguistic as well as social theories would provide the field with a better understanding of the processes and dynamics related to issues of power and inequality in blue-collar workplaces.

Further Reading

Working from a shared frame of migration under neoliberal economies and focusing on work and institutional settings, the ethnographic chapters in Duchêne, Moyer, and Roberts (2013) all demonstrate how language plays a powerful role in the professional and social placing of migrants.

Goldstein (1997) is a core reading for anyone interested in language and blue-collar work. By studying the speech economy of a Canadian factory with primarily Portuguese workers, Goldstein shows how language influences professional opportunities as well as social relations of cultural tensions.

Holmes and Stubbe (2015) uses naturally occurring data to examine how considerations of power and politeness influence a wide range of interactions in both white- and blue-collar workplaces.

Related Topics

Relational talk; Gender; Intercultural communication; Multilingualism; Men's talk in women's work; Professional identity construction; Learning language on-the-job

Acknowledgement

The authors would like to thank Bent Preisler, Meredith Marra, Anne Fabricius, Marta Kirilova, Jan Svennevig, and the other participants at the LINGCORP 2015 workshop for valuable comments and critique of a previous version of this chapter.

Note

1   One has German as L1, one has Faroese as L1, the rest Danish.

References

Allan, Kori. 2013. "Skilling the Self: The Communicability of Immigrants as Flexible Labour." In *Language, Migration and Social Inequalities: A Critical Sociolinguistic Perspective on Institutions and Work*, edited by Alexandre Duchêne, Melissa Moyer, and Celia Roberts, 56–78. Bristol: Multilingual Matters.

Baxter, Judith, and Kieran Wallace. 2009. "Outside In-Group and Out-Group Identities? Constructing Male Solidarity and Female Exclusion in UK Builders' Talk." *Discourse & Society* 20: 411–429.

Brannan, Rebecca. 2000. "When the Pig Is in the Barnyard, Not the Parlor: Should Courts Apply a 'Coarseness Factor' in Analyzing Blue-Collar Hostile Work Environment Claims?" *Georgia State University Law Review* 17 (3): Article 7.

Bremer, Katharina, Celia Roberts, Marie-Thérèse Vasseur, Margaret Simonot, and Peter Broeder. 1996. *Achieving Understanding: Discourse in Intercultural Encounters*. London: Longman.

Cohen-Goldner, Zarit, and Zvi Eckstein. 2008. "Labor Mobility of Immigrants: Training, Experience, Language, and Opportunities." *International Economic Review* 49: 837–872.

Daly, Nicola, Janet Holmes, Jonathan Newton, and Maria Stubbe. 2004. "Expletives as Solidarity Signals in FTAs on the Factory Floor." *Journal of Pragmatics* 36: 945–964.

Duchêne, Alexandre. 2011. "Neoliberalism, Social Inequalities, and Multilingualism: The Exploitation of Linguistic Resources and Speakers" [Translated from Néolibéralisme, inégalités sociales et plurilinguisme: L'exploitation des ressources langagières et des locuteurs]. *Langage et Société* 2: 81–108.

Duchêne, Alexandre, and Monica Heller, Eds. 2012. *Language in Late Capitalism: Pride and Profit*. New York: Routledge.

Duchêne, Alexandre, Melissa Moyer, and Celia Roberts, Eds. 2013. *Language, Migration and Social Inequalities: A Critical Sociolinguistic Perspective on Institutions and Work*. Bristol, UK: Multilingual Matters.

Erickson, Frederick, and Jeffrey Schultz. 1982. *The Counselor as Gatekeeper: Social Interaction in Interviews*. New York: Academic Press.

Franziskus, Anne. 2013. "Getting by in a Multilingual Workplace: The Language Practices, Ideologies and Norms of Cross-Border Workers in Luxembourg." PhD diss., University of Luxembourg.

Gibson, Melissa K., and Michael J. Papa. 2000. "The Mud, the Blood, and the Beer Guys: Organizational Osmosis in Blue-collar Work Groups." *Journal of Applied Communication Research* 28: 68–88.

Goldstein, Tara. 1997. *Two Languages at Work: Bilingual Life on the Production Floor*. Berlin: Walter de Gruyter.

Halle, David. 1984. *America's Working Man: Work, Home, and Politics among Blue-Collar Property Owners*. Chicago, IL: University of Chicago Press.

Holmes, Janet, and Meredith Marra. 2002. "Having a Laugh at Work: How Humour Contributes to Workplace Culture." *Journal of Pragmatics* 34: 1683–1710.

Holmes, Janet, and Maria Stubbe. 2015. *Power and Politeness in the Workplace. A Sociolinguistic Analysis of Talk at Work*. 2nd ed. Oxon, UK: Routledge.

Holmes, Janet, and Jay Woodhams. 2013. "Building Interaction: The Role of Talk in Joining a Community of Practice." *Discourse & Communication* 7: 275–298.

Juhász, Dávid. 2013. "Re-Routing in Europe: The Key to Successful Communication as a Truck Driver with Limited Language Competence." *Working Papers in Language Pedagogy* 7: 100–114.

Kraft, Kamilla. 2017. "Constructing Migrant Workers: Multiingualism and Communication in the Transnational Construction Site." PhD diss., University of Oslo.

Lederer, Muriel. 1987. *Blue-Collar Jobs for Women*. New York: New York Books.
Lønsmann, Dorte. 2014. "Linguistic Diversity in the International Workplace: Language Ideologies and Processes of Exclusion." *Multilingua* 33: 89–116.
Lønsmann, Dorte. 2015. "Language Ideologies in a Danish Company with English as a Corporate Language: 'It Has to be English'." *Journal of Multilingual and Multicultural Development* 36: 339–356.
Lønsmann, Dorte. 2016. "Negotiating Positionality in Ethnographic Investigations of Workplace Settings: Student, Consultant or Confidante?" In *The Ins and Outs of Business and Professional Discourse Research: Reflections on Interacting with the Workplace*, edited by Glen Michael Alessi, and Geert Jacobs, 13–36. Basingstoke, UK: Palgrave Macmillan.
Lucas, Kristen. 2011. "Blue-Collar Discourses of Workplace Dignity: Using Outgroup Comparisons to Construct Positive Identities." *Management Communication Quarterly* 25: 353–374.
Lucas, Kristen, and Patrice M. Buzzanell. 2004. "Blue-Collar Work, Career, and Success: Occupational Narratives of *Sisu*." *Journal of Applied Communication Research* 32: 273–292.
Nelson, Marie. 2014. "'You Need Help as Usual, Do You?': Joking and Swearing for Collegiality in a Swedish Workplace." *Multilingua* 33: 173–200.
Piller, Ingrid, and Loy Lising. 2014. "Language, Employment, and Settlement: Temporary Meat Workers in Australia." *Multilingua* 33: 35–59.
Roberts, Celia. 2013. "The Gatekeeping of Babel: Job Interviews and the Linguistic Penalty." In *Language, Migration and Social Inequalities: A Critical Sociolinguistic Perspective on Institutions and Work*, edited by Alexandre Duchêne, Melissa Moyer, and Celia Roberts, 81–94. Bristol, UK: Multilingual Matters.
Savage, Mike, Fiona Devine, Niall Cunningham, Mark Taylor, Yaojun Li, Johs Hjellbrekke, Brigitte Le Roux, Sam Friedman, and Andrew Miles. 2013. "A New Model of Social Class? Findings from the BBC's Great British Class Survey Experiment." *Sociology* 47: 219–250.
Strömmer, Maiju. 2015. "Affordances and Constraints: Second Language Learning in Cleaning Work". *Multilingua* 35: 697–721.
Tallichet, Suzanne E. 1995. "Gendered Relations in the Mines and the Division of Labor Underground." *Gender & Society* 9: 697–711.
Tranekjær, Louise. 2015. *Interactional Categorization and Gatekeeping: Institutional Encounters with Otherness*. Bristol, UK: Multilingual Matters.

13
Language in Legal Settings
Bronwen Innes

Introduction

In legal circles it is often believed that "the law" is objective and independent of ordinary interaction. Modern linguists see it differently. We ask how language constitutes and shapes the law, and how it operates as the tool for getting legal work done. The legal context is seen as being created by the goals, activities, and identities constructed in interaction across the range of legal settings, which come in great variety: formal/informal, spoken/written, traditional/alternative.

It is well established that spoken language in legal settings draws on the techniques and structures of everyday conversation, albeit altered according to the activities, participants (legal and lay) and goals relevant to those settings (e.g., Atkinson and Drew 1979). Much talk in legal settings is dialogic, predominantly question-answer sequences, e.g., between lawyers and witnesses. Courtrooms also include monologic talk by judges and lawyers, often to juries. While juries may not speak in court they are an integral part of the interaction; more than just ratified overhearers (Heritage and Clayman 2010), they are the "true" addressees (Olsson and Luchjenbroers 2014, 241).

Alongside the spoken interaction often comes written material (police records, witness statements, judges' rulings, statutes). The creation and co-construction of that material involves "the interweaving of text and talk" (Eades 2010, 194) as part of legal workplace activity. Records are kept and documents produced in preparation for hearings; while it is often assumed that these represent talk, in fact the talk has often been changed substantially. A consequence of this can be that lay participants' voices become distorted or even lost. Written language is also often the basis for legal talk; e.g., when police read rights to suspects. Further, people working in the law appear to assume that written language carries more weight than spoken (Eades 2010); e.g., transcripts may be given more weight than the audio or video recordings that are in fact the evidence (with potentially important consequences).

Two significant characteristics of legal language are its formality and complexity (see e.g., Melinkoff 1963; Gibbons 2003; Coulthard and Johnson 2007). However there are ongoing moves advocating plain language in the law, leading, for example, to changes in courtrooms and statutes in England, Wales, Australia, and New Zealand (Eades 2010; Heffer 2005). Despite that, legal language remains a major challenge for lay people. People still feel disadvantaged, even intimidated, by courtroom language, often believing that lawyers manipulate language to suit their legal goals. Many lay people encountering legal settings are not familiar with or skilled in the use of language there, in either legal or pragmatic senses.

First Encounters: Police–Lay Interaction

People's first encounter with the law is often with police. They are at a clear disadvantage, not always aware that interview purposes are both investigative (discovering the facts) and evidential (concerned with proof). Issues arising include people's understanding of what is being said, the (sometimes hostile) interview process, and the production of written statements. The system assumes an ideal situation where interviewees can answer questions freely and provide whatever information they wish. But this is clearly not the case, given controlling questioning and unequal power among the participants. Police interview practices have received increasing attention (e.g., Eades 2010; Rock 2007; Cotterill 2005), with comment on coercive and complex questioning techniques, as well as audience design (e.g., Haworth 2013). Shuy (1998) suggests that if police were to use a more informal register and simple direct questions, it might alleviate interviewees' stress. This may not be easy: they often have to follow a pre-set framework and "police speak" can creep into both their talk and the written witness statements which result from interviews.

Of particular concern is the communication of rights (to silence, to seek legal advice), known as cautions or Miranda warnings (e.g., Ainsworth 2008; Mason 2013), where legal motivations can be in conflict with lay people's need to understand (Heffer, Rock, and Conley 2013). Done at the beginning of interviews, this is "a constitutive, formal mechanism which frames the interview, marking and delimiting it for the legal institution" (Rock 2010, 129). In the UK, police are required to ask suspects whether they understand the cautions; this is problematic because self-evaluations are often inaccurate (Olsson and Luchjenbroers 2014). Cotterill (2005) states that the rights were delivered inadequately in 42 per cent of the cases she studied, which may result in suspects not understanding their rights fully.

"Verballing", where police either invent a confession or "help" the interviewee to produce a statement, has created injustice, sometimes with severe consequences. Less deliberately dangerous, perhaps, is the process of turning interview questions and responses into a "single-authored narrative" (Eades 2010, 196), concealing how questioning has shaped the information obtained. This is done, for example, with lexical and phrasal choices, syntactic structures, and cultural aspects; it can have serious consequences further down the legal road. Haworth (2010) calls the result contaminated evidence and comments that this is very different from the treatment of physical evidence, the integrity of which is paramount.

Rock (2007, 2010) discusses this transformation in terms of recontextualization and control, now termed textual travel (Heffer, Rock, and Conley 2013). The interviewee's story is recontextualized during the interview as the participants go through it several times, changing it each time. The written statements produced after the interview become "the main reference text" and "shape" the next stages in the process (Rock 2010, 134). The transformation, however, while "constitutive and purposive" (135), is not visible to the participants. Nor is it acknowledged by the legal system (Haworth 2010). Haworth discusses the Harold Shipman case, where the statement produced in court was different from what Shipman had said in his interview. A related issue is that interview transcripts are not always entirely accurate. Haworth refers to the UK practice of transcripts being read aloud in court by a police witness (as the interviewer) and the prosecution lawyer (as the defendant), rightly calling it bizarre.

Recontextualization becomes even more significant here as it can result in the prosecution story being privileged over the suspect's story (Heydon 2005).

Second Encounters: Lawyer–Lay Interaction

Lawyer–client interactions are different again: they are less structured and formal, and they are private and confidential. Eades (2010) characterizes them as interpreting (between clients and the law) and puzzle-solving. Here too we have the interweaving of talk and text (Halldorsdottir 2006; Scheffer 2006), with the talk based to some extent on written text and producing written outcomes, including, for example, affidavits and court submissions. Eades concludes that this is "even more central" (2010, 189) than in other legal settings. Kashimura (2015) shows how lawyers and clients collaborate and orient to each other's goals in coming to understand the story.

The lawyers are in control, using both legal strategies and ordinary techniques (e.g., yes–no questions, interruption) to achieve institutional goals. They tend to focus on legal and objective matters (e.g., financial details, specific incidents) while clients focus more on social and emotional issues (e.g., what spouses said and what went wrong). By often ignoring the latter, lawyers silence their clients (another exercise of power—Eades 2010). Trinch (2007) shows that women's reports of resisting abusers were often ignored (they might be construed as evidence of participation in violence), despite this being a dangerous omission (such reports are necessary in proving women have not consented to abuse). On the other hand, clients are not entirely powerless, as lawyers have professional obligations towards them; power relations can therefore be dynamic, sometimes changing from turn to turn in an interaction (Sarat and Felstiner 1989).

Third Encounters: Courtroom Interaction

The courtroom is perhaps the most studied legal setting (much of the work concerning adversarial courtrooms), with most attention being given to questioning phases. Its sub-genres vary (e.g., lawyers' opening/closing statements, direct/cross-examination, judges' summings up), both shaping and being shaped by the participants' roles and goals. It has often been described in terms of storytelling (e.g., Stygall 1994; Heffer 2005), with a tension between legal argument on the one hand and everyday narratives and ordinary reasoning on the other. This reflects the notions both that interaction constructs legal practice and that legal professionals and lay participants use different frameworks. Conley and O'Barr (1990) characterize these frameworks as rule-orientation (legal framework) versus relational orientation (relationships with people). Olsson and Luchjenbroers (2014) describe lawyer–witness/defendant interaction as a "fictive" dynamic, where the lawyers are acting a role, presenting the jury with stories to decide between.

Conversation analysis has illuminated courtroom practice, beginning with Atkinson and Drew (1979). In summary, the conversational practices of one person speaking at a time and sequences of adjacency pairs continue in the courtroom. Differences include that turns are pre-allocated and predominantly controlled by the lawyers in a generally orderly process with little overlap or interruption. Courtroom questioners often know the answers to their questions and tend not to provide the usual conversation receipt markers (perhaps because it is the jury or the judge who is the real audience). The requirement for an answer to be directed to the questioner can create a difficulty unusual in everyday conversation: to whom should a witness address their answer: the questioner, the judge, the jury? (Lane 1990; Heffer 2005). Extended question–answer sequences, rare in conversation, are heard frequently in court (e.g., Lane 1990; Innes 2001; Fărcașiu 2012).

Lawyers use questioning to achieve their legal goals through exerting control over topics and answers (e.g., Drew 1992; Heffer 2005; Berk-Seligson 1999), with the line of questioning being as important as individual questions (Mooney 2014). Questions, particularly yes–no questions, tag questions, and confirmation questions, are used for a variety of functions in addition to eliciting information: accusation, blame, assertion, challenge, creating empathy, and establishing authority, trustworthiness, and reliability. Syntactic complexity adds to this, for example through the placement of significant information in embedded clauses (named "smuggling" by Aldridge and Luchjenbroers 2007), which witnesses find themselves unable to refute (which clause do they answer?). Lexical choices similarly evince questioner control (Loftus 1979; Danet 1980). Cotterill (2003) shows how lawyers in the O. J. Simpson trial used metaphors to foreground or silence talk about particular people or events. Others have commented on the importance of reported speech (e.g., Matoesian 2000; Galatolo 2007) and presenting contrasts and alternative versions of events (Holt and Johnson 2010). Drew (1992) also recognizes that witnesses can resist lawyers' control through techniques such as denial, saying "I don't remember", avoidance or proffering a different scenario. Johnson (2002) reports a slightly different perspective in child interviews, where questions are used to help children by scaffolding their answers.

Lawyers often choose different approaches in direct and cross-examination. In direct examination lawyers seek to let witnesses tell their stories, due partly to the need to avoid leading questions at this stage of the process. In cross-examination, on the other hand, lawyers tend to present the story themselves using declaratives and tag questions, attempting to coerce the witness into confirming the lawyers' version; such fragmented testimony may be evaluated less positively, as may witnesses' choices of powerless language styles (O'Barr 1982), with potentially serious consequences. The lawyer's goal here is to "trap the witness into giving, or giving off, information which undermines their own testimony" (Heffer 2005, 126). Heffer notes the lack of research on the effect of such lawyer's "testimony" on jurors.

Lawyers' closing arguments are their opportunity to present their "'master narrative' of the crime, investigation, and the trial" (Gibbons 2003, 155), i.e., to persuade the judge or jury. As with questioning, we see the multi-faceted nature of lawyers' courtroom identity, representing authority on the one hand (e.g., Bogoch 1997) and solidarity with ordinary people on the other (e.g., Stygall 1994). Heffer (2005) and Rosulek (2010) both note counsel's use of the first person pronouns *we/I* in establishing solidarity with jurors (contrast Danet [1980] who says that they do this to portray lawyers and judges as being in agreement, i.e., to establish authority). This works to silence jurors' doubts as well as "to construct jurors as equal participants" (Rosulek 2010, 222). Rosulek calls for more work here, including on how far lawyers are aware of recontextualization and how far their strategies affect jurors.

Jury deliberations are the least studied of the courtroom genres and the closest to ordinary conversation. A critical issue is whether jurors understand what they are hearing. Charrow and Charrow's (1979) classic US study provided an early alert to this problem, as did Stygall (1994). Research in New Zealand (Young, Cameron, and Tinsley 1999, 2001) and Australia (Ogloff *et al.* 2006) has found similar problems. Even though believing that summings-up were clear, New Zealand jurors had "fairly fundamental misunderstandings of the law" (Tinsley 2001, 1470). Heritage and Clayman (2010, 199), however, conclude that juries are "highly resourceful", "creative", and "knowledgeable" in dealing with the legal framework and their task.

In inquisitorial systems, e.g., Germany, France, the Middle East, and Japan, it is judges who control the floor and do most of the questioning, which tends to be more exploratory. This suggests that the questioning styles might vary between the adversarial and inquisitorial systems. Bednarek (2014) finds that Polish defendants/witnesses are given free rein in their often highly-elaborated answers. Fărcașiu (2012) says that rather than the "question cascade" approach seen in American courtrooms, questioning in Romanian courtrooms relies more on multi-unit questions, "making the question more explicit to the witness" (111). Wodak (1985) finds in traffic offence trials in Germany that high-status witnesses were permitted to give their evidence in narrative form, unlike other witnesses. Komter (2013) shows the textual travel of a suspect's initial statement to police in its transformation into a case note, relied on by Dutch judges in arriving at their verdicts.

Judicial Language

Judges have three roles in court: i) to ensure an orderly and fair hearing; ii) to sum up the case in jury trials (including jury directions); iii) to deliver judgments and sentences. Heffer (2005) characterizes the judge as a helper for juries in dealing with the law. During the evidential phase, the judge may ask questions and intervene to ensure fairness (e.g., to disallow a question) or to clarify a question or response.

There is evidence that juries sometimes struggle with judges' directions. Charrow and Charrow (1979), Tiersma (2000) and Dumas (2000) all deal with pattern instructions in the USA where what the judge can say is heavily prescribed. Significant misunderstandings occur, arising from technical language, convoluted word order, excessive embedding, multiple negation, and passive verbs in subordinate clauses. Despite strenuous efforts to improve instructions (e.g., Tiersma 2010), Stygall (2014) comments that they remain very difficult for jurors, especially those concerning the death penalty.

Judges in some other countries (e.g., UK, Australia, New Zealand) have more flexibility when summing up. As noted above, however, some jurors in New Zealand and Australia express difficulties, as do some in England. Heffer (2005, 181) suggests that judges are "too divergent from the narrative mode thought and speech patterns of the average juror", and recommends they use a more narrative mode. A New Zealand project illustrates how some judges do exactly that (Innes 2016).

Reviewing evidence in summing up necessarily entails taking a viewpoint, with judges attempting to influence the jury and be impartial at the same time (Heffer 2005). Metaphor, repetition, sarcasm, euphemism, innuendo, extraneous comments, rhetorical questions, connotations, modal auxiliaries, and presuppositions have all been demonstrated as playing a part here. Non-verbal and paralinguistic behaviour are also important. Epistemic modality is particularly important: stating baldly suggests influence, while intensifying, normalizing, hedging, attributing, and disclaiming suggest impartiality. Judges create influence through "position[ing] themselves as intersubjectively reading the mind of the jurors" (Heffer 2005, 200), for example, saying "for you" (a matter for you) or "you may think". While the possibility of directionality may cause concern, Heffer (2005, 206) says that judges "would argue that some cases are simply much 'stronger' from a legal perspective" and that this does not constitute bias. He also points out, however, that we do not know how far it may affect verdicts.

From a different perspective, Tracy and Parks (2012) discuss talk between legal professionals in court, namely questioning of lawyers by appeal court judges. The judges' ideological stance was reflected in the questioning they employed, with "tough questioning" (including, for example, interruptions, sequences of more than one question on a point and disagreement markers) being used more by those who had voted against allowing same-sex marriages. They note the judges' use of argument metalanguage (e.g., "claim", "arguably"), neutrality claims, and citation of case law to claim authority and objectivity.

In the bilingual jurisdiction of Hong Kong, judges adjust their style according to whether English or Cantonese is being used in court (Leung 2012). Judicial English used in the higher courts has traditionally been extremely formal, avoiding colloquialism and cultural reference in the interests of preventing misunderstandings. Cantonese-speaking courtrooms are less formal, judges there expressing more emotion, culture, and personal views, acting as a scolding parent, educator, scholar, and godfather. While this may be thought to decrease judges' authority, Leung comments that only the judge has the authority to act in this way. She suggests that "legal bilingualism in Hong Kong is providing us a window on the deconstruction of the imaginary boundary between judgeliness and humanness, and that between legal and non-legal discourses and ideologies" (255). Micro-level conversation analysis of such interchanges would be interesting (Leung's data are media reports).

Alternative Settings

Arbitration and mediation are examples of alternative dispute resolution, a markedly less formal process where an independent facilitator helps people to resolve their disputes. Mediation is a collaborative process through which the parties arrive at the solution. In adjudication, the adjudicator provides a binding and enforceable decision.

Mediation practices stem from an explicit professional stance, i.e., mediator neutrality. Initial approaches were facilitative, with the mediator attempting to help disputants to arrive at a solution acceptable to them all. Over time, more models have been added, resulting in a continuum of mediator intervention. They include a more judicial approach (commenting on the merits of disputants' positions), transformative mediation (attempting to repair relationships), and narrative mediation (attempting to create a single story). The research outlined below mainly concerns facilitative models; investigations of the other models may reveal different language practices.

Where earlier practice was to direct talk through the mediator (Garcia 1991), Greatbatch and Dingwall (1999) find a more flexible pattern, with disputants often speaking to each other directly, and both mediators and disputants orienting to mediator neutrality. They call for research on how far mediators' social values, organization policy, and aspects of the particular cases affect neutrality and potentially the result. Heritage and Clayman (2010) show how a mediator's involvement transforms (recontextualizes) position statements so as to emphasize concessionary aspects and thus contributes to achieving successful compromises. Turn-taking is not pre-allocated, and there is less topic control than in formal courtrooms. Questions are again a major tool, here allowing the mediator "to avoid personally committing to any particular suggestion" (Eades 2010, 218). Minimal and neutral responses can be used to avoid affiliating/disaffiliating but, on the other hand, they can facilitate one party's viewpoint over the other's (Greatbatch and Dingwall 1999).

Atkinson (1992) looks at informal arbitration proceedings. Questions are the major tool here too, and extended question–answer sequences are frequent. Unlike formal courtrooms, the arbitrator often acknowledged what a disputant said, which contributed to a less intimidating atmosphere and greater certainty for the witness. Arbitrators often allowed elaborated answers, again unlike formal court where speakers may be silenced. Like mediators, arbitrators used neutral responses rather than assessments to avoid affiliating/disaffiliating with what has been said, aiming for fairness.

Restorative justice, used in determining penalties, is a relatively new approach most frequently used in youth and family matters. As opposed to traditional, retributive sentencing, it focuses on goals of moral education, healing, and restoration or reparation (Eades 2010), with the aim of reintegrating offenders into their community. This too uses an informal conferencing or collaborative approach. Once again questions are the major tool, used by the convenor to organize, structure, and control the talk. Therapeutic courts are further recent initiatives dealing similarly with penalties and compliance for those in drug courts, family violence courts, and mental health courts. Representatives from community and government organizations are often involved, as well as judges and police officers.

Indigenous sentencing courts (e.g., in USA, Canada, Australia), also use alternative approaches in legal settings, focusing on the need to restore balance to the community. They demonstrate a range of formality. In Australia such hearings involve indigenous elders or respected persons who play an active role, enabling the hearings to operate in a more culturally appropriate context. Complex legal language is eschewed in favour of ordinary conversation and a comfortable atmosphere encourages participants to speak.

Language and Disadvantage

Along with the challenges for lay people in dealing with legal language, there is long-standing awareness that courtroom and police practices create extra disadvantage for certain vulnerable participants, e.g., children/young people, people from minority cultures or who do not speak the courtroom's language fluently, deaf people, those who are disabled physically or mentally, victims.

In recognition of children's language skills it is intended that children in police interviews should be able to tell their stories in their own way (Aldridge and Luchjenbroers 2007; Heydon 2005). These are different from adult interviews in being less formal and with interviewers aiming for a neutral stance. Despite that, the resulting statements and testimonies may be even more a product of police construction than those of other witnesses. Four major issues arise here. First, children are often seen as inherently unreliable (therefore not believable). Second, witnesses who change their evidence are similarly thought unreliable, yet lawyers and judges often tell children that "it's ok to change your mind" (Olsson and Luchjenbroers 2014, 272). Third, children often offer inconsistent information which "muddies the victim frame" (Olsson and Luchjenbroers 2014, 272). Fourth, questioning, whether in interviews or in court, is even more fraught with danger for children because they may not have adult understanding. Police in England now receive training in how to question children, interviews are video-recorded, and the recordings become the witness's evidence-in-chief in court. However such measures still assume that children can function in an essentially adult way (Aldridge and Luchjenbroers 2007). Eades (e.g., 2010) and Brennan (1994) have found similar issues for Aboriginal children in Australia, with the added dimension of cultural difference.

A further initiative introduced recently in the UK and New Zealand is to provide young people with mediators in court to help them in understanding and dealing with the interaction (Plotnikoff and Woolfson 2015). This was used in New Zealand for the first time to my knowledge in 2015 to aid a youth being tried for murder, with significant success according to the mediator (personal communication).

Miscommunication caused by cultural and linguistic difference also creates disadvantage in encounters with the law, e.g., for Australian Aboriginals (Eades 2010). Differences there include: a cultural requirement to speak indirectly; silence is valued; certain information may not be spoken in general contexts (e.g., a deceased person's name; men's versus women's business), alternative questions, wh-questions (Aboriginals tend not to use quantifying expressions); gender distinctions, and lexical differences. Cultural context may not be carried into courtroom records (Liberman 2015). A catch-22 situation arises for Aboriginals in land tribunal hearings. If Aboriginal witnesses are articulate in English, they are seen as less traditional, whereas if they are less articulate it is more difficult for the tribunal to assess their claims. Eades produced a handbook in 1992 aimed at helping lawyers to understand Aboriginal English. Sadly, she reports (2004) that some used it to increase miscommunication for their own purposes, an unlooked-for danger in linguists' efforts to help.

The use of interpreters to address communication difficulties can be problematic (see Raymond this volume). Various issues have been described with interpreting in legal settings, including specifically linguistic matters (e.g., Hale 1999; Berk-Seligson 1999; Cheung 2014) but also concerning choices between speaker intent and accuracy, interpreters' understanding of legal issues including their role (Nakane 2014), interpreter attitudes, and the dangers of relying on translations in transcripts of evidence (Eades 2010). Another issue here is that code-switching in court is frowned upon, both by legal and lay participants, and can affect defendants' and witnesses' credibility negatively (Angermeyer 2015).

New technology raises new issues. Licoppe and Verdier (2013) consider interpreting in French video-conferences where the defendants are in prison while the interpreters are in court. The authors say that interpreters perform a greater role here than in conventional courtrooms. Further, judges intervene, either to reformulate the prosecutor's talk or to collaborate with the interpreter, so that the judge's voice is heard in a manner not normally appropriate in court. Also, the defendant, who cannot see all the cues (including gesture) available in the courtroom, may hear an opportunity to self-select and may be judged for speaking out of turn. This study raises another important question: to whom is the interpreter orienting, the defendant, the prosecutor or the judge?

Testing asylum-seekers' claims to particular language origins is another legal-type activity where speakers of minority languages can be disadvantaged (e.g., Eades 2010; Patrick 2012) as they are often simply disbelieved and "the burden of proof is much greater than in mainstream courts" (Olsson and Luchjenbroers 2014, 276). Further, if they have been in refugee camps they often learn aspects of other languages and then code-switch. This is then used as evidence that they are lying about their origins. Other issues relate to whether assessors have the relevant background, both in the language or dialect concerned and in their ability to understand variation within a community.

Conclusion and Future Directions

The work outlined in this chapter reveals common themes emerging in research from the different theoretical approaches used and the variety of legal workplaces examined. One major theme is the control exerted by participants on the institutional side, seen in both the interactions themselves and their outcomes. Despite moves to reduce the impact of this, and a recognition that lay participants are not always entirely powerless, recent work shows that even with efforts to reduce legal jargon and complexity, power and control remain firmly in legal institutions' hands. A second major theme is a micro-analytical lens on how that control is achieved, principally through questioning but also through other linguistic (including pragmatic) features. Why does it matter? The effects of the interactional strategies used are clearly significant in impeding lay people's access to justice.

Some directions for future research include work on newer kinds of legal settings such as restorative justice and indigenous courts: how is interaction there similar to and different from what has been demonstrated for more formal courts? Another direction is to look at how far strategies by lawyers and judges affect juries' deliberations, as well as whether judges' accommodation to perceived needs of juries in fact makes any difference. In addition, there is room for much more work in countries other than those traditionally investigated for legal language, for example China and the Middle East.

Some linguists seek to develop and work within a framework of partnering with institutions, rather than creating a snapshot of workplace settings to be published in academic circles. Working *with* workplace professionals and laypeople means research emerges from and identifies with their goals and then creates pathways for that research to be applied practically. One of the fundamental aspects of this is respect for all stakeholders involved and for the needs of those workplaces to be paramount in any research we undertake. It is all very well to be able to describe what happens in legal settings, but that is of little use unless it can help improve justice.

Further Reading

Atkinson and Drew (1979) is a classic work applying the rigour of conversation analysis to show how language operates in both systematic and strategic ways in court.

Eades (2010) shows how sociolinguistics can be applied in many different areas of people's interactions with legal systems, including a particular focus on Australia.

Olsson and Luchjenbroers (2014) outlines the discipline of forensic linguistics, combining the science of phonetics and the analysis of texts (spoken and written) with their practical application in the law.

Finally, *The International Journal of Speech, Language and the Law* is an excellent source of articles in this area, covering a wide range of issues.

Related Topics

Conflict talk; Argumentation; Interpreting; Intercultural communication

References

Ainsworth, Janet. 2008. "'You Have the Right to Remain Silent . . . But Only if You Ask for It Just So': The Role of Linguistic Ideology in American Police Interrogation Law." *The International Journal of Speech, Language and the Law* 15: 1–22.

Aldridge, Michelle, and June Luchjenbroers. 2007. "Linguistic Manipulations of Witness Testimonies: Framing Questions and 'Smuggling' Information?" *International Journal of Speech, Language and the Law* 14: 83–107.

Angermeyer, Philip. 2015. *Speak English or What: Codeswitching and Interpreter Use in New York City Courts*. Oxford: Oxford University Press.

Atkinson, J. Maxwell. 1992. "Displaying Neutrality: Formal Aspects of Informal Court Proceedings." In *Talk at Work: Interaction in Institutional Settings*, edited by Paul Drew and John Heritage, 119–211. Cambridge: Cambridge University Press.

Atkinson, J. Maxwell, and Paul Drew. 1979. *Order in Court: The Organisation of Verbal Interaction in Judicial Settings*. London: Macmillan.

Bednarek, Grazyna Anna. 2014. *Polish vs American Courtroom Discourse*. Basingstoke, UK: Palgrave Macmillan.

Berk-Seligson, Susan. 1999. "The Impact of Court Interpreting on the Coerciveness of Leading Questions." *International Journal of Speech, Language and the Law* 6: 30–56.

Bogoch, Bryna. 1997. "Gendered Lawyering: Difference and Dominance in Lawyer-Client Interaction." *Law and Society Review* 31: 672–712.

Brennan, Mark. 1994. "Cross-Examining Children in Criminal Courts: Child Welfare under Attack." In *Language and the Law*, edited by John Gibbons, 199–216. London: Longman.

Charrow, Robert, and Veda Charrow. 1979. "Making Legal Language Understandable: A Psycholinguistic Study of Jury Instructions." *Columbia Law Review* 79: 1306–1374.

Cheung, Andrew. 2014. "The Use of Reported Speech and the Perceived Neutrality of Court Interpreters." *Interpreting* 16: 191–208.

Conley, John, and William O'Barr. 1990. *Rules versus Relationships*. Chicago, IL: University of Chicago Press.

Cotterill, Janet. 2003. *Language and Power in Court: A Linguistic Analysis of the OJ Simpson Trial*. New York: Palgrave Macmillan.

Cotterill, Janet. 2005. "'You Do Not Have to Say Anything . . .': Instructing the Jury on the Defendant's Right to Silence in the English Criminal Justice System." *Multilingua* 24: 7–24.

Coulthard, Malcom, and Alison Johnson, Eds. 2007. *An Introduction to Forensic Linguistics*. London: Routledge.

Danet, Brenda. 1980. "'Baby' or 'Fetus'? Language and the Construction of Reality in a Manslaughter Trial." *Semiotica* 32: 187–220.

Drew, Paul. 1992. "Contested Evidence in Courtroom Cross-Examination: The Case of a Trial for Rape." In *Talk at Work: Interaction in Institutional Settings*, edited by Paul Drew and John Heritage, 470–520. Cambridge: Cambridge University Press.

Dumas, Bethany K. 2000. "US Pattern Jury Instructions: Problems and Proposals." *Forensic Linguistics* 7: 49–71.

Eades, Diana. 1992. *Aboriginal English and the Law: Communicating with Aboriginal English Speaking Clients: A Handbook for Legal Practitioners*. Brisbane: Queensland Law Society.

Eades, Diana. 2004. "Understanding Aboriginal English in the Legal System: A Critical Sociolinguistics Approach." *Applied Linguistics* 25: 491–512.

Eades, Diana. 2010. *Sociolinguistics and the Legal Process*. Great Britain: Multilingual Matters.

Fărcaşiu, Marcela Alina. 2012. "Language in the Courtroom: A Comparative Study of American and Romanian Criminal Trials." *The International Journal of Speech, Language and the Law* 19: 109–112.

Galatolo, Renata. 2007. "Active Voicing in Court." In *Reporting Talk: Reported Speech in Interaction*, edited by Elizabeth Holt, and Rebecca Clift, 195–220. Cambridge: Cambridge University Press.

Garcia, Angela. 1991. "Dispute Resolution without Disputing: How the Organization of Mediation Hearings Minimizes Argument." *American Sociological Review* 56: 818–835.

Gibbons, John. 2003. *Forensic Linguistics*. Oxford: Blackwell.

Greatbatch, David, and Robert Dingwall. 1999. "Professional Neutralism in Family Mediation." In *Talk, Work and Institutional Order: Discourse in Medical, Mediation and Management Settings*, edited by Srikant Sarangi, and Celia Roberts, 271–292. Berlin: Walter de Gruyter.

Hale, Sandra. 1999. "Interpreter's Treatment of Discourse Markers in Courtroom Questions." *Forensic Linguistics* 6: 57–82.

Halldorsdottir, Iris. 2006. "Orientations to Law, Guidelines and Codes in Lawyer-Client Interaction." *Research on Language and Social Interaction* 39: 263–301.

Haworth, Kate. 2010. "Police Interviews in the Judicial Process." In *Routledge Handbook of Forensic Linguistics*, edited by Malcolm Coulthard, and Alison Johnson, 169–194. Abingdon, UK: Routledge.

Haworth, Kate. 2013. "Audience Design in the Police Interview: The Interactional and Judicial Consequences of Audience Orientation." *Language in Society* 42: 45–69.

Heffer, Chris. 2005. *The Language of Jury Trial: A Corpus-Aided Analysis of Legal-Lay Discourse*. Basingstoke, UK: Palgrave Macmillan.

Heffer, Chris, Frances Rock, and John Conley. 2013. *Legal-Lay Communication: Textual Travels in the Law*. Oxford: Oxford University Press.

Heritage, John, and Steven Clayman. 2010. *Talk in Action: Interactions, Identities and Institutions*. Malden, MA: Wiley-Blackwell.

Heydon, Georgina. 2005. *The Language of Police Interviewing: A Critical Analysis*. Basingstoke, UK: Palgrave Macmillan.

Holt, Elizabeth, and Alison Johnson. 2010. "Legal Talk." In *Routledge Handbook of Forensic Linguistics*, edited by Malcolm Coulthard, and Alison Johnson, 21–36. Abingdon, UK: Routledge.

Innes, Bronwen. 2001. *Speaking Up in Court: Repair and Powerless Language in New Zealand Courtrooms*. PhD diss., University of Auckland. https://researchspace.auckland.ac.nz/handle/2292/366.

Innes, Bronwen. 2016. "Summing Up in Jury Trials as Interactive Discourse—One Plank in the New Zealand Judiciary's Effort to Improve Communication with Juries." In *Sociolinguistic Research: Impact and Application*, edited by Robert Lawson, and Dave Sayers, 132–150. Oxford: Routledge.

Johnson, Alison. 2002. "*So* . . .?: Pragmatic Implications of *So*-Prefaced Questions in Formal Police Interviews." In *Language in the Legal Process*, edited by Janet Cotterill, 91–110. Basingstoke, UK: Palgrave Macmillan.

Kashimura, Shiro. 2015. "Hearing Client's Talk as Lawyers' Work." In *Law at Work*, edited by Badouin Dupret, Michael Lynch, and Tim Berard, 139–162. Oxford: Oxford University Press.

Komter, Martha. 2013. "Travels of a Suspect's Statement." In *Legal-Lay Communication: Textual Travels in the Law*, edited by Chris Heffer, Frances Rock, and John Conley, 126–146. Oxford: Oxford University Press.

Lane, Chris. 1990. "The Sociolinguistics of Questioning in District Court Trials." In *New Zealand Ways of Speaking English*, edited by Allan Bell, and Janet Holmes, 221–251. Wellington: Victoria University Press.

Leung, Janny. 2012. "Judicial Discourse in Cantonese Courtrooms in Postcolonial Hong Kong: The Judge as Godfather, Scholar, Educator and Scolding Parent." *The International Journal of Speech, Language and the Law* 19: 239–261.

Liberman, Kenneth. 2015. "Producing Records of Testimony." In *Law at Work*, edited by Badouin Dupret, Michael Lynch, and Tim Berard, 115–137. Oxford: Oxford University Press.

Licoppe, Christian, and Maud Verdier. 2013. "Interpreting, Video Communication and the Sequential Reshaping of Institutional Talk in the Bilingual and Distributed Courtroom." *The International Journal of Speech, Language and the Law* 20: 247–275.

Loftus, Elizabeth. 1979. *Eyewitness Testimony*. Cambridge, MA: Harvard University Press.

Mason, Marianne. 2013. "Can I Get a Lawyer? A Suspect's Use of Indirect Requests in a Custodial Setting." *The International Journal of Speech, Language and the Law* 20: 203–227.

Matoesian, Gregory. 2000. "Intertextual Authority in Reported Speech: Production Media in the Kennedy Smith Rape Trial." *Journal of Pragmatics* 32: 879–914.

Melinkoff, David. 1963. *The Language of the Law*. Boston: Little, Brown and Company.

Mooney, Anabelle. 2014. *Language and Law*. Basingstoke, UK: Palgrave Macmillan.

Nakane, Ikuko. 2014. *Interpreter-Mediated Police Interviews*. Basingstoke, UK: Palgrave Macmillan.

O'Barr, William. 1982. *Linguistic Evidence: Language, Power, and Strategy in the Courtroom*. San Diego, CA: Academic Press.

Ogloff, James, Jonathan Clough, Jane Goodman-Delahunty, and Warren Young. 2006. *The Jury Project: Stage 1—A Survey of Australian and New Zealand Judges*. Melbourne: Australian Institute of Judicial Administration.

Olsson, John, and June Luchjenbroers. 2014. *Forensic Linguistics*. London: Bloomsbury.

Patrick, Peter. 2012. "Language Analysis for Determination of Origin: Objective Evidence for Refugee Status Determination." In *Oxford Handbook of Language and Law*, edited by Peter Tiersma, and Lawrence Solan, 535–546. Oxford: Oxford University Press.

Plotnikoff, Joyce, and Richard Woolfson. 2015. *Intermediaries in the Criminal Justice System*. Bristol, UK: Policy Press.

Rock, Frances. 2007. *Communicating Rights: The Language of Arrest and Detention*. Basingstoke, UK: Palgrave Macmillan.

Rock, Frances. 2010. "Witnesses and Suspects in Interviews. Collecting Oral Evidence: The Police, the Public and the Written Word." In *Routledge Handbook of Forensic Linguistics*, edited by Malcolm Coulthard, and Alison Johnson, 126–138. Abingdon, UK: Routledge.

Rosulek, Laura Felton. 2010. "Prosecution and Defense Closing Speeches." In *Routledge Handbook of Forensic Linguistics*, edited by Malcolm Coulthard, and Alison Johnson, 218–230. Abingdon, UK: Routledge.

Sarat, Austin, and William L. F. Felstiner. 1989. "Lawyers and Legal Consciousness: Law Talk in the Divorce Lawyer's Office." *The Yale Law Journal* 98: 1663–1688.

Scheffer, Thomas. 2006. "The Microformation of Criminal Defense: On the Lawyer's Notes, Speech Production and a Field of Presence." *Research on Language and Social Interaction* 39: 303–342.

Shuy, Roger W. 1998. *The Language of Confessions, Interrogation and Deception*. London: Sage.

Stygall, Gail. 1994. *Trial Language: Differential Discourse Processing and Discursive Formation*. Philadelphia, PA: John Benjamins.

Stygall, Gail. 2014. "Death Penalty Instructions to Jurors." *Language and Law/Languagem e Direito* 1: 95–108.
Tiersma, Peter. 2000. "Rocky Road to Legal Reform: Improving the Language of Jury Instructions." *Brooklyn Law Review* 66: 1081.
Tiersma, Peter. 2010. "Redrafting California's Jury Instructions." In *Routledge Handbook of Forensic Linguistics*, edited by Malcolm Coulthard, and Alison Johnson, 251–264. Abingdon, UK: Routledge.
Tinsley, Yvette. 2001. "Juror Decision-Making: A Look Inside the Jury Room." *British Society of Criminology Conference Proceedings* Vol. 4: 1464–1488.
Tracy, Karen, and Russell Parks. 2012. "'Tough Questioning' as Enactment of Ideology in Judicial Conduct: Marriage Law Appeals in Seven US Courts." *The International Journal of Speech, Language and the Law* 19: 1–25.
Trinch, Shonna. 2007. "The Pragmatic Use of Gender in Latina Women's Legal Narratives of Abuse." *The International Journal of Speech, Language and the Law* 14: 51–83.
Wodak, Ruth. 1985. "The Interaction between Judge and Defendant." In *Discourse Analysis in Society*. Vol. 4 of *Handbook of Discourse Analysis*, edited by Teun van Dijk, 181–191. London: Academic Press.
Young, Warren, Neil Cameron, and Yvette Tinsley. 1999. *Juries in Criminal Trials*. Wellington: New Zealand Law Commission.
Young, Warren, Neil Cameron, and Yvette Tinsley. 2001. *Jury Trials In New Zealand—A Survey Of Jurors*. Wellington: New Zealand Law Commission.

14
Service Encounters

J. César Félix-Brasdefer

Introduction

Service Encounters (SEs) are broadly defined as everyday interactions in which some kind of commodity, be it goods, information, or both, is exchanged between a service provider and a service seeker. The participants in SEs may be physically present at a designated public setting (face-to-face encounters), or the transaction can be carried out by telephone or online. SE settings include markets, small shops, grocery stores, convenience stores, travel agencies, library front-desks, bookshops, commercial, and government settings, as well as online shopping (e.g., eBay, Amazon, Craigslist).

Independent of the various settings, SEs belong to the same genre, as they share structural, functional, and stylistic features, as well as content (Swales 1990, 58). The genre of SEs comprises the following four characteristics:

1. Setting: Although SEs may occur at non-designated sites (e.g., a person asking a policeman for information on the street, or buying candy from a street vendor), face-to-face SEs take place at designated settings (e.g., small shops, information centres, and market places). In e-service encounters buyers and sellers negotiate service in a variety of online environments;
2. Goal or task-orientation: Interactions in SEs show an orientation by at least one of the participants toward some task/goal that is conventionally related to the setting (Drew and Heritage 1992, 22);
3. Participants' roles: The roles of the participants are institutionalized, and each participant is expected to play a specific role (service provider or service seeker);
4. Constrained topic: in SEs the topic is constrained by what participants consider to be allowable for the sales transaction (Drew and Heritage 1992, 22).

It is the sharing of these aspects, specifically, their communicative purpose in seeking and giving goods and services that represents the main criterion for the definition of this genre. While transactional talk predominates in SEs (e.g., sales transaction or negotiation of service), non-transactional talk (e.g., small talk, metalinguistic comments) is also important for the outcome of the interaction because it promotes and maintains interpersonal relations between the participants (see Félix-Brasdefer 2015, Chap. 7; Placencia and Mancera Rueda 2011).

Previous Research

This section offers a selective account of research on SEs from different theoretical and methodological perspectives, and in different settings. It includes studies that adopt either a top-down (organizational/discourse structure) or a bottom-up (micro-analytic analysis of social action) approach, or both; research on SEs in multilingual and intercultural contexts, as well as the emerging field of e-service encounters.

Top-Down Approach: Macro-Analysis and Discourse Organization

A top-down approach is characterized by the analysis of discourse patterns (phases of the transaction), the generic structure (obligatory elements), and discourse strategies (e.g., repair, politeness). A number of earlier studies took this approach to SEs, focusing on the generic structure of transactional talk, with little attention to the sequential organization of transactional and non-transactional talk. For example, Mitchell (1957) focused on the language of buying and selling in Cyrenaica (Libya) (Arabic). He examined the social actions that occurred in three types of encounters: (i) market sales transactions; (ii) market auctions; and (iii) shop transactions. He identified four stages of market auctions: (i) the auctioneer's opening; (ii) the investigation of the object for sale; (iii) bidding, and (iv) conclusion. With regard to market (non-auction) and shop transactions, Mitchell identified five stages: (i) salutation; (ii) inquiry as to the object for sale; (iii) investigation of the object for sale; (iv) bargaining; and (v) conclusion. Using an integrated model of discourse coherence Merritt (1976) identified four stages in the structure of SEs in over 1000 interactions at a self-service convenience store: (i) the customer's presence which summons the vendor; (ii) the decision stage (e.g., "can I have ..."); (iii) the exchange of product and money; and (iv) the closing stage. She examined the data through pragmatic inferences with regard to the assumptions, contextual presuppositions, and appropriateness required during the interpretation of a speech act sequence.

From a Systemic Functional Linguistics perspective, Halliday and Hasan (1980) and Hasan (1985) looked at the generic structure of SEs in small shops selling fruit. The authors concluded that the genre of SEs is defined by obligatory elements: sale request, sale compliance, sale, purchase, and purchase closure (Hasan 1985, 60). Further, Ventola (1987) examined the conversational structure of SEs. She proposed a generic structure with the following elements: greeting, attendance-allocation (e.g., "who's next?"), service bid (e.g., "can I help you?"), service (e.g., "could I have ..."), resolution (i.e., decision to buy or not to buy), goods handover, payment, closing, and goodbye. Although Ventola's (1987) work predominantly employed a top-down model, she also analysed SEs from a bottom-up perspective (e.g., focusing on speech act sequences or exchange structures locally managed by the participants). In her more recent work, Ventola (2005) argues for an interdisciplinary approach to SEs, including the multimodal analysis of verbal and non-verbal actions.

Bottom-Up Approach: Micro-Analysis of Social Action

A bottom-up approach focuses on the micro-analysis or sequential organization of social action in SE interactions in different languages and in a wide variety of settings. The PIXI project (Pragmatics of Italian/English Cross-Cultural Interaction) (Aston 1988) is an applied linguistic investigation of the pragmatics of Public Service Encounters (PSE) in two settings (bookshops in Southern England and Northern Italy) which took this approach. The project's main objective was to identify similarities and differences in the social practices, pragmalinguistic forms, and structural patterns of bookshop encounters (e.g., openings, closings, request-response sequences, role of laughter, preference/dispreference). Although the focus was on transactional talk, some aspects of non-transactional talk were examined. The seminal work of Aston (1988) and his collaborators advanced our understanding of SEs in contrastive pragmatics. Their work also examines cross-cultural differences with regard to the participants' roles (e.g., information seeker and information provider).

Researchers in Lyons, France (e.g., Kerbrat-Orecchioni and Traverso 2008) and Geneva, Switzerland (e.g., Filliettaz 2004) have also made significant contributions to the field of SEs through their data collected in bakeries, butcher shops, jewellery stores, and at newspaper stands. For instance, Kerbrat-Orecchioni and Traverso (2008) investigated politeness practices and the sequential organization (e.g., openings, closings, requests-response sequence) of transactions in small shops. Their model of analysis looks at the overall organization of the encounter (generic structure) (top-down approach) as well as the sequential structure of social actions (e.g., openings and closings, request–response sequence) (bottom-up approach). Further, Filliettaz (2004) and his collaborators examined SEs in bookshops and small stores in Geneva from a multimodal perspective (mainly transactional talk). His model includes the analysis of linguistic and non-verbal actions (e.g., gesture, presence of the interlocutors).

Traverso has also made important contributions to contrastive pragmatics and the understanding of non-transactional talk in SEs with her work in regions of France and Syria (Traverso 2006). The negotiation of service (request for service-response sequences) has also been analysed in a few varieties of Spanish in regions of Mexico (Félix-Brasdefer 2012, 2015; Merino-Hernández 2016; Solon 2013), Ecuador (Placencia 2005, 2008), Argentina (Yates 2016), and Spain (Bataller 2015). In general, these studies focus on the micro-analytic dimension of transactional talk and the participants' roles in different sociocultural contexts. They examine the sequential structure of the joint-actions necessary to accomplish the sales transaction, including presence/absence of greetings, offer-response sequences, the co-construction of request for service-response, bargaining sequences, and closing sequences. These studies adopt general concepts of conversation analysis to examine the realization of social action in face-to-face interaction.

SEs in Multilingual Contexts

The negotiation of service in intercultural and inter-ethnic settings has been examined in multilingual contexts. Using written field notes, Callahan (2009) examined English and Spanish bilingual encounters in New York City (cafés, pharmacies, grocery stores, convenience stores, delicatessens, clothing, and shoe stores). The author focused on the patterns of language choice and code-switching among Hispanics. In a butcher shop in France, Hmed (2008) examined bilingual interactions between native speakers of French and Arabic-speaking immigrants from Tunisia. In bilingual encounters, direct requests, and informal address forms were expressed in Arabic in order to express solidarity and involvement with the interlocutor. With regard to code-switching, bilingual speakers chose French to perform the transaction. Further, Solon (2013) examined interactions in SEs between handicraft and souvenir vendors and their tourist customers at the archaeological zone of Chichén Itzá (Yucatán, Mexico). The vendors interacted with tourists in both Spanish and English. As in Hmed's (2008) study, the interactions in Solon's study are representative of code-switching and language choice. Finally, Torras and Gafaranga (2002) examined language alternation in trilingual settings in Barcelona, Spain (Spanish, Catalan, and English). The data were collected at a student exchange office (university campus) and in two Anglo-Celtic pubs. In these settings, language selection served to establish social identity; specifically, the choice of language was employed to open the interaction, repair, and make a request.

SEs in Intercultural and Learning Contexts

Research on SEs has been conducted in settings where customers (with different L1 backgrounds) interact in English with members of a second culture. Bailey (1997) examined 25 (video-taped) interactions at a liquor store between US immigrant Korean retailers (owners) and African American customers. The African Americans showed an orientation towards involvement (e.g., joking, interpersonal meaning), while the Korean retailers showed an orientation towards restraint politeness and they appeared to feel uncomfortable when exchanging interpersonal talk. Korean immigrant shopkeepers and African American customers were also the focus of research by Ryoo (2005, 2007), who investigated interactions at beauty salons. The author examined in-group identity markers (e.g., joking), compliments, small talk, and solidarity attitudes. Using principles of Conversation Analysis, David (1999) investigated interethnic interactions between immigrant store owners of different backgrounds (e.g., Korean, Chinese, Arab, or Chaldean) and African American customers in convenience stores in the Detroit metropolitan area. This study focused on interethnic humour (e.g., jokes, anecdotes, rumours, legends) and small talk.

With regard to SEs and learners, Shively investigated SEs between seven US learners of Spanish and service providers (native Spanish speakers) in Toledo, Spain (e.g., local stores, banks, information desks). In her 2011 study the author focused on transactional talk (e.g., requests, openings, and closings), while in her 2013 article she examined the pragmatic function of small talk. The main objective of these studies was to identify developmental patterns with regard to the politeness practices and interactional patterns of L2 learners of Spanish during a semester abroad.

E-service Encounters

Researchers have begun to examine different dimensions of the discourse structure of the e-service encounter genre. E-service encounters have been broadly defined as web-based services or interactive services that are delivered through online technology, such as a website. Rowley (2006) offers a critical overview of e-service encounters in commercial and non-commercial settings.

Current research in e-service encounters includes the negotiation of meaning through online service in a variety of online environments, including commercial and non-commercial interactions in web-mediated SEs (e.g., Bou-Franch 2015), online buying and selling in a Mexican market through FaceBook (Merino-Hernández 2016), e-commerce and selection of forms of address in an Ecuadorian market (Placencia 2015), the negotiation of service through hyperlinks (Stommel and te Molder 2015), and requests for service through personal ads in *Vivastreet* (Zahler 2016). In these studies, Computer-Mediated Discourse (Herring and Androutsopoulos 2015) is the predominant framework utilized to examine the e-service encounter discourse, and Garcés-Conejos Blitvich (2015) proposes an agenda for examining the linguistic structure of the e-service encounter genre.

An Integrative Model for The Analysis of Service Encounters

In this section I present an integrated model that examines the structure of SEs from a pragmatic-discursive perspective (Félix-Brasdefer 2015). The proposed framework is influenced by two perspectives of social interaction, namely, variational pragmatics (Barron and Schneider 2009; Schneider and Barron 2008) and rapport management (Spencer-Oatey 2000; see Fletcher this volume). The discourse approach I adopt to examine SE interactions is interdisciplinary. It includes theoretical and methodological notions from Goffman (1961, 1971, 1981) (face-to-face encounters and changes in footing), Speech Act Theory, Discourse Analysis, and Conversation Analysis. The current framework includes eight levels. Although these levels closely resemble those utilized in Variational Pragmatics (e.g., Schneider 2010; Schneider and Barron 2008), the present framework differs methodologically with regard to the type of data selected and the context, that is, interactions in natural settings, including both face-to-face SEs and e-service encounters. To illustrate each of the levels in the model, I will draw on the example below, as well as referencing other research on SEs.

Example 14.1[1]

Context: Negotiation of service at a US visitor information centre (female visitor; male clerk)

01		((visitor enters the centre and looks at the clerk))	
02	Visitor:	I was looking for:: um a walking tour—	
03		I wanted to see the Thomas Hart Benton Murals ↑	
04	Clerk:	oh:: ok.	Transactional talk
05	Visitor:	park and then walk ↑	
06	Clerk:	uh yeah, you could park right here	
07	Visitor:	oh, it's the Auditorium	
08	Clerk:	yeah	
09	Visitor:	ok, thank you ↓	
10	Visitor:	are you going to school here?	
11	Clerk:	uh I did as an undergraduate, and I will be starting the fall	
12	Visitor:	what year?	
13	Clerk:	I'm gonna be starting my Master's in Informatics	
14	Visitor:	my daughter is great at math but decided not—	Relational talk
15		she's getting a <u>major</u> in it ↑ but I don't think she	
16		wants to do anything with it. Are you gonna do anything with it ↑	
17	Clerk:	yeah—and well with undergrad I'm I'm actually doing	
18		my emphasis right now on anthropology	
19	Visitor:	oh coo::l =	
20	Clerk:	= and then with informatics I don't know	
21	Visitor:	good luck	Closing sequence
22	Clerk:	thank you.	

In this exchange, the visitor opens the interaction with a request for information, followed by the clerk's acknowledgement (lines 02–04). Notice the absence of a greeting exchange, which reflects a sociocultural expectation and a focus on task-orientedness in this US service setting. The first part of the interaction includes the negotiation of transactional talk through coordinated joint actions (negotiation of information) (lines 01–09). Then, the visitor shifts alignment to relational talk (small talk), which is reciprocated by the clerk (lines 10–20). In this exchange, relational talk establishes a rapport between the interlocutors, enhances solidarity politeness, and shows involvement with the interlocutor (for a detailed analysis of this sequence, see Félix-Brasdefer 2015, Chap. 6).

Formal Level

This level concerns the formal analysis of linguistic expressions with regard to form, function, and force in specific contexts. It includes the analysis of discourse markers, epistemic expressions, and backchannels. An example of this is the examination of discourse markers such as "OK", "oh", "yes", or "well" in bookshops (Mansfield 1988) and self-service stores (Merritt 1984). In the exchange in Example 14.1, the discourse marker "OK" is used as an acceptance response after the elongated acknowledgement marker "oh::" to signal continuation of the request for service (line 04).

Actional Level

This level comprises the analysis of the pragmalinguistic strategies used in speech acts (e.g., requests, offers, greetings). For example, a request consists of a "head act" (e.g., "can I have a half a pound of ham?") which may include internal modification (e.g., "*could* I *please* have a half a pound of ham?"). The aim at this level is to provide an analysis of the pragmalinguistic expressions used to convey the illocutionary force of the action. Issues of directness or indirectness, or politeness or impoliteness can also be analysed at this level. For instance, Kerbrat-Orecchioni (2006) looked at politeness practices when making requests in small shops in France.

The actional level is often examined through an analysis of request types (the request for service), following Blum-Kulka, House, and Kasper (1989) classification of request strategies and internal modification, such as lexical (e.g., "please", "probably") and syntactic (e.g., conditional, aspect, past tense) downgraders. Focusing on the actional level, Taylor (2016) examined the different ways of expressing a request for service in Starbucks SEs with regard to the modality of the interaction, face-to-face vs drive-through microphone. In Example 14.1, the request for service is realized by means of a "want statement" ("I wanted to see . . .") with a final rising intonation ↑ (line 03).

Interactional Level

This level focuses on the analysis of speech act sequences or joint-social actions. It employs tools of Conversation Analysis (Schegloff 2007; see Toerien this volume) to examine sequential patterns in the organization of speech actions jointly produced by the customer and the server. It consists of an examination of openings, closings, and request-response sequences. Examples of this include Aston's (1995a, 1995b) analysis of openings and closings in bookshop SEs, Merritt's (1976) analysis of questions following questions, or elliptical questions-responses in small store transactions, and Filliettaz's (2008) co-construction of request–response sequences. In Example 14.1, the request–response sequence is realized across seven turns (lines 02–09). The request for service (line 03) is prefaced by a pre-sequence (line 02). The request is followed by an additional clarification request and the successful response on the part of the clerk closing the sequence (lines 05–09).

Stylistic Level

This level focuses on the stylistic aspects of an interchange. It is influenced by Goffman's (1981) notions of frame and footing (Goodwin 1996); for example, shifting from business talk (e.g., buying and selling) to a friendly tone (e.g., joking or small talk). It also includes the choice of forms of address used to open, close, and negotiate a business transaction, or shifting from formal (V) to informal (T) styles to express involvement or camaraderie. For example, Placencia (2005) showed how Spaniards shifted alignment from a business transaction to relational talk, while Ylänne-McEwen (2004) analysed the shifts of alignment from business to interpersonal talk (phatic exchanges) during the negotiation of service in travel agencies. An example of shift of alignment can be seen in Example 14.1. After the request for information is completed (lines 01–09), the visitor engages in non-transactional talk, asking the clerk about his status as a university student (lines 10–22). Non-transactional (i.e., relational talk) enhances the interlocutor's involvement and links of solidarity.

Topic Level

This level is concerned with discourse content throughout the interaction. It includes topic selection, topic management, topic abandonment, topic shift, and re-introduction of topics. It is concerned with knowing which topics are appropriate or inappropriate to bring up in a conversation, or the choice and management of sensitive topics. For instance, James (1992) examined the role of topic control during the negotiation of service at a convenience store; specifically, topic selection, topic shifts, topic development, and whether the topic is initiated by the customer or the seller. In Félix-Brasdefer's (2015) corpus, clerks and customers engaged in small talk shifting from one topic to another (e.g., weather, politics, health, vacation). Instances of relational sequences were embedded in the sales transaction and at the end of the transaction to enhance links of solidarity between the interlocutors.

Organizational Level

This level centres on the organization of turn-taking in conversation and is influenced by conversation analysis (e.g., Schegloff 2007; see Toerien this volume). It addresses aspects of turn-taking, overlap, interruption, silence, and preference organization. For instance, in an examination of dispreferred responses in bookshop encounters among Britons and Italians, Gavioli (1995) analysed turn-taking procedures for the presence of laughter as a repair device in turn-initial and turn-final position. In Example 14.1, the negotiation of service takes place without overlap or interruption during the first part of the interaction (transactional talk), with a fixed adjacency-pair system (lines 01–09). In contrast, instances of overlap are observed in the second part of the interaction during non-transactional talk that resembles colloquial conversation (lines 19–20).

Non-Verbal Level

This level consists of social actions performed through gesture. Kendon (2010, 1) refers to gestures as "visible acts" when uttering actions, such as body movement, hand movement, or gaze direction. More specifically, gesture is used

> to show what kinds of actions we are taking with our utterances: with gestures we can, among other things, show agreement or disagreement, affirmation or denial. We can show that we are asking a question or begging another's indulgence, that we are doubtful of something or that what we are saying is hypothetical.
>
> (2010, 1)

Further, Kidwell (2000) showed the primacy of non-verbal communication in accomplishing the action of requesting (in the absence of verbal actions) in front-desk encounters. In Example 14.1, an instance of non-verbal behaviour is observed during the opening sequence with the visitor entering the centre and looking at the clerk (line 01). The visitor looking at the clerk represents the summons for service.

Prosodic Level

Prosody is a pragmatic resource used to express interpersonal or marked meaning. This level focuses on pragmatic meaning that is conveyed through prosodic information: intonation (e.g., low or high pitch), stress, loudness, duration, and timing (e.g., rhythm and rate of speech). These prosodic resources function as "contextualization cues" (Gumperz 1982), i.e., signals that allow the interlocutor to draw an inference from the speaker's message. In bookshop SEs, Mansfield (1988) examined different pragmatic functions of the intonation (rising or falling) of requests, offers, and minimal exchanges, and Félix-Brasdefer (2015) looked at the interpersonal functions of duration and low and high terminals during the realization of the request for service.[2] In Example 14.1, the request for service is realized with a final rising intonation (↑) to ensure the clerk's response (lines 03–04).

The model presented here provides researchers with a framework for examining different dimensions of transactional and non-transactional talk in both formal and non-formal settings. The proposed model is contrastive, empirical, and aims at examining one or more levels of pragmatic analysis in comparable sociocultural settings, or in one or more varieties of the same language. The eight levels are aimed at examining verbal and non-verbal aspects of social interaction in both face-to-face interaction and in a variety of online environments. Finally, it is important to note that a detailed analysis of the prosodic and the non-verbal levels requires quality of the audio- and video-recordings in different naturalistic contexts.

Future Directions

There are many possible areas that could be explored in future research on SEs. Comprehensive analysis of bodily actions that are part of a joint activity (using video-taped data) are needed for the interpretation of gestures as expressive acts (Kendon 2010). Using the dimensions of transactional and relational talk, other types of encounters (commercial and non-commercial) are also needed in other regions (e.g., exploring intra-lingual pragmatic variation) and in situations of languages in contact, such as in Mexico (Maya-Spanish), Bolivia (Quechua and

Aymara in contact with Spanish), Paraguay (Guaraní-Spanish), or the United States (English and Spanish). In particular, research is needed on the dynamics of SEs in multilingual contexts and where one language is used as a lingua franca of the speech community (post-colonial pragmatics), such as French spoken in Senegal in formal contexts and Wolof in informal (familiar) contexts (Johns and Félix-Brasdefer 2015). In addition to the audio- and video-recorded data, researchers should consider triangulation of the data, such as Likert scales to examine perception of service on the part of the clerk (see Fink and Félix-Brasdefer 2015) or interviews with the clerks and customers.

A more fine-grained instrumental analysis of prosody is also needed to examine the expressive functions of vocal effects during the negotiation of service (e.g., timing, loudness, pitch) (Selting 2010). Likewise, given the ubiquitous nature of online service via the internet, more research on the negotiation of e-service is needed to improve our understanding of this particular genre, using theoretical and methodological tools from computer-mediated communication (Herring, Stein, and Virtanen 2013). Finally, while most research in SEs has been conducted among adult service providers and service seekers, studies of SEs with child customers are starting to emerge (Merritt 2015), with a view to examining the developmental process and sociocultural expectations of children during the negotiation of service. This promises to be another fruitful area for research on SEs.

Further Reading

Callahan (2009) examines English and Spanish bilingual encounters in New York City, exploring patterns of language choice and code-switching among Hispanics in the US.

Grounded in naturally occurring face-to-face interactions and drawing on a pragmatic-discursive approach, Félix-Brasdefer (2015) offers a comprehensive account of SEs in commercial and non-commercial settings in the United States and Mexico. This book length study takes a close look at the structure of these interactions on different pragmatic/discourse levels, including the actional (speech acts), sequential, prosodic, stylistic, and organizational levels, with particular attention to variation by gender.

Kerbrat-Orecchioni (2006) examines the realization of politeness and the sequential structure of social action in small shops in France. She takes a close look at the linguistic structure of the request for service, presence and absence of internal modification, and politeness practice in French SEs.

Merritt (1976) examines social action between customers and servers who negotiate service in face-to-face interactions. She adopts a cognitive and a discursive approach to social interaction and examines the sequential structure of joint actions during the negotiation of service.

Placencia (2008) examines intra-lingual pragmatic variation in SEs in Quito and Manta (Ecuador), focusing on the realization of the request for service, the sequential structure of the request, presence/absence of internal modification, and stylistic variation in small talk.

Related Topics

Interactional sociolinguistics; Conversational analysis; (Im)politeness theory; Genre theory; Call centre discourse; Relational talk; Intercultural communication

Notes

1. The transcription notation used in this example is as follows:
   = Equal signs indicate no break-up or gap. They are placed when there is no interval between adjacent utterances and the second utterance is linked immediately to the first.
   : A colon marks a lengthened syllable or an extension of a sound. More colons (:::) prolong a sound or syllable.
   ↑↓ The up and down arrows mark sharp rises or falls in pitch.
   — A dash marks a short untimed pause within an utterance.
   Word Underlining is used to indicate some form of stress or emphasis, either by increased loudness or higher pitch.
2. Studies analyzing prosodic resources used during the negotiation of service can utilize the *Praat* software program (Boersma and Weenink 2013).

References

Aston, Guy, Ed. 1988. *Negotiating Service: Studies in the Discourse of Bookshop Encounters*. Bologna: Editrice.
Aston, Guy. 1995a. "In Reference to the Role of Openings in Service Encounters." *Cahiers de Linguistique Française* 16: 89–112.
Aston, Guy. 1995b. "Say 'Thank You': Some Pragmatic Constraints in Conversational Closings." *Applied Linguistics* 16: 57–86.
Bailey, Benjamin.1997. "Communication of Respect in Interethnic Service Encounters." *Language in Society* 26: 327–356.
Barron, Anne, and Klaus Schneider. 2009. "Variational Pragmatics: Studying the Impact of Social Factors on Language Use in Interaction." *Intercultural Pragmatics* 6: 425–442.
Bataller, Rebeca. 2015. "Pragmatic Variation in the Performance of Requests: A Comparative Study of Service Encounters in Valencia and Granada (Spain)." In *A Multidisciplinary Approach to Service Encounters*, edited by Maria de la O Hernández-López, and Lucía Fernández-Amaya, 113–137. Boston, MA: Brill.
Blum-Kulka, Shoshana, Juliane House, and Gabriele Kasper, Eds. 1989. *Cross-Cultural Pragmatics: Requests and Apologies*. Norwood, NJ: Ablex.
Boersma, Paul, and David Weenink. 2013. *Praat: Doing Phonetics by Computer. Version 5.3.77*. Amsterdam: University of Amsterdam. Accessed on July 13, 2016 (www.praat.org).
Bou-Franch, Patricia. 2015. "The Genre of Web-Mediated Service Encounters in Not-for-Profit Organizations: Cross-Cultural Study." In *A Multidisciplinary Approach to Service Encounters*, edited by Maria de la O Hernández-López, and Lucía Fernández-Amaya, 65–83. Boston, MA: Brill.
Callahan, Laura. 2009. *Spanish and English in U.S. Service Encounters*. New York: Palgrave Macmillan.
David, Gary. 1999. "Intercultural Relationships across the Counter: An Interactional Analysis of In-Situ Service Encounters." PhD diss., Wayne State University.
Drew, Paul, and John Heritage, Eds. 1992. "Analyzing Talk at Work: An Introduction." In *Talk at Work: Interaction in Institutional Settings*, edited by Paul Drew, and John Heritage, 3–65. Cambridge: Cambridge University Press.
Félix-Brasdefer, J. César. 2012. "Pragmatic Variation by Gender in Market Service Encounters in Mexico." In *Pragmatic Variation in First and Second Language Contexts: Methodological Issues*, edited by J. César Félix-Brasdefer, and Dale Koike, 17–48. Amsterdam: John Benjamins.
Félix-Brasdefer, J. César. 2015. *The Language of Service Encounters: A Pragmatic-Discursive Approach*. Cambridge: Cambridge University Press.
Filliettaz, Laurent. 2004. "The Multimodal Negotiation of Service Encounters." In *Discourse and Technology: Multimodal Discourse Analysis*, edited by Philip Le Vine, and Ron Scollon, 88–100. Washington, DC: Georgetown University Press.
Filliettaz, Laurent. 2008. "La co-construction de requêtes: Le cas du service à la clientèle dans les grandes surfaces" [The Co-Construction of Requests: The Case of Customer Service in Supermarkets]. In *Les interactions en site commercial: Invariants et variations* [Interactions in Commercial Sites: Invariants and Variations], edited by Catherine Kerbrat-Orecchioni, and Véronique Traverso, 77–103. Lyon: Ens Éditions.

Fink, Lisa and J. César Félix-Brasdefer. 2015. "Pragmalinguistic and Gender Variation in U.S. Café Service Encounters." In *Researching Sociopragmatic Variability: Perspectives from Variational, Interlanguage and Contrastive Pragmatics*, edited by Kate Beeching, and Helen Woodfield, 19–48. Basingstoke, UK: Palgrave Macmillan.

Garcés-Conejos Blitvich, Pilar. 2015. "Setting the Linguistics Research Agenda for the E-service Encounters Genre: Natively Digital versus Digitized Perspectives." In *A Multidisciplinary Approach to Service Encounters*, edited by Maria de la O Hernández-López, and Lucía Fernández-Amaya, 15–36. Boston, MA: Brill.

Gavioli, Laura. 1995. "Turn-Initial and Turn-Final Laughter: Two Techniques for Initiating Remedy in English/Italian Bookshop Service Encounters." *Discourse Processes* 19: 369–384.

Goffman, Erving. 1961. *Encounters: Two Studies in the Sociology of Interaction*. Indianapolis, IN: Bobbs-Merrill.

Goffman, Erving. 1971. *Relations in Public: Micro Studies of the Public Order*. New York: Basic Books.

Goffman, Erving. 1981. *Forms of Talk*. Philadelphia, PA: University of Pennsylvania Press.

Goodwin, Marjorie H. 1996. "Shifting Frame." In *Social Interaction, Social Context, and Language: Essays in Honor of Susan Ervin-Tripp*, edited by Dan I. Slobin, Julie Gerhardt, Amy Kyratzis, and Jiansheng Guo, 71–82. Mahwah, NJ: Lawrence Erlbaum.

Gumperz, John. 1982. *Discourse Strategies*. Cambridge: Cambridge University Press.

Halliday, Michael A. K., and Ruqua Hasan. 1980. "Text and Context: Aspects of Language in a Social-Semiotic Perspective." *Sophia Linguistica* 6: 4–107.

Hasan, Ruqua. 1985. "The Structure of a Text." In *Language, Context, and Text: Aspects of Language in a Social-Semiotic Perspective*, edited by Michael A. K. Halliday, and Ruqua Hasan, 52–69. Oxford: Oxford University Press.

Herring, Susan, and Jannis Androutsopoulos. 2015. "Computer-Mediated Discourse 2.0." In *Handbook of Discourse Analysis*. 2nd ed., edited by Deborah Tannen, Heidi E. Hamilton, and Deborah Schiffrin, 127–151. Malden, MA: Wiley-Blackwell.

Herring, Susan, Dieter Stein, and Tuija Virtanen. 2013. *Pragmatics of Computer-Mediated Discourse*. Berlin: Mouton de Gruyter.

Hmed, Neijete. 2008. "Analyse comparative d'interactions dans des petits commerces Français, Tunisiens et Franco-Maghrébins" [Comparative Analysis of Interactions in Small French, Tunisian, and Franco-North African shops]. In *Les interactions en site commercial: Invariants et variations* [Interactions in Commercial Sites: Invariants and Variations], edited by Catherine Kerbrat-Orecchioni, and Véronique Traverso, 254–276. Lyon: Ens Éditions.

James, Trevor H. 1992. "Facework, Power Displays, and Transaction Activities in a Public Service Encounter." PhD diss., University of North Carolina.

Johns, Andrew, and J. César Félix-Brasdefer. 2015. "Linguistic Politeness and Pragmatic Variation in Request Production in Dakar French." *Journal of Politeness Research* 11: 131–164.

Kendon, Adam. 2010. "Some Topics in Gesture Studies." In *Fundamentals of Verbal and Nonverbal Communication and the Biometric Issue*, edited by Anna Esposito, Maja Bratanic, Eric Keller, and María Marinaro, 3–19. Amsterdam: IOS Press.

Kerbrat-Orecchioni, Catherine. 2006. "Politeness in Small Shops in France." *Journal of Politeness Research* 2: 79–103.

Kerbrat-Orecchioni, Cathérine, and Véronique Traverso. 2008. "Les interactions en site commercial: Des interactions polies" [Interactions in Commercial Sites: Polite Interactions]. In *Les interactions en site commercial: Invariants et variations* [Interactions in Commercial Sites: Invariants and Variations], edited by Catherine Kerbrat-Orecchioni, and Véronique Traverso, 105–137. Lyon: Ens Éditions.

Kidwell, Mardi. 2000. "Common Ground in Cross-Cultural Communication: Sequential and Institutional Contexts in Front Desk Service Encounters." *Issues in Applied Linguistics* 11: 17–37.

Mansfield, Gillian. 1988. "The Supportive Role of Intonation in Service Encounters." In *Negotiating Service: Studies in the Discourse of Bookshop Encounters*, edited by Aston Guy, 203–231. Bologna: CLUEB.

Merino-Hernández, Laura Margarita. 2016. "*Tianguis Friki*: Intracultural Pragmatic Variation of E-service Encounters in a Northern Mexican Community." *IULC Working Papers* 15: 159–180. (www.indiana.edu/~iulcwp/wp)

Merritt, Marilyn. 1976. "On Questions Following Questions in Service Encounters." *Language in Society* 5: 315–357.

Merritt, Marilyn. 1984. "On the Use of Okay in Service Encounters." In *Language in Use: Readings in Sociolinguistics*, edited by John Baugh, and Joel Sherzer, 294–304. Englewood Cliffs, NJ: Prentice Hall.

Merritt, Marilyn. 2015. "Service Encounters in the Natural World: Bringing Children Along." In *A Multidisciplinary Approach to Service Encounters*, edited by Maria de la O Hernández-López, and Lucía Fernández-Amaya, 191–201. Boston, MA: Brill.

Mitchell, T. F. (1957) 1975. "The Language of Buying and Selling in Cyrenaica: A Situational Statement." *Hesperis*, 26. Reprinted in *Principles of Firthian Linguistics*, edited by T. F. Mitchell, 167–200. London: Longman.

Placencia, María Elena. 2005. "Pragmatic Variation in Corner Store Interactions in Quito and Madrid." *Hispanic* 88: 583–98.

Placencia, María Elena. 2008. "Requests in Corner Shop Transactions in Ecuadorian Andean and Coastal Spanish." In *Variational Pragmatics: A Focus on Regional Varieties in Pluricentric Languages*, edited by Klaus Schneider, and Anne Barron, 307–332. Amsterdam: John Benjamins.

Placencia, María Elena. 2015. "Address Forms and Relational Work in E-commerce: The Case of Service Encounter Interactions in Mercado Libre Ecuador." In *A Multidisciplinary Approach to Service Encounters*, edited by Maria de la O Hernández-López, and Lucía Fernández-Amaya, 37–64. Boston, MA: Brill.

Placencia, María Elena, and Ana Mancera Rueda. 2011. '¡Vaya, ¡qué chungo!' Rapport-Building Talk in Service Encounters: The Case of Bars in Seville at Breakfast Time." In *Spanish at Work: Analyzing Institutional Discourse across the Spanish-Speaking World*, edited by Nuria Lorenzo-Dus, 192–207. New York: Palgrave Macmillan.

Rowley, Jennifer. 2006. "An Analysis of the E-service Literature: Towards a Research Agenda." *Internet Research* 16: 339–359.

Ryoo, Hye-Kyung. 2005. "Achieving Friendly Interactions: A Study of Service Encounters between Korean Shopkeepers and African-American Customers." *Discourse & Society* 16: 79–105.

Ryoo, Hye-Kyung. 2007. "Interculturality Serving Multiple Interactional Goals in African American and Korean Service Encounters." *Pragmatics* 17: 23–47.

Schegloff, Emanuel. 2007. *Sequence Organization in Interaction: A Primer in Conversation Analysis I*. Cambridge: Cambridge University Press.

Schneider, Klaus. 2010. "Variational Pragmatics." In *Variation and Change: Pragmatic Perspectives*, edited by Mirjam Fried, 239–267. Amsterdam: John Benjamins.

Schneider, Klaus, and Anne Barron, Eds. 2008. *Variational Pragmatics: A Focus on Regional Varieties in Pluricentric Languages*. Amsterdam: John Benjamins.

Selting, Margret. 2010. "Prosody in Interaction: State of the Art." In *Prosody in Interaction*, edited by Dagmar Barth-Weingarten, Elisabeth Reber, and Margret Selting, 3–40. Amsterdam: John Benjamins.

Shively, Rachel L. 2011. "L2 Pragmatic Development in Study Abroad: A Longitudinal Study of Spanish Service Encounters." *Journal of Pragmatics* 43: 1818–1835.

Shively, Rachel L. 2013. "Out-of-Class Interaction during Study Abroad: Service Encounters in Spain." *Spanish in Context* 10: 53–91.

Solon, Megan. 2013. "Cross-Cultural Negotiation: Touristic Service Encounters in Yucatán, Mexico." In *Selected Proceedings of the 15th Hispanic Linguistics Symposium*, edited by Chad Howe, Sarah E. Blackwell, and Margaret Lubbers Quesada, 252–268. Somerville: Cascadilla Proceedings Project.

Spencer-Oatey, Helen. 2000. *Culturally Speaking: Managing Rapport through Talk across Cultures*. London: Continuum.

Stommel, Wyke, and Hedwig te Molder. 2015. "Counseling Online and Over the Phone: When Preclosing Questions Fail as a Closing Device." *Research on Language and Social Interaction* 48: 281–300.

Swales, John M. 1990. *Genre Analysis: English in Academic and Research Settings*. Cambridge: Cambridge University Press.

Taylor, Jenna. 2016. "I Need a Coffee: Pragmalinguistic Variation of Starbucks Service Encounter Requests According to Interaction Modality." *IULC Working Papers* 15: 33–61. (www.indiana.edu/~iulcwp/wp)

Torras, María-Carmen, and Joseph Gafaranga. 2002. "Social Identities and Language Alternation in Non-Formal Institutional Bilingual Talk: Trilingual Service Encounters in Barcelona." *Language in Society* 31: 527–548.

Traverso, Véronique. 2006. "Aspects of Polite Behaviour in French and Syrian Service Encounters: A Data-Based Comparative Study." *Journal of Politeness Research* 2: 105–122.

Ventola, Eija. 1987. *The Structure of Social Interaction: A Systemic Approach to the Semiotics of Service Encounters*. London: Frances Pinter.
Ventola, Eija. 2005. "Revisiting Service Encounter Genre—Some Reflections." *Folia Linguistica* 39: 19–43.
Yates, Allison. 2016. "Pragmatic Variation in Service Encounters in Argentine Spanish." *IULC Working Papers* 15: 128–158. (www.indiana.edu/~iulcwp/wp)
Ylänne-McEwen, Virpi. 2004. "Shifting Alignment and Negotiating Sociality in Travel Agency Discourse." *Discourse Processes* 6: 517–533.
Zahler, Sara Louise. 2016. "Pragmalinguistic Variation in Electronic Personal Ads from Mexico City and London." *IULC Working Papers* 15: 208–230. (www.indiana.edu/~iulcwp/wp/issue/view/25)

15
Call Centre Discourse
Jon S. Y. Hui

Introduction

Technological innovations and social change since the end of the last century have had a direct influence on the way we interact with each other in every sphere of life, including in the workplace. As a result of these changes, new forms of text and discourse have emerged, with new resources for establishing interpersonal relationships and constructing identities (Goodman and Graddol 2001). Call centre discourse, set in one of the newer service-oriented, technology-enabled professional environments, is a prime example of technological, social, and economic progress in recent years. This "technicalization" of human contact creates a unique kind of discourse, located within the area of professional communication and workplace discourse (Gunnarsson 2013).

As an example of the Information Technology Enabled Services (ITES) industry, call centres are where modern technology interfaces meet the complexity of the human interface. Millions and millions of data records and documents are centralized, ready to be retrieved by customer service representatives (CSRs) while they are managing conversations with customers who could be local, but are more likely to be in another part of the country or even in another country altogether. In operational terms, a call centre is where information services are produced and delivered to the public through the interface of CSRs, who are supported by a host of technological innovations, including advanced telecommunication and call-management systems. Inevitably, this development influences the way we interact, communicate, and "talk" in this unique workplace.

Call centres, sometimes labelled contact centres, have become an integral part of companies' marketing and customer service strategies (Sawyerr, Srinivas, and Wang 2009) and have become the most common avenue for customer contact since they became part of the customer service scene in the early 1990s. They have become essentially what I term the "virtual front desk" of companies and organizations (Hui 2014).

Types of Call Centres and Their Functions

Call centres may broadly be classified into two categories: "in-house" and "service bureaux", with CSRs—sometimes labelled agents (Belt, Richardson, and Webster 2002)—answering enquiries from their customers via telephone systems. Those that are "in-house" form part of a company, whereas the "service bureaux" are contracted companies. These outsourced companies may handle the business of a single company or multiple companies. The in-house call centres usually interface with end-users within the company and outside the company in the form of support and after-sales service. From time to time, outbound calls may be made in response to requests from customers. Examples of this type are call centres located in banks or large institutions. Another form of "outbound" calling is when CSRs ring potential customers and perform the role of sales and marketing executives. This type of call is often labelled "telemarketing". The functions of call centres range therefore from answering product enquiries to resolving administrative issues, from clarification of contracts to technical support, and from handling complaints to making cold sales calls.

Call centres can also be categorized by their location. "Onshore" refers to operations within a country where CSRs are usually local employees, whereas "offshore" refers to when the call centre operation has been subcontracted to a bureaux type company located in another country, usually a developing one such as India or the Philippines. CSRs of these offshore operations are from a very different linguistic and cultural background than their callers. Therefore, language related research topics can be quite different from those relevant in onshore call centres.

In the following sections, I will outline the unique nature of call centre discourse, review some common language research topics and discuss additional language issues which mainly pertain to offshore workplaces. Research methods and suggestions for future research directions complete the chapter.

Call Centre Discourse

Multiple issues have been analysed since call centres became synonymous with customer service in the early 1990s. Research on organizational, occupational, and technical aspects of call centres began to emerge in the late 1990s. These studies not only raised questions about the general working conditions of the professionals in this industry, they also highlighted the organizational and occupational aspects of call centres. These factors invariably influence the way in which CSRs communicate with their customers, for instance, the inability of CSRs to express emotions freely because of excessive call-scripting (Roberts 2010).

At the heart of the call centre setting as a workplace, the use of language is intimately linked to the transactions between CSRs and their callers/customers. These transactions in turn are influenced by the kind of tasks and goals that need to be achieved. For instance, the way the CSR interacts with his/her caller of an inbound call enquiry is quite different from a telemarketing agent calling a potential customer. Nevertheless, there are a number of common topics that can be broadly discussed.

Call Structure

Despite research on the language used in call centres being a decade or so old, there are not many studies on the overall structure of calls. Among the three examples below, one is based on offshore and two are based on onshore call centre data.

Probably the first of its kind, Forey and Lockwood (2007) investigated communication breakdown in an offshore call centre in the Philippines and suggested a generic call structure consisting of six obligatory stages: Opening, Purpose, Gathering of information, Purpose, Service, and Closing, with one optional stage—Summarizing—wedged between Service and

Closing. Their analysis was based on calls to an insurance company and interactions between native English (NE) speaking North Americans and non-native English (NNE) speaking Filipino CSRs.

In Xu *et al.* (2010) an onshore centre was the focus with data collected from a Chinese telecommunication products technical support call centre where both interactants are Chinese native speakers. Xu *et al.* (2010) proposed a three-stage generic structure (Opening, Servicing, and Closing) which fans out to five generic exchanges: Greeting exchange (Opening), Purpose, Information, Service exchanges (servicing), and Farewell exchange (Closing). In turn these exchanges may involve up to 23 interactional steps. The rationale behind the two proposed structures in Forey and Lockwood (2007) and Xu *et al.* (2010) seems very similar. Both suggest the opening as a simple greeting exchange and the main part as a transactional service, where the exchange is dominated by "help and information" provided by the CSRs.

Viewed from a more interpersonal relationship and collaborative perspective, Hui (2014) proposed a four-stage generic structure: Opening, Request for Assistance, Solution Negotiation, and Closing, based on his data from an essentially onshore call centre in New Zealand. Request for Assistance is highlighted as rich pragmatic data, as is expected in this stage. Also, this structure sees the "solution" to the request or stated problem as a negotiation process between the customer and the CSR. More often than not, information flows both ways, and may involve modification by both interactants before a resolution is arrived at.

While these three proposed structures are the result of analysing data from a small number of call centres, they reflect the diversity and complexity of call centre study and point to the existence of a generic structure, at least within particular contexts.

Politeness Markers and Communication Strategies

One of the prominent issues in call centre discourse is politeness, as the encounters are between people who do not in general know each other and who engage in exchanging information by face-threatening acts such as requests and refusals. One way of reducing potential tension in this situation is the employment of politeness markers. Research has shown that politeness is regarded as an important strategy in call centre interaction both in onshore and offshore operations (Adolphs *et al.* 2004; Friginal 2008).

Indeed, from a UK-based call centre, Brown and Crawford (2009) found multiple layers of politeness markers when health-care professionals solicit sensitive and personal information from callers. Three main strategies were identified. A three-part politeness structure is the first strategy. This consists of "a request for permission to ask a question", followed by another "request for permission to ask a question", then a rising tone "please" tag. The researchers suggest that the occurrence of this call-opening politeness phenomenon can be explained by the aim of establishing the right kind of rapport at the beginning of the call, reducing the imposition of asking personal details, framing for more questions to come, and minimizing the awkwardness of an unexpected opening sequence. The second politeness strategy is the employment of a "pre-sequence": the act of asking a question about the upcoming question (Schegloff 1988). The function of a "pre-sequence" or "meta-question" is to forewarn the caller and mitigate the imposition (Brown and Crawford 2009). The third politeness strategy is to carefully place a token of "self-referential deixis" preceding the sensitive question to minimize the intrusion. This prepackaging of the question has the effect of deflecting the origin of the question and hence mitigates the question's potential offensiveness (Brown and Crawford 2009).

Investigating data from an offshore call centre, different frequencies in the use of politeness and respect markers by CSRs and their callers feature prominently in Friginal's study (2008).

Among other findings, addressee-focused politeness respect markers occurred consistently in all situations while the CSRs' total number of politeness markers is notably higher than that of the callers (Friginal 2008). The nature of the CSRs' job requires a courteous style, since call centres are there to serve their customers and CSRs are expected to be helpful, courteous and polite.

Other strategies have also been found to facilitate communication in call centre interaction. These include "work aloud" (Houtkoop, Jansen, and Walstock 2005), repetition (Kaur 2010), metaphoric expressions (Kraan 2005) and accommodation (Lockwood 2013).

Language and Power

Language and power in call centre discourse has been examined from two primary perspectives: applying a critical lens at a macro level to view the top-down power exerted by management in the form of control of talk in call exchanges; and viewing from a micro level the interactional power enactment between CSRs and callers as evident in talk. The former is illustrated by the phenomenon of language "styling".

The Globalization of Styling Talk

The power of management to exert global corporate branding, explicitly or otherwise, to "style" workers in call centres has caused noticeable concern (Cameron 2000). CSRs in call centres are often required to adhere to a predetermined script when they interact with their customers. While the rationale behind the conformity is claimed to be "standardization", leading to "better" quality assurance and greater cost effectiveness, in offshore call centres it adds to "location masking" strategies in addition to "accent neutralization" and "cultural training". Large US international companies for example are keen to offer the same kind of service experience to their customers as if they were interacting with a domestic call centre. The ripple effect is that the corporate cultural identities of these large corporations, predominantly US companies, are being exported and enforced on call centre workers.

In an attempt to see how the "call centre style" is being taken up globally, Hultgren (2011) examined data from four call centres, one each in Britain and Denmark, Hong Kong and the Philippines. She found that there is a remarkable similarity in the prescribed materials across the board. In further investigation and comparison between British and Danish interactional data, a difference in the uptake of such a style was found, with Danish CSRs seeming to exhibit the prescribed style to a lesser extent than their British counterparts. Differences in cultural associations with business were suggested as the reason.

The exportation of such styles of interaction, usually associated with "informalization", could backfire. As Elias (2010) observed, one caller was annoyed when an offshore CSR addressed him by his first name. This shows resistance to the style existing at the CSR level in Hultgren's (2011) case and at the customer level in Elias' (2010) case. Nevertheless, there is a clear indication of a spread of a globalized style within the call centre genre; and styling of workers' language in call centres is being seen as "commodification of language" (Heller 2010) and as a form of exploitation.

Perhaps one of the most talked about topics regarding language and power in call centres is the application of pre-assigned scripts. Following up on earlier work (Cameron 2000) and collecting data from an onshore call centre in the UK, Cameron (2008) examines the power relation between institutions and their employees by demonstrating how highly regulated and standardized use of language imposed by their management restricts the ability of CSRs to perform their work effectively. She suggests that this imposition might do more harm than good in the name of efficiency.

However, other research has argued that working in call centres can empower CSRs in terms of language proficiency (Woydack and Rampton 2015). Although Woydack and Rampton's data was also obtained from an onshore UK call centre, English is mostly the second or foreign language of the CSRs. These CSRs were making and receiving calls in English in addition to their native tongue and other proficient languages in order to serve the European Union. By being involved in the conception, creation and revision of the operational scripts, these CSRs gain access, knowledge, and learning in relation to the use of English at their workplace. The researchers further reported that CSRs treat the script as a "workplace tool", where it can be applied, refashioned, and repersonalized skilfully. This suggests language policy in a call centre can be perceived as detrimental or beneficial depending on the context.

Power Display Through Naming and Professional Identity

At the micro level, a display of power can be seen to arise within interactions between callers and CSRs in the act of naming (Hood 2010) and through invoking professional identity (Hui 2014). Actual language use in call centre interactions can unpack the complexity of interpersonal relations between the two interlocutors. As Hood (2010) has shown in her study, names by which people choose to address each other can display the intricate relationship of power and status of the CSRs and their callers. In an offshore call centre in the Philippines, where CSRs are local Filipinos speaking English as their second or foreign language and serving NE speakers from the USA, the interactants assess each other's status, calibrate power, and build solidarity or distance, through their conscious choice of names as the exchanges unfold (Hood 2010). Exploring power and identity in call centre interactions, Hui (2014) examines the calls of an onshore call centre. One common form of power display is through the invocation of professional identity by stating job titles, work organizations and professional status. Invariably, these displays are influenced by institutional and cultural factors owing to the unique contexts in which the call centre is situated. Nevertheless, naming and invoking professional identity are resources for creating deference or solidarity, shifting strategically, and displaying status and power (Hood 2010; Hui 2014).

Intercultural Language Issues

Setting up an offshore call centre in a developing country where operation costs are relatively low (e.g., India and the Philippines) to serve a developed country (e.g., US/North America, UK) may make economic sense for a large corporation or organization. However, linguistic and cultural differences will inevitably create a host of language related issues, for instance, communication breakdown, training and assessment of CSRs.

Communication Breakdown

A breakdown in communication between a CSR and a customer may occur for a number of professional, linguistic, and cultural reasons. Forey and Lockwood (2007) analysed authentic data from a "service bureau" type call centre in the Philippines where the interactions occurred between NNE speaking CSRs, and NE speaking customers. Their study indicated that poor interactional and discourse skills contributed to communication breakdown.

The telephone interaction between NE and NNE speakers brings the cultural aspect to the forefront and adds a new dimension to the determining factors. This is particularly relevant in Tomalin's study (2010) based on his research of an offshore call centre in India doing contracted work for the outsourcing industry in the UK. He categorized the factors which may lead to a communication breakdown into two categories: "linguistic" and "culture and empathy". Under linguistic factors, accent, stress, vocabulary, pitch and intonation, speed and pacing, and Indianism (localized expressions) were further identified. Essentially, except for the case of Indianisms, these highlight the linguistic differences between the language systems of English and the Indian CSR's mother tongue. Under the heading of culture and empathy, the different concept of formal and informal, and application of empathy are the key areas that exacerbate the vast cultural gulf between the two nations.

Similarly, Lockwood, Forey, and Price (2008) examined data from an offshore call centre in the Philippines, analysing it at the following four levels: phonological aspects of call centre communication, language accuracy and range, discourse competence, and interactive and sociolinguistic competence. Their analysis shows that deviation of phonemic and prosodic features in Philippine English from "standard" varieties of English causes potential misunderstandings between CSRs and their callers. In contrast, minor grammatical errors do not seem to affect communication. At the discourse level, the offshore call centre CSRs in their dataset seemed to lack strategies for explaining product details unambiguously. The researchers suggested that this may be due to the different rhetorical structure of the CSRs' culture and mother tongue. Weak interactive and sociolinguistic competence is another factor to cause communication breakdown between the CSRs and the callers in their data. When the callers become irate and agitated in particular, the CSRs appear to be ineffective or reluctant to deal with confrontation. Silence or formulaic responses often occur in this kind of situation, and it was suggested that cultural and linguistic factors are at play here.

The role of silence was also seen in a study comparing the ways CSRs handle complaints in a Hong Kong trilingual call centre (Cantonese, English, and Mandarin). Lam and Yu (2013) reported that silence was employed when Cantonese native-speaker CSRs handle English-speaking highly emotionally charged customers, though not in their interactions with Cantonese speakers. They found that silence was not well received in that context, but did not elaborate further. The function of silence is often misunderstood in a cross-cultural and linguistic context. As Hui (2015) observed in his study of an essentially monolingual (English) call centre, silence can be used as a "power-exerting" tool to demand services as well as a rapport-building strategy where the CSR lets the customer vent their frustrations.

Training of CSRs

Training has been perceived as a way to help CSRs handle the various situations that the job demands. In an onshore environment where CSRs and callers mostly share a common mother tongue, communication skills appears to be the most appropriate area of training. However, the need for language proficiency (in English, in particular) and cultural awareness, in addition to communication skills, adds an extra burden to the training in native/non-native or offshore situations.

Early training programmes in the call centre industry put the emphasis on product and procedure training. The so-called "soft skills" side of CSR development was later included in order to help build effective relationships with customers and to promote the ability to listen actively, defuse confrontational situations, maintain positivity, deviate from pre-script at the appropriate moment, and solve problems that the customers deem to be equally if not more important (Crome 1998).

In the offshore outsourced context, call-takers are usually NNE speakers in developing countries serving NE callers mainly from the USA, UK, Australia, and New Zealand. As extra variables are introduced into the CSRs and customers' interface, domestic training programmes often fail when applied to NNE and NE environments (Lockwood, Forey, and Elias 2009). The communication skills, so valued as an indication of the CSR's professional competence, are now complicated by the further elements of a need for English proficiency and cultural knowledge of the target customer's country.

While there is a perception that adding English and cultural training to an existing programme will serve the purpose of preparing CSRs in these outsourced call centres, training in this context has its own unique demands. Conventional language-teaching programmes tend to put the emphasis on grammatical accuracy and language competence (Lockwood, Forey, and Elias 2009), but research has shown that minor grammatical inaccuracy does not seem to create misunderstanding in call exchanges (Lockwood, Forey, and Price 2008). Materials that asked students to imitate the target language accents do not always work (Cowie and Murty 2010), and the presentation of isolated cultural artefacts in cultural training lessons only pays lip service to the actual needs of the students (Tomalin 2010). The real problem is the lack of a pedagogical framework in these programmes (Elias 2010). Predictably, such courses do not serve the industry well and the trained CSRs are not as effective as expected.

Researchers in the applied linguistics field have been advocating specific English-training courses and assessment to address the workplace needs of outsourced call centres (Friginal 2013; Lockwood 2015). For instance, emphasis on enhanced listening skills (Lockwood 2013) and teaching an intelligible-sounding English catering for an international audience (Bolton 2013), including NNE-NNE interactions (Lockwood 2013), rather than presenting discrete cultural items in cross-cultural training courses, may serve the purpose better for future intercultural encounters.

An added consideration is that English proficiency is not necessarily the most important focus of training in the outsourced call centre environment. Rapport management has been highlighted as an important aspect of communication in such settings (Friginal 2007), since interacting with clients occupies a good portion of CSRs' daily activities. Unfortunately, the role of rapport management seems to have somewhat escaped management's attention. Instead, call centre management seems to adhere to the notion that language- and accent-training is key to improving the performance of CSRs, as demonstrated by the willingness of outourced call centre companies in India to send their prospective employees to "accent training" courses (Cowie 2007) in an attempt to mask the identity of their employees. Accent neutralisation for the purpose of "masking" (Pal and Buzzanell 2013), with the aim to deceive callers into thinking the call centre is a domestic one, is a controversial subject in India. The "manipulation" of workers' accents amounts to the "manipulation" of their identities as well.

Assessment of CSR Performance

Training has attracted a considerable amount of research interest. However, the same cannot be said of studies devoted to the assessment of CSR performance. Evaluating the oral performance of CSRs is not an easy task. Among a handful of papers, two very diverse approaches have been utilized.

First, adapting an existing framework, Friginal (2013) applied an instrument based on the Melbourne Medical Students' Diagnostic Speaking Scale. The rubric of the assessment is broadly divided into two categories: Task Criteria and Linguistic Criteria. Under task criteria, the performance is evaluated on Adequacy of Support and Interpersonal Skills. Under linguistic criteria, the performance is evaluated on Language and Production (Friginal 2013, 29–30). According to the researcher's pilot study, the instrument seems reliable and easy to apply. The emphasis on interpersonal communication skills is particularly useful in assessing the CSR's ability to engage and build rapport with the caller.

Second, separating assessment at the "recruitment" phase from the "working" phase, Lockwood (2015) has developed assessment tools and a set of procedures for appraising spoken performance in the offshore call centre context. A "weak" version is applied to the recruitment phase and a "strong" version to the working phase. The differences include an added item "Task Fulfilment/Business Solutioning" and the overall weighting proportion leans towards this added item in the "strong" version. The rater of the recruitment version is typically an experienced communication trainer and the "on-the-job" version is assessed by internal industry experts from the field. This evaluation framework has been described as an "end-to-end" solution for the workplace context (Lockwood 2015, 11).

As the offshore call centre industry expands, there is a need for a systemic instrument and process for oral assessment. The involvement of industry experts, as in Lockwood's study (2015), can enhance the validity of the tools and the feedback loops of these studies can certainly inform training programmes.

Methods in Call Centre Discourse Research

A host of research approaches have been employed in investigating call centre discourse. Corpus Linguistics has been favoured by some to provide an overall picture of the language used (e.g., Friginal 2008). Conversation Analysis is the natural choice for dealing with specific pragmatics used in calls (e.g., Reiter 2008). Critical Discourse Analysis has been employed to unpack language and power relations in the workplace (e.g., Cameron 2008). Systemic Functional Linguistics (SFL) has been successful in explaining the language choices of the interaction (e.g., Hood and Forey 2008). Some researchers have opted for a combination of qualitative and quantitative methods (e.g., Stacey *et al.* 2005) and some research has used an Interactional Sociolinguistics approach (e.g., Grieve and Seebus 2008) to improve reliability of their data interpretation.

No matter what approach has been adopted, it seems that contextual information can be an essential element in understanding the motivation behind certain linguistic realizations. The importance of contextual cues (Gumperz 2001) in call centre discourse can be demonstrated in the following example from my own research, which employed a mixed methods approach within an Interactional Sociolinguistics framework (see Hui 2014). In this example, there is information mismatch between the caller (Ca2) and the CSR (CS5). The caller thinks that she has filed a document online that is required to extend her affiliation with the organization. However, she receives a termination warning letter. She rings up because she wants to check why she has received a warning letter after having filed the required document properly. In the course of the call, it emerges that there is no record of the document in the system.

This interaction could be easily interpreted as indicating that there is a problem with the electronic filing system, a failure of memory by the caller, or incompetence on the part of the individual CSR in extracting the record. However, thanks to a period of observation in

> **Example** (from Hui 2014, 65–66)
>
> | Line | | |
> |---|---|---|
> | 1 | Ca2 | and I have filed online my account |
> | 2 | CS5 | and you've got through confirmation |
> | 3 | | that they were all filed [rising tone] |
> | 4 | Ca2 | I can't remember I mean it uploaded |
> | 5 | | and it told me it's done everything . . . |
> | 17 | Ca2 | yeah that's the same day I uploaded them |
> | 18 | CS5 | but we haven't received the account . . . |

the call centre, I gained a good understanding of the way the call centre operates in receiving calls and was aware of the common confusion with technical terms that occurs in this particular section of the organization, as well as of the responsibilities of individual CSRs. This offered a different interpretation. It is likely that there is a mismatch in the meaning making of the term "account" in this particular context. Three pieces of information gathered through various ethnographic methods support this interpretation. First, in this particular section of the organization, the word "account" refers to a "report"—not the usual interpretation as a "financial statement". This information comes from listening to over 100 calls and listening to expert CSRs in this particular section giving explanations to numerous confused callers. Second, CS5's usual responsibility is in another section of the call centre and this section is not her "assigned" area. This piece of information comes from the interview with the CSR. Third, the reason that she picked up the call is probably because of the call centre's undertaking to respond to callers within a certain number of rings. When one particular section's line is ringing, any unengaged CSR must pick up the call after three rings even if they are not familiar with that particular section's operation. This information comes from observation of the workplace and interviews with the CSRs, trainers, and managers. So, given that this CSR (CS5) operated outside her own area and encountered very easily confused terms, it is not hard to explain the confusion and misunderstanding. This example demonstrates that information gathered through ethnographic methods can help to reconstruct the contexts in multiple strands and provide vital clues in interpreting complex interactions (see Wilson this volume).

Future Directions

While there are a number of macro-level studies examining the relation of language used and power in onshore call centres, the focus has been mainly on the enactment of power from management in relation to employees, resulting in "styling" of talk by enforcing standard scripts. At the micro-level, the importance of attending to the relational aspect of call interactions has been highlighted in the implementation of training programmes and assessment of CSRs' performance, especially in offshore operations, and a lot more research could be done in this area to support training and assessment.

Looking ahead, more research needs to examine authentic call exchanges. Authentic call exchange data are hard to obtain due to confidentiality and company reputation issues and many studies have been based on observational data and offsite interviews. Many of the issues discussed above, however, deserve further study using authentic call exchanges. On the topic of generic call structure, more work on covering a wider range of call centres (e.g., telemarketing) is required to uncover the genre. In addition, research on the rapport management, construction of identity and its associated power as dynamically realized in call exchanges are certainly areas worth investigating. Not only can this enhance the development of English for Specific Purposes (ESP) materials for training purposes, it will also provide a clearer insight into professional discourse in the call centre context.

Further Reading

Archer and Jagodziński (2015) deconstruct the notion of (im)politeness in the context of call centre exchanges where agents are at the receiving end of verbal aggression. The concepts of institutional sanctioning and instrumentality have been applied in the discussion of call centre discourse.

Perhaps Friginal (2009) is the first comprehensive study of call centre language of an offshore operation. A corpus-based approach was adopted providing an overall linguistic landscape as well as particular language usage of the workplace.

Hultgren and Cameron (2010) examine power relations between callers and agents; in particular the form of question and response exchanges. Casting a critical lens over the call data, the researchers also raise the question of the influence of the interactions by the inflexible policies of the call centre regime.

Analysing authentic call exchanges related to the topic of offshoring, Kahlin and Tykesson (2016) examine identity negotiation of Moldovan agents working in an offshore call centre servicing Swedish speaking customer calling from Sweden. A mixed method of data collection was adopted and the interactional data was analysed through conversation analysis and membership categorization analysis.

Tracking the curriculum development of an ESP training and assessment project of an offshore call centre, Lockwood (2012) traced the needs analysis, the design of the syllabus and the evaluation of communication breakdown causes. It also explored training and assessment of offshore call centre agents.

Related Topics

Interactional sociolinguistics; Conversation analysis; (Im)politeness theory; Service encounters; Intercultural communication

References

Adolphs, Svenja, Brian Brown, Ronald Carter, Paul Crawford, and Opinder Sahota. 2004. "Applying Corpus Linguistics in a Health Care Context." *Journal of Applied Linguistics* 1: 9–28.
Archer, Dawn, and Piotr Jagodziński. 2015. "Call Centre Interaction: A Case of Sanctioned Face Attack?" *Journal of Pragmatics* 76: 46–66.
Belt, Vicki, Ranald Richardson, and Juliet Webster. 2002. "Women, Social Skill and Interactive Service Work in Telephone Call Centres." *New Technology, Work and Employment* 17: 20–34.
Bolton, Kingsley. 2013. "World Englishes and International Call Centres." *World Englishes* 32: 495–502.
Brown, Brian, and Paul Crawford. 2009. "Politeness Strategies in Question Formulation in a UK Telephone Advisory Service." *Journal of Politeness Research* 5: 73–91.
Cameron, Deborah. 2000. "Styling the Worker: Gender and the Commodification of Language in the Globalized Service Economy." *Journal of Sociolinguistics* 4: 323–347.
Cameron, Deborah. 2008. "Talk from the Top down." *Language & Communication* 28: 143–155.
Cowie, Claire. 2007. "The Accents of Outsourcing: The Meanings of "Neutral" in the Indian Call Centre Industry." *World Englishes* 26: 316–330.

Cowie, Claire, and Lalita Murty. 2010. "Researching and Understanding Accent Shifts in Indian Call Centre Agents." In *Globalization, Communication and the Workplace: Talking across the World*, edited by Gail Forey, and Jane Lockwood, 125–144. London: Continuum.

Crome, Matthew. 1998. "Call Centres: Battery Farming or Free Range?" *Industrial and Commercial Training* 30: 137–141.

Elias, Neil. 2010. "Reconceptualizing Culture for Workplace Communication." In *Globalization, Communication and the Workplace: Talking across the World*, edited by Gail Forey, and Jane Lockwood, 159–171. London: Continuum.

Forey, Gail, and Jane Lockwood. 2007. "'I'd Love to Put Someone in Jail for This': An Initial Investigation of English in the Business Processing Outsourcing (BPO) Industry." *English for Specific Purposes* 26: 308–326.

Friginal, Eric. 2007. "Outsourced Call Centers and English in the Philippines." *World Englishes* 26: 331–345.

Friginal, Eric. 2008. "Linguistic Variation in the Discourse of Outsourced Call Centers." *Discourse Studies* 10: 715–736.

Friginal, Eric. 2009. *The Language of Outsourced Call Centers: A Corpus-Based Study of Cross-Cultural Interaction*. Amsterdam: John Benjamins.

Friginal, Eric. 2013. "Evaluation of Oral Performance in Outsourced Call Centres: An Exploratory Case Study." *English for Specific Purposes* 32: 25–35.

Goodman, Sharon, and David Graddol. 2001. *Redesigning English: New Texts, New Identities*. London: Routledge.

Grieve, Averil, and Ingrid Seebus. 2008. "G'day or Guten Tag?: A Cross-Cultural Study of Australian and German Telephone Openings." *Journal of Pragmatics* 40: 1323–1343.

Gumperz, John. 2001. "Interactional Sociolinguistics: A Personal Perspective." In *The Handbook of Discourse Analysis*, edited by Deborah Schiffrin, Deborah Tannen, and Heidi Hamilton, 215–228. Oxford: Blackwell.

Gunnarsson, Britt-Louise. 2013. "Multilingualism in the Workplace." *Annual Review of Applied Linguistics* 33: 162–189.

Heller, Monica. 2010. "The Commodification of Language." *Annual Review of Anthropology* 39: 101–114.

Hood, Susan. 2010. "Naming and Negotiating Relationships in Call Centre Talk." In *Globalization, Communication and the Workplace: Talking across the World*, edited by Gail Forey, and Jane Lockwood, 88–105. London: Continuum.

Hood, Susan, and Gail Forey. 2008. "The Interpersonal Dynamics of Call-Centre Interactions: Co-Constructing the Rise and Fall of Emotion." *Discourse & Communication* 2: 389–409.

Houtkoop, Hanneke, Frank Jansen, and Anja Walstock. 2005. "Collaborative Problem Description in Help Desk Calls." In *Calling for Help: Language and Social Interaction in Telephone Helplines*, edited by Carolyn D. Baker, Michael Emmison, and Alan Firth, 63–90. Amsterdam: John Benjamins.

Hui, Jon S. Y. 2014. "Analysing Interpersonal Relations in Call-Centre Discourse." PhD diss., Victoria University of Wellington.

Hui, Jon S. Y. 2015. "When Not Talking Is Talking: The Function of Silence." In *Proceedings of the 17th Conference of the Pragmatics Society of Japan* 10: 191–197. Kyoto: Pragmatic Society of Japan.

Hultgren, Anna Kristina. 2011. "'Building Rapport' with Customers across the World: The Global Diffusion of a Call Centre Speech style." *Journal of Sociolinguistics* 15: 36–64.

Hultgren, Anna Kristina, and Deborah Cameron. 2010. "'How May I Help You?' Questions, Control, and Customer Care in Telephone Call Center Talk." In *"Why Do You Ask?" The Function of Questions in Institutional Discourse*, edited by Alice Freed, and Susan Ehrlich, 322–342. Oxford: Oxford University Press.

Kaur, Jagdish. 2010. "Achieving Mutual Understanding in World Englishes." *World Englishes* 29: 192–208.

Kahlin, Linda, and Ingela Tykesson. 2016. "Identity Attribution and Resistance among Swedish-Speaking Call Centre Workers in Moldova." *Discourse Studies* 18: 87–105.

Kraan, Wilbert. 2005. "The Metaphoric Use of Space in Expert-Lay Interaction about Computing Systems." In *Calling for Help: Language and Social Interaction in Telephone Helplines*, edited by Carolyn D. Baker, Michael Emmison, and Alan Firth, 91–108. Amsterdam: John Benjamins.

Lam, Marvin, and Carol Yu. 2013. "English and Cantonese in a Bilingual Call Centre in Hong Kong." *World Englishes* 32: 521–535.

Lockwood, Jane. 2012. "Developing an English for Specific Purpose Curriculum for Asian Call Centres: How Theory Can Inform Practice." *English for Specific Purposes* 31: 14–24.

Lockwood, Jane. 2013. "International Communication in a Technology Services Call Centre in India." *World Englishes* 32: 536–550.

Lockwood, Jane. 2015. "Language for Specific Purpose (LSP) Performance Assessment in Asian Call Centres: Strong and Weak Definitions." *Language Testing in Asia* 5. https://languagetestingasia.springeropen.com/articles/10.1186/s40468–014–0009-6.

Lockwood, Jane, Gail Forey, and Neil Elias. 2009. "Call Center Communication: Measurement Processes in Non-English Speaking Contexts." In *English for Specific Purposes in Theory and Practice*, edited by Diane Belcher, 143–164. Ann Arbor, MI: University of Michigan Press.

Lockwood, Jane, Gail Forey, and Helen Price. 2008. "English in Philippine Call Centers and BPO Operations: Issues, Opportunities and Research." In *Philippine English: Linguistic and Literary Perspectives*, edited by Maria Lourdes S. Bautista, and Kingsley Bolton, 219–241. Hong Kong: Hong Kong University Press.

Pal, Mahuya, and Patrice M. Buzzanell. 2013. "Breaking the Myth of Indian Call Centers: A Postcolonial Analysis of Resistance." *Communication Monographs* 80: 199–219.

Reiter, Rosina Márquez. 2008. "Intra-Cultural Variation: Explanations in Service Calls to Two Montevidean Service Providers." *Journal of Politeness Research* 4: 1–30.

Roberts, Celia. 2010. "Language Socialization in the Workplace." *Annual Review of Applied Linguistics* 30: 211–227.

Sawyerr, Olukemi O., Shanthi Srinivas, and Sijun Wang. 2009. "Call Center Employee Personality Factors and Service Performance." *Journal of Services Marketing* 23: 301–317.

Schegloff, Emanuel A. 1988. "Presequences and Indirection: Applying Speech Act Theory to Ordinary Conversation." *Journal of Pragmatics* 12: 55–62.

Stacey, Dawn, Ian D. Graham, Annette M. O'Connor, and Marie-Pascale Pomey. 2005. "Barriers and Facilitators Influencing Call Center Nurses' Decision Support for Callers Facing Values-Sensitive Decisions: A Mixed Methods Study." *Worldviews on Evidence-Based Nursing* 2: 184–195.

Tomalin, Barry. 2010. "India Rising: The Need for Two Way Training." In *Globalization, Communication and the Workplace: Talking across the World*, edited by Gail Forey, and Jane Lockwood, 172–189. London: Continuum.

Woydack, Johanna, and Ben Rampton. 2015. "Text Trajectories in a Multilingual Call Centre: The Linguistic Ethnography of a Calling Script." *Tilburg Papers in Culture Studies* 124.

Xu, Xunfeng, Yan Wang, Gail Forey, and Lan Li. 2010. "Analyzing the Genre Structure of Chinese Call-Center Communication." *Journal of Business and Technical Communication* 24: 445–475.

16
Genetic Counselling
Olga Zayts

Introduction

This chapter focuses on one specific workplace setting in a medical context, namely genetic counselling. This context presents an important and flourishing area of investigation for scholars working on language and communication in the workplace for several reasons.

First, genetic counselling activity is predominantly communication-based. It typically accompanies genetic testing,[1] and may be provided before or after the test. While genetic counselling is typically conducted in a clinical setting, it is distinctively different from other medical encounters as it is aimed at providing information and support rather than medical treatment (Clarke, Parsons, and Williams 1996). A counselling encounter normally involves genetic professionals (e.g., genetic counsellors, geneticists or genetic nurses) and clients[2] who discuss diagnostic and clinical aspects of a genetic condition, family and pedigree information, inheritance patterns, the clients' risks, and available options of genetic testing. Professionals also provide psychosocial support to clients and the family, and facilitate clients' decision-making regarding genetic tests, management of a genetic condition and disclosure of information about one's genetic status to family and others (Clarke 1997; Harper 2010).

Second, while genetic counselling has previously mainly concerned clients at risk of or diagnosed with a genetic condition, it is becoming increasingly applicable to a broader group of the general population. With many recent scientific advances in genetics and genomic medicine, more people are already making (or will be making) decisions about their health and well-being that (will) involve at least some genetic considerations (Ashida *et al.* 2011). Convincing emerging evidence links even the most common health conditions (e.g., obesity, diabetes, heart conditions) with our genetic make-up. The need for genetic counselling and communication of genetic information, therefore, is spreading to healthcare specialties beyond genetics and genomic medicine, subsequently presenting more opportunities for research.

Third, with the scientific advances, the general population is increasingly exposed to genetic information through a range of medical (e.g., medical consultation) and non-medical (e.g., popular fiction, media) sources, and the quality of that information varies considerably. For example, the direct-to-consumer genetic testing (or DCT) that involves marketing and distributing genetic tests directly to consumers foregoing specialist medical consultation is getting more attention with even the US Food and Drug Administration (FDA) authorizing this type of genetic testing.[3] While some DCT companies offer counselling to their clients to explain the test results and address clients' questions, this service is not always available or explicitly recommended. In this context, however, counselling becomes particularly important as understanding of genetic information and potential implications of genetic knowledge for one's personal health impacts whether and how this information is used. Counselling also ensures that health-related decisions that individuals make and that involve considerations of genetics are *informed* decisions, i.e., that they are based on good quality reliable information, and are not coerced by successful marketing strategies. Moreover, more complex tests enabled by modern technologies may also produce incidental (i.e., unexpected, additional) or uncertain test results that may need interpretation by a professional. Communication once again plays a crucial role in this process of understanding genetic information.

In sum, there are many compelling reasons why genetic counselling as a workplace context presents an important area of investigation for language and communication scholars. There are also several specific contexts for investigation, namely genetic counselling clinics, other medical settings (e.g., in primary or secondary health care), and DCT testing. This chapter first outlines existing research on communication in medical and genetic counselling contexts and highlights some gaps in that research and introduces some critical issues. Focusing on non-English dominant contexts, two examples of prenatal screening consultations for Down syndrome in Hong Kong are then presented. These analyses focus on decision-making and the impact of participants' diverse sociocultural and linguistic backgrounds on how decisions are made. The chapter concludes with some recommendations for professional practice and suggested directions for future research.

Communication Studies in Medical and Genetic Counselling Contexts

While there is a rich research tradition on communication in healthcare in medical, sociological, educational and anthropological literature, much of that research has focused on the "outcomes" of medical encounters (such as patients' satisfaction with provided services, or patients' adherence to medical recommendations). Language- and discourse-oriented studies, in contrast, have foregrounded the actual communication "processes" and how various outcomes of medical encounters are negotiated and achieved in the "on-going talk-in-interaction".

In genetic counselling, language- and discourse-oriented studies have mainly been qualitative in nature, although there are also studies that have utilized quantitative and mixed methods (for a systematic review see Paul *et al*. 2015). A common quantitative method is the Roter Interaction Analysis System (RIAS) where talk is categorized using a pre-determined set of codes. Studies that have used qualitative methods (such as discourse analysis, conversation analysis, interactional sociolinguistics and linguistic ethnography) have shown that communication processes in genetic counselling are complex and nuanced, and coding these processes does not capture the interactional dynamics of genetic counselling encounters in full detail. A mixed methods approach allows combining micro-level analyses of selected sets of interactions, and macro-level analysis of larger datasets, thus making the findings potentially more generalizable.

In terms of the specific contexts of investigation, the majority of studies on genetic counselling have been conducted in genetic counselling clinics. These studies have examined a wide range of genetic conditions (e.g., various types of cancer; Huntington's disease). Other contexts of genetic counselling (e.g., non-genetic healthcare sites, DCT) have not yet received much attention. The bulk of earlier studies has been carried out in English-dominant contexts, such as the USA (e.g., Benkendorf *et al*. 2001) and the UK (e.g., Pilnick 2002; Clarke, Sarangi, and Verrier-Jones 2011) although more recently published research has expanded the focus to other, non-English dominant contexts, for example, Northern Europe (e.g., Thomassen, Sarangi, and Skolbekken 2015) and Hong Kong (e.g., Zayts and Schnurr 2014; Zayts and Pilnick 2014; Zayts and Sarangi 2013; Zayts et al. 2013) and emphasized the importance of investigating intercultural communication in genetic counselling.

Studies in English-dominant contexts have contributed to our understanding of genetic counselling activity from structural, interactional, and thematic viewpoints. They have emphasized three crucial activities of genetic counselling: information-giving, advice management, and decision-making. In these studies genetic counselling has been described as a "hybrid" activity that resembles mainstream medical encounters and other counselling/therapy settings (e.g., psychotherapy, HIV/AIDS counselling, social work encounters, and family mediation) (Sarangi 2000). From the interactional viewpoint, the following interactional features have been highlighted as characteristic of genetic counselling: process- (or interaction-) orientation being more significant than outcome- (or topic-) orientation; professionals' withholding direct advice to clients; professionals' use of reflective and hypothetical questions to elicit the clients' perspectives on past, present and future scenarios, etc. (Sarangi 2013). Among the main themes addressed in these studies are risk communication and uncertainty, (non)directiveness/professional neutrality, client autonomy, information-giving and advice-giving, and client reassurance (e.g., Arribas-Ayllon, Sarangi, and Clarke 2008a, 2008b, 2009; Sarangi 2002).

Building and expanding on research in English-dominant contexts, studies in other contexts have begun to highlight that the specific nature of genetic counselling communication may differ considerably across different cultural settings (e.g., Zayts et al. 2013). These differences range from what is understood by genetic counselling in different parts of the world to stark communicative differences. Research in intercultural and non-English dominant contexts has, therefore, focused on describing these communicative differences at the micro-level of an interaction, linking the analyses to broader social and cultural contexts. For example, studies in Hong Kong have shown that the introduction of aspects of clients' different sociocultural backgrounds into consultations (by both professionals and clients) has strong implications for decision-making, particularly whether decisions by clients are accepted or contested by professionals. When clients' decisions are contested by professionals, this compromises the nondirective nature of genetic counselling (e.g., Pilnick and Zayts 2012; Zayts and Pilnick 2014). Another example is when professionals assume the relevance of clients' sociocultural backgrounds and tailor the information delivery to these clients accordingly, at times at the expense of the quality or the quantity of provided information. These and other issues of communication in genetic counselling in intercultural and non-English dominant contexts require more systematic and in-depth research.

Decision-Making in Genetic Counselling and Prenatal Screening

As noted above, decision-making is one of three crucial activities of genetic counselling identified in previous research. In genetic counselling, decision-making involves several interrelated and complementary, or at times competing, processes. First, the clients need to consider medical aspects of testing, such as specific types of test(s), family medical history, etc. For example, in prenatal screening for Down syndrome in Hong Kong in a public sector, women are offered the options of screening tests (such as nuchal translucency and maternal blood tests) or diagnostic tests (CVS or amniocentesis), or they can opt out of testing. Screening tests present a safer option, because diagnostic testing carries a small risk of miscarriage (0.5 to 1 per cent). Diagnostic testing, however, has a higher detection rate. Moreover, screening can only give a probabilistic rather than a definitive or diagnostic result.

Second, genetic testing raises profound social, moral, and ethical issues. In prenatal screening, for example, the discussion of pregnancy termination or having a child with Down syndrome is part of these consultations and the decision-making process, because termination is generally the only available medical "intervention" if fetal anomalies are confirmed (Pilnick and Zayts 2012).

Third, medical professionals must balance their professional expert knowledge and women's autonomy in decision-making. Traditionally, genetic counselling has been governed by the principle of nondirectiveness, which stipulates that professionals should withhold direct advice to clients and present information in a value-free, neutral manner (Kessler 1997). The principle, however, has been the crux of much debate among both professional and academic communities, who question its ideological background and practical application (for a detailed discussion see Zayts, Wake, and Schnurr 2012; Zayts and Schnurr 2012). Among the common criticisms are a conflict between upholding nondirectiveness and ensuring the best possible support to clients, as well as potential lack of responsiveness and empathy to clients' needs. Communication studies have shown that attempts to be nondirective by professionals may actually achieve undesirable outcomes, such as worsened client understanding of provided information. For example, clients may find it difficult to differentiate between general information and specific references to themselves when professionals use such generic nouns as "some people" or "most people" (see Zayts and Pilnick 2014).

Next, decision-making in prenatal screening is further complicated by the fact that arguably it concerns the family to a greater extent than in other genetic counselling contexts. While a woman as a child-bearer may be seen as the primary decision-maker (that is a woman primarily makes a decision for *herself*), that decision also has direct implications for *others* (immediate and distant family members, husband/partner, existing and future children). Women are also typically accompanied to these consultations by husbands/partners/other family members who participate in decision-making. Previous research in counselling contexts suggests that the presence of a third party impacts communication. For example, Ellington *et al.* (2005, 381) in a quantitative study (using RIAS) of communication in counselling for BRCA1 gene note that communication between professionals and companions "largely parallels" communication with a client and mostly consists of medical or psychosocial statements. The companions use fewer "receptive statements", because communication is primarily directed at clients, and they tend to ask more questions than clients. In another quantitative study (also using RIAS), Aalfs *et al.* (2006) observe a positive impact of a companion on clients' psychosocial state: the clients feel fewer negative emotions like anger or irritation. Aalfs *et al.* also note a general paucity of studies on the impact of companions on clinical interactions.

In the context of prenatal screening, Wake (2006) (drawing on Goffman 1974) identifies four types of husbands'/partners' involvement in different types of activities: (1) ratified by-standing; (2) indirect participation; (3) co-participation; and (4) leading participation. The author maintains that in this context a husband/partner is a "secondary patient" and a "co-decision-maker". Ratified by-standing refers to when a husband/partner, who is a ratified participant, refrains from participation in the actual prenatal screening activities, for example, during history-taking phase of the consultations that are typically dyadic interactions between professionals and pregnant women. Indirect participation refers to when a husband/partner discusses questions asked by a professional with the woman (and not directly with a professional), or responds to questions that the woman addresses to him directly. Co-participation refers to mutual engagement by a pregnant woman and her husband/partner into a counselling process. When a husband/partner plays a leading role in the counselling process, he communicates with a professional directly. In her study, Wake makes a strong assertion that a husband's/partner's presence and the mode of participation in counselling has a direct impact on counselling results, including the decisions that are made.

In examples of prenatal screening consultations analysed in this chapter the husbands/partners are ratified participants. They are explicitly invited to participate in the consultations, for example, when a medical professional invites them to sign various forms alongside pregnant women. Of particular interest in this chapter is the level of husbands'/partners' engagement in the decision-making process, and more specifically, whether and why they take the stance of by-standing, indirect participation, co-participation, or leading participation.

In intercultural contexts decision-making may yet be further complicated by the fact that participants may not share a native language and, therefore, they may use a lingua franca. In these cases collaborative decision-making involving a husband/partner and a woman may take on a form of interpreting, whereby a more proficient companion interprets for the other party, less proficient in a language. Another aspect of decision-making is participants' different cultural backgrounds (Zayts and Schnurr 2014).

Figure 16.1 summarizes the multiple dimensions of decision-making in genetic counselling and prenatal screening contexts.

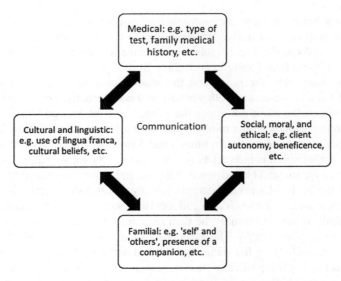

Figure 16.1 Multiple dimensions of decision-making in genetic counselling and prenatal screening contexts

Family Decision-Making Regarding Testing: Cases from Prenatal Screening Consultations in Hong Kong

In this section, examples are presented from a large scale communication study of prenatal screening for Down syndrome in Hong Kong that was conducted in 2006–2011.[4] The study involved collaboration between linguistic and communication scholars at the University of Hong Kong and Prenatal Diagnostics and Counselling Departments of a public hospital.

It drew on qualitative research methods of discourse analysis, conversation analysis, interactional sociolinguistics, and ethnographic methods (such as participant observation and interviews with participants prior to and after the consultations; consulting a range of organizational documents that regulate the provision of prenatal screening services). The analyses presented here use conversation analysis (ten Have 2007) that is concerned with "*the interactional accomplishment of particular social activities*" (Drew and Heritage 1992, 17; original emphasis). These activities are analysed with regards to their context, social organization, and alternative means of accomplishment (ibid.). The prenatal consultations were video recorded and transcribed using Jeffersonian transcription conventions traditionally used in conversation analytic research (see Zayts and Schnurr 2012 and Pilnick and Zayts 2014 for more details of the project).

The complexity of interactional analysis of decision-making lies in the fact that decision-making is not easily defined and identifiable in the data: as Atkinson (1995, 58) writes, it is "dispersed" in both time and space, or fragmented in the data. For example, in prenatal screening clients may make a decision prior to seeing a medical professional, or change their decision in the course of the consultation after receiving information from a medical professional. A decision may be clearly marked in the data with a direct degree of lexicalization (e.g., "we have discussed it and decided that . . ."), or it may be more implicit. Moreover, not every decision-making sequence leads to a decision being made; the decision may be deferred or not made at all.

The examples below present decision-making sequences that occur after the medical professional (in both cases, a nurse, N) has delivered all information about available tests, their benefits and risks to the clients (abbreviated in the transcripts as W—pregnant woman; H—husband). The couple in Example 16.1 come from Japan.

In this interaction, both the nurse and the woman construct the husband as a ratified participant and co-decision-maker both verbally and non-verbally. For example, in turn 1 in eliciting the decision the nurse addresses the woman and the husband and looks at both of them. The woman responds with a minimal acknowledgement ("Mm:", turn 2) and does not announce the decision immediately. In turns 3 and 5 the husband code-switches to Japanese. The husband's participation is indirect as he engages with the nurse's question by discussing it with his wife in Japanese. The code-switching, the indirect participation in the interaction, are displays of the husband's insufficient proficiency in English. In discussing the decision with his wife, the husband frames it as a collaborative activity by using a collective pronoun "we" ("What shall we do?" in turn 3); he then re-frames it as the woman's decision ("What do (you) want to do?" in turn 5). The woman looks at her husband while he is asking the questions thus acknowledging his status as a ratified participant. It appears that the woman has a higher level of English proficiency as she responds to the nurse's question with a choice of one of the screening options, namely a blood test (turn 6). In announcing the decision, the woman includes her husband as a co-decision-maker ("we just take the blood"), and although in line 8 she switches to the first person pronoun ("I don't do ultrasound"), this statement is an expansion of the collective decision that the woman has announced earlier in turn 6 and it deals with a procedural aspect of testing (doing the blood test that does not include taking the ultrasound as well).

From turn 9 onwards the husband continues to talk to his wife in Japanese. He asks her about a particular type of blood test that his wife prefers to take. The woman's hesitation in turn 10 is followed by the nurse's question in English whether the woman prefers a blood test that will be performed later, or a blood test that will be performed on the day of the consultation. Interestingly, before responding to the nurse's question, the woman code-

Genetic Counselling

Example 16.1

1	N:	So, what's your choice? ((looks at W first and then H))
2	W:	Mm:
3	H:	どうしようか？
		dou shiyou ka?
		What shall we do?
4	W:	((looks at H))
5	H:	どうしたい？
		dou shi tai?
		What do (you) want to do?
6	W:	We just take the blood.
7	N:	Blood test.
8	W:	I don't do ultrasound.
9	H:	((inaudible, speaks Japanese)) Test C?
10	W:	え
		e
		er
11	N:	You want to have this one .h er later? Or this one, blood test today?
12	W:	これでいいよ。
		korede ii yo
		This is good
		だって、ドクターでも(とこがねる)の。
		datte, doctor demo (toko ga neru no)
		because (we can also do that with) the doctor
13	H:	あ、そう？
		a, sou?
		Oh, really?
14	W:	Actually we went to the- we go to the private [doctor as well]. And then he re-check that- so maybe this one ((pointing to the test description in front of the nurse))
15	N:	[OK. Alright.]
16	H:	OK.

switches to Japanese and responds to her husband first, confirming what test she would prefer (a test taken on the day), and also informing her husband that they could do the other test with their private doctor. In turn 14 the woman responds to the nurse, confirming the type of test, and informing the nurse that they also see a private doctor who would "re-check" the results of the test. Once again, the woman uses a collective pronoun *we* ("we went to the- we go to the private doctor as well"), thus constructing the husband not only as a co-decision-maker but also as a co-participant of prenatal care more generally.

Of particular interest to us is the code-switching strategy, or more specifically the specific point in the interaction where the code-switching occurs—immediately after the nurse's question that elicits the couple's decision. Auer and Eastman (2010, 100) observe that code-switching is "strongly linked to face-work". The switch to Japanese, the language that the nurse does not speak, is a face-threatening and disaffiliate action that also threatens "the established language of interaction", English (Auer and Eastman 2010, 100). It renders the nurse a non-participant of that part of the interaction. In relation to the husband, however, the code-switching is an affiliative action that accommodates to the husband's insufficient competence in English ("competence-related code-switching"; Auer and Eastman 2010, 100) and allows him to fully participate in the decision-making. The woman alternates between the two codes to communicate in English with the nurse and in Japanese with her husband. In the analysed context the code-switching acquires an additional communicative meaning. In particular, by excluding the nurse from the interaction, it ensures that the decision that the couple are making is autonomous. Code-switching thus contributes to nondirectiveness of the decision-making process.

The couple in Example 16.2 are French. Example 16.2 starts with the nurse eliciting the couple's decision. The woman announces the decision to take the screening test followed up by amniocentesis. The woman frames the decision as collaborative by using a collective pronoun "we" (turns 2, 4, and 6). Rather than accepting this decision, the nurse responds with a minimal token ("Hmmm", turn 7) that signals her resistance to the couple's decision. She then provides further information regarding the couple's decision. Her response is indirect (that may be an attempt to adhere to non-directiveness), as she uses hypothetical framing, "if the screening test is normal . . ." and generalization, "usually". The nurse's response, however, is not neutral: the use of the "it + (to be) + adjective+ infinitive clause" structure ("it is not worthwhile to go for further test"), is typically used to express one's opinion or advice, and it foregrounds the information about being "not worthwhile". The adjective "worthwhile" carries a strong evaluative meaning as well. Thus the use of indirect language does not preclude the nurse from being directive (see also Zayts and Pilnick 2014). In turns 11 and 13, following the woman's clarification question, the nurse reiterates the information, this time personalizing a test result to the woman's circumstances, "if the report is normal . . . you risk of having Down syndrome's baby is small . . .". The personalization strategy is typically used in these consultations to render the information more understandable to a client.

In the first part of this example the woman displays some difficulty in reproducing and understanding the information that the nurse is providing (e.g., in turn 4 she tries to pronounce "amniocentesis"; and in turn 10 she acknowledges that she has not understood what the nurse said). These difficulties may, however, not be due to the woman's improficiency in English; the complex medical issues that the participants are discussing and the medical jargon may contribute to misunderstanding as well. From turn 19 onwards the woman code-switches to French. Similar to Example 16.1, the code-switch excludes the nurse from the interaction and allows the couple to discuss their decision autonomously. The woman first clarifies with the husband what the nurse said (turns 19 and 20). Interestingly, in turn 21 the woman's utterance "it looks like she is questioning that what we do is up to us" highlights the issue of autonomous decision-making, and that in this case the woman's code-switch may indeed be not so much the case of competence-related switch but a deliberate and strategic attempt on the part of the woman to exclude the nurse from decision-making. In turn 23 the woman code-switches back to English and asks the nurse about doing the amniocentesis again. Following the nurse's suggestion about doing the amniocentesis without a prior screening test, the woman again clarifies with the husband in French what the nurse means. The husband then confirms with the nurse that the couple cannot do both tests (turns 27 and 28). The consultation concludes with the couple agreeing to take the screening test and discuss amniocentesis after the test results become available (not shown in Example 16.2).

Example 16.2

1	N:	So, what do you think?
2	W:	What we would like to do is to do the screening first,
3	N:	Yes.
4	W:	And, also the ani-amnio[centesis]
5	N:	[Amnio]centesis.
6	W:	Mm:, even if the risk is low, because we would like to be sure.
7	N:	Hmmm. In that case, usually if the screening test is normal, then it is not worthwhile to go for further test.
8	W:	It is not what?
9	N:	Worthwhile. Because mm:: [with the report],=
10	W:	[Sorry, sorry] I didn't understand.
11	N:	=If the report is normal,
12	W:	Yes,
13	N:	It suggests that your risk of having Down syndrome's baby is small. So::, mm:, usually it is not indicated for further invasive testing.
14	W:	OK, but what if we want?

((4 turns are omitted))

19	W:	Elle est en train de dire que ce ne serait peut-être pas grave, ce n'est pas important tout ça . . . ((Inaudible))? ((talking to H))
		Is she saying that ((inaudible))? ((talking H))
20	H:	Non elle est en train de dire que les risques . . .
		No, she is saying that ((inaudible)) the risks.
21	W:	Oui oui d'accord mais elle n'a pas répondu à ma question qu'est-ce qu'on fait si nous on veut. C'est ça.
		Yes, yes, alright but it looks like she is questioning that what we do is up to us. That is so.
22	H:	Qui.
		Yes.
23	W:	OK. And eh: what about if we want to do amniocentesis eh even if there is some risk? ((talking to N))
24	N:	So maybe we can have the amniocentesis directly without the screening test because the::
25	W:	T'as compris est-ce qu'elle a dit ((inaudible))? ((talking to H))
		Did you understand, is she saying ((inaudible))? ((talking to H))
26	H:	Oui elle te dit de passer directement à l'amniosynthèse sans passer par ((inaudible)) ((talking to W))
		Yes, she is telling you to directly have amniocentesis without having the screening test ((talking to W))
27	H:	We cannot do both? ((talking to N))
28	N:	Em: we usually arrange one. Because ninety-five of the women will have normal reports.

Examples 16.1 and 16.2 demonstrate the complexity of the decision-making process. Both examples present triadic interactions that include a nurse, a pregnant woman and her husband. The women actively orient to "self" and "other" (i.e., the husbands) in the decision-making. The husbands are ratified participants and co-decision makers, and the specific type of husband's participation appears to depend on the participants' language proficiency. More specifically, the husbands participate indirectly when their proficiency in English is not sufficient (as in Example 16.1); and both indirectly (allowing the woman to be a primary decision-maker) and directly when their language proficiency is adequate. In both examples the women act as primary decision-makers; this observation is in line with the previous studies on prenatal screening for Down syndrome in other countries (e.g., Wake 2006). In Example 16.2, the decision-making is exacerbated by the complexity of medical information and medical jargon. To address this, the clients employ a number of strategies, such as clarification questions and code-switching.

Code-switching in both examples allows for a proficient speaker to accommodate to a less proficient interlocutor (Sussex 2012). In Example 16.1, code-switching is instigated by the husband, and it allows him to extend his communicative competence to be included in the decision-making. In this case, code-switching is mainly competence-related, whereas in Example 16.2 it appears more deliberate and strategic as it allows the woman who instigates the code-switching to exclude the nurse from the decision-making. This discursive "exclusion", unlike in other social contexts where it is typically analysed as the strategy of social segregation, inequality, and even oppression, performs a positive function in prenatal screening. More specifically, it allows the couples to avoid any imposition by the nurse in the decision-making. The code-switching thus facilitates an autonomous decision by the couples.

Conclusion

This chapter has examined one specific workplace context of genetic counselling. It has highlighted that intercultural and non-English dominant healthcare contexts more generally, and the genetic counselling context in particular, present a rich area for further studies of language and communication in the workplace. As an example of research in non-English dominant contexts the chapter examined prenatal screening in Hong Kong, focusing on the decision-making activity. It has shown that in analysing intercultural encounters researchers need to avoid the temptation of narrowing down their analyses to cultural and linguistic aspects. While a non-native language proficiency may indeed be important, as the participants utilize a range of communicative strategies to accommodate speakers with a lower language proficiency other contextual factors may also play a role in how these interactions unfold.

Language- and discourse-oriented research in non-English dominant contexts has strong implications for professional practice. For example, this chapter provides empirical grounds for the discussion of a concept of "multicultural competence" that has been prominent in genetic counselling and medical sociological and educational literature in recent years (see Zayts and Pilnick 2014). In particular, it shows that when participants come from different sociocultural and linguistic backgrounds they do not necessarily miscommunicate. In other words, culture and language may not impact communication unless participants themselves actively orient to their cultural and linguistic differences. In that sense, Examples 16.1 and 16.2 may be considered prototypical examples of "when language and culture" do matter, as the participants actively orient to their non-native status through code-switching. However, as discussed in this chapter, professionals also need to be aware of other contextual factors (e.g., complex medical jargon; the presence of a companion) that also have an impact on interaction. The situated analyses of the participants' interactional behaviour has much to contribute to professional training and the development of critical analytic and reflective skills among professionals.

Further Reading

Sarangi (1994) discusses the main strands of intercultural communication research, while Sarangi (2000) describes the main features of genetic counselling activity in English-dominant contexts. Zayts and Pilnick (2014) discuss genetic counselling in the multilingual and multicultural context of Hong Kong, focusing on clients' language proficiency and its impact on professionals' involvement in decision-making.

Related Topics

Interactional sociolinguistics; Conversation analysis; Linguistic ethnography; Intercultural communication; Multilingualism

Notes

1. Genetic tests may cover general population screening (e.g., screening of newborns for certain genetic conditions), prenatal screening of pregnant women (e.g., Down syndrome screening) or a test for a genetic condition that may occur within an individual's lifespan (in childhood, adolescence or adult life).
2. While in general literature on health communication the term "patients" is commonly used, in genetic counselling contexts the term 'clients' is preferred to refer to people at risk of or diagnosed with a genetic disorder.
3. In 2015 the FDA authorized the use of some of genetic tests offered by the US-based DCT company 23andMe.
4. The research reported here was fully supported by a grant from the Hong Kong Research Grants Council of the Hong Kong Special Administrative Region, China (project no. HKU 754609 H). Thanks are due to all participants of and to the medical colleagues on the project, in particular to Ms. Vivian Chan, Dr. H. Y. M. Tang, and Dr. C. P. Lee, Dr. Anita S. Y. Kan. I would also like to thank Ms. Hyacintha Olaitan Faustino and Dr. Janet Lorraine Borland for proofreading the examples included in this chapter.

References

Aalfs, Cora M., Frans J. Oort, Hanneke C. J. M. de Haes, Nico J. Leschot, and Ellen M. A. Smets. 2006. "Counselor–Counselee Interaction in Reproductive Genetic Counseling: Does a Pregnancy in Counselee Make a Difference?" *Patient Education and Counseling* 60: 80–90.

Arribas-Ayllon, Michael, Srikant Sarangi, and Angus Clarke. 2008a. "Managing Self-Responsibility through Other-Oriented Blame: Family Accounts of Genetic Testing." *Social Science and Medicine* 66: 1521–1532.

Arribas-Ayllon, Michael, Srikant Sarangi, and Angus Clarke. 2008b. "The Micropolitics of Responsibility vis-à-vis Autonomy: Parental Accounts of Childhood Genetic Testing and (Non)disclosure." *Sociology of Health and Illness* 30: 255–271.

Arribas-Ayllon, Michael, Srikant Sarangi, and Angus Clarke. 2009. "Professional Ambivalence: Accounts of Ethical Practice in Childhood Genetic Testing." *Journal of Genetic Counselling* 19: 173–184.

Ashida, S., M. Goodman, C. Pandya, L. M. Koehly, C. Lachance, J. Stafford, and K. A. Kaphingst. 2011. "Age Differences in Genetic Knowledge, Health Literacy and Causal Beliefs for Health Conditions." *Public Health Genomics* 14: 307–316.

Atkinson, Paul. 1995. *Medical Talk and Medical Work*. London: Sage.

Auer, Peter, and Carol M. Eastman. 2010. "Code-Switching." In *Society and Language in Use*, edited by Jürgen Jaspers, Jan-Ola Östman, and Jef Vershueren, 84–112. Amsterdam: John Benjamins.

Benkendorf, Judith L., Michele B. Prince, Mary A. Rose, Anna De Fina, and Heidi E. Hamilton. 2001. "Does Indirect Speech Promote Nondirective Genetic Counselling? Results of a Sociololinguistic Investigation." *American Journal of Medical Genetics* 106: 199–207.

Clarke, Angus. 1997. "Introduction." In *Culture, Kinship and Genes: Towards Cross-Cultural Genetics*, edited by Angus Clarke, and Evelyn Parsons, 1–26. Basingstoke, UK: Macmillan.

Clarke, Angus, Evelyn Parsons, and Allison Williams. 1996. "Outcomes and Process in Genetic Counselling." *Clinical Genetics* 50: 462–469.

Clarke, Angus, Srikant Sarangi, and Kate Verrier-Jones. 2011. "Voicing the Lifeworld: Parental Accounts of Responsibility in Genetic Consultations for Polycystic Kidney Disease." *Social Science & Medicine* 72: 1743–1751.

Drew, Paul, and John Heritage. 1992. "Analyzing Talk at Work: An Introduction." In *Talk at Work: Interaction in Institutional Settings*, edited by Paul Drew and John Heritage, 3–65. Cambridge: Cambridge University Press.

Ellington, Lee, Debra Roter, William N. Dudley, Bonnie J. Baty, Renn Upchurch, Susan Larson, Jean E. Wylie, Ken R. Smith, and Jeffrey R. Botkin. 2005. "Communication Analysis of BRCA1 Genetic Counseling." *Journal of Genetic Counseling* 14: 377–386.

Goffman, Erving. 1974. *Frame Analysis*. New York: Harper & Row.

Harper, Peter. 2010. *Practical Genetic Counseling*. 7th ed. London: Hodder Arnold.

Have, Paul ten. 2007. *Doing Conversation Analysis: A Practical Guide*. 2nd ed. London: Sage.

Kessler, Seymour. 1997. "Psychological Aspects of Genetic Counseling. XI. Nondirectiveness Revisited." *American Journal of Medical Genetics* 72: 164–171.

Paul, Jean, Sylvia Metcalfe, Lesley Stirling, Brenda Wilson, and Jan Hodgson. 2015. "Analyzing Communication in Genetic Consultations—A Systematic Review." *Patient Education and Counselling* 98: 15–33.

Pilnick, Alison. 2002. "What 'Most People' Do: Exploring the Ethical Implications of Genetic Counselling." *New Genetics and Society* 21: 339–350.

Pilnick, Alison, and Olga Zayts. 2012. "'Let's Have It Tested First': Directiveness, Culture and Decision-Making Following Positive Antenatal Screening in Hong Kong." *Sociology of Health and Illness* 34: 266–282.

Pilnick, Alison, and Olga Zayts. 2014. "'It's Just a Likelihood': Uncertainty as Topic and Resource in Conveying 'Positive' Results in an Antenatal Screening Clinic." *Symbolic Interaction* 37: 187–208.

Sarangi, Srikant. 1994. "Intercultural or Not? Beyond Celebration of Cultural Differences in Miscommunication Analysis." *Pragmatics* 4: 409–427. Republished in *The Language and Intercultural Communication Reader*, edited by Zhu Hua, 261–276 (2011). London: Routledge.

Sarangi, Srikant. 2000. "Activity Types, Discourse Types and Interactional Hybridity: The Case of Genetic Counselling." In *Discourse and Social Life*, edited by Srikant Sarangi, and Malcolm Coulthard, 1–27. London: Pearson.

Sarangi, Srikant. 2002. "The Language of Likelihood in Genetic Counselling Discourse." *Journal of Language and Social Psychology* 21: 7–31.

Sarangi, Srikant. 2013. "Genetic Counselling Communication: A Discourse-Analytical Approach." In *Encyclopaedia of Life Sciences*. Chichester, UK: John Wiley & Sons.

Sussex, Roland. 2012. "Switching in International English." In *English as an International Language in Asia: Implications for Language Education*, edited by Andy Kirkpatrick, and Roland Sussex, 175–187. London: Springer.

Thomassen, Gøril, Srikant Sarangi, and John-Arne Skolbekken. 2015. "Negotiating Parental/Familial Responsibility in Genetic Counselling." In *Discourse and Responsibility in Professional Contexts*, edited by Jan-Ola Östman, and Anna Solin, 67–95. London: Equinox.

Wake, Virginia Yelei. 2006. "The Triad in Prenatal Genetic Counseling." PhD diss., Georgetown University.

Zayts, Olga, and Alison Pilnick. 2014. "Genetic Counseling in Multilingual and Multicultural Contexts." In *Routledge Handbook of Language and Health Communication*, edited by Heidi E. Hamilton, and Wen-ying Sylvia Chou, 557–572. London: Routledge.

Zayts, Olga, and Srikant Sarangi. 2013. "Modes of Risk Explanation in Telephone Consultations between Nurses and Parents for a Genetic Condition." *Health, Risk and Society* 5: 194–215.

Zayts, Olga, Srikant Sarangi, Meow-Keong Thong, Brian Hon-yin Chung, Ivan Fo-man Lo, Anita Sik-yau Kan, Juliana Mei-Har Lee *et al.* 2013. "Genetic Counseling/Consultation in South-East Asia: A Report from the Workshop at the 10th Asia Pacific Conference on Human Genetics." *Journal of Genetic Counseling* 22: 917–924.

Zayts, Olga, and Stephanie Schnurr. 2012. "'You May Know Better Than I Do': Negotiating Advice-Giving on Down Syndrome Screening in a Hong Kong Prenatal Hospital." In *Advice in Discourse*, edited by Holger Limberg, and Miriam A. Locher, 195–212. Amsterdam: John Benjamins.

Zayts, Olga, and Stephanie Schnurr. 2014. "More Than 'Information Provider' and 'Counselor': Constructing and Negotiating Roles and Identities of Nurses in Genetic Counseling Sessions." *Journal of Sociolinguistics* 18: 345–369.

Zayts, Olga, Virginia Yelei Wake, and Stephanie Schnurr. 2012. "Chinese Prenatal Genetic Counseling Discourse in Hong Kong: Health Care Providers' (Non)directive Stance, or Who is Making the Decision." In *Chinese Discourse and Interaction: Theory and Practice*, edited by Yuling Pan, and Dániel Z. Kádár, 228–247. London: Equinox.

Part III
Key Areas of Workplace Talk

17
Directives in Workplace Discourse

Junko Saito and Haruko Minegishi Cook

Introduction

Workplace discourse is characterized by a high frequency of directives, as workers, particularly those in authoritative positions, need to achieve institutional objectives. On the other hand, directives require the intricate and delicate crafting of discourse to maintain good working relationships with receivers. In other words, when people issue directives they need to consider a situation's transactional and interpersonal aspects. Close examination of directives in workplace interaction allows us to observe various aspects of a specific workplace or community of practice (Wenger 1998), such as social relationships between the directive-giver and the directive-receiver and even a directive-receiver's work experience. Focusing on directives also contributes to the interpretation of meanings encoded in workplace talk (Holmes and Woodhams 2013).

This chapter provides an overview of research on directives in workplaces. First, general issues of importance to research on directives are delineated, and then research on directives in the workplace in relation to gendered language and politeness is discussed. In the final section, we suggest future directions for research on directives.

Directive Speech Acts: Definitions, Terminology, and Taxonomy

Research on directives has been extensive; but the topic is complex and ambiguities abound in definitions, taxonomy, and terminology. Searle (1976, 11) defines directives as "attempts ... by the speaker to get the hearer to do something". Jones (1992, 429) slightly extends this definition: a speaker's attempts "to get a hearer to do (or refrain from doing) some action". Craven and Potter (2010, 420) narrow it down to an "action where one participant *tells* another to do something" (original emphasis), arguing that Searle leaves the boundary between directives and requests blurry. Nevertheless, a substantial number of researchers (e.g., Ervin-Tripp 1976; Goodwin 2001; Koester 2010; Mullany 2007; Takano 2005) define directives as "getting an addressee to do something". However, many authors (e.g., Holmes 2006; Holmes and Woodhams 2013; Mondada 2014; Shin 2003; Smith 1992; Sunaoshi 1994; Weigel and Weigel 1985) do not provide explicit definitions, perhaps because the definition of directives is somewhat taken for granted.

Likewise, the terminology used to refer to directives varies from researcher to researcher. As Vine (2004) points out, using different terms to label what appears to be the same linguistic phenomenon generates confusion and complexity in the literature on directives. For example, Blum-Kulka, Danet, and Gherson (1985), as well as Shin (2003), employ the term "requests" to refer to what others call "directives". In fact, Shin, in an investigation of "requests" on Korean TV dramas, utilizes "request" and "directive" interchangeably.

The variation in terminology is confusing; however, what makes the literature more complicated is that researchers largely adopt the term "directive" without clearly stating what they count as such. Even within the literature specifically on workplace discourse, taxonomies for directives vary depending on researchers. Holmes and Stubbe (2003), Saito (2011), and Weigel and Weigel (1985) identify requests as a category of directives, whereas Koester (2010) and Mondada (2014) distinguish directives from requests. Shin (2003) treats them as interchangeable.

How the social acts of directives and requests are conceptualized seems to be crucial in these different classifications. Levels of politeness and directness play important roles in many scholars' judgements of whether a specific social act should be construed as a directive or a request (Craven and Potter 2010). Craven and Potter (2010, 420) explain that this "approach tends to treat requests and directives as versions, of varying politeness, of the same action". In contrast, Craven and Potter draw on Curl and Drew's (2008) notions of entitlement and contingency to provide an insightful perspective[1]: a request's speaker orients to the addressee's contingencies; in contrast, a directive's speaker orients entirely to the addressee's compliance. The addressee's contingencies are "removed and managed in conjunction with issuing the directives" (Craven and Potter 2010, 426). In other words, addressees have little choice but to comply with a directed action; in this sense, the directive-giver's entitlement is high. Based on the differences in entitlement and contingency between directives and requests, Craven and Potter suggest that participants perceive requests and directives as different acts rather than variations of the same act.

Taking another approach, Vine (2004, 28) considers two factors to conceptualize directives and requests: status differences between speaker and addressee, and the addressee's right of refusal. Table 17.1 illustrates Vine's distinction between directives and requests. While Vine perceives directives and requests as separate social acts, she nevertheless claims that they are very similar, and categorizes them both as control acts (directing control acts).[2]

As this overview of the current state of the research on directives suggests, researchers on the topic could help avoid further confusion and complexity by stating their own positions explicitly. Concrete definitions and taxonomies should be considered basic in this field. It is particularly essential that researchers clearly explain how their work treats directives and requests.

Table 17.1 Factors differentiating directives, requests, and advice

Control acts		Speaker higher status	Hearer has right of refusal	Benefit to speaker
Directing	Directive	yes	no	yes
	Request	no	yes	yes
Suggesting	Advice	maybe	yes	no

Source: Vine 2004, 31; reproduced with permission from John Benjamins

Directives in the Workplace

Much research on workplace discourse explores correlations between the speaker's choice of directive forms/strategies and social variables. Social status, power relations, the addressee's work duties, and the purpose of the interaction or genre (e.g., Holmes and Stubbe 2003; Koester 2010; Saito 2009; Vine 2009) are often regarded as influential factors in the speaker's choice of directive forms. Some research (e.g., Mullany 2007; Saito 2011; Smith 1992; Sunaoshi 1994; Takano 2005) also considers gender, usually in terms of gender inequality in the public sphere, to empirically examine gendered styles of directive-giving in the course of interaction. Much research likewise considers the role of politeness in directive usage. Directives are theoretically considered face-threatening acts (FTAs) (Brown and Levinson 1987); speakers tend to issue them carefully to mitigate their illocutionary force. Furthermore, gender and politeness interact in directive-giving behaviours (e.g., Mullany 2007; Saito 2009; Sunaoshi 1994; Takano 2005) because stereotypical women's language is associated with politeness. Given this theoretical background and the previous research's demonstration of the interconnections between gender and politeness in directive discourse, we discuss directives in workplace settings in relation to gendered language and politeness.

Directives and Gendered Language

Normative Gendered Styles of Directives

Recent research on workplace discourse (e.g., Holmes 2006; Mullany 2007; Saito 2011; Takano 2005) documents detailed and subtle variations in how male and female individuals manipulate gendered ways of giving directives in the course of interaction. This line of research explores what people *do* with directives in terms of normative gendered interactional styles. In normative terms, masculine ways of issuing directives are direct, contestive, assertive, and authoritative, whereas feminine ways are polite, indirect, collaborative, and mitigated (Holmes 2006; Mullany 2007). Examples of masculine directive forms are imperatives and "need" statements; examples of feminine forms include hedges such as "I wonder if", modal verbs such as "may", "could", "would", and the pronoun "we" (Holmes 2006).

Holmes (2006) illustrates how female professionals in managerial positions in New Zealand employ normative masculine and feminine styles to project different institutional identities. In her study, a female professional utilizes masculine styles of giving directives to present herself as a confident and authoritative leader, while another female superior employs indirect forms such as "I wonder if you wouldn't mind", constructing an identity as a considerate and empathetic manager. Holmes demonstrates that, regardless of their gender, leaders use a wide range of directive forms or strategies to achieve communicative goals in given contexts.

Mullany (2007), who examines linguistic practices of workers in managerial positions at international corporations in the UK, also reports that both male and female managers utilize speech styles stereotypically associated with the other gender. For example, she demonstrates how a male director issues directives in a normatively feminine way with the use of the pronoun "we" and a hedge "just", choices that minimize status differentials between other employees and himself. Mullany argues that both discourse context and social context, including relative power, status, and role responsibility, contribute to speakers' choices of directive strategies.

Polite Styles in Japanese Directives

In the Japanese scholarship, Takano (2005) scrutinizes professional Japanese women's use of directives and compares it to male directive usage through quantitative and qualitative analyses of female data (630 directives) collected from naturally occurring interactions and male data (122 directives) collected from TV documentaries. As Table 17.2 shows, female superiors tend to use more polite and indirect styles, such as Verb root+*te kudasai* "please do X", *onegai shimasu* "I ask you a favour", and N *wa*/Verb root *-te ii desu* "N/doing N is alright", than their male counterparts. In contrast, male superiors frequently use rough, coarse-sounding directives, Verb root+*ro* "Do X", which is never utilized by female superiors. In the qualitative analysis, Takano finds that such "polite language, an apparently powerless marker", enables the female superiors to empower themselves and control the power dynamics of the workplace (657). Takano contends that giving directives in the polite form allows these female superiors to detach themselves from the group of employees and perform their institutional role as superiors.

Takano also construes polite language as a "property of Japanese women's language" (658). His arguments suggest that politeness is associated with women's language and powerlessness in Japanese. However, as shown in Table 17.2, male superiors in Takano's study also adopt polite styles, such as Verb root+*te kudasai* "Please do X" and N *wa*/Verb root *-te ii desu* "N/doing N is alright". Other empirical studies (e.g., Cook 2011; Okamoto 1998) likewise demonstrate that in formal situations like workplaces, men use honorifics in the same way as women do, and their use of honorifics contributes to these men's construction of professional or institutional identities rather than a gendered identity. Male superiors in Takano's study may also utilize polite styles to perform their institutional identities. The following example, adapted from Saito (2011), similarly illustrates how a Japanese male superior issues directives in non-honorific and honorific forms to index different types of identities. Directives are in bold throughout the examples.[3]

Table 17.2 Distribution of directive forms

Rank	Women	%	Rank	Men	%
1	Verb root+ *te kudasai* "Please do X."	23.0	1	Verb root +*ro* "Do X."	15.6
2	Verb root + *te* (*ne*/*yo*) "Do X."	8.3	2	Verb root+ *te kudasai* "Please do X."	10.7
3	*Onegai shimasu*/ *itashimasu* "I ask you a favour."	5.2	3	Verb root + *te* (*ne*/*yo*) "Do X."	7.4
4	N *wa*/Verb root –*te ii*/*yoroshii*/*kamawanai*/ *kekkoo desu* "N/doing N is alright."	4.9	4	Verb stem + *nai to dame*/*ikan* "It wouldn't work well unless you do X."	6.6
5	Verb root + *te moraeru?*/ *moraemasu?*/ *moraemasen?*/*itada kemasu ka?* "Could I have you do X?"	4.4	5	N *wa*/Verb root –*te ii*/*yoroshii*/*kamawanai*/ *kekkoo desu* "N/doing N is alright."	6.6

Source: adapted from Takano 2005, 642; with permission from Elsevier.

> **Example 17.1**
>
> Context: At a dental laboratory, both Ueda (superior) and Tani (male subordinate) are dental lab technicians, possessing governmental licenses to make dentistry products.
>
> 1 Ueda: *koko un. kono enshin no resuto dake nokoshite hoshii n da yo.*
> 2 °*un.* °*kono hooryuu toka koo kezutte ii kara.*
> "Here, yeah. **I want you to** only keep a metallic projection for this distal side of a tooth. Yeah. It is okay to shave off this swell of the denture."
>
> ((Lines 3–5 omitted: After a 1-minute pause, Tani acknowledges Ueda's directive.))
>
> 6 Tani: *(.) e↑>boku de< daijoobu na n desu ka↑*
> "What? Is it alright for me to do it?"
> 7 Ueda: *daijoobu jan. nande. kocchi kezuru dake jan. ano. fuan nattara ( )*
> 8 *ano: motte kureba ii kara.*
> "It's alright, right? Why? You just shave off here, right? Well, if you get worried ( ), well: you can bring it (the denture) to me, so"
> 9 Tani: *hai.*
> "Yes."
>
> ((Lines 10–18 omitted: Ueda repeats his instructions.))
>
> 19 Ueda: *yoroshii desu ka↑*
> "Is it alright?"
> 20 Tani: *hai.*
> "Yes."
> 21 Ueda: *fuan ga aru yoo dattara motte kite kudasai.*
> "If you ever get worried, **please bring it to me**."
> 22 Tani: *hai.*
> "Yes."

In line 1, with the "want" statement in the non-honorific form, Ueda issues a directive to Tani. In addition, he uses *n da* and the particle *yo* in conjunction with the directive form. The combination of *n da* and *yo* indicates the speaker's non-challengeable (Iwasaki 1985), authoritative stance (Morita 2002). Thus, along with the co-occurring linguistic features, the directive form in line 1 can be construed as direct and authoritative. However, when Tani challenges Ueda by speculating on his own ability to carry out Ueda's directive (line 6), Ueda shifts his stance and displays his consideration of Tani's face demands by saying *fuan nattara* "if you get worried" (line 7). After re-stating the instructions, Ueda shifts his speech style, delivering an utterance in the honorific form: *yoroshii desu ka↑* "Is it alright?" (line 19), thus wrapping up the interaction. Ueda further attends to the interpersonal aspect (*fuan ga aru yoo dattara* "If you ever get worried") and ends a final directive in the honorific form in line 21. In Example 17.1, Ueda's direct way of giving a directive in the non-honorific form contributes to his construction of an identity as an authoritative and knowledgeable superior, whereas his use of honorific forms enables Ueda to construct an institutional identity of a professional lab technician, who formally makes a request to Tani, another professional lab technician.

As mentioned earlier, in the Western scholarship, normative masculine styles are characterized as direct and authoritative, whereas feminine forms are characterized as indirect and polite. In the Japanese scholarship, however, it is too simplistic to associate polite language, particularly honorifics, with women's speech. Honorifics are employed to construct a professional/institutional identity in the workplace (e.g., Cook 2011), while non-honorific, rough lexical items can be used to index masculinity. In Japanese, gendered language largely manifests in the informal speech style (Sreetharan 2004). As illustrated in Example 17.1, men also use honorifics to index professional/institutional identity. Furthermore, honorifics in Japanese are not necessarily powerless, as they can index professional identity. When analysing data, therefore, researchers should not simply associate polite language with powerlessness or women's language.

Directives and Politeness

Contextual Factors

As noted in section 1, the workplace is an ideal site to examine how power dynamics influence the ways in which directives are used. Researchers have examined how indirectly (politely) or directly directives are issued among co-workers.

A range of contexts affect how directly or indirectly people in power give directives. Research indicates that the nature of the employment (whether the subordinate is a temporary worker or not), the length of a relationship, the nature of the task (routine or non-routine task), and/or the setting (whether the speaker is talking to a group of co-workers or engaging in one-to-one conversation) make a difference. By analysing a large corpus of workplace discourse in New Zealand (the Wellington Language in the Workplace Project), Holmes and Stubbe (2003) show that context and setting, the nature and length of relationships, and/or the nature of the required task affect how people in power in the workplace issue directives to their subordinates. For example, a production team leader changes forms of directives depending upon the speech context. She uses direct forms when urging factory workers to be more efficient and accurate in their work in a team briefing meeting, whereas she mitigates her directives in one-to-one conversation with one of the factory workers when conveying the same message. A superior tends to use more indirect forms to someone who is a peripheral member (e.g., a temporary worker), but her directives may become more direct once the two become more comfortable with one another. Also, a superior's directives become more polite when asking her subordinate to perform a non-routine task.

Holmes and Woodhams (2013) suggest that directives index degrees of a worker's familiarity with the work and assimilation into a workplace. Their study, which analysed interactions among blue-collar construction workers in New Zealand, reveals that due to their unfamiliarity with the work, more explicit and detailed directives are issued to newcomers to the workplace. Vine (2004) also studied how directives are issued between managers and their staff as well as between peers using data from the Wellington Language in the Workplace Project. Her study demonstrates co-workers' preference to attend to one another's feelings. Directives exchanged between equals are always mitigated, and managers soften their directives to their subordinates. In addition, the managers try to minimize status differences. In sum, these studies demonstrate that directives in the workplace are not static but dynamic and complex. Directives are linguistic resources which people in power use in order to manage the balance between getting things done and keeping a good relationship with their subordinates. Through "community of practice" (Wenger 1998; see King this volume), the members of a company develop their ways of giving and interpreting different forms of directives in their workplace.

Types of Directives

Cook (in press), who analysed superiors' directives in new employee orientation sessions in a Japanese company, investigated another contextual factor—whether or not directives require immediate compliance. This distinction is referred to as "NOW and LATER" (Vine 2004), and "procedural" and "non-procedural" directives (Jones 1992).[4] In Cook's study, superiors' directives were categorized into "procedural" and "non-procedural" directives, and the two were tabulated separately. The findings are that almost 80 per cent of all of the superiors' procedural directives are expressed in three linguistic forms—one is the term of address and the other two are typical or default request forms in Japanese (-*te kudasai* "please do X" and *onegai shimasu* "I ask you a favour"). Example 17.2 illustrates procedural directives encoded in the default request forms.

Example 17.2

Context: The lesson is a writing exercise. Superior Hata is telling the new employees, Kato and Nishi, to write a short sentence.

1	Hata:	*boku wa bikkuri shimashita mitai na mono o katte ni **kaite kudasai***
2		*seikai wa nai node.*
		"Please write freely (a sentence such as) 'I am surprised'. There is no correct answer."
3	Kato:	*hai.*
		"Yes."
4	Hata:	***onegai shimasu.***
		"I ask you to do so."
5	Kato:	*moo kaite ii n desu ka*↑
		"Is it OK to write now?"
6	Hata:	*hai kaite kudasai.*
		"Yes, please write."

Procedural directives are low in imposition because the preparatory condition of the directive (request) is "the hearer is able to perform the act" (Searle 1969), and the kinds of act that the hearer can perform in the immediate speech context are rather limited. In Example 17.2, the superior's request to write a sentence requires immediate compliance, and his request is a normal procedure of an orientation session, and thus expected. The superior uses *kaite kudasai* "please write" twice and *onegai shimasu* "I ask you to do so" once.

The imposition level of non-procedural directives is high in this set of data because non-procedural directives ask for the subordinates' compliance in almost all aspects of their life and personal habits. For instance, in the examples below, Hata asks the new employees to state the conclusion first in expressing their opinions (Example 17.3) and urges them to check email messages every day and respond to them right away (Example 17.4). To mitigate the high imposition, the superiors use a wide range of politeness strategies when giving non-procedural directives. In Examples 17.3 and 17.4, in which Hata is issuing non-procedural directives, he is utilizing positive and negative politeness strategies (Brown and Levinson 1987), respectively.

Example 17.3

Context: Superior Hata is telling the new employees, Kato and Nishi, how to communicate in a business setting.

1	Hata:	*juuyoo na hatsugen o suru sa- sai ni wa ketsuron kara saki ni iu yoo ni*
2		***kokorogakemashoo.***
		"When saying something important, let's try to state the conclusion first."

Example 17.4

Context: Superior Hata is instructing the new employees, Kato and Nishi, how to manage email messages.

1	Hata:	*meeru (.) saitee demo ichinichi ikkai wa mite (.) henshin ga hitsuyoo*
2		*na mono wa dekiru dake hayaku henshin o suru yoo ni suru to (.) ii*
3		***desu yo.***
		"As for email messages, check them at least once a day. For those that require a response, it is good if you respond to them as soon as possible."

In Example 17.3, the superior uses the *mashoo* form "let's", which includes the speaker in the activity. In this sense, this is a positive politeness strategy. In Example 17.4, the superior employs the conditional *to* clause "if clause" to make his request tentative, which is a negative politeness strategy. Furthermore, Hata's short pauses index the hesitant manner in which he speaks.

Cultural Differences

How politely superiors talk to their subordinates may differ from culture to culture. In contrast to the West where egalitarianism is a societal value, Pan's study (1995) suggests such a concern is not important in mainland China. Pan's study, which analysed government officials' meetings in mainland China, found that superiors' directives are very direct and unmitigated. Pan argues that this practice is due to different politeness behaviour in mainland China, where a hierarchical relation is the norm between superiors and subordinates, and it is neither necessary nor desirable to treat subordinates as if they are equal in status.

A few studies explored cross-cultural differences between the East and West, collecting data from companies in Hong Kong, where the influence of Western culture is strong. Kong

(2006), using email exchanged within a company in Hong Kong, investigated the frequency, semantic type, and sequencing of accounts that accompany directives. Three categories of relationships (peer to peer, subordinate to superior, and superior to subordinate) were examined.[5] The paper found that subordinates most frequently use accounts when making a request to their superiors. Also, managers justify their requests to their subordinates more frequently than peers justify requests among themselves. The paper identified seven semantic types of accounts, and reason as an account has the highest frequency among the seven types. As for the sequencing of the accounts, the majority of the accounts are placed before directives, but the superior-to-subordinate group exhibits a more balanced distribution of the two positions. In contrast to Pan's research (1995), Kong's study (2006) showed that superiors' speech to subordinates is mitigated, which, he explains, is due to a cultural difference between mainland China and Hong Kong.

Bilbow (1995) examined the speech act of request for cooperation in weekly meetings of a company in Hong Kong to test if the following two hypotheses are true: (i) as transactional discourse is typically more direct (Blum-Kulka, House, and Kasper 1989), requests in business meetings are made in a direct fashion, and (ii) there are differences between Chinese and Western workers in terms of politeness judgments in business meetings. The meetings were attended by both native speakers of English and non-native speakers of English who were native speakers of Chinese. The study found that the first hypothesis is untenable. The Chair used a wide range of request forms including a number of conventionally indirect requests. The second hypothesis was not proven due to a lack of instances of requests made by non-native speakers of English.

Directives and Brown and Levinson's Politeness Theory

Brown and Levinson's seminal theory of politeness (1987) contends that directives (including requests, advice, and suggestions) are FTAs that threaten the hearer's negative face and that their weightiness influences a pragmatic choice the speaker makes. The formula that calculates the weightiness of an FTA involves three social variables—distance between the speaker and the hearer, power that the hearer has over the speaker, and the rank of imposition. The sum of these three variables contributes to the seriousness of an FTA. Research of directives in the workplace, however, reveals that Brown and Levinson's formula alone cannot account for the actual use of directives in the workplace.

Using three institutional settings in England (magistrate-defendant, doctor-patient, and police-member of community) as data, Harris (2003) explored how politeness strategies are realized in these settings where power relations are inherent. In particular, she examined how requests are made by people in a less powerful position and how they are responded to by people in power. Brown and Levinson's formula for calculating the weightiness of an FTA would predict that a person in power would be less likely to mitigate his/her refusal to a request made by a person in a less powerful position because the weight of the FTA is relatively lower. The analysis of data shows that contrary to their prediction, even those in power when rejecting a request made by a person in a less powerful position utilize various politeness strategies. The result in Harris' study, thus, cannot be adequately explained solely by Brown and Levinson's formula and suggests that even in a power-laden interaction, relational work is important.

Vine (2009) also showed that Brown and Levinson's formula for predicting the seriousness of an FTA is only partially tenable and that actual practices are much more complex. Her study investigated the influence of contextual factors on the frequency and expression of directives in two government departments in New Zealand. All the directives are issued by three managers to subordinates in one-to-one interactions. The study demonstrates that a person receiving the most direct forms may also receive the least direct form in the same interaction, which suggests that power and distance are not the sole social factors that influence the managers' choice of directives. The paper identified the goal of interaction and discourse context as factors that affect the managers' pragmatic choices. The goal of interaction influences the frequency and density of directives and the way in which they are expressed, while discourse context affects the form of directives. For example, imperatives were used (i) at the end of a long discussion; (ii) when there are multiple tasks; and (iii) when directly elicited.

While many studies on directives and politeness show that superiors display politeness to subordinates when issuing directives (Bilbow 1995; Harris 2003; Holmes and Stubbe 2003; Kong 2006; Vine 2004, 2009), it is assumed that in hierarchical organizations such as the military and hospitals, superiors' directives are on-record without politeness strategies (see Ervin-Tripp 1976). The military particularly keeps strict power relations among its members. Halbe (2011) investigated how directly or indirectly the members of different ranks (commissioned officers, sergeants first class, sergeants, and junior soldiers) in the military give directives, based on 42 questionnaires and 19 interviews collected from different ranks of a US army battalion. The study found that power and social distance play a role in the choice of a linguistic form as proposed by Brown and Levinson's politeness theory. Directives are most frequently used by superiors to subordinates, less to peers, and the least to superiors. The most polite form ("Can you do") is used most with superiors and peers, and for subordinates the most common forms are "need" statements followed by imperatives and mitigated imperatives (Imperative + "please"). All ranks had a preference for "need" statements toward subordinates. A limitation of this study, however, is the use of questionnaires and interviews as data, which does not always uncover how subjects actually behave. If naturally occurring data are collected from the military, we may obtain different results.

Summary and Future Directions

This chapter has discussed directives in the workplace and has reviewed prior research. Most research in the workplace has focused on gender and/or politeness. Recent research on workplace discourse that focuses on gendered language has revealed that people at work utilize a range of gendered interactional styles according to discourse and social contexts for pragmatic effects, such as identity construction and minimization of status differentials or power. Social and discourse contexts play a significant part in our understanding of "what people do with gendered directives" in the course of interaction. Furthermore, we have argued that polite language, in particular honorifics, can index a formal or professional dimension and may not necessarily be gendered or powerless. The association between polite language and powerlessness/women's language proposed by the Western scholarship needs to be reconsidered.

Directives are one of the linguistic resources available to people at work for attaining the goals of the workplace. Although superiors tend to give direct and explicit directives, they often mitigate their directives in order to maintain collegiality. The research shows that contextual factors largely affect whether or not superiors use politeness strategies when issuing directives. Settings, the nature and length of relationships, and/or the nature of the required tasks, among other factors, affect how politely directives are expressed. Furthermore, it is shown that superiors' directive use changes when giving different sub-types of directives.

Finally, the foregoing discussion suggests directions for future research. It has already been clear from previous research (e.g., Holmes 2006; Mullany 2007; Saito 2011) that men and women use both normative masculine and feminine ways of giving directives as linguistic resources. Instead of exploring the correlation between gender and the speaker's choice of directive strategies, future research should further focus on how people use normative gendered directives to convey social meanings in the course of interaction. Intra-status interactions have particularly been paid less scholarly attention. It would be interesting if research explored how gendered directives are used in intra-status interactions.

The topic of cross-cultural differences in superiors' directive use is also an interesting area for future research. In Western societies, settings, the nature and length of relationships, and/or the nature of the tasks are factors that affect the degree of politeness superiors encode. To date, there are few studies that directly address cross-cultural differences in directive use in the workplace. Although Pan's study (1995) suggests that there are cultural variations, it is not clear to what extent such variations exist in workplaces across cultures. In East Asian societies, for example, age is an important social variable. Traditionally, superiors in the workplace in East Asian societies are older than their subordinates, but in recent years this situation is changing, and more young but capable people hold higher positions in companies. Future research could investigate in what ways superiors who are younger than their subordinates issue directives. Furthermore, due to globalization, many companies have branch offices in other countries, or companies and organizations have become multinational. How directives are issued in such a multicultural environment is an important area to explore, for the findings could help solve miscommunication due to different cultural assumptions.

Future research should also investigate sub-types of directives. As noted by Vine (2004), the distinction of NOW and LATER directives is an important one. In the literature, the distinction between these two sub-types is largely ignored with the exception of a few studies (e.g., Cook in press; Mulholland 1994; Trosborg 1994). Because these two sub-types may be realized in different linguistic forms (see Cook forthcoming), future research needs to pay close attention to these sub-types when analysing directives at work.

Further Reading

Holmes (2006) deals with diverse topics in New Zealand workplaces. Chapter 2 analyses the relationship between directives and gender.

Saito (2011) on Japanese directive discourse demonstrates how male managers manipulate gendered language.

Vine (2004) is highly informative regarding various concepts that researchers should attend to when conducting directive research.

Related Topics

Interactional sociolinguistics; (Im)politeness theory; Rapport management; Social constructionism; Communities of practice; Relational talk; Gender; Leadership

Transcription Conventions

(.)   Micro pause
:   Prolongation of the immediately prior sound; multiple colons indicate
            a more prolonged sound

↑	A rising intonation
.	A falling intonation
-	A cut-off of the previous sound
> <	Relatively slower than the surrounding talk
( )	The transcriber's inability to hear what was said
°	Relatively quieter than the surrounding talk

Notes

1 Curl and Drew's (2008) notion of "entitlement" refers to "the speaker's right to make the request and to expect compliance" (Craven and Potter 2010, 429), while "contingency" indicates "the recipient's ability or willingness to grant the request" (421).
2 Vine (2004, 27) defines control acts as "attempt[s] to get someone to do something."
3 The term "directive" in the examples includes directives and requests, following Vine's (2004, 31) definition of "directing control acts."
4 The two sub-types are also called "internal and external" (Mulholland 1994) and "request-now and request-then" (Trosborg 1994).
5 Kong does not clearly mention that the email messages in this company are written in English, but judging from some examples, we assume they are written in English.

References

Bilbow, Grahame. 1995. "Requesting Strategies in the Cross-Cultural Business Meeting." *Pragmatics* 5: 45–56.
Blum-Kulka, Shoshana, Brenda Danet, and Rimona Gherson. 1985. "The Language of Requesting in Israeli Society." In *Language and Social Situations*, edited by Joseph P. Forgas, 113–139. New York: Springer-Verlag.
Blum-Kulka, Shoshana, Juliane House, and Gabriele Kasper. 1989. *Cross-Cultural Pragmatics: Requests and Apologies*. Norwood, NJ: Ablex.
Brown, Penelope, and Stephen C. Levinson. 1987. *Politeness: Some Universals in Language Usage*. Cambridge: Cambridge University Press.
Cook, Haruko M. 2011. "Are Honorifics Polite? Uses of Referent Honorifics in a Japanese Committee Meeting." *Journal of Pragmatics* 43: 3655–3672.
Cook, Haruko M. In press. "Superior's Directives in the Japanese Workplace: Are They All Strategies?" In *Recent Advances in Japanese Grammar and Discourse*, edited by Mutsuko Endo Hudson, Yoshiko Matsumoto, and Junko Mori. Amsterdam: John Benjamins.
Craven, Alexandra, and Jonathan Potter. 2010. "Directives: Entitlement and Contingency in Action." *Discourse Studies* 12: 419–442.
Curl, Traci S., and Paul Drew. 2008. "Contingency and Action: A Comparison of Two Forms of Requesting." *Research on Language and Social Interaction* 42: 129–153.
Ervin-Tripp, Susan. 1976. "Is Sybil There? The Structure of Some American English Directives." *Language in Society* 5: 25–66.
Goodwin, Marjorie. 2001. "Organizing Participation in Cross-Sex Jump Rope: Situating Gender Differences within Longitudinal Studies of Activities." *Research on Language and Social Interaction* 34: 75–106.
Halbe, Dorothea. 2011. "Language in the Military Workplace between Hierarchy and Politeness." *Text & Talk* 31: 315–334.
Harris, Sandra. 2003. "Politeness and Power: Making and Responding to 'Requests' in Institutional Settings." *Text* 23: 27–52.
Holmes, Janet. 2006. *Gendered Talk at Work*. Malden, MA: Blackwell.
Holmes, Janet, and Maria Stubbe. 2003. *Power and Politeness in the Workplace: A Sociolinguistic Analysis of Talk at Work*. London: Longman.
Holmes, Janet, and Jay Woodhams. 2013. "Building Interaction: The Role of Talk in Joining a Community of Practice." *Discourse & Communication* 7: 275–298.

Iwasaki, Shoichi. 1985. "Cohesion, Nonchallengeability, and the *-n desu* Clause in Japanese Spoken Discourse." *Journal of Asian Culture* 9: 125–142.
Jones, Kimberly. 1992. "A Question of Context: Directive Use at a Morris Team Meeting." *Language in Society* 21: 427–445.
Koester, Almut. 2010. *Workplace Discourse*. London: Continuum.
Kong, Kenneth. 2006. "Accounts as a Politeness Strategy in the Internal Directive Documents of a Business Firm in Hong Kong." *Journal of Asian Pacific Communication* 16: 77–105.
Mondada, Lorenza. 2014. "Instructions in the Operating Room: How the Surgeon Directs their Assistant's Hands." *Discourse Studies* 16: 131–161.
Morita, Emi. 2002. "Stance Marking in the Collaborative Completion of Sentences: Final Particles as Epistemic Markers in Japanese." In *Japanese/Korean Linguistics*. Vol. 10, edited by Noriko Akatsuka, and Susan Strauss, 220–234. Stanford, CA: CSLI.
Mulholland, Joan. 1994. "Multiple Directives in the Doctor–Patient Consultation." *Australian Journal of Communication* 21: 74–85.
Mullany, Louise. 2007. *Gendered Discourse in the Professional Workplace*. Basingstoke, UK: Palgrave Macmillan.
Okamoto, Shigeko. 1998. "The Use and Non-Use of Honorifics in Sales Talk in Kyoto and Osaka: Are They Rude or Friendly?" In *Japanese/Korean Linguistics*. Vol. 7, edited by Noriko Akatsuka, Hajime Hoji, Shoichi Iwasaki, Sung-Ock Sohn, and Susan Strauss, 141–157. Stanford, CA: CSLI.
Pan, Yuling. 1995. "Power behind Linguistic Behavior: Analysis of Politeness Phenomena in Chinese Official Settings." *Journal of Language and Social Psychology* 14: 462–481.
Saito, Junko. 2009. "Gender and Linguistic Ideology: A Re-Examination of Directive Usage by Japanese Male Superiors in the Workplace." PhD diss., University of Hawai'i at Mānoa.
Saito, Junko. 2011. "Managing Confrontational Situations: Japanese Male Superiors' Interactional Styles in Directive Discourse in the Workplace." *Journal of Pragmatics* 43: 1689–1706.
Searle, John R. 1969. *Speech Acts*. Cambridge: Cambridge University Press.
Searle, John R. 1976. "A Classification of Illocutionary Acts." *Language in Society* 5: 1–23.
Shin, Jeeweon. 2003. "Politeness and Discourse Strategies by Korean Women in Non-Traditional Authority Positions." *Acta Koreana* 6: 25–54.
Smith, Janet S. 1992. "Women in Charge: Politeness and Directives in the Speech of Japanese Women." *Language in Society* 21: 59–82.
Sreetharan, Cindi Sturtz. 2004. "Students, *Sarariiman* (pl.), and Seniors: Japanese Men's Use of 'Manly' Speech Register." *Language in Society* 33: 81–107.
Sunaoshi, Yukako. 1994. "Mild Directives Work Effectively: Japanese Women in Command." In *Cultural Performances: Proceedings of the Third Berkeley Women and Language Conference*, edited by Mary Bucholtz, A. C. Liang, Laurel A. Sutton, and Caitlin Hines, 678–690. Berkeley, CA: University of California.
Takano, Shoji. 2005. "Re-Examining Linguistic Power: Strategic Uses of Directives by Professional Japanese Women in Positions of Authority." *Journal of Pragmatics* 37: 633–666.
Trosborg, Ann. 1994. *Interlanguage Pragmatics: Requests, Complaints and Apologies*. Berlin: Mouton de Gruyter.
Vine, Bernadette. 2004. *Getting Things Done at Work: The Discourse of Power in Workplace Interaction*. Amsterdam: John Benjamins.
Vine, Bernadette. 2009. "Directives at Work: Exploring the Contextual Complexity of Workplace Directives." *Journal of Pragmatics* 41: 1395–1405.
Weigel, Margaret M., and Ronald M. Weigel. 1985. "Directive Use in a Migrant Agricultural Community: A Test of Ervin-Tripp's Hypotheses." *Language in Society* 14: 63–79.
Wenger, Etienne. 1998. *Communities of Practice: Learning, Meaning, and Identity*. Cambridge: Cambridge University Press.

18
Relational Talk at Work

Julien C. Mirivel and Ryan Fuller

Introduction

The way people communicate—what they say and how—makes a difference in the workplace. As Lutgen-Sandvik, Riforgiate, and Fletcher (2011, 16) explain, organizations are "not simply places where people gather to complete tasks, they are social arenas." In contrast to core business talk, which is focused, on-task and high-information talk (Holmes 2000), small talk is "non-obligatory talk" (McCarthy 2000, 84) that builds rapport. Across studies, researchers have found that social talk at work makes a difference: it "oils the social wheels" and helps people manage important relationships at work and creates collegiality.

During task-based talk, there are also ways people can attend to relational aspects of interaction. What specific behaviours make a difference in this type of talk? What communicative acts are most critical in practice? And what forms of relational talk matter most across contexts? In this chapter, we review the literature on relational talk at work to reveal the communication practices that function positively in workplace interaction. To do so, we draw on a model of positive communication proposed by Mirivel (2014) and argue that six communication practices are especially critical in creating effective and productive workplace interaction. To proceed, we introduce the model. Then, we use the model to synthesize our review.

A Model of Positive Communication

In *The Art of Positive Communication: Theory and Practice*, Mirivel (2014) introduced a heuristic model of positive communication that is grounded in theory and research. The model contributes to a larger movement in the field of communication that focuses on the positive side of interpersonal communication (see Socha and Beck 2015; Socha and Pitts 2012, 2013). It was originally created to synthesize basic principles of human communication and as a call to action. The model is both descriptive of communication practices that function positively and normative. It highlights communicative acts that produce high-quality relationships, create a sense of vitality, positive regard, and felt mutuality (Stephens *et al*. 2013). The model also foregrounds behaviours that foster a positive workplace culture in which individuals and

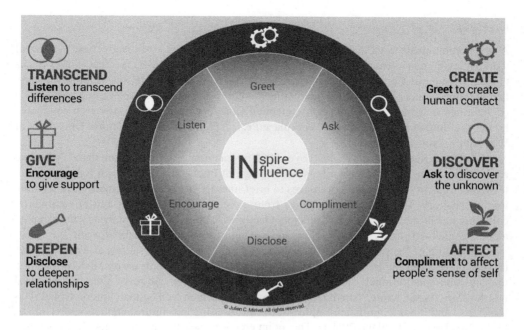

Figure 18.1 Mirivel's (2014) *model of positive communication*

organizations can flourish (Browning, Morris, and Kee 2011; Lutgen-Sandvik, Riforgiate, and Fletcher 2011). Consider Mirivel's (2014) proposal (see Figure 18.1).

The model identifies six communicative acts that contribute positively to human interaction. These acts are greeting, asking, complimenting, disclosing, encouraging, and listening. Connected to these six practices are the functions they serve, respectively: to "create", to "discover", to "affect", to "deepen", to "give", and to "transcend". Every act serves many functions, sometimes simultaneously. Communication is not just a way of transmitting information; it creates meaning, serves as a way to discover new information, affects people's identities, deepens intimacy, and more. For the purposes of the model, though, the behaviours and the functions of those behaviours are connected to form a principle to guide interaction:

> Greeting creates human contact
> Asking discovers the unknown
> Complimenting affects the self
> Disclosing deepens relationships
> Encouraging gives support
> Listening transcends differences

When these behaviours are practiced, communicators can influence and inspire others in a positive direction. They are making choices that will naturally impact others, shape the direction of interaction, and help to co-create better social worlds at home or at work.

Having introduced the model briefly, we now draw on it to synthesize our review of the literature on relational talk at work. We focus on the six communication behaviours at the heart of the model to integrate the findings from empirical research.

Greeting

A first communicative act that serves positive social functions at work is greeting. Across all workplaces, human interaction often begins with a greeting sequence—a fact that Harvey Sacks (1992), founder of Conversation Analysis, explored in his lectures. In this section, we show that greeting sequences are critical in creating human contact and that the presence or absence of greetings at work is especially consequential. Consider, for example, research conducted by the Wellington Language in the Workplace Project (LWP) based at Victoria University of Wellington, New Zealand.

Since 1996, the LWP has recorded over 2000 interactions, involving more than 700 people across more than 30 different workplaces. A range of interactions have been recorded, from team meetings in white collar workplaces to brief interactions between workers on a packing line in a factory. The organizations range from government departments and private white-collar organizations to factories and eldercare facilities. Using discourse analysis, ethnography, as well as thematic analysis, researchers have examined how people talk at work.

One finding of the project is the importance of small talk conversations at work. Holmes (2000, 2003), for example, showed that through small talk, participants accomplish collegiality, manage their institutional roles, and shape and reshape the nature of their professional relationship. As she wrote, "small talk is one means by which we negotiate interpersonal relationships" and it has "significant implications for on-going and future interactions" (Holmes 2000, 33; also see Coupland 2000a). This point emerged clearly when Holmes (2003) studied interactions with workers with disabilities. In exploring those interactions, she found that their inability to engage effectively in greeting sequences or to "do" small talk affected their ability to build and maintain relationships and to succeed at work.

The presence or absence of greetings is especially significant in the workplace. In one study, for example, Waldvogel (2007) investigated two contrasting organizations: a manufacturing plant and an educational organization. She found a striking difference in the form and content of emails and the culture of these organizations. At the educational organization, emails were short without warm greetings or closings. This organization suffered from low morale, conflict across departments, and poor social cohesion. In the manufacturing plant, however, the majority of emails featured friendly openings and closings. As a result, the organization had a culture where managers and staff were "more in harmony and supportive of each other" (473). In the article, Waldvogel wrote:

> Does the absence or presence of greetings and closings in an organization's emails provide insight into its culture? The findings presented here suggest that it does [. . .] The much greater use made of greetings and closing in [the manufacturing plant] suggests that staff members are concerned to establish a friendly tone in their interactions and maintain good interpersonal relationships.
>
> (473)

The LWP has shown that the presence or absence of greetings and the following small talk interactions that occur are crucial to an organization's culture. Research in other contexts have suggested similar results: the presence or absence of greetings affects student learning (e.g., Weinstein *et al.* 2009), correlates with patient satisfaction in health care interaction (e.g., Comstock *et al.* 1982), and serves important functions in business settings. Across contexts, researchers have shown that greeting serves positive identity, relational, and organizational functions. Greeting, thus, is a communicative act that does relational work.

Asking

In one of his lectures, Sacks (1992, 49) said "[t]here looks to be a rule that a person who asks a question has a right to talk again afterwards. And that rule can provide a simple way of generating enormous masses of sequences of talk: question, talk, question, talk, etc., etc.". Sacks' point permeates talk at work since to conduct business, professionals have to ask questions. But it turns out that the form of questioning also matters. Our review suggests that open-ended questions rather than closed-ended questions function more positively on a relational level in workplace interaction.

As Heritage (2003) explained, questions are powerful because they set the agenda for the next turn of talk. Questions shape the "topical domain as the appropriate or relevant domain of responses" (66). They frame the actions that the interviewee "should perform in relation to the topical domain" (67) and define how narrow or broad the responses should be. The way a question is asked also often embodies "presuppositions with varying degrees of explicitness" (71). With this mind, scholars have often made a useful distinction between questions that are open-ended or closed-ended.

By definition, closed-ended questions are narrow in focus and control the next response. Open-ended questions, on the other hand, are expansive, focus on the person's experience, and give freedom to the respondent. Although closed-ended questions are often used in workplace settings (e.g., Drew 1992), research in language and social interaction reveals that open-ended questions are often most effective.

A wide body of scholarship, for example, shows that physicians who ask open-ended questions can attend to patients' concerns more deeply and that such questions are a hallmark of effective patient-centred care (e.g., du Pré 2002). In news interviews, open-ended questions promote discovery and produce less conflict (Heritage 2003). In education, the best teachers use open-ended questions to lead students' learning (Bain 2004). In performance appraisals, open-ended questions allow employees to reflect on their jobs and explore important aspects of their work, and give them "a sense of pride in their work" (Van De Mieroop and Vrolix 2014, 167). In one study, Marrs (2007) explored conversations-gone-bad at work. There, she found that as participants improved their communication, they moved toward asking open-ended questions. Asking questions is a hallmark of workplace interaction, but open-ended questions function most positively on a relational level in talk at work.

Complimenting

Communication affects people's sense of self. Theories such as Symbolic Interactionism (Mead 1934) and Coordinated Management of Meaning (Pearce 1994) suggests that what people say and do has consequences on others' sense of self—in the present and in the future. One communicative act that impacts a person's identity is complimenting. In this section, we explore the use of compliments and how it serves relational functions at work.

There is a large body of work that has examined complimenting in interaction (for a review see Golato 2003). An often-cited article is the work of Pomerantz (1978). Another is Holmes' (1986) study of compliments in New Zealand in which she found that 65 per cent of compliment exchanges expressed positive affect. In one study, Holmes (1988) showed the different functions that complimenting may serve across gender as well as the ways in which complimenting can be threatening to a person's sense of self. As Holmes (2005, 355) explained "[t]here are more or less acceptable ways of responding to compliments. Many Asian cultures prescribe overt modesty, including denials and disagreements as appropriate responses to compliments, whereas western cultures tend to prescribe a gracious acceptance of some kind."

By definition, a compliment is a "speech act which explicitly or implicitly attributes credit to someone other than the speaker; usually the person addressed, for some 'good' (possession, characteristic, skill, etc.) which is positively valued by the speaker and the hearer" (Telaumbanua 2012, 34). Across key studies, scholars have shown that complimenting impacts human behaviour and has tangible outcomes. For example, a study by Seiter (2007) on the effect of complimenting on customers showed that "food servers received significantly higher tips when complimenting their customers than when not complimenting them" (478). Holmes and Marra (2004a; 2004b) revealed that compliments made in passing, off-record, before or after a meeting helped to create team spirit and to construct good working relationships. In education, researchers have found that "positive statements (praise) have been found to be more beneficial than verbal criticism" in giving instructional feedback (Burnett 2002, 5). Similarly, Trees, Kerssen-Griep, and Hess (2009) found that feedback that communicates respect, liking and mitigates threat, is better received by students and directly affects their learning. Complimenting serves positive functions across workplace contexts, but it is especially important when it is practiced by leaders and supervisors.

Communicating well is at the heart of leadership and managing staff (see Cameron 2013). Complimenting employees and staff contributes to creating trust and facilitates a positive workplace environment. Several studies demonstrate that complimenting or criticizing affects relationship quality and work climate. A study by Huseman, Hatfield, and Miles (1987) revealed that employees perceive that their supervisors overestimate the amount of positive verbal recognition they give, while supervisors report giving less criticism than employees report receiving. The greater the perceived gap between supervisors and supervisees, the lower employees' satisfaction with supervision and overall job satisfaction. Willemyns, Gallois, and Callan (2003), for example, found that conveying that an employee is valued through praise or inclusion in decisions, in addition to other behaviours, leads to "positive relationships and increased trust between managers and employees" (124). In their research, Lutgen-Sandvik, Riforgiate, and Fletcher (2011) collected critical incidents of positive experiences at work. They found that the most frequent experience evoking positive emotion were compliments for a "job well done", and "being singled out for doing my job, going above and beyond what was expected of me, in front of my colleagues" (Lutgen-Sandvik, Riforgiate, and Fletcher 2011, 12).

Disclosing

A fourth behaviour that serves positive relational functions at work is the act of disclosing. For researchers, disclosing private information is critical to the development and maintenance of relationships. As Mirivel (2014) explains, disclosing deepens relationships. This claim is well-supported by communication theories such as Social Penetration Theory (Altman and Taylor 1973), Relational Dialectics Theory (Montgomery and Baxter 1998), and Communication Boundary Management Theory (Petronio 2002), all of which have revealed the importance and challenges of self-disclosure in intimate relationships. But disclosure is also critical at work, where it serves both relational and institutional functions.

Consider again the article by Willemyns, Gallois, and Callan (2003). In their study, the authors found that self-disclosure, "where the manager discloses relatively personal information about themselves, or their feelings about issues or other people" (122) helps to create trust in the manager–employee relationship. According to Pearce and Sharp (1973, 420), a general principle of self-disclosure is that it occurs in the context of positive social relationships. Self-disclosing includes surface level information about a person as well as more personal or intimate features. The ways in which people negotiate both breadth and depth of disclosure reflects the degree of intimacy that people will experience. But altogether the research is reasonably clear: the act of disclosing serves social functions at work and creates high-quality relationships that are built on "trust, respect, and a willingness to share information, resources, and perspectives" (Phillips, Rothbard, and Dumas 2009, 710).

Crisis communication scholars, for example, have found that in a time of crisis, the most effective leaders will disclose relevant information to stakeholders, be open and honest about the crisis and share appropriate knowledge with the public (e.g., Ulmer, Sellnow, and Seeger 2014). One exemplary case of an ethical response to a crisis is Aaron Feuerstein, owner and manager of Malden Mills, a textile producer. In 1995, "The plant exploded resulting in 36 injuries" (Seeger and Ulmer 2001, 371). The facility was destroyed thereby leaving many employees without a job. In response, and as Seeger and Ulmer (2001) showed in their case study, Feuerstein immediately communicated with the public, reduced uncertainty about the future by continuing to pay his employees and providing health benefits, and committed the organization to stay local. In one public address, Aaron Feuerstein revealed not just information but also deeply held personal values of people before profits (see Seeger and Ulmer 2001).

Issues of disclosure permeate the workplace. Physicians who disclose personal information during a visit support patients' understanding of an illness, build rapport, serve their patients more effectively, and increase patient satisfaction (e.g., Beach *et al.* 2004; du Pré 2002). In the context of teaching, researchers have shown that teacher self-disclosure "is a powerful tool in the classroom" (Cayanus 2004, 6–7) in that it is linked to several positive student outcomes such as student interest, affective learning, and understanding of material (see e.g., Goldstein and Benassi 1994; Sorensen 1989). Disclosing is part of small talk that extends beyond greetings, so as noted earlier, research in this area has shown how this can serve a wide variety of positive functions in the workplace (Holmes 2000).

Encouraging

Encouraging simply means to give courage—to provide the strength and support to another person so that they can enact their potential. Encouraging exemplifies a person's ability to provide social support. By definition, social support refers "to verbal and nonverbal communication between recipients and providers that reduces uncertainty about a situation, the self, the other, or the relationships and functions to enhance a perception of personal control in one's experience" (Albrecht and Adelman 1987, 19).

Across contexts, researchers have shown that social support has a range of positive impacts including positive physiological and mental consequences on both recipients and providers. As Caplan and Samter (1999, 245) wrote, "[S]ocially supportive interactions are related to a variety of positive outcomes including reducing stress (e.g., moderating emotional and psychological distress), enhancing esteem, and providing tangible assistance with stressful experiences" (also see MacGeorge *et al.* 2012, 212). In this section, we first describe the nature of social support and its significance in the workplace. Then, we focus specifically on the importance of encouraging at work.

Supportive communication has three forms. First is instrumental support. By definition, instrumental support is communication that provides information to assist another person. Advice-giving sequences exemplify best this form of social support. In the literature, researchers have examined advice-giving between managers and staff (Stubbe *et al.* 2003; Vine 2004) and in health care interaction (e.g., Heath 1986; Heritage and Maynard 2006).

Overall, we know that advice giving is especially meaningful at work. As Knapp, Stohl, and Reardon (1981) revealed, most memorable messages come from interaction at work, especially from a supervisor.

The second form is emotional support. By definition, emotional support includes any communication behaviour that is designed to reduce emotional distress. In the workplace, emotional support reduces job stress and burnout (e.g., Dignam and West 1988). As Amason, Allen, and S. Holmes (1999, 314) explained, "supportive intraorganizational relationships have been linked to reduced uncertainty, increased job satisfaction and job security, increased satisfaction with supervisors and individual self-worth, decreased job stress and burnout, and increased worker health". Emotional support, whether it unfolds as comforting communication (MacGeorge et al. 2012) or as affection (see Floyd 2002), serves positive functions at work.

The last form of support is esteem support. MacGeorge et al. (2012, 221) define this concept as communicative actions, verbal or nonverbal, that are designed to "enhance how recipients feel about themselves" and therefore can be seen to relate to complimenting. In the workplace, we know that forms of social support "play an important role in mitigating intention to quit" (172) and can reduce staff turnover (see Firth et al. 2004).

Mirivel's (2014) emphasis on the act of encouraging is a way to synthesize the concept of social support and calls on professionals across contexts to find opportunities to be supportive. In the business setting, researchers have shown that "subordinates prefer supervisory communication that is accepting and encouraging rather than neutral or negative" (see Redding and Tompkins 1988, 229). Put simply, encouraging is a hallmark of effective managerial communication. In the classroom, scholars have found that teacher encouragement affects students' self-efficacy and motivation (Tuckman and Sexton 1991). Encouragement also matters in coach–athlete relationships (Smoll and Smith 2006). In medical interaction, encouragements from physicians can enhance patients' adherence to treatment and affect patient satisfaction and overall health (see Heritage and Maynard 2006; Brown, Stewart, and Ryan 2003). In Vine, Holmes, and Marra (2012), the ways two mentors support their migrant interns is discussed, and the way this facilitates the transition into the workplace for the migrants.

Listening

The last communication behaviour in Mirivel's model is listening. In terms of communication competence, listening is "*the* quintessential positive interpersonal communication behaviour as it connotes an appreciation of and an interest in the other" (Bodie 2012, 109; original emphasis). As we show here, it is a behaviour that is critical in workplace interaction.

In a review of the literature, Haas and Arnold (1995, 124) wrote that "listening ability, or the perception of effective listening, is inextricably linked to effective individual performance in organizations". In that same article, the authors found that "listening well was the most frequently mentioned attribute associated with communication competence" (131). In small group research, scholars have found, for example, that "leaders typically exhibit more effective listening skills in group meetings" (Johnson and Bechler 1998, 464) and that emergent leaders "exhibit superior listening skills" (467). Managerial listening can promote open dialogue between supervisors and supervisees, contribute to support, trust and motivation, and lead to important outcomes for the organization such as increased productivity and lower absenteeism (Stine, Thompson, and Cusella 1995). As Flynn and Faulk (2008) argue, effective listening is not simply the skills that people have, but is also enabled or constrained by the listening environment. Listening environment, or the perceptions of conditions that help with listening in the organization, can promote understanding, reduce conflict, and build relationships.

In turn, such a listening environment can improve performance and satisfaction (Cooper 1997), and positively influence an employee's intention to stay with the organization (Crittenden and Crittenden 1985). Simply put, effective listening has a range of positive outcomes. As Dutton (2003, 38) argued, effective listening has "real payoff in terms of creating and sustaining high-quality relationships both within and across work organizations."

Limitations of the Model and Future Research Directions

In this chapter, we have reviewed literature on relational talk at work through the theoretical lens of Mirivel's model of positive communication. Across workplace contexts, and in light of that model, we have argued that greeting, asking, complimenting, disclosing, encouraging, and listening are communicative acts that exemplify positive communication and serve important social, relational, and institutional functions at work. In this section, we describe the limitations of the model and call for future research.

Although Mirivel's model provides a useful synthesis of relational talk at work, it does not account for a number of other interactional practices that can also have an impact in the workplace. The use of humour, for instance, can also be used to do relational work (see Holmes, Marra, and Vine 2011, chap. 5). The model could thus be strengthened by including some of these practices and taking account of such strategies as humorous or affectionate greetings, playful disclosure or encouragement.

One value of the model is that it provides an integrative framework through which to examine the impact and functions of multiple communicative acts across workplaces. This is helpful in part because research on language and social interaction in the workplace is diffused and is often reviewed in light of the context or the method that is being used, but not the actions that make a difference. Future research can draw on this model as a way to synthesize scholarly findings so that scholars can learn more about how certain communication behaviours function in the workplace and their value in terms of human connection.

More importantly, the model of positive communication is a call to action for professionals. Given the evidence provided in this review, we find that the six areas highlighted—greeting, asking, complimenting, disclosing, encouraging, and listening—all play an important role across a range of workplace settings. Physicians, managers, supervisors, teachers and professors, as well as nurses, lawyers, and the people they interact with all benefit from these behaviours. The question of how individuals can *intentionally* create a positive workplace culture through communication is complex, but calling attention to details in everyday talk is one way researchers in Language and Social Interaction can contribute. Future research needs to examine what happens when individuals and professionals are taught these communicative competencies and engage in them. Can one leader who practices positive communication break a culture of hostility? Can a physician who engages in these behaviours affect her patients' health, their satisfaction, and their adherence to treatment? Can managers trained in positive communication make a difference? These questions and others are worth further exploration.

Much of the research outlined in this chapter has been conducted in Western contexts. Another fruitful area of research would be to explore more fully other cultures, for example Asian cultures, and how different cultural norms relate to relational practice (see Fletcher this volume; Holmes this volume).

Workplace contexts are created by the conversations that people have and the ways in which they engage with one another. It matters to patients if they are greeted. It matters to an organizational culture if people encourage one another. It makes a difference when teachers listen deeply to their students. Every moment of interaction is significant. As we have shown in this chapter, positive communication can help create positive organizational climates, high-quality relationships, and affect a wide range of outcomes such as health, learning, or morale. The way people communicate at work—simply said—makes a difference. With this impulse, research on relational talk at work can therefore strengthen professionals' competencies and inspire them to connect more effectively.

Further Reading

Coupland (2000b) is a nice introduction to the literature on small talk and its significance across contexts.

Dutton (2003) gives a business focus on how to create high quality connections at work.

Holmes, Marra, and Vine (2011, chap. 5) explores the connection between relational talk and leadership.

Mirivel (2014) provides a theoretically grounded and heuristic model of positive communication.

Vine (2004) captures how power is discursively managed in interaction at work.

Related Topics

(Im)politeness theory; Rapport management; Social constructionism; Directives; Humour; Narratives; Leadership

References

Albrecht, Terrance L., and Mara B. Adelman. 1987. "Communicating Social Support: A Theoretical Perspective." In *Communicating Social Support*, edited by Terrance L. Albrecht, and Mara B. Adelman, 18–39. Newbury Park, CA: Sage.

Altman, Irwin, and Dalmas Taylor. 1973. *Social Penetration: The Development of Interpersonal Relationships*. New York: Holt, Rinehart and Winston.

Amason, Patricia, Myria Watkins Allen, and Susan Holmes. 1999. "Social Support and Acculturative Stress in the Multicultural Workplace." *Journal of Applied Communication Research* 27: 310–334.

Bain, Ken. 2004. *What the Best College Teachers Do*. Cambridge, MA: Harvard University Press.

Beach, Mary Catherine, Debra Roter, Haya Rubin, Richard Frankel, Wendy Levinson, and Daniel E. Ford. 2004. "Is Physician Self-Disclosure Related to Patient Evaluation of Office Visits?" *Journal of General Internal Medicine* 19: 905–910.

Bodie, Graham D. 2012. "Listening as Positive Communication." In *The Positive Side of Interpersonal Communication*, edited by Thomas J. Socha, and Maggie J. Pitts, 109–125. New York: Peter Lang.

Brown, Judith B., Moira Stewart, and Bridget L. Ryan. 2003. "Outcomes of Patient–Provider Interaction." In *Handbook of Health Communication*, edited by Teresa L. Thompson, Alicia M. Dorsey, Katherine I. Miller, and Roxanne Parrott, 141–161. Mahwah, NJ: Lawrence Erlbaum.

Browning, Larry D., G. H. Morris, and Kerk F. Kee. 2011. "The Role of Communication in Positive Organizational Scholarship." In *Handbook of Positive Organizational Scholarship*, edited by Kim Cameron, and Gretchen Spreitzer, 566–578. Oxford: Oxford University Press.

Burnett, Paul C. 2002. "Teacher Praise and Feedback and Students' Perceptions of the Classroom Environment." *Educational Psychology* 22: 5–16.

Cameron, Kim. 2013. *Practicing Positive Leadership: Tools and Techniques that Create Extraordinary Results*. Berrett-Koehler Publishers.

Caplan, Scott E., and Wendy Samter. 1999. "The Role of Facework in Younger and Older Adults' Evaluations of Social Support Messages." *Communication Quarterly* 47: 245–265.

Cayanus, Jacob L. 2004. "Using Teacher Self-disclosure as An Instructional Tool." *Communication Teacher* 18: 6–9.

Comstock, Loretto M., Elizabeth M. Hooper, Jean M. Goodwin, and James S. Goodwin. 1982. "Physician Behaviors that Correlate with Patient Satisfaction." *Academic Medicine* 57: 105–12.

Cooper, Lynn O. 1997. "Listening Competency in the Workplace: A Model for Training." *Business Communication Quarterly* 60: 75–84.

Coupland, Justine. 2000a. "Introduction: Sociolinguistic Perspectives on Small Talk." In *Small Talk*, edited by Justice Coupland, 1–25. Harlow, UK: Longman.

Coupland, Justine, Ed. 2000b. *Small Talk*. Harlow, UK: Longman.

Crittenden, William F., and Victoria L. Crittenden. 1985. "Listening—A Skill Necessary for Supervisory Success." *Supervision* 47: 3–5.

Dignam, John T., and Stephen G. West. 1988. "Social Support in the Workplace: Tests of Six Theoretical Models." *American Journal of Community Psychology* 16: 701–724.

Drew, Paul. 1992. "Contested Evidence in Courtroom Cross-Examination: The Case of a Trial for Rape." In *Talk at Work: Interaction in Institutional Settings*, edited by Paul Drew and John Heritage, 470–520. Cambridge: Cambridge University Press.

du Pré, Athena. 2002. "Accomplishing the Impossible: Talking about Body and Soul and Mind during a Medical Visit." *Health Communication* 14: 1–21.

Dutton, Jane E. 2003. *Energize your Workplace: How to Create and Sustain High-Quality Connections at Work*. San Francisco, CA: John Wiley & Sons.

Firth, Lucy, David J. Mellor, Kathleen A. Moore, and Claude Loquet. 2004. "How Can Managers Reduce Employee Intention to Quit?" *Journal of Managerial Psychology* 19: 170–187.

Floyd, Kory. 2002. "Human Affection Exchange: V. Attributes of the Highly Affectionate." *Communication Quarterly* 50: 135–152.

Flynn, Jan, and Larry Faulk. 2008. "Listening in the Workplace." *Kentucky Journal of Communication* 27: 15–31.

Golato, Andrea. 2003. "Studying Compliment Responses: A Comparison of DCTs and Recordings of Naturally Occurring Talk." *Applied Linguistics* 24: 90–121.

Goldstein, Gary S., and Victor A. Benassi. 1994. "The Relation between Teacher Self Disclosure and Student Classroom Participation." *Teaching of Psychology* 21: 212–216.

Haas, John W., and Christa L. Arnold. 1995. "An Examination of the Role of Listening in Judgments of Communication Competence in Co-workers." *Journal of Business Communication* 32: 123–139.

Heath, Christian. 1986. *Body Movement and Speech in Medical Interaction*. Cambridge: Cambridge University Press.

Heritage, John. 2003. "Designing Questions and Setting Agendas in the News Interview." In *Studies in Language and Social Interaction: In Honor of Robert Hopper*, edited by Phillip J. Glenn, Curtis D. LeBaron, and Jenny Mandelbaum, 57–90. Mahwah, NJ: Lawrence Erlbaum.

Heritage, John, and Douglas Maynard. 2006. "Introduction: Analyzing Primary Care Encounters." In *Communication in Medical Care: Interactions between Primary Care Physicians and Patients*, edited by John Heritage, and Douglas Maynard, 1–21. Cambridge: Cambridge University Press.

Holmes, Janet. 1986. "Compliments and Compliment Responses in New Zealand English." *Anthropological Linguistics* 28: 485–508.

Holmes, Janet. 1988. "Paying Compliments: A Sex Preferential Positive Politeness Strategy." *Journal of Pragmatics* 12: 445–465.

Holmes, Janet. 2000. "Doing Collegiality and Keeping Control at Work: Small Talk in Government Departments." In *Small Talk*, edited by Justine Coupland, 32–62. Harlow, UK: Longman.

Holmes, Janet. 2003. "Small Talk at Work: Potential Problems for Workers with an Intellectual Disability." *Research on Language and Social Interaction* 36: 65–84.

Holmes, Janet. 2005. "When Small Talk is a Big Deal: Sociolinguistic Challenges in the Workplace." In *Second Language Needs Analysis*, edited by Michael L. Long, 344–372. Cambridge: Cambridge University Press.

Holmes, Janet, and Meredith Marra 2004a. "Leadership and Managing Conflict in Meetings." *Pragmatics* 14: 439–462.

Holmes, Janet, and Meredith Marra 2004b. "Relational Practice in the Workplace: Women's Talk or Gendered Discourse?" *Language in Society* 33: 377–398.

Holmes, Janet, Meredith Marra, and Bernadette Vine. 2011. *Leadership, Discourse and Ethnicity*. Oxford: Oxford University Press.

Huseman, Richard C., John D. Hatfield, and Edward W. Miles. 1987. "A New Perspective on Equity Theory: The Equity Sensitivity Construct." *Academy of Management Review* 12: 222–234.

Johnson, Scott D., and Curt Bechler. 1998. "Examining the Relationship between Listening Effectiveness and Leadership Emergence: Perceptions, Behaviors, and Recall." *Small Group Research* 29: 452–471.

Knapp, Mark L., Cynthia Stohl, and Kathleen K. Reardon. 1981. "'Memorable' Messages." *Journal of Communication* 31: 27–41.

Lutgen-Sandvik, Pamela, Sarah Riforgiate, and Courtney Fletcher. 2011. "Work as a Source of Positive Emotional Experiences and the Discourses Informing Positive Assessment." *Western Journal of Communication* 75: 2–27.

MacGeorge, Erina L., Bo Feng, Kristi L. Wilkum, and Eileen E. Doherty. 2012. "Supportive Communication: A Positive Response to Negative Life Events." In *The Positive Side of Interpersonal Communication*, edited by Thomas Socha, and Maggie J. Pitts, 212–228. New York: Peter Lang.

Marrs, Paige C. 2007. "The Enactment of Fear in Conversations-Gone-Bad at Work." PhD. diss., Fielding Graduate University.

McCarthy, Michael. 2000. "Mutually Captive Audiences: Small Talk and the Genre of Close-Contact Service Encounters." In *Small Talk*, edited by Justine Coupland, 84–109. Harlow, UK: Longman.

Mead, George Herbert. 1934. *Mind, Self and Society: From the Standpoint of a Socialist Behavorist*. Chicago, IL: University of Chicago Press.

Mirivel, Julien C. 2014. *The Art of Positive Communication: Theory and Practice*. New York: Peter Lang.

Montgomery, Barbara M., and Leslie A. Baxter. 1998. "Dialogism and Relational Dialectics." In *Dialectical Approaches to Studying Personal Relationships*, edited by Barbara M. Montgomery, and Leslie A. Baxter, 155–183. Mahwah, NJ: Lawrence Erlbaum.

Pearce, W. Barnett, and Stewart M. Sharp. 1973. "Self-Disclosing Communication." *Journal of Communication* 23: 409–425.

Pearce, W. Barnett. 1994. *Interpersonal Communication: Making Social Worlds*. New York: Harper Collins.

Petronio, Sandra. 2002. *Boundaries of Privacy: Dialectics of Disclosure*. New York: State University of New York Press.

Phillips, Katherine W., Nancy P. Rothbard, and Tracy L. Dumas. 2009. "To Disclose or Not to Disclose? Status Distance and Self-Disclosure in Diverse Environments." *Academy of Management Review* 34: 710–732.

Pomerantz, Anita. 1978. "Compliment Responses: Notes on the Co-operation of Multiple Constraints." In *Studies in the Organization of Conversational Interaction*, edited by Jim Schenkein, 79–112. New York: Academic Press.

Redding, W. Charles, and Phillip K. Tompkins. 1988. "Organizational Communication: Past and Present Tenses." In *Handbook of Organizational Communication*, edited by Gerald M. Goldhaber, and George A. Barnett, 5–33. Norwood, MA: Ablex.

Sacks, Harvey. 1992. *Lectures on Conversation, Volumes I and II*. Edited by Gail Jefferson with Introductions by Emanuel Schegloff. Oxford: Blackwell.

Seeger, Matthew W., and Robert R. Ulmer. 2001. "Virtuous Responses to Organizational Crisis: Aaron Feuerstein and Milt Colt." *Journal of Business Ethics* 31: 369–376.

Seiter, John S. 2007. "Ingratiation and Gratuity: The Effect of Complimenting Customers on Tipping Behavior in Restaurants." *Journal of Applied Social Psychology* 37: 478–485.

Smoll, Frank L., and Ronald E. Smith. 2006. "Enhancing Coach–Athlete Relationships: Cognitive-Behavioral Principles and Procedures." In *The Sport Psychologist's Handbook: A Guide for Sport-Specific Performance Enhancement*, edited by Joaquin Dosil, 19–37. Hoboken, NJ: John Wiley & Sons.

Socha, Thomas J., and Gary A. Beck. 2015. "Positive Communication and Human Needs: A Review and Proposed Organizing Conceptual Framework." *Review of Communication* 15: 173–199.

Socha, Thomas. J., and Maggie J. Pitts. 2012. "Toward a Conceptual Foundation for Positive Interpersonal Communication." In *The Positive Side of Interpersonal Communication*, edited by Thomas J. Socha, and Maggie J. Pitts, 1–15. New York: Peter Lang.

Socha, Thomas J., and Maggie J. Pitts. 2013. "Coda: Apples and Positive Messages: Towards Healthy Communication Habits and Wellness." In *Positive Communication in Health and Wellness*, edited by Maggie J. Pitts, and Thomas J. Socha, 299–304. New York: Peter Lang.

Sorensen, Gail. 1989. "The Relationship among Teachers' Self-Disclosive Statements, Students' Perceptions, and Affective Learning." *Communication Education* 38: 259–276.

Stephens, John Paul, Emily D. Heaphy, Abraham Carmeli, Gretchen M. Spreitzer, and Jane E. Dutton. 2013. "Relationship Quality and Virtuousness: Emotional Carrying Capacity as a Source of Individual and Team Resilience." *Journal of Applied Behavioral Science* 49: 13–41.

Stine, Mary, Teresa Thompson, and Louis Cusella. 1995. "The Impact of Organizational Structure and Supervisory Listening Indicators on Subordinate Support, Trust, Intrinsic Motivation, and Performance." *International Journal of Listening* 9: 84–105.

Stubbe, Maria, Chris Lane, Jo Hilder, Elaine Vine, Bernadette Vine, Meredith Marra, Janet Holmes, and Ann Weatherall. 2003. "Multiple Discourse Analyses of a Workplace Interaction." *Discourse Studies* 5: 351–388.

Telaumbanua, Yohannes. 2012. "Complimenting as a Conversation Opener: A Strategy in Teaching English Speaking Proficiency." *Journal Polingua Scientific Journal of Linguistic, Literature and Education* 1: 32–38.

Trees, April R., Jeff Kerssen-Griep, and Jon A. Hess. 2009. "Earning Influence by Communicating Respect: Facework's Contributions to Effective Instructional Feedback." *Communication Education* 58: 397–416.

Tuckman, Bruce W., and Thomas L. Sexton. 1991. "The Effect of Teacher Encouragement on Student Self-Efficacy and Motivation for Self-Regulated Performance." *Journal of Social Behavior and Personality* 6: 137–146.

Ulmer, Robert R., Timothy L. Sellnow, and Matthew W. Seeger. 2014. *Effective Crisis Communication*. Thousand Oaks, CA: Sage.

Van De Mieroop, Dorien, and Eveline Vrolix. 2014. "A Discourse Analytical Perspective on the Professionalization of the Performance Appraisal Interview." *International Journal of Business Communication* 51: 159–182.

Vine, Bernadette. 2004. *Getting Things Done at Work: The Discourse of Power in Workplace Interaction*. Amsterdam: John Benjamins.

Vine, Bernadette, Janet Holmes and Meredith Marra. 2012. "Mentoring Migrants: Facilitating the Transition to the New Zealand Workplace." In *Advice in Discourse*, edited by Holger Limberg, and Miriam A. Locher, 145–165. Berlin: Mouton de Gruyter.

Waldvogel, Joan. 2007. "Greetings and Closings in Workplace Email." *Journal of Computer-Mediated Communication* 12: 456–477.

Weinstein, Lawrence, Antonio Laverghetta, Ralph Alexander, and Megan Stewart. 2009. "Teacher Greetings Increase College Students' Test Scores." *College Student Journal* 43: 452–453.

Willemyns, Michael, Cynthia Gallois, and Victor J. Callan. 2003. "Trust Me, I'm Your Boss: Trust and Power in Supervisor-Supervisee Communication." *International Journal of Human Resource Management* 14: 117–127.

19
Humour in the Workplace
Bernie Chun Nam Mak

Introduction

Humour was condemned as unproductive at work half a century ago due to the (rationalist) view that the workplace should be a serious setting (see Westwood and Johnston 2013). However, there are numerous studies propounding the advantages of using humour in the workplace. Early studies found that humour could provide informal catharsis to alleviate routine and unavoidable problems at work (see e.g., Bradney 1957; Collinson 1988). Later research concentrated on investigating employees' bottom-up use of humour (see e.g., Ackroyd and Thompson 1999), for example, to challenge superiors in a socially-acceptable way (Taylor and Bain 2003). In the past decade, scholars have taken the view that humour should be deemed functional to achieving a variety of short- and long-term workplace goals (see e.g., Ladegaard 2009), such as boosting creativity (Holmes 2007) and socializing newcomers (Schnurr and Mak 2009).

With the gathering of momentum in research, humour has been defined differently across scholarly fields (see Ladegaard 2009 for a review). This chapter employs Holmes' (2000, 163) definition, considering humour instances to be "utterances that are identified by the analyst, on the basis of paralinguistic, prosodic, and discoursal clues, as intended by the speakers to be amusing and perceived to be amusing by at least some participants." This definition highlights the interactional nature of humour and differentiates it from what psychologists call "the sense of humour", a cognitive ability. Holmes' notion of "utterances" can usefully be extended to include all forms of communication including non-verbal interaction online (Cooper 2008).

The diverse definitions of humour are matched by various theories of humour. Different theories or frameworks serve to emphasize various aspects of humour (see Plester 2016). This chapter adopts classic Incongruity Theory, which takes the view that humour occurs when participants are amused by the overt inconsistencies between the expected interpretation and the unexpected encounter via the process of conversational implicature (Ellithorpe, Esralew, and Holbert 2014). In other words, humour occurs when an unexpected event invites participants to move from serious schemas to a fantasy assimilation in order to understand the underlying meaning to be communicated (Gray and Ford 2013).

Humour in Face-to-Face Workplace Communication

The phenomenon of using humour strategically at work originates from its inherent indirectness which enables colleagues to communicate face-threatening messages without causing offence (Taylor and Bain 2003), and its amusing nature which allows them to maintain or develop (superficial) harmony and solidarity (Holmes and Marra 2006). Self-deprecating humour, for managers, is found to be useful in mitigating top-down workplace talk (Holmes and de Bres 2012). For subordinates, it can attenuate the embarrassment due to inappropriate actions (Holmes, Marra, and Burns 2001). Hostile teasing, sometimes quite aggressive in nature, can implicate important disagreement (Schnurr and Zayts 2011) and criticism for work incompetency (Collinson 1988). Even innuendo can consolidate the bonding among colleagues (Vine *et al.* 2009), while humorous irony allows low-ranked employees to enact spiritual superiority (Watts 2007). Among the subtypes of humour, playful teasing seems to be widely used in defusing mental tension in critical moments (Koester 2010). Example 19.1 provides an example of how playful teasing can also be conducive to and indicative of the socialization process of a workplace newcomer.

Example 19.1[1]

Context: Emma,[2] a migrant worker from the Philippines, is a newcomer to the Hong Kong office of Sunflower Holdings Limited. Gavin and David, the assigned mentors, are teaching her to use a computer programme for business.

1	Emma:	oh I under-tick the ( ) box
2	David:	what? /this\
3	Emma:	/yeah\ yeah I find out the problems (.) oh
4	David:	oh you tick it ( ) give you zero (point) one minute
5	Gavin:	you make it /Hah\
6	David	/Hah\
7	Emma:	/oh HELP\ (5) I leave that flower box blank is it?
8	Gavin:	yeah
9	Emma:	no more (.) no more other
10	David:	no more /other\
11	Gavin:	/this\ this two all first (.) and then just (.) just keep this
...		
13	Gavin:	( ) this for for future (.) if the customer want to ( )
14	Emma:	some seems MO2 (.) not marked
15	Gavin:	yes
16	Emma:	okay ( ) other (.) two minute
17	Gavin:	two minutes
18	David:	Hah thirty (.) second
19	Gavin:	twenty sec twenty seconds
20	David:	Hah thirty Hah oh not more than twenty
21	Emma:	ten times of it /Hah\
22	Gavin:	/Hah\
23	David:	/Hah\

David's suggestion for Emma's fixing the problem in "zero point one minute", echoed by Gavin's encouragement "you make it" and laughter (lines 3–5), is playful teasing. Emma responds to their humour by yelling "oh help", but this yields a five-second silence (line 7). However, similar teasing on the theme of time-allowed is picked up by the two mentors again (lines 19–21). This time Emma plays along with it by jesting that she needs "ten times" their suggested time (line 22), which provokes laughter from the two mentors. Humour taking place within such a mentoring activity for Emma not only creates light heartedness for learning, but also provides her with an opportunity to reach a milestone of socialization. Conversely, her failure to respond humorously in the first instance illustrates her newcomer status that occasionally deprives her of full participation.

The analysis of Example 19.1 is consistent with Vinton (1989) who testified that humour could be a catalyst for integration into the workplace. Example 19.2, however, shows that hostile teasing which is elicited inappropriately may have the opposite effect.

Example 19.2

Context: Kevin, a new senior ship engineer to Cosmos Marine Engineering Services Limited, is hanging around a mechanical ship to follow the working progress of his team. Peter is a crew member who is experienced in technical work on the ship. They are arguing about the angle of a searchlight on the deck.[3]

1	Kevin:	what're you /setting\?
2	Peter:	/setting\ up those lights
3	Kevin:	all on?
4	Peter:	yes all /on\
5	Kevin:	/all\ on but why don't you bow this down?
6	Peter:	not bow it down and cast light on the ship surface (.) now it
7		also casts light on that side
8	Kevin:	you want to use it for fishing don't you? Hah
9	Peter:	no just on the ship surface (.) it's useless ( ) that place is
10		blocked from fishing
11	Kevin:	do you want it for fishing? Hah
12	Peter:	no
		((Peter keeps explaining why he does not bow the light down. Finally Kevin gives up.))

Kevin attempts to order Peter to bow down the searchlight using the indirect structure "why don't you" (line 5). When Peter seriously explains his reason for keeping it horizontal (lines 6–7 and 9–10), Kevin playfully asks him with laughter if he wants to fish twice (lines 8 and 11). This question is hostile teasing in the form of nonsense in that they are working in the profession of marine engineering, overtly contrasting with the indigenous field of fishery in Hong Kong. The meaning of Kevin's question cannot be taken literally (Dynel 2014). It implicitly carries Kevin's negative evaluation of Peter's refusal to bow down the searchlight. The top-down humour is rejected probably due to the fact that Peter, a technician, considers that he knows more about practical things, while Kevin (only) knows theoretical and supervisory work. Peter's stance may also be due to Kevin's new membership, a factor which may outweigh his superiority in the official ranking.

Example 19.2 indicates that workplace humour does not *always* work (Mallett and Wapshott 2014). Inappropriate play may not only fail to convey a superior's intention but also cause negative consequences to management (Pundt and Herrmann 2015). Only when the joker behaves appropriately and other participants decode correctly will a humorous exchange end productively. The uses and misuses of humour in face-to-face workplace interaction are however not limited to those discussed and exemplified above (see e.g., Butler 2015; Gunnarsson 2009; Holmes and de Bres 2012 for overviews). I now turn to an investigation of humorous exchanges among colleagues through instant-messaging and microblogging.

Humour in Instant-Messaging and Microblogging Workplace Communication

Few studies have investigated online humour, and even fewer the use of it when colleagues interact on computers. A handful of earlier research studies investigated the violations of traditional linguistic rules (e.g., Gricean Maxims, adjacency pairs) for playful communication in chatrooms (Herring 1997). More recently, works centred on Facebook are on the increase, looking into teachers' humorous posts for educational purposes (Imlawi and Gregg 2014), students' canned jokes to reshape identities in the aftermath of a political event (Moalla 2015), organizations' pages created to ridicule existing language policy (Sherman and Svelch 2015), and users' perceptions of sexist humour (Strain, Saucier, and Martens 2015). Some concentrate on the humorous (anti)racist messages on forums (Malmqvist 2015); others examine humour about the relation between human beings and IT in the broader online context (Shifman and Blondheim 2010) and rebellious jokes against the political correctness of mass media that circulate among Web 2.0 (Blank 2013). While these studies provide insights into the role of humour in the Digital Age, there is a need for more discussion of the use of online humour within a workplace's Community of Practice (CofP) (see King this volume).

Humour in Instant-Messaging Among Colleagues

Instant messengers had gained popularity among young teenagers with the development of ICQ in 1996, but the leisure pursuits faded out when many of them (e.g., MSN, AIM) were developed with a more formal interface and introduced into the workplace in the 2000s (Handel and Herbsleb 2002). Instant messengers are software that supports users to exchange one-on-one and one-on-many messages instantly with their contacts over the Internet (Baron 2004; Crystal 2006). Many have been integrated (or developed) into social-network sites where the technical affordances are more flexible and multifaceted than the early protocols (Jones 2010). Researchers have argued that instant messengers are upstaging workplace talk (e.g., Darics 2010; Stephens, Cowan, and Houser 2011), for instance, through providing an extra means for colleagues' work reminders (Quan-Haase, Cothrel, and Wellman 2005), small talk (Chung and Nam 2007), and formation of an online community (Debbabi and Rahman 2004).

The additional arena provided by instant messengers in the workplace often engenders the use of humour among colleagues online. Example 19.3 provides a wordplay instance that could only occur in the computer context.

Key Areas of Workplace Talk

Example 19.3

Context: In Superstar Electronics Holdings, Martin and Tommy are at the managerial rank albeit working in different areas. Martin cleans the database for marketing in an upcoming industrial fair, and finds that the model 9407 has become out-dated. He informs Tommy of this in Windows Live Messenger.

1	Martin	we used to make money by this model and 9407 . . . . .
2		when w98 was popular everywhere
3	Tommy	computer tech is like this . . . .
4		as we always look forward the new . . . . .
5		but I still keep a sony 3.5' and maxell 5.25' fds
6	Martin	really? still have the drives to read them?
7	Tommy	no just for memories and history
8	Martin	we loved them when we still used dos 6.2
9		dir/w/p
10		copy a:*.gif c:\photos
11	Tommy	yes I still remember some commands
12		cd . . .
13	Martin	c:\rename a:\install.exe uninstall.exe
14	Tommy	Hahahaaaaaa
15		those days we thought dos was more convenient than w3.1
16	Martin	yes but w95 changed everything

When the topic changes from the old items to development of computers (lines 1–4), Martin and Tommy evoke nostalgia by creating a cultural world where MS-DOS jargon still had overt prestige in computing (lines 5–12). The imagined MS-DOS era is extended from the work-related frame, but results in humour using DOS commands. Martin types "C:\rename a:\install.exe uninstall.exe" (line 13), a silly command that will replace the name of a file to install a program with the name of a file to uninstall thereby triggering massive errors whenever these files are opened afterwards. The suggestion evokes a prolonged written expression of laughter from Tommy indicated by "hahaha" followed by a series of "a" (line 14). The jargon-based humour (McGhie 1991) grants them an identity as part of a generation that had grown up working with MS-DOS.

While the humour in Example 19.3 depends upon cognitive symbolic behaviour, the wordplay in Example 19.4 appears to rely on exploitation of the norms of instant messaging to tease and engage in banter.

Charles plays with ellipsis dots and the connectivity between the pronoun "you" and its possessive form "your" to construct a flirtation (lines 3–7). Scholars of computer-mediated communication have agreed that in order to type fast to maintain a sense of instantaneity, instant-messenger users tend to split continuous utterances into several smaller units by pressing the enter key after typing each segment (e.g., Baron 2004; Chung and Nam 2007). Each press results in a single line or fragment of a message on the receiver's window. Moreover, to avoid interruption, the sender will use ellipsis dots to signal that the utterance remains unfinished (Mak 2014). These norms are adapted by Charles for use in wordplay making fun

> **Example 19.4**
>
> Context: Jenny, a new merchandising trainee to Superstar Electronics Holdings, went to the Hong Kong Trade Development Council (TDC) for some registration work for the upcoming industrial fair. Charles, an integral member of the team, greets her when he sees her online in Windows Live Messenger again.
>
> | 1 | Charles | jenny |
> |---|---|---|
> | 2 | Jenny | ? |
> | 3 | Charles | when you went to the tdc today ..... |
> | 4 | | do you know how much I miss you .... |
> | 5 | Jenny | ha?! |
> | 6 | Charles | do you know how much I miss you .... |
> | 7 | | .... r buyer who confirmed the order with 5000 bk010a last week? |
> | 8 | Jenny | .... |
> | 9 | Charles | wakakaaa surprised? |
> | 10 | Jenny | fortunately, you miss my buyer only, not me! |
> | 11 | | but the buyer is a man |
> | 12 | | are you gay? |
> | 13 | Charles | (lol) |
> | 14 | | good job today? |

of Jenny, who initially seems surprised as shown by the combination of question and exclamation marks (line 5). When Jenny realizes the truth, she counters with a clever innuendo that imposes a "gay" identity on Charles (lines 10–12), which elicits a "lol" (laugh out loud) response (line 13). Here Jenny's response could be considered a bantering technique indicating her ability to collaborate in constructing mischievous humour on a slippery topic, just like Charles.

The technical affordances of instant messengers and the Internet play a critical role in the humour instances from my dataset. In addition to the traditional elements such as the head icon, user nickname and status message, the latest instant messengers are preloaded with animated emoticons, the function of previewing an uploaded file or a hyperlink, and extension to the user profile or blog. My participants are found to exploit these affordances, together with the innovative use of Internet slang, to do humour with colleagues. Such humour has diffused into the backroom online talk within a professional context, which normatively involves politic communication.

Humour in Microblogging Among Colleagues

A microblog is a broadcasting device similar to the traditional blog, but the content is usually shorter, more casual and impromptu (Jansen *et al.* 2009; Lee 2011). Some famous examples of microblogs are Twitter and Facebook Status Update. Status Updates enable users to "share what they do and/or think 'at the moment' through short messages ... with or without embedded multimedia" (Mak and Chui 2013, 96). The post will be broadcasted on the first page of their friends, who can respond, share, or "like" (see Appendix). A microblog post can convey many emotions to different participants, and may express many emotions simultaneously.

Microblogs have been used by organizations to interact with the general public, potential partners, and customers (Zhao and Rosson 2009). However, in the context of Facebook, status updates may be used internally by colleagues as a medium of communication beyond the constraints of work hours and physical distance. Below is an exemplar of the use of a status update in consolidating a presumption within a CofP.

Example 19.5

Context: Edmund, the assistant manager, is supposed to work in the manager's room. Because of a shortage of front-line crew, he has often temporarily been required to take over the cashier role to help them. He is good at "fast trade" (persuading customers to buy extra food after they have ordered what they initially wanted), and here he broadcasts this on his Facebook Status Update.

1	[photo]	**Edmund**
2		my colleagues about to refuse to work with me la
		Friday at 0:21
		[You, Emily, Wilson and other 4 persons like this!]
3	[photo]	**Wilson** absolutely, i will be the 1st! u try not to go to
4		the cashier! everytime you go bills q up
		Friday at 0:22 [1 person likes this]
5	[photo]	**Mike** so serious
		Friday at 1:04
6	[photo]	**Edmund** they said everytime I work the biz will be better
		Friday at 1:10 [1 person likes this]
7	[photo]	**Wilson** this is the proof from my experience with u!
		Friday at 1:10
8	[photo]	**Jerry** then you need think yourself! cashier will explode
		Friday at 1:35
9	[photo]	**Derek** haha~ morning shift with you biz really very gd
		Friday at 1:36

The reason that Edmund's colleagues are about to refuse to work with him is that his fast-trade skills have led to busy work (lines 1–4, 6–7). The "la" in line 2 is a transliteration of the Cantonese exclamation "啦" to imply the speaker's (fake) disappointment. This joking remark not only is recognized through the number of "likes" on Facebook, but also attracts (superficially) criticizing responses. They should be interpreted as mock impoliteness for friendliness (Culpeper 1996) based on the assumption that more orders point to better development of business (biz). This is evidenced by Edmund's grand self-confession of the meaning of his post (line 6). Following the non-serious frame, Jerry performs playful teasing by warning Edmund that the "cashier will explode" (line 8), and then Derek responds to the humour in sing-song laughter with explicit compliments for Edmund's fast-trade skills, which are "really very gd" (good) (line 9). This marks a positive end to the back-and-forth humour appreciating Edmund's transactional accomplishments.

The content of the self-deprecating humour in Example 19.5, which is strange from a management viewpoint in Hong Kong culture, allows Edmund to present himself as more accessible to his subordinates while engaging the workforce (Pundt and Herrmann 2015). It is deep down a playful exchange after work that recapitulates the discourse of individual business performance in the fast-food catering field. The humour refers to on-site business issues in office hours, but takes place after midnight when everyone is off duty and has left the workplace.

Humour in the Workplace in the Digital Age

The topic of humour in the workplace has been explored over the past three decades. Before the popularization of the Internet, colleagues tended to joke face to face. Such humour could be conducive to optimization of business accomplishments and the development of collaborative relationships, but simultaneously it might have adverse effects if inappropriately initiated or decoded. Humour has become part of professionalism in some industries (Tanay, Wiseman, and Roberts 2014). Owing to the adaptability of humour and its potential to bend official codes or neutralize institutionalized power distance for resolving workplace problems, acquisition and practice of it constitute the establishment of membership, enactment of expertise, and exercise of judgement within the professional CofP, as Examples 19.1 and 19.2 illustrated. Effective users of workplace humour demonstrate intellectual skill in employing humour strategies to enact both professional knowledge and interpersonal skills in their workplace roles.

Humour and the Decline in Social Etiquette in the Workplace

When taking place in instant messaging and microblogging among colleagues, humour appears in the creative forms of wordplay, innuendo, and mixed teasing. Although colleagues are still constrained by the existing norms of the shared repertoires of doing humour in a CofP, digital devices that allow diverse topical choices, rapid topical shifts but slow pace create little social pressure for participants to conform (Crystal 2006). The informal nature of computer-mediated communication provides vast possibilities to joke depending upon their own preferences or perceived intimacy with others. As shown in the examples, humour may be task-oriented, entertainment-directed, rapport-aimed, problem-based, or a mix of these. Instant messengers and microblogs have seemingly escalated heterogeneity, ambiguity and multiplicity of humour and its functions in the workplace. Colleagues' online humour is more than a discursive strategy to minimize the feeling of dehumanization resulting from computer work nowadays.

The Blending of the Form of Humour with Workplace Discourse

Humour that occurs in instant messaging and microblogging is characterized by heterogeneous uses of punctuation, emoticons, acronyms, etc. as clues. These symbolic, semio-graphic, phonographic, and logographic cues have been identified in studies of synchronous computer-mediated communication (Djordjilovic 2012). They are not only intended to maintain spontaneity and brevity in online communication (Darics 2010), but also to portray a humorous frame that signals participants to suspend normal interpretations (cf. Grugulis 2002). Example 19.3 displayed the typographic use of computer language for humour. Equally important is the ready-made functions afforded by instant messengers and microblogs. Example 19.4

indicated the normative division of instant messages could be adapted for humour. These pre-designed functions stimulate their users to explore their potential to be employed flexibly and creatively (Barton and Lee 2013). The capacity to perform humour in this way leads to plural intertextuality and multimodality as the conversation unfolds (see Jones 2010). The interpenetrative instances also encompass textual, visual, and audio modes to form an aesthetic experience (Bezemer and Kress 2008), thereby blending or redefining the broader workplace context.

Humour as a Tool to Reconstruct Offline Identity and Power in the Workplace

When colleagues convey humour through instant messengers and microblogs, the involved identity construction often accretes in an intangible state of flux. Since they also meet and know each other face to face in the workplace, there may be little motivation for them to fake or modify their characteristics as these are already well known to their colleagues (Handel and Herbsleb 2002). Instead, they tend to wield or reshape their perceived offline images or characteristics by behaving in an unstable humorous manner on the platforms that do not officially require them to operate inside their shared repertoires. Humour in itself encourages personalization (Holmes 2006), while use of the two digital devices needs a personal account that invites individualization (cf. Anandarajan *et al.* 2010). Colleagues in this way may feel free to joke about whatever they think comfortable, thereby revealing many associated or conflictual characteristics. The large (sense of) autonomy reduces the demarcations among different identities, blending them into a hybridized and complicated construct. As shown in Examples 19.3 and 19.4, colleagues could joke around generation, gender, and work-related issues at the same time. This finding echoes scholars (Schnurr 2013; Vine *et al.* 2009) who demonstrated that colleagues nowadays tend to enact different characteristics simultaneously reflecting the complexities and permeability of workplace interaction, and then subsequently produce a synthesis of identities.

The reconstruction of power through instant messaging and microblogging among colleagues is manifested and controlled by their intellectual and information technology skills. As humour challenges the standards and inertia of professional communication, power is always negotiated when it occurs in workplace interaction (Taylor and Bain 2003; Vine *et al.* 2009). Through their manipulation of digital devices, colleagues reveal personal cleverness by taking control of content, language, symbols, numbers, and the preloaded functions, as partially indicated in Example 19.4. Their use is refined by the norms of instant messaging and microblogging: time lags between exchanges are tolerated, so colleagues have more time to manage their thoughts; the instant message or microblog is not displayed until the sender presses the enter key or the "post" button, so users enjoy greater freedom to edit the (humorous) message without the need to improvise (Crystal 2006). The devices even enable colleagues to jump from the online to the offline, the present to the past, the global to the local, or to roam between them, thereby providing more resources with which to scaffold alternative interpretation and intellectual stimulation. This is demonstrated by Example 19.5 where the manager reinstated the importance of (his) fast trade humorously. Due to the large potential pool of resources, humour in instant messaging and microblogging can be elaborate, infotaining, and effective, which results in enrichment in the power of intelligence and information fluency for work- or workplace-related purposes.

Conclusion

The increasing needs of computer work may limit the humour among some colleagues, but they can still be playful using digital devices. This chapter started from a general discussion on humour in the workplace, and moved into examining several examples of authentic data from face-to-face workplace settings to instant messaging and microblogging in Hong Kong. The analyses and inferences indicated that humour could be a tool to be employed purposefully for various transactional and relational purposes, and that when introduced to online platforms it could be manifested more or less differently from its offline counterparts. Electronic devices have added to the quality of extra but erratic temporal, spatial, and psychological spaces to perform humour, which helps extend the work relationship beyond normal work hours and the physical site. Therefore, scholars are recommended to look at any innovative use of humour and the involved computer-related processes in the Information Age. As humour involves risk-taking (and is face-threatening) despite the cheery surface, future research should pay more attention to the miscommunication caused by colleagues' use of it on the Internet where clues are not always sufficient and contextual information is fluctuating for participants at different receipt settings. Subtypes of humour like innuendo and ironic humour can be used maladaptively or (mis)interpreted as sexual harassment or personal attack. By and large, employees and senior management could consider the speech event openly but handle it carefully, particularly in Asian societies where face, relationship, and networking are deemed exceedingly crucial at work.

Further Reading

Plester (2009) draws on empirical data from a three-year study to investigate the influence of humour on workplace well-being, for example to alleviate tension and soften harsh directives. Plester (2016) starts from an investigation of classic humour theories, discussing the bright and dark sides of organizational humour using data collected from ethnographic research and extracts selected from published sources over a period of 12 years. Furtado, Carrieri, and Bretas (2014) examine the use of online humour to protest against resignations and outsourcing and to ridicule official discourse and decisions.

Related Topics

Rapport management; Corporate settings; Relational talk; Narratives; Leadership

Appendix

Transcription conventions for the audio-recorded examples

HELP	Capitals indicate emphatic stress
Hah	Laughter
(.)	Minor pause (of up to one second)
(3)	Longer pause (of up to two seconds or above; the number inside the brackets indicates the length of the pause)
.../...\...	
.../...\...	Overlap (which originates from simultaneous speech)
( )	Unclear or inaudible utterance

?	A question or rising intonation
I see bu-	Incomplete or cut-off speech
((Chris joins in))	Transcriber's additional information in double round brackets

Transcription conventions for the instant messaging examples

lol	
that guy	
no help	Chunks of an utterance sent by the same user
((One hour passed))	Transcriber's additional information in double round brackets

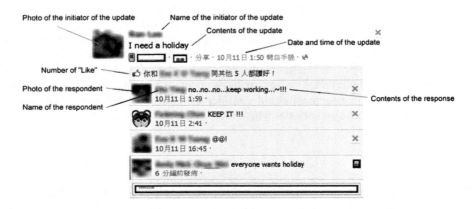

Figure 19.1 Sample of a Facebook status update

Notes

1 The examples in this chapter come from a dataset of 25 hours of face-to-face organizational talk, a pool of 78,000 English words of workplace instant messaging, and a database of over 100 microblogs posted by the colleagues of a company. They were collected from eight Hong Kong workplaces. See Appendix for Transcription Conventions.
2 All names of people and organizations used in the examples are pseudonyms.
3 This conversation was originally in Cantonese. The transcription was translated into English and double-checked by a native English speaker.

References

Ackroyd, Stephen, and Paul Thompson. 1999. *Organizational Misbehaviour*. London: Sage.
Anandarajan, Murugan, Maliha Zaman, Qizhi Dai, and Bay Arinze. 2010. "Generation Y Adoption of Instant Messaging: An Examination of the Impact of Social Usefulness and Media Richness of Use Richness." *IEEE Transactions on Professional Communication* 53: 132–143.
Baron, Naomi S. 2004. "See You Online: Gender Issues in College Student Use of Instant Messaging." *Journal of Language and Social Psychology* 23: 397–423.
Barton, David, and Carmen Lee. 2013. *Language Online: Investigating Digital Texts and Practices*. London: Routledge.
Bezemer, Jeff, and Gunther Kress. 2008. "Writing in Multimodal Texts: A Social Semiotic Account of Designs for Learning." *Written Communication* 25: 166–195.

Blank, Trevor J. 2013. *The Last Laugh: Folk Humor, Celebrity Culture, and Mass-Mediated Disasters in the Digital Age*. Madison, WI: The University of Wisconsin Press.
Bradney, Pamela. 1957. "The Joking Relationship in Industry." *Human Relations* 10: 179–187.
Butler, Nick. 2015. "Joking Aside: Theorizing Laughter in Organizations." *Culture and Organization* 21: 42–58.
Chung, Donghun, and Chang S. Nam. 2007. "An Analysis of the Variables Predicting Instant Messenger Use." *New Media and Society* 9: 212–234.
Collinson, David. 1988. "Engineering Humour: Masculinity, Joking and Conflict in Shopfloor Relations." *Organization Studies* 9: 181–199.
Cooper, Cecily. 2008. "Elucidating the Bonds of Workplace Humor: A Relational Process Model." *Human Relations* 61: 1087–1115.
Crystal, David. 2006. *Language and the Internet*. 2nd ed. Cambridge: Cambridge University Press.
Culpeper, Jonathan. 1996. "Towards an Anatomy of Impoliteness." *Journal of Pragmatics* 25: 349–367.
Darics, Erika. 2010. "Relational Work in Synchronous Text-Based CMC of Virtual Teams." In *Handbook of Research on Discourse Behavior and Digital Communication: Language Structures and Social Interaction*, edited by Rotimi Taiwo, 830–851. Hershey, PA: IGI Global.
Debbabi, Mourad, and Mahfuzur Rahman. 2004. "The War of Presence and Instant Messaging: Right Protocols and APIs." In *Proceedings of the 2004 Consumer Communications and Networking Conference*, 341–346. Los Alamitos, CA: IEEE Press.
Djordjilovic, Olga. 2012. "Displaying and Developing Team Identity in Workplace Meetings—A Multimodal Perspective." *Discourse Studies* 14: 111–127.
Dynel, Marta. 2014. "Isn't It Ironic? Defining the Scope of Humorous Irony." *Humor* 27: 619–639.
Ellithorpe, Morgan, Sarah Esralew, and Lance Holbert. 2014. "Putting the 'Self' in Self-Deprecation: When Deprecating Humor about Minorities is Acceptable." *Humor* 27: 401–422.
Furtado, Raquel Alves, Alexandre de Padua Carrieri, and Paula Fernandes Furbino Bretas. 2014. "Humor on the Internet: Workers Employ New Strategy to Protest against Resignations and Outsourcing." *Revista de Administração (São Paulo)* 49: 33–44.
Gray, Jared A., and Thomas E. Ford. 2013. "The Role of Social Context in the Interpretation of Sexist Humor." *Humor* 26: 277–293.
Grugulis, Irena. 2002. "Nothing Serious? Candidates' Use of Humour in Management Training." *Human Relations* 55: 387–406.
Gunnarsson, Britt-Louise. 2009. *Professional Discourse*. London: Continuum.
Handel, Mark, and James D. Herbsleb. 2002. "What is Chat Doing in the Workplace?" In *Proceedings of the 2002 ACM Conference on Computer Supported Cooperative Work and Social Computing*, 1–10. New York: ACM Press.
Herring, Susan C. 1997. "Humor That Binds: Joking and Coherence in Internet Relay Chat." Paper presented at *The International Society for Humor Studies Conference*, July 13. University of Oklahoma.
Holmes, Janet. 2000. "Politeness, Power and Provocation: How Humour Functions in the Workplace." *Discourse Studies* 2: 159–185.
Holmes, Janet. 2006. "Sharing a Laugh: Pragmatic Aspects of Humour and Gender in the Workplace." *Journal of Pragmatics* 38: 26–50.
Holmes, Janet. 2007. "Making Humour Work: Creativity on the Job." *Applied Linguistics* 28: 518–537.
Holmes, Janet, and Julia de Bres. 2012. "Ethnicity and Humour in the Workplace." In *Routledge Handbook of Discourse Analysis*, edited by James P. Gee, and Michael Handford, 494–508. London: Routledge.
Holmes, Janet, and Meredith Marra. 2006. "Humour and Leadership Style." *Humor* 19: 119–138.
Holmes, Janet, Meredith Marra, and Louise Burns. 2001. "Women's Humour in the Workplace: A Quantitative Analysis." *Australian Journal of Communication* 28: 83–108.
Imlawi, Jehad, and Dawn Gregg. 2014. "Engagment in Online Social Networks: The Impact of Self-Disclosure and Humor." *International Journal of Human-Computer Interaction* 30: 106–125.
Jansen, Bernard J., Mimi Zhang, Kate Sobel, and Abdur Chowdury. 2009. "Micro-Blogging as Online Word of Mouth Branding." In *Proceedings of the 27th International Conference Extended Abstracts on Human Factors in Computing System*, 3859–3864. Boston, MA: ACM Press.
Jones, Rodney. H. 2010. "Cyberspace and Physical Space: Attention Structures in Computer Mediated Communication." In *Semiotic Landscapes: Language, Image, Space*, edited by Adam Jaworski, and Crispin Thurlow, 151–167. London: Continuum.
Koester, Almut. 2010. *Workplace Discourse*. London: Continuum.

Ladegaard, Hans J. 2009. "Politeness, Power and Control: The Use of Humour in Cross-Cultural Telecommunications." In *Professional Communication: Collaboration between Academics and Practitioners*, edited by Winnie Cheng, and Kenneth C. C. Kong, 191–209. Hong Kong: Hong Kong University Press.

Lee, Carmen K. M. 2011. "Microblogging and Status Updates on Facebook: Texts and Practices." In *Digital Discourse: Language in the New Media*, edited by Crispin Thurlow, and Kristine Mroczek, 110–128. New York: Oxford University Press.

Mak, Bernie C. N. 2014. "Instant Messaging in Office Hours: Use of Ellipsis Dots at Work and Hong Kong Culture." *International Journal of Language Studies* 8: 25–50.

Mak, Bernie C. N., and Hin-leung Chui. 2013. "Colleagues' Talk and Power after Work Hours: A Community of Practice in Facebook Status Updates?" *Discourse, Context and Media* 2: 94–102.

Mallett, Oliver, and Robert Wapshott. 2014. "Informality and Employment Relationships in Small Firms: Humour, Ambiguity and Straight-Talking." *British Journal of Management* 25: 118–132.

Malmqvist, Karl. 2015. "Satire, Racist Humour and the Power of (Un)laughter: On the Restrained Nature of Swedish Online Racist Discourse Targeting EU-Migrants Begging for Money." *Discourse and Society* 26: 733–753.

McGhie, Caroline. 1991. "The Jargon of Wellington Taxi Dispatchers." *Wellington Working Papers in Linguistics* 3: 20–35.

Moalla, Asma. 2015. "Incongruity in the Generation and Perception of Humor on Facebook in the Aftermath of the Tunisian Revolution." *Journal of Pragmatics* 75: 44–52.

Plester, Barbara 2009. "Healthy Humour: Using Humour to Cope at Work." *New Zealand Journal of Social Sciences Online* 4: 89–102.

Plester, Barbara. 2016. *The Complexity of Workplace Humour*. New York: Springer.

Pundt, Alexander, and Felicia Herrmann. 2015. "Affiliative and Aggressive Humour in Leadership and Their Relationship to Leader-Member Exchange." *Journal of Occupational and Organizational Psychology* 88: 108–125.

Quan-Haase, Anabel, Joseph Cothrel, and Barry Wellman. 2005. "Instant Messaging for Collaboration: A Case Study of a High-Tech Firm." *Journal of Computer-Mediated Communication* 10. Retrieved from http://jcmc.indiana.edu/vol10/issue4/quan-haase.html.

Schnurr, Stephanie. 2013. *Exploring Professional Communication: Language in Action*. London: Routledge.

Schnurr, Stephanie, and Bernie C. N. Mak. 2009. "Humor as an Indicator of Workplace Socialization." In *Language for Professional Communication: Research, Practice and Training*, edited by Vijay K. Bhatia, Winnie Cheng, Bertha Du-Babcok, and Jane Lung, 131–145. Hong Kong: The Hong Kong Polytechnic University.

Schnurr, Stephanie, and Olga Zayts. 2011. "Be(com)ing a Leader: A Case Study of Co-Constructing Professional Identities at Work." In *Constructing Identities at Work*, edited by Jo Angouri, and Meredith Marra, 40–60. London: Palgrave Macmillan.

Sherman, Tamah, and Jaroslav Svelch. 2015. "Grammar Nazis Never Sleep: Facebook Humor and the Management of Standard Written Language." *Language Policy* 14: 315–334.

Shifman, Limor, and Menaham Blondheim. 2010. "The Medium is the Joke: Online Humor about and by Networked Computers." *New Media and Society* 12: 1348–1367.

Stephens, Keri K., Renee L. Cowan, and Marian L. Houser. 2011. "Organizational Norm Congruency and Interpersonal Familiarity in E-Mail: Examining Messages from Two Different Status Perspectives." *Journal of Computer-Mediated Communication* 16: 228–249.

Strain, Megan, Donald Saucier, and Amanda Martens. 2015. "Sexist Humor in Facebook Profiles: Perceptions of Humor Targeting Women and Men." *Humor* 28: 119–141.

Tanay, Mary A., Theresa Wiseman, and Julia Roberts. 2014. "A Time to Weep and a Time to Laugh: Humour in the Nurse-Patient Relationship in an Adult Cancer Setting." *Support Care Cancer* 22: 1295–130.

Taylor, Phil, and Peter Bain. 2003. "'Subterranean Worksick Blues': Humour as Subversion in Two Call Centres." *Organization Studies* 24: 1487–1509.

Vine, Bernadette, Susan Kell, Meredith Marra, and Janet Holmes. 2009. "Boundary-Marking Humour: Institutional, Gender and Ethnic Demarcation in the Workplace." In *Humor in Interaction*, edited by Neal R. Norrick, and Delia Chiaro, 125–139. Amsterdam: John Benjamins.

Vinton, Karen L. 1989. "Humor in the Workplace—It is More Than Telling Jokes." *Small Group Behavior* 20: 151–166.

Watts, Jacqueline. 2007. "Can't Take a Joke? Humour as Resistance, Refuge and Exclusion in a Highly Gendered Workplace." *Feminism and Psychology* 17: 259–266.
Westwood, Robert I., and Allanah Johnston. 2013. "Humor in Organization: From Function to Resistance." *Humor* 26: 219–247.
Zhao, Dejin, and Mary B. Rosson. 2009. "How and Why People Twitter: The Role That Microblogging Plays in Informal Communication at Work." In *Proceedings of the ACM 2009 International Conference on Supporting Group Work*, 243–252. Sanibel Island, FL: ACM Press.

20
Workplace Narratives
Hans J. Ladegaard

Introduction

Telling stories is an important part of our social and professional life. In fact, storytelling is so fundamental to human experience that it has been labelled as "the beginning of consciousness" (Damasio 1999), and as a human universal that applies across all social and cultural groups (Bruner 1986). Storytelling accomplishes a variety of interactional goals. We tell stories to entertain, provide information, make accusations or complaints, compete for power, justify our actions, and to build social organization and (re)align social order (Goodwin 1997; Holmes 2006). But narratives also serve a deeper psychological function. People use them to make sense of themselves and their world. As Cortazzi (2001, 388) argues: "through life stories individuals and groups make sense of themselves; they tell what they are or what they wish to be, as they tell so they become, they *are* their stories." Because people are so intimately connected with their stories, narrative and life-story research also becomes a way to study people, their lives and experiences, and their hopes and aspirations. As Riessman (2003, 7) cogently puts it, "[w]e 'become' the stories through which we tell our lives . . . Telling stories configures the 'self-that-I-might-be.'"

This chapter explores the form and function of narratives in the workplace. First, it outlines how narratives have been defined and the various narrative genres we find in workplace talk, and it explains why the therapeutic aspect of storytelling should be included in work on workplace narratives. Selected excerpts from a number of workplaces are then analysed. They illustrate some of the well-documented functions of storytelling in workplace settings, but they also explore some lesser-known functions, such as establishing corporate values and exposing abusive employers.

Narrative Form and Characteristics

Sociolinguistics has proposed influential conceptual models of narratives, and most studies refer to Labov's (1972) seminal work on narrative structure to identify the key components of an oral narrative. His prototypical narrative consists of six key components:

1   Abstract: a brief summary of the general propositions the story will make; it usually occurs at the beginning of the story
2   Orientation: essential background information like time, place and people involved in the story
3   Complicating action: the key events of the story
4   Evaluation: highlighting and evaluating the point of the story
5   Resolution: how the crisis/complicating action was resolved
6   Coda: closing or concluding remarks.

More recently, Toolan (2001, 4–6) argues that (some of) the following characteristics should allow us to distinguish narratives from more spontaneous conversations:

1   A narrative contains a certain degree of "constructedness" that we do not find in spontaneous talk
2   Narratives tend to have a certain degree of prefabrication: they contain elements we have heard before
3   Narratives have a trajectory; they "go somewhere", or are expected to go somewhere, which means some degree of narrative development is usually involved
4   Most narratives have discourse units we can identify as beginning, middle and end
5   Narratives must have a teller and the teller is always important
6   Narratives usually make use of displacement; they refer to events that are removed, in space and time, from the speaker and addressee(s).

The telling of personal narratives in the workplace is usually a joint discursive accomplishment where individual narrators' input should be seen as an integral part of the story. Ochs and Capps (2001) propose a continuum between what they call the "default narrative" with only one active teller at the one end of the continuum, and a dynamic co-constructed narrative with multiple tellers at the other end. They argue that the "default narrative", which has been the object of most research, is in fact quite rare in natural conversation. And even when there is seemingly only one storyteller, other group members are in fact also taking part in the construction of the story. By using subtle linguistic or paralinguistic means, audience members become co-participants in the development and interpretation of individual (workplace) narratives (Fasulo and Zucchermaglio 2008).

Another characteristic feature of narratives that has been identified by many scholars is tellability (Ochs and Capps 2001). In order for a story to avoid the "so-what" reaction and not be deemed pointless, it must be tellable. This means it must somehow deviate from expected norms. Bruner (1991) calls it a breach from the unmarked script of everyday life: for a story to be deemed tellable, it must explore the boundary between the ordinary and the exceptional. Or, as argued by Thornborrow and Coates (2005, 11), to achieve tellability, "a story needs to reach a moment where the unexpected and unusual erupts from out of the mundane and predictable." In abuse narratives, tellability is not an issue. By their very nature, these stories breach the unmarked script of everyday life and will therefore always be deemed tellable. The only caveat is that tellability is compromised by the unacceptability of the events (Shuman 2005), but a trauma narrative can never be deemed pointless or irrelevant.

Narrative Genre and Functions

Linde (1993) proposes a distinction between narratives and life stories. While narratives can be anything from mundane stories about trivial everyday activities to horrifying accounts of near-death experiences, a life story is usually a discontinuous discourse unit that is told in separate stories over an extended period of time. It expresses the teller's sense of self: who we are in relation to others and how we came to be what we are. This means life stories are used to claim and negotiate group membership(s), but they also serve therapeutic functions in that they help the narrator understand and come to terms with his/her past and create a sense of coherence. Landmark events such as "choice" of profession (voluntary or enforced), marriage, divorce, and religious conversion would often be important themes in life stories. The migrant worker narratives in this chapter could be referred to as life stories. They deal with identity and notions of "self" and "other", and with notions of belonging, or not belonging, and what it means to (not) have a "home" and be confined to a diasporic life separated from your loved ones.

Scholars have pointed to at least five key functions of storytelling (Medved and Brockmeier 2008). First, it creates coherence in that it "synthesizes personal experiences and sensations that may otherwise be disconnected and random" (61). Second, narratives serve a distancing function. As Bruner (2002, 89) argues, "we distance ourselves from the immediacy of events by converting what we've encountered into story form." Third, narratives serve a communicative function. They connect the teller to his/her audience so that the narrator's universe becomes shared and all participants become engaged in the construction of narrative events. Fourth, narratives serve an evaluative function in that they provide a framework for evaluating past events. They give perspective but also an opportunity to re-evaluate and suggest alternative interpretations and an alternative course of action. Finally, narratives serve an explorative function and allow us to explore two sides of human experience: the real and the possible. As Medved and Brockmeier (2008, 67) argue, "the explorative function of narrative is about probing and extending the horizon of human possibilities."

Marra and Holmes (2004, 64) have identified a variety of functions that apply particularly to workplace narratives. They found that stories are used to entertain, educate, socialise, and inform, and to express individual employees' preoccupations, perspectives and feelings. Workplace narratives also contribute to individual and group identity formation, they express solidarity and face needs, and they mark social boundaries. Holmes (2006) has identified anecdotes as particularly salient in workplace talk. Anecdotes often appear in the form of (welcome) digressions from core business talk, and they typically function as a means for negotiating the public-private interface. Other narrative genres in workplace talk include habitual narratives in which tellers embark on events that happened (repeatedly) in their past. Habitual narratives tend to be less dramatic and would sometimes be used to explain or legitimize a certain course of action. Argumentative narratives are also common in workplace talk. They usually deviate from prototypical narratives and their function is to put forward an opinion, or to challenge somebody's point of view (see De Fina and Georgakopoulou 2012 for an overview of narrative genres).

De Fina (2003, 11) argues that the characteristic features of the narrative genre make it "particularly apt to become the locus of expression, construction and enactment of identity". Among the narrative features that add something important to discourse-based theories of identity is temporality (Linde 1993). Narratives create a sense of identity coherence because they tend to include connectedness and temporal unity (Benwell and Stokoe 2006). Bruner (1990) notes that during the 1970s and 1980s, psychologists began to see the "self" as a storyteller and focus their attention on the narrative construction of identity. Part of this new narrative movement is also the realization that the "self" is not a static unit but a social discursive construction that emerges in narrative form. Narratives thus become essential in the interpretation of human experience "because experience itself becomes intelligible to humans only when they narrate it" (De Fina 2003, 17).

Therapeutic Narratives

A key assumption behind narrative therapy is that we live storied lives (White 1995). People are encouraged to tell their stories to make sense of their experiences because our stories constitute us and shape our lives and relationships (Brown and Augusta-Scott 2007). Narrative therapy is influenced by post-structuralism, social constructionism, and Foucault's (1984) essays on power and knowledge. It focuses on identity as socially constructed in the narrative context, and it claims that all individual stories are social stories, shaped by dominant ideologies of power and cultural conventions. It refers to Foucault to show how people in positions of power construct dominant stories that allow them to remain in power. This echoes with some of the narratives in this chapter in which migrant women tell how their employers construct them as stupid, poor and vulnerable. This means their stories are circumscribed by the employer and workplace narratives therefore become a means for migrant workers to challenge dominant stories and co-author more helpful ones (Brown and Augusta-Scott 2007).

A justification for combining narrative therapy with a sociolinguistic approach to narrative analysis is that both approaches emphasize the use of language. White (1995) cautions that language is fraught with ambiguity and misinterpretation; it is full of culturally derived meanings that may distort how people see themselves (Payne 2006). Narrative therapy takes conscious effort to escape these meanings and can therefore help people who have been abused or bullied in the workplace to become aware of how they have internalized their employers' or colleagues' demeaning discourses (Ladegaard 2017; Simons and Mawn 2012).

A problem-saturated description of past events—the narrator shares his/her story and thus externalizes the problem—is essential in narrative therapy. The aim of using "externalizing language" is for the teller to separate his/her identity from the problem, and to reconstruct the trauma/bullying as an external event. It is a common reaction for abused migrant workers to turn the problem inwards and argue that they have been mistreated because they are "unworthy to be respected" (Ladegaard 2013). In such cases, storytelling serves to repair damaged identities (Nelson 2001) and propose alternative stories.

Workplace Narratives

Narratives as Icebreakers and Entertainment

One function of workplace narratives is their role as icebreakers, or as entertaining diversions from the tediousness of business talk, as in Example 20.1.[1]

Because of his role as support team leader, Nigel would often chair meetings and teleconferences. He is from the UK and he fully lives up to the stereotype that the British love to talk about the weather. In meetings, particularly if new colleagues are involved (as in Example 20.1), he would engage in small talk first. The story he tells to illustrate his point (lines 9–11) is very short and yet, has most of the components Labov (1972) proposes as essential in narrative. It has the **orientation** ("all my friends from England", line 9), the **complicating action** ("this conception they have about Denmark", "you'll get a white Christmas", lines 10–11), and the **evaluation/resolution** ("no probably not", line 11). We could also argue that the additional information about the likelihood of a white Christmas (lines 13–15) constitutes the **coda**.

> **Example 20.1**
>
> Nigel, IT support team leader in a Danish IT Service Centre and
> Carola, IT supporter in the Finnish daughter company, in a
> Same-Time Teleconference. They introduce themselves and then
> they engage in small talk before the business talk is initiated (original in English)
>
> | 1 | Nigel: | how is the weather up where you are? |
> |---|---|---|
> | 2 | Carola: | eh: I've left today |
> | 3 | Nigel: | sorry (1.0) yeah, it's pretty ugly here |
> | 4 | Carola: | it's raining and it's eh: so grey, I eh: took [went] home it's the same |
> | 5 | Nigel: | well yes, it's intolerable here, there's no other word for it, terrible |
> | 6 | Carola: | well I don't think we'll have a white Christmas |
> | 7 | Nigel: | you don't? |
> | 8 | Carola: | no, eh: not fully |
> | 9 | Nigel: | it's a problem this conception all my friends from England have |
> | 10 | | about Denmark (1.0) they'll go like 'so oh, you'll get a white |
> | 11 | | Christmas this year' (1.0) 'no, probably not' |
> | 12 | Carola: | [laughs] |
> | 13 | Nigel: | on the news they do this eh: percentage chance of a white Christmas |
> | 14 | | and at one point about two weeks ago they were talking about 20%, |
> | 15 | | and er: now it's gone down to 5% |
> | 16 | Carola: | okay [laughs] |

The anecdote about British people's misperception of Denmark is triggered by Carola's remark in line 6 that there won't be a white Christmas in Finland. It elaborates on a point that has been made, as well as filling a gap during the initial stages of the teleconference. The colleagues do not know each other and the anecdote and the small talk therefore also work as an icebreaker. Nigel is trying to establish rapport with a colleague who initially is not very talkative. Carola's laughter (line 12, 16) suggests that the anecdote has worked and a quiet, slightly reticent colleague is slowly warming up to conversation.

Example 20.2 shows how workplace narratives may be used to entertain and create a more relaxed atmosphere. The colleagues are discussing what they do when they get a service request from somebody they do not know in one of the company's subsidiaries.

Prior to and in this example, the colleagues discussed how difficult it is to communicate with a faceless global citizen. They need markers of national or ethnic identity in order to frame their communication, and the colleagues thus refute the idea that global business communication is uniform and "neutral" and can be directed at anybody. Lucas' story consists of two personal anecdotes, which illustrate how important gender is when you communicate with unidentified colleagues in the virtual workplace. While the anecdotes make an important contribution to the discussion—that national and gender stereotypes are used to provide orientation in virtual communication—their function is to entertain more than anything. As Holmes (2006, 169) argues, "like humour and small talk (with which they frequently overlap), they provide relief from the core business of the workplace".

The evidence that Lucas' story functions as intended is the frequent use of laughter (lines 4, 6, 7, 12, 14). Lucas often takes on the role as the entertainer in meetings and other

> **Example 20.2**
>
> Lucas and Britt, IT controllers in the IT Service Centre of a global business corporation. Five more colleagues were in this focus group interview, which was set up to discuss work practices and conventions (original in Danish)
>
> | 1 | Lucas: | if I get a service call from somebody I really don't know, well |
> | --- | --- | --- |
> | 2 | | then I know that John he knows this person well so I'll ask him |
> | 3 | | what he or she is like . . . I've actually communicated once with |
> | 4 | | an Italian thinking that it was a really nice girl [someone laughs] |
> | 5 | | and then when I came down to Italy it turned out it a man with |
> | 6 | | curly hair [general laughter] it wasn't actually very funny |
> | 7 | Britt: | is that really true? [laughs] |
> | 8 | Lucas: | in fact I tried the same thing in the old job I had (1.0) for about |
> | 9 | | half a year I communicated with a German, and because of the |
> | 10 | | name I'd imagined that this person was a very beautiful black |
> | 11 | | girl or something like that, and then when I came down there |
> | 12 | | [somebody laughs] it was a giant negro [sic] and he just said |
> | 13 | | 'G'day Lucas' [general laughter] I hadn't understood a damn |
> | 14 | | thing [general laughter] |
> | 15 | Britt: | it's important to meet people |
> | 16 | Lucas: | but what I do now is I go [to the intranet] and check their |
> | 17 | | photographs sometimes |

business-related activities in this workplace. Therefore, his story is expected to be funny and prior to both anecdotes, a colleague laughs even before there is any indication that this will be funny (lines 4, 12). Lucas adorns his story with entertaining details, such as "a man with curly hair" (lines 5–6) and "a giant negro" who just said "G'day Lucas" (lines 12–13). The information is not particularly relevant to the storyline but it serves an important intragroup function by adding humour to a business-related discussion. The colleagues recognize this by laughing loudly (lines 6, 13), and this recognition may be the cue that encourages Lucas to present himself as the anti-hero and admit that he "hadn't understood a damn thing" (lines 13–14). He ridicules himself and in subsequent lines not reported here, he tells the group how he was flirting with these presumed good-looking female colleagues in writing, only to discover that they were both men. Therefore, the coda of the story is important: that Lucas now checks the photographs of new colleagues on the intranet before he communicates with them. The story shows how workplace anecdotes may serve an important socio-pragmatic function and contribute to workplace culture.

Reinforcing Ingroup Cohesion

Another important function of workplace narratives is that they reinforce ingroup cohesion. They bring colleagues together as a group, often in contrast to colleagues in comparable outgroups (Tajfel and Turner 1986).

Example 20.3

Nigel, IT support team leader; Anna and Jesper, IT supporters.
Four more colleagues were in this focus group interview,
which was set up to discuss work practices (original in English).

1	Nigel:	I'd say I certainly have experienced that where I, I sent an email
2		to somebody in Germany (1.0) and then I was approached by
3		somebody else, from the, from [Company A] Germany to say (0.5)
4		they didn't understand what you've written in the email
5	Anna:	yeah
6	Jesper:	mhm
7	Nigel:	so there I had to resend it with (0.5) as you said, not baby
8		English//
9	Anna:	//no no//
10	Nigel:	//but a lot more simple
11	Anna:	yeah [general laughter]

Example 20.3 is part of a discussion about the use of English as corporate language. The colleagues agree that communication problems are caused by "the other", not by them. Nigel, who is from the UK, tells the group how his language is perceived as incomprehensible by his German colleagues so he is being asked to simplify it. The term "baby English" was introduced earlier by Anna who explains: "when you know they're on a lower level, I put my level down when I know that they're not that well in English" (original in English). Anna is Danish and although her English is perfectly comprehensible, it is far from grammatically correct. Yet, she sees her English language skills as superior to those of her Southern European colleagues with whom she allegedly "puts her English down". Nigel's anecdote (which is also argumentative in nature) serves to confirm this stereotype. Despite being a native speaker of English, he is being asked to simplify his language to accommodate to the German colleagues' subpar language skills. German colleagues are discursively constructed as linguistically inferior, and Nigel's story provides the evidence. This leaves the colleagues in the Danish company as superior and Nigel's story therefore also serves to reinforce a positive ingroup identity (Hogg and Abrams 2003; Ladegaard 2011a).

Reinforcing Workplace Culture and Corporate Values

Storytelling in the workplace also serves as a means to share and disseminate cultural norms and corporate values. Natalie is Head of Sales and Project Proposals in the headquarters of a large multinational entrepreneurial company. She talks to two colleagues who complain that the company has made a statement that they would prioritise certain issues, but has done nothing to address the problems.

Natalie is "doing being a leader" in this example (Ladegaard 2011b) and her story takes the form of an argumentative narrative, which is told to back up claims that may be seen as controversial or disputable (Schiffrin 1994). The company's senior management is being criticized for being inactive, so Natalie tells a story to counter the evidence presented by the

Example 20.4

Natalie, Head of Sales of Project Proposals; Peter and Niels are both engineers and work in another department (original in Danish)

1	Natalie:	there's something I'd like to tell you, you know I lost this guy
2		Hans Christian Nissen, he worked for me, you know the guy
3		who died
4	Peter:	really? (0.5) oh my goodness
5	Natalie:	Sunday it was (0.5.) didn't you see it on the news channel?
6	Niels:	yes I did see it but then I thought //
7	Peter:	//yes I did think (0.5)
8	Natalie:	ah: his wife called me Monday morning (0.5) yesterday it was
9		(0.5) and she told me he was dead
10	Peter:	okay
11	Natalie:	and she was confused of course, right and didn't know who
12		she should talk to, she'd like to talk to somebody from PFA
13		[Pension Fund], you know so I promised I'd call HR and ask,
14		and you know HR were just absolutely amazing, they just
15		took over completely
16	Niels:	really?
17	Natalie:	and found the names and took care of everything, you know
18		Bodil Sørensen and Carina Nordtoft, they just took care of it
19		and they would call the wife and everything
20	Peter:	okay

two colleagues. Note how she refers to the deceased colleague: "I lost this guy", "he worked for me" (lines 1–2). She personifies the company and when somebody passes away, it is a personal loss. The point of the story is presented in line 14: "HR were absolutely amazing." A company that is criticized for not caring for their employees is positioned through storytelling as caring and considerate. Thus, Natalie's story is constructing a workplace culture and disseminates corporate values to colleagues. As evidenced by other examples in the dataset, the company is working to portray the image of a caring organization and Natalie's story works towards consolidating this image. So, rather than openly disagreeing with her two male colleagues in their criticism of the company, Natalie uses storytelling as an indirect disagreement strategy, and she uses her personal experience as evidence because personal stories are difficult to refute (Tusting, Crawshaw, and Callen 2002). Holmes (2006, 186) argues that storytelling provides a "legitimate and acceptable, but unofficial and off-record, outlet for dissatisfaction, jealousy, or irritation in the workplace." Natalie's story illustrates this point as she uses it to counter her colleagues' criticism.

The next example also illustrates how storytelling can be used to disseminate corporate values and workplace culture. Paul is IT Support Team Leader, and he is discussing with a group of IT supporters why some European colleagues are more difficult to work with than others.

> **Example 20.5**
>
> Paul, IT support team leader during a focus group discussion
> with his support team (original in Danish)
>
> | 1 | Paul: | I can provide a very specific example from France where I |
> |---|---|---|
> | 2 | | was in a meeting with 3–4 colleagues and their boss, and we |
> | 3 | | were discussing how they could estimate prices when they sell |
> | 4 | | to their customers, and eh: of course I had to know how they |
> | 5 | | wanted that done so I could set up the system to handle all the |
> | 6 | | regulations they had and eh: it was the boss who eh: presented their |
> | 7 | | eh: terms and conditions and told me how everything worked, types |
> | 8 | | of customers etc etc, and those 3–4 colleagues they just sat there |
> | 9 | | nodding and were completely passive, and eh: he was very |
> | 10 | | convincing and I was like 'okay', I took notes and then he left |
> | 11 | | and the four colleagues stayed behind and then they told me |
> | 12 | | 'now we'll tell you how it **really** is', and then we started all |
> | 13 | | over [general laughter] and I noted down and then I was in |
> | 14 | | a dilemma because how should I develop the system? According |
> | 15 | | to what the boss had said or how it was in the real world? |

Paul's question in lines 14–15 is rhetorical, and the answer (which is never explicitly stated) underlines the point of this argumentative narrative: they need to respond to "the real world", not to what an autocratic leader in France says. This story is used to convey negative outgroup stereotypes but it is also used to identify power difference as a major problem in their external communication. As evidenced in other types of data, the colleagues are proud of working for an organization that has a flat anti-hierarchical management structure where everybody is allegedly treated the same, and secretaries and CEOs alike are called by their first name. Therefore, the power difference between the French employees (representing "the real world") and their CEO becomes an obstacle to successful intergroup communication.

The French colleagues are implicitly mocked: "they just sat there nodding and were completely passive" (lines 8–9), and the assumption behind this statement is that "we" are not like "them" (Ladegaard 2011a). The story presents hierarchical organizational structures as problematic and thus, indirectly hails an anti-hierarchical management structure as effective. After Paul's story, Lucas sums up the moral by saying: "but that's the thing with French culture [...] they have great respect for their boss and they don't contradict [him]". A specific management problem is perceived as a cultural issue (Schnurr and Zayts 2012). National culture becomes a universal explanation for all behaviour, thus ignoring other potentially significant explanations.

Narratives of Denigration and Humiliation

I now turn to a different type of narrative about the workplace, which has received less attention in the literature. However, abusive employers and workplace bullying are increasingly recognized as a significant problem so there are good reasons for examining therapeutic work-related narratives.

Migrant workers arriving at a church shelter in Hong Kong,[2] are interviewed by caseworkers, and invited to share their stories in a session with other migrant women. Domestic migrant worker (DMW) narratives would often be in the form of habitual narratives in which a narration of past events (like recurrent abuse and bullying) is used to explain their current predicament.

Example 20.6

Vera and Ruth, both Filipino migrant workers, and a
male interviewer/volunteer (Int). One more migrant worker
was in this sharing session (original in English)

1	Vera:	they [the employers] always get mad at me (2.0) I don't know
2		how to speak English [laughs] I don't know how to speak
3		English fluent
4	Int.:	don't worry, it's fine
5	Vera:	because I'm only a high school graduate [laughs]
6	Int.:	don't worry, that's fine
7	Vera:	so after two days, my employer, my employer's always
8		getting mad at me, and the third day, she hit me in my back
9		because she's (1.5) I don't know (1.5.) and then
10	Int.:	so she hit you with what?
11	Vera:	she hit me with her hand
12	Int.:	okay, for doing what?
13	Vera:	I just keep quiet
14	Int.:	yeah
15	Vera:	because I don't want to (1.0) go home because I have many
16		(1.0) *utang*
17	Ruth:	yeah, she has a lot of loan
18	Int.:	so debt again, yeah
19	Vera:	until until (3.0) because from January 3rd to January 12th, she
20		hit me two times and she even dragged me three times, but I
21		don't complain because I don't want to go home, I don't have
22		money to go home, and at the night of January 12th she come
23		home and she's getting mad at me (0.5) just because of a simple
24		mistake I did not put the food on the table when she come home
25		from the office, and then she (0.5) speak bad words she's always
26		telling me 'poor Filipino, stupid Filipino, go home', she always
27		act like that since I came here

Vera's story provides a typical example of the way DMWs position themselves through narrative (Wortham and Gadsden 2006). Vera's self-presentation makes sense in a culturally hegemonic society where migrant workers are consistently marginalized and the objects of blatant discrimination (Constable 2007; Ladegaard 2017). As Schiffrin (1996, 170) argues, "our identities as social beings emerge as we construct our own individual experiences as a way to position ourselves in relation to social and cultural expectations." Thus, our narrative self-construction is closely intertwined with predominant attitudes and stereotypes in the society in which we live. Therefore, Vera denigrates herself; she apologizes for her alleged inability to speak proper English (lines 1–3) despite the fact that she is perfectly fluent, and she positions herself as a lowly high school graduate (line 5).

Vera's self-presentation as inferior is probably also the reason she does not defend herself when she is being assaulted (line 13). Constable (2007, 51) argues that physical assault reflects how DMWs historically have been, and in many ways still are, perceived in Hong Kong (and elsewhere). They are seen as household commodities, who/which can be "inspected, bought, traded, owned, [and] generally objectified", and this may explain why physical assault is still shockingly common. Domestic battering is usually explained by reference to power and control: one party in a domestic dispute is trying to gain power and control over another by means of violence (Augusta-Scott 2007). However, it is also possible that physical abuse is used in lieu of language. Communication problems are often reported in DMW narratives. It is usually the Chinese women of the household who deal with domestic workers and they often do not speak (much) English. DMWs do not speak (much) Chinese and in the absence of a common language, it is more likely that employers may resort to violence.

Although she knows she has done nothing wrong, Vera keeps quiet when she is assaulted (line 13) because she does not want to go home (line 15), and for fear of retaliation (lines 23–24). Her story portrays the identity of the subservient maid who tolerates her employer's abusive behaviour because she is in debt (lines 15–16). She took out loans to pay the extortionate agency fees and when the contract is terminated prematurely, she has two concerns: first, that she cannot pay her agency fees, and second, that she cannot provide for her family. As Yeoh and Huang (2000, 422) argue, "far from eroding notions of family ties, diasporic existence often serves to strengthen women's gendered identifications as sacrificial sisters, daughters, mothers, and wives."

Vera's narrative also shows how references to poverty and stupidity are used to denigrate DMWs. The reference to poverty reiterates the fact that power and access to financial resources are intrinsically linked, so mocking DMWs for their poverty is a reminder of their vulnerability (Bales 2012). They do not put up a fight against abusive employers because they cannot afford to lose their jobs (Simons and Mawn 2012). The reference to stupidity is ironic because Filipina DMWs tend to be better educated than their lower-middle-class female employers in Hong Kong. However, as other narratives have shown, the reason for individuals or groups to voice negative outgroup stereotypes may be to emphasize intergroup differentiation (Hogg and Abrams 2003).

Therapeutic Narratives

An important aspect of workplace narratives is that they serve a therapeutic function. Employees, who have suffered under the hands of abusive employers, or from bullying from fellow colleagues, may use storytelling as a means to come to terms with what happened and receive help from their audience to construct more helpful counter-narratives. In Example 20.7, Ayu's friends show their support and sympathy through single words, exclamations and minimal response. In line 3, Nadia shows her support through a loud ironic exclamation, "seven only", followed by laughter from other participants. The laughter in line 7 suggests that the women find the employer's demand—that Ayu should smile after they hit her—outrageous, even hilarious. Siti's brief comment, "Crazy" (line 8), and Rina's question

Example 20.7

Ayu, Nadia, Siti, and Rina, all Indonesian migrant workers,
and a male interviewer/volunteer (Int). Four more migrant workers
were in this sharing session (original in Bahasa)

1	Ayu:	I, I worked in my employer's house as a housekeeper, I clean
2		seven cars
3	Nadia:	**seven only** //[general laughter]//
4	Ayu:	//seven cars// seven cars, then the only thing I don't
5		like about them is, even though I wasn't wrong, instead of
6		clarifying they just beat me (1.0) and then after they hit me they
7		ask me to smile [general laughter]
8	Siti:	crazy
9	Aya:	and then and then, everything is tough, they count all my work
10		by the minute
11	Rina:	they time all your work?
12	Ayu:	yes, their house is quite big (2.0) there are seven people in that
13		house (2.0) there are four floors, seven cars, the only domestic
14		helper there is me (1.5) if I made a mistake and apologised I'll be
15		beaten instead, that's why I can't stand working there and finally
16		I ran away (0.5) reported to the police . . . there were two
17		children in the house (3.0) but I never touched them, they forbid
18		me to touch them, they said I'm dirty
19	Siti:	mm: race discrimination
20	Ayu:	then I usually sleep at 2:30 at night and begin working again at
21		8 o'clock in the morning
22	Siti:	2:30 in the morning?
23	Ayu:	yes
24	Nadia:	**2:30 *lah:***

"they time all your work?", also suggest indignation and outrage and encourage Ayu to continue her story. She tells her peers that she was not allowed to touch her employer's children because she was accused of being dirty (lines 17–18), a comment which leads Siti to label the employers as racist (line 19). And when she tells the group that she worked until 2:30 am, Siti's question suggests disbelief (line 22) and Nadia's loud exclamation, including the Cantonese sentence-final particle *lah:* (line 24), suggests shock. In Cantonese, *lah:* signifies the end of a turn, but when DMWs use it, the semantic implication has changed to something like "No kidding!"

Throughout Ayu's story, the feedback from her peers helps her to reinterpret the events so that she comes to see herself as a victim. The feedback provides the moral and emotional support she needs to reconstruct a counter-narrative, which labels her employers as racist and abusive. Because our stories constitute us and shape our lives (Brown and Augusta-Scott 2007), it is essential that Ayu gets support to question the abusive discourses she was subjected to in her employer's house. As we get to the end of the sharing session and the women are asked what they intend to do, Ayu is committed to pursuing a case against her employer. Thus, storytelling may help employees to question taken-for-granted dominant stories and reconstruct a different narrative that will help them become agents in their own life stories.

Discussion and Conclusion

Holmes (2006) argues that narratives are generally regarded as "dispensable, irrelevant, or peripheral, and in some cases even distracting in the workplace context". The evidence that supports this point is the fact that colleagues would often use discourse markers, such as "to get back to the point", or "enough (of that)", after the narrative is completed. However, the fact that workplace anecdotes are often off-topic digressions from core business does not mean that they are dispensable. Teambuilding and relational work are essential in any organization (Fletcher 1999) and storytelling plays an essential role in these processes. In her analysis of job interviews for low-status positions in the UK, Roberts (2013) shows that applicants with an immigrant background are usually not successful because they are unable to produce narratives during the interview which conform to Anglo-American conventions of storytelling. And Holmes (2015) shows that a significant problem for new immigrants in New Zealand workplaces is that they do not know how to tell stories and respond appropriately to small talk during coffee and lunch breaks. Thus, we may assume that storytelling is peripheral, but research shows that when employees do not master the skills of telling and interpreting workplace narratives, they are likely to suffer exclusion or marginalization.

If we consider the therapeutic component of narrative, it becomes even more pertinent that workplace narratives should not be perceived as dispensable and peripheral. For DMWs who have suffered under the hands of abusive employers, or for colleagues who have been belittled through bullying by their colleagues (Hoel and Einarsen 2015), storytelling may be a way for them to come to terms with traumatic workplace experiences and get support from their peers to question the demeaning discourses they have been subjected to, and propose more helpful stories that will help the victim to regain self-confidence. Trauma destroys the self (Herman 1997) and employees who have been subjected to abuse or bullying need to rediscover their own resources and potential. The therapeutic use of narratives may provide people with "experiences in which they can give voice to their traumas, evaluate their interpretations, reconsider their identity conclusions, and re-author their lives from victimhood to survival and beyond" (Duvall and Béres 2007, 233).

One of the most important potentials of workplace narratives is arguably their ability to bridge the gap between the personal and professional dimensions of our identity (Holmes 2006). They provide a legitimate outlet for negative emotions, they entertain and contribute to teambuilding, they reinforce ingroup identity, and communicate corporate values. But they are also instigators of change, both at the personal and the corporate levels, because as people tell, they *become* their stories.

Further Reading

De Fina and Georgakopoulou (2015) provides comprehensive coverage of the latest advances in narrative analysis, from work on social media and organizational and classroom narratives to small stories research.

Thornborrow and Coates (2005) analyses the use and functions of narratives in a wide range of socio-cultural contexts. One chapter (Holmes and Marra 2005) deals with workplace narratives.

Brown and Augusta-Scott (2007) provides a compilation of current narrative therapy research in a range of therapeutic contexts.

Shuman (2005) discusses a number of potentially problematic issues in narrative research, including empathy with the teller and entitlement claims.

Related Topics

Linguistic ethnography; Social constructionism; Relational talk; Humour; Leadership

Note

1 Narratives presented come from research conducted in both Denmark and Hong Kong (see Ladegaard 2007, 2011a, 2011b and 2017).

Transcription conventions
Bold = pronounced with stress/emphasis
Italics = Tagalog/Cantonese
[it's a] = word(s) inserted by the transcriber to ease comprehension
, = short pause, less than 0.5 second
(2.0) = pause in seconds
'give me that' = reporting direct speech
: (as in ah:) = the vowel sound is prolonged
xx = incomprehensible
// = interruption; //as I said// = overlapping speech
? = question/rising intonation
... turn(s) left out

2 From a database recorded over a 4-year period in sharing sessions held at Bethune House, a charity run by the Mission for Migrant Workers, which is part of the Anglican Church in Hong Kong (see http://www.migrants.net).

References

Augusta-Scott, Tod. 2007. "Conversations with Men about Women's Violence. Ending Men's Violence by Challenging Gender Essentialism." In *Narrative Therapy. Making Meaning, Making Lives*, edited by Catrina Brown, and Tod Augusta-Scott, 197–210. Thousand Oaks, CA: Sage.

Bales, Kevin. 2012. *Disposable People: New Slavery in the Global Economy*. Berkeley, CA: University of California Press.

Benwell, Bethan, and Elizabeth Stokoe. 2006. *Discourse and Identity*. Edinburgh: Edinburgh University Press.

Brown, Catrina, and Tod Augusta-Scott. 2007. "Introduction: Postmodernism, Reflexivity, and Narrative Therapy." In *Narrative Therapy. Making Meaning, Making Lives*, edited by Catrina Brown, and Tod Augusta-Scott, ix-xlii. Thousand Oaks, CA: Sage.

Bruner, Jerome. 1986. *Actual Minds, Possible Worlds*. Cambridge, MA: Harvard University Press.

Bruner, Jerome. 1990. *Acts of Meaning*. Cambridge, MA: Harvard University Press.

Bruner, Jerome. 1991. "The Narrative Construction of Reality." *Critical Inquiry* 18: 1–21.

Bruner, Jerome. 2002. "Narrative Distancing: A Foundation of Literacy." In *Literacy, Narrative and Culture*, edited by Jens Brockmeier, Min Wang, and David R. Olson, 86–93. Richmond, UK: Curzon Press.

Constable, Nicole. 2007. *Maid to Order in Hong Kong. Stories of Migrant Workers*. 2nd ed. Ithaca, NY: Cornell University Press.

Cortazzi, Martin. 2001. "Narrative Analysis in Ethnography." In *Handbook of Ethnography*, edited by Paul Atkinson, Amanda Coffey, Sara Delamont, John Lofland, and Lyn Lofland, 384–394. London: Sage.

Damasio, Antonio. 1999. *The Feeling of What Happens: Body and Emotion in the Making of Consciousness*. New York: Harcourt Brace.
De Fina, Anna. 2003. *Identity in Narrative. A Study of Immigrant Discourse*. Amsterdam: John Benjamins.
De Fina, Anna, and Alexandra Georgakopoulou. 2012. *Analyzing Narrative. Discourse and Sociolinguistic Perspectives*. Cambridge: Cambridge University Press.
De Fina, Anna, and Alexandra Georgakopoulou, Eds. 2015. *The Handbook of Narrative Analysis*. Chichester, UK: Wiley Blackwell.
Duvall, Jim, and Laura Béres. 2007. "Movement of Identities. A Map for Therapeutic Conversations about Trauma." In *Narrative Therapy. Making Meaning, Making Lives*, edited by Catrina Brown, and Tod Augusta-Scott, 229–250. Thousand Oaks, CA: Sage.
Fasulo, Alessandra, and Cristina Zucchermaglio. 2008. "Narratives in the Workplace: Facts, Fictions, and Canonicity." *Text & Talk* 28: 351–376.
Fletcher, Joyce K. 1999. *Disappearing Acts: Gender, Power and Relational Practice at Work*. Cambridge, MA: MIT Press.
Foucault, Michel. 1984. "Space, Knowledge, and Power." In *The Foucault Reader*, edited by Paul Rabinow, 239–256. New York: Pantheon Books.
Goodwin, Marjorie Harness. 1997. "Toward Families of Stories in Conext." *Journal of Narrative and Life Stories* 7: 107–112.
Herman, Judith. 1997. *Trauma and Recovery*. New York: Basic Books.
Hoel, Helge, and Ståle Einarsen. 2015. "Workplace Bullying." *Wiley Encyclopedia of Management* 5: 1–3.
Hogg, Michael A., and Dominic Abrams. 2003. "Intergroup Behaviour and Social Identity." In *Sage Handbook of Social Psychology*, edited by Michael A. Hogg, and Joel Cooper, 407–431. Thousand Oaks, CA: Sage.
Holmes, Janet. 2006. "Workplace Narratives, Professional Identity and Relational Practice." In *Discourse and Identity*, edited by Anna De Fina, Deborah Schiffrin, and Michael Bamberg, 166–187. Cambridge: Cambridge University Press.
Holmes, Janet, and Meredith Marra. 2005. "Narrative and the Construction of Professional Identity in the Workplace." In *The Sociolinguistics of Narrative*, edited by Joanna Thornborrow, and Jennifer Coates, 193–213. Amsterdam: John Benjamins.
Holmes, Prue. 2015. "'The Cultural Stuff around How to Talk to People': Immigrants' Intercultural Communication during Pre-Employment Work-Placement." *Language and Intercultural Communication* 15: 109–124.
Labov, William. 1972. *Language in the Inner City*. Philadelphia, PA: University of Pennsylvania Press.
Ladegaard, Hans J. 2007. "Global Culture—Myth or Reality? Perceptions of 'National Cultures' in a Global Corporation." *Journal of Intercultural Communication Research* 36: 139–163.
Ladegaard, Hans J. 2011a. "Stereotypes and the Discursive Accomplishment of Intergroup Differentiation: Talking about 'the Other' in a Global Business Organization." *Pragmatics* 21: 85–109.
Ladegaard, Hans J. 2011b. "'Doing Power' at Work: Responding to Male and Female Management Styles in a Global Business Corporation." *Journal of Pragmatics* 43: 4–19.
Ladegaard, Hans J. 2013. "Beyond Ethics and Equity? Depersonalisation and Dehumanisation in Foreign Domestic Helper Narratives." *Language and Intercultural Communication* 13: 44–59.
Ladegaard, Hans J. 2017. *The Discourse of Powerlessness and Repression: Life Stories of Domestic Migrant Workers in Hong Kong*. London: Routledge.
Linde, Charlotte. 1993. *Life Stories: The Creation of Coherence*. New York: Oxford University Press.
Marra, Meredith, and Janet Holmes. 2004. "Workplace Narratives and Business Reports: Issues of Definition." *Text & Talk* 24: 59–78.
Medved, Maria I., and Jens Brockmeier. 2008. "Talking about the Unthinkable. Neurotrauma and the 'Catastrophic Reaction'." In *Health, Illness and Culture: Broken Narratives*, edited by Lars-Christer Hydén, and Jens Brockmeier, 54–72. New York: Routledge.
Nelson, Hilde Lindemann. 2001. *Damaged Identities, Narrative Repair*. Ithaca, NY: Cornell University Press.
Ochs, Elinor, and Lisa Capps. 2001. *Living Narrative: Creating Lives in Everyday Storytelling*. Cambridge, MA: Harvard University Press.
Payne, Martin. 2006. *Narrative Therapy*. 2nd ed. London: Sage.

Riessman, Catherine Kohler. 2003. "Performing Narratives in Illness Narratives: Masculinity and Multiple Sclerosis." *Qualitative Research* 3: 5–33.
Roberts, Celia. 2013. "The Gatekeeping of Babel: Job Interviews and the Linguistic Penalty." In *Language, Migration and Social Inequalities*, edited by Alexandre Duchene, Melissa Moyer, and Celia Roberts, 81–94. Bristol, UK: Multilingual Matters.
Schiffrin, Deborah. 1994. *Approaches to Discourse*. Oxford: Blackwell.
Schiffrin, Deborah. 1996. "Narrative as Self-Portrait: Sociolinguistic Constructions of Identity." *Language in Society* 25: 167–203.
Schnurr, Stephanie, and Olga Zayts. 2012. "'You Have to be Adaptable, Obviously'. Constructing Professional Identities in Multicultural Workplaces in Hong Kong." *Pragmatics* 22: 279–299.
Shuman, Amy. 2005. *Other People's Stories. Entitlement Claims and the Critique of Empathy*. Urbana, IL: University of Illinois Press.
Simons, Shellie, and Barbara Mawn. 2012. "Bullying in the Workplace. A Qualitative Study of Newly Licensed Registered Nurses." In *(Re)thinking Violence in Health Care Settings. A Critical Approach*, edited by Dave Holmes, Trudy Rudge, and Amélie Perron, 177–188. Burlington, VT: Ashgate.
Tajfel, Henri, and John Turner. 1986. "The Social Identity of Intergroup Behavior." In *Psychology of Intergroup Relations*. 2nd ed., edited by Stephen Worchel, and William G. Austin, 7–24. Chicago, IL: Nelson-Hall.
Thornborrow, Joanna, and Jennifer Coates. 2005. "The Sociolinguistics of Narrative: Identity, Performance, Culture." In *The Sociolinguistics of Narrative*, edited by Joanna Thornborrow, and Jennifer Coates, 1–16. Amsterdam: John Benjamins.
Toolan, Michael J. 2001. *Narrative. A Critical Linguistic Introduction*. 2nd ed. London: Routledge.
Tusting, Karin, Robert Crawshaw, and Beth Callen. 2002. "'I Know 'Cos I Was There': How Residence Abroad Students Use Personal Experience to Legitimate Cultural Generalizations." *Discourse & Society* 13: 651–672.
White, Michael. 1995. *Re-Authoring Lives: Interviews & Essays*. Adelaide: Dulwich Centre.
Wortham, Stanton, and Vivian Gadsden. 2006. "Urban Fathers Positioning Themselves through Narrative: An Approach to Narrative Self-Construction." In *Discourse and Identity*, edited by Anna de Fina, Deborah Schiffrin, and Michael Bamberg, 314–341. Cambridge: Cambridge University Press.
Yeoh, Brenda S. A., and Shirlena Huang. 2000. "'Home' and 'Away': Foreign Domestic Workers and Negotiations and Diasporic Identity in Singapore." *Women's Studies International Forum* 23: 413–429.

21
Miscommunication at Work
Maria Stubbe

Introduction

Miscommunication is widely regarded as an occupational hazard in workplaces. Organizational textbooks and training programmes routinely offer advice on communication issues arising from linguistic and cultural diversity, workplace culture, information complexity or organizational change. Areas of concern are wide-ranging, and include aspects of spoken, written and electronic communication, interpersonal or intergroup relations, team work, and higher-level organizational communication processes. Direct observation of workplace interactions also provides evidence that people orient to miscommunication as an actual or potential source of trouble. This is most often implicit in the detail of how a given interaction unfolds, but is sometimes made explicit, as we will see later in this chapter.

Given the complexity of human interaction, it is unsurprising that communication problems occur regularly at work. In most cases these are relatively minor and easily repairable interruptions to the smooth and efficient flow of interaction between colleagues and are not especially consequential in and of themselves. Nevertheless, in workplace settings there is a greater risk than elsewhere that either ineffective or problematic communication will have visible and costly negative outcomes. In certain high stakes settings like health care, aviation or emergency management, an apparently trivial incident of miscommunication can potentially lead to disastrous outcomes including injury or loss of life. But in any workplace, even a minor misunderstanding inevitably comes at some cost.

Despite this, precisely what is meant by terms such as "miscommunication" or "communication problem" is seldom clearly articulated in workplaces, where they are often used rather loosely to gloss more general relational or systemic issues. Where communication is the primary focus, lay descriptions typically focus narrowly on the transfer or expression of information, as in commonly heard phrases like "not getting the message across" or "not speaking the same language" (Janicki 2010; Stubbe 2010), or they might draw on very general dictionary-style definitions such as "failure to communicate clearly, fully, or accurately" (OED-Online 2010). Such characterizations understate the true nature and complexity of problematic communication. They are thus of limited value when trying to make sense of how and why a particular real world interactional problem has arisen or could be resolved. The more nuanced approaches to analysing miscommunication developed within academic disciplines such as interactional sociolinguistics, conversation analysis (CA), pragmatics and critical discourse analysis (CDA) therefore have a great deal to offer anyone with a practical interest in understanding and addressing problematic interactions in workplace settings (Jones and Stubbe 2004; Auer and Roberts 2011).

Historical Perspectives

There is a substantial amount of research relevant to miscommunication in workplace settings dating back at least 30 years. However, this is by no means a unified field, with relevant studies in various domains of theoretical and applied academic inquiry. These include specific disciplines (e.g., linguistics, psychology, sociology), as well as cross-disciplinary communities of interest (e.g., intercultural miscommunication, language and gender, organizational studies). Health communication research provides a classic example of how academic silos have developed. Here, a well-developed research literature on problematic communication from social science and humanities sits alongside a body of more applied research on managing practical communication challenges in the clinical, health services and medical education literatures. However, these two research traditions (themselves multi-disciplinary) have only started to connect with one another relatively recently (Sarangi 2004). This lack of coherence is typical of workplace miscommunication research, and makes it difficult for both practitioners[1] and applied researchers to determine when and how different (and sometimes incommensurable) theoretical models might be applied to practical real world instances of problematic workplace discourse (Stubbe et al. 2003).

Interactional Research

A significant body of micro-analytic interactional research explores institutional and workplace miscommunication. The primary focus is on describing the discursive practices used to negotiate the asymmetrical (and thus inherently problematic) relationships typical of institutional settings, and/or mismatches between the communicative norms of different groups. Spoken interaction is viewed instrumentally as the primary medium for getting work done or managing interpersonal relationships. The kinds of issues examined range from relatively straightforward instances of misunderstanding (e.g., cases where the propositional content or "message" has not been adequately conveyed), through to the management of face and competing goals in inherently problematic interactional activities such as disagreement, criticism, advice-giving, complaints, directives, refusals and conflict talk, or the sequential co-construction and repair of interactional misalignment and "trouble".

Earlier research of this kind was mostly concerned with analysing interactions in relatively formal "front stage" (Goffman 1959) (more public) institutional or professional settings. Examples include several classic volumes that canvass topics such as health encounters, courtroom cross-examination, and inter-ethnic job interviews (e.g., Drew and Heritage 1992; Gumperz 1992; Roberts, Davies, and Jupp 1992). Later influential volumes include collections of work on discourse in medical, mediation and management settings (Sarangi and Roberts 1999); workplace negotiation and problem-solving (Firth 1995); intercultural misunderstanding in "high stakes" events (House, Kasper, and Ross 2003); and more recently an overview of CA research into institutional talk (Heritage and Clayman 2010).

An important strand of this research continues to examine problematic aspects of more specialized occupational or professional discourse such as healthcare consultations (e.g., Heritage and Maynard 2006; Roberts et al. 2005; Watson et al. 2015; White and Cartmill

2016), telephone helplines (e.g., Hepburn, Wilkinson, and Butler 2014), and dispute resolution (e.g., Jacobs 2002; Sikveland and Stokoe 2016). Such studies often have a strong focus on solving real-world problems, particularly in relation to professional quality and safety issues. In the last decade or so, advances in video-recording and analytic technology have allowed researchers to investigate the fine detail of communication in various socio-technical settings and, increasingly, to take interactional analysis into the multimodal arena. Relevant examples include problematic aspects of exchanges between pilots and air traffic controllers (e.g., Garcia 2016; Howard 2008), in operating theatres (e.g., Korkiakangas *et al.* 2016), vocational education (Fillieataz 2012), and in complex interaction with tools and technology (e.g., Carroll, Iedema, and Kerridge 2008).

Since the late 1990s there has been growing interest in moving behind the scenes to study informal and less predictable "back stage" interactions between colleagues as they undertake everyday tasks, engage in routine workplace meetings or socialise in the tearoom. The Wellington Language in the Workplace Project (LWP) is an early example of this type of research (Holmes and Stubbe 2015). Similar approaches have been used to study intercultural miscommunication in factory and professional settings (e.g., Măda and Săftoiu 2012), problematic communication in gendered settings (see Mullany and Yoong this volume; Baxter this volume), and more general team communication issues in professional workplaces (e.g., Angouri 2012; Richards 2006).

Critical discourse analysts are primarily interested in how people in workplaces negotiate or contest asymmetries in power and status relationships (Wodak 1996). For instance, analysts might examine how the operation of power is masked by the way a particular discourse or specific interaction is constructed, including coercion, manipulation, silencing, exclusion, and resistance. "Repressive discourse" (Fairclough 1992) is one example of this, where the language forms used are superficially friendly and polite, but the underlying message is manipulative, observably aimed at getting the addressee(s) to conform or agree to do something which they do not necessarily wish to. The analytic approach taken in CDA is to integrate macro-level analysis of organizational communication practices and processes with close analysis of interactional and/or textual data (see Koller this volume) in an attempt to identify as precisely as possible what the various sources of miscommunication or "disorders of discourse" are in particular contexts (Wodak 1996).

Organizational Communication Research

By contrast, organizational communication research usually focuses on macro-level observational and textual data rather than close analysis of naturally-occurring interaction. Relevant methodologies include systemic approaches to problems relating to human error or occupation safety, and genre or activity theories. Studies using systemic approaches take an organization- or team-wide perspective on institutional processes, including problematic communication. Here, localized phenomena are seen in the context of the system as an integrated whole (Sligo and Bathurst 2005). Genre analysis explores the discursive management of activities such as troubleshooting a workplace problem or negotiating roles and identities, and how information and relationships get (re)interpreted over time (Bazerman and Russell 2003). A more recent development is the emergence of complexity theory as a framework for studying problems in organizational communication, for example in the health quality and safety literature (e.g., van Beurden *et al.* 2011).

Critical Issues

The research summarized above offers useful insights and tools to inform the analysis of workplace communication issues. Another important contribution is the seminal volume, *Miscommunication and Problematic Talk*, which includes a first attempt at an "integrative model" of miscommunication incorporating different analytic perspectives and levels (Coupland, Giles, and Wiemann 1991). Although not tailored specifically to miscommunication in the workplace, the underlying principles have provided a useful starting point for subsequent applied studies (e.g., Watson *et al.* 2015). However, 25 years on, some important theoretical and analytic issues remain unresolved. First, in the words of Coupland, Wiemann, and Giles (1991, 11), miscommunication is "an interesting and slippery concept", one that still resists straightforward definition or classification. Moreover, miscommunication and problematic talk are dynamic, multi-faceted phenomena, not static and clearly bounded speech events, which raises some tricky methodological problems. Most fundamentally, we still lack a coherent and practical analytic framework that takes account of the highly complex, intertextual and situated nature of miscommunication and problematic talk in real workplaces.

Problems of Definition and Classification

The most basic issue that any analysis must address is delineation of the phenomenon of interest. Defining precisely what "counts" as miscommunication or problematic discourse, and how the relevant phenomena should be categorized in relation to one another is no straightforward task. This is reflected in an inconsistent use of terminology. Coupland, Wiemann, and Giles (1991) suggested "miscommunication and problematic talk" as an umbrella term to encompass a range of more localized occurrences such as "misunderstandings" or "mismatches", while Linell (1995, 177) sees "miscommunication" as a subset of "problematic talk" that includes "non-deliberate unclarity of expression, misrepresentations, mishearings, misunderstandings, misconstruals of others' utterances, misquotes, misattributions ... talk at cross-purposes", but excludes deliberate discrepancies such as lies, misleading, evasiveness or strategic silence. Finer level distinctions are found in some pragmatics research, where the term "misunderstanding" refers to a single turn or exchange (e.g., Bazzanella and Damiano 1999), and a "miscommunication" is a sustained misunderstanding that persists for several turns (e.g., Weigand 1999).

Miscommunication can also be viewed through different analytic "lenses". In talk-in-interaction research, miscommunication might be seen as a product of speaker-based mis(re)presentations or hearer-based misunderstandings (Bell 1991), or as one result of interactional "trouble" with the co-constructed negotiation of meaning (e.g., Garrod and Pickering 2009; Schegloff 1987). Alternatively, or as well, problematic talk may be seen to arise from systematic socio-cultural differences or patterns (e.g., House and Rehbein 2004; Sarangi 2009). Miscommunication can be characterized as a localized, discrete event embedded in a linear process (Tzanne 2000), or as a global miscommunication "characteristic of a whole interaction or a phase of its discourse" (Linell 1995, 190). At another level, problematic discourse can be seen as part of the largely invisible "discursive fabric" of institutions (Smart 2003).

Further definitional issues arise from variable factors such as intentionality, perspective, awareness, multifunctionality, and intertextuality. For example, some writers view only unintentional lapses as miscommunication (Linell 1995), while others contend that we cannot necessarily assume that interlocutors intend to be clear, or that they do always have shared goals (Coupland, Wiemann, and Giles 1991). Second, apparently problematic talk can also fulfil positive functions. Ambiguity, indirectness, or the selective imparting of information may better accomplish the relational or political ends of one or more parties than completely clear and honest communication would (Mustajoki 2012), or may function as a face saving device (Tzanne 2000). Conversely, unambiguously clear, concise, and "honest" communication may cause relational difficulties, and in any case does not often reflect the reality of everyday workplace interaction (Holmes and Stubbe 2015).

To further complicate matters, seemingly mundane or unproblematic sequences of events or interactions can be "deceptively adequate" (Coupland, Wiemann, and Giles 1991, 7), but may actually involve some degree of miscommunication that may or may not ever surface. Linell (1995) distinguishes between "latent", "covert", and "overt" miscommunication. An example of a latent event would be inadvertent cross talk between people from different sociocultural backgrounds where participants (mis)attribute a perceived problem to some other factor such as personality, attitude or intention (e.g., Morgan 2013; Roberts 2009). In "covert" cases, participants might perceive a difficulty but these would not emerge overtly in the discourse itself. It is far from clear where we should draw the line analytically in each of these cases.

Unsurprisingly, analysts from different research traditions routinely disagree on what counts as evidence that an "instance of miscommunication" has occurred. Conversation analysts do not assume that a sequence of talk involves any kind of misunderstanding or "trouble" unless participants observably orient to it. Researchers from other traditions will admit different kinds of contextual information or interpretive frameworks to the analysis. The ways in which these constructs are conceptualized and defined inevitably determines what kinds of data are examined and what is identified as an "instance" of miscommunication.

Methodological Issues

The dynamic, intertextual, and situated nature of miscommunication makes it very challenging to systematically locate and "capture" instances for analysis. Workplace conversations can often be fully understood only as connected episodes in an ongoing dialogue, and miscommunication is seldom a discrete event amenable to purely localised analysis. Even if a particular episode is clearly problematic, it can still be tricky to determine whether and how this fits into a wider sequence of events. An earlier trigger (probably not available for analysis) may influence how subsequent utterances or behaviours are (mis)interpreted by all or some of the present interlocutors, and subsequent misunderstandings may build upon one another and become mutually reinforcing. Such scenarios are very common and are at the heart of many workplace disputes, disagreements, and relationship difficulties. However, it can be very difficult indeed, if not impossible, to unravel them.

In addition, as an outsider, the analyst may "see" an apparent problem where none exists, or fail to recognize an instance of problematic discourse or a possible trigger for miscommunication because they lack the requisite insider knowledge or have access to only partial data. Workplace participants may also fail to recognise latent or covert problems, or may evaluate aspects of interaction (such as digressions in meetings or overlapping talk) as being problematic from their perspective, when from the discourse analyst's perspective these are perfectly normal phenomena.

These issues highlight the importance of undertaking a "thick description" (Geertz 1973), encompassing both fine-grained linguistic and sequential analysis of individual interactions, and more macro-level, ethnographic descriptions of the communicative patterns and systems observed in a particular workplace (see Wilson this volume). Many interactional researchers studying workplace miscommunication do incorporate ethnographic methods and data and/or a critical dimension into their analysis of problematic talk. However, the data commonly consist of unconnected interactions, with few studies to date that systematically "track" related interactions and texts or explicitly consider how communication issues relate systemically to the wider organizational context.

Conversely, a common limitation of research in the organizational or professional research domains is a tendency to focus on communication as a linear flow of information, and to identify features of "unsuccessful" communication at an unhelpfully global or abstract level. Language-in-use is often ignored or given a fairly superficial and mechanistic treatment. This can result in a narrow skills-deficit view of problematic talk which does not recognize either the complex reality of how such cases evolve, or the sophisticated interactional resources routinely used by people to manage their communicative tasks, for the most part sucessfully.

Problems of Practical Relevance

In order to have true practical relevance, an analytic model of miscommunication in the workplace needs to go beyond providing a purely theoretical framework for application by researchers. Rather it must accommodate a degree of "joint problematisation" (Roberts and Sarangi 1999, 473). In real life, unlike in academia, people do not often have the luxury of looking in depth at just one little "slice" of a complex issue or episode in any detail. Instead, they want to be able to "solve the problem" and work out "what's happened here?" in a holistic way, often in real time, as they attempt to get their jobs done while at the same time managing their workplace relationships. It is the tensions between these sometimes conflicting roles and imperatives that often render workplace talk problematic, rather than specific aspects of the interactions themselves.

Moreover, from a practical perspective, the context of the problem at hand is crucial in deciding which aspect of miscommunication it is important for analysts or the participants themselves to focus on at a given time. For an airline pilot trainer or crash investigator, for example, the immediate context of the talk and a fairly microscopic approach to how and why a misunderstanding could arise is not only appropriate but essential, although at some point, systems factors might also come into focus in such a case. For a manager in an organization faced with conflict or other dysfunctional patterns of communication, the immediate focus is likely to be at a different level of detail. In such a context, the most useful model is likely to be one that focuses on intergroup relationships and/or on how communication becomes distorted (or not) over time and across multiple interactions.

Because different phenomena are highlighted depending on the conceptual framework applied, some researchers have argued for a pluralistic and situated approach to analysis of workplace miscommunication. This allows us to "capitalize on the complexity of in situ practices rather than reduce it to abstracted models or simplified case studies" (Carroll, Iedema, and Kerridge 2008, 381). What is needed is an integrated framework and set of analytic tools that will allow communication researchers and practitioners alike to "think practically and look locally" (Eckert and McConnell-Ginet 1992) as they attempt to understand and deal with actual instances of miscommunication and problematic talk.

A Multi-Dimensional Analytic Framework

Design Principles

As we have seen, there is great diversity in the theoretical approaches available to investigate problematic communication; each defines miscommunication in different ways and teases out different aspects. This presents a particular challenge for researchers or practitioners who are interested mainly in the situated examination of whole cases or episodes.

The multi-dimensional model presented here is a heuristic tool for analysing "real world" cases of miscommunication and problematic talk. It extends Coupland, Wiemann, and Giles' (1991) integrative model by drawing on different theoretical approaches to miscommunication within a unifying framework of critical interactional sociolinguistics. Taking this approach accommodates the application of fine-grained interactional analysis within a broader ethnographic and socio-cultural context, and acknowledges the reality that specific utterances and interactions do not stand alone, but are produced within a complex adaptive system characterized by intertextuality, interdiscursivity, and the co-construction of meaning, one where problematic talk is an inevitable aspect of normal communication processes. The overarching aim for this analytic framework is to be sufficiently flexible and spacious to allow the rigorous application of a range of relevant tools and perspectives to the messy, complex reality of actual cases.

This framework grew organically out of the insights gained by looking across a large set of workplace interactions and ethnographic data in an iterative process (Stubbe 2010). This involved analysing and reflecting on many individual interactional sequences, as well as examining a number of more extended and complex cases of problematic communication tracked over multiple interactions. Dialogue with the workplace participants themselves was an integral part of the process, and in fact produced some of the most interesting and revealing insights.

Figure 21.1 provides a summary overview of this "working model". This is designed to help tease out the many possible overlapping dimensions and levels of analysis. It is not a rigid prescription for a stepwise analytic process, nor is it intended as a "grand theory" of miscommunication. The remainder of this section briefly explains the scope of the main components of this analytic framework.

"Candidate episodes" or cases of miscommunication and problematic talk may include superficially straightforward and localized misunderstandings through to more complex and extended instances of problematic discourse that relate to the ongoing negotiation of workplace tasks, processes and relationships. It may be clear from the discourse itself that participants themselves are orienting to some aspect of problematic communication, or there may be other evidence from related interactions or from ethnographic information.

The six "analytic actions" (scan, describe, define, locate, diagnose, and evaluate) have been arranged in a logical but not necessarily chronological sequence. The bi-directional arrows indicate that there may be multiple entry points for the processes of identification and analysis, and are also reflective of the iterative and overlapping nature of these analytic actions.

Corresponding to each "analytic action", are six sets of "analytic dimensions or levels". These are drawn from various sources and represent a synthesis of descriptive analytic tools and/or heuristic frameworks from the existing literature that have proved helpful in answering the questions noted underneath each of the six analytic actions.

There are three inter-related sets of analytic dimensions that are "omni-relevant" in the sense that they have global significance and may enter the analysis at any point: 1) awareness and repairability; 2) intentionality, perspective, and agency; and 3) multi-functionality and intertextuality.

Miscommunication at Work

	Candidate episode of miscommunication or problematic talk	
Analytic action	*Analytic dimensions or levels**	
Scan What 'traces' or other indications of 'problems' are evident in the data?	**Nature of evidence** **Interactional:** *observable issue or 'trouble' (micro-analytic features, immediate context)* **Intertextual:** *'thread' to or from linked interactions* **Ethnographic:** *clue(s) from historical or background information (observations, reports, documents)*	
Describe What is happening here? Where, when, how, why? Who is involved?	**'Situation':** *setting, time, context* [*1] **'Participants':** *individuals/relationships* **'Ends':** *goals and outcomes- interactional/concrete* **'Actions/activity sequences':** *content/design/structure* **'Keys':** *tone/manner, footing* **'Instrumentalities':** *channel, media, linguistic code/style* **'Norms':** *interactional and interpretative 'rules'/practices* **'Genres':** *types, sets, networks/systems*	
Define What is the nature of the 'problem' or issue? What is at stake? Is the problem primarily (i) a communication issue; (ii) a problematic issue of some other kind (mediated through discourse); or (iii) a mixed case?	**Referential:** *Information content, knowledge* **Instrumental:** *Goals and outcomes* **Affective:** *Perceived intent, attitudes* **Relational:** *Power, solidarity, identity, face* **Discourse-internal** *Interactional incident or process at one or more levels (non-verbal, paralinguistic, pragmatics, turn design, sequential organisation, coherence, genre, linguistic code)*	**Contextual** [*(2:188)] *Mismatches or gaps in background knowledge or understandings Aspect of setting or situation (e.g. work environment, systemic issues, a practical or interpersonal problem)*
Locate Where does the observed episode 'fit' (in time and sequentially)? Does it have defined boundaries, and what is its extent?	**Localised:** *a 'focused' one-off incident which originates, develops and is resolved within a single sequence or interaction* [*(2:190)] **Global:** *an 'unfocused' problem, characteristic of a whole sequence, interaction, or a series of encounters* [*(2:190)] **Multiplex:** *one of a series of episodes in a longer sequence/process, or a surfacing or 'trace' of a past event*	
Diagnose What is the underlying cause or origin of the problem? Is it possible to identify a source or trigger?	**1: Flawed 'transfer' or negotiation of meaning** [*3] » localised breakdowns » minor misunderstandings » misreading of intentions or attitude *'Not getting the message (across)'* **2 Goal conflict or failure to achieve goals** [*3] » resistance » non-alignment » 'strategic' miscommunication (misleading, withholding, masking) *'Talking at cross-purposes'*	
Evaluate What are the likely outcomes (actual or potential), and how consequential are they? What strategies have been/could be used (if any) to mitigate and/or resolve the matter?	**3 Differing group/sociocultural norms/practices** [*3] » 'crosstalk' (misalignment, misunderstandings, misattribution) » exclusion » discrimination/inequalities *'Talking past each other'* **4 Competing/hegemonic discourses or ideologies** [*3] » repressive discourse, masking » coercion » silencing » conflict » marginalisation/exclusion *'Conflict or disempowerment'*	

Left margin: *Identify* ↕ *Analyse*

Right margin: § Awareness § Repairability § Intentionality § Agency § Perspective(s) § Multi-functionality § Intertextuality §
Omni-relevant dimensions of analysis

* A number of the analytic concepts and terms used in this framework have been adapted from previous models (as marked):
[*1] Hymes (1974): 'SPEAKING' grid; [*2] Linell (1995:188-90); [*3] Coupland, Wiemann and Giles (1991): 'integrative model'

Figure 21.1 Multi-dimensional analytic framework (from Stubbe 2010)

Sample Analysis

> **Candidate Episode:**
>
> Two colleagues troubleshoot a workflow issue:
>
> Jan: it hasn't been signed by Philip because he wanted that information included
> Heke: all right okay (.) hhh oh look I'm <u>drea</u>dfully sorry about that
> Jan: oh well, just check out to see what happened. 'cause there was clearly some miscommunication somewhere

This brief exchange[2] comes towards the end of a lengthy meeting between Jan (a senior manager of New Zealand European ethnicity) and Heke (a Māori team leader within Jan's section). Philip is the CEO. In the discussion below, **bold** text signals the relevant analytic action; *italics* signal the analytic dimension or level being referred to (see Figure 21.1).

An **initial scan** provides local *evidence* of at least two *observable "troubles"*: Heke's apology, and Jan's explicit mention of miscommunication. To satisfactorily **define the nature and location of the problem, evaluate** its import, and **diagnose its underlying origins** however, it is necessary to **describe** and more closely examine both *the wider context* and *interactional features* of the focus excerpt.

The earlier part of this meeting had focused on a number of misunderstandings and differing work expectations within Heke's team, and was hearably tense at times. In the first line of the excerpt above, Jan indicates how the last of these problems should be resolved (Heke's team need to provide the missing information), preceded by a justification (so that the CEO will sign off). Heke acknowledges and aligns with Jan's *directive* in the first part of his succeeding turn with "all right okay", but then shifts to a new action, formulated as a very fulsome *apology*, which on the surface at least treats Jan's utterance as also embodying a *complaint* (thus making an *apology* relevant). However, the rather exaggerated delivery of this apology (initiated with a dramatic sigh and the recognition marker "oh look", followed by an emphatic "I'm <u>drea</u>dfully sorry about that") suggests an alternative interpretation: namely that Heke is positioning Jan's utterance (instead or as well) as a *criticism*, an analysis that is consistent with patterns observed in earlier parts of this same meeting. With her points apparently accepted, Jan's response is to simply acknowledge the apology with a neutrally produced "oh well", before offering the *face-saving suggestion* that "there was clearly some miscommunication somewhere". This plays down the seriousness of the problem and/or the degree to which her previous comment should be heard as being critical of Heke and his team.

Upon further analysis, this apparently straightforward example begins to reveal further layers. A *mooted instance of miscommunication* has surfaced explicitly as the **underlying cause** of a practical work problem—because certain essential information was omitted from a letter the CEO had declined to sign it off, causing a delay in a project, and also potential embarrassment for Jan. The **substantive problem** is therefore a mixed case. What is foregrounded is a *practical (instrumental) matter* **diagnosed** by Jan as a relatively *minor lapse or breakdown in communication (not identified at the time)*, and **evaluated** implicitly as not consequential in the long term.

At the same time, there is *interactional evidence* that a number of *tricky relational and identity issues* are at stake here. Both parties orient to preserving their longer term working relationship and their own personal positions within the organization. Jan's *complaint* and the implicit *criticism* of the performance of Heke's team (and hence, by extension, of his own effectiveness as their immediate line manager) are *potentially face-threatening* to Heke, challenging his *professional identity* as a competent team leader. Jan, on the other hand, indexes her own close working relationship with Philip, the CEO, by the way she uses his first name and is able to report directly what he wanted. This, together with her explicit instruction to Heke to "check out ... what happened", *foregrounds her status* as a senior manager and introduces an element of *coercion*. Such explicit *indexing of her managerial authority* was unusual for Jan, who more typically downplayed status differences with her subordinates. Jan's *non-threatening formulation* of her directive, mitigated with the hedge "just", along with her *alternative account* of the **cause of the problem** both work to balance this assertion of status, arguably reinforcing her *identity* as a firm but fair manager.

In just these few lines, then, we can see Jan and Heke negotiating several problematic aspects of workplace talk: the downstream practical consequences of the omission of information from a letter, the difference in their status, protecting their personal "face" and their positions within the organizational hierarchy, while at the same time working to maintain an amicable personal and working relationship.

What makes this example especially interesting is the way in which the lay concept of miscommunication is used as a resource for managing these other tricky issues. Attributing the problem to "miscommunication" provides Jan with a convenient strategy for tabling her expectation that the issue should not recur, while at the same time managing a potential relational difficulty. In addition, Jan's vague formulation, "some miscommunication somewhere", indexes the difficulty of locating the precise point at which an instance of problematic talk has occurred and leaves open who was responsible, thus implying that she considers it unimportant to understand the exact nature and provenance of the supposed miscommunication.

This example succinctly illustrates the important point that, at a fundamental level, discourse analysts and workplace participants face somewhat similar problems in trying to understand a given instance of miscommunication or problematic talk. The first requirement of course is to recognize that an interactional problem has in fact occurred (or has the potential to unfold). The second is to describe and analyse what happened: to define the issue at stake, how or where it arose and how consequential it is, taking account as far as possible of all relevant dimensions or factors. In the case of workplace practitioners, a third task is to select appropriate communicative strategies for dealing with any problems identified within the dynamic and contingent environment of an ongoing interaction, and to align these strategies with longer term transactional and relational goals.

Discussion and Conclusions

As a "working model" to guide the analysis of possible instances of miscommunication, the integrated analytic framework presented here has a number of strengths. It provides the analyst with a set of heuristics against which to test initial identifications, systematically create descriptions and develop alternative readings of data. As illustrated above, it also facilitates the teasing out of different layers and dimensions of observed or reported episodes of miscommunication and problematic talk and detailed analysis of the interactional strategies used by workplace participants to manage these, thus allowing a more nuanced analysis. By offering multiple "entry points" into the analysis of a candidate episode, it is also possible to accommodate the intertextuality and context-embeddedness of workplace communication, making it possible to identify complexities which may otherwise remain occluded.

Naturally, there are also limitations to be noted. First, this is an analytic resource, not an integrated theory or methodological approach. Rather, I have sought to provide a logical framework to accommodate a range of existing perspectives and tools in a coherent working model for analysing miscommunication and problematic talk, so that these can be applied in a rigorous and useful way. Second, for this approach to work to best advantage, it requires a particular kind of research design and data collection methodology. This includes a mix of ethnographic and interactional data which allows the tracking of intertextual and inter-contextual links, and ideally some kind of participatory or action research component to facilitate a close engagement between researchers and workplace participants (see Holmes and Stubbe 2015).

A unifying conceptual framework for such a pluralistic, multi-paradigm approach that shows some promise is complexity theory. Complexity theorists take it as read that there will be multiple valid representations of the same complex system. An analytic framework that is sufficiently flexible to tolerate potentially contradictory approaches is far more powerful than a model that attempts to somehow integrate or compress different approaches into a single "grand theory" that is ultimately reductionist and insensitive to the nuances of particular situations (Richardson 2008). As noted earlier, the modelling of organizations as complex adaptive systems is gaining currency, largely in relation to more generic issues of teamwork and error management. Complexity thinking has not as yet been widely applied to the study of language and communication (cf. Larsen-Freeman and Cameron 2008), but its applicability to the study of miscommunication and problematic talk in workplaces is an exciting avenue that is ripe for further exploration.

Further Reading

For those readers interested in exploring research on miscommunication and problematic talk further, I would recommend starting with Coupland, Giles, and Wiemann (1991), Heritage and Clayman (2010) and House, Kasper, and Ross (2003).

Related Topics

Interactional sociolinguistics; Conversation analysis; Critical discourse studies; Linguistic ethnography; (Im)politeness theory; Rapport management; Conflict talk

Acknowledgement

I am grateful for the invaluable input of the original research participants and my colleagues and research assistants from the LWP. Any errors or infelicities are my own responsibility.

Notes

1. The term "practitioner" is used here to refer to people in workplaces and to organisational training and management professionals to distinguish these groups from academic researchers and commentators on workplace communication (Jones and Stubbe 2004).
2. Data from LWP (Stubbe 2010). Names used are pseudonyms.

References

Angouri, Jo. 2012. "Managing Disagreement in Problem Solving Meeting Talk." *Journal of Pragmatics* 44: 1565–79.

Auer, Peter, and Celia Roberts. 2011. "Introduction—John Gumperz and the Indexicality of Language." *Text & Talk* 31: 381–393.
Bazerman, Charles, and David R. Russell, Eds. 2003. *Writing Selves/Writing Societies: Research from Activity Perspectives*. Fort Collins, CO: WAC Clearinghouse.
Bazzanella, Carla, and Rossana Damiano. 1999. "The Interactional Handling of Misunderstanding in Everyday Conversations." *Journal of Pragmatics* 31: 817–836.
Bell, Allan. 1991. "Hot Air: Media, Miscommunication and the Climate Change Issue." In *Miscommunication and Problematic Talk*, edited by Nikolas Coupland, Howard Giles, and John M. Wiemann, 259–282. London: Sage.
Carroll, Katherine, Rick Iedema, and Ross Kerridge. 2008. "Reshaping ICU Ward Round Practices Using Video-Reflexive Ethnography." *Qualitative Health Research* 18: 380–390.
Coupland, Nikolas, Howard Giles, and John M. Wiemann, Eds. 1991. *"Miscommunication" and Problematic Talk*. London: Sage.
Coupland, Nikolas, John M. Wiemann, and Howard Giles. 1991. "Talk as 'Problem' and Communication as 'Miscommunication': An Integrative Analysis." In *"Miscommunication" and Problematic Talk*, edited by Nikolas Coupland, Howard Giles, and John M. Wiemann, 1–17. London: Sage.
Drew, Paul, and John Heritage, Eds. 1992. *Talk at Work. Interaction in Institutional Settings*. Cambridge: Cambridge University Press.
Eckert, Penelope, and Sally McConnell-Ginet. 1992. "Think Practically and Look Locally: Language and Gender as Community-Based Practice." *Annual Review of Anthropology* 21: 461–490.
Fairclough, Norman. 1992. *Critical Language Awareness*. London: Longman.
Fillieataz, Laurent. 2012. "The Linguistic Demands of Workplace Learning: Power and Miscommunication in Vocational Interactions." In *Globalisierung, Migration und Fremdsprachenunterricht*, edited by Marcus Bär, Andreas Bonnet, Helene Decke-Cornill, Andreas Grünewald, and Adelheid Hu, 315–326. Hamburg: Schneider Verlag Hoengehren.
Firth, Alan, Ed. 1995. *The Discourse of Negotiation: Studies of Language in the Workplace*. Oxford: Pergamon.
Garcia, Angela Cora. 2016. "Air Traffic Communications in Routine and Emergency Contexts: A Case Study of Flight 1549 'Miracle on the Hudson'." *Journal of Pragmatics* 106: 57–71.
Garrod, Simon, and Martin J. Pickering. 2009. "Joint Action, Interactive Alignment, and Dialog." *Topics in Cognitive Science* 1: 292–304.
Geertz, Clifford. 1973. *The Interpretation of Cultures*. New York: Basic Books.
Goffman, Erving. 1959. *The Presentation of Self in Everyday Life*. New York: Doubleday.
Gumperz, John. 1992. "Interviewing in Intercultural Situations." In *Talk at Work: Interaction in Institutional Settings*, edited by Paul Drew, and John Heritage, 302–327. Cambridge: Cambridge University Press.
Hepburn, Alexa, Sue Wilkinson, and Carly W. Butler. 2014. "Intervening with Conversation Analysis in Telephone Helpline Services: Strategies to Improve Effectiveness." *Research on Language and Social Interaction* 47: 239–254.
Heritage, John, and Douglas W. Maynard. 2006. *Communication in Medical Care: Interaction Between Primary Care Physicians and Patients*. Cambridge: Cambridge University Press.
Heritage, John, and Steven Clayman. 2010. *Talk in Action. Interactions, Identities, and Institutions*. Malden, MA: Wiley-Blackwell.
Holmes, Janet, and Maria Stubbe. 2015. *Power and Politeness in the Workplace*. 2nd ed. Abingdon, UK: Routledge.
House, Juliane, and Jochen Rehbein, Eds. 2004. *Multilingual Communication*. Amsterdam: John Benjamins.
House, Juliane, Gabriele Kasper, and Steven Ross, Eds. 2003. *Misunderstanding in Social Life: Discourse Approaches to Problematic Talk*. London: Longman.
Howard, John W. 2008. "'Tower, Am I Cleared to Land?': Problematic Communication in Aviation Discourse." *Human Communication Research* 34: 370–391.
Hymes, Dell. 1974. *Foundations in Sociolinguistics: An Ethnographic Approach*. Philadelphia, PA: University of Pennsylvania Press.
Jacobs, Scott. 2002. "Maintaining Neutrality in Dispute Mediation: Managing Disagreement while Managing Not to Disagree." *Journal of Pragmatics* 34: 1403–1426.
Janicki, Karol. 2010. "Lay People's Language Problems." *International Journal of Applied Linguistics* 20: 73–94.

Jones, Deborah, and Maria Stubbe. 2004. "Communication and the Reflective Practitioner: A Shared Perspective from Sociolinguistics and Organisational Communication." *International Journal of Applied Linguistics* 14: 185–211.

Korkiakangas, Terhi, Sharon-Marie Weldon, Jeff Bezemer, and Roger Kneebone. 2016. "'Coming up!':Why Verbal Acknowledgement Matters in the Operating Theatre." In *Communication in Surgical Practice*, edited by Sarah J. White, and John A. Cartmill, 234–256. Sheffield, UK: Equinox.

Larsen-Freeman, Diane, and Lynne Cameron. 2008. *Complex Systems and Applied Linguistics*. Oxford: Oxford University Press.

Linell, Per. 1995. "Troubles with Mutualities: A Dialogical Theory of Misunderstanding and Miscommunication." In *Mutualities in Dialogue*, edited by Ivana Markovà, Carl F. Graumann, and Klaus Foppa, 176–213. Cambridge: Cambridge University Press.

Măda, Stanca, and Răzvan Săftoiu, Eds. 2012. *Professional Communication across Languages and Cultures*. Amsterdam: John Benjamins.

Morgan, Sonya. 2013. "Miscommunication between Patients and General Practitioners: Implications for Clinical Practice." *Journal of Primary Health Care* 5: 123–128.

Mustajoki, Arto. 2012. "A Speaker-Oriented Multidimesional Approach to Risks and Causes of Miscommunication." *Language and Dialogue* 2: 216–243.

OED-Online. 2010. "Oxford English Dictionary." Oxford University Press.

Richards, Keith. 2006. *Language and Professional Identity*. Basingstoke, UK: Palgrave Macmillan.

Richardson, Kurt A. 2008. "Managing Complex Organizations: Complexity Thinking and the Science and Art of Management." *E:CO Emergence: Complexity & Organization* 10: 13–26.

Roberts, Celia, Becky Moss, Val Wass, Srikant Sarangi, and Roger Jones. 2005. "Misunderstandings: A Qualitative Study of Primary Care Consultations in Multilingual Settings, and Educational Implications." *Medical Education* 39: 465–475.

Roberts, Celia, Evelyn Davies, and Thomas Cyprian Jupp. 1992. *Language and Discrimination: A Study of Communication in Inter-Ethnic Workplaces*. London: Longman.

Roberts, Celia. 2009. "'Mince' or 'Mice'? Clinical Miscommunication and Patient Safety in a Linguistically Diverse Community." In *Health Care Errors and Patient Safety*, edited by Brian Hurwitz, and Sheikh Aziz, 112–128. Oxford: Blackwell.

Roberts, Celia, and Srikant Sarangi. 1999. "Hybridity in Gatekeeping Discourse: Issues of Practical Relevance for the Researcher." In *Talk, Work and Institutional Order. Discourse in Medical, Mediation and Management Settings*, edited by Srikant Sarangi, and Celia Roberts, 473–503. Berlin: Mouton de Gruyter.

Sarangi, Srikant, and Celia Roberts, Eds. 1999. *Talk, Work, and Institutional Order: Discourse in Medical, Mediation, and Management Settings*. Berlin: Mouton de Gruyter.

Sarangi, Srikant. 2004. "Editorial: Towards a Communicative Mentality in Medical and Healthcare Practice." *Communication & Medicine* 1: 1–11.

Sarangi, Srikant. 2009. "Intercultural or Not? Beyond Celebration of Cultural Differences in Miscommunication Analysis." *Pragmatics* 4: 409–427.

Schegloff, Emanuel A. 1987. "Some Sources of Misunderstanding in Talk-in-Interaction." *Linguistics* 25: 201–18.

Sikveland, Rein, and Elizabeth Stokoe. 2016. "Dealing with Resistance in Initial Intake and Inquiry Calls to Mediation: The Power of 'Willing'." *Conflict Resolution Quarterly* 33: 235–254.

Sligo, Frank, and Ralph Bathurst. 2005. *Communication in the New Zealand Workplace: Theory and Practice*. Wellington: Software Technology NZ.

Smart, Graham. 2003. "A Central Bank's 'Communications Strategy': The Interplay of Activity, Discourse Genres, and Technology in a Time of Organizational Change." In *Writing Selves, Writing Societies: Research from Activity Perspectives*, edited by Charles Bazerman, and David R. Russell, 9–61. Fort Collins, CO: WAC Clearinghouse.

Stubbe, Maria. 2010. "'Was That My Misunderstanding?' Managing Miscommunication and Problematic Talk at Work." PhD diss., Victoria University of Wellington. http://hdl.handle.net/10063/1462.

Stubbe, Maria, Chris Lane, Jo Hilder, Elaine Vine, Bernadette Vine, Meredith Marra, Janet Holmes, and Ann Weatherall. 2003. "Multiple Discourse Analyses of a Workplace Interaction." *Discourse Studies* 5: 351–388.

Tzanne, Angeliki. 2000. *Talking at Cross-purposes: The Dynamics of Miscommunication*. Amsterdam: John Benjamins.

van Beurden, Eric, Annie M. Kia, Avigdor Zask, Uta Dietrich, and Lauren Rose. 2011. "Making Sense in a Complex Landscape: How the Cynefin Framework from Complex Adaptive Systems Theory Can Inform Health Promotion Practice." *Health Promotion International* 28: 73–83.

Watson, Bernadette M., Elizabeth Manias, Fiona Geddes, Phillip Della, and Dorothy Jones. 2015. "An Analysis of Clinical Handover Miscommunication Using a Language and Social Psychology Approach." *Journal of Language and Social Psychology* 34: 687–701.

Weigand, Edda. 1999. "Misunderstanding: The Standard Case." *Journal of Pragmatics* 31: 763–785.

White, Sarah J., and John A. Cartmill, Eds. 2016. *Communication in Surgical Practice*. Sheffield, UK: Equinox.

Wodak, Ruth. 1996. *The Disorders of Discourse*. London: Longman.

22
Conflict Talk
Almut Koester

Introduction

Maintaining good relationships with co-workers and customers is seen as important for business and for the smooth running of organizational processes in the workplace. How this is achieved through talk has been the subject of many studies of workplace interaction (e.g., Holmes and Stubbe 2003; Koester 2006; Schnurr 2013). People working together invest considerable effort into managing problems and avoiding conflict (Holmes and Stubbe 2003, 137–163). At the same time, such activities as problem-solving and negotiating, in which differing views may be expressed or opposing goals pursued, occur frequently in the workplace (Firth 1995; Holmes and Stubbe 2003; Koester 2006). In such situations, disagreement, or even conflict, may arise. Another feature of workplace interactions is that they are frequently marked by relationships of asymmetry (Heritage 1997). While the power dynamic of such asymmetrical relationships may lead to the suppression of disagreement or conflict, if such power relations are resisted or challenged, this can also result in conflict (Culpeper 2008, 39).

Given these features of workplace discourse, exploring how conflicts unfold and are handled in workplace interactions should provide a rich vein of enquiry, complementing the extensive research on how co-operation is achieved. This chapter aims to give an overview of research to date into conflictual talk at work. A brief literature review is followed by a discussion of theoretical and methodological issues in which "conflict talk" is defined in comparison to related phenomena, such as "disagreement" and "impoliteness". The remainder of the chapter is devoted to exploring conflictual discourse in a variety of workplace contexts. The chapter concludes with recommendations for further research.

Literature Review

While naturally-occurring spoken discourse has been the object of research for at least four decades, studies of conflictual discourse are more recent. William Labov was one of the first sociolinguists to focus attention on talk that was competitive and sometimes conflictual in his analyses of inner-city Black Vernacular English (Labov 1972a, 1972b). But it was not until the 1980s that conflict talk became the object of study in its own right, culminating in the publication of a collection of studies by linguists, sociologists and anthropologists on *Conflict Talk* (Grimshaw 1990). A few years earlier, Schank and Schwitalla (1987) had published a collection of papers on conflict in conversations among German speakers, attesting to the interest in this topic across national borders.

Many of these early studies focused on conflict talk among children and adolescents (e.g., Corsaro and Rizzo 1990; Goodwin 1990; Eder 1990), perhaps partly because such data was more readily available than conflictual discourse among adults, who might be more reluctant to display such behaviour in a recording situation.

With regard to how "grown-ups" argue, there is surprisingly little research focusing specifically on conflict talk at work, especially given the potential for disagreement and conflict in workplace interactions. Conflict is, of course, at the heart of legal discourse; indeed two of the chapters in Grimshaw's (1990) landmark volume deal with talk during trials (Conley and O'Barr 1990; Philips 1990). However, this does not mean that all legal discourse is conflictual, as the extensive literature on legal and forensic discourse has shown (see Innes this volume; Coulthard and Johnson 2010). Trial discourse and police interviews have both been widely studied (e.g., Thornborrow 2002, 37–59; Holt and Johnson 2010) and have been shown to be highly orderly and rule-governed with specialized turn-taking systems and involving a range of genres, such as narratives, cross-examination, and closing arguments. Negotiations also involve institutionally sanctioned forms of arguing, following schematic structures and displaying specific strategic and discursive characteristics, as demonstrated in the extensive literature, for example, on business or union-management negotiations (e.g., Firth 1995; Walker 1995; Koester 2014).

A number of studies carried out specifically to study conflictual or "impolite" discourse have used data taken from "fly-on-the-wall" television documentaries of police work or military training (Bousfield 2008a; Limberg 2008), discourse types in which aggressive or confrontational behaviour might be expected. Other media data targeted to analyse conflict talk include news interviews (Greatbatch 1992), live TV discussions (Gruber 1996) or political interviews (Locher and Watts 2008). The fact that so many studies of conflictual or impolite discourse draw on media sources, rather than naturally-occurring spoken discourse, points to the difficulty of obtaining conflictual data from ordinary conversation or non-mediated workplace settings. As conflicts in interaction are not generally planned, getting hold of naturally-occurring conflict talk is largely a matter of chance, not to mention the difficulty of obtaining permission to use such data.

Apart from these specialized workplace contexts (e.g., police work, trials) or genres (e.g., negotiating, mediation), we find only a few studies of conflict talk in workplace encounters, for example in public sector meetings between labour and management (O'Donnell 1990), a supplier–customer encounter (Handford and Koester 2010) or emergency phone calls (Svennevig 2012). However, two related areas of research focusing on disagreement and impoliteness have received considerable attention, and here one also finds studies of workplace interactions, for example, Mullany (2008), Angouri (2012), Marra (2012) and Choi and Schnurr (2014). Research on conflict talk has been carried out mainly within a conversation analytical framework, whereas impoliteness research has its origins in pragmatics. Drawing on these distinct research traditions, the next section explores the intersection between "conflict talk", "disagreement", and "impoliteness".

What is Conflict Talk? Conflict, Disagreement, and Impoliteness

Conflict and Disagreement

According to one definition from the organizational behaviour literature, "conflict is a process that begins when an individual or group perceives differences and opposition between oneself and another individual or group about interests, beliefs or values that matter to them" (De Dreu, van Dierendonck, and Dijkstra 2004, 8). But conflict as such should be distinguished from "conflict talk". As Gruber (1996, 54) points out, verbal conflict is just one mode among others to carry out conflict, and, therefore, he uses the term "disagreement sequence" (following Kotthoff 1993). The end of a disagreement sequence does not necessarily mean the conflict itself has been resolved. Instead, it simply indicates the re-establishment of a non-conflictual mode of talk: "Verbal conflict ends when the oppositional turns cease and other activities are taken up" (Vuchinich 1990,118).

Other terms used are "conflict talk" (Grimshaw 1990) and "conversational arguing" (Muntigl and Turnbull 1998). Conversational arguing, according to Muntigl and Turnbull (1998, 225) "involves the conversational interactivity of making claims, disagreeing with claims, countering disagreements, and the processes by which such disagreements arise, are dealt with, and resolved."

As the above definitions show, conflict talk involves disagreement; however Angouri (2012) argues that it is important to distinguish between disagreement and conflict. Angouri sees conflict as negatively marked (from the point of view of the conflicting parties), involving linguistic behaviour that breaches the norm and affects rapport between the interlocutors. Disagreement, on the other hand, involves "opposing views" and is not inherently negative or damaging to rapport (1567–1568). As Angouri points out, problem-solving or decision-making is a central activity in workplace interactions (see also Koester 2006), and disagreeing is a normal and necessary part of finding solutions to problems. Other discourse analysts researching both everyday and workplace interactions have also challenged the view that disagreement is necessarily linked to conflict (Schiffrin 1984; Tannen 1984; Marra 2012; Sifianou 2012). In their introduction to a special edition of the *Journal of Pragmatics* dedicated to the topic of disagreement in discourse, Angouri and Locher (2012b, 1549) argue that "disagreeing cannot be seen as an a priori negative act" and furthermore that "certain practices are prone to disagreement so that this speech act is expected rather than the exception." The latter is, of course, particularly the case for certain workplace contexts and genres, as discussed above.

One important distinguishing feature between conflictual and non-conflictual disagreements can be drawn on the basis of whether they are aimed at the task at hand or at the person addressed; in other words whether the disagreement is content-oriented or relationally-oriented (Gruber 1996, 51–54). In the meeting talk analysed by Angouri (2012), there was a preference towards task rather than person-oriented argumentation. In fact, the participants themselves, when interviewed after the meetings, did not see this problem-solving talk as conflictual. However, as Gruber (1996, 53–54) points out, it may not be possible when analysing conflictual talk to distinguish clearly between these two levels of content versus relationship, as disagreement about content has an impact on the relationship between the interlocutors. Nevertheless, it is important to take into account speaker relationships when analysing disagreement and conflict, as these may influence the speakers' behaviours and interpretations in a number of ways. How long the participants have known each other, the degree of intimacy between them and whether the relationship is friendly or antagonistic may all affect the tolerance of disagreement and the likelihood of conflict (O'Donnell 1990; Sifianou 2012).

Impoliteness

There is some consensus in the literature that an attack on the interlocutor's face, which impacts rapport negatively, is a clear sign of disagreement having turned to conflict (Gruber 1996; Angouri 2012, 1567; Sifianou 2012, 1559). This takes us into the realm of politeness and impoliteness research, in which notions of "face" and "face threatening acts" (FTAs) have been widely discussed (Brown and Levinson 1987; Watts 2003). Impoliteness research has emerged as an area of study in its own right within the established field of politeness research (Bousfield 2008a; Dynel 2015; Haugh and Watanabe this volume), and is of particular relevance for a discussion of conflict talk. The key theoretical premises and findings from research on impoliteness can only be summarised briefly here, and only to the extent that they relate to the issue of conflict talk.[1]

Miriam Locher and Richard Watts have proposed a framework of "relational work" (Locher 2004; Locher and Watts 2008) which attempts to account for the spectrum of judgements that interactants can make about the politeness or impoliteness of an utterance or other communicative act. According to this framework, impolite behaviour, defined as inappropriate, non-politic and negatively marked, is evaluated negatively by interactants and may lead to conflict, as "[p]eople respond quite forcefully when the level of relational work does not match their expectations" (Locher and Watts 2008, 79). Culpeper (2008, 36) defines impoliteness as involving "communicative behaviour intended to cause the 'face loss' of a target or perceived by the target to be so."

Interpretations of impoliteness depend critically on interlocutors' intentions and perceptions. Determining intentionality is, of course, notoriously difficult, therefore many researchers prefer to define acts of politeness and impoliteness on the basis of interlocutors' perceptions of communicators' intentions, not the intentions themselves (Locher and Watts 2008; Mullany 2008; Terkourafi 2008).

Another issue related to impoliteness, disagreement and conflict is power. Power is defined as the restriction of freedom of action, according to a number of politeness researchers (Watts 1991, 60; Locher 2004, passim). Locher (2004, 323) sees disagreement as restricting the addressee's freedom of action, and thus involving power, and she argues, furthermore, that committing a serious FTA is a way of exercizing power. In the literature on impoliteness, power is thus seen as emergent from the interaction rather than as externally determined by status or hierarchy.

Issues of speaker relationship and power are particularly important for understanding instances of impoliteness in workplace interactions. Due to the institutional hierarchies in most organizations, workplace relations are often asymmetrical and embody certain power structures. Nevertheless, power should not be seen as static, but as something that can be reinforced, contested or negotiated in interactions. An interesting example of how relationship and power can impact conflictual discourse is discussed by O'Donnell (1990) in her analysis of meetings between labour and management in a municipal department. O'Donnell interprets the style of arguing of two managers on the basis of their relationship: "long-term relations between these two managers allow them to disagree in a far less formal way and with greater reciprocity. The solidarity semantic tempers power differentials" (218).

Most research on impoliteness in the workplace also considers the role of the community of practice to be central. The notion of community of practice (CofP), developed from a social constructionist framework, is frequently used by sociolinguists to describe teams or groups of people who work together (see King this volume). According to Wenger (1998, 72–73) a CofP is defined by three criteria: mutual engagement, joint enterprise and a shared repertoire.

As argued in a number of studies (e.g., Schnurr, Marra, and Holmes 2008; Marra 2012), what counts as polite or impolite is crucially dependent on the shared practices of the CofP. Schnurr, Marra and Holmes use Locher and Watts' (2008) relational work framework to analyse impolite and overly polite behaviour in three workplaces. They conclude that whether particular utterances are considered polite or impolite depends on the norms of the CofP as well as on the specific discursive context. This means that utterances which appear impolite could be "politic" or even face-enhancing, for example the use of insults as solidarity markers in a factory team (see also Holmes and Stubbe 2003, 126–129). Conversely, superficially polite contributions might have a contestive or subversive message, and thus be considered over-polite and negatively marked (Schnurr, Marra, and Holmes 2008).

Conflict Talk

Based on the discussion so far, can we say that the presence of disagreement in conversation perceived as impolite (i.e., as negatively marked and face-threatening or aggravating) means that the interaction is conflictual? Not necessarily, as instances of such impoliteness might not be challenged, as in the case of the training of army recruits discussed by Bousfield (2008a, 2008b). For an interaction to be conflictual, negatively marked disagreement must involve two participants and extend over a number of turns, as reflected in Vuchinich's (1990, 118) definition: "In verbal conflict, participants oppose the utterances, actions, or selves of one another in *successive turns at talk*" [my emphasis].

While acts of impoliteness or disagreement can involve single speech acts, conflict talk unfolds across a disagreement sequence.[2] Furthermore, studies of conflictual talk have identified a number of key structural properties of such disagreement sequences (Coulter 1990; Goodwin 1990; Kotthoff 1993; Muntigl and Turnbull 1998). These will be illustrated using an extract from a conflictual workplace meeting discussed in Koester (2006, 122–135) and Handford and Koester (2010). In this meeting from a small printing company, Val, the office manager, and her boss, Sid, the owner of the company, discuss how to solve a problem with a customer who has a complaint about a printing job and does not want to pay.

In turns 1 and 3 of Example 22.1, Val reports the contents of a telephone conversation she has just had with the customer, and Sid immediately disputes the factual content of both utterances in his next turns, 2 and 4 respectively. This corresponds to the typical structure of an argument sequence, according to Muntigl and Turnbull (1998, 227), where speaker A makes a claim, which is then disputed by speaker B.

Example 22.1

1	Val	Well. . . she said she had conversations with you her*self*, →
2	Sid	⌊ No she didn't.
3	Val	→ and so did *Patricia*. =
4	Sid	= No she didn't.
5	Val	So-
6	Sid	⌊ If that's the case, why didn't she /??/.
7	Val	↑ She didn't- because it all went to the: i- it was all according to the *art*work. she said it went down through to NPL,

Another typical feature of turn structures in disputes, according to Kotthoff (1993), is that the usual preference structure is reversed. According to conversation analysis (CA), refusals or disagreements are "dispreferred" responses ("second pair parts", in CA terms) in non-conflictual talk (Levinson 1983; Pomerantz 1984). This means that such responses are less frequent than "preferred" second pair parts (i.e., acceptance or agreement) and tend to have more complex turn shapes, such as delays, hedges, and accounts, than preferred responses. Sid's responses in Example 22.1 clearly do not conform to this pattern. Turns 2 and 4 are direct and unhedged ("No she didn't") and there is no delay; in fact quite the opposite: Sid interrupts Val in turn 2, and there is "latching" (i.e., no gap) between turns 3 and 4. What we find is a reversal of the usual preference structure of consensual discourse, with disagreement and opposition having become preferred (Kotthoff 1993, 201).

Sid's interruption of Val in turn 2 (also in turn 6), illustrates another feature of conflictual talk, namely that speaker change occurs not at transition relevance place (TRP), which marks the end of a turn construction unit (Sacks, Schegloff, and Jefferson 1974), but at "disagreement relevance place" (Gruber 1996, 60–61). This means that speakers interrupt at points where they want to disagree, rather than waiting for the (potential) end of the current speaker's turn.

Finally, Example 22.1 also displays another structural property of disputes identified by Kotthoff (1993): an "opposition format". Here a speaker "co-opts the opponent's expression or point, and uses it for his or her own side" (201). We see this in Val's response to Sid in turn 7, where the beginning of her turn ("She didn't- because") echoes the end of Sid's prior turn: "If that's the case, why didn't she /??/." Kotthoff notes that the occurrence of opposition formats signals a very high level of divergence or "aggravated dissent" (203). Such aggravated dissent can be seen clearly in Example 22.2, taken from a later stage of Val and Sid's meeting, where the conflict seems to have reached a peak:

Example 22.2

1	Sid	No I'm sorry, I don't accept all this. If you give somebody an order, you give a give them an order with the sizes on it.
2	Val	⌊ ↑ Well Sid, it's no good talking to me about it then.
3	Sid	What?
4	Val	'Cause she's gonna stand her ground. So. . .
5	Sid	⌊ And I'm standing mine, too.

In turn 5, Sid reuses an idiom employed by Val ("she's gonna stand her ground"), reformulating it to oppose her (whom he sees as representing the customer's side in the dispute) and reinforce his own stance ("And I'm standing mine, too"). These two turns also illustrate a linguistic characteristic of conflictual workplace talk identified by Handford and Koester (2010): the frequent use of idioms and metaphors. An analysis of conflictual meetings in two different workplace contexts showed that these meetings had a high density of idioms and metaphors compared to non-conflictual encounters in the two data sets. While idioms and metaphors frequently have a convergence function (Moon 1998; Carter 2004), examples such as Example 22.2 show that when combined with a lack of vagueness and the use of performatives (e.g., turn 1: "I don't accept all this") they can also show divergence (Koester 2006; Handford and Koester 2010). Koester (2006, 122–135) also found that conflictual discourse was characterized by a high density of "markers of subjective stance", including strong modals, evaluative lexis, and idioms, as well as intensifiers, exclamations, and expletives.

It has been strongly argued by researchers working with a CofP framework that whether an interaction is considered conflictual depends on the norms of the CofP (Locher and Watts 2008; Schnurr, Marra, and Holmes 2008; Angouri 2012). While the role of the CofP is no doubt important for the interpretation of any instance of workplace talk, the similarities in the structural and linguistic characteristics of conflictual talk (e.g., reversal of preference, opposition formats, "markers of subjective stance") across a range of workplace contexts indicates that conflict talk does display some stability beyond specific CofPs.

Disagreement, Impoliteness, and Conflict in Workplace Discourse

In the last section, the differences between conflict, disagreement, and impoliteness were established, along with the main characteristics of conflict talk. This next section explores conflict talk at work in more detail. Research on divergent interactions at work has dealt with various degrees of divergence from unmarked disagreement (Angouri 2012), impolite behaviour (Schnurr, Marra, and Holmes 2008; Mullany 2008) to full-blown conflict (O'Donnell 1990; Handford and Koester 2010). Different workplace contexts have also been investigated, such as business-to-business meetings (Handford and Koester 2010), internal meetings (Mullany 2008; Handford and Koester 2010; Choi and Schnurr 2014), factory work (Schnurr, Marra, and Holmes 2008) or telephone service encounters (Fauzi, Ibrahim, and Maros 2014; Archer and Jagodziński 2015).

In terms of methodology, research on conflict at work is largely carried out through interactional analysis of naturally-occurring talk. Dominant methodologies employed are CA (e.g., Greatbatch 1992; Svennevig 2012), social constructionist approaches incorporating a CofP framework (e.g., Marra 2012; Choi and Schnurr 2014), and Locher and Watts' (2008) framework of relational work developed within (im)politeness research (e.g., Schnurr, Marra, and Holmes 2008; Archer and Jagodziński 2015).

The studies reviewed in more detail below illustrate the range from unmarked disagreement to face-aggravating conflict. In doing so, a number of issues identified as key above for understanding disagreement and conflict at work will also be addressed: the role of power and the CofP, as well as the nature of the relationship between the dissenting parties. Particularly interesting cases are those where the occurrence of impoliteness or the escalation (or suppression) of conflict is found to be directly linked to particular workplace practices.

Unmarked disagreements occur in situations where the interlocutors eventually reach a resolution or consensus. Choi and Schnurr (2014) look at how disagreements are resolved in leaderless research teams in a university setting. In these meetings, speakers' disagreements often display typical features of conflictual talk, such as preference reversal and opposition formats, but are ultimately resolved smoothly after everyone has had a chance to disagree. In this CofP, quite explicit and direct ways of disagreeing are part of the established discursive norms, and negotiating consensus is seen as the responsibility of the team.

Angouri (2012) also found disagreements to be unmarked in the context of problem-solving meetings in two workplaces in the private sector. Here too, disagreements sometimes displayed typical features of conflictual discourse, but were not perceived as conflictual by the participants. Again, knowledge of the CofP is important, for example, the long history of working together of the two main speakers in one meeting sanctioned the expression of dissonant views (see the example from O'Donnell 1990 discussed earlier). Similarly, in

Examples 22.1 and 22.2, the long work relationship history of the two speakers allows Val to argue with Sid (her superior) on an equal footing, despite the asymmetry in the relationship. However, in contrast to the participants in Angouri's study, comments made by both speakers show that they see this interaction as conflictual; in fact the problem remains unsolved by the end of the meeting. Reaching a resolution, or some kind of positive outcome, thus seems to be another key factor in distinguishing "disagreement" from "conflict", as shown in Koester's (2006, 122–135) comparison of two decision-making encounters involving disputes.

Between such unmarked disagreement and full-blown conflict, a number of studies have focused on acts of impoliteness or verbal aggression occurring in workplace encounters. Mullany (2008) takes a social constructionist approach to investigating impoliteness and gender. She analysed examples of women managers being strategically impolite to enact power over male colleagues, thereby challenging stereotypical views of women's interaction styles (249). While the discourse in the examples discussed was not overtly conflictual, the performance of face-threatening impoliteness over a stretch of talk marked it as divergent and conflict-laden. Taking a participants' view, Fauzi, Ibrahim, and Maros (2014) used ethnographic interviews to study perceptions of impoliteness in service encounters between staff and international students in the international office of a Malaysian university. They found that certain working conditions and work procedures, including understaffing and the filing method, contributed to impoliteness by staff. Other factors included lack of language proficiency of the students and cultural differences. In studying another type of service encounter, call centre interactions, Archer and Jagodziński (2015) contend that impoliteness and verbal aggression on the part of callers to agents constitute a form of institutional sanctioning of face attacks. When irate callers are impolite or aggressive, agents are expected to keep calm and remain polite, which means that these conflicts are very one-sided. Due to the constraints under which the agents operate, the linguistic and interactive resources to "do conflict" are unevenly distributed in favour of the callers, and therefore typical conflictual sequences (reversal of preference structure/opposition formats) do not usually occur. Archer and Jagodziński found that while for some agents the customers' verbal aggression is neutralized, this is not the case for all. Sanctioned aggressive facework also occurs in institutional settings such as police interviews and military training camps (Bousfield 2008a; Limberg 2008), and here too, as Culpeper (2008, 28–31) argues, such impoliteness may be perceived as inappropriate by those at the receiving end, even if it is expected.

Examples of full-blown conflictual talk at work in the literature are rare. Example 22.3 (discussed in Handford and Koester 2010) is from a meeting between the operations director of a pub chain (Peter) and the estates manager of a multinational brewer (John). It shows a dispute arising from Peter's attempt to resist the conditions of the brewer's contract with the pub chain requiring them to buy beer from John's company.

Example 22.3[3] (from Handford and Koester 2010, 31)

1	Peter:	And the rent's (1 second) stupid. So.
2	John:	Not as stupid as I was trying to make it.
3	Peter:	It's ridiculous already. The the the amount you were trying to make it was absolutely erm (1 second) beyond any business sense whatsoever.

This brief exchange displays all the typical characteristics of conflictual discourse: disputing claims, preference for disagreement, opposition formats (the repetition of "stupid" in turns 1 and 2) and strongly evaluative lexis and intensifiers ("stupid", "ridiculous", "absolutely", "whatsoever"). Moreover, Peter's accusation that the rent is "stupid" and "ridiculous" is unequivocally impolite. While the rent, not the addressee, is characterized as "stupid", the use of the pronoun "you" in turn 3 makes the accusation sound personal and intentionally face-attacking with no attempt to separate the task from the relationship. The extreme conflictual nature of the discourse, compounded by impoliteness, is all the more surprising as this is the first meeting of the interlocutors. In contrast to the other examples discussed in this section, there is no relationship history which could sanction such conflictual behaviour.

A further rare example of aggravated conflict in a workplace setting is found in Svennevig's (2012) analysis of a series of emergency calls, where misalignments between the caller and two different operators leads to "spiraling hostility". Misalignments occur, for example, when operators withhold displays of acceptance, and, instead, continue interrogating the caller. Svennevig concludes that these misalignments occur in part as a result of operators following routine procedures, but also because of errors in the way they respond to an emotionally upset caller. Thus there appear to be structural problems in the way these calls are handled, which in this particular case leads to fatal consequences.

Conclusions and Future Directions

In the examples discussed above, disagreement or conflict is linked to the pursuit of transactional work-related goals, for example trying to solve a problem, dealing with a complaint or getting emergency help. This focus on workplace goals or procedures is perhaps the main distinguishing feature of conflict at work compared to private settings. Nevertheless, as the examples above show, the relationship (or "mutual engagement" in CofP terms) of the co-workers is always affected in some way as well. This can involve an effort to maintain a good relationship, despite a disagreement regarding the task (e.g., Angouri 2012), an enactment of power through impoliteness (e.g., Mullany 2008) or a threat or even damage to the relationship through the escalation of conflict (Example 22.3). Further research into disagreement, impoliteness and conflict talk at work, and the links between them, should provide a rich and multi-faceted picture of the ways in which people working together manage divergence affecting both tasks and relationships within the CofP.

As disagreeing is a central and necessary part of problem-solving, it is likely that much disagreement at work is unmarked and non-conflictual, as argued by Angouri (2012). While outright conflict (as seen in Examples 22.1, 22.2 and 22.3) may be rare, given the imperative of getting the work done, impoliteness may afford co-workers more or less subtle ways (short of outright conflict) of showing dissent or exercizing and challenging power. The case of call centres is a striking example of employees' being actively discouraged from "doing conflict" when interacting with irate customers (Archer and Jagodziński 2015). In contrast, some studies have found certain workplace conditions (e.g., understaffing) or practices (e.g., the handling of emergency calls) to contribute to impoliteness or conflict. As poignantly shown by Svennevig's (2012) case study of a conflictual emergency call ending fatally, research on conflict talk at work has relevance for practitioners. Further research on ways in which impoliteness or conflict may be linked to particular workplace practices could provide other valuable insights for improving workplace practices.

Further Reading

Grimshaw's (1990) landmark edited volume sets out the agenda for researching "conflict talk" and first establishes it as a research field in its own right.

The special issue of the *Journal of Pragmatics* edited by Angouri and Locher (2012a) reappraises the notion of disagreement in relation to conflict and (im)politeness and includes contributions on workplace discourse.

Related Topics

(Im)politeness theory; Social constructionism; Communities of practice; Legal settings; Blue-collar workplaces; Service encounters; Call centre discourse; Miscommunication; Argumentation

Transcription Conventions

. . .	noticeable pause or break of less than 1 second within a turn
-	sound abruptly cut off, e.g. false start
italics	emphatic stress
→	speaker's turn continues without interruption
/?/	inaudible utterances
⌊	overlapping or simultaneous speech
,	slightly rising intonation at end of tone unit
?	high rising intonation at end of tone unit
.	falling intonation at end of tone unit
↑	A step up in pitch (higher key)
=	latching: no perceptible inter-turn pause
:	elongated vowel

Notes

1 For an in-depth discussion of impoliteness see Bousfield 2008a; Bousfield and Locher 2008; Dynel 2015.
2 Nevertheless, "conflict" and "disagreement" do overlap and the terms are often used interchangeably in the literature (see Dynel 2015).
3 Example 22.3: parentheses (1 second) show pauses of 1 second or longer. Data originally from CANBEC (the Cambridge and Nottingham Spoken Business English Corpus). Used with permission of Cambridge University Press.

References

Angouri, Jo. 2012. "Managing Disagreement in Problem Solving Meeting Talk." *Journal of Pragmatics* 44: 1566–1579.
Angouri, Jo and Miriam A. Locher, Eds. 2012a. "Theorising Disagreement." Special issue, *Journal of Pragmatics* 44.
Angouri, Jo, and Miriam A. Locher. 2012b. "Theorising Disagreement." *Journal of Pragmatics* 44: 1549–1554.
Archer, Dawn, and Piotr Jagodziński. 2015. "Call Centre Interaction: A Case of Sanctioned Face Attack?" *Journal of Pragmatics* 76: 46–66.
Bousfield, Derek. 2008a. *Impoliteness in Interaction*. Amsterdam: John Benjamins.

Bousfield, Derek. 2008b. "Impoliteness in the Struggle for Power." In *Impoliteness in Language: Studies on its Interplay with Power in Theory and Practice*, edited by Derek Bousfield, and Miriam A. Locher, 127–153. Berlin: Mouton de Gruyter.

Bousfield, Derek, and Miriam A. Locher, Eds. 2008. *Impoliteness in Language: Studies on its Interplay with Power in Theory and Practice*. Berlin: Mouton de Gruyter.

Brown, Penelope, and Stephen C. Levinson. 1987. *Politeness: Some Universals in Language Usage*. Cambridge: Cambridge University Press.

Carter, Ronald. 2004. *Language and Creativity: The Art of Common Talk*. London: Routledge.

Choi, Seongsook, and Stephanie Schnurr. 2014. "Exploring Distributed Leadership: Solving Disagreements and Negotiating Consensus in a 'Leaderless' Team". *Discourse Studies* 16: 3–24.

Conley, John M., and William M. O'Barr. 1990. "Rules Versus Relationships in Small Claims Disputes." In *Conflict Talk*, edited by Allen D. Grimshaw, 178–196. Cambridge: Cambridge University Press.

Corsaro, William A., and Thomas Rizzo. 1990. "Disputes in the Peer Culture of American and Italian Nursery-School Children". In *Conflict Talk*, edited by Allen D. Grimshaw, 21–66. Cambridge: Cambridge University Press.

Coulter, Jeff. 1990. "Elementary Properties of Argument Sequences." In *Interaction Competence*, edited by George Psathas, 181–203.

Coulthard, Malcolm, and Alison Johnson. 2010. *Routledge Handbook of Forensic Linguistics*. London: Routledge.

Culpeper, Jonathan. 2008. "Reflections on Impoliteness, Relational Work and Power." In *Impoliteness in Language: Studies on its Interplay with Power in Theory and Practice*, edited by Derek Bousfield, and Miriam A. Locher, 17–44. Berlin: Mouton de Gruyter.

De Dreu, Carsten K.W., Dirk van Dierendonck, and Maria T. M. Dijkstra. 2004. "Conflict at Work and Individual Well-Being." *International Journal of Conflict Management* 15: 6–26.

Dynel, Marta. 2015. "The Landscape of Impoliteness Research." *Journal of Politeness Research* 11: 329–354.

Eder, Donna. 1990. "Serious and Playful Disputes: Variation in Conflict Talk among Female Adolescents." In *Conflict Talk*, edited by Allen D. Grimshaw, 67–84. Cambridge: Cambridge University Press.

Fauzi, Wan J., Noraina Ibrahim, and Marlyna Maros. 2014. "Perception of Impoliteness in Counter Service Discourse." *Procedia—Social and Behavioral Sciences* 118: 118–125.

Firth, Alan, Ed. 1995. *The Discourse of Negotiation: Studies of Language in the Workplace*. Oxford: Pergamon.

Goodwin, Marjorie Harness. 1990. *He-said-she-said: Talk as Social Organisation among Black Children*. Bloomington, IN: Indiana University Press.

Greatbatch, David. 1992. "On the Management of Disagreement between News Interviewees." In *Talk at Work: Interaction in Institutional Settings*, edited by Paul Drew, and John Heritage, 268–301. Cambridge: Cambridge University Press.

Grimshaw, Allen D., Ed. 1990. *Conflict Talk*. Cambridge: Cambridge University Press.

Gruber, Helmut. 1996. *Streitgespräche: Zur Pragmatik einer Diskursform*. Opladen: Westdeutscher Verlag.

Handford, Michael, and Almut Koester. 2010. "'It's not Rocket Science': Metaphors and Idioms in Conflictual Business Meetings." *Text & Talk* 30: 27–51.

Heritage, John. 1997. "Conversation Analysis and Institutional Talk". In *Qualitative Research: Theory, Method and Practice*, edited by David Silverman, 161–182. London: Sage.

Holmes, Janet, and Maria Stubbe. 2003. *Power and Politeness in the Workplace*. London: Longman.

Holt, Elisabeth, and Alison Johnson. 2010. "Socio-Pragmatic Aspects of Legal Talk: Police Interviews and Trial Discourse." In *Routledge Handbook of Forensic Linguistics*, edited by Malcolm Coulthard, and Alison Johnson, 21–36. London: Routledge.

Koester, Almut. 2006. *Investigating Workplace Discourse*. London: Routledge.

Koester, Almut. 2014. "'We'd Be Prepared to Do Something, Like if You Say . . .' Hypothetical Reported Speech in Business Negotiations." *English for Specific Purposes* 36: 35–46.

Kotthoff, Helga. 1993. "Disagreement and Concession in Disputes: On the Context Sensitivity of Preference Structures." *Language in Society* 22: 193–216.

Labov, William. 1972a. *Language in the Inner City: Studies in the Black English Vernacular*. Philadelphia, PA: University of Pennsylvania Press.

Labov, William. 1972b. "Rules for Ritual Insults." In *Studies in Social Interaction*, edited by David Sudnow, 120–169. New York: Free Press.

Limberg, Holger. 2008. "Threats in Conflict Talk: Impoliteness and Manipulation." In *Impoliteness in Language: Studies on its Interplay with Power in Theory and Practice*, edited by Derek Bousfield, and Miriam A. Locher, 155–179. Berlin: Mouton de Gruyter.

Levinson, Stephen. 1983. *Pragmatics*. Cambridge: Cambridge University Press.

Locher, Miriam A. 2004. *Power and Politeness in Action: Disagreements in Oral Communication*. Berlin: Mouton de Gruyter.

Locher, Miriam, and Richard Watts. 2008. "Relational Work and Impoliteness: Negotiating Norms of Linguistic Behavior." In *Impoliteness in Language: Studies on its Interplay with Power in Theory and Practice*, edited by Derek Bousfield, and Miriam A. Locher, 77–99. Berlin: Mouton de Gruyter.

Marra, Meredith. 2012. "Disagreeing without Being Disagreeable: Negotiating Workplace Communities as an Outsider." *Journal of Pragmatics* 44: 1580–1590.

Moon, Rosamund. 1998. *Fixed Expressions and Idioms in English: A Corpus-Based Approach*. Oxford: Clarendon Press.

Mullany, Louise. 2008. "'Stop Hassling Me!' Impoliteness, Power and Gender Identity in the Professional Workplace". In *Impoliteness in Language: Studies on its Interplay with Power in Theory and Practice*, edited by Derek Bousfield, and Miriam A. Locher, 232–251. Berlin: Mouton de Gruyter.

Muntigl, Peter, and William Turnbull. 1998. "Conversational Structure and Facework in Arguing." *Journal of Pragmatics* 29: 225–256.

O'Donnell, Katherine. 1990. "Difference and Dominance: How Labor and Management Talk Conflict." In *Conflict Talk*, edited by Allen D. Grimshaw, 210–240. Cambridge: Cambridge University Press.

Philips, Susan U. 1990. "The Judge as Third Party in American Trial-Court Conflict Talk." In *Conflict Talk*, edited by Allen D. Grimshaw, 197–209. Cambridge: Cambridge University Press.

Pomerantz, Anita. 1984. "Agreeing and Disagreeing with Assessments: Some Features of Preferred/Dispreferred Turn Shapes." In *Structures of Social Action*, edited by John M. Atkinson, and John Heritage, 57–102. Cambridge: Cambridge University Press.

Sacks, Harvey, Emanuel A. Schegloff, and Gail Jefferson. 1974. "A Simplest Systematics for the Organisation of Turn-Taking for Conversation." *Language* 50: 696–735.

Schank, Gerd, and Johannes Schwitalla, Eds. 1987. *Konflikte in Gesprächen*. Tübingen: Gunter Narr Verlag.

Schiffrin, Deborah. 1984. "Jewish Argument as Sociability." *Language in Society* 13: 311–335.

Schnurr, Stephanie. 2013. *Exploring Professional Communication. Language in Action*. London: Routledge.

Schnurr, Stephanie, Meredith Marra, and Janet Holmes. 2008. "Impoliteness as a Means of Contesting Power Relations in the Workplace." In *Impoliteness in Language: Studies on its Interplay with Power in Theory and Practice*, edited by Derek Bousfield, and Miriam A. Locher, 211–229. Berlin: Mouton de Gruyter.

Sifianou, Maria. 2012. "Disagreements, Face and Politeness." *Journal of Pragmatics* 44: 1554–1564.

Svennevig, Jan. 2012. "On Being Heard in Emergency Calls. The Development of Hostility in a Fatal Emergency Call." *Journal of Pragmatics* 44: 1393–1412.

Tannen, Deborah.1984. *Conversational Style*. Norwood, NJ: Ablex.

Terkourafi, Marina. 2008. "Toward a Unified Theory of Politeness, Impoliteness and Rudeness." In *Impoliteness in Language: Studies on its Interplay with Power in Theory and Practice*, edited by Derek Bousfield, and Miriam A. Locher, 45–74. Berlin: Mouton de Gruyter.

Thornborrow, Joanna. 2002. *Power Talk: Language and Interaction in Institutional Discourse*. London: Pearson Education.

Vuchinich, Samuel. 1990. "The Sequential Organization of Closing in Verbal Family Conflict." In *Conflict Talk*, edited by Allen D. Grimshaw, 118–138. Cambridge: Cambridge University Press.

Walker, Elisabeth. 1995. "Making a Bid for Change: Formulations in Union/Management Negotiations." In *The Discourse of Negotiation: Studies of Language in the Workplace*, edited by Alan Firth, 101–140. Oxford: Pergamon.

Watts, Richard. 1991. *Power in Family Discourse*. Berlin: Mouton de Gruyter.

Watts, Richard. 2003. *Politeness*. Cambridge: Cambridge University Press.

Wenger, Etienne. 1998. *Communities of Practice: Learning, Meaning and Identity*. Cambridge: Cambridge University Press.

23
Argumentation in the Workplace
Jérôme Jacquin

Introduction and Definition

Anyone wishing to examine *Argumentation in the Workplace* faces a variety of issues, the first being the very meaning of the word *argumentation* in English. Unlike in other Indo-European languages (e.g., French, German, Italian, Spanish, Dutch), *argumentation* is not a neutral term in English, but often has negative connotations. It is associated with "having an argument", which challenges the possibility of using the word in a scientific context and as a descriptive category. Another crucial difference is that the English word places a special emphasis on the process (i.e., the activity of arguing), rather than balancing, like in the aforementioned languages, argumentation as production and argumentation as product (i.e., the result of such activity).[1] This complexity justifies beginning this chapter with a scientific definition of what argumentation is or can be. "Argumentation is a verbal and social activity of reason aimed at increasing (or decreasing) the acceptability of a controversial standpoint for the listener or reader, by putting forward a constellation of propositions intended to justify (or refute) the standpoint before a rational judge" (van Eemeren, Grootendorst, and Snoeck Henkemans 1996, 5).

Such a definition requires additional explanation. First, argumentation arises in a situation of disagreement (see also Doury 2012; Plantin 2005), which can be *in praesentia* (i.e., the opposing positions are defended by two different interacting participants) or *in absentia* (i.e., at least one speaker argues against a position that no other participant in the interaction defends). Second, argumentation is not taken to be the verbal activity of persuading people in order to *solve* the disagreement. As has been examined by Angenot (2008) and Plantin (2012), persuasion is a bad candidate for a general definition, even if, in some cases, argumentation is—actually and systematically—oriented to persuading the addressee (e.g., in the legal context). Instead of persuasion, the definition given above highlights the importance of the two complementary goals that Angenot (2008) identifies as being the core features of argumentation: people argue to *justify* a standpoint and to *position* it in the disagreement. Third, as a "verbal activity" that requires the speaker to produce a "constellation of propositions", argumentation can be analysed from a linguistic and descriptive point of view, by examining the way justification and positioning are grounded in language, discourse, and interaction (Jacquin and Micheli 2012).

Argumentation Theory is a relatively young scientific field. However, as argumentation is now considered as one of the verbal underpinnings of reasoning and decision-making in ordinary and institutional settings, it has become a popular topic in human and social sciences. In much the same way as classical Rhetoric, argumentation is viewed as the skeleton of democracy, where citizens are expected not only to *hold* an opinion, but also to *support* it with arguments (Danblon 2004; van Eemeren 2015, chap. 45). The same can be said about private companies and public institutions, where decisions are increasingly expected to be made dialectically (i.e., by taking others' points of view into account).

The aim of this chapter is to provide a general overview of argumentation as being part of the analysis of language in the workplace. This includes surveying studies which examine talk *at work*, i.e., studies that explicitly and reflectively address, from a language-oriented perspective, relevant topics in workplace studies, such as leadership, decision-making, workflows, and professional and employable identities. Such a scope goes beyond what happens in private companies; it also concerns the work done by the representatives of organizations and institutions, both internally and externally, i.e., in the public sphere (e.g., constitutions and laws, parliamentary debates, awareness and election campaigns, presidential addresses, press conferences). In other words, *argumentation at work* is understood here as argumentation provided in a professional context, i.e., where at least one arguer assumes a professional identity (e.g., lawyer, manager, sales assistant, president of the United States) in a professional setting (e.g., court, doctor's office, parliament, press conference).

I begin by providing historical perspectives in Argumentation Theory, followed by an introduction to the main research methods that are relevant for a language-oriented study of argumentation at work as well as examples of current contributions. Main crucial issues and topics related to argumentation at work are then discussed and the chapter concludes with a discussion of future directions of research.

Historical Perspectives

As van Eemeren *et al.* pointed out, "a great many of the theoretical concepts as well as a large part of the terminology used in present-day approaches to argumentation are adopted from or inspired by the classical disciplines of dialectic, logic, and rhetoric" (2014, 52). Aristotle (384–322 BC) has certainly been the most influential thinker in the field. Aristotle's *Logic* introduces the universal, logical patterns that the speaker can use to establish the truth of a statement; his *Dialectic* gathers the techniques for reasoning and decision-making through critical discussion; while his *Rhetoric* is the art of persuading an audience in context. Logic, dialectic, and rhetoric were part of the then-emerging democracy and public organization of citizenship in ancient Greece. During Late Antiquity (Cicero and Quintilian) and Early Middle Ages (St. Augustine and Boethius), logic became progressively part of dialectic. As a consequence, the rhetorical and (logical-)dialectical perspectives were clearly separated and even opposed during the 16th and 17th centuries.

In 1958, two books made crucial contributions to the emergence and consolidation of Argumentation Theory as an independent field and as a method for going beyond formal logic, which emerged in the 19th century, and beyond the classical opposition between dialectic and rhetoric, by tackling argumentation as a practical and situated phenomenon. These books are *The Uses of Argument* by Toulmin (1958) and *La nouvelle rhétorique, traité de l'argumentation* [The New Rhetoric. A Treatise on Argumentation] by Perelman and Olbrechts-Tyteca (1958, translated into English in 1969).

Toulmin's book is well-known for its description of the argumentation layout, which schematizes the practical procedure and its constitutive steps that allow the arguer to draw a conclusion or "claim" (e.g., person P must be helped) from a fact or "data" (e.g., person P is threatened). This procedure highlights the importance of the "warrant", which is the general rule or value that is applied to the case and which often remains implicit (e.g., one must provide assistance to people in danger). In some cases, the warrant can be legally consolidated by a "backing" (e.g., as stated in law L). By using a "modal qualifier" the arguer can also display the degree of certainty of the claim (e.g., "maybe"), while the "rebuttal" is a way to provide for an exception to the procedure (e.g., unless person P is threatening someone else). Toulmin's layout not only systematizes notions such as warrant, claim or rebuttal, but it also provides a general framework for the analysis of natural argumentation and practical reasoning, as it is used in a wide diversity of contexts. Contrasting with formal logic, this is consistent with what Toulmin says about evaluation criteria: while the layout is universal, the norms that are used to evaluate argumentation are contextual and historical and "[they] depend on the nature of the problem at issue" (van Eemeren *et al.* 2014, 211). The context-dependency of such "non-idealized practical logic" (212) calls for empiricism, as a way to tackle the diversity of the—professional and non-professional—spheres, situations, and types of dialogue. Because of the different aspects of argumentation it covers, Toulmin's account has impacted various subfields in Argumentation Theory, and some language-oriented approaches to argumentation have re-examined Toulmin's argumentative layout from a linguistic perspective (see below).

The wish to move beyond formal logic we find in Toulmin's work can also be taken to underlie Perelman and Olbrechts-Tyteca's *New Rhetoric*. Drawing from Aristotle's *Dialectic* and *Rhetoric*, the authors examine argumentation as a way of justifying practical decisions and actions, rather than as a means to support abstract and decontextualized reasoning. Such context-dependency highlights the crucial importance of the audience, to which the arguer must adapt in order to increase the persuasiveness of argumentation or the intensity of adherence. This does not mean that the audience is independent from the argumentative performance: in order to be persuasive, the speaker needs both to strategically construct the audience and to adapt to it accordingly (e.g., categorizing recipients as patriots in a declaration of war, or addressing judges as parents in a trial on child murder). Argumentation is then intrinsically dialectical—even when the audience remains silent and no explicit interaction emerges—as the arguer must anticipate potential objections or agreements from the strategically addressed audience. Perelman and Olbrechts-Tyteca make a distinction between argumentation based on the structure of reality (facts, truths, presumptions), which target a universal audience, and argumentation based on the preferable, which target a particular audience by mobilizing shared values. As in Toulmin's model, context-dependency calls for descriptive empiricism, and classical rhetoric is thus extended—beyond the political and legal spheres—to the analysis of ordinary and professional argumentation, be it embedded in written texts or in oral interaction.[2]

Main Research Methods and Current Contributions

I now introduce four language- and corpus-oriented approaches to argumentation that emerged from classical and post-classical studies and that are currently used in the analysis of argumentative practices at work. Three are grounded in linguistics and take a descriptive stance,[3] while the last is associated with communication studies and is critical and normative. Each approach is exemplified by a selection of monographs, edited books, and doctoral dissertations—mostly in French and English—that illustrate current contributions and research on various professional domains or spheres where argumentation plays a crucial role (see also van Eemeren and Garssen 2012).

The first approach to be mentioned is the discursive model *Argumentation dans le discours* [Argumentation in Discourse] (Amossy 2009; Amossy 2010). This model draws on both French Discourse Analysis and Perelman's New Rhetoric in order to analyse the "argumentative orientation" of discourses (Amossy 2005). Particular attention is paid to genres, stereotypes, identities, and emotions in a large variety of domains, whether literary or non-literary (on media talk and political communication, see Amossy and Burger 2011; Bonhomme and Rossari 2013; on diplomatic correspondence, see Cohen-Wiesenfeld 2007). In this framework, argumentation is defined as a verbal method for influencing people by modifying their beliefs and representations. The model stresses the importance of dialogism (i.e., reported speech, polyphony, and intertextuality) in order to capture the coexistent argumentative voices and the state of controversies that surround the arguer.

The second approach is the *Modèle dialogal de l'argumentation* [Dialogical Model of Argumentation], also known as the Question→AnswerS Model (Plantin 2005; Plantin 2012). It examines argumentation as it is linguistically and sequentially implemented in written or oral talk-in-interaction. Argumentation is not defined in terms of its potential, external effect or orientation (e.g., persuading or influencing someone), but in terms of its internal dynamics (i.e., justification and positioning; Jacquin and Micheli 2012) and as a verbal means, among others, of managing disagreements and conflicts. In this sense, argumentation emerges when a difference of opinion not only arises, but "crystallizes" (Traverso 2005) through the linguistic, discursive, and interactional construction and consolidation of opposing positions with respect to a controversial question (Doury 1997; Jacquin 2014). The model has been applied to various political contexts, such as parliamentary (Micheli 2010), televised (Doury 1997), and public debates (Jacquin 2014). The analysis of the way politicians justify standpoints and position themselves in the disagreement gives insights into the role of argumentation in the vitality of the public sphere, in the emergence and organization of democracy, and in the discussion of political topics, values, and ideologies. Multimodality has recently been integrated into the model, with a focus on the role of gestures and shifts in gaze direction in segmenting argumentative moves (Jacquin forthcoming) and in making reference to the contested position (Jacquin 2015).

The third approach is the Argumentum Model of Topics (Rigotti and Greco Morasso 2009; Rigotti and Greco Morasso 2010). This model combines classical Rhetoric and modern approaches to argumentation schemes (e.g., Perelman and Olbrechts-Tyteca 1958; Walton, Reed, and Macagno 2008; see also below) in order to model and elicit the complete picture of the "inferential configuration" that connects the argument with the standpoint. The model also integrates a semantic analysis of keywords and modals in order to gain access to the linguistic underpinnings—or indicators—of argumentative structures (Rigotti and Rocci 2005). The model has been used to analyse argumentation in various domains, with a focus on financial communication about takeover bids (Palmieri 2014) and dispute mediations in companies and institutions (Greco Morasso 2011). Recent studies investigate argumentation in news production workflows, examining how decisions regarding editorial choices are expressed and justified in the newsroom (Zampa 2015; Andone and Rocci 2016).

Finally, the Pragma-Dialectical Model of Amsterdam is a well-known and influential approach to argumentation, which it defines as the way in which arguers aim to "resolve [a] difference of opinion by achieving agreement on the acceptability or unacceptability of the standpoint(s) involved through the conduct of a regulated exchange of views" (van Eemeren and Grootendorst 2004, 58). The model ascribes equal importance to the analysis and the evaluation of argumentation. In order to fulfil this goal, "rules for a critical discussion" have been established and applied as an ideal framework to analyse actual communicative practices.[4] Particular attention is paid to what the model calls "reconstruction", which is an analytical step where empirical argumentation is simplified and summarized by the analyst as a method for drawing a general picture of the speech event. The model has recently incorporated some linguistic observations (on "argumentative indicators", see van Eemeren, Houtlosser, and Snoeck Henkemans 2007) as well as a rhetorical component (on "strategic manoeuvring", see van Eemeren 2010), but the normative and communication-oriented stance of the approach remains central and the Pragma-Dialectical Model should be distinguished—from this perspective—from empirical, descriptive language-oriented approaches. In the domain of political argumentation, much has been done on strategic manoeuvring in various genres of political deliberation (Lewiński and Mohammed 2015), such as parliamentary debates (Tonnard 2011; Mohammed 2009) and political interviews (Andone 2013). The model has also been applied to law and available studies in legal argumentation focus on the way guilt is discursively established, punishment justified, testimony contested, decisions made, and convictions handed down in various legal cultures (Feteris 2005; Feteris 1999; Dahlman and Feteris 2013). In the health sector (Rubinelli and Snoeck Henkemans 2012), recent studies have focused on argumentation in health brochures (van Poppel 2013) and medical consultations (Pilgram 2015; Labrie 2013).

Critical Issues and Topics

From the overview provided in the previous section, it is now possible to summarize five critical issues and topics that are of particular interest for a language-oriented analysis of argumentation at work. While the first topic, "from disagreeing to decision-making", tackles the whole process in which argumentation plays a crucial role, the others are adapted from Arisotle's Rhetoric, which, as mentioned above, has been crucially influential for current methods and contributions about argumentation in professional contexts. "Genre" provides the general outline for the participants to tackle the disagreement in an argumentative way. The other three are connected to Aristotle's rhetorical proofs: "argumentation schemes and structures (logos)", "authority and credibility (ethos)", and "emotions (pathos)".

From Disagreeing to Decision-Making

Since disagreement is the starting point of argumentation, it is of particular interest to examine how it is expressed, polarized, and managed in context. The first task is to identify the relevant roles of the argumentative situation: "the proponent engages in a discourse of proposition; the opponent, in a counterdiscourse, or discourse of opposition; the third party takes responsibility for the topic of the argument" (Plantin 2002, 363). Such roles can be taken by one, two, three or more speakers, varying from inner dialogue to complex, multi-party argumentative situations (Doury 2012; Plantin 1996). The analyst may wish to examine the presence or absence of politeness, mitigation, and mediation strategies in the expression and management of disagreement and to evaluate to what extent it relates to the professional status of the participants (i.e., employer, employee, colleague). Examples of other relevant questions are: Does the disagreement emerge during a specific phase of the speech event (e.g., introduction of a new topic, brainstorming, decision-making)? Does the disagreement concern only the writers/speakers or do the participants refer, through reported speech or polyphonic markers, to other points of view or voices that are expressed by absent persons or non-represented institutions (e.g., Fløttum, Dahl, and Kinn 2006, chap. 6)?

At the other end of the chain, decisions can be viewed as results to be achieved by professional workflows, whether they are in companies, institutions, or the public sphere (e.g., democratic elections or votes). Decision-making is then crucial for the study of argumentation in the workplace. Depending on the genre (see below), argumentation can be oriented to disagreement resolution, be it through persuasion/alignment (the decision is made as soon as people are convinced) or simply justification (the decision has already been made but it has to be justified in order to be better accepted). The analyst should pay particular attention not only to the arguments that are used and to the order in which they are introduced, but also to the linguistic resources that have been selected to express the decision (e.g., Gunnarsson 2006; see Rieke, Sillars, and Peterson 2013 for a communication-oriented perspective).

Genre

Genres, such as parliamentary debates, press conferences, constitutional texts, judicial reviews, advertisements, or management meetings, are crucial since they provide the general framework to tackle the complexity of argumentation structures as they emerge in empirical data, whether they are written texts, oral speeches, or polylogues (on "genre", see Bhatia 1993; File this volume). Analysing a decontextualized argumentative sequence of three sentences is one thing, but drawing the entire argumentative picture of a speech event is another. When the different positions in the disagreement are defended by more than one person, coalitions of people (or "parties") defending the same position can occur, while splitting and disagreeing on subtopics (Jacquin 2014; Lewiński and Aakhus 2014). From a language-oriented perspective, it is thus of particular relevance to consider the sequentiality of both spoken and written argumentation. This allows one to examine the "interpretation" of the argumentative moves from the participants' point of view (i.e., "emic" perspective, following Pike 1954), and not only as a purely *a posteriori* "reconstruction" by the analyst (on the difference between argumentation interpretation and argumentation reconstruction in Pragma-Dialectics, see van Rees 2001). As they provide the canvas for the argumentative structure, genres are also crucial when considering the formal and functional complexity of multimodal argumentation, i.e., argumentation based on a combination of various semiotic resources, such as language, gestures, gaze, images, documents, or movies (e.g., Birdsell and Groarke 1996; Tseronis and Forceville forthcoming; Van Belle *et al.* 2013).

Genre also relates to the degree to which argumentation is oriented towards persuasion (e.g., Amossy 2009; van Eemeren 2010; Walton 1998). For example, in televised or parliamentary debates, although the debaters do not try to persuade each other, the viewer may be targeted, especially when a decision is pending (e.g., during referendums or election campaigns). However, when the decision has already been made, argumentation provides only reasons justifying a standpoint against another, most often without any orientation to persuasion.

Finally, and as already noted by Toulmin (see above), genres are of crucial importance when examining the norms, values, and evaluation criteria that are in use to assess in context the quality or acceptability of argumentation provided. In other words, norms are indexical, since they pertain to specific genres (Goodwin 2005; Plantin 2005). For instance, "The *scientific inquiry* . . . requires that proof proceed only from premises that either are axiomatic or can be established by methods of inference accepted by standards in a particular branch of scientific knowledge" (Walton 1998, 32; original emphasis).

Argumentation Schemes and Structures (Logos)

Argumentation schemes consist of the different "forms of argument (structures of inference)" (Walton, Reed, and Macagno 2008, 1) or reasoning strategies that the arguer can use to draw a conclusion from an argument. For instance, the "argument from positive consequences" is based on "causal reasoning": "A should be brought about" because "if A is brought about, then good consequences will occur" (101). This "practical reasoning" differs from other schemes, such as "argumentation from values" or "argument from rules". It is therefore relevant to identify the schemes that are used and the way they contribute to the disagreement. For instance, two managers can disagree on whether or not to fire employee E by selecting and putting forward different kinds of argumentation schemes. While the first manager claims that firing E would lower the operating costs (argument from positive consequence), the second argues that E should not be fired since that would contradict the company's ethics, which state that people are more important than benefits (argument from values). Argumentation schemes thus provide a window on various modes of reasoning as well as on the hierarchy of values and ideologies that are at stake in a professional context or culture. Argumentation schemes also help the analyst not only to segment the talk into argumentative moves, but also to examine argumentation structures, i.e., how arguments and conclusions are coordinated in such a way as to strengthen the defended position in the disagreement.

Authority and Credibility (Ethos)

Credibility and authority are crucial dimensions of workplace studies. Authority, on one hand, relates to the professional status of the speaker (e.g., employer versus employee; expert versus lay) or the person, group or organization upon whom the arguer bases their argumentation (i.e., in the case of arguments from a "position to know", such as appeal to expert opinion or testimony; Walton, Reed, and Macagno 2008; Zemplén and Kutrovátz 2011). On the other hand, credibility is derived from the rhetorical performance in context (on the distinction between authority and credibility in argumentation, see Charaudeau 2009). Credibility relates to *ethos*, being the image of the self that the arguer displays, through talk-in-interaction, in order to strengthen their argumentation. *Ethos* can be challenged by *ad hominem* arguments, which are attacks on the arguer's credibility (e.g., by highlighting a logical inconsistency between two incompatible arguments put forward by the arguer). Leadership is an example of a relevant in-between category: depending on the situation (e.g., management meeting versus peer collaboration), the authority of the leader can be based on a professional status, but the credibility of the leader always needs to be established in context, through their discursive and interactional ability to justify their opinions, position him/herself in the disagreement and, sometimes, argumentatively mediate emerging conflicts.

Emotions (Pathos)

Beside *ethos*, *pathos* is another rhetorical means by which the arguer can strengthen the argumentation. Classic examples of *pathos* are appeals to shame, fear or pity. In those cases, emotion functions as a support for the ongoing argumentation. Emotions can also become objects of argumentation. This is the case when the relevance of expressing a specific emotion in context—such as feeling pity for victims—is disputed (e.g., Micheli 2010 on French parliamentary debates on the abolition of death penalty; see Plantin 2004 for a general introduction to the topic). Such rationality of emotions is important in the workplace: how are emotions verbally expressed by the participants and how are they articulated with the defended standpoint? What is the role of such rationalized emotions in the structure of the text, the organization of the interaction, or, more generally, the workflow?

Future Directions

Coming to the end of this chapter, it should be noted that even if various language-oriented approaches to argumentation have been applied to different professional settings, no study in Argumentation Theory precisely defines workplace discourses and interactions or grounds its observations in workplace studies. In other words, no matter the setting that is analysed, work-related issues are not addressed as such and it is very unusual to read studies on argumentation that are based on an explicit method or theory for the analysis of workplace language and interaction. In addition, while many workplace studies in Argumentation Theory focus on written or spoken monologues, few exist on argumentative talk-in-interaction. Developing the theoretical, methodological, and analytical dimensions of the study of *Argumentation in the Workplace* therefore still remains a challenge. And there is much to be done on the relationship between argumentation and gender, power, or ideology at work.

Further Reading

van Eemeren *et al* (2014) provides an extensive overview of the historical roots, theoretical backgrounds and current contributions in Argumentation Theory.

Doury and Moirand (2004) brings together different perspectives on what argumentation is and how it can be analysed from a language-oriented point of view.

van Eemeren and Garssen (2012) gathers essays examining argumentation in a wide variety of professional contexts, including politics, law, health and the media.

Related Topics

(Im)politeness theory; Genre theory; Corporate settings; Legal settings; Directives; Narratives; Conflict talk; Leadership

Acknowledgements

The author has been supported in 2014 and 2015 by the Swiss National Science Foundation [P2LAP1_155110]. He is most grateful to Bernadette Vine, Steve Oswald, and two anonymous reviewers for their helpful comments on a previous version of this paper and to Keely Kidner for correcting his English.

Notes

1 For a more in-depth overview of the meaning of the word *argumentation* in different languages, see Plantin (2002, 344–346) and van Eemeren *et al*. (2014, 3–5).
2 The formal-dialectical approach to argumentation introduced by Hamblin (1970) is another post-classical study that has been important for the development of Argumentation Theory. Hamblin's "formal dialectic" is logical since it aims to define and systematize different "dialectical systems", which are regulated speech-exchange patterns with specific rules and properties. Such systems are introduced as a way of tackling the difficult issue of analyzing fallacies. Because it is formal and logical, Hamblin's model has been less crucially influential for the development of the language-oriented approaches to argumentation.

3   As noted by van Eemeren *et al.* (2014), the linguistic approaches to argumentation are grounded in studies by French scholars (see also Doury and Moirand 2004); first of all Anscombre and Ducrot's semantic approach *Argumentation dans la langue* [argumentation in language] (1983) and Grize's semio-cognitive approach *Logique naturelle* [natural logic] (1982). Both approaches have been very influential in the development of the language-oriented models mentioned in the present section. However, they are not outlined here in more depth, since they do not aim to analyse argumentation in context and examine it as a specific verbal practice: while Anscombre and Ducrot's radical perspective on argumentation consists of examining the argumentative orientation that is embedded in all the words of a given language, Grize associates argumentation with the general principle of influence (i.e., the modification of beliefs and representations through communication).
4   These rules have been incorporated in Critical Discourse Analysis by Reisigl and Wodak (2001) and Fairclough and Fairclough (2012).

References

Amossy, Ruth. 2005. "The Argumentative Dimension of Discourse." In *Argumentation in Practice*, edited by Frans H. van Eemeren, and Peter Houtlosser, 87–98. Amsterdam: John Benjamins.

Amossy, Ruth. 2009. "Argumentation in Discourse: A Socio-Discursive Approach to Arguments." *Informal Logic* 29: 252–267.

Amossy, Ruth. 2010. *L'argumentation dans le discours*. 3rd ed. Paris: Armand Colin.

Amossy, Ruth, and Marcel Burger, Eds. 2011. "Polémiques médiatiques et journalistiques. Le discours polémique en question(s)." Special issue, *Semen 31*.

Andone, Corina. 2013. *Argumentation in Political Interviews: Analyzing and Evaluating Responses to Accusations of Inconsistency*. Amsterdam: John Benjamins.

Andone, Corina, and Andrea Rocci, Eds. 2016. "Argumentation in Journalism: Professional Practices and the Public Sphere." Special issue, *Journal of Argumentation in Context* 5 (1).

Angenot, Marc. 2008. *Dialogues de sourds: Traité de rhétorique antilogique*. Paris: Mille et une nuits.

Anscombre, Jean-Claude, and Oswald Ducrot. 1983. *L'argumentation dans la langue*. Bruxelles: Mardaga.

Bhatia, Vijay K. 1993. *Analysing Genre: Language Use in Professional Settings*. London: Longman.

Birdsell, David S., and Leo Groarke. 1996. "Toward a Theory of Visual Argument." *Argumentation and Advocacy* 33: 1–10.

Bonhomme, Marc, and Corinne Rossari. 2013. "L'argumentation dans le discours politique." *Argumentation & Analyse du Discours* 10. https://aad.revues.org/1424.

Charaudeau, Patrick. 2009. "L'argumentation dans une problématique d'influence." *Argumentation et analyse du discours* 1. http://aad.revues.org/193.

Cohen-Wiesenfeld, Sivan. 2007. "Le discours diplomatique—Analyse de la correspondance diplomatique entre la France et l'Allemagne entre 1871 et 1914." PhD diss., Tel Aviv University.

Dahlman, Christian, and Eveline T. Feteris, Eds. 2013. *Legal Argumentation Theory: Cross-Disciplinary Perspectives*. Dordrecht: Springer.

Danblon, Emmanuelle. 2004. *Argumenter en démocratie*. Bruxelles: Labor.

Doury, Marianne. 1997. *Le débat immobile. L'argumentation dans le débat médiatique sur les Parasciences*. Paris: Kimé.

Doury, Marianne. 2012. "Preaching to the Converted. Why Argue When Everyone Agrees?" *Argumentation* 26: 99–114.

Doury, Marianne, and Sophie Moirand, Eds. 2004. *L'argumentation aujourd'hui: Positions théoriques en confrontation*. Paris: Presses Sorbonne Nouvelle.

Fairclough, Isabela, and Norman Fairclough. 2012. *Political Discourse Analysis*. London: Routledge.

Feteris, Eveline T. 1999. *Fundamentals of Legal Argumentation. A Survey of Theories on the Justification of Judicial Decisions*. Dordrecht: Springer.

Feteris, Eveline T., Ed. 2005. "Schemes and Structures of Legal Argumentation." Special issue, *Argumentation* 19 (4).

Fløttum, Kjersti, Trine Dahl, and Torodd Kinn. 2006. *Academic Voices: Across Languages and Disciplines*. Amsterdam: John Benjamins.

Goodwin, Jean. 2005. "Designing Premises." In *Argumentation in Practice*, edited by Frans H. van Eemeren and Peter Houtlosser, 99–114. Amsterdam: John Benjamins.

Greco Morasso, Sara. 2011. *Argumentation in Dispute Mediation: A Reasonable Way to Handle Conflict.* Amsterdam: John Benjamins.
Grize, Jean-Blaise. 1982. *De la logique naturelle à l'argumentation.* Genève: Droz.
Gunnarsson, Magnus. 2006. "Group Decision-Making—Language and Interaction." PhD diss., Göteborg: Göteborg University.
Hamblin, Charles L. 1970. *Fallacies.* London: Methuen.
Jacquin, Jérôme. 2014. *Débattre. L'argumentation et l'identité au coeur d'une pratique verbale.* Bruxelles: De Boeck.
Jacquin, Jérôme. 2015. "Multimodal Counter-Argumentation in the Workplace: The Contribution of Gesture and Gaze to the Expression of Disagreement." In *GESPIN 4 Proceedings*, 155–160.
Jacquin, Jérôme. Forthcoming. "Embodied Argumentation in Public Debates. The Role of Gestures in the Segmentation of Argumentative Moves." In *Multimodal Argumentation and Rhetoric in Media Genres*, edited by Assimakis Tseronis, and Charles Forceville. Amsterdam: John Benjamins.
Jacquin, Jérôme, and Raphaël Micheli. 2012. "Entre texte et interaction: Propositions méthodologiques pour une approche discursive de l'argumentation en Sciences du Langage." In *Actes Du CMLF 2012— 3ème Congrès Mondial de Linguistique Française*, edited by Franck Neveu, Valelia Muni Toke, Peter Blumenthal, Thomas Klingler, Pierluigi Ligas, Sophie Prévost, and Sandra Teston-Bonnard, 599–611. Lyon: EDP Sciences.
Labrie, Nanon. 2013. "For the Sake of Argument: Considering the Role, Characteristics, and Effects of Argumentation in General Practice Consultation." PhD diss., Università della Svizzera italiana, Lugano.
Lewiński, Marcin, and Mark Aakhus. 2014. "Argumentative Polylogues in a Dialectical Framework: A Methodological Inquiry." *Argumentation* 28: 161–185.
Lewiński, Marcin, and Dima Mohammed, Eds. 2015. *Argumentation in Political Deliberation.* Amsterdam: John Benjamins.
Micheli, Raphaël. 2010. *L'émotion argumentée. L'abolition de la peine de mort dans le débat Parlementaire Français.* Paris: Le Cerf.
Mohammed, Dima. 2009. "The Honourable Gentleman Should Make up His Mind. Strategic Manoeuvring with Accusations of Inconsistency in Prime Minister's Question Time." PhD diss., University of Amsterdam.
Palmieri, Rudi. 2014. *Corporate Argumentation in Takeover Bids.* Amsterdam: John Benjamins.
Perelman, Chaïm, and Lucie Olbrechts-Tyteca. 1958. *La nouvelle rhétorique. Traité de l'argumentation.* 2 vols. Paris: PUF.
Pike, Kenneth L. 1954. *Language in Relation to a Unified Theory of the Structure of Human Behavior.* Part 1. Glendale: Summer Institute of Linguistics.
Pilgram, Roosmaryn. 2015. "A Doctor's Argument by Authority: An Analytical and Empirical Study of Strategic Manoeuvring in Medical Consultation." PhD diss., University of Amsterdam.
Plantin, Christian. 1996. "Le trilogue argumentatif. Présentation de modèle, analyse de cas." *Langue Française* 112: 9–30.
Plantin, Christian. 2002. "Argumentation Studies and Discourse Analysis: The French Situation and Global Perspectives." *Discourse Studies* 4: 343–368.
Plantin, Christian. 2004. "On the Inseparability of Emotion and Reason in Argumentation." In *Emotions in Dialogic Interactions*, edited by Edda Weigand, 265–275. Paris: Presses Sorbonne Nouvelle.
Plantin, Christian. 2005. *L'argumentation: Histoire, théories et perspectives.* Paris: PUF.
Plantin, Christian. 2012. "Persuasion or Alignment?" *Argumentation* 26: 83–97.
Reisigl, Martin, and Ruth Wodak. 2001. *Discourse and Discrimination: Rhetorics of Racism and Antisemitism.* London: Routledge.
Rieke, Richard D., Malcolm O. Sillars, and Tarla Rai Peterson. 2013. *Argumentation and Critical Decision Making.* 8th ed. Boston, MA: Pearson Education.
Rigotti, Eddo, and Sara Greco Morasso. 2009. "Argumentation as an Object of Interest and as a Social and Cultural Resource." In *Argumentation and Education*, edited by Nathalie Muller Mirza, and Anne-Nelly Perret-Clermont, 9–66. Dordrecht: Springer.
Rigotti, Eddo, and Sara Greco Morasso. 2010. "Comparing the Argumentum Model of Topics to Other Contemporary Approaches to Argument Schemes: The Procedural and Material Components." *Argumentation* 24: 489–512.
Rigotti, Eddo, and Andrea Rocci. 2005. "From Argument Analysis to Cultural Keywords (and Back Again)." In *Argumentation in Practice*, edited by Frans H. van Eemeren, and Peter Houtlosser, 125–142. Amsterdam: John Benjamins.

Rubinelli, Sara, and Francisca Snoeck Henkemans, Eds. 2012. *Argumentation and Health*. Amsterdam: John Benjamins.

Tonnard, Yvon M. 2011. "Getting an Issue on the Table. A Pragma-Dialectical Study of Presentational Choices in Confrontational Strategic Maneuvering in Dutch Parliamentary Debate." PhD diss., University of Amsterdam.

Toulmin, Stephen E. 1958. *The Uses of Argument*. Cambridge: Cambridge University Press.

Traverso, Véronique. 2005. "Cristallisation des désaccords et mise en place de négociations dans l'interaction: Des variations situationnelles." In *La négociation au travail*, edited by Michèle Grosjean, and Lorenza Mondada, 43–69. Lyon: PUL.

Tseronis, Assimakis, and Charles Forceville, Eds. Forthcoming. *Multimodal Argumentation and Rhetoric in Media Genres*. Amsterdam: John Benjamins.

Van Belle, Hilde, Paul Gillaerts, Baldwin Van Gorp, Dorien Van De Mieroop, and Kris Rutten, Eds. 2013. *Verbal and Visual Rhetoric in a Media World*. Amsterdam: Leiden University Press.

van Eemeren, Frans H. 2010. *Strategic Maneuvering in Argumentative Discourse: Extending the Pragma-Dialectical Theory of Argumentation*. Amsterdam: John Benjamins.

van Eemeren, Frans H. 2015. *Reasonableness and Effectiveness in Argumentative Discourse*. Dordrecht: Springer.

van Eemeren, Frans H., and Bart Garssen, Eds. 2012. *Exploring Argumentative Contexts*. Amsterdam: John Benjamins.

van Eemeren, Frans H., Bart Garssen, Erik C. W. Krabbe, Francisca Snoeck Henkemans, Bart Verheij, and Jean H.M. Wagemans. 2014. *Handbook of Argumentation Theory*. Dordrecht: Springer.

van Eemeren, Frans H., and Robert Grootendorst. 2004. *A Systematic Theory of Argumentation: The Pragma-Dialectical Approach*. Cambridge: Cambridge University Press.

van Eemeren, Frans H., Robert Grootendorst, and Francisca Snoeck Henkemans, Eds. 1996. *Fundamentals of Argumentation Theory: A Handbook of Historical Backgrounds and Contemporary Developments*. New York: Routledge.

van Eemeren, Frans H., Peter Houtlosser, and A. Francisca Snoeck Henkemans, Eds. 2007. *Argumentative Indicators in Discourse: A Pragma-Dialectical Study*. Dordrecht: Springer.

van Poppel, Lotte. 2013. "Getting the Vaccine Now Will Protect You in the Future! A Pragma-Dialectical Analysis of Strategic Maneuvering with Pragmatic Argumentation in Health Brochures." PhD diss., University of Amsterdam.

van Rees, M. Agnès. 2001. "Argument Interpretation and Reconstruction." In *Crucial Concepts in Argumentation Theory*, edited by Frans H. van Eemeren, 165–199. Amsterdam: Sic Sat.

Walton, Douglas. 1998. *The New Dialectic: Conversational Contexts of Argument*. Toronto: University of Toronto Press.

Walton, Douglas, Christopher Reed, and Fabrizio Macagno. 2008. *Argumentation Schemes*. Cambridge: Cambridge University Press.

Zampa, Marta. 2015. "News Values as Endoxa of Newsmaking. An Investigation of Argumentative Practices in the Newsroom." PhD diss., Università della Svizzera italiana, Lugano.

Zemplén, Gabor Á., and Gabor Kutrovátz, Eds. 2011. "Rethinking Arguments from Experts." *Argumentation* 25 (3).

24
Interpreting in the Workplace
Chase Wesley Raymond

Introduction

Interpreting is commonly conceptualized as a relatively simple, cut-and-dried procedure: just take what's said in one language and say the same thing in another language. Indeed, this lay understanding of how interpreting works affects both who serves as interpreters, as well as how interpreting is realized in a variety of workplace settings across the globe. Nonetheless, given the complexity of language use in *non*-interpreted contexts, it should come as no surprise that brokering interactions between two or more individuals whose linguistic, social, and cultural views and experiences differ, generates a site of language use that is particularly complex and multifarious.

This chapter provides an overview of some of the major themes in workplace interpreting. While interpreters serve a wide range of distinct workplace settings, each with its own considerations and nuances, here the focus is primarily on medical and legal settings. Moreover, while various issues related to interpreting have been pursued by researchers (see the Further Reading section below), the scope of this chapter is dedicated to the actual *doing* of interpreting—that is, the ground-level use of language by interpreters in context.

To begin, the myth of verbatim translation is discussed in order to set up the interpreter as an active participant in interaction. With this essential foundation in place, I will then turn to a discussion of some critical issues and topics, focusing specifically on who interpreters are, and how their identities and roles can affect the linguistic and discursive practices involved in interpreting. Once interpreters are understood to have their own identities and to be contributors to the ongoing interaction, this naturally invites the question as to what specific contributions they can (or should/should not) bring into the talk, which has been the primary focus of recent research in the field. I will then reference and describe some of the research methods that have proven effective in the examination of workplace interpreting, before suggesting possible avenues for future research.

Historical Perspectives

Early studies of interpreting posited a simple transfer or "conduit" model of translation from one language to the other (see Reddy 1979). According to such a theory, the interpreter's role is solely that of a conduit which allows information to pass, *unchanged*, from one interactant to the other. Moreover, any deviation between the source language and the recipient language is viewed as a threat to the neutral, non-participant identity that the interpreter is meant to embody—in other words: "Translate, don't interpret" (Morris 1995). As researchers began to investigate the real-time use of language in interpreting contexts, however, it became apparent that a conduit-like model was unable to account for the micro-level details involved in interpreters' practices (e.g., Wadensjö 1998). On the contrary, interpreters' use of language can profoundly impact interactions, and thus those who interpret talk must be viewed as active co-participants (as opposed to invisible non-participants).

Despite the inadequacy of the conduit theory to explain interpreters' moment-by-moment use of language in authentic interactional contexts, it is nonetheless an important concept for researchers to bear in mind. This is because many institutions (see e.g., Morris 1995) as well as interpreters themselves (see e.g., Dysart-Gale 2005; Hsieh 2009) strive for interpreter invisibility in interaction, viewing a conduit-like role as their ideal and preserving the myth of verbatim/exact translation (see Hale 2007 on "direct" versus "mediated" approaches to interpreting). The frequent mismatch between interpreters' self-perceptions/goals and the reality of interpreter-mediated talk, often the result of the pedagogical techniques used in training programs, therefore cannot be ignored when studying interpreting in the workplace.

Critical Issues and Topics

Who Are Interpreters?

In studying interpreting, it is of crucial importance to distinguish between the different "sorts" of individuals who serve as interpreters in different environments, as this has a profound impact on how the interpreting is actually realized. Although the laws vary from country to country, numerous settings require interpreters that are specially trained in the lexicon and institutional procedures particular to the context—legal and medical settings being typical examples (see Angelelli *et al.* 2004 and Hertog *et al.* 2004 for discussion of concrete cases in the US and the EU). Courtrooms, for instance, have strict protocols with regard to when and how talk is produced (see Innes this volume), and the same scrutiny is often applied to individuals brought in to interpret for plaintiffs, defendants, and witnesses who are put on the stand to testify. In the following example, taken from Berk-Seligson (1990), a district attorney uses a negative interrogative in questioning a witness, which the interpreter proposes reformulating in the affirmative.

Heritage (2002) argues that negative interrogatives, although seemingly seeking information, exist at the limit of "questioning" due to their being produced and treated as assertions.

Example 24.1 (adapted from Berk-Seligson 1990, 257)

01	DA:	And isn't it true that this was for, this money was for the purchase of airline tickets and expenses for you?
02	I:	Um, I'm going to change that to the...uh, to the affirmative. Is that, sir, is that all right, sir, instead of "isn't"?
03	DA:	I want the question exactly as I stated it.

In Example 24.1, the district attorney pressures the interpreter to preserve the assertiveness of the question's design by maintaining the negative formulation of the utterance in the translation, which has been designed in this way to fit the trajectory of questioning being undertaken in this cross-examination (see also Berk-Seligson 2009). We are thus able to observe that it is not only surface-level informational content that is expected to be preserved in certain interpreting contexts, but also the more pragmatic and context-based dimensions of language use such as assertiveness, style, register, and so on.

Medical interpreters are frequently subject to similar training requirements that equip them with knowledge of the medical procedures and terminology to which they will be exposed. Interpreting of medical terminology can include not only specifically biomedical lexical items like "methylmalonic acid" (Raymond 2014b, 432), which might otherwise be unfamiliar to general interpreters without specific medical training, but also the reformulation of lengthy patient narratives into concise, medically relevant categories. For instance, an extended sequence describing chest pain caused by physical work, exercise, walking, and so on might be synthesized for the doctor with the single, diagnosis-relevant turn that the symptoms are "exertion-related" (Bolden 2000, 400–401). For these context-particular reasons, some countries require legal and medical interpreters to possess additional training and certification beyond that of a "general" interpreter.

The training requirements for interpreters in other workplace contexts often differ from the comparatively strict requirements placed on legal and medical interpreters. Companies like Language Line, for instance, are available remotely via telephone and provide "general" interpreters that can be used in a variety of interactions.[1] When the need for an interpreter arises, Language Line is contacted, at which point the operator connects the caller with an interpreter who is certified in the requested language, and interpreting begins. What this means in practice, then, is that the same English–Mandarin interpreter, for example, may telephonically interpret for a business meeting between executives in Beijing and Washington, and then be contacted to interpret for an emergency-service (911) call in the US between a monolingual English-speaking dispatcher and a monolingual Mandarin-speaking caller in need of assistance (see Raymond 2014a). General interpreters of this sort are thus less specialized with regard to a particular workplace context, but are often more readily accessible and monetarily feasible than context-specific interpreters, and thus they must be flexible and adaptable to the contingencies of a diverse array of settings.

What has been described thus far might best be described as the institutional ideal with regard to who engages in interpreting in various contexts. However, who is actually called in to interpret when the (often sudden) need arises does not always conform to this ideal. Orellana, Dorner, and Pulido (2003, 507) cite Harris and Sherwood (1978, 155) as the first researchers to analyse "translating done in everyday circumstances by people who have no special training in it", their focus being on children who act as interpreters for their monolingual family members (see section below). Indeed, it is not only formally trained interpreters who perform the role of interpreter in the workplace; a host of other individuals—ranging from fully bilingual friends, family members, and workplace staff, to *less-than*-fully-bilingual friends, family members, and staff—are frequently recruited to interpret for others in various workplace settings. This may be due to practical contingencies (e.g., time or money; Raymond 2014a), or it may be an active decision based on institutional or other objectives (e.g., Berk-Seligson 2009; see also Martínez-Gómez 2015). Moreover, there are often competing preferences and pressures from each side of the interactional divide in terms of who is "best qualified" to render interpreting services. In the case of medicine, patients have been reported to prefer that family members or friends interpret for them, while hospital officials often prefer on-staff, medically trained interpreters or even bilingual nurses (see e.g., Fadiman 1997; Kuo and Fagan 1999), a discrepancy which Raymond (2014c) suggests may exist because both patients and healthcare providers wish to ensure that their "own" perspective on the medical issue at hand will be prioritized by the interpreter.

The regulations on what sorts of individuals are able to provide interpreting services in various workplace settings are primarily intended to ensure the accuracy of the services rendered, and therefore preserve the rights of all parties involved. As a range of researchers have illustrated, numerous problems can arise when untrained individuals "double" as interpreters. In a study of 21 medical visits in which nurses served as interpreters, Elderkin-Thompson, Cohen Silver and Waitzkin (2001, 1343) report that "approximately half of the encounters had serious miscommunication problems that affected either the physician's understanding of the symptoms or the credibility of the patient's concerns". Flores *et al.* (2003) report similar findings in their study of pediatric visits, namely that ad-hoc interpreters are significantly more likely to produce translation errors that can have clinical consequences—e.g., omitting questions about drug allergies and inaccurately conveying treatment recommendations. Indeed, countless studies of this sort exist in the literature, with ample evidence of the dangers of mistranslation.

It must be noted that interpreting by particular individuals, and in particular ways, may also be less of an "error" and more of a strategic decision. In her study of police interrogations, Berk-Seligson (2009) argues that officers who double as interpreters create "a speech situation that lends itself to coerced confessions", which she contends is the linguistic equivalent of police misconduct. The author demonstrates how officer-interpreters consistently shift between the roles of interpreter and interrogator, thereby biasing the interaction in the police's favour such that the ultimate on-record "translation" fits the police's understanding of the incident in question.

On the whole, then, the identity of the interpreter (including institutional affiliation, alignment/positioning, background, training, and relationship to the parties) is a significant factor affecting how interpreting is done in the workplace.

What do Interpreters do?

Throughout the discussion so far, I have made reference to the interpreter's role as an active participant in mediated interactions. Interpreters are not simply "translating", but rather they are "interpreting" the messages being conveyed. Indeed, through their involvement, interpreters have been shown to enact a variety of roles, including cultural liaison, clarifier, gatekeeper, advocate, social actor, interrogator, and co-diagnostician (e.g., Bancroft and Rubio-Fitzpatrick 2005; Berk-Seligson 2009; Bolden 2000; Davidson 2000; Hsieh 2007, 2009; Ozolins 2015; Vilela Biasi 2003), thereby embodying what Hsieh and Kramer (2012) call "smart technology". Much recent research has therefore been dedicated to the investigation of this work that interpreters do beyond "just translating".

One important topic that has received significant attention is language and culture "brokering". When interpreters engage in brokering, they actively take into consideration the linguistic and cultural knowledge that each party possesses in order to structure the "translation" in ways that will be comprehensible to recipients. In the case of "language brokering", interpreters reshape specific linguistic terms from the source language when equivalent concepts do not exist in the receiving language. This is often inextricably linked to "culture brokering", which can be necessary when the parties significantly diverge in their belief systems and worldviews. Both concepts are seen in Kaufert and Koolage's (1984) study of Cree and Saulteau medical interpreters in Canada: How is a diagnosis of appendicitis linguistically conveyed to a patient whose language does not possess terminology for internal organs? And how can the doctor's recommendation for immediate surgery be conveyed to the patient's family who insists that a weeklong healing ritual is the more appropriate course of action? It is in these environments that brokering is often considered essential.

The relevance of interpreters' linguistic and cultural knowledge is also seen in the ethnographic account offered by Haffner (1992, 258), who provides the following example:

Example 24.2 (from Haffner 1992. Used with permission of Linda Haffner.)

Next I am called to the Emergency Department. When I arrive, the room is full of physicians and nurses. Among them is an x-ray technician busily taking an x-ray film of a man's leg. The patient, a 38-year-old Mexican gardener, had fallen out of a 10-ft high tree. After I introduce myself, the physicians and I ask the patient routine questions. The man keeps repeating, "*Mi canilla, mi canilla.*" Somebody else in the room knew a little Spanish, which explains to me why the technician is taking x-ray films of the man's leg. I tell them that he means his wrist, which turns out to be broken. In most Spanish-speaking countries, *canilla* means shinbone and the use of *canilla* for the wrist is a little unusual—except in certain parts of Mexico where the word means wrist.

Interpreters as language- and culture-brokers find themselves in the middle of such negotiations, "occurring in real-time", and therefore must be able to swiftly mobilize their linguistic and cultural knowledge if the encounter is to be mediated effectively. As Haffner (1992, 259) concisely concludes: "The situation always is bicultural and not merely bilingual", and thus "translation is not enough". Nonetheless, it should be noted that some researchers warn that interpreting practices risk becoming "*over*-culturalized". Such scholars have therefore argued in favour of the development of more standardized methods of (and materials for) dealing with cultural differences (see e.g., Hale 2007; Skaaden 2013).

Recent research has proposed an additional form of brokering that functions at the interactional level. "Epistemic brokering" refers to the discursive steps taken by interpreters to ensure that linguistically discordant doctors and patients are socially aligned at each step in the ongoing interaction by facilitating the establishment of common ground (Raymond 2014b, 2014c). That is, interpreters-as-epistemic-brokers are seen to be taking into account not solely the basic transfer of informational content between the interactants but also the specific discursive formats mobilized to do so, thereby finessing the inherent asymmetries of knowledge in patient–provider encounters, along with interactional contingencies that can arise during an ongoing medical encounter. In Example 24.3,[2] taken from a pediatric genetics consultation between an English-speaking dietician and a Spanish-speaking parent of a child diagnosed with a genetic disorder, Mom asks how best to prepare store-bought macaroni and cheese for her daughter so that it has less protein (one of the child's dietary restrictions). Observe how the dietician's "over-supposing and under-telling" (Heritage 2013) directive response about alternatives in lines 14–21 is reformulated into an epistemically more appropriate informing action by the interpreter in lines 22–24/26.

Example 24.3 (from Raymond 2014b: 434–435)

```
1    MOM:         Y:: entonce- (.) para darle yo los macarrones así,
                  and so for to-give-her I the macaroni like-that
                  A::nd so- (.) for me to give her macaroni like that,
2                 Con menos pro- (.) Qué es lo que no le tengo que poner.=
                  with less    pro- what is it that no to-her I-have that to-put
                  With less    pro- (.) What is it that I shouldn't put in.=
3                 =El queso:? (0.3) o::: °qué.°=
                    the cheese or what
                  =The chee:se? (.3) or::: what.=
4    INT:         =U::h If she wants to giveuh er macaroni an cheese,=
5                 =and doesn't want (.) as much protein,
6                 What does she- m:like leave out. The chees::e?
7                 (0.7)
8    DIET:        tch If you wanna give er macaroni an cheese?
9                 (.)
10   INT:         [(Yes)
11   MOM:         [Yeah
12   DIET:        [Is'at what you mean?=
13   MOM:         =Yes °yeh.°
14   DIET:        .h Then you'd have to u::s:e (.)
15                Either jus give a very small amount or: u- u:m:
16         →      Use the low protein (.)
17         →      macaroni er *the low* protein cheese,
18                (.)
19                And so it doesn't have that much.
20                (0.2)
21                In it.
22   INT:   →     Hacen: macarone: especial con menos queso,<o con queso
                  they-make macaroni special with less cheese or with cheese
                  They ma:ke special macaroni: with less cheese,<or with cheese
23         →      que no tiene tanta proteína,=
                  that no has much protein
                  that doesn't have as much protein,=
24         →      =También hacen otro tipo de mac[arone con queso,
                  also they-make other type of macaroni with cheese
                  =They also make another type of macaroni with cheese,
25   MOM:   →                                    [Ah.
26   INT:   →     que tiene menos proteína.
                  that has less protein
                  that has less protein.
27   MOM:   →     S:í...
                  yes
                  Ye:ah...
```

In this case, there are no linguistic or cultural discrepancies that would prevent the interpreter from directly translating "Use the low protein (.) macaroni er *the low* protein ch<u>ee</u>se" (lines 15–16) as a directive, complete with the definite article "the", in the way that it was produced in English by the dietician. Nonetheless, this response is epistemically ill-fitted to Mom's question, which betrayed no knowledge of a low-protein macaroni and cheese option; after all, Mom suggested leaving some of the cheese out of the original recipe as a method for rendering the dish lower in protein. The dietician's over-supposing and under-telling response may therefore not only fail to provide the medically relevant information to Mom, but may also risk casting Mom's inquiry as inapposite. The interpreter's reformulation of this turn as an overt informing—*Hacen: macaroni especial . . .* ("They make special macaroni . . .") (line 22)—no longer holds Mom accountable for knowledge of this specific product, which, because it is "special", legitimately lies outside of Mom's epistemic domain. Not only does this interactional move better convey medically relevant information to Mom (note the change-of-state token in line 25, suggesting that this was indeed new information for her; Heritage 1984), but it also promotes her active participation in the medical encounter by legitimizing her initial question. Interpreting the epistemic landscape between parties is thus another dimension of the brokering work that interpreters often perform.

Yet another way that interpreters do more than translate is through their enactment of institutional roles, such as co-diagnostician in a medical visit. Bolden (2000), for example, illustrates how experienced medical interpreters go beyond turn-for-turn translation, instead orienting to the medical end-goal of the interaction by actively taking steps to get there as quickly and efficiently as possible, as seen in Example 24.4 between a Russian-speaking patient, an English-speaking doctor, and a bilingual interpreter.

Example 24.4 (from Bolden 2000, 406–7; reproduced with permission from Sage Publishing)

1	D2	N<u>o</u>:w- can she: y'think sh- c'n she wa:lk up some s-stai:rs or things like that[t
2	I	[По лестнице можете подниматься? on stairs you+can climb [*Can you climb some <u>s</u>tairs?*
((several lines omitted))		
16	I	<So on the second s- uh fl<u>oo</u>r: (.)
17		she needs to make three sto:ps.
18		(0.5)
19	D2	(Becau:se there)
20		(0.2)
21	I	Из-за чего вы останавливаетесь? because + of what you stop *Wh<u>y</u> do you stop?*
22		(0.8)
23	P	Ну с<u>е</u>рдце не дает. well heart not allow *Well my h<u>e</u>art doesn't let me.*
24		(1.2)

```
25 → I    Отды:шка              или  боль в  сердце.
          shortness + of + breath or  pain in heart
          Shortness of breath or heart pain.
26 → I    Или о[ба.
          or  both
          Or  bo[th.
27   P         [Боль.
               [Pain.
28             (0.5)
29   P    Бо[ль.
          Pa[in.
30   I    [Боль в  сердце. <Отдышки          нет, да?
          pain in heart   shortness + of + breath no  right
          [Heartpain. No shortness of breath, right?
31        (0.8)
32   I    Pain.
33        (0.5)
34   I    Not- not adispia, just- pain.
```

In this excerpt, the interpreter reports an answer to the doctor's question (lines 16–17). Following this, though, the interpreter authors four questions of his own (lines 21, 25, 26, 30), thereby demonstrating his orientation to the objective of the history-taking phase as moving toward diagnosis. Then, in lines 32 and 34, the specifically diagnosis-relevant information is passed on to the doctor. It is through the interpreter's use of language in the interaction that he is able to accomplish the role of co-diagnostician alongside the doctor.[3]

Current Contributions and Research

The Issue of Accuracy

One topic currently under debate in the research literature on interpreting is the issue of accuracy, or more specifically, *can* the accuracy of interpreting be assessed, and if so, *how*? Just from the handful of examples seen in the previous sections, one can see why this is a debatable issue: for instance, did the interpreter in Example 24.3 "accurately" translate "Use the low-protein macaroni or the low-protein cheese", when she produced it as *Hacen macarone especial con menos queso,* . . . ("They make special macaroni with less cheese . . .")? Did the interpreter in Example 24.4 translate the entire back-and-forth sequence she had with the patient "accurately" when she said to the doctor simply "Pain (0.5) Not- not adispia, just- pain"? While omissions and reformulations did not seem to be undesirable in those cases, we have also seen quantitative findings describing interpreter omissions (and other practices) that were indeed categorized as "errors" (Berk-Seligson 2009; Elderkin-Thompson, Cohen Silver, and Waitzkin 2001; Flores *et al.* 2003). This illustrates concretely that much of the difficulty involved in assessing the accuracy of interpreting arises as a result of ambiguities in what specifically we mean by "accuracy", especially when we bear in mind that if any and all deviations from exact/verbatim translation were conceptualized as inaccuracies, then nearly every turn-at-talk produced by an interpreter would be deemed "inaccurate". Moreover, given the preceding section's description about the positive potential of various brokering practices, should accuracy even be the primary objective or concern?

The situation complicates itself further when one considers interpretation of some of the more finely grained features of participants' linguistic production. For instance, Hale (2002, 25) examines hedges/fillers, discourse markers, and hesitations in court proceedings and concludes that "interpreters tend to accurately interpret only the content of witnesses' answers, but constantly alter the style of testimony, either favourably or detrimentally, thus potentially changing the outcome of the case". This sort of work suggests that accuracy might best be understood as a multi-dimensional phenomenon, different aspects of which may be more or less accurate than others.

Children as Interpreters

As alluded to previously, children are often the ones who are called on to provide interpreting services for family members in a variety of workplace settings, but especially in public-service contexts. In fact, somewhere between 84–90 per cent of immigrant youth are reported to have brokered at least once (Tse 1995; Chao 2006; Trickett and Jones 2007), which may explain the continued interest in child interpreters over the years.

In addition to investigating the particular linguistic practices of child interpreters, researchers have also become interested in the effects that these brokering events can have on children socially, psychologically, intellectually, and so on. Initially, the use of children in these contexts was considered a negative. Haffner (1992, 257) describes a case in which a 7-year-old girl was used as an interpreter during her mother's ultrasound examination, "and was told to tell her mother that the baby (her little brother-to-be) [was] dead" in her mother's womb. It therefore comes as no surprise that child interpreters have been reported to experience psychological symptoms, a sense of burden, and premature adultification, in addition to a disruption of the overall family dynamic (Buriel, Love, and DeMent 2006; Chao 2006; Hall and Sham 2007; Jones and Trickett 2005). Nonetheless, recent research has also focused on the positive effects that interpreting can have on children who perform the task. In addition to finding positive correlations with academic achievement and literacy skills among child language brokers (Buriel *et al.* 1998; Dorner, Orellana, and Li-Grining 2007; McQuillan and Tse 1995), researchers have also reported that these individuals frequently feel a strong sense of self-efficacy (Buriel *et al.* 1998; Wu and Kim 2009) as they are able to facilitate access to a range of goods and services which would otherwise be largely inaccessible to their monolingual family members (Orellana, Dorner, and Pulido 2003).

There are several context- and topic-based differences that account for these mixed adaptive/maladaptive findings regarding the use of children as interpreters. That is, the psychosocial contingencies and pressures are not the same when a child interprets a quick back-and-forth between her mother and an employee at the post office regarding how to mail a letter abroad, versus when she is forced to relay to her father that he has been diagnosed with stage IV lung cancer and likely has only a few months left to live. Future research may consider analytic methods for disaggregating these contingencies and pressures.

Research Methods

A wide range of methods have been used to conduct research on interpreting. Angelelli and Baer (2016) include chapters on: action research, bibliometric studies, case studies, conversation analysis, corpus-based studies, critical discourse analysis, ethnography of communication, experimental research, *histoire croisée*, interviews and focus groups, narrative analysis, observations, and survey-based studies. Indeed, several of these have been used to arrive at the findings reported throughout this chapter. Below I outline three major themes that can be used to conceptualize these and other methods for studying interpreting.

Some methods (e.g., discourse/conversation analysis, ethnography of communication, [participant] observation) make use of naturally occurring interpreter-mediated interactions as their source of data. When these data are video- and/or audio-recorded, the researcher is able to examine how interpreting actually unfolds on a moment-by-moment basis in authentic contexts, thereby opening up the possibility of investigating more micro-level features of the talk that one would not be able to analyse with other sources of data. The above-referenced study by Hale (2002), for instance, reports 220 hedges and fillers in her dataset (125 in the original Spanish, and 95 in the interpreted English), which she uses to investigate the issue of style. It would have been impossible for Hale to interview interpreters and simply ask them to list each of the occasions in which they had produced "Uh's" and "Uhm's" during a given mediated interaction. Rather, the use of recorded, naturalistic data was essential to the issue Hale was interested in.

Other methods (e.g., interviews, focus groups, surveys) are designedly retrospective and used "after" interpreted interactions have taken place, for different sorts of inquiries. Here, the emphasis is less frequently placed on specific features of the talk and more on issues related to participants' thoughts, experiences, and preferences. Kuo and Fagan (1999) used a survey to investigate patients' versus medical professionals' satisfaction with professional versus ad-hoc interpreters, and Rose *et al.* (2010) did the same to analyse physicians' use of different sorts of in-person versus remote (telephonic) interpreters. Interviews have proven particularly useful in examining the perspective of the interpreters themselves. Orellana, Dorner, and Pulido (2003) organized semi-structured group interviews with children, asking them "how they feel in their positions as translators and what they do when they encounter problems", routinely "following up on their responses with questions that probed for details" (510). Thus, retrospective methods are often most fruitful when the researcher's objective is to gain access to participants' inner thoughts and feelings regarding the interpreting process.

Lastly, various experimental methods (e.g., oral or written translation tasks, role plays) can be used to investigate how interpreters would hypothetically or ideally interpret specific sorts of utterances. Researchers must bear in mind, though, that these responses may differ from how those same utterances would be interpreted by those same individuals in naturally occurring talk.

In sum, then, there is no "better" or "worse" method for studying interpreting in the workplace, although there are certainly "better" and "worse" methods for answering particular sorts of questions about interpreting in the workplace. As with any linguistic inquiry, it is best for researchers to first think of the question(s) that they are interested in answering, and use that as the guide for planning the research project: As a certain sort of data will be better equipped than others to provide answers to those questions, an appropriate method for *gathering* such data will also be driven by the research question.

Future Directions

One avenue for future research on interpreting in the workplace concerns the limits of the various roles that were described earlier. As discussed, interpreters wear many hats as they mediate interactions, which invites the question as to whether some of these roles are inappropriate, and if so, which ones, when, and where? An interpreter who acts as an advocate for a patient in a medical visit or a witness in a courtroom, for example, might on the one hand be conceptualized as doing positive or beneficial social work. But can too much advocacy generate inappropriate biases that actually hinder a social institution's ability to serve the public? Similarly, despite the positive work that brokering can accomplish (be it language, culture, or epistemic), can "too much" brokering actually end up negatively affecting the outcome of an interpreter-mediated encounter? And again, if so, how much is "too much"? These questions as to the "limits" of the different identities that interpreters routinely enact are prime areas for future research (see Hale 2007; Ozolins 2015).

In addition, advances in technology have changed the landscape of options available for interpreting. Various remote services (e.g., telephonic systems, text-to-talk translation technology, video-based systems for the deaf) are now available in many workplace settings across the globe. Precisely how this shifted landscape affects interpreting in the workplace—including who serves as interpreters, how the interpreting is realized, what preferences the participants have about those options—is a matter for future research to investigate.

Further Reading

Pöchhacker and Shlesinger (2002) includes excerpts from foundational studies in interpreting research from the 1950s through the early 2000s, while Angelelli and Baer (2016) provides an up-to-date overview of the field, as well as various chapters on how different methods can be used for translation/interpreting research. Mikkelson and Jourdenais (2015) offers chapters on the history of interpreting, different modes of interpreting (e.g., sight, signed), various settings, as well as current issues and debates in the field. In addition, John Benjamins publishes a series of edited volumes under the heading *Benjamins Translation Library* (BTL), which "aims to stimulate research and training in translation and interpreting studies."

There are also several peer-reviewed journals on interpreting and translation, for example: *Interpreting: International Journal of Research and Practice in Interpreting* and *The Translator*. Articles on interpreting can also be found in various other journals that publish research on language in society, and language in social interaction (e.g., *Discourse Studies*, *Journal of Sociolinguistics*, *Language in Society*).

Related Topics

Conversation analysis; Linguistic ethnography; Legal settings; Genetic counselling; Miscommunication; Intercultural communication; Multilingualism

Notes

1 For an overview of remote interpreting, see Braun (2015).
2 See Jefferson (2004) for transcription conventions.
3 Note that the ethics of engaging in such practices is a highly debated issue in the literature (just as is the case for the various other forms of "brokering", discussed above), with some scholars viewing these interactional moves as important and necessary, and others viewing them as unethical. See Ozolins (2015) for an overview.

References

Angelelli, Claudia V., Niels Agger-Gupta, Carola E. Green, and Linda Okahara. 2004. "The California Standards for Healthcare Interpreters: Ethical Principles, Protocols and Guidance on Roles and Intervention." In *The Critical Link 4: Professionalisation of Interpreting in the Community*, edited by Cecilia Wadensjö, Birgitta Englund Dimitrova, and Anna-Lena Nilsson, 167–177. Philadelphia, PA: John Benjamins.

Angelelli, Claudia V., and Brian James Baer, Eds. 2016. *Researching Translation and Interpreting*. New York: Routledge.

Bancroft, Marjory A., and Lourdes Rubio-Fitzpatrick. 2005. *The Community Interpreter: A Comprehensive Training Manual*. Columbia: Culture & Language Press.

Berk-Seligson, Susan. 1990. *The Bilingual Courtroom: Court Interpreters in the Judicial Process*. Chicago, IL: University of Chicago Press.

Berk-Seligson, Susan. 2009. *Coerced Confessions: The Discourse of Bilingual Police Interrogations*. New York: Mouton de Gruyter.

Bolden, Galina B. 2000. "Toward Understanding Practices of Medical Interpreting: Interpreters' Involvement in History Taking." *Discourse Studies* 2: 387–419.

Braun, Sabine. 2015. "Remote Interpreting." In *Routledge Handbook of Interpreting*, edited by Holly Mikkelson, and Renée Jourdenais, 352–367. New York: Routledge.

Buriel, Raymond W., Julia A. Love, and Terri L. DeMent. 2006. "The Relationship of Langauge Brokering to Depression and Parent-Child Bonding among Latino Adolescents." In *Acculturation and Parent-Child Relationships*, edited by Marc H. Bornstein, and Linda R. Cote, 249–270. Mahwah, NJ: Lawrence Erlbaum.

Buriel, Raymond W., William Perez, Terri L. DeMent, David V. Chavez, and Virginia R. Moran. 1998. "The Relationship of Language Brokering to Academic Performance, Biculturalism, and Self-Efficacy among Latino Adolescents." *Hispanic Journal of Behavioral Sciences* 20: 283–297.

Chao, Ruth K. 2006. "The Prevalence and Consequences of Adolescents' Language Brokering for Their Immigrant Parents." In *Acculturation and Parent-Child Relationships*, edited by Marc H. Bornstein, and Linda R. Cote, 271–296. Mahwah, NJ: Lawrence Erlbaum.

Davidson, Brad. 2000. "The Interpreter as Institutional Gatekeeper: The Social-Linguistic Role of Interpreters in Spanish-English Medical Discourse." *Journal of Sociolinguistics* 4: 379–405.

Dorner, Lisa M., Marjorie Faulstich Orellana, and Christine P. Li-Grining. 2007. "'I Helped My Mom' and It Helped Me: Translating the Skills of Language Brokers into Improved Standardized Test Scores." *American Journal of Education* 113: 451–478.

Dysart-Gale, Deborah. 2005. "Communication Models, Professionalization, and the Work of Medical Interpreters." *Health Communication* 17: 91–103.

Elderkin-Thompson, Virginia, Roxanne Cohen Silver, and Howard Waitzkin. 2001. "When Nurses Double as Interpreters: A Study of Spanish-Speaking Patients in a US Primary Care Setting." *Social Science & Medicine* 52: 1343–1358.

Fadiman, Anne. 1997. *The Spirit Catches You and You Fall Down: A Hmong Child, Her American Doctors, and the Collision of Two Cultures*. New York: Farrar, Straus, and Giroux.

Flores, Glenn, M. Barton Laws, Sandra J. Mayo, Barry Zuckerman, Milagros Abreu, Leonardo Medina, and Eric J. Hardt. 2003. "Errors in Medical Interpretation and Their Potential Clinical Consequences in Pediatric Encounters." *Pediatrics* 111: 6–14.

Haffner, Linda. 1992. "Translation Is Not Enough." *Western Journal of Medicine* 157: 255–259.

Hale, Sandra. 2002. "How Faithfully Do Court Interpreters Render the Style of Non-English Speaking Witnesses' Testimonies? A Data-Based Study of Spanish-English Bilingual Proceedings." *Discourse Studies* 4: 25–47.

Hale, Sandra. 2007. *Community Interpreting*. Basingstoke, UK: Palgrave Macmillan.

Hall, Nigel, and Sylvia Sham. 2007. "Language Brokering as Young People's Work: Evidence from Chinese Adolescents in England." *Language and Education* 21: 16–30.

Harris, Brian, and Bianca Sherwood. 1978. "Translating as an Innate Skill." In *Language Interpretation and Communication*, edited by David Gerver, and H. Wallace Sinaiko, 155–170. New York: Plenum.

Heritage, John. 1984. "A Change-of-State Token and Aspects of Its Sequential Placement." In *Structures of Social Action*, edited by J. Maxwell Atkinson, and John Heritage, 299–345. Cambridge: Cambridge University Press.

Heritage, John. 2002. "The Limits of Questioning: Negative Interrogatives and Hostile Question Content." *Journal of Pragmatics* 34: 1427–1446.

Heritage, John. 2013. "Asymmetries of Knowledge in Patient-Provider Encounters: Three Studies Adopting Conversation Analysis." *Patient Education and Counseling* 92, 1–2.

Hertog, Erik, Ann Corsellis, Kirsten Wolch Rasmussen, and Yolanda Vanden Bosch. 2004. "From Aequitas to Aequalitas: Establishing Standards in Legal Interpreting and Translation in the European Union." In *The Critical Link 4: Professionalisation of Interpreting in the Community*, edited by Cecilia Wadensjö, Birgitta Englund Dimitrova, and Anna-Lena Nilsson, 151–165. Philadelphia, PA: John Benjamins.

Hsieh, Elaine. 2007. "Medical Interpreters as Co-Diagnosticians: Overlapping Roles and Services between Providers and Interpreters." *Social Science & Medicine* 64: 924–937.

Hsieh, Elaine. 2009. "Bilingual Health Communication: Medical Interpreters' Construction of a Mediator Role." In *Communicating to Manage Health and Illness*, edited by Dale E. Brashers, and Daena J. Goldsmith, 135–160. New York: Routledge.

Hsieh, Elaine, and Eric Mark Kramer. 2012. "Medical Interpreters as Tools: Dangers and Challenges in the Utilitarian Approach to Interpreters' Roles and Functions." *Patient Education and Counseling* 89: 158–162.

Jefferson, Gail. 2004. "Glossary of Transcript Symbols with an Introduction." In *Conversation Analysis: Studies from the First Generation*, edited by Gene Lerner, 13–23. Amsterdam: John Benjamins.

Jones, Curtis J, and Edison J. Trickett. 2005. "Immigrant Adolescents Behaving as Culture Brokers: A Study of Families from the Former Soviet Union." *The Journal of Social Psychology* 145: 405–427.

Mikkelson, Holly, and Renée Jourdenais, Eds. 2015. *Routledge Handbook of Interpreting*. New York: Routledge.

Kaufert, Joseph M., and William W. Koolage. 1984. "Role Conflict among 'Culture Brokers': The Experience of Native Canadian Medical Interpreters." *Social Science and Medicine* 18: 283–286.

Kuo, David, and Mark J. Fagan. 1999. "Satisfaction with Methods of Spanish Interpretation in an Ambulatory Clinic." *Journal of General Internal Medicine* 14: 547–550.

Martínez-Gómez, Aída. 2015. "Non-Professional Interpreters." In *Routledge Handbook of Interpreting*, edited by Holly Mikkelson, and Renée Jourdenais, 417–431. New York: Routledge.

McQuillan, Jeff, and Lucy Tse. 1995. "Child Language Brokering in Linguistic Minority Communities: Effects on Cultural Interaction, Cognition, and Literacy." *Language and Education* 9: 195–215.

Morris, Ruth. 1995. "The Moral Dilemmas of Court Interpreting." *The Translator* 1: 25–46.

Orellana, Marjorie Faulstich, Lisa Dorner, and Lucila Pulido. 2003. "Immigrant Youth's Work as Family Translators or 'Para-Phrasers'." *Social Problems* 50: 505–524.

Ozolins, Uldis. 2015. "Ethics and the Role of the Interpreter." In *Routledge Handbook of Interpreting*, edited by Holly Mikkelson, and Renée Jourdenais, 319–336. New York: Routledge.

Pöchhacker, Franz, and Miriam Shlesinger, Eds. 2002. *The Interpreting Studies Reader*. New York: Routledge.

Raymond, Chase Wesley. 2014a. "Entitlement to Language: Calling 911 without English." *Language in Society* 43: 33–59.

Raymond, Chase Wesley. 2014b. "Epistemic Brokering in the Interpreter-mediated Medical Visit: Negotiating 'Patient's Side' and 'Doctor's Side' Knowledge." *Research on Language & Social Interaction* 47: 426–446.

Raymond, Chase Wesley. 2014c. "Conveying Information in the Interpreter-Mediated Medical Visit: The Case of Epistemic Brokering." *Patient Education and Counseling* 97: 38–46.

Reddy, Michael J. 1979. "The Conduit Metaphor: A Case of Frame Conflict in Our Language about Language." In *Metaphor and Thought*, edited by Andrew Ortony, 284–310. Cambridge: Cambridge University Press.

Rose, Danielle E., Diana M. Tisnado, Jennifer L. Malin, May L. Tao, Melinda A. Maggard, John Adams, Patricia A. Ganz, and Katherine L. Kahn. 2010. "Use of Interpreters by Physicians Treating Limited English Proficient Women with Breast Cancer: Results from the Provider Survey of the Los Angeles Women's Health Study." *Health Services Research* 45: 172–194.

Skaaden, Hanne. 2013. "Assessing Interpreter Aptitude in a Variety of Languages." In *Assessment Issues in Language Translation and Interpreting*, edited by Dina Tsagari, and Roelof van Deemter, 35–50. Frankfurt: Peter Lang.

Trickett, Edison J., and Curtis J. Jones. 2007. "Adolescent Culture Brokering and Family Functioning: A Study of Families from Vietnam." *Cultural Diversity and Ethnic Minority Psychology* 13: 143–150.

Tse, Lucy. 1995. "Language Brokering among Latino Adolescents: Prevalence, Attitudes, and School Performance." *Hispanic Journal of Behavioral Sciences* 17: 180–193.

Vilela Biasi, Edith. 2003. "Court Interpreters as Social Actors: Venezuela, a Case Study." In *The Critical Link 3: Interpreters in the Community*, edited by Louise Brunette, Georges Bastin, Isabelle Hemlin, and Heather Clarke, 239–245. Philadelphia, PA: John Benjamins.

Wadensjö, Cecilia. 1998. *Interpreting as Interaction*. London: Longman.

Wu, Nina H., and Su Yeong Kim. 2009. "Chinese American Adolescents' Perceptions of the Language Brokering Experience as a Sense of Burden and Sense of Efficacy." *Journal of Youth and Adolescence* 38: 703–718.

Part IV
Identity and the Workplace

25
Gender and the Workplace
Louise Mullany and Melissa Yoong

Introduction

Research investigating the interplay between language and gender in the workplace has been a rapidly expanding field of academic enquiry since the 1990s. The vast majority of this research tends to be feminist in orientation, in that the work has an overall commitment to redressing gender inequalities in workplace settings. These inequalities include: the long-standing problem of a lack of women in senior leadership positions, often referred to as the "glass ceiling" (Morrison, White, and Van Velsor 1987) (i.e., the metaphorical barrier preventing women globally from breaking through into the higher echelons of power); the global gender pay gap (World Economic Forum 2016) with women being paid lower than men on average for fulfilling exactly the same role; and the overwhelming predominance of women in low-paid, low-status jobs. The role that linguistic analysis can play in assessing, evaluating, and attempting to rectify these socio-political problems often forms the basis and motivation for the research that emerges in this area of workplace studies (e.g., West 1990; Cameron 2000; Holmes 2006; Mullany 2007; Baxter 2011).

Historical Perspectives

To trace the development of studies investigating gender and language in the workplace, it makes sense to provide an historical overview of the theoretical advances in the field of language and gender more broadly, as these developments clearly map onto empirical workplace studies. Earlier studies on gender and language treated gender as a fixed, static category, coterminous with sex (e.g., Zimmerman and West 1975; Fishman 1980). Women and men were perceived as separate, homogeneous groups. The aim of these initial studies was to uncover the differences between female and male linguistic behaviour by contrasting women's talk to men's talk. Analyses of gender differences in workplace settings focused on questions such as whether men or women held the floor longer during meetings (e.g., Edelsky 1981; Schick Case 1988; Woods 1988; James and Drakich 1993) and who interrupted more (e.g., Tannen 1994a). As more women gained access to managerial positions, there was a shift from a predominant focus on professional–lay person exchanges (e.g., West 1990; Pizzini 1991; Kendall and Tannen 1997) to a greater focus on the discursive resources used by women leaders (e.g., Horikawa, Mickey, and Miura 1991; Tannen 1994b). Early scholarly work in this area identified features that characterized different gendered leadership language, claiming, for example, that men managers were authoritative and assertive in their speech, while women leaders adopted more facilitative and collaborative speech styles.

During the 1990s, a paradigm shift to social-constructionist perspectives was clearly evident in language and gender studies and this approach is still dominant in current research. Drawing on Butler's (1990, 2004) theoretical model of performativity, social constructionists view gender as dynamic and fluid, and as something enacted and worked out within interaction, as opposed to something that pre-exists in interaction. Numerous studies examining workplace discourse have since drawn upon Butler's model of gender, such as Mulholland's (2006) study of advisor–client interaction, Metcalfe's (2006) examination of multiple gender performances in international business communication, and Holmes's (2000, 2006) analysis of gender in a multitude of different workplaces in New Zealand. There has been an observable wave of research on gender, language, and leadership using social constructionist perspectives. These studies reject the essentialist view that confines a leader by their definition as a "woman" or a "man", challenging the polarization of speech and management styles as "male" or "female" (Holmes 2006; Mullany 2007; Baxter 2008; Baxter and Al A'ali 2014). A great deal of empirical evidence has emerged from this body of research demonstrating that men and women leaders skilfully switch between stereotypically masculine and feminine discourse strategies, depending on their context, objectives, and audience. This is often referred to as adaptable leaders making best use of a "wide-verbal-repertoire" (cf. Marra, Schnurr, and Holmes 2006; Mullany forthcoming). It is clearly time to break down the deeply ingrained myth of men and women speaking in different styles at work (cf. Cameron 2007) and instead look to models with more context-sensitivity and more sophisticated approaches to identity construction (see below).

Researchers favouring social-constructionist approaches point out that the linguistic strategies used by individuals are not a completely free choice, without evaluation or consequence, but instead conform to a "rigid regulatory frame" (Butler 1990, 33), governing the way we evaluate and judge one another, thus constraining the ways in which gender can be accomplished. Structural constraints that impinge on participants and predispose them to certain ways of interacting in the workplace occur at multiple levels, from the norms of the specific workplace community of practice to which they belong, to the workplace culture of their organization, to wider societal expectations regarding how women and men should speak and behave at work (Holmes and Marra 2011).

There are two further theoretical developments that are often integrated at a more macro level into the social constructionist approach to investigating gender and language at work: Ochs's (1992) notion of "indexicality" and research influenced by Foucauldian notions of discourses (Foucault 1972), where broader societal discourses, held in place by powerful gender ideologies, are analysed as a form of social practice.

Ochs's model has been invaluable in bridging local linguistic analyses with global considerations. According to Ochs, very few lexical items directly index gender. More commonly, gender is indirectly indexed through speech styles that have come to be encoded with gendered meaning through regular association with either women or men. These stereotypical gendered expectations of male and female speech patterns, held in place by powerful gender ideologies, dictate our language preferences when interacting and affect how we are assessed. Likewise, there are ways of talking which have become indices of leadership (Mullany 2007; Holmes and Marra 2011). Certain linguistic features that index leadership are associated with particular stances (e.g., authoritative, consultative), which, in turn, are associated with dominant hegemonic masculinity or femininity (Bucholtz and Hall 2005). For example, transactional behaviours that "primarily aim at getting things done, solving problems and achieving set goals" are stereotypically coded as "masculine" whereas more relationally-oriented behaviours are traditionally seen as "feminine" (Schnurr and Mak 2011, 347). In other words, "the same way of speaking signifies both a professional identity and a gendered identity, and in practice these are difficult to separate: the two meanings co-exist, and both of them are always potentially relevant" (Cameron and Kulick 2003, 58).

Ochs's theory of indexicality and its reconceptualization of linguistic behaviour as ideologically prescribed have much in common with Foucauldian models of discourse. The rigid regulatory frame can be applied here to include a series of powerful discourse positions that result in women being evaluated and judged more harshly than their male counterparts (Mullany 2007, see below). Sunderland's (2004) concept of "gendered discourses" is often integrated into empirical studies of this nature. Sunderland (2004, 3) coined the term "gendered discourses" to describe systems which "carry" ideology and regulate appropriate gendered behaviour in society, following Foucault's (1972) discourse theory. The concept of gendered discourses has been applied in gender and workplace research across disciplines including management studies, organizational studies, and sociology (e.g., Fitzsimons 2002; Olsson and Walker 2003). Mullany's (2007) ethnographic investigation into gender and language examined gendered discourses to assess the effects of gender ideologies on how women leaders were evaluated in relation to their construction of their identities. The following section will review two critical issues that have emerged from research applying the theoretical frameworks discussed above.

Critical Issues and Topics

The Double Bind

Traditionally, typical behaviours and discourses associated with "effective" leadership have been indexed for masculinity, while relational practices have been undervalued due to their strong association with a more feminine stance (Fletcher 1999). However, over the years, more stereotypically "feminized" workplace cultures that recognize the value of relational skills in leadership have developed in multinational corporations (Cameron 2000). As a result, stereotypical "feminine" speech styles are being institutionalized as part of a range of professional and managerial discourse strategies that all business leaders are expected to acquire (Holmes 2006; Baxter 2008). For example, Baxter's (2008, 210) linguistic analysis of interviews with male managers showed that they tried to distance themselves from the masculinized stereotype of leadership that is "direct, adversarial, self-promoting and competitive" and consciously constructed a "caring" and "open" identity. Nevertheless, this did not imply a stronger preference for "feminine" discourse styles when doing leadership. Rather, the leaders constructed themselves as "complex, multi-skilled professionals, who could draw upon a range of communicative strategies as required by audience, purpose and context" (2008, 210).

Despite the shift away from a masculinized notion of leadership, leadership researchers Eagly and Carli (2007) argue that women in authority face challenges in their enactment of leadership because women and men are assessed unequally for adopting the same strategies. This is clearly evidenced in the findings from many language and gender studies. While senior men are commended for their appropriation of more feminine communicative strategies and tolerated or admired if they speak in an authoritative manner (Baxter 2008), women in leadership roles are subject to what has become known as the "double bind": they are judged to be less competent if they display linguistic characteristics that are deemed too feminine, yet perceived as overly authoritative if they adopt a more stereotypically masculine style of speech (Holmes 2006; Litosseliti 2006a; Mullany 2007). Furthermore, by conforming to long-established expectations of leadership, women "violate conventions concerning appropriate female behaviour" (Grabe and Shibley Hyde 2006, 194). In other words, women cannot win.

Women leaders often devise a range of strategies "with which to observe, regulate, police, review and repair the way they appear and sound to their colleagues" to avoid being stereotyped or negatively evaluated, including making use of "rigorous preparation, warmth of manner, humour, an acceptance of being teased, mitigated commands, and forms of politeness such as apology" (Baxter 2008, 217) or "by drawing on discourse strategies associated with acceptable feminine leadership roles, such as the 'mother', which licence women to behave in authoritative ways" (Holmes and Marra 2011, 318). Litosseliti's (2006b, 49) analyses of argumentative interactions demonstrated that women conducted "additional conversational work" in order to prevent being typecast as "irrational females". Baxter (2008, 217) argues that the adoption of these self-regulatory strategies may "dilute the force or impact of words spoken" and undermine the women's authority as leaders. Hence, the role of language in maintaining the glass ceiling can be clearly seen.

Intersectionality

Earlier language and gender research has been critiqued for foregrounding gender as the most salient social identity category, with other influential facets being overlooked (see Mills and Mullany 2011). More recent empirical studies have integrated gender with other variables that may be relevant in specific research (Wodak 2015), such as class, religion, culture, race, and ethnicity. Within this approach, termed intersectionality, identity is conceptualized not only as dynamic and fluid (Butler 1990) but also as multidimensional, where different components of social identities are instantiated in interaction and conveyed indirectly via an array of stances indexed by linguistic and discursive features in accordance with the interactional context and goals (Holmes and Marra 2011).

The complex integration of social categories can lead to the identification of hybridized social identities in empirical research (Holmes and Marra 2011). While Lemke (2008, 33) claims that "hybridity represents a compromise by the individual among the pressures and forces of multiple cultures and institutions which are seeking to control our identities", Holmes and Marra (2011) believe that hybridity can be an innovative and constructive force in culturally diverse and gendered institutional contexts. They illustrate how a female Māori Managing Director linguistically negotiates the dimensions of gender, leadership, and ethnicity to forge a complex, hybridised identity while satisfactorily performing her diverse identities as a Māori woman, a Māori leader, and a female. This intersectionality allows her to achieve goals in a society where the discourse norms stereotypically associated with masculinity and the majority ethnic group, Pākehā (people of European origin), are both dominant. Their study demonstrates that, while gender is significant in shaping the performance of leadership, a Māori woman enacts leadership differently from a Pākehā woman, due to differing sociocultural expectations. Such findings clearly show the value of the intersectional approach and the diversity within groups of women in the workplace. This will be further demonstrated in the next section.

Current Contributions and Research

Early research on language and gender tended to focus on the Western world, with most studies taking place in the UK, North America, and New Zealand. One of the most crucial issues in the field at present is the need for empirical evidence in a much broader range of geographical settings and cultural contexts, to ensure that gender inequalities in workplaces in under-researched countries and contexts are far better represented. Here, we provide an overview of the diverse range of research on language and gender in the workplace that has started to emerge from Asia, Africa, and the Middle East in recent years.

There is a small yet increasing body of language and gender research in Asian professional settings, including Japan (Yoshida 2001; Ohara 2004; Inoue 2007; Saito 2013), Hong Kong (Schnurr 2010; Schnurr and Chan 2011; Schnurr and Mak 2011), Mainland China (Zhang 2007), Malaysia (Mullany and Yoong 2016; Yoong 2017), and India (Iyer 2009). Some of this research reflects global trends relating to gender politics and neoliberalism. For example, drawing on ethnographic research in a Tokyo corporate office in the early 1990s, Inoue (2007) found that, rather than problematizing institutionalized sexist practices within the company, women employees' communication skills were instead targeted for change, illustrating how neoliberalism can de-radicalize the linguistic construction of identity in the workplace.

Studies in Asia have also investigated how culturally-governed ideological expectations about masculinity inform the linguistic practices of men. In Japan, men's linguistic practices have been considered unmarked in the public sphere, whereas women's discursive practices are viewed as deviant, leading to a gap in the examination of the former in the scholarship of Japanese language and gender (Saito 2013). Saito's analysis of interactions between male superiors and their male subordinates in a Japanese workplace demonstrates that the male superiors utilized less male-associated language in interactions where male-associated stylistic features are otherwise used. On the other hand, they used a linguistic form strongly associated with normative men's language in exchanges that otherwise involve feminine-associated stylistic features. This endorses the findings of previous studies conducted in the Western world: men's language is not monolithic and male leaders skilfully utilize linguistic and stylistic features indexed for both masculinity and femininity. However, Saito's discussion of the use of the ideologically masculine linguistic form illustrates the importance of situating the findings within the socio-cultural context in which the interlocutors negotiated their professional and gender identities—in Japanese society, a man needs to prove his masculinity to other men (Nakamura 2010), and therefore, it is likely that the male superiors in the study used stereotypically male language in their interactions to index a dominant hegemonic masculine identity. Additionally, since normative men's language occurs only in male groups (Nakamura 2010), it is also possible that the male superiors in this study were attempting to establish homosociality with their male subordinates.

In addition to analysing spoken discourse, Schnurr and Mak (2011, 363) examine the discourse patterns of internal emails to explore how a woman leader in Hong Kong enacts power and gender identity online. They found that the participant presented different linguistic behaviours in the three interactional contexts examined: she adopted a stereotypically masculine leadership style in her email; her behaviour in one-to-one conversations indexed for femininity and her speech style in meetings contained a combination of both masculine and feminine elements, though it was closer to the masculine end of the discourse continuum. Schnurr and Mak thus make the case that, in addition to the sociocultural context, the specific interactional context in which leadership is enacted must also be considered to produce a nuanced analysis of discourse-based sociocultural practices.

In addition to corporate business contexts, language and gender research in Asia has also investigated how professional identities are constructed in other domains, including politics. Mullany and Yoong (2016) examine texts from Malaysian online media data sources, exploring a Malay-Muslim politician's self-construction of her identities alongside the media's representations of her. The findings show how gender and professional identity categories intersect with age, race, religion, and sexuality to create powerful subject positions for both the female politician and her male competitor. These work to position her as a less able and less suitable candidate in a parliamentary by-election campaign. The salience of her religion and ethnicity, in particular, as crucial components intersecting with her gendered identity construction is central to the Malaysian political context. Once again, the importance of the localized socio-cultural context in producing a thorough examination of the subtleties and nuances of gendered discourses in particular settings is emphasized.

In Africa, there has also been research on women's political participation, though few studies have examined gender issues in political life from a linguistic perspective. Here, we will compare the findings of two studies from the same country, Cameroon, to illustrate how opposing discourses work to construct traditional and resistant identities for women politicians within the same sociopolitical context, in particular one where women are perceived as "just good at domestic chores and called to be silent in public" (Jiogo Ngaufack 2013). Atanga (2012) examined the discursive construction of what she terms a "model Cameroonian woman" in the Cameroonian parliament and found that the gendered discourses articulated by the male members of parliament were mainly traditional and subject positioned women parliamentarians as mothers, carers, and wives, reflecting the conservative stance within the wider society. Nevertheless, several women subverted these identity constructions by producing emancipatory discourses—"an indication of the changing roles of Cameroonian women, away from tradition and towards a greater degree of autonomy in a globalising world" (2012, 40). Jiogo Ngaufack's (2013) analysis of Cameroonian mass media also pointed to a movement towards the empowerment of women as political leaders in the country. In written media texts, women in politics were represented positively as effective leaders and as the hope for Africa's political change; this contrasted with their male counterparts who were portrayed as uncaring and dictatorial.

There is a limited yet growing literature on gender, language, and leadership in the Middle East (e.g., Sadiqi 2003; Metcalfe 2007; Baxter and Al A'ali 2014). In Baxter and Al A'ali's (2014) analyses of how a Middle Eastern (ME) woman and a Western European (WE) woman index leadership in management meetings in largely male-dominated companies, they found that both women performed the "unmarked" interactional style of feminized relational practices to navigate their leadership roles with colleagues. However, despite the Western perspective that ME women face more barriers than WE women due to cultural and religious pressures, the ME leader made greater use of an authoritative and confident interactional style stereotypically associated with masculinity, while the WE leader was more evasive and uncertain. This was mainly because the ME leader had established long-term relationships with her colleagues, whereas the WE leader was in a less secure position due to major restructuring within her company, demonstrating that gender is not always the only salient aspect in the enactment of leadership. It clearly illustrates the importance of examining the construction of gender and leadership identities within a specific workplace community of practice as well as the need for more empirical research in this region to refute ingrained cultural stereotypes.

Research Methods

Research on gender and language in the workplace has drawn upon a variety of research methods, including quantitative, qualitative, and mixed-methodological approaches. Overall, qualitative research has tended to be the most dominant over the last two decades. Arguably this is related to the observable theoretical shift within gender and language studies more broadly towards smaller-scale research examining workplaces through the lens of communities of practice (see King this volume). This shift to the communities of practice approach followed Eckert and McConnell-Ginet's (1992) seminal paper to "look locally", to avoid the re-production of overgeneralizations about the behaviour of all women and men in workplaces, as if they were two homogeneous groups of automata, with no variation among them.

A proportion of qualitative-based workplace research has been ethnographic (e.g., Mullany 2007; Baxter 2011; Chalupnik 2015), with researchers entering workplace sites over a period of time to produce detailed descriptions of gender and language using the widest variety of data sources available. For example, Mullany (2007) used audio-recordings of business meetings, semi-structured interviews, field-notes, and analyses of written documents (e.g., meeting agendas, minutes, mission statements) to develop a detailed account of gendered language practices in UK-based commercial organizations.

Despite the advantages of the production of "thick descriptions" that can be gained by workplace ethnographies (Sarangi and Roberts 1999), they are notoriously lengthy to conduct and access is difficult to negotiate. Other researchers have demonstrated the value of alternative methods, and another successful approach has been where the researcher is not present during data recording. For example, the Language in the Workplace team in New Zealand (Holmes 2000, 2006; Holmes and Marra 2011; Holmes and Schnurr 2006) favour giving recording equipment to participants themselves, thus placing them in charge of the recording process. As well as minimizing some of the effects of the observer's paradox that are undeniably exacerbated by the researcher's presence, this method enables larger datasets to be recorded. Arguably this method can make the data collection process a more empowering experience for those being researched and it increases the chances of the findings being of applied practical value to those being studied, with analysts accessing interactions that those being researched think are the most significant for them. Although there is an undeniable risk of valuable ethnographic data being lost, practically speaking, research subjects are more likely to agree to this method as it does not involve having a researcher present in what are often sensitive contexts that make participants uneasy, despite the number of reassurances given by research teams and ethics protocols (see Chalupnik 2015).

Arguably a key reason for the plethora of research drawing upon qualitative methods is due to data access issues. Gaining access to workplaces is notoriously difficult, particularly when researchers are looking to investigate the politically-sensitive role that gender plays in affecting day-to-day workplace communication and the language practices of a business or organization in general (see Mullany 2008 for detailed consideration of methodological challenges).

Quantitative research can be very useful in particular for identifying overall patterning in data samples, and the establishment of broad patterns can then be followed up by more detailed qualitative research (Mullany forthcoming). Koller's (2004) analysis of written business media discourse took a mixed-methodological approach. She focused on gendered metaphors, by neatly combining quantitative techniques from corpus linguistics to survey the overall sample, followed by micro-level, qualitative analyses of texts where stretches of discourse had been highlighted as being particularly salient by the corpus analysis.

In terms of the different types of linguistic data that have been examined in gender and the workplace research, spoken language has dominated, with a key emphasis on recordings of interactions taking place, particularly in the context of business meetings. That said, studies of written discourse have been conducted, examining genres including letters of recommendation for promotion (Trix and Psenka 2003) and business magazines (Koller 2004; Iyer 2009). More recently, with the increasing use of digital communication in everyday workplace discourse, a handful of studies of emails and other forms of electronic communication have emerged, already highlighted above with Schnurr and Mak's (2011) work.

Recommendations for Practice

One key recommendation for practice is the importance of explicitly raising awareness of stereotypes of gendered interactional norms in workplaces globally, particularly focusing upon how gendered linguistic stereotypes can play an (often unconscious) role in maintaining and reifying gender imbalances in terms of how workplace members are judged and evaluated. With the dominance of gender differences discourses clearly hampering the success of women in the workplace (cf. Cameron 2007), it is time to break down the deeply ingrained global myth of men and women speaking in different styles at work.

Other recommendations for practice that we believe should be considered to help eradicate gender bias from written workplace language include interventions such as producing best practice guides for referees writing letters of reference for job and promotion applications, to ensure that an (un)conscious gender bias is not entering into the selection process. For example, the University of Nottingham (our own workplace), has recently designed one of these guides for best practice for reviewers of academic promotion applications across all the University's campuses (in the UK, Malaysia, and China). This draws in particular upon the original linguistic findings of Trix and Psenka (2003) and aims to address the gender imbalances at senior levels of the University's management and academic structures, via its equality and diversity network. This is just one small example, but in our view, the more that academic linguistic findings can get into the public domain and inform workplace practitioners and policymakers working to eradicate gender inequality, the better in terms of understanding, addressing and then hopefully changing future behaviours. In October 2015, the Civil Service in the UK announced that it was going to name-blind all CVs to prevent gender bias from unconsciously creeping into the shortlisting process for job recruitment. The UK's University and Colleges Admissions System (UCAS) will also follow suit from 2017.

Other interventions include linguistically-informed training to help those in the professions to be able to identify gendered discourse norms in their own organizations and raise awareness of the deeply entrenched gendered discourse styles that may be holding people back in their careers. Learning key concepts from the research field, such as the double bind, and encouraging people to reflect upon their own evaluations and value judgements of others based upon gendered language norms can help those being researched and wider populations recognize and understand gendered workplace norms, and ultimately change their behaviours. The emergence of dedicated initiatives such as the "Linguistic Profiling for Professionals" research consultancy (based at the University of Nottingham in the UK and in Ningbo, China), have been designed to facilitate knowledge exchange with those being researched and with wider populations, encouraging engagement in consciousness raising of gendered linguistic norms and how these can seriously affect career progression. Such consciousness-raising activity by itself cannot break down deeply entrenched gendered systems, but it can empower people to reflect upon their own communicative prejudices and norms and critically assess these, alongside unpicking the attitudes, evaluations and judgements that go along with these hegemonic norms.

Future Directions

One of the most important future directions for the field, in our opinion, is to continue with the expansion of research across different cultural contexts, ensuring that probing political questions of gender inequality are asked across the widest range of workplace research sites globally. As a key part of this, and to make the field more representative, there is a need to examine languages other than English, alongside ensuring that intersectionality is fully taken into account. Researchers need to consider race, ethnicity, sexuality, religion, and the fullest range of relevant intersectional subject positions, alongside gender, to produce a nuanced analysis reflecting the complexities of language and gender in the world of work.

Further Reading

Holmes (2006) draws on authentic recorded workplace interactions collected by the Wellington Language in the Workplace Project over seven years and examines how women and men construct their gender and professional identities by employing "feminine" and "masculine" discursive strategies.

Mullany (2007) is an interactional sociolinguistic study focusing on the interplay between language and gender in everyday workplace interactions, using ethnographic methods. It focuses on whether evaluations and judgements of women based on gendered language norms are key factors in preventing women from breaking through the glass ceiling.

Zhang (2007) explores the interplay between language, gender, and the workplace in China as it transitions from a state-controlled economy to a globalised market economy.

Related Topics

Linguistic ethnography; Social constructionism; Communities of practice; Corporate settings; Directives; Leadership; Men's talk in women's work; Enabling women leaders

References

Atanga, Lilian. 2012. "The Discursive Construction of a 'Model Cameroonian Woman' Within the Cameroonian Parliament." *Gender and Language* 6: 21–45.
Baxter, Judith. 2008. "Is It All Tough Talking at the Top? A Post-Structuralist Analysis of the Construction of Gendered Speaker Identities of British Business Leaders within Interview Narratives." *Gender and Language* 2: 197–222.
Baxter, Judith. 2011. *The Language of Female Leadership*. Basingstoke, UK: Palgrave.
Baxter, Judith, and Haleema Al A'ali. 2014. "'Your Situation is Critical . . .': The Discursive Enactment of Leadership by Business Women in Middle Eastern and Western European Contexts." *Gender and Language* 8: 91–116.
Bucholtz, Mary, and Kira Hall. 2005. "Identity and Interaction: A Sociocultural Linguistic Approach." *Discourse Studies* 7: 585–614.
Butler, Judith. 1990. *Gender Trouble: Feminism and the Subversion of Identity*. New York: Routledge.
Butler, Judith. 2004. *Undoing Gender*. New York: Routledge.
Cameron, Deborah. 2000. *Good to Talk?: Living and Working in a Communication Culture*. London: Sage.
Cameron, Deborah. 2007. *The Myth of Mars and Venus: Do Men and Women Really Speak Different Languages?* Oxford: Oxford University Press.

Cameron, Deborah, and Don Kulick. 2003. *Language and Sexuality*. Cambridge: Cambridge University Press.
Chalupnik, Malgorzata. 2015. "Beyond Politeness: Shifting Focus to the Management of Relations and Tasks in the Analysis of Workplace Discourse." PhD diss., University of Nottingham.
Eagly, Alice H., and Linda L. Carli. 2007. *Through the Labyrinth: The Truth About How Women Become Leaders*. Boston, MA: Harvard Business School Press.
Eckert, Penelope, and Sally McConnell-Ginet. 1992. "Think Practically and Look Locally: Language and Gender as Community-Based Practice." *Annual Review of Anthropology* 21: 461–490.
Edelsky, Carole. 1981. "Who's Got the Floor?" *Language in Society* 10: 383–421.
Fishman, Pamela. 1980. "Interactional Shitwork." *Heresies* 2: 99–101.
Fitzsimons, Annette. 2002. *Gender as a Verb: Gender Segregation at Work*. Aldershot, UK: Ashgate.
Fletcher, Joyce K. 1999. *Disappearing Acts: Gender, Power and Relational Practice*. Cambridge, MA: MIT Press.
Foucault, Michel. 1972. *The Archaeology of Knowledge*. London: Routledge.
Grabe, Shelly, and Janet Shibley Hyde. 2006. "Impact of Gender on Leadership." In *Gender, Race and Ethnicity in the Workplace: Issues and Challenges for Today's Organizations*. Vol. 2: *Legal, Psychological, and Power Issues Affecting Women and Minorities in Business*, edited by Margaret Foegen Karsten, 183–198. London: Prager.
Holmes, Janet. 2000. "Women at Work: Analysing Women's Talk in New Zealand Workplaces." *Australian Review of Applied Linguistics* 22: 1–17.
Holmes, Janet. 2006. *Gendered Talk at Work*. Oxford: Blackwell.
Holmes, Janet, and Meredith Marra. 2011. "Leadership Discourse in a Māori Workplace: Negotiating Gender, Ethnicity and Leadership at Work." *Gender and Language* 5: 317–342.
Holmes, Janet, and Stephanie Schnurr. 2006. "Doing Femininity at Work: More Than Just Relational Practice." *Journal of Sociolinguistics* 10: 31–51.
Horikawa, Randy Y., Jeffrey Mickey, and Steven Miura. 1991. "Effects of Request Legitimacy on the Compliance-Gaining Tactics of Male and Female Managers." *Communication Monographs* 58: 421–436.
Inoue, Miyako. 2007. "Language and Gender in an Age of Neoliberalism." *Gender and Language* 1: 79–91.
Iyer, Radha. 2009. "Entrepreneurial Identities and the Problematic of Subjectivity in Media-Mediated Discourses." *Discourse & Society* 20: 241–263.
James, Deborah, and Janice Drakich. 1993. "Understanding Gender Differences in Amount of Talk." In *Gender and Conversational Interaction*, edited by Deborah Tannen, 281–312. Oxford: Oxford University Press.
Jiogo Ngaufack, Caroline S. 2013. "A Representation of Political Agents in Cameroon's Newspapers." In *Perspectives of Gender and Language in Cameroonian Contexts*, edited by Lilian Lem Atanga, 141–165. Bamenda: Langaa RPCIG.
Kendall, Shari, and Deborah Tannen. 1997. "Gender and Language in the Workplace." In *Gender and Discourse*, edited by Ruth Wodak, 81–105. London: Sage.
Koller, Veronika. 2004. *Metaphor and Gender in Business Media Discourse: A Critical Cognitive Study*. Basingstoke, UK: Palgrave.
Lemke, Jay L. 2008. "Identity, Development and Desire: Critical Questions." In *Identity Trouble: Critical Discourse and Contested Identities*, edited by Carmen Rosa Caldas-Coulthard, and Rick Iedema, 17–43. New York: Palgrave.
Litosseliti, Lia. 2006a. *Gender and Language: Theory and Practice*. London: Hodder & Arnold.
Litosseliti, Lia. 2006b. "Constructing Gender in Public Arguments: The Female Voice as Emotional Voice." In *Speaking Out: The Female Voice in Public Contexts*, edited by Judith Baxter, 40–58. Basingstoke, UK: Palgrave.
Marra, Meredith, Stephanie Schnurr, and Janet Holmes. 2006. "Effective Leadership in New Zealand Workplaces: Balancing Gender and Role." In *Speaking Out: The Female Voice in Public Contexts*, edited by Judith Baxter, 240–260. Basingstoke, UK: Palgrave.
Metcalfe, Beverly D. 2006. "Gender, Communication and International Business." In *Gender and Communication at Work*, edited by Mary Barrett, and Marilyn J. Davidson, 95–110. Aldershot, UK: Ashgate.
Metcalfe, Beverly D. 2007. "Gender and Human Resource Management in the Middle East." *International Journal of Human Resource Management* 18: 54–74.

Mills, Sara, and Louise Mullany. 2011. *Language, Gender and Feminism: Theory, Methodology and Practice*. Oxon, UK: Routledge.
Morrison, Ann M., Randall P. White, and Ellen Van Velsor 1987. *Breaking the Glass Ceiling: Can Women Reach the Top of America's Largest Corporations?* Reading, MA: Addison-Wesley.
Mulholland, Joan. 2006. "Gender and Advisor-Client Communication." In *Gender and Communication at Work*, edited by Mary Barrett, and Marilyn J. Davidson, 84–94. Aldershot, UK: Ashgate.
Mullany, Louise. 2007. *Gendered Discourse in the Professional Workplace*. Basingstoke, UK: Palgrave.
Mullany, Louise. 2008. "Negotiating Methodologies: Making Language and Gender Relevant in the Professional Workplace." In *Gender and Language Research Methodologies*, edited by Kate Harrington, Lia Litosseliti, Helen Sauntson, and Jane Sunderland, 43–55. Basingstoke, UK: Palgrave.
Mullany, Louise. forthcoming, 2017. *The Sociolinguistics of Gender in Public Life*. Basingstoke, UK: Palgrave.
Mullany, Louise, and Melissa Yoong. 2016. "Language, Gender and Identities in Political Life: A Case Study from Malaysia." In *Routledge Handbook of Language and Identity*, edited by Sian Preece, 428–442. Oxon, UK: Routledge.
Nakamura, Momoko. 2010. "Women's and Men's Languages as Heterosexual Resource: Power and Intimacy in Japanese Spam E-mail." In *Femininity, Feminism and Gendered Discourse*, edited by Janet Holmes, and Meredith Marra, 125–144. Cambridge: Cambridge Scholars.
Ochs, Elinor. 1992. "Indexing Gender." In *Rethinking Context: Language as an Interactive Phenomenon*, edited by Alessandro Duranti, and Charles Goodwin, 335–358. Cambridge: Cambridge University Press.
Ohara, Yumiko. 2004. "Prosody and Gender in Workplace Interaction: Exploring Constraints and Resources in the Use of Japanese." In *Japanese Language, Gender, and Ideology: Cultural Models and Real People*, edited by Shigeko Okamoto, and Janet Smith, 222–239. Oxford: Oxford University Press.
Olsson, Su, and Robyn Walker. 2003. "Through a Gendered Lens? Male and Female Executives' Representations of One Another." *Leadership and Organization Development* 24: 387–396.
Pizzini, Franca. 1991. "Communication Hierarchies in Humor: Gender Differences in the Obstetrical Gynaecological Setting." *Discourse & Society* 2: 477–488.
Sadiqi, Fatima. 2003. *Women, Gender and Language in Morocco*. Leiden: Brill.
Saito, Junko. 2013. "Gender and Facework: Linguistic Practices by Japanese Male Superiors in the Workplace." *Gender and Language* 7: 231–260.
Sarangi, Srikant, and Celia Roberts, Eds. 1999. *Talk, Work and Institutional Order: Discourse in Medical, Mediation and Management Settings*. Berlin: Mouton de Gruyter.
Schick Case, Susan. 1988. "Cultural Differences, Not Deficiencies: An Analysis of Managerial Women's Language." In *Women's Careers: Pathways and Pitfalls*, edited by Suzanna Rose, and Laurie Larwood, 41–63. New York: Praeger.
Schnurr, Stephanie. 2010. "'Decision Made—Let's Move On': Negotiating Gender and Professional Identity in Hong Kong Workplaces." In *Language in its Socio-cultural Context: New Explorations in Global, Medial and Gendered Uses*, edited by Markus Bieswanger, Heiko Motschenbacher, and Susanne Muehleisen, 111–135. Frankfurt am Main: Peter Lang.
Schnurr, Stephanie, and Angela Chan. 2011. "Exploring Another Side of Co-leadership: Negotiating Professional Identities Through Face-work in Disagreements." *Language in Society* 40: 187–209.
Schnurr, Stephanie and Bernie Mak. 2011. "Leadership in Hong Kong: Is Gender Really Not an Issue?" *Gender and Language* 5: 343–371.
Sunderland, Jane. 2004. *Gendered Discourses*. Basingstoke, UK: Palgrave.
Tannen, Deborah. 1994a. *Gender and Discourse*. Oxford: Oxford University Press.
Tannen, Deborah. 1994b. *Talking from 9 to 5: Women and Men at Work*. New York: William Morrow.
Trix, Frances, and Carolyn Psenka. 2003. "Exploring the Color of Glass: Letters of Recommendation for Female and Male Medical Faculty." *Discourse & Society* 14: 191–220.
West, Candace. 1990. "Not Just Doctor's Orders: Directive-Response Sequences in Patients' Visits to Women and Men Physicians." *Discourse and Society* 1: 85–112.
Wodak, Ruth. 2015. "Gender and Language: Cultural Concerns." In *International Encyclopedia of the Social & Behavioral Sciences*. 2nd ed., Vol. 9, edited by James D. Wright, 698–703. Oxford: Elsevier.
Woods, Nicola. 1988. "Talking Shop: Sex and Status as Determinants of Floor Apportionment in a Work Setting." In *Women in their Speech Communities*, edited by Jennifer Coates, and Deborah Cameron, 141–157. London: Longman.

World Economic Forum (2016) The Global Gender Gap Report 2016. Switzerland: World Economic Forum. www3.weforum.org/docs/GGGR16/WEF_Global_Gender_Gap_Report_2016.pdf.

Yoong, Melissa. 2017. "Men and Women on Air: Gender Stereotypes in Humour Sequences in a Malaysian Radio Phone-in Programme." *Gender and Language* 11: 30–50.

Yoshida, Mitsuhiro. 2001. "Joking, Gender, Power and Professionalism Among Japanese Inn Workers." *Ethnology* 40: 361–369.

Zhang, Qing. 2007. "Cosmopolitanism and Linguistic Capital in China: Language, Gender and the Transition to a Globalized Market Economy in Beijing." In *Words, Worlds, and Material Girls: Language, Gender and Globalization*, edited by Bonnie McElhinny, 404–422. Berlin: Mouton de Gruyter.

Zimmerman, Don H., and Candace West. 1975. "Sex Roles, Interruptions and Silences in Conversation." In *Language and Sex: Difference and Dominance*, edited by Barrie Thorne, and Nancy Henley, 105–129. Rowley, MA: Newbury House.

26
Leadership
Stephanie Schnurr

Introduction: What Is Leadership?

This chapter provides a brief overview of a particularly interesting aspect of language in the workplace, namely leadership. The topic of leadership has long been of interest to researchers from different disciplines, including, for example, organizational sciences, political sciences, management studies, psychology, and, more recently, linguistics. In this chapter, however, I will mainly focus on this last aspect and write about leadership from a linguistics perspective.

But what exactly is leadership? This, of course, is a rather complex question, and as Bass (1981, 7), a prominent leadership researcher, has famously noted, there are "almost as many different definitions of leadership as there are people who have attempted to define the concept". This multitude of definitions is perhaps not surprising given the attention this topic has received from scholars across different disciplines. Earlier scholarship conceptualized leadership as innate traits (as reflected in the assumption that certain people were born as leaders) or learnable or trainable behaviours. More recent research—across different disciplines— understands leadership as a process or a performance, that is, as something that people *do* (e.g., Tourish and Jackson 2008b). Based on this perception of leadership as an activity, and considering the general agreement between scholars and practitioners that leadership is closely related to influencing others, in this chapter leadership is defined as a process through which people are influenced to work towards a common goal in ways that typically combine transactional and relational behaviours. Transactional behaviours aim at getting things done and achieving outcomes, while relational behaviours aim at enhancing interpersonal relationships and creating a positive working atmosphere (Dwyer 1993; Robbins *et al.* 1998). Both behaviours are equally important aspects of leadership, and as I will illustrate below in more detail, they are often closely intertwined with each other and occur simultaneously (Ferch and Mitchell 2001).

In the next sections, I first outline historical perspectives of leadership and mention a few critical issues and topics, before briefly introducing one of the main research methods often used by researchers in the field, namely discursive leadership (Fairhurst 2007). I then discuss some of the most interesting and most recent developments in leadership research, and provide a short illustration of leadership discourse in action. The chapter ends by mentioning some meeting points between leadership research and practices, and by outlining some suggestions for avenues for future research.

A Very Brief Overview of Research on Leadership and Language

Since it is impossible, within the word limit of this chapter, to provide a detailed overview of leadership research taking into account the enormous number of research studies and conceptual papers and books that were (and currently are) written on this topic by scholars from different academic disciplines, in line with the overall aim of this handbook, I mainly concentrate on research that specifically looks at leadership and language. A lot of this research has been conducted in linguistics but it is also important to mention some non-linguistic research on leadership in business and management studies, communication studies and organizational sciences which also increasingly acknowledges and investigates the crucial role that language plays in leadership (see e.g., the contributions in Tourish and Jackson 2008b; Grint 2000).

However, in spite of this interest in leadership and language, it was not before the late 1990s, early 2000s that discourse analysts started to more systematically approach the topic. One of the earliest studies to analyse leadership discourse in situ, i.e., the ways in which designated leaders use language, is a study by Ruth Wodak on Austrian school principals (Wodak 1997). She observed that the school leaders skilfully disguised their criticism with praise, avoided conflict by creating a general consensus and emphasizing cooperation, and they also created a sense of solidarity among interlocutors. In addition to this study on leadership discourse in a school setting, several studies on leadership in New Zealand workplaces were conducted by Janet Holmes and her colleagues from the Wellington Language in the Workplace Project (e.g., Holmes 2000; Holmes, Schnurr, and Marra 2007; Marra, Schnurr, and Holmes 2006; Schnurr 2009). These studies also found that leaders played a crucial role in meeting management—for example, they were in charge of opening and closing the meeting, they kept the discussion on track, summarized progress, as well as dominated the talking time, and managed and controlled the contributions of others. At around the same time, but taking a slightly different, conversational analytic approach (see below), Jonathan Clifton wrote several seminal research papers outlining the multiple benefits that discourse analytical approaches bring to the study of leadership (e.g., Clifton 2006, 2009, 2012).

Over the past decade or so, the topic of leadership discourse at work has continuously attracted the attention of linguistics researchers around the globe, and several monographs, as well as research articles have been published on leadership discourse in a variety of different workplaces. This research has largely focused on various white-collar workplaces (e.g., Schnurr 2009; Holmes, Marra, and Vine 2011), but has also looked at NGOs (e.g., Schnurr and Mak 2011), educational settings (e.g., Choi and Schnurr 2014), government departments (e.g., Goebel 2014), manufacturing companies (e.g., Svennevig 2011; Schnurr and Chan 2009), and a factory outlet (Ladegaard 2012). Although leadership discourse has been researched in different countries, such as, for example, Austria (Wodak 1997), Australia (Wodak, Kwon, and Clarke 2011), New Zealand (Holmes, Marra, and Vine 2011; Schnurr 2009), Hong Kong (Ladegaard 2012; Schnurr and Mak 2011), Indonesia (Goebel 2014), Japan (e.g., Saito 2011), Greece (Angouri 2011), Malaysia, Dubai, and Spain (Svennevig 2011), Norway (Skovholt 2015), France (e.g., Clifton forthcoming), the US (e.g., Kathlene 1995), and the UK (Baxter 2010; Clifton 2006), most of these studies work with English data.

Moreover, most of this continuously increasing body of research uses qualitative methodologies, as outlined in more detail below, to identify and describe some of the discursive processes through which leadership is enacted in the specific professional and socio-cultural context in which it occurs. In the next section I will outline in more detail some of the critical issues and topics this research engages with.

Some Critical Issues and Topics

The question of what leadership is and how it is "done" has been and still is at the heart of much research. In addressing this question from a linguistic perspective, researchers have identified and described various transactional and relational behaviours that are indexed for leadership, such as getting things done (e.g., Schnurr and Mak 2011), solving disagreements (e.g., Choi and Schnurr 2014; Holmes and Marra 2004), managing meetings (e.g., Holmes 2000), and creating a positive working atmosphere in a team (e.g., Schnurr 2009). Since these behaviours are typically associated with the notions of power, authority and influence, by performing them, interlocutors do leadership. The following short examples briefly illustrate this.

Example 26.1 (Schnurr 2010, 120–121; shortened)

Context: A weekly meeting at an NGO in Hong Kong chaired by Sabitha, the CEO. During a relatively elaborate discussion about the length of the company's lease agreement, Sabitha cuts in and brings the ongoing discussion to an end.

1	Sabitha:	okay fine made the decision let's move on
2		I don't want to think about this anymore
3		I've spend talked about this with Betty so many times
4	Beth:	okay

[*the team then move on to discuss another topic*]

In this example Sabitha is clearly the one in charge. She interrupts the other team members' discussion and brings it to an end—presumably because they have discussed the topic of the company's lease agreement thoroughly in the past (see her comment in lines 2 and 3). Her utterance initial *okay* (line 1) facilitates this and prepares the topic shift which is about to come (after line 4). Noteworthy is also the reply of Betty, one of the team members, who accepts Sabitha's display of power and authority without question (line 4). While the behaviour displayed by Sabitha can be described as mainly transactional (as it is mainly oriented towards achieving her transactional objectives, namely to move on with the meeting), the next, slightly longer, example illustrates how transactional and relational behaviours are often inextricably interwoven with each other.

Example 26.2 was recorded at an IT company in New Zealand. This example nicely illustrates how Donald combines transactional and relational behaviours in his leadership performance. When he finds out that Ann is reluctant to write the letter of offer, he does not force her to do it but rather teasingly reminds her of her duties as a project manager (line 5). The teasing together with the subsequent shared laughter can be interpreted as relational behaviours which aim at creating positive relationships and a productive working atmosphere. This is highly effective here as it enables Ann to tell Donald exactly what her problem is (line 7). Donald then gives her some advice (i.e., to use a standard letter in line 9) and more explicitly spells out what she needs to do (lines 13–16). These are transactional objectives which ultimately aim at making sure the letter of offer gets written and Ann knows what she needs to do. However, rather than providing this information explicitly, Donald uses several discursive

Example 26.2 (Schnurr 2009, 28–29)

Context: The excerpt below occurred during an interaction between Donald, the CEO, and Ann, a project manager, after a job interview that they just had with Beverley. They would like to offer her the job and since she will join Ann's team Donald asks Ann to prepare the letter offering her the job.

1	Donald:	yep + okay alright
2		do you wanna write do up a letter of offer
3	Ann:	no //[laughs]\
4	Donald:	/[laughs]\\
5		(are) you the project manager
6		//[laughs]\
7	Ann:	/how do i\\ do that
8	Donald:	eh? [laughs]
9		there's standard templates
10	Ann:	for letters of offers?
11	Donald:	yep
12	Ann:	oh hell
13	Donald:	so but what you're gonna have to do is work out
14		what you're asking her to do and what the
15		what the position is +
16		cos we don't have a position for (her) + [laughs]
17	Ann:	okay so what's that then

strategies to perform relational behaviours, including humour and laughter, while at the same time achieving his transactional aims. His final humorous remark "cos we don't have a position for (her)" (line 16) is a good illustration of this: he makes it clear that he still expects Ann to write the letter of offer, while at the same time lightening the situation and reinforcing solidarity with Ann (by making fun of possible job titles for the new employee). Ann's final comment "okay so what's that then" (line 17) signals that Donald's leadership was successful and that he has indeed managed to convince her to write the letter of offer as intended.

Examples 26.1 and 26.2 have illustrated some of the ways in which certain behaviours provide insights into an understanding of how these people do leadership, such as bringing a discussion to an end and telling people what to do. The leadership displayed by Sabitha in Example 26.1 was rather decisive and autocratic, and she did not leave much room for her subordinates to contribute to this decision making (but see Schnurr and Mak 2011 for further examples of her leadership behaviour in different situations). In Example 26.2, on the other hand, Donald displayed a rather relaxed and participative leadership style, allowing his subordinate Ann to contribute to the discussion and to utter her concerns. Thus, while Sabitha seemed to display her power and authority rather overtly, Donald used influence and put more emphasis on convincing (rather than forcing) Ann to write the letter.

There are clearly many different ways of doing leadership and of performing the various behaviours that are associated with power, authority and influence, and hence leadership. But, as I discuss in more detail below, often these leadership behaviours are not performed by an individual (i.e., the leader) but are actually collaboratively enacted among various members (see Example 26.3).

Research in linguistics is also particularly interested in the wider context in which leadership takes place, and in better understanding the role of this context for leadership performance. To date, some of the more widely researched contextual factors that have been found to have an effect on leadership performance are gender (e.g., Baxter 2010; Marra, Schnurr, and Holmes 2006; Ladegaard 2012; Schnurr and Mak 2011) and culture and ethnicity (e.g., Schnurr and Chan 2009; Schnurr *et al.* forthcoming; Holmes, Marra, and Vine 2011). Research on leadership and gender explores, for example, how specific leadership behaviours are gendered and how the same behaviour may be perceived differently when it is enacted by a man as opposed to a woman. Several recent studies lament the fact that in spite of the so-called feminization of leadership (i.e., the general acknowledgement that several behaviours which are typically associated with feminine behaviours/speech styles are actually beneficial for leadership), leadership remains a predominately masculine concept (e.g., Baxter 2010; Schnurr 2008). As a consequence of this masculine bias, women often experience specific difficulties as they climb up the organisational ladder—also known as the infamous glass ceiling and the double-bind (see Mullany and Yoong this volume).

Recent research on leadership and culture and ethnicity increasingly takes a critical stance towards earlier essentialist assumptions (as for example proposed by the seminal GLOBE study—House *et al.* 2004) and problematizes often stereotypical claims about the impact of culture or ethnicity on leadership performance. Rather than assuming that culture-specific leadership styles exist a priori, this research explores how leadership is enacted dynamically in a specific context taking into consideration not only the socio-cultural macro-context but also more locally negotiated norms and practices that emerge, for example, on the level of the specific working team in which the leadership takes place (cf. community of practice—see King this volume). This research also illustrates that there is not only one way of doing leadership in a specific socio-cultural context but rather that a lot of diversity exists (e.g., Schnurr *et al.* forthcoming).

Discursive Leadership

Although a myriad of different theoretical and methodological approaches to leadership exist, I will outline here only one of them, namely discursive leadership. This approach, which was proposed by Fairhurst (2007) is based on a dynamic understanding of leadership as outlined above, and acknowledges the crucial role of language in the leadership process (see also Tourish and Jackson 2008b). Discursive leadership thus explores how leadership is *done* with a particular focus on the role of discourse. Research in this tradition conducts mainly qualitative research, often involving case studies (such as a specific team in an organization) with the aim to understand the specific (discursive) processes through which leadership is enacted. Discursive leadership research is *not* interested, however, in establishing "grand theories of leadership" but rather focuses on how leadership is done on the mirco-level of interaction (e.g., Clifton 2006).

Discursive leadership is often set in opposition to what Fairhurst (2007) refers to as leadership psychology (see also Chen 2008). While leadership psychology is mostly concerned with the perceptions and self-reflections of leaders, discursive leadership focuses on language *in use* and explores the specific process through which leadership is actually communicated and accomplished in (and through) discourse (e.g., Schnurr and Chan 2011; Choi and Schnurr 2014). Discursive leadership acknowledges the crucial role of language on the performance of leadership and thus utilizes tools and methods developed by discourse analytic approaches (such as conversation analysis, e.g., Clifton 2006; Svennevig 2008, or Interactional Sociolinguistics, e.g., Schnurr 2009) to analyse the specific processes through which leadership is done at the micro-level of interaction. Discursive leadership research thus aims at gaining "a better understanding of the everyday practices of talk that constitute leadership and a deeper knowledge of how leaders use language to craft 'reality'" and to construct meaning (Clifton 2006, 203), rather than attempting "to capture the experience of leadership by forming and statistically analysing a host of cognitive, affective, and conative variables and their casual connections" (Fairhurst 2007, 15), as is typical for most research in leadership psychology. It is precisely this ability of discursive leadership to provide insights into the actual practice of leadership (rather than its recounted perception or post-experience evaluation) that has the potential to make important contributions to leadership research by generating new insights into how leadership is actually *done*.

Current Trends in Leadership Research

Based on the definition of leadership as a process described above and building on previous research in leadership and management studies, recent linguistic research on leadership is increasingly moving towards exploring alternative, non-hierarchical, non-top down leadership constellations. For example, Vine *et al.* (2008) and Schnurr and Chan (2011) analyse co-leadership constellations in a range of New Zealand and Hong Kong workplaces, respectively, and demonstrate how the leaders and their second in commands share the leadership responsibilities with each of them being responsible for a more or less defined aspect of the leadership role. Vine *et al.* (2008), for example, observed that while one member of the co-leadership constellation generally makes sure that the team reach their transactional objectives, another member mainly performs relational functions and ensures team members are happy and the morale stays high.

In a study on a research project team in a UK higher education institution, Choi and Schnurr (2014) analyse leadership in a leaderless team. They show how team members do leadership collaboratively in situations of disagreement and conflict. In this team, which does not have an officially assigned chair or "leader", various members, regardless of their hierarchical position within the team, contribute to the leadership performance. Example 26.3 briefly illustrates this.

Although the extract shown here is taken from a much longer sequence in which meeting participants are engaged in a heated discussion (and mostly disagree with each other—see Choi and Schnurr 2014 for a more detailed discussion of the disagreement), even by just looking at the beginning of the excerpt, the different viewpoints among participants become clear. At this point in the discussion, although there is some agreement (e.g., between Dan and Ylva, line 4), the discussion is rather stuck. It is then Sarah, one of the most junior people on the team who (in line 8) picks up a suggestion and proposes this as the solution to the disagreement. After having received some agreement by Dan and Bee (in lines 9–12), she formulates a very clear solution to the problem: "It's just a matter of showing that they're consistently greater than the time point zero" (lines 13–14). This proposal generates general agreement among participants (Dan, Bee, and Ylva) and gets further elaborated and thereby ratified by Dan, one of the most senior people on the team (lines 20–23). In this example then, it is mainly Sarah, one of the most junior people in the team, and Dan, one of the most senior people, who collaboratively solve the disagreement and find a solution to which the entire team agrees. However, Sarah's leadership is emergent rather than pre-determined, and may be due to the

Example 26.3 (Choi and Schnurr 2014, 9–11; shortened)

Context: A project research team at a university consisting of members from different departments. Sarah is a postdoctoral researcher in mathematics, Dan is a professor in mathematics and one of the co-investigators on the project, Bee is an associate professor and also a co-investigator on the project, and Ylva is an associate professor in biology and the principal-investigator on the project. Prior to this excerpt Dan has heavily disagreed with Sarah's proposal (supported by Bee and Ylva) to include certain 'plots' into a research paper that they are currently writing up.

1	Dan:	no but I think this sort of thing this got a lot more interesting
2		information
3	Sarah:	it's just a correlation of //(xxx) figure\
4	Ylva:	/no agreed\\ agreed
5	Dan:	so I think er Sarah should think about how to that into a the
6		figure and put it in the paper
7	Sarah:	yes

[*11 turns of further discussion omitted*]

| 8 | Sarah: | then we can do it this way |

[*22 turns of more discussion omitted*]

9	Dan:	yeah I wouldn't mind (that) too much.
10	Bee:	//mm\
11	Dan:	/you got\\ (xxx) next to each other so that's fine
12	Bee:	yeah yeah
13	Sarah:	it's just a matter of showing that they're consistently greater
14		than the time point zero
15	Dan:	mm
16	Bee:	mm
17	Sarah:	and you get the last (xxx)
18	Dan:	mm
19	Ylva:	yeah
20	Dan:	yeah that's ok I don't think that's a problem i- i- that's very
21		informative I think + because it gets over the idea that if
22		we get all six even if we (xxx) small thing
23		//(xxx) small probability of\
24	Sarah:	/yeah that's + spot on time job\\
25	Dan:	(xxx)
26	Ylva:	mmhm

leaderless character of this team. In this team, as this example illustrates, various team members, regardless of their status within the team and the wider organization in which this exchange took place, perform leadership behaviours and thus contribute to the leadership performance (see Choi and Schnurr 2014 for more examples).

With a focus on leader*ship* rather than individual leaders, more recent research studies, as in the study from which this example is taken, clearly demonstrate the benefits of discursive approaches to leadership. Focusing on the discourse of leadership and analysing how specific leadership behaviours are enacted and by whom, provides important insights into leadership as it enables researchers to better understand the specific processes through which leadership is accomplished in a specific situation. This research is thus very much in line with recent trends in (non-linguistic) leadership which "challenge the traditional orthodoxies of leadership and following" by questioning "the hegemonic view that leaders are the people in charge and followers are the people who are influenced" (Jackson and Parry 2011, 83). Findings from these discourse analytic studies thus make an important contribution to leadership scholarship in other disciplines and provide further empirical support for recent conceptualisations of leadership as collaboratively constituted and co-produced among leaders and followers (Collinson 2005, 1419).

Leadership Research and Practice

Although "most practitioners readily identify superior communication skills as being the primary attribute required by effective leaders" (Tourish and Jackson 2008a, 220), and although several researchers spell out the practical applications of their research and provide suggestions, for example, on "how to achieve an effective language of leadership" (Baxter 2010), direct and continuous engagement and collaboration between linguistic researchers and practitioners (e.g., via trainers or coaches) is relatively rare. This is particularly surprising given that leadership training courses typically include communication as one of the topics in their programmes and that a relatively large amount of practitioner oriented books exist on the topic of leadership and communication, such as *Effective Communication Skills: How to Improve Your Communication Skills to Become a Confident and Inspiring Leader* (Jones 2014).

One of the researchers who puts an emphasis on using the findings of her academic enquiries into advice for practice is Judith Baxter (see Baxter this volume). In her monograph *The Language of Female Leadership* (Baxter 2010) she outlines several "strategies and contexts which might enable senior women to use language as effectively as possible to achieve their business goals", and she also mentions some "strategies which corporations can use to counter negative evaluations made against senior women" (147). She proposes that senior women should try and become "linguistic role models" to their junior colleagues by combining the following three aspects of language use: doing authority, doing politeness, and doing humour. The corporate linguistic strategies that she outlines include, for example, the assignment of "linguistic champions" whose role it is to "help colleagues to develop a greater linguistic awareness, and to provide expertise and advice" (155). Other possibilities include raising awareness of the negative effects of gendered discourses which often discriminate against women. This could be achieved, for example, by contesting the use of sexist language (e.g., replacing generic *he* with gender neutral forms such as *s/he* in all documents), and challenging the uncritical use of often derogatory terms to describe women (e.g., as "corporate transvestites", even if used humorously).

In addition to these specific guidelines for practitioners, another channel for communicating research findings on leadership to lay audiences is via increasingly popular professional skills modules, i.e., modules which are taught at a university and which are specifically devised for particular professions, such as engineering (e.g., www2.warwick.ac.uk/fac/sci/eng/study/pg/degree/msc/mscmodules/es97i). Participants in these programmes typically have considerable work experience and are funded by their companies to attend these sessions. This trend of making research findings on leadership discourse available to professionals and to communicate them in relatively easily accessible and non-expert ways is also reflected in some recent publications on leadership discourse which are specifically targeted at practitioners *and* (business) students (e.g., Walker and Aritz 2014).

Avenues for Future Research

In spite of the increasing attention that leadership has been, and still is, receiving from researchers across different disciplines, it is very likely that leadership will remain a topic of interest for some time to come. The theoretical and methodological approaches, and the current trends and topics as outlined above, show the increasing interest in leadership from a linguistic perspective. This line of research, as I have shown throughout this chapter, constitutes an important aspect of current leadership scholarship. Indeed, both the findings and theoretical and methodological advances made in the past few years in this branch of leadership research have contributed considerably, and are likely to make further important contributions, to the ways in which leadership is conceptualized and approached—both by academics and practitioners. And while the possibilities, and indeed the need, for future research on leadership are quite literally unlimited, I outline just a few specific avenues here which I think are particularly important and capture current trends.

First, future research needs to continue to focus on the processes of leadership and to pay more attention to understanding the intricate and often complex ways in which leadership is actually put into practice. In other words, research should continue to explore how leadership is *done*—often collaboratively among various people—and it should move away from an often exclusive focus on the behaviour of individual leaders. It is this focus on non-traditional and alternative leadership constellations, as outlined above, where I believe future research taking discourse analytical approaches will make important contributions to leadership scholarship. These observations will crucially contribute to the quest towards a better understanding of what exactly leadership is, how it is done, how it is perceived, and ultimately, how it can be improved.

The second avenue for future research concerns the context in which most previous and current research is placed. Most studies on leadership discourse to date are based on data collected in English-speaking workplaces—albeit around the world—and very little attention is currently paid to leadership discourse in non-English speaking workplaces (but see for example Goebel 2014; Saito 2011; Schnurr *et al.* forthcoming). This lack of focus on non-English data constitutes a significant gap which needs to be addressed urgently. Future research addressing this dearth could, perhaps more systematically than is currently the case, explore what kinds of behaviours are indexed for leadership in these contexts, and how these leadership behaviours are enacted. Insights gained through such studies could then make important contributions towards overcoming the often lamented "Western bias" of much current leadership research (e.g., Jackson and Parry 2011), and could provide the data and insights necessary to facilitate a debate about global or more local notions of leadership.

In addition to the need for more research on non-English speaking workplaces, there is also a clear need for more research on leadership (and other aspects of language at work) to analyse interactional contexts other than the relatively easily accessible but relatively widely researched business meeting. These other, equally important, contexts provide crucial sites for future research on leadership. In addition to looking, for example, at one-to-one interactions (long) before and after a meeting (e.g., Schnurr 2009), it is equally important to explore leadership discourse in the context of online communication—both internal and external—such as emails, WhatsApp posts, Facebook and Twitter messages. Given the increasingly virtual nature of professional communication and the use of social media (Darics 2015), an important avenue for future research is leadership in virtual teams (e.g., Skovholt 2015)—for example with the aim of identifying potential genre-specific ways of doing leadership.

Further Reading

Since leadership is an extremely complex and widely researched topic, any attempt at compiling a list of further readings is an almost impossible task. This difficulty is further intensified by the fact that leadership research is conducted in a diversity of disciplines. Nevertheless, in the list below I have tried to incorporate both seminal texts as well as more recent research articles to reflect some of the issues discussed above.

Baxter (2010) is an engaging book-length read on leadership and gender.

Choi and Schnurr (2014) illustrates how leadership is performed in a leaderless team. It also outlines some of the benefits of discourse analytical approaches for the study of leadership.

Clifton (2006) is a seminal text for anyone interested in understanding leadership discourse. It demonstrates some of the benefits of approaching leadership by using conversation analytical tools and practices. Clifton (2012) is also very useful in this respect.

Fairhurst (2007) provides a comprehensive discussion of discursive leadership and provides several illustrations of how this approach can be used within different theoretical frameworks.

Holmes, Marra, and Vine (2011) is a book-length account of the relationship between leadership and ethnicity.

Ilie and Schnurr (forthcoming) is a collection of research articles that challenge existing leadership stereotypes—pertaining for example to power, gender, and culture.

Jackson and Parry (2011) is a general, very readable introduction on the topic of leadership from the perspective of business studies. It provides an excellent comprehensive overview of leadership research and outlines current trends and debates.

Schnurr (2009) is one of the first research monographs on leadership discourse in a workplace context. It approaches the topic of leadership through the lens of humour.

Related Topics

Communities of practice; Corporate settings; Directives; Relational talk; Gender; Enabling women leaders

Transcription Conventions

[laughs]	Paralinguistic features in square brackets
+	Pause of up to one second
. . . //. . . . . .\ . . .	Simultaneous speech
. . . /. . . . . . .\\ . . .	
(hello)	Transcriber's best guess at an unclear utterance
(xxx)	unintelligible utterance

?	Rising or question intonation
-	Incomplete or cut-off utterance
[comment]	Editorial comments italicized in square brackets

All names used in the examples are pseudonyms.

References

Angouri, Jo. 2011. "'We Are in a Masculine Profession ...': Constructing Gender Identities in a Consortium of Two Multinational Engineering Companies." *Gender & Language* 5: 365–394.

Bass, Bernard. 1981. *Stogdill's Handbook of Leadership. A Survey of Theory and Research.* Revised and expanded. New York: Free Press.

Baxter, Judith. 2010. *The Language of Female Leadership.* Basingstoke, UK: Palgrave Macmillan.

Chen, Ling. 2008. "Leaders or Leadership: Alternative Approaches to Leadership Studies". *Management Communication Quarterly* 21: 547–555.

Choi, Seongsook, and Stephanie Schnurr. 2014. "Exploring Distributed Leadership: Solving Disagreements and Negotiating Consensus in a 'Leaderless' Team." *Discourse Studies* 16: 3–24.

Clifton, Jonathan. 2006. "A Conversation Analytical Approach to Business Communication." *Journal of Business Communication* 43: 202–219.

Clifton, Jonathan. 2009. "Beyond Taxonomies of Influence. 'Doing' Influence and Making Decisions in Management Team Meetings." *Journal of Business Communication* 46: 57–79.

Clifton, Jonathan. 2012. "A Discursive Approach to Leadership Doing Assessments and Managing Organizational Meanings." *Journal of Business Communication* 49: 148–168.

Clifton, Jonathan. Forthcoming. "Taking the (Heroic) Leader out of Leadership. The In Situ Practice of Distributed Leadership in Decision-Making Talk." In *Challenging Leadership Stereotypes. Discourse and Power Management*, edited by Cornelia Illie and Stephanie Schnurr. London: Springer.

Collinson, David. 2005. "Dialectics of Leadership." *Human Relations* 58: 1419–1442.

Darics, Erica. 2015. *Digital Business Communication.* Basingstoke, UK: Palgrave.

Dwyer, Judith. 1993. *The Business Communication Handbook.* 3rd ed. New York: Prentice Hall.

Fairhurst, Gail. 2007. *Discursive Leadership: In Conversation with Leadership Psychology.* London: Sage.

Ferch, Shann, and Matthew Mitchell. 2001. "Intentional Forgiveness in Relational Leadership: A Technique for Enhancing Effective Leadership." *The Journal of Leadership Studies* 7: 70–83.

Goebel, Zane. 2014. "Doing Leadership through Signswitching in the Indonesian Bureaucracy." *Journal of Linguistic Anthropology* 24: 193–215.

Grint, Keith. 2000. *Leadership. A Very Short Introduction.* Oxford: Oxford University Press.

Holmes, Janet. 2000. "Women at Work: Analysing Women's Talk in New Zealand Workplaces." *Australian Review of Applied Linguistics* 22: 1–17.

Holmes, Janet, and Meredith Marra. 2004. "Leadership and Managing Conflict in Meetings." *Pragmatics* 14: 439–462.

Holmes, Janet, Meredith Marra, and Bernadette Vine. 2011. *Leadership, Discourse, and Ethnicity.* Oxford: Oxford University Press.

Holmes, Janet, Stephanie Schnurr, and Meredith Marra. 2007. "Leadership and Communication: Discursive Evidence of a Workplace Culture Change." *Discourse and Communication* 1: 433–451.

House, Robert J., Paul J. Hanges, Mansour Javidan, Peter W. Dorfman, and Vipin Gupta. 2004. *Culture, Leadership, and Organizations. The GLOBE study of 62 societies.* Thousand Oaks, CA: Sage.

Ilie, Cornelia, and Stephanie Schnurr, Eds. Forthcoming. *Challenging Leadership Stereotypes. Discourse and Power Management.* London: Springer.

Jackson, Brad, and Ken Parry. 2011. *A Very Short, Fairly Interesting and Reasonably Cheap Book About Studying Leadership.* 2nd ed. Los Angeles, CA: Sage.

Jones, Daniel. 2014. *Effective Communication Skills: How to Improve Your Communication Skills to Become a Confident and Inspiring Leader.* Kindle Edition.

Kathlene, Lyn. 1995. "Position Power Versus Gender Power: Who Holds the Floor?" In *Gender Power, Leadership, and Governance*, edited by Georgina Duerst-Lahti, and Rita Mae Kelly, 167–193. Ann Arbor, MN: University of Michigan Press.

Ladegaard, Hans J. 2012. "Rudeness as a Discursive Strategy in Leadership Discourse: Culture, Power and Gender in a Hong Kong Workplace." *Journal of Pragmatics* 44: 1661–1679.

Marra Meredith, Stephanie Schnurr, and Janet Holmes. 2006. "Effective Leadership in New Zealand Workplaces: Balancing Gender and Role." In *Speaking Out: The Female Voice in Public Contexts*, edited by Judith Baxter, 240–260. Basingstoke, UK: Palgrave.

Robbins, Stephen P, Bruce Millett, Ron Cacioppe, and Terry Walters-Marsh. 1998. *Organisational Behaviour. Leading and Managing in Australia and New Zealand*. 2nd ed. Sydney: Prentice Hall.

Saito, Junko. 2011. "Managing Confrontational Situations: Japanese Male Superiors' Interactional Styles in Directive Discourse in the Workplace." *Journal of Pragmatics* 43: 1689–1706.

Schnurr, Stephanie. 2008. "Surviving in a Man's World with a Sense of Humour. An Analysis of Women Leaders' Use of Humour at Work." *Leadership* 4: 299–319.

Schnurr, Stephanie. 2009. *Leadership Discourse at Work: Interactions of Humour, Gender and Workplace Culture*. Basingstoke, UK: Palgrave Macmillan.

Schnurr, Stephanie. 2010. "'Decision Made—Let's Move On'. Negotiating Gender and Professional Identity in Hong Kong Workplaces". In *Language in its Socio-Cultural Context: New Explorations in Gendered, Global and Media Uses*, edited by Markus Bieswanger, Heiko Motschenbacher, and Susanne Mühleisen, 111–136. Berlin: Peter Lang.

Schnurr, Stephanie, and Angela Chan. 2009. "Leadership Discourse and Politeness at Work. A Cross Cultural Case Study of New Zealand and Hong Kong." *Journal of Politeness Research* 5: 131–157.

Schnurr, Stephanie, and Angela Chan. 2011. "Exploring Another Side of Co-Leadership: Negotiating Professional Identities through Face-Work in Disagreements." *Language in Society* 40: 187–210.

Schnurr, Stephanie, Angela Chan, Joelle Loew, and Olga Zayts. Forthcoming. "Leadership and Culture: When Stereotypes Meet Actual Workplace Practice." In *Challenging Leadership Stereotypes. Discourse and Power Management*, edited by Cornelia Ilie and Stephanie Schnurr. London: Springer.

Schnurr, Stephanie, and Bernie Mak. 2011. "Leadership and Workplace Realities in Hong Kong. Is Gender Really *Not* an Issue?" *Gender and Language* 5: 337–364.

Skovholt, Karianne. 2015. "Doing Leadership in a Virtual Team: Analysing Addressing Devices, Requests and Emoticons in a Leader's Email Messages." In *Digital Business Communication*, edited by Erica Darics, 101–121. Basingstoke, UK: Palgrave.

Svennevig, Jan. 2008. "Exploring Leadership Conversations." *Management Communication Quarterly* 21: 529–536.

Svennevig, Jan. 2011. "Leadership Style in Managers' Feedback in Meetings." In *Constructing Identities at Work*, edited by Jo Angouri, and Meredith Marra, 17–39. Basingstoke, UK: Palgrave Macmillan.

Tourish, Dennis, and Brad Jackson. 2008a. "Communication and Leadership: An Open Invitation to Engage." *Communication and Leadership* 4: 219–225.

Tourish, Dennis, and Brad Jackson, Eds. 2008b. "Leadership." Special issue, *Communication and Leadership* 4 (3).

Vine, Bernadette, Janet Holmes, Meredith Marra, Dale Pfeifer, and Brad Jackson. 2008. "Exploring Co-Leadership Talk through Interactional Sociolinguistics." *Leadership* 4: 339–60.

Walker, Robyn, and Jolanta Aritz. 2014. *Leadership Talk. A Discourse Approach to Leader Emergence*. New York: Business Expert Press.

Wodak, Ruth. 1997. "'I Know We Won't Revolutionize the World with This, But...': Styles of Female Leadership in Institutions." In *Communicating Gender in Context*, edited by Helga Kotthoff and Ruth Wodak, 335–370. Amsterdam: Benjamins.

Wodak, Ruth, Winston Kwon, and Ian Clarke. 2011. "'Getting People on Board'. Discursive Leadership for Consensus in Teams." *Discourse & Society* 22: 592–644.

27
Intercultural Communication in the Workplace
Janet Holmes

Introduction

Workplaces in many countries are increasingly diverse, attracting employees from many different ethnic groups and nations. The results enrich workplace interaction linguistically and culturally, but also provides communicative challenges to many employers and co-workers who are members of the majority group. Intercultural communication is thus not only a fascinating research area but also one with the potential for raising awareness of the complexities of interaction in diverse workplace contexts.

Piller (2012, 9) points out that intercultural communication has been the focus of many textbooks in areas such as Business and Organisation Studies, Management Studies, Communication Studies, and Psychology, but that, surprisingly, the central role of language in communication is not always recognized or acknowledged. And the important role of power and control in terms of who defines what is relevant or irrelevant in interaction, or what is deemed appropriate behaviour, is equally obfuscated in many intercultural research studies (Piller 2012, 12). In this chapter, I review a range of research which focuses on specific workplace contexts, and examine some of the underlying assumptions and ideological presuppositions which underpin instances of successful and less successful intercultural interaction in specific workplace contexts.

But first a couple of definitions are in order. It is useful for research purposes to clarify the distinction between cross-cultural and intercultural interaction. Where researchers accept such a distinction, they generally define cross-cultural communication research as *comparative* research which contrasts the communicative practices of distinct cultural groups, while intercultural communication research focuses on interaction *between* two distinct cultural groups (e.g., Gudykunst 2002, 175–6; Bargiela-Chiappini and Nickerson 2003). Hence research which compares the discourse norms for opening a meeting between Japanese participants in a business setting in Tokyo with the norms for opening a business meeting in New York, would qualify as a cross-cultural study, while an analysis of a business meeting involving both Japanese and American participants would be classified as intercultural research. As Piller (2007, 2012) notes, however, both these approaches assume that group membership and identity can be clearly attributed to participants. Following Scollon and Scollon (2001) and Blommaert (2005), she argues for a more dynamic, social constructionist approach which asks "how culture and intercultural communication are produced in discourse" (Piller 2012, 8), and which focuses on "discourses where 'culture' is indeed important, whether explicitly or implicitly, [asking] by whom, for whom in which contexts, for which purposes" (Piller 2012, 14). Similarly Liebscher (2006, 155) argues for a more positive focus stating that "interculturality is negotiated by speakers themselves" while "utilizing different cultural and interactional resources", and "that these negotiations reflect an understanding, rather than a misunderstanding, of participants' perspectives."

These points are well illustrated by video-recordings we collected of meetings in a New Zealand government organization where group boundaries were constantly being drawn and re-drawn along a range of dimensions which included institutional, gender, and ethnicity (Vine et al. 2009). The organization had established two working groups, one comprising only Māori women and the other comprised of predominantly Pākehā (majority group) women.[1] In the following exchange which involved just the Māori group, ethnicity is explicitly invoked as the women use humour to express their rejection of the bureaucratic demands of the Pākehā organization.

Example 27.1 [2]

1	Tracey:	it's always been like that though eh ( )
2		//I don't know\ how many reviews there's been
3	Hera:	/it's a political issue\\
4	Ripeka:	just like the Māoris
		[*people smile and look amused*]
5	Hera:	it's a political issue not a not an issue
6		it's not it's not it's got nothing to do with logic
7	Tracey:	no

In lines 1–2 Tracey refers to a situation they have been discussing which keeps surfacing and attracting criticism. The standard political response in such a situation is to set up a review. Hence her comment "I don't know how many reviews there's been" (line 2). Hera makes the point quite explicit "it's a political issue" (line 3), implying that the lack of progress has nothing to do with logic, a point she spells out explicitly in lines 5–6. In between these comments Ripeka inserts an ironic remark "just like the Māoris" (line 4), drawing on a familiar negative stereotype of Māori interactional style in which, in the New Zealand popular imagination, political tension and fractious argument are considered to be major features of Māori communication (Belich 2014). These negative allusions can be derived without any effort by the women at the meeting for whom such a remark serves as a compressed shorthand for the dominant group's predictable prejudices about Māori behaviour. As members of the minority group, Māori participants are sensitive to potentially discriminatory behaviours, and very aware of the pervasiveness of unequal treatment (Holmes and Hay 1997). This illustrates well how interpretation of such remarks is extremely context-sensitive. Ripeka's remark is perfectly acceptable when made by a Māori person among other Māori, where it clearly signals in-group solidarity and shared knowledge of damaging racist stereotypes. Uttered by a non-Māori person in the same context, it would almost certainly be interpreted as insulting and racist. By contrast, there are no such examples, nor even a hint of humour in the Pākehā meetings referring to their position as members of the dominant culture. As noted in Holmes and Hay (1997, 135):

> Minority groups are much more sensitive to areas of difference between their norms and those of other groups than are those in power. Powerful groups take their norms for granted; they are "given", assumed, unquestioned and even unconscious. Members of minority groups are generally much more attuned to areas of cultural difference between their own patterns of interaction and those of the majority group.

Hence, intercultural discourse must be examined in context in order to appreciate the diverse ways in which cultural norms regarding ways of doing things are constantly being constructed, reinforced or contested in workplace interaction.

Previous Research

The field of intercultural communication is rich in theoretical material (e.g., Liddicoat 2009; Holliday 2011; Piller 2011; Bardhan and Orbe 2012; Scollon, Scollon, and Jones 2012; Kecskes 2014; Tranekjær 2015), and many researchers pay specific attention to the workplace as a research site (e.g., Cook-Gumperz 2001; Ting-Toomey and Oetzel 2001; Geluykens and Kraft 2008; Hua 2014). Spencer-Oatey and Franklin (2009), for example, outline an interdisciplinary theoretical approach to intercultural interaction, and then explore its application in professional and educational contexts, while Hua (2014) reviews research on real world intercultural negotiations in the classroom, the family and travel, as well as in workplace and business meetings. Sharifian and Jamarani (2013) further broaden the scope of intercultural research with a collection that examines intercultural communication in contexts such as chat rooms, emails, personal weblogs, Facebook, Twitter, and mobile text messaging, as well as multinational classrooms and workplaces.

Conversely, those researching workplace discourse often focus attention on intercultural interaction. Clyne's (1994) pioneering research in this area, examined speech acts and communication patterns in a multicultural factory in Melbourne, making an invaluable contribution to intercultural theorizing as well as to methodology. Candlin and Gotti (2004) is a rich collection of research on intercultural communication in specialist fields, including the legal, commercial, political and institutional discourse used in particular workplaces. The contributions explore to what extent intercultural pressure leads to particular discourse patternings, and the extent to which textual re-encoding and recontextualization alter the pragmatic value of the texts taken into consideration. Focusing on power asymmetries, Cook-Gumperz (2001) seeks to illuminate how "the apparent positive image and lack of conflict that has become the dominant concern of late modern society, requires a great deal of work on the part of participants" (137). Much of this "work" is concerned with concealing the power asymmetry characteristic of service encounters and she notes that "intercultural differences exist as unmarked parts of managed, interpersonal exchanges and it is not until breakdown occurs that cultural differences are regarded as having any special significance" (137).

Considering the role of English as an international language at work, Koester (2010) notes how speech accommodation, and convergence in particular, are common strategic features of business interaction in international settings where the focus is on conveying meaning effectively, as well as establishing good working relations. With a focus on successful intercultural interaction, Bolden (2012) examines repairs where someone with expertise is enlisted as a language broker to resolve a problem, as well as situations where participants themselves act as language brokers "to mediate an actual or potential understanding problem" (107–108). In a factory context, Sunaoshi (2005) demonstrates that despite severely limited knowledge of the other group's language and sociolinguistic norms, Japanese and American factory workers creatively exploit available communicative resources and effectively co-construct meaning in interaction. Hartog (2006) also questions the tendency to equate intercultural interaction with misunderstanding, problematizing in particular the relationship between interculturality and institutional discourse. She argues that "all is not intercultural at all times in discourse simply because persons of different cultures meet" (185). Institutional discourse needs to be considered outside of culture in order to properly understand when and where interculturality plays a role.

The research of the Language in the Workplace Project (LWP) team has also focused on many positive aspects of intercultural workplace discourse, including humour (Marra and Holmes 2007), politeness (Holmes and Marra 2011), leadership (Holmes, Marra, and Vine 2011), and professional identity construction (Holmes and Riddiford 2010). The discussion below draws on some of this research.

Theoretical Perspectives

As noted in the previous section, intercultural research focusing on discourse and interaction has been undertaken using a number of different theoretical perspectives. This section discusses just three of these focusing on their importance for intercultural research, namely Interactional Sociolinguistics, Politeness Theory, and Rapport Management Theory.

John Gumperz was undoubtedly a pioneer in analysing the role of language in intercultural interaction. His Interactional Sociolinguistics framework provided a rich and fruitful means of understanding how people convey and interpret meaning, and especially social meaning, in interaction (see Gordon and Kraut this volume). Attending to a range of features, Interactional Sociolinguistics provides techniques for identifying how we interpret what is meant from what is said.

When conversational partners bring different socio-cultural and linguistic experiences to an interaction, there is the potential for misunderstanding. People tend to assume shared interactional rules for speaking and hence they may make inaccurate inferences when this is not the case. An utterance which was intended as a compliment may be misinterpreted as offensive or presumptuous if the addressee does not share the assumption that it is acceptable to compliment a more experienced and statusful colleague in the work setting. Some cultural groups expect speakers to be allowed to complete their contributions to a debate uninterrupted. Example 27.2 demonstrates how this may lead to misunderstanding when such rules for speaking are not shared by other interlocuters. The excerpt is from a meeting of a sub-committee of the New Zealand National Museum Planning Committee, and focuses on a central issue for the Board, namely, how the museum will represent and reflect the relationship between the two major cultural groups in New Zealand, the indigenous Māori people and the Pākehā settlers. The museum is to include within it a *marae*, a traditional Māori meeting house and surrounding area for speech-making, for which Cliff Whiting, the Māori Chief Executive Officer of the Museum, is responsible. Most traditional New Zealand marae are built by and for Māori, and located in particular tribal areas, though there are also some urban marae which are non-tribal. The planned museum marae is unusual in that it will be clearly visible and public. Cliff Whiting is responding to a statement from Ron Trotter, the Chair of the Planning Committee, about how he sees the museum marae as being a place where Pākehā as well as Māori will feel comfortable.

> **Example 27.2**[3]
>
> 1 Cliff: there are two <u>main</u> (0.2) fields that have to be explored (0.2)
> 2   and er (0.1) the one that is <u>most</u> important is its <u>cus</u>tomary role
> 3   in the first place? because (0.2) marae <u>comes</u> (<u>on</u>) and it comes from
> 4   (0.4) the tangata whenua who are Māori
> 5   //(0.7) to change it\
> 6 Ron: /but it's not just\\ for Māori=
> 7 Cliff: =no=
> 8 Ron: =it it you <u>must</u> get that if it is a Māori institution and nothing more
> 9   <u>this</u> [*bangs table*] marae has failed (0.2)
> 10   and they <u>must</u> [*bangs table*] get that idea

Cliff Whiting states that there are two fields to be explored (line 1), from which a listener might infer that he has two points to make. He speaks slowly and deliberately, with regular pauses, as is customary in formal Māori oratory. At line 6, Ron Trotter overlaps Cliff Whiting with a statement that challenges Cliff's focus on Māori. The overlap is positioned at a Transition Relevant Point (TRP), a point where it would be reasonable for Ron Trotter to assume Cliff Whiting had completed his turn if it were not for the fact that, first, Cliff has given notice that he had two points to make, and, second, that he is speaking slowly and deliberately with regular pauses between clauses. In these circumstances, Ron Trotter's overlap can be interpreted as a disruptive interruption, especially since he proceeds to take over the floor and to state his position with great emphasis accompanied by banging on the table. After one brief response "no" (line 7) (which could be a protest or could be agreeing with Ron Trotter's statement), Cliff Whiting is silent thereafter, and on the video of this excerpt he can be seen to physically withdraw and look down, while Ron Trotter's table banging invades his physical space.

The excerpt clearly illustrates how misunderstandings may arise when participants orient to different rules for speaking, a point which was supported in subsequent interviews with the participants. In relatively formal Māori cultural contexts, speakers typically expect to complete even relatively long turns without interruption. In many Pākehā business meetings, however, especially in normatively "masculine" workplaces (Baxter 2010; Holmes 2014), interruption is a perfectly acceptable strategy for challenging a position one disagrees with. Consequently, Cliff Whiting's withdrawal from the debate was a response to what he considered rude and disruptive behaviour, while Ron Trotter expected him to engage in continued discussion of the point at issue.

Another approach, quite compatible with Interactional Sociolinguistics, is a Politeness framework which is concerned with affective aspects of interaction ("the use of language to promote, maintain or threaten harmonious social relations" (Spencer-Oatey 2008, 4), and which focuses on the ways in which interaction addresses (or fails to address) people's face needs (Geyer 2008). This is currently found in many forms ranging from the classic Leech (1983) and Brown and Levinson (1987) models through approaches focusing on interpersonal relations (e.g., Holmes and Schnurr 2005; Locher and Watts 2005; Spencer-Oatey 2008) to post-modern frameworks (e.g., Mills 2003; Arundale 2006) which emphasize the negotiated, co-constructed, and indeterminate nature of meaning in interaction, and question the proposition that people necessarily agree on what constitutes polite behaviour (see Haugh and Watanabe this volume). Interaction is regarded as a dynamic discursive struggle, with the possibility that different participants may interpret the same interaction quite differently with obvious implications for analysing intercultural interaction in workplace contexts.

Politeness could be considered the heart of successful intercultural communication. Getting one's message across effectively, and without causing unintended offence to interlocuters from different cultural backgrounds, entails familiarity with a range of communicative norms (global focus), and the ability to draw on them appropriately and negotiate meaning (including social meaning) in specific workplace contexts (local focus). Interpreting Example 27.2 through a Politeness Theory framework highlights the ways in which Ron Trotter's disregard of Cliff Whiting's rules for speaking can be interpreted as face-threatening, and impolite (albeit unintentionally). While Ron Trotter's rules for speaking might be appropriate in cut-throat debate among industrial barons, they were not considered acceptable by the Māori cultural expert in a small meeting intended to negotiate a thorny intercultural issue.

A third approach to analysing intercultural interaction, Rapport Management Theory (RMT), was developed by Helen Spencer-Oatey (2000, 2008) to address what she considered the western bias in Politeness Theory, the focus on the individual, and the lack of attention to larger discourse segments (see Fletcher this volume). RMT includes the concepts of sociality rights and obligations (concerns relating to fair treatment, social inclusion, and respect, which differ in different socio-cultural contexts), and consideration of people's interactional goals (both transactional and relational) in a specific exchange. Moreover, as Spencer-Oatey and Xing (2003, 43–44) point out "rapport is clearly managed through multiple domains, particularly the discourse and non-verbal domains".

Illustrating this approach, Spencer-Oatey and Xing (2008) analysed a 10-day visit to a British engineering company by a group of six Chinese business people representing an organization who had negotiated a contract with the British firm. The meetings were video-recorded and the participants were subsequently interviewed to gain their perceptions and interpretations of the meetings. This triangulation of the data provided invaluable information concerning the different ways in which the "same" behaviours were interpreted by each group. The analysis focused on reasons why both the British hosts and the Chinese delegates were unhappy at the end of the visit.

Spencer-Oatey and Xing identify a range of factors which contributed to the Chinese delegates feeling that their face needs were inadequately attended to. They considered, for example, that the seating arrangements for the meetings conveyed a message which indicated lack of respect for their social identities and status. Similarly, the amount of time allocated to the welcome event and to different speakers, in particular, was considered inadequate, and thus disrespectful. The British hosts, on the other hand, (mistakenly) felt that the Chinese would prefer to be treated informally, since there had been many previous delegations and "formalities have really eroded" over time according to the British chairman (2008, 263). They were irritated that the Chinese seemed so dissatisfied with their arrangements. RMT highlights the fact that different groups have different expectations concerning how their sociality rights should be recognized, and about what constitutes an adequate demonstration of respect for their social identities in a formal context.

Research Methods

As the discussion in the previous sections has implied, the data collection methods most favoured by those interested in intercultural communication at work involve audio and video recording of workplace interactions in context, usually enriched by interviews and ethnographic observations. The undoubted pioneers in this field were John Gumperz (1982) and Celia Roberts (Gumperz, Jupp, and Roberts 1979; Roberts, Davies, and Jupp 1992) and Michael Clyne (1994), who observed and recorded authentic interaction in the workplace, and followed up with interviews asking participants for their interpretations of specific interactions. Supplementing recorded interaction with preliminary ethnographic observation to establish workplace norms and subsequent interviews with participants is a valuable way of checking and warranting particular interpretations, and these methods are now used by many current researchers in the area of workplace discourse (see Marra 2008; Holmes, Marra, and Vine 2011 for further discussion). Observation can provide useful information on a range of relevant local patterns, including the norms for social talk, interactional behaviour at morning tea and lunchtimes, the prevalence of corridor talk, and so on. Interviews after recording are similarly invaluable in assisting interpretation. An interview with Cliff Whiting after the excerpt discussed in Example 27.2, for instance, validated the interpretation of his response to Ron Trotter's interruption as inappropriate and disruptive.

Interviews with Pākehā employees working in Māori "ethnicized" workplaces (Schnurr, Marra, and Holmes 2007) similarly illuminate their perceptions of particular intercultural interactions, and highlight the point that in the wider society, it is Pākehā norms that dominate and are taken for granted. Gretel, for example, a Pākehā manager working in a Māori company, pseudonymed Kiwi Productions, indicates through her discourse, both in interview and in interaction, that she is very aware of the omni-relevance of ethnicity in the company's business, and the implications of this for what constitutes appropriate and effective behaviour on her part in a range of situations. In interview, for example, she articulated her perceptions of her role as follows.

Example 27.3[4]

1	Gretel:	I think the two biggest things are er
2		knowing what you don't know
3		or at least having an inkling of what you don't know
4		I mean you never know everything you don't know
5		and knowing knowing when to sit down and shut up
6		actually knowing when your input
7		when your direct input is not appropriate is very helpful

This reflection is illuminating—and unusual. In the wider society, it is generally those from cultural backgrounds other than the majority Pākehā group who are expected to make adjustments, and learn to interact appropriately according to Pākehā norms. Similarly, Paula, another Pākehā member of Kiwi Productions, commented that she too had learned not to parade her knowledge in meetings, even when the discussion was in an area in which she was hired for her expertise. This is very different behaviour from that observed in meetings in Pākehā organizations where it is usual for people to offer, and indeed to be expected to offer, explicit comments based on their knowledge and expertise. Interview data can thus provide useful additional insights which assist in interpreting what is going on in intercultural interaction.

Analysing Intercultural Interaction At Work

As Koester (2010, 126) notes, a good deal of research on intercultural communication in the workplace tends to focus on problematic communication. This is understandable since such interaction is "marked" or noticeable, and moreover this is where researchers often feel they can make a contribution. As applied sociolinguists, our own work has sometimes adopted this approach, often with the goal of providing guidance to new immigrants to New Zealand (e.g., Holmes and Riddiford 2009; see also www.victoria.ac.nz/lwp/resources/). However, we have also consistently adopted an "appreciative enquiry" (Cooperrider, Whitney, and Stavros 2003) approach to workplace interaction. In this section, I draw on the research of the LWP team to briefly discuss three examples of effective intercultural workplace communication.

The first example involves a skilled migrant, Isaac, whose mentor, Leo was helping him acquire the interactional norms of the New Zealand workplace he had joined as an intern for six weeks. At the beginning of his internship Leo was very shy and did not join in the social talk which is so crucial to integration in New Zealand workplaces. Small talk is almost obligatory at the beginning and end of the day, and in many workplaces the morning tea break and lunch time provide additional regular sites for social exchanges (Holmes 2000). In Example 27.4, Leo is encouraging Isaac to participate.

Example 27.4

1	Leo:	try and integrate yourself more with everyone . . .
2		but also the learning is to sit with people at lunch time
3		and learn the language and listen to the jokes
4		and then and participate

Leo is encouraging Isaac to join in more with social interaction in the workplace and he gives examples of how Isaac can do this: he should sit at lunch with his workmates (line 2) and *listen to the jokes . . . and participate* (lines 3–4). Isaac is a keen learner and by the end of his internship he demonstrates that he has learned the social norms of this particular workplace when he offers to bring cake for his farewell morning tea, a well-established custom in many New Zealand white collar workplaces.

Example 27.5

1	Isaac:	tomorrow I will bring a cake a cake at morning tea time
2		and I would like to share it with all the colleague
3	Leo:	that's very nice we'll look forward to eating it
4	Isaac:	[laughs] okay thank you
		[*When Isaac brings the cake Leo jokes that he can't use chopsticks on it*]
5	Leo:	that's part of Isaac's training
		[*Teasing him about earlier having trouble using a fork instead of chopsticks*]

Leo here confirms that Isaac has learned the local ways of doing things, but he also teases him about his earlier preference for chopsticks, indicating humorously that both sides have learned something about the other's culture in the period of Isaac's internship. The evident good humour developed in the relationship is testimony to successful intercultural interaction. But it is worth noting that the measure of success is Isaac's acquisition of New Zealand workplace norms. The power relationship means that it is the migrant who must accommodate, not the New Zealanders. Accommodation to Isaac's cultural norms seems never to be considered (see Holmes 2015 for further discussion of this issue).

In another New Zealand workplace, Ava, the skilled migrant, is a Chinese accountant who has very valuable experience which has led to her placement with a particular company. Her mentor is Chris and in Example 27.6 he listens to Ava's rather direct criticism of the organization's accounting system.

Example 27.6

1	Ava:	if er if they're overdue that mean um
2		firstly that mean probably user don't want to use it
3		and not update correctly and er timely
4		and another reason if the this other system is not er
5		the interface is not quite er friendly
6	Chris:	mm
7	Ava:	and er also some function a functionality
8		cannot meet the users' requirement
9		so they think always it's a waste of time waste my time
10		or probably they will think they don't want to use it . . .
11	Chris:	yeah no this looks excellent
12		and um I mean y- you- you do raise
13		some um very valid valid points there

It is noticeable that Ava is very direct, a style of interaction we identified as typical among Chinese professionals interacting at work, and she makes a number of very critical remarks about the inadequacies of the system (lines 2, 5, 7–10). Chris's response is affirming and appreciative and equally direct (lines 11–13), positively responding to Ava's interactional style in this professional context. There is no hint of defensiveness and he provides a high evaluation of her work. This is promising evidence of the willingness of some mentors to accept and respond positively to alternative interactional norms in workplace contexts.

The opening of meetings in New Zealand are also often sites of intercultural interaction, with Māori formalities often introduced in Pākehā workplaces where Māori people are employed. In one government workplace, Greg, a Māori manager, structured his team meetings with a formal opening section which included a Māori component. Greg used this as an opportunity to teach his team (who did not know much Māori language) the meaning of a *whakataukī* or Māori proverb each week. We have analysed many meetings in Māori workplaces (see e.g., Holmes and Marra 2011), and the standard meeting opening is a *karakia*, a prayer, or recitation in Māori by the meeting chair. As described in Holmes and Vine (forthcoming), Greg chose to use something slightly different in this case, designating another staff member, Marama, to read the proverb, and then discussing its meaning with the team members. The *whakataukī* served not just as a formal means of opening the meeting, but also as a way of promoting thinking about Māori values. Greg used the opportunity provided by the opening of the meeting to extend his team members' understanding of Māori language and Māori cultural values, providing another example of the creative negotiation of intercultural norms in a specific workplace context.

Future Directions

It is clear from the number of edited collections and monographs, as well as journal articles which have appeared in the last decade that intercultural communication in workplace discourse is a steadily growing research area. New theoretical approaches are regularly emerging and more reliable methodologies are progressively developing.

Current research focuses on the dynamic negotiation of meaning in interaction and successful and effective communication is increasingly attracting as much attention as miscommunication and misunderstanding (cf. Stadler 2011). Effective methodologies are also expanding to include more multimodal analysis with insights regarding the ways in which such features as gaze, gesture and facial expression can facilitate (or hinder) intercultural understandings (e.g., Jewitt 2009; Kuśmierczyk 2011, 2013).

Finally, research on the perspective of minority group members is an area which is in need of more attention in the study of intercultural workplace interaction. The taken-for-granted status of majority norms and the accompanying assumptions and presuppositions often result in a very skewed perception of intercultural interaction. When minority group norms are privileged, majority group members gain new insights into alternative ways of doing things. There is abundant scope for turning the tables in intercultural interaction and for majority group members to designate themselves as the learners, familiarizing themselves with the norms of the "other" culture, rather than always expecting the accommodation to be in their direction.

Further Reading

On theory see Scollon, Scollon, and Jones (2012) and Ting-Toomey and Chung (2014). On methodology and analysis see Clyne (1994), Holmes, Marra, and Vine (2011) and Roberts, Davies, and Jupp (1992).

Related Topics

Interactional sociolinguistics; Linguistic ethnography; (Im)politeness theory; Rapport management; Miscommunication; Multilingualism; Language preparation; Language learning on-the-job

Transcription Conventions

[laughs]	Paralinguistic features in square brackets
(0.2)	Timed Pause
...//......\...	Simultaneous speech
.../.......\\...	

=	Latching, i.e., where there is not even the smallest pause between utterances
(hello)	Transcriber's best guess at an unclear utterance
( )	Unintelligible word or utterance
?	Rising intonation but not necessarily a question; i.e., a high rising terminal (HRT)
[comment]	Editorial comments italicized in square brackets
<u>yes</u>	Stressed syllable

All names used in the examples are pseudonyms.

Acknowledgements

I would like to express my appreciation to other members of the Language in the Workplace team for ongoing support for the research described in this paper, and especially Keely Kidner who provided excellent assistance with a literature survey. I also appreciate the helpful suggestions from the reviewer and the editor.

Notes

1. Pākehā is the New Zealand term for people of European (mainly British) origins. Pākehā are the majority group (about 70%) in the New Zealand population.
2. This example is discussed in more detail in Vine *et al.* (2009). See transcription conventions.
3. *tangata whenua* refers to the indigenous Māori people.
4. This example is taken from Holmes, Marra, and Vine (2011, chap. 8), where these issues are discussed in more detail.

References

Arundale, Robert B. 2006. "Face as Relational and Interactional: A Communication Framework for Research on Face, Facework, and Politeness." *Journal of Politeness Research* 2: 193–217.
Bardhan, Nilanjana, and Mark P. Orbe, Eds. 2012. *Identity Research and Communication: Intercultural Reflections and Future Directions*. Lanham, MD: Lexington Books.
Bargiela-Chiappini, Francesca, and Catherine Nickerson. 2003. "Intercultural Business Communication: A Rich Field of Studies." *Journal of Intercultural Studies* 24: 3–16.
Baxter, Judith. 2010. *The Language of Female Leadership*. Basingstoke, UK: Palgrave Macmillan.
Belich, James. 2014. "European Ideas about Māori—Modern Racial Stereotypes." *Te Ara—The Encyclopedia of New Zealand*. www.TeAra.govt.nz/en/european-ideas-about-maori/page-6.
Blommaert, Jan. 2005. *Discourse: A Critical Introduction*. Cambridge: Cambridge University Press.
Bolden, Galina B. 2012. "Across Languages and Cultures: Brokering Problems of Understanding in Conversational Repair." *Language in Society* 41: 97–121.
Brown, Penelope, and Stephen C. Levinson. 1987. *Politeness*. Cambridge: Cambridge University Press.
Candlin, Christopher N., and Maurizio Gotti, Eds. 2004. *Intercultural Aspects of Specialized Communication*. Bern: Peter Lang.
Clyne, Michael. 1994. *Intercultural Communication at Work*. Cambridge: Cambridge University Press.
Cook-Gumperz, Jenny. 2001. "Cooperation, Collaboration and Pleasure in Work." In *Culture in Communication: Analyses of Intercultural Situations*, edited by Aldo di Luzio, Suzanne Gunthner, and Franca Orletti, 117–139. Amsterdam: John Benjamins.
Cooperrider, David L., Diana Whitney, and Jacqueline M. Stavros. 2003. *Appreciative Inquiry Handbook*. Bedford Heights, OH: Lakeshore Communications.
Geluykens, Ronald, and Bettina Kraft. 2008. *Institutional Discourse in Cross-Cultural Contexts*. Muenchen: Lincom Europa.
Geyer, Naomi. 2008. *Discourse and Politeness: Ambivalent Face in Japanese*. London: Continuum.

Gudykunst, William B. 2002. "Issues in Cross-Cultural Communication Research." In *Handbook of International and Intercultural Communication*. 2nd ed., edited by William B. Gudykunst, and Bella Mody, 165–179. Thousand Oaks, CA: Sage.

Gumperz, John J. 1982. *Discourse Strategies*. Cambridge: Cambridge University Press.

Gumperz, John. J., Thomas Cyprian Jupp, and Celia Roberts. 1979. *Crosstalk*. London: National Centre for Industriual Language Training.

Hartog, Jennifer. 2006. "Beyond 'Misunderstandings' and 'Cultural Stereotypes': Analysing Intercultural Communication." In *Beyond Misunderstanding: Linguistic Analyses of Intercultural Communication*, edited by Kristin Bührig, and Jan D. ten Thije, 175–188. Amsterdam: John Benjamins.

Holliday, Adrian. 2011. *Intercultural Communication and Ideology*. London: Sage.

Holmes, Janet. 2000. "Doing Collegiality and Keeping Control at Work: Small Talk in Government Departments." In *Small Talk*, edited by Justine Coupland, 32–61. London: Longman.

Holmes, Janet. 2014. "Language and Gender in the Workplace." In *Handbook of Language, Gender and Sexuality*. 2nd ed., edited by Susan Ehrlich, Miriam Meyerhoff, and Janet Holmes, 433–451. New York: John Wiley & Sons.

Holmes, Janet. 2015. "Joining a New Community of Workplace Practice: Inferring Attitudes from Discourse." In *Intersections: Applied Linguistics as a Meeting Place*, edited by Elke Stracke, 2–21. Newcastle-upon-Tyne: Cambridge Scholars.

Holmes, Janet, and Jen Hay. 1997. "Humour as an Ethnic Boundary Marker in New Zealand Interaction." *Journal of Intercultural Studies* 18: 127–151.

Holmes, Janet, and Meredith Marra. 2011. "Relativity Rules: Polite Talk in Ethnicised Workplaces." In *Situated Politeness*, edited by Bethan L. Davies, Michael Haugh, and Andrew John Merrison, 27–52. London: Continuum.

Holmes, Janet, Meredith Marra, and Bernadette Vine. 2011. *Leadership, Discourse and Ethnicity*. Oxford: Oxford University Press.

Holmes, Janet, and Nicky Riddiford. 2009. "Talk at Work: Interactional Challenges for Immigrants." In *Language for Professional Communication: Research, Practice and Training*, edited by Vijay K. Bahtia, Winnie Cheng, Bertha Du-Babcock, and Jane Lung, 217–234. Hong Kong: The Hong Kong Polytechnic University.

Holmes, Janet, and Nicky Riddiford. 2010. "Professional and Personal Identity at Work: Achieving a Synthesis through Intercultural Workplace Talk." *Journal of Intercultural Communication* 22. www.immi.se/intercultural/.

Holmes, Janet, and Stephanie Schnurr. 2005. "Politeness, Humour and Gender in the Workplace: Negotiating Norms and Identifying Contestation." *Journal of Politeness Research* 1: 121–149.

Holmes, Janet, and Bernadette Vine. Forthcoming. "'That's Just How We Do Things Round Here': Researching Workplace Discourse for the Benefit of Employees." In *Crossing Boundaries: Interdisciplinarity in Language Studies*, edited by Vander Viana. Amsterdam: John Benjamins.

Hua, Zhu. 2014. *Exploring Intercultural Communication: Language in Action*. London: Routledge.

Jewitt, Carey, Ed. 2009. *Routledge Handbook of Multimodal Analysis*. London: Routledge.

Kecskes, Istvan. 2014. *Intercultural Pragmatics*. Oxford: Oxford University Press.

Koester, Almut. 2010. *Workplace Discourse*. London: Continuum.

Kuśmierczyk, Ewa. 2011. "English-Background and Non-English Background Speakers' Perceptions of Gaze and Bodily Movements in Academic Interactions." *University of Sydney Papers in TESOL* 6: 71–96.

Kuśmierczyk, Ewa. 2013. *"The Only Problem is Finding a Job"—Multimodal Analysis of Job Interviews in New Zealand*. PhD diss., Victoria University of Wellington.

Leech, Geoffrey. 1983. *Principles of Pragmatics*. London: Longman.

Liebscher, Grit. 2006. "Perspectives in Conflict: An Analysis of German-German Conversations." In *Beyond Misunderstanding: Linguistic Analyses of Intercultural Communication*, edited by Kristin Bührig, and Jan D. ten Thije, 155–174. Amsterdam: John Benjamins.

Liddicoat, Anthony J. 2009. "Communication as Culturally Contexted Practice: A View from Intercultural Communication." *Australian Journal of Linguistics* 29: 115.

Locher, Miriam A., and Richard J. Watts. 2005. "Politeness Theory and Relational Work." *Journal of Politeness Research* 1: 9–33.

Marra, Meredith. 2008. "Recording and Analyzing Talk across Cultures." In *Culturally Speaking: Culture, Communication and Politeness Theory*, edited by Helen Spencer-Oatey, 304–321. London: Continuum.

Marra, Meredith, and Janet Holmes. 2007. "Humour across Cultures: Joking in the Multicultural Workplace." In *Handbook of Intercultural Communication*, edited by Helga Kotthoff, and Helen Spencer-Oatey, 153–172. Berlin: Mouton de Gruyter.
Mills, Sara. 2003. *Gender and Politeness*. Cambridge: Cambridge University Press.
Piller, Ingrid. 2007. "Linguistics and Intercultural Communication." *Language and Linguistics Compass* 1: 208–226.
Piller, Ingrid. 2011. *Intercultural Communication: A Critical Introduction*. Edinburgh: Edinburgh University Press.
Piller, Ingrid. 2012. "Intercultural Communication: An Overview." In *Handbook of Intercultural Discourse and Communication*, edited by Christina Bratt Paulston, Scott F. Kiesling, and Elizabeth S. Rangel, 3–18. Oxford: Blackwell.
Roberts, Celia, Evelyn Davies, and Thomas Cyprian Jupp. 1992. *Language and Discrimination: A Study of Communication in Multiethnic Workplaces*. London: Longman.
Scollon, Ron, and Suzanne Wong Scollon. 2001. "Discourse and Intercultural Communication." In *The Handbook of Discourse Analysis*, edited by Deborah Schiffrin, Deborah Tannen, and Heidi E. Hamilton, 538–547. Oxford: Blackwell.
Scollon, Ron, Suzanne Wong Scollon, and Rodney H. Jones. 2012. *Intercultural Communication: A Discourse Approach*. 3rd ed. Chichester, UK: John Wiley & Sons.
Schnurr, Stephanie, Meredith Marra, and Janet Holmes. 2007. "Being (Im)polite in New Zealand Workplaces: Māori and Pākehā Leaders." *Journal of Pragmatics* 39: 712–729.
Sharifian, Farzad, and Maryam Jamarani, Eds. 2013. *Language and Intercultural Communication in the New Era*. New York: Routledge.
Spencer-Oatey, Helen. 2000. "Introduction: Language, Culture and Rapport Management." In *Culturally Speaking: Managing Rapport through Talk across Cultures*, edited by Helen Spencer-Oatey, 1–10. London: Continuum.
Spencer-Oatey, Helen. 2008. "Face, (Im)politeness and Rapport." In *Culturally Speaking: Culture, Communication and Politeness Theory*, edited by Helen Spencer-Oatey, 11–47. London: Continuum.
Spencer-Oatey, Helen, and Peter Franklin. 2009. *Intercultural Interaction*. Basingstoke, UK: Palgrave Macmillan.
Spencer-Oatey, Helen, and Jianyu Xing. 2003. "Managing Rapport in Intercultural Business Interactions: A Comparison of Two Chinese-British Welcome Meetings." *Journal of Intercultural Studies* 24: 33–46.
Spencer-Oatey, Helen, and Jianyu Xing. 2008. "Issues of Face in a Chinese Business Visit to Britain." In *Culturally Speaking: Culture, Communication and Politeness Theory*, edited by Helen Spencer-Oatey, 258–273. London: Continuum.
Stadler, Stefanie. 2011. "Intercultural Communication and East Asian Politeness." In *Politeness in East Asia*, edited by Sarah Mills, and Dániel Kádár, 98–124. Cambridge: Cambridge University Press.
Sunaoshi, Yukako. 2005. "Historical Context and Intercultural Communication: Interactions between Japanese and American Factory Workers in the American South." *Language in Society* 34: 185–218.
Ting-Toomey, Stella, and Leeva C. Chung. 2014. *Understanding Intercultural Communication*. 2nd ed. New York: Oxford University Press.
Ting-Toomey, Stella, and John G. Oetzel. 2001. *Managing Intercultural Conflict Effectively*. London: Sage.
Tranekjær, Louise. 2015. *Interactional Categorization and Gatekeeping: Institutional Encounters with Otherness*. Bristol, UK: Multilingual Matters.
Vine, Bernadette, Susan Kell, Meredith Marra, and Janet Holmes. 2009. "Boundary Marking Humour: Institutional Gender and Ethnic Demarcation." In *Humor in Interaction*, edited by Neal R. Norrick, and Delia Chiaro, 125–141. Amsterdam: John Benjamins.

28
Identity in the Workplace in a Context of Increasing Multilingualism

Georges Lüdi

Introduction

Human societies have always been multilingual despite the raising of monolingual ideologies fostered by the world-wide processes of nation-building and the elaboration of national languages. However, the growing mobility of the world's population has led to a further interpenetration of language communities drawing on what Vertovec (2007) calls "super-diversity" in plural post-modern societies. This entails multiple forms of individual plurilingualism and social multilingualism.[1]

Companies operating across language borders are responding to this challenge by adopting a "corporate (linguistic) identity", i.e., by choosing various language regimes (Vandermeeren 1998). Some of these correspond to monolingual modes of communication (standardization by imposing the language of their home country or a "neutral" language like English as a corporate language) and some to multilingual modes (in particular, institutional multilingualism and what Lavric [2007] calls "mixed strategies").

But linguistic identity is also and mainly an attribute of individuals. Some say: "Let me hear how you speak, and I'll tell you who you are." However, the maxim should better read: "Let me hear how you speak, and I'll tell you who you want to be." Indeed, speakers have a certain freedom in their choice of a language/variety which is always also an "act of identity" (Le Page and Tabouret-Keller 1985) expressing a desired affiliation to a linguistic group.

In a context of increasing labour mobility and linguistic diversity, the relationship between language and identity can be observed in individual language choices in linguistically mixed meetings and teams that contribute substantially to processes of employees' identity construction. This raises the question, among others, of the divisibility of social identities and the possibility of a plurilingual identity. However, language choices are partly determined by regulations in the form of language regimes set by the company's management based on a monolingual or multilingual corporate identity to which employees are urged to accommodate.

In fact, employees cope with linguistic diversity by developing plurilingual repertoires and by inventing a range of techniques to maintain communication. Myriad forms of monolingual and plurilingual speech transpose language regimes set up by the management, or differ from and contrast with them, in external communication with stakeholders and internal communication between employees. Tensions appear at a number of levels: between the language prevalent in the local context (e.g., German in Basel) and the corporate language decided upon by the management (e.g., English in a global pharmaceutical company headquartered in Basel); between different strata of language management (e.g., by managers at the headquarters and at the French branch of a Japan based producer of cars); between a monolingual language regime and plurilingual practices in everyday work; and between what people say ("our corporate language is English") and what they do (e.g., by using a hybrid *lingua franca* deeply influenced by other languages). At both the macro- and the micro-level, all these phenomena are intrinsically linked to the exercise of power (in the sense of "power of language" as well as in the sense of "language of power") and to identity-laden processes.

This chapter will explore linguistic identity and power in the framework of multilingualism by drawing on empirical research conducted by a team from the University of Basel as part of the large-scale DYLAN-project from the European Union's Sixth Framework Programme (see Berthoud, Grin, and Lüdi 2013 for detail). This project's approach to the question of linguistic identity and power in the workplace was basically ethnographic, but also multimethodological. Semi-directed interviews[2] and official documents were analysed, along with actual language use at work.

Language Choice and Power

Within companies operating in a context of multilingualism the use of particular languages is not neutral but linked in various ways to the exercise of power. As stated by Fairclough ([1989] 2001), language is a tool in the creation and recreation of power. In the tradition of critical discourse analysis, he sees language as a social practice and focuses on the way in which sociopolitical domination is reproduced by means of texts and discourses. With regard to institutional structures, we might thus look at such phenomena as access to information depending on the language used, freedom of language choice or, on the contrary, the imposition of languages by management for certain forms of communication (e.g., for writing reports). These phenomena enhance or reduce the status of a language and thus the power of its speakers. With regard to language practice, we might focus on particular features that are indicators of inclusion or exclusion and therefore, the exercise of power in face-to-face interaction. These features include turn-taking behaviour, length of turns, interruption and correction, and code-switching.

In multilingual workplaces, a key dimension of this power play is the choice of language either as it is imposed by the company or negotiated in interaction. "Power is neither given, nor exchanged, nor recovered, but rather exercised, and . . . it only exists in action" (Foucault 1980, 89). Following Foucault, we adopt a conception of power as consisting of a force which certain groups or individuals exert on others in situations in which various forms of action or reaction are possible. Holding or constructing a position of power primarily means being able to choose (or impose) one variety, out of all those that make up the individuals' social repertoires, that is deemed "legitimate" at a given moment and in terms of a mutually acknowledged value system. This may be the majority language in a society, or a language that is acknowledged to have more prestige, such as the company's corporate language. Thereby, the superiority of one language over another is not based on linguistic arguments, but on a set of beliefs about the legitimacy of authorised speakers (Bourdieu and Thompson, 2001). This can lead both to the enhancement and reduction of the status of languages. At the headquarters of a Swiss national company, for example, the choice of German enhances the status of Switzerland's majority language and hence reduces the status of the other national languages.

In contrast, the status of English is enhanced in some companies, and the status of other languages, including the national one, is reduced. This is based on wide-spread social representations: English is valued as "a symbol of modernity . . . [and] of the company's success, evidence of its dynamism and its ability to anticipate change" (Bothorel-Witz and Tsamadou-Jacoberger 2009, 53).

The enhancement and the reduction of the status of languages occurs frequently. From a macro perspective, the reduction of status can be due to employment or promotion policies (people who do not speak language X are not employed or promoted), or management measures adopted by the institution, e.g., the abovementioned "standardization", i.e., the imposition of one single language throughout a company. Institutions may, on the contrary, allow employees to choose the language in which they wish to communicate, and thus seek alternatives to a culture of domination by reducing or even eliminating discrimination in the interest of fairness in the framework of a philosophy of inclusion. Inclusion and exclusion may or may not be perceived as such by the people involved, but are measurable from outside (for instance in statistics on the representation of linguistic minorities in certain national companies in Switzerland in general and on their executive boards in particular). From a micro perspective, one observes ways of interaction that belong to a "culture of domination" or, in contrast, sets of strategies to prevent discrimination or remedy it during interaction (Mondada and Nussbaum 2012). A "reduction of status" occurs not only when an institution decides not to use certain languages spoken by its employees (e.g., the local national language), but also whenever a speaker's language is denigrated (e.g., by laughter or disparaging comments). In contrast, "enhancement of status" is evident when the value attached to a language is raised by measures that impose it on employees as well as by speakers' comments justifying its use.

These phenomena can be illustrated by data from a Swiss department store, Example 28.1. This excerpt comes from a meeting of HR representatives from all language regions at the headquarters of the department store. The company's language philosophy is clearly inclusive: the rule "everyone speaks his or her own language" explicitly includes all three major national languages. Most of the participants in the meeting are German-speaking, a small minority are French-speaking, and there are also a few Italian-speakers (who refrain from using their own language despite the fact that they could). All participants can speak all three languages. The various presenters display different communication strategies. The comments and reactions of the minority indicates that some strategies are perceived as more exclusive (e.g., monolingual German presentation), and some as more inclusive (e.g., documentation in two languages, bilingual presentation, multimodality, interpretation, repair strategies, negotiation sequences on the choice of languages). Thus, after a long period of monolingual presentations in German, the dominant role of the majority language is challenged by a kind of subversive act by one of the participants.[3]

In order to (re)negotiate the language, FC symbolically switches to French, the reduced-status language. He deliberately employs a strategy that includes MG, a French-speaking participant, but stigmatises him at the same time (see the references to him falling asleep in lines 3 and 7 and the laughter this causes). Yet the German-speaking majority do not agree to a change of language and the presenter (FG) postpones the use of French to the next presentation. The general laughter seems to indicate that the decision to stick to German and reduce the status of French once more is validated, despite MG's disillusioned reaction (line 13). Choosing the other language would in turn have meant an additional effort for the presenter and the majority.

The use of the terms "enhancement of status" and "reduction of status" does not mean that individuals do not have choices. In fact, there is room to manoeuvre here, i.e., for individuals'

Example 28.1[4]

1	FC:	also (..) wobei (ich) wir müssen jetzt aufpassen dass
		((German)) so (..) i mean (i) we must make sure
2		wir nicht (hier) die ganze zeit auf deutsch sprechen
		not to talk in german (here) the whole time
3		weil sonst (.) schlaft (MG) ein und=
		or else (.) (MG) will fall asleep and=
4	RS:	=ja ist schade ja
		=yes that's a pity yes
5		((laughter and murmuring))
		((. . .))
6	FC:	quand même un petit peu en français peut-être sinon tu
		((French)) perhaps a little bit of French after all otherwise
7		vas t'endormir (.) hein? (4) ehm ist es ok wenn wir
		you'll fall asleep (.) won't you (4) ((German)) er is it ok if we
8		auf französisch weitermachen? (1) also nicht weil
		carry on in french? (1) well not because
9		jetzt ehm [(xxx)]
		now er [(xxx)]
10	FG:	[wenn wir zum]
		[when we]
11		nächsten thema kommen gerne!
		move to the next topic gladly!
12		((general laughter)) (3)
13	MG:	c'est un peu tard (h) (2)
		((French)) it's a bit late (h) (2)
14	FC?:	also machen wir auf deutsch fertig
		((German)) so let's finish off in german

freedom to cope with the practical problems they face in specific instances. As Gaibrois (2015, 54) notes "individuals in power relations (as opposed to repression or dominance) are seen as 'free' in the sense that they are confronted with a field of possibilities from which to act—this might include resistance, but also other, more creative forms of action."

In an ideal world, all those taking part in a meeting are automatically legitimate, ratified listeners. Yet this is frequently not the case. If not all participants understand a particular language, choosing that language "has the effect of excluding part of the audience and making it an overhearing audience" (Mondada 2001, 41). This helps to explain two specific situations:

(a) when the language changes when the constellation of people attending a meeting changes (someone arrives or leaves who does not understand a language);
(b) when a person who is physically present but does not speak the chosen language is excluded, gets "overhearer" status, but can be reincorporated (with the status of a ratified, designated listener), involving a change of participatory mode, for example by means of participant-related code-switching.

It may be concluded from all this that being plurilingual in a set of relevant languages at a given moment means having some freedom of choice and being in a position of power, while someone who does not speak the language chosen for a communication event is excluded and powerless. The very frequent occurrence of asymmetrically plurilingual speakers having to use a non-preferred language or one they do not know well is particularly interesting. Given the closer attention and increased cognitive processing effort required, they may feel ill at ease, discriminated against or excluded. In contrast, speakers may also choose strategies that tend to reduce discrimination, i.e., to reincorporate people who are actually or potentially excluded. As we will see later on, one form of potentially inclusive behaviour between people with asymmetrical skills consists of avoiding to choose between variety A or variety B, i.e., in using plurilingual speech in a plurilingual mode (Lüdi and Py 2009, 2013).

Let us add that the hierarchical position of the participants within the institution or a specific activity is important, but by no means decisive. Sometimes, a superior imposes a language on speakers of other languages, who may or may not resist this. For example, in the meeting of the editorial board of the internal magazine of Pharma A, the entrance of the superior, who does not speak German, entails an immediate switch by all the other members from German to English. Other settings are far less clearly determined by hierarchical relationships, however, and involve accommodation in all directions, including by superiors towards their subordinates. In Laboratory B, for example, we see that Jamal, who has very limited skills in German, encourages his subordinates to use this language. As stated by Schmitt (2002, 113 ff.), formal hierarchies may be of relevance in structuring action, but this must be actively realized by the participants, who again have some room for manoeuvring. In Goffmanian terms, the people in charge of a meeting play a key role in organizing participatory modes, but the way in which a meeting unfolds, including the choice of languages, is ultimately the result of collaboration between all the participants (see Goffman 1981; Gordon and Kraut this volume). Indeed, the ethnography of communication enables us to identify a whole fabric of relationships between the communicative surface and the respective institutional framework. The context in which an interaction takes place is a shifting one; it is not given *a priori*, but is configured by the way in which actors organise interactions and focus on this or that aspect of the situation that has thus been made relevant (Mondada 2001).

The kind of "subversive" promotion of local languages in contrast to standardized corporate languages draws not only on matters of power, but seeks also to avoid side effects of a monolingual language policy and ideology, including a possible lack of creativity, loss of information and the appearance of fractures between science and society (Berthoud, Grin, and Lüdi 2013). A sense of well-being and feeling secure is created by using one's own language, as noted by an HR manager at Agro A who said "I speak differently in my own language, more freely, more openly, with more self-confidence and more security." This is the point where considerations concerning power give way to questions of identity.

Language Practices and the Construction of Identity

Among other dimensions of an economic and communicative nature, aspects of power and of identity are interconnected when it comes to deciding language management measures and language choice in the world of work. First, "identity" serves to create stability where everything seems to be in a constant state of flux. Acknowledging that every individual is changing more or less basically with time, the concept serves to grasp the successive manifestations of the same individual as an actor in different places, times and social roles.

However, "identity" not only serves to single out somebody as an invididual, but also to assign him to a category of linguistic, ethnic or social order. This happens on the basis of a set of patterns which characterise the respective category, either directly or indirectly (Marra and Angouri 2011). According to Giles, Scherer, and Taylor (1979) linguistic variables such as certain varieties, words, expressions, style, form one of the most important clues to the identity of a speaker. Jamal, a Moroccan ex-pat based in Basel, for example, is a Moroccan, male, a scientist, part of middle management, and plurilingual, and these aspects of his identity are all evident in his interactions.

If certain linguistic variables point to identity components such as age, gender and social origin that are not subject to the control of the individual, others "assume salience . . . in marking our beliefs about and attitudes towards . . . social categories" (Giles, Scherer, and Taylor 1979, 344). Therefore, one can distinguish between involuntarily manifested identity and claimed identity, for instance through language choice. In a non-essentialist sense, identity is (as are power relations) constructed in interaction. Thus, in German-speaking Switzerland choosing Swiss German is often perceived to be an explicit claim for "Swissness". The *Basel Dialect Association* claims that "the dialect form is the special regional mode of expression— a cultural inheritance, an anchor of the identity" (www.igdialekt.ch/Dialekt.htm, accessed 08.07.2016).

We find a trace of such an attitude in an interview with Tobias, a senior manager at Pharma A, who regrets the dominance of English in his company.

Example 28.2

Tobias: in <Pharma A, International> the national or the languages linked to the [sc. local] market- ehm ehm are completely turned off so in <International> everybody speaks only English ehm and practically well I say if I can chair a meeting in German there is almost need for a ceremony isn't it because this is wonderful (.) and a meeting in Swiss German dialect once a month at the outmost

---

More generally, different observable discursive phenomena may be read as identity markers. Tobias marks his identity, for example, at the level of content in what he says about English, German and Swiss German. Phenomena of a formal nature such as plurilingual speech play a similar role. As mentioned earlier, Le Page and Tabouret-Keller (1985) introduced the concept of "act of identity". They understand linguistic behavior as a chain of acts with which the interlocutors exploit the amount of freedom they have and choose the (social) identity to which they aspire.

Language practices play a crucial role in articulating the different facets of a speaker's identity, but also in actively constructing it as speakers make choices in favour of some varieties over others. It has been suggested that consistent patterns of both conscious and unconscious language choices made by speakers at the micro-level may entail language management measures at a macro-level (Nekvapil and Sherman 2015). In the case of Tobias, we observe a correspondance between what he says is desirable and the language management measures he takes, Example 28.3.

> **Example 28.3**
>
> Tobias: it is kind of a struggle I have to go through <in my function [anonymized]>, so languages, the minimum we use is German, French, English; you have to say it again and again because those from the holding company pressure us for everything to be in English, but well I insist upon two national languages so it is always also in German and French, that is the way it is done

But the main way of manifesting identity does not always consist of choosing (or switching to) one language instead of another even if such choices are a very powerful tool for actively shaping identity. The alternative to one language is not necessarily another one, e.g., a local language, but choosing mixed ways of implementing the participants' plurilingual repertoires (Lüdi and Py 2013). This corresponds to what we observed at Laboratory B. Jamal, the head of the laboratory, draws on his own broad repertoire and creates a deeply plurilingual communicative culture at his workplace, Example 28.4.

> **Example 28.4**
>
> Jamal: in your daily work, you don't realize how you juggle with the languages. The aim is really to bring the message through and to be efficient. We have no time to waste. (. . .) She [Mara] needs to understand the message in the shortest time possible. It's useless to speak English and then I have to explain it again, to tell it again, to wait for somebody to translate, so I try to be a translator myself. So here, it is really to facilitate things, that is to make everyone feel at ease, everyone understands, everyone at the same level, and that is it, efficiency means in fact, immediately, when a meeting is finished, everyone already knows the message

The key words in his explanation are "shortest time possible", "facilitate", "feel at ease" and "efficiency"—precisely those notions frequently associated with the use of English. In a team meeting in his research laboratory, Jamal (his repertoire comprises Arabic, French, Dutch, English, and a bit of German), Mara, the Hungarian lab assistant mentioned above and three German-speaking laboratory assistants/technicians with a rather good command of English meet to present, discuss and correct an experience protocol. Because the protocol is written in German, and to make Marianne (ML) feel more comfortable, Jamal asks her to present it in German (Example 28.5, line 26).

In lines 32–33, Marianne hesitates about the right concept and ends up with the English "correction factor" in a strategy of code-mixing. English as the dominant scientific language of the company (and of science) weighs heavily on terminological choices even when another language is spoken. The English term in a German utterance is felt as being the right word, a choice that is confirmed by other members of the team.

> **Example 28.5**
>
> | | | |
> |---|---|---|
> | 22 | JH: | (. . .) so we start with this |
> | 23 | | protocol |
> | 24 | NS: | mmh |
> | 25 | JH: | if you have feedback (. . .) who wants maybe |
> | 26 | | marianne you can summarize in german ya what's |
> | 27 | | eh you did |
> | 28 | ML: | mmh |
> | 29 | JH: | and what you expect |
> | 30 | ML: | mmh (. . .) also wir haben jetzt das rpmi |
> | 31 | | protokoll (.) aufgemöbelt (.) aufdatiert (.) und |
> | 32 | | zwar haben wir diesen faktor (.) diesen |
> | 33 | | verdünnungs- eh fakt- correction factor noch |
> | 34 | | reingegeben= |
>
> *mmh so we now have pepped up updated this rpmi protocol, i.e., we have added this factor this dilution eh fact- correction factor*

Such examples of plurilingual speech are in no way restricted to encounters between people with limited language skills and/or subordinate roles at the workplace. Thus, Tobias (the senior manager quoted in Example 28.3), recalls the following experience:

> **Example 28.6**
>
> Tobias: . . . I had to run a meeting with (. . .) ten completely new people, so you bring them together and find a language, and er it's a mixture of Basel dialect, standard German and English, and if you like this was the Esperanto we worked out between us (. . .) our creative processes really got going and we discussed the whole thing in our Esperanto gibberish

Alert to his employees' needs and practices, Tobias is fully aware of the fact that on many occasions language use is hybrid. Some may reject any form of linguistic mixing on the basis of monolingual language ideologies where hybrid forms of speech usually occupy a very low position on a prestige scale. However, many accept this phenomenon as typical of plurilinguals' language behaviour, and emblematic of a plural identity (Gogolin and Lüdi 2015). This is clearly the case in the workplace settings we investigated.

The notion of "plural identities" and therefore the challenge to the existence of something like a unified, homogeneous linguistic identity, is in line with new views of "plurilingual repertoires" and their use. An important part of the DYLAN-project consisted of a fine-grained examination of numerous interactions in order to understand how the very diverse linguistic repertoires of speakers operating in increasingly multilingual environments develop and how actors make the best use of their repertoires and adapt them skilfully to different objectives and conditions (Berthoud, Grin, and Lüdi 2013). Our research confirmed the contrast between what Grosjean (1985) had called monolingual or plurilingual modes, but also the shift from "additive" to "integrated" views of individual plurilingualism: a set of skills in different languages, from perfect to very partial, is seen as an integrated whole which is more than the sum total of its parts. Such a "multicompetence" (Cook 2008) or "plurilingual repertoire" (Gumperz 1982; Moore and Castellotti 2008; Lüdi and Py 2009) represents a set of "resources" that are shared and jointly mobilized by speakers. Careful observation of speakers' plurilingual practices revealed finely tuned communicative strategies drawing on a wide range of different languages, including various forms of mixed speech[5] (Berthoud, Grin, and Lüdi 2013). In extreme exolingual-plurilingual settings such as a medical consultation between a Swiss doctor (M) and a Portuguese patient (P), the boundaries between the languages (Spanish, Italian, and Portuguese) may vanish (see Lüdi, Höchle Meier, and Yanaprasart 2016).

Example 28.7

11	P:	eh tengo mAle . a la cabeza?
		I have headache
12	M:	mmh
13	P:	eh duo-dolores y e (bri tisas)?
		and pain and ((incomprehensible word, maybe drawing on "vertigems"))
14	M:	mmh
15	P:	y me doile tambem moito la la spalda.
		and I feel also heavy pains in the the shoulder ((mixture of Portuguese, Spanish and Italian))
16	M:	la columna! due[le.]
		you feel pain in your back
17	P:	[la]columna me doi molto! y e: (..) e +<cui> un poco+
		I feel heavy pain in my back and a little here ((language mixing; touches her neck))

Having to find ways to manage the corresponding linguistic repertoires also has, of course, an identity dimension. In particular, forms of plurilingual speech are heavily identity-laden (see Auer 1998). In extreme cases, the conflict between the roles of different languages in a person's repertoire can be experienced as traumatizing as illustrated in a text by Birol Denizeri ("Das verlorene Gesicht", in *In zwei Sprachen leben*, DTV1983, 16–18).

Example 28.8

Then she [Saniye] started integrating. In the meantime, her German had become very good and she often asked herself whether one noticed that she was a foreigner. (. . .) Her nightmares became more and more frequent. She saw again and again hands that were tearing off her face (our translation from German)

But in most cases, a fluid, mixed or plural identity is experienced as an enrichment as in the case of Ural Tufan, a Swiss historian with Turkish roots. Ural calls himself a "best-of-program" with respect to all the dimensions of his composite identity, saying that "if identities are hats, there will soon be no more place on my hat rack" (Basler Zeitung 13.09.2006, 18 second@schweiz).

In practice, identity can be a matter of choice. Benjamin, for instance, section head at Public Service A, manages a meeting in a plurilingual mode very often using English in contradiction to the company's regime.

Example 28.9

1	BH:	Guet (.) also (.) tschuldigung wänn ich da s wort
		((Swiss German)) Right (.) well (.) sorry if i
2		ergri:fe =wenn ich das wort ergreife auf hochdeutsch
		spe:ak ((German)) =if i speak standard german
3		si je prends la parole en français I take the lead (.)
		((French)) if i speak french ((English))
4		in english (..)

The code-switching from Swiss German to standard German (lines 1–2) marks the official start of the meeting. He continues with two code-switches from German to French and from French to English, deploying his plurilingual repertoire. Benjamin is proud of his English skills and feels at ease speaking the language. Some of his utterances seem curious, however. Contrary to what he seems to believe, "I take the lead" is not a translation of *je prends la parole* (he could have said "I'll start (off) in English" or "I'll get the ball rolling in English"), but has a quite different meaning. In addition, the parallel syntactic construction "verb in present + noun phrase" resembles more a transfer from Swiss German or French respectively (in English the future would be compulsory) than an original English utterance (Kevin Cook, personal communication). Benjamin draws on various linguistic resources.

This example confirms the status of ELF (English as *lingua franca*) as "a multilingual mode". In other words, the use of a *lingua franca* does not differ categorically from other forms of plurilingual speech, but constitutes a borderline case (Berthoud, Grin, and Lüdi 2013). Obviously the identity value of English does not rely here on native speaker competency. As confirmed in interview, by choosing English Benjamin expresses a desire to enact leadership and to belong to a global English-speaking business community. This confers a new meaning on the notion of "corporate language" manifesting a "corporate identity".

Conclusion

Organizations must meet the manifold challenges of linguistic diversity for the purposes of internal and external communication, collaboration in mixed teams, and the transmission and construction of knowledge. Together with their stakeholders, they must find ways to manage plural linguistic repertoires, which include countries' official languages, migrant languages, and English. Languages' demo- and sociolinguistic importance influence language choice, along with dominating ideologies about a language's legitimacy. Language choices, be it at the macro-level of language management measures taken by a company or at the micro-level of communication strategies used by speakers during interaction, are strongly related to the exercise of power, but also to the construction and negotiation of personal and corporate identities (Pavlenko and Blackledge 2004). Tensions between the macro- and the micro-level, but also between different facets of plural identities, reveal that statements like "the language of (international) business is English" only cover a small part of the reality. In fact, international business is multilingual and many of its members are plurilingual and manifest plural and often overlapping identities. The resulting complex interrelationships between actual language practices, people's representations about plurilingualism, their declared choices, and the myriad contexts in which people are confronted with linguistic diversity demand more and more sophisticated, empirical methods of investigation. The DYLAN-project was a path-opener in this respect; a path which is already being followed and broadened by other researchers around the world, enriching our understanding of the complex nature of the way people enact plurilingual identities.

Further Reading

Berthoud, Grin, and Lüdi (2012) addresses the meanings and implications of multilingualism, as well as the use of plurilingual repertoires and the many challenges this poses to political institutions, universities, and private-sector companies. It examines at close range how these repertoires develop, and how actors skilfully adapt their use to different objectives and conditions.

A considerable number of recent publications have revealed the broad interest of scientific research in questions about multilingualism in the workplace. The 2014 *Multilingua* special issue on multilingualism at work, with an introduction by Angouri, represents an important landmark in this respect. A paper by Angouri and Miglbauer (2014) analyses the dynamic linguistic ecology of multinational workplaces in an approach quite similar to the one used in DYLAN. For a recent survey of research on multilingualism at work in European environments, Gunnarsson has an excellent state-of-the-art article in this special issue (Gunnarsson 2014).

Related Topics

Interactional sociolinguistics; Conversation analysis; Social constructionism; Communities of practice; Corporate settings; Blue-collar workplaces; Directives; Interpreting; Intercultural communication; Language learning on-the-job

Appendix

Transcription Conventions

For the transcription of the interviews, normal orthography has been maintained. For the transcription of interaction, the following transcription symbols have been used.

Speaker	A:
Overlapping sequences	[text] start and end of overlapping
Truncation, interruption	te-
Lengthened vowel	te:xt, te::xt
Non-verbal behaviour	((coughing))

Laughter	(h) or ((laughter))
Transcriber's comments	((comments))
Slower speech	<text>
Short pause	(.)
Medium pause	(..)
Long pause	(...)
Longer pause (duration)	(3.5)
Start and end of movement or gaze	+concernedsegment+
Unclear sound, guess; incomprehensible sound	(text), (XXX)
Continuity of sound production, latching	ma=me

Notes

1 Following the tradition of the Council of Europe, a distinction is made here between *multi*lingualism, i.e., the coexistence of different languages in the social and public sphere (institutional multilingualism and multilingual social repertoires), and *pluri*lingualism which focuses on the individuals' repertoire.
2 The interviews were conducted in the interviewee's preferred language (mostly German and Swiss German, some in French and English); the excerpts quoted have been translated into English.
3 He is a German Swiss HR manager who has worked for many years in Geneva.
4 All names of people and companies are pseudonyms. See Appendix for transcription conventions.
5 There are many terms for denominating a range of ways of simultaneously using different languages. Some authors talk about "plurilingual speech" (Auer 1984, 1999; Lüdi and Py 2009, 2013), others prefer "translanguaging" (García and Wei 2014), "multilanguaging" (Makoni and Makoni 2010) or "plurilanguaging" (Berthoud, Grin, and Lüdi 2013).

References

Angouri, Jo, and Marlene Miglbauer. 2014. "'And Then We Summarise in English for the Others': The Lived Experience of the Multilingual Workplace." *Multilingua* 33: 147–172.
Auer, Peter. 1984. *Bilingual Conversation*. Amsterdam: John Benjamins.
Auer, Peter, Ed. 1998. *Code-Switching in Conversation: Language, Interaction and Identity*. New York: Routledge.
Auer, Peter. 1999. "From Code-Switching via Language Mixing to Fused Lects. Toward a Dynamic Typology of Bilingual Speech." *International Journal of Bilingualism* 3: 309–332.
Berthoud, Anne-Claude, François Grin, and Georges Lüdi. 2012. *The DYLAN Project Booklet. Dylan Project, Main Findings*. www.dylan-project.org/Dylan_en/dissemination/final/booklet/booklet.php.
Berthoud, Anne-Claude, François Grin, and Georges Lüdi, Eds. 2013. *Exploring the Dynamics of Multilingualism. The DYLAN project*. Amsterdam: John Benjamins.
Bothorel-Witz, Arlette, and Irini Tsamadou-Jacobsberger. 2009. "Les processus de minoration et de majoration dans le discours sur les langues et les pratiques dans des entreprises à vocation internationale (implantées en Alsace)." In *Langues régionales, culture et développement. Etudes de cas en Alsace, en Bretagne et en Provence*, edited by Dominique Huck, and René Kahn, 43–91. Paris: L'Harmattan.
Bourdieu, Pierre, and John Thompson. 2001. *Langage et Pouvoir Symbolique*. Paris: Seuil.
Cook, Vivian. 2008. *Second Language Learning and Language Teaching*. London: Arnold.
Fairclough, Norman. (1989) 2001. *Language and Power*. London: Longman.
Foucault, Michel. 1980. *Power/Knowledge: Selected Interviews and Other Writings 1972–1977*, edited by Gordon Colin. New York: Pantheon.
Gaibrois, Claudine. 2015. *Power at Work: The Discursive Constructing of Power Relations in Multilingual Organizations*. Bamberg: Difo-Druck GmbH.
García, Ofelia, and Li Wei. 2014. *Translanguaging: Language, Bilingualism and Education*. Basingstoke, UK: Palgrave Macmillan.

Giles, Howard, Klaus Scherer, and Donald M. Taylor. 1979. "Speech Markers in Social Interaction." In *Social Markers in Speech*, edited by Klaus Scherer, and Howard Giles, 343–381. Cambridge: Cambridge University Press, and Paris: Éditions de la Maison des Sciences de l'Homme.

Goffman, Erving. 1981. *Forms of Talk*. Philadelphia, PA: University of Pennsylvania Press.

Gogolin, Ingrid, and Georges Lüdi. 2015. "Multilingualism: Multilingualism in Everyday Life. Mixing and Switching between Languages." *Sprache*. (www.goethe.de/en/spr/mag/20492250.html)

Grosjean, François. 1985. "The Bilingual as a Competent but Specific Speaker-Hearer." *Journal of Multilingual and Multicultural Development* 6: 467–477.

Gumperz, John. 1982. *Discourse Strategies*. Cambridge: Cambridge University Press.

Gunnarsson, Britt-Louise. 2014. "Multilingualism in European Workplaces." *Multilingua* 33: 11–33.

Lavric, Eva. 2007. "Code Choice and Face." *Lodz Papers in Pragmatics* 3: 23–35.

Le Page, Robert, and Andrée Tabouret-Keller. 1985. *Acts of Identity*. Cambridge: Cambridge University Press.

Lüdi, Georges, Katharina Höchle Meier, and Patchareerat Yanaprasart. Eds. 2016. *Managing Plurilingual and Intercultural Practices in the Workplace. The Case of Multilingual Switzerland*. Amsterdam: John Benjamins.

Lüdi, Georges, and Bernard Py. 2009. "To Be or Not to Be . . . a Plurilingual Speaker." *International Journal of Multilingualism* 6: 154–167.

Lüdi, Georges, and Bernard Py. 2013. *Etre bilingue*. 4e édition ajoutée d'une postface. Berne: Peter Lang.

Makoni, Sinfree, and Busi Makoni. 2010. "Multilingual Discourses on Wheels and Public English in Africa. A Case for 'vague linguistique'." In *Routledge Companion to English Language Studies*, edited by Janet Maybin, and Joan Swann, 258–270. London: Routledge.

Marra, Meredith, and Jo Angouri. 2011. "Investigating the Negotiation of Identity: A View from the Field of Workplace Discourse." In *Constructing Identities at Work*, edited by Jo Angouri and Meredith Marra, 1–16. Basingstoke, UK: Palgrave Macmillan.

Mondada, Lorenza. 2001. "Intervenir à distance dans une opération chirurgicale: l'organisation interactive d'espaces de participation." *Bulletin VALS-ASLA* 74: 33–56.

Mondada, Lorenza, and Luci Nussbaum, Eds. 2012. *Interactions cosmopolites. L'organisation de la participation plurilingue*. Limoges: Lambert Lucas.

Moore, Danièle and Véronique Castellotti, Eds. 2008. *La compétence plurilingue: Regards francophones*. Berne: Peter Lang.

Nekvapil, Jiří, and Tamah Sherman. 2015. "An Introduction: Language Management Theory in Language Policy and Planning." *IJSL* 232: 1–12.

Pavlenko, Aneta, and Adrian Blackledge, Eds. 2004. *Negotiation of Identities in Multilingual Settings*. Bristol, UK: Multilingual Matters.

Schmitt, Reinhold. 2002. "Hierarchie in Arbeitsgruppen als stilbildender Aspekt." In *Soziale Welten und Kommunikative Stile*, edited by Inken Keim, and Wilfried Schütte, 113–135. Tübingen: Narr.

Vandermeeren, Sonja. 1998. *Fremdsprachen in europäischen Unternehmen. Untersuchungen zu Bestand und Bedarf im Geschäftsalltag mit Empfehlungen für Sprachenpolitik und Sprachunterricht*. Waldsteinberg: Heidrun Popp.

Vertovec. Steven. 2007. "Super-Diversity and Its Implications." *Ethnic and Racial Studies* 30: 1024–1054.

29
Men's Talk in Women's Work
Doing Being a Nurse
Joanne McDowell

Introduction

The construction of the labour market has changed over time with more women, once assigned to the private world of the home, crossing into the public domain of business and commerce (Barrett 2004; Baxter 2010). Despite this, many occupations continue to be categorized as more suitable for one gender (Nilsson and Larsson 2005; Britton 2000), with women traditionally working in jobs that adhere to the feminine stereotypes of women as caring and nurturing and that focus on building supportive social relationships (Holmes 2006). Male dominated jobs by contrast are typically perceived as encapsulating normative masculine qualities such as assertiveness and competitiveness (Hendel, Fish, and Galon 2005; Trauth 2002; Williams 1995b). Society views people who step out of this gender construct into "non-traditional" lines of work, as deviant to the mainstream: they become demasculinized or defeminized. The dichotomy has also contributed to an androcentric view of gender, where male behaviour is the unmarked norm and women's behaviour has been devalued (see Mullany and Yoong's discussion of the Double Bind, this volume).

Describing a setting as mainly feminine or masculine, however, treats just one aspect of that workplace setting as an important influence on all activities within that setting (Sidnell 2003). In light of this, the match of a gendered profession to gendered behaviour has warranted further investigation. Accordingly, studies have examined women's experiences within what are considered traditionally male dominated occupations (e.g., engineering, police, military), and the barriers and challenges they face in performing a feminine identity in such occupational roles. Women were often reported to adopt masculine linguistic styles in order to adapt to their work environment and perform their work role in these contexts (Rhoton 2011; Powell, Bagilhole, and Dainty 2008; Priola 2004; Miller 2004; Thimm, Koch, and Schey 2003; McElhinny 1995). However, few scholars have focused on men who cross into traditionally female occupations, with the language used by men in such environments attracting even less exploration (Holmes 2006; Nilsson and Larrson 2005). This chapter examines the language of male and female nurses within nurse-nurse interactions. While previous studies have examined task-based talk during nurse-patient interaction (Holmes and Major 2003), talk *between* nurse colleagues has not received much attention. What happens when nurses are discussing work related issues, or moreover, making small talk?

Background and Critical Issues

Men Who Work In "Non-Traditional Jobs"

Many women's work activities are perceived to have lesser status, and therefore are less valued, than men's (Eckert and McConnell-Ginet 2003). Consequently, men who cross over into women's jobs are often considered abnormal, and constitute a challenge to the traditional ideas of appropriate gender behaviour (Williams 1995a, 1995b). A small number of researchers have explored what happens when men work in so-called "women's jobs", i.e., as librarians, primary school teachers, hairdressers, and nurses (Cross and Bagilhole 2006; Simpson 2004; Whittock and Leonard 2003; Brown, Nolan, and Crawford 2000). They have examined the implications of men's non-traditional career choices for the construction of their gender identity, and investigated how they manage possible gender identity conflict in such contexts. Often regarded as different from "real" men who confirm their masculine identity by doing so-called "men's" work, men in "women's" jobs are accused of failing to measure up to a "real man's" role. These men are stereotyped as wimpy, homosexual, and passive, especially those who work within a caring role such as nursing. As a result, these men frequently face several challenges to their masculine identity and in response have developed strategies to enhance and emphasise it (see e.g., Cross and Bagilhole 2006; Whittock and Leonard 2003; Evans 1997; Alvesson 1998; MacDougall 1997; Williams 1995b). This *doing* masculine gender is found to be much more explicit in female dominated work contexts than in traditional male occupational roles (Heikes 1991; Williams 1992, 1995a, 1995b).

Nursing: A "Feminine" Occupation?

A job is often classed as feminine or masculine when its staff composition consists of more than 70 per cent of a particular sex (see Huppatz and Goodwin 2013). Women in nursing currently make up more than 88 per cent of the staff population (UK Nursing and Midwifery Council 2015). Gendered workplaces are also often built on characteristics deemed necessary by the nature of the work role (Ku 2011). Sex role segregation is also visible *within* workplaces. Within nursing, for example, men tend to work within the more "masculine" areas such as on emergency wards or in psychiatric nursing, rather than in midwifery or elderly care (Brown, Nolan, and Crawford 2000; Bird 1996; Isaacs and Poole 1996). This is further illustrated by Berkery, Tiernan, and Morley's (2014) research which demonstrated that male nurses regard management positions as masculine, and therefore view them as positions suitable only for men.

However, defining nursing in terms of only feminine characteristics creates misleading job stereotypes, often causing male nurses to worry about their masculine image (Schilt 2006) or even suggesting that male nurses cannot adequately perform a caring role (MacDougall 1997). Furthermore, the expectation that management roles in nursing are better carried out by males could deny women equal access to such positions (Berkery, Tiernan, and Morley 2014). Instead, it is more fruitful to explore the kinds of linguistic resources people use to construct their identity (be it gendered or professional), and the extent to which the context and job role influence the language utilized. Therefore, it is important to examine the context in which identity performance takes place.

Community of Practice

Workplaces consist of groups of people who work together, who share a work purpose and a common goal based on work related knowledge. These aspects are captured in the concept of Community of Practice (CofP) (Wenger 1998; see King, this volume). Arguably then, workplace groups can be CofPs (Eckert and McConnell-Ginet 2003), each with their own linguistic repertoire used to negotiate meaning, and help develop and display belonging. This allows members to retain an effective work relationship, which can increase work productivity and ensure work is completed efficiently (Fletcher 1999). Not surprisingly then, this paradigm is now widely employed within sociolinguistic research in relation to workplace discourse (McDowell 2015a, 2015b; Holmes and Schnurr 2006; Mullany 2007; Holmes and Marra 2011; Holmes and Meyerhoff 1999), and scholars stress the importance of looking for linguistic patterns in relation to the particular CofP (e.g., workplace and job role) to identify the established speech norms which may become part of the member's communicative style (Eckert and McConnell-Ginet 2003). In non-traditional occupations this may allow men and women to step away from the stereotypical gendered manner in which society expects them to behave, and enable them to perform by accommodating to the requirements of their job (McDowell 2015b; Holmes and Schnurr 2006; McElhinny 1995). It is therefore possible to examine how people produce or resist gender arrangements in their communities, and explore how gender intertwines with other components of a speaker's identity.

The Role of Language in the Workplace

As gender and language research moved away from essentialist approaches towards social constructionist frameworks, gender identity was analysed as "socially constructed, highly contextualised, hence fluid and variable" (Coates 1997, 19). In short, gender identity is not fixed and language is one resource that people draw upon to construct an appropriate gender identity. Over time, various linguistic resources have become normatively linked to particular gender identities. However, people can challenge gendered expectations, giving language a very important position in the study of the performance of gender practices (Holmes 2006). This makes the workplace an especially interesting research context as the performance of one's gender may not be the overriding goal. Constructing and demonstrating one's professional identity may be more important.

We all perform different identities in different contexts, which may involve behaving in ways normatively associated with the other gender (McDowell 2015a, 2015b; Kendall 2004; Thimm, Koch, and Schey, 2003). Therefore, speakers might not necessarily choose linguistic strategies in order to enact a masculine or feminine persona, but rather another identity altogether (Kendall 2004; Holmes and Schnurr 2006). However, pinpointing the reason behind a speaker's use of language is not an easy task as identities are often intertwined. For example, performing one's professional identity may be enacted through the use of the same linguistic features that can be used to express a gendered identity. Furthermore, professional and gendered identity may be even more entwined within a gendered CofP, making the performance of the two harder to separate (Holmes 2006). Indeed, Holmes and Schnurr (2006) argue that gender is always present and therefore relevant in workplace interaction: it can constrain our behaviour and how we interpret the behaviour of others. As a result, workplaces can reinforce gender stereotypes, especially in professions based on gendered characteristics where speakers conform to certain behaviour. The gendering of a job can affect the language used within it, and participants need to learn the linguistic repertoire to gain acceptance professionally and socially in that community. Indeed, as Holmes and Schnurr state, "any individual is likely to be heavily influenced and even constrained by ... the gendered interactional norms of their specific community of practice" (2006, 137). Research has illustrated how women who infiltrate "male" professions often adopt "masculine" behaviours (Rhoton 2011; McElhinny 1995) while men in "female" professions tend to interact in ways that contribute to viewing a workplace as "feminine" (McDowell 2015b). Hence in certain CofPs, performing a particular professional identity may be inextricably linked to performing a particular gender identity (Holmes and Schnurr 2006).

Earlier research indicates that speakers are flexible in their discourse practices and many workplaces draw on a mixture of normatively masculine and feminine practices. Holmes and Schnurr (2006) point out that just because a workplace is described as gendered in a particular way does not mean that all participants will behave in that gendered manner all the time. They may deviate from the norm, or even challenge it. But "doing being a nurse" tends to be associated with feminine attributes, and if men choose to separate themselves from these and to exploit their masculinity, scholars have suggested that this could be at the expense of satisfactorily enacting a caring role (MacDougall 1997). So, what happens when one's gendered identity is threatened as often reported by men working in non-traditional occupations? (Cross and Bagilhole 2006)

Performing a Nursing Identity

This section examines some empirical data collected by three male ward nurses working in a hospital in Northern Ireland (for more details see McDowell 2015a, 2015b). I focus in particular on the relevance of their linguistic choices in the construction of gender identity and professional identity in communicating with other members of their team.[1] The examples selected represent typical linguistic strategies evident in the corpus from which they are drawn, and involve interactions in mixed-sex and single-sex groups from a larger case study of the identity construction of men in nursing. The context is a very high involvement one, and the features found were consistent with the normatively feminine end of the style continuum, described by Holmes in her study of "feminine" CofPs (Holmes 2006, 2014). The main patterns found in the data (illustrated in the examples below) demonstrate that participants employ a variety of strategies to construct their professional identity as a nurse and to form an in-group collective identity.

The discursive construction of an "us" versus "them" binary in the nurses' communication emphasizes the difference between their particular nursing group in opposition to "others". This is an important means by which nurses demarcate their CofP from other CofPs in the medical profession (e.g., doctors, surgeons, and other types of nurses). All nurses took great pride in the ward in which they worked, and often expressed reluctance to work elsewhere (see McDowell 2015a, 283–284). Often, the nurses talked about others in a negative, critical manner, demonstrating a collective feeling of exasperation towards them and their actions. Example 29.1 illustrates how male and female nurses use language to present their own group's opinion in a positive way while the others, in this case community nurses, are portrayed in a negative way.

Joe's recurrent use of the inclusive pronouns "we" and "us" constructs an alliance between all three participants (lines 4–6, 9 and 12), while the district nurses are referred to repeatedly as "they" (lines 2, 4, 9, 12–14, and 18). This demarcates two distinct groups; insiders and outsiders. The two male nurses clearly define the outside group with which they are all annoyed as the "community people", also referred to as "the district nurses" (lines 1, 4). District nurses

> **Example 29.1** (from McDowell 2015a, 281)[2]
>
> Context: Two male nurses, Joe and Mike, and one female nurse, Amy, are talking about a patient who needs extra treatment.
>
> | | | |
> |---|---|---|
> | 1 | Joe: | surely the community nurses have to provide the pressurising |
> | 2 | | mattress wouldn't they/ |
> | 3 | Amy: | yeah |
> | 4 | Mike: | the district nurses <?> have they nothing better to do than ring us |
> | 5 | | up asking us when was the last time we had seen the patient/ |
> | 6 | | I rang them back on the phone and says we are enquiring . . . |
> | 7 | | [and] <?> will need a a mattress when goes home from [here] |
> | 8 | Joe: | [ay] [I know] |
> | 9 | | if someone went home with me they would soon ring [us] |
> | 10 | Mike: | [oh] definitely |
> | 11 | Joe: | wouldn't they/ why did this patient (.) why weren't we informed |
> | 12 | Amy: | but I suppose then maybe they wouldn't know if it was there or |
> | 13 | | not would they\ in this case or not (.) because they would have |
> | 14 | | no reason to see it |
> | 15 | Mike: | <?> |
> | 16 | Amy: | yeah |
> | 17 | Mike: | cause then the family weren't letting them into the house for |
> | 18 | | while [either] |
> | 19 | Amy: | [where they not/] |
> | 20 | Mike: | no |
> | 21 | Joe: | that would make it very difficult like (.) you know/ |

have a partially different occupational role than that of ward nurses and based on this difference, the ward nurses in this example form an alliance, and openly criticize the "community people" as the "other" that are causing problems in regards to a particular patient. By highlighting the unison of the speakers in the group, Joe is creating a sense of mutual agreement (shared anger at the community group), reducing the likelihood of offending his listeners when making negative comments. The use of "we" (lines 5, 6, 11) is a relational indicator; it allows the discursive construction of group identity through bonding allowing group consensus and decision. The speakers' selection of "we" rather than the personal pronoun "I" or "you" is important here as the choice of this particular pronoun has certain sociological meaning (Oddo 2011; Wodak 2011). Using the personal pronoun "I" means the speaker claims sole responsibility for a task or an opinion. "We", however, is a collective pronoun and its use here allows the speakers to construct themselves as part of a collective, sharing responsibility for actions or comments.

The speakers, especially Joe, also make argumentative appeals to their shared knowledge acquired through the job. This is a common strategy within "us" versus "them" discussions used to build an in-group, creating consensus between the group members especially when criticizing others, making decisions on what to do, or deciding to act on a problem (Wodak 2011). In this process, the nurses mitigate their opinions and their criticisms toward the outside group (line 2, 12, 21) as a precautionary measure (in case a group member is affronted) while simultaneously seeking consolidation from and establishing collegial relationships with their fellow group members (Coates 2004). Joe's tag question "wouldn't they" (line 2) seeks agreement with his suggestion that the "community people" should be providing the equipment needed for the patient (cf. Holmes 1982, 1990).

Collaborative agreement is apparent in the nurses' use of simultaneous turns throughout the conversation (lines 6–10; 17–19). The two males in particular partly coincide with each other to show their agreement and support for one another's comments, especially when negative remarks are made. This is evidence of relational practice, where speakers collaboratively take turns and facilitate each other's comments (Fletcher 1999; Holmes 2006). The female however, remains relatively quiet until line 12. At this point, she attempts to provide an excuse for the community nurses' behaviour. She introduces her thoughts with two hedges to soften her opinion in case her two colleagues disagree: "but *I suppose* then *maybe* they wouldn't know if it was there or not *would they*" (lines 12–15).

As well as gossip to create this in-group, the nurses regularly attributed shared knowledge that could only have been acquired through their work as a nurse (i.e., medical knowledge; lack of beds; being short staffed; feeling overworked). Example 29.2 is a typical example: nurses complaining about their work load and disparaging their shift rota. Long days (12 hour shifts) were common, and one group in particular felt that they were always scheduled to work on public holidays. As well as allowing the nurses to vent their annoyance at their workload, these conversations allowed them to use their shared experience of being a nurse to connect with one another, bonding over their negative feelings towards being over-worked and underappreciated.

Example 29.2

Context: Two female nurses, Bea and Ruth, and one male nurse, Bob, complain about the rota and how often they have to work. Extract has been shortened.

1	Ruth:	I'm tired
2	Bea:	well its only (1.0) half 10/\
3	Bob:	I'm tired too
4	Ruth:	I've got a [long day] tomorrow as well (.)
5	Bea:	[I'm on a long day]
6	Bea:	<?> he's tired (.) he's going to have a long day (.)
7	Bob:	<laughs>
8	Ruth:	but I think we're psychologically traumatized because of a
9		long day (1.0) we wouldn't be this tired if we were off at two
10	Bea:	no (.) it's a while going in (.) see when it hits 3 o'clock on our ward
11		I hate it (.) from about 3 to 5 is [terrible]
12	Ruth:	[<?>]
13	Bea:	I know (.)
14	Ruth:	I remember one day last week when I was doing the pills
15		and I was trying to talk to people on the phone and listen to the
16		voice and I was trying to listen <?> it's like what/ what did you say/
17	Bob:	<laughs> <?> <laughs> (3.0) that's right (.) and of course
18		looks who's working on Monday (1.0) and on a bank holiday (1.0)
19		it just seems like we're always working (.) on holidays [<?>]

This example demonstrates a recurring pattern in the data which supports the analysis of the participants as members of a CofP: their frequent use of the inclusive pronoun "we" (lines 8, 9, 19). A discussion that begins with one individual's expression of tiredness "I'm tired" (line 1) quickly progresses to a unified discussion of others feeling the same, and a discussion of why this could be "long days" (lines 4–5). Ruth even goes as far as classifying the group as "psychologically traumatized" due to the tiredness brought on by such long shifts (line 8). Bob adds to the complaints by reminding the group they are working on yet another bank holiday. This group are the "usual suspects" for working on holidays (lines 17–19) which acts to strengthen their little in-group on the ward. What the nurses are doing here goes beyond simply complaining. Venting in this manner (although it changes nothing) allows them to negotiate their solidarity with one another. Being over-worked and tired is part and parcel of being a nurse. Therefore, complaining about it aids nurses in the construction of their professional identities, establishes co-membership, and builds rapport with the other community members.

Nurses also enacted their professional expertise through another type of shared knowledge: the use of technical language related to patient illnesses, surgical procedures and appropriate aftercare:

Example 29.3

Context: Male charge nurse, Tim, and a female nurse, Deb, are talking about a surgical procedure a patient in their care requires.

```
1  Tim:  [yeah] Heldon has er (.) Heldon has (.) I don't think he has a J pouch as such
2        (.) he's got I'm not sure but part of the anastomosis has blown and it caused a
3        fistula that tracked right up to here to the side of his stomach and caused a big
4        abscess
5  Deb:  for god's sake
6  Tim:  so they're going to have to probably abort the whole thing and just give
7        him a permanent stoma.
8  Deb:  mhm (.) so a fistula from there right up to to [the] outside of the stomach
9  Tim:  [yeah]
10       Yeah (.) it just takes the path of least resistance apparently and comes out
11       on the surface (.) you know/ and it's this pus and all leaking into his pouch
12       that's why he has a catheter in it to allow all the stuff to drain out. [The other]
13       problem that happens after when the pouch is formed and they have a new
14       ileostomy (.) the second part of the surgery (.) I've seen it a couple of times
         . . .
```

Example 29.4 offers a brief insight into a further type of shared knowledge found in the data: the use of in-group humour, a key characteristic in creating and maintaining an in-group (Holmes 2006). This example reflects a well-known fact (and in-joke) among the nurses: that they "talk about" their patients. This "talk" does not however, refer to the on-task behaviour of talking about a patient's care, but rather refers more to "gossip", when they joke and laugh about their patients. This demonstrates shared knowledge, and is perhaps used as a form of

Identity and the Workplace

Example 29.4

Context: Tim is discussing moving their staff room into another room and jokes with two female nurses, Cathy and Bev, that this is a good idea so they can gossip about patients in there without anyone over-hearing.

1	Tim:	I'll tell you what we should do (.) move one into Shona's room and
2		get that big bench out of there. Shona's going to be away for six months.
3	Cathy:	aye right enough
4	Bev:	aye
5	Tim:	I'll have a wee look at [that later].
6	Bev:	Why do you have to move it to the other room
7		<some laughter is heard>
8	Tim:	because (.) if we're in there chatting there there'll
		[be people sitting outside] (.)
9		you know/
10	Bev:	[and they'll hear us]
11	Tim:	they'll hear us.
12	Cathy:	Ah so better to talk quiet then <laughs>
13	Tim:	aye but it'll be quieter to... you may be able to hear that sort of thing
14		but us sitting laughing and joking and talking about patients [probably] you know
15	Cathy:	<laughs and says in feigned shocked tone> we don't do that.
16		<All laugh>

release from the emotional stresses and strains of the job. Laughing is evident throughout the chat (lines 12–16), and the nurses build a collaborative floor to share the joke through overlapping speech. Bev finishes Tim's turn "and they'll hear us" (line 10), evidence that she is aware of where he is going with his point "there'll be people sitting outside" (line 8). Tim indicates agreement by repeating her utterance (line 11), causing laughter among the group. His use of the hedge "probably" followed by "you know" (line 14), indicates a humorous jibe toward his staff. Cathy adopts an offended tone when she disagrees with Tim's accusation, "we don't do that" (line 15) to show that not only is she not offended, but is joining in the humour and acknowledging that yes, this is something that staff do. More laughter ensues as a result (line 16).

Discussion and Conclusion

The examples presented above demonstrate nurses (both male and female) expressing collegiality and group membership through their linguistic behaviour: nurses appear to use language to bind themselves to other nurses in their CofP (Oddo 2011; Wenger 1998). The men in this study did not use typical "masculine" linguistic indices to emphasize their masculinity or to separate themselves from their female nurse colleagues. Instead, they used linguistic resources (often classed as feminine) to build and maintain a nursing CofP and enact their identity as a nurse. In contrast then with research that reports that men in feminized jobs construct their identities in contrast to their female colleagues to underline their masculine difference (Cross and Bagilhole 2006; Simpson 2004), these interactions show the male nurses participating appropriately in their CofP and demonstrating their in-group nursing identity. The male nurses do not orient to hegemonic norms of masculinity or what is classed as "acceptable maleness" (Coates 2003, 196).

The male (and female) nurses' linguistic performance could be to some extent determined by their workplace culture, with the context, work role, and shared linguistic repertoire of their setting influencing their linguistic choices (Angouri 2011; Holmes and Marra 2011; Vine 2004). Perhaps these nurses are negotiating their identity in relation to the dominant discourse of the environment (see Pullen and Simpson 2009; Holmes, 2006). These findings are similar to previous research concerning women in masculinized jobs, where women embrace masculine characteristics in order to perform their job as they are aware of the threat potential of using language inappropriately in their CofP (Barrett 2004; Rhoton 2011; Baxter 2012). It can be argued that the discourse used by these men is used not to construct a feminine identity, but rather a *nursing* identity to align themselves with their workplace, which just happens to be feminized (Milani 2011). Most research in the field of nursing focuses on nurse–patient communication and although these findings cannot be assumed to extend to inter-professional communication among nurses and their colleagues, the ideology underlying nursing may have an effect on what is considered appropriate behaviour among nursing staff in order to maintain rapport. Communication is a vital tool in nursing as it can affect the standards of the care given and consequently patient well-being (see Grohar-Murray and DiCroce 1997). Arguably then, maintaining a harmonious nursing group is an important element of the ward environment as nurses often work in teams to address work-related problems using their combined knowledge and expertise. Indeed, Timmens and McCabe (2005, 66) suggest that "being isolated, disliked or punished, by nurse colleagues was a barrier to assertive behaviour". Nurse-nurse harmony is vital, and nursing managers need skills to negotiate internal conflicts to create collective teams. Nilsson and Larsson (2005) report for example that female head nurses felt that adopting a masculine controlling attitude to leadership would be counterproductive and ineffective, creating problems and collision between staff. This is supported by Hendel, Fish, and Galon (2005, 138) who noted that good leadership skills encompass the provision of "encouragement and support, releases tensions, harmonises misunderstanding and deals with disruptive or aggressive behaviour". The stereotypically dominant, aggressive strategies of "masculine" speech may not be the most effective to use in nursing contexts. Furthermore, the stereotypical "feminine" abilities; i.e. the ability to multi-task, support and nurture others, build solidarity through communication skills, and create a sense of teamwork, have been described as good qualities for any worker (Barrett 2004; Priola 2004; Cameron 2007).

The analysis of the language in this chapter is not representative of all male nurses' behaviour. Moreover, it cannot be claimed that the men who took part in this current study do not "do" traditional masculinity in non-linguistic ways while at work. What is evident however is that these men are not struggling to preserve their masculinity at the expense of the nursing collective. The analysis provides further evidence that there are many similarities in the discursive behaviour of men and women in particular contexts (Holmes and Schnurr 2006). So, a final important point emerges here: better terminology is needed to classify nursing language behaviour. The suggestion that men use "feminine" strategies strengthens gendered linguistic stereotypes. They are not "doing femininity" but rather using the discursive practices that are associated with and most appropriate for their CofP. As men and women are both capable of doing any type of work, jobs such as nursing and indeed the linguistic repertoire used within them, need to be de-gendered. Only then may we see more men taking up such professional occupations.

Further Reading

Baxter (2012) explores the challenges that women often face when they become leaders in a "masculine" workplace.

Heikes (1991) offers a discussion of men as "tokens" in the nursing environment.

MacDougall (1997) asks whether men can truly "care" and therefore questions whether they can be nurses due to hegemonic masculine characteristics.

McDowell (2015a) and (2015b) explore the language used by male and female nurses in the workplace, and demonstrates how a) they all demonstrate belonging to their CofP and b) use stereotypical "feminine" language to do so.

Related Topics

Interactional sociolinguistics; Rapport management; Social constructionism; Communities of practice; Directives; Relational talk; Humour; Gender; Leadership; Professional identity construction

Appendix

Transcription Conventions

=	Turn latching
[ ]	Overlapping speech
<?>	Indecipherable speech
//	Point at which speech is interrupted
(.)	Very brief pause
(1.0)	Longer pause with length in seconds
/	Rising intonation on word or part or syllable
:	Lengthening/drawing out of final syllable/sound
(( ))	Paralanguage

All names are pseudonyms.

Notes

1. To warrant data analysis and interpretation, I have consulted with other researchers in this area of study, as well as using relevant ethnographic material and interviews recorded during the data collection period. This triangulation of data is a valid way to warrant data analysis and interpretation (Holmes 2014).
2. See Appendix for transcription conventions.

References

Alvesson, Mats. 1998. "Gender Relations and Identity at Work: A Case of Masculinity and Femininity in an Advertising Agency." *Human Relations* 51: 969–1005.

Angouri, Jo. 2011. "'We Are in a Masculine Profession . . .': Constructing Gender Identities in a Consortium of Two Multinational Engineering Companies." *Gender and Language* 5: 373–404.

Barrett, Mary. 2004. "Should They Learn to Interrupt? Workplace Communication Strategies Australian Women Managers Forecast as Effective." *Women in Management Review* 19: 391–403.

Baxter, Judith. 2010. *The Language of Female Leadership*. Basingstoke, UK: Palgrave Macmillan.

Baxter, Judith. 2012. "Survival or Success? A Critical Exploration of the Use of 'Double-Voiced Discourse' by Women Business Leaders in the UK." *Discourse and Communication* 5: 231–245.

Berkery, Elaine, Siobhan Tiernan, and Michael Morley. 2014. "The Relationship between Gender Role Stereotypes and Requisite Managerial Characteristics: The Case of Nursing and Midwifery Professionals." *Journal of Nursing Management* 22: 707–719.

Bird, Sharon. 1996. "Welcome to the Men's Club: Homosociality and the Maintenance of Hegemonic Masculinity." *Gender and Society* 10: 120–132.

Britton, Dana M. 2000. "The Epistemology of the Gendered Organisation." *Gender and Society* 14: 418–434.

Brown, Brian, Peter Nolan, and Paul Crawford. 2000. "Men in Nursing: Ambivalence in Care, Gender and Masculinity." *International History of Nursing Journal* 5: 4–13.

Cameron, Deborah. 2007. *The Myth of Mars and Venus: Do Men and Women Really Speak Different Languages?* Oxford: Oxford University Press.

Coates, Jennifer. 1997. "One-at-a-Time: The Organisation of Men's Talk." In *Language and Masculinity*, edited by Sally Johnson, and Ulrike Hanna Meinhof, 107–130. Oxford: Blackwell.

Coates, Jennifer. 2003. *Men Talk: Stories in the Making of Masculinities*. Oxford: Blackwell.

Coates, Jennifer. 2004. *Women, Men and Language: A Sociolinguistic Account of Gender Differences in Language*. 3rd ed. Harlow, UK: Pearson Longman.

Cross, Simon, and Barbara Bagilhole. 2006. "'It Never Struck Me as Female': Investigating Men's Entry into Female Dominated Occupations." *Journal of Gender Studies* 15: 35–48.

Eckert, Penelope, and Sally McConnell-Ginet. 2003. *Language and Gender*. Cambridge: Cambridge University Press.

Evans, Joan. 1997. "Men in Nursing, Issues of Gender Segregation and Hidden Advantage." *Journal of Advanced Nursing* 26: 226–231.

Fletcher, Joyce K. 1999. *Disappearing Acts: Gender, Power and Relational Practice at Work*. Cambridge, MA: MIT Press.

Grohar-Murray, Mary Ellen, and Helen R. DiCroce. 1997. *Leadership and Management in Nursing*. 2nd ed. Upper Saddle River, NJ: Prentice Hall.

Heikes, E. Joel. 1991. "When Men Are in the Minority: The Case of Men in Nursing." *Sociological Quarterly* 32: 389–401.

Hendel, Tova, Miri Fish, and Vered Galon. 2005. "Leadership Style and Choice of Strategy in Conflict Management among Israeli Nurse Managers in General Hospitals." *Journal of Nursing Management* 13: 137–146.

Holmes, Janet. 1982. "Functions of Tag Questions." *English Language Research Journal* 3: 40–65.

Holmes, Janet. 1990. "Hedges and Boosters in Women's and Men's Speech." *Language and Communication* 10: 185–205.

Holmes, Janet. 2006. *Gendered Talk at Work. Constructing Social Identity through Work Place Interaction*. Oxford: Blackwell.

Holmes, Janet. 2014. "Language and Gender in the Workplace." In *Handbook of Language, Gender and Sexuality*. 2nd ed., edited by Susan Ehrlich, Miriam Meyerhoff, and Janet Holmes, 433–451. Malden, MA: John Wiley & Sons.

Holmes, Janet, and Meredith Marra. 2011. "Leadership Discourse in a Maori Workplace: Negotiating Gender, Ethnicity and Leadership at Work." *Gender and Language* 5: 317–343.

Holmes, Janet, and George Major. 2003. "Talking to Patients: The Complexity of Communication on the Ward." *Vision: A Journal of Nursing* 11: 4–9.

Holmes, Janet, and Miriam Meyerhoff. 1999. "The Community of Practice: Theories and Methodologies in the New Language and Gender." *Language in Society* 28: 173–183.

Holmes, Janet, and Stephanie Schnurr. 2006. "Doing Femininity at Work: More Than Just Relational Practice." *Journal of Sociolinguistics* 20: 31–51.

Huppatz, Kate, and Susan Goodwin. 2013. "Masculinised Jobs, Feminised Jobs and Men's 'Gender Capital' Experiences: Understanding Occupational Segregation in Australia." *Journal of Sociology* 49: 291–308.

Isaacs, Dallas, and Marilyn Poole. 1996. "Being a Man and Becoming a Nurse: Three Men's Stories." *Journal of Gender Studies* 5: 39–47.

Kendall, Shari. 2004. "Framing Authority: Gender, Face and Mitigation at a Radio Network." *Discourse and Society* 15: 55–79.

Ku, Manwai C. 2011. "When Does Gender Matter? Gender Differences in Speciality Choice among Physicians." *Work and Occupations* 38: 221–262.

MacDougall, Graham. 1997. "Caring—A Masculine Perspective." *Journal of Advance Nursing* 25: 809–813.
McDowell, Joanne. 2015a. "Masculinity and Non-Traditional Occupations: Men's Talk in Women's Work." *Gender, Work and Organization* 22: 273–291.
McDowell, Joanne. 2015b. "Talk in Feminised Occupations: Exploring Male Nurses' Linguistic Behaviour." *Gender and Language* 9: 365–389.
McElhinny, Bonnie S. 1995. "Challenging Hegemonic Masculinity: Female and Male Police Officers Handling Domestic Violence." In *Gender Articulated: Language and the Socially Constructed Self*, edited by Kira Hall, and Mary Bucholtz, 217–247. New York: Routledge.
Milani, Tommaso M. 2011. "Recasting Language and Masculinities." *Gender and Language* 5: 175–186.
Miller, Gloria E. 2004. "Frontier Masculinity in the Oil Industry: The Experience of Women Engineers." *Gender, Work and Organisation* 11: 47–73.
Mullany, Louise. 2007. *Gendered Discourse in Professional Communication*. Basingstoke, UK: Palgrave.
Nilsson, Kerstin, and Ullabeth Sätterlund Larsson. 2005. "Conceptions of Gender: A Study of Female and Male Head Nurses' Statements." *Journal of Nursing Management* 13: 179–186.
Oddo, John. 2011. "War Legitimisation Discourse, Representing 'Us' VS. 'Them' in Four US Presidential Addresses." *Discourse Society* 22: 287–314.
Powell, Abigail, Barbara Bagilhole, and Andrew Dainty. 2008. "How Women Engineers Do and Undo Gender: Consequences for Gender Equality." *Gender, Work and Organisation* 16: 412–428.
Priola, Vincenza. 2004. "Gender and Feminine Identities: Women as Managers in a UK Academic Institution." *Women in Management Review* 19: 421–430.
Pullen, Alison, and Ruth Simpson. 2009. "Managing Difference in Feminized Work: Men, Otherness and Social Practice." *Human Relations* 62: 561–587.
Rhoton, Laura A. 2011. "Distancing as a Gendered Barrier: Understanding Women Scientists' Gender Practices." *Gender and Society* 25: 696–716.
Schilt, Kristen. 2006. "Just One of the Guys: How Transmen Make Gender Visible at Work." *Gender and Society* 20: 465–490.
Sidnell, Jack. 2003. "Constructing and Managing 'Male-Only' Conversations." In *Handbook of Language and Gender*, edited by Janet Holmes, and Miriam Meyerhoff, 327–353. Oxford: Blackwell.
Simpson, Ruth. 2004. "Masculinity at Work: The Experiences of Men in Female Dominated Occupations." *Work, Employment and Society* 18: 349–368.
Thimm, Caja, Sabine C. Koch, and Sabine Schey. 2003. "Communicating Gendered Professional Identity: Competence, Cooperation, and Conflict in the Workplace." In *Handbook of Language and Gender*, edited by Janet Holmes, and Miriam Meyerhoff, 528–529. Oxford: Blackwell.
Timmens, Fiona, and Catherine McCabe. 2005. "How Assertive are Nurses in the Workplace? A Preliminary Pilot Study." *Journal of Nursing Management* 13: 61–67.
Trauth, Eileen M. 2002. "Odd girl out: An Individual Differences Perspective on Women in the IT Profession." *Information Technology and People* 15: 96–118.
UK Nursing and Midwifery Council. 2015. *Statistical analysis of the register 1 April 2007 to 31 March 2015*. Available at www.nmc.org.uk/. . ./freedom-of-information-disclosure-log-2015.xls. Retrieved on 1st October 2016.
Vine, Bernadette. 2004. *Getting Things Done at Work. The Discourse of Power in Workplace Interaction*. Amsterdam: John Benjamins.
Wenger, Etienne. 1998. *Communities of Practice: Learning, Meaning, and Identity*. Cambridge: Cambridge University Press.
Whittock, Margaret, and Laurence Leonard. 2003. "Stepping Outside the Stereotype: A Pilot Study of the Motivations and Experiences of Males in the Nursing Profession." *Journal of Nursing Management* 11: 242–249.
Williams, Christine L. 1992. "The Glass Escalator: Hidden Advantages for Men in the 'Female Professions'." *Social Problems* 39: 253–267.
Williams, Christine L. 1995a. "Hidden Advantages for Men in Nursing." *Nursing Administration Quarterly* 19: 63–70.
Williams, Christine L. 1995b. *Still a Man's World: Men Who do "Women's" Work*. Berkeley, CA: University of California Press.
Wodak, Ruth. 2011. "Language, Identity, Power." *Language Teaching* 45: 215–233.

30
Professional Identity Construction
Cabin Crew Discourse
Barbara Clark

Introduction

Bucholtz and Hall (2005, 585) note that identity is "a social and cultural rather than primarily internal psychological phenomenon" and from a linguistic perspective identity is evident in talk. In terms of professional identity, this discursive construction of identity refers to the occupationally-relevant discourse by members of a profession incorporating notions of that profession, including institutionally and non-institutionally sanctioned ways of talking about and interacting as members of a profession (cf. Cotter and Marschall 2006; Holmes 2006; Mullany 2007).

The cabin crew profession has existed for over a century. Core professional duties include safety, service, and, owing to the 11 September, 2001 US terror attacks (i.e., 9/11) and other terrorist-related events, a greater emphasis than ever on security tasks and practices. Cabin Crew (i.e., Flight Attendants) use language in most aspects of their profession, yet have historically received limited academic attention, in particular on the discursive construction of professional identity. This chapter contributes to work on discursive professional identity construction, discussing professional Flight Attendant (FA) identity construction in the discourse of inflight incident reports and online discussion forums.

Approaching the Discursive Construction of Identity

As noted by Holmes (2006, 12), a range of approaches to identity "emphasize the dynamic aspects of interaction, and the constantly changing and developing nature of social identities." Research in this vein has considered different aspects of identity such as gender identity (e.g., McElhinny 1995; Bucholtz and Hall 2004, 2005; Holmes 2006), leadership identity (e.g., Schnurr 2009; Holmes, Marra, and Vine 2011) and professional identity in different occupations (e.g., Dyer and Keller-Cohen 2000; Ashcraft 2007; Baxter and Wallace 2009).

In this chapter I draw in particular on the work of Bucholtz and Hall (2004, 2005), who provide a framework for analysing the discursive construction of identity. Here I briefly examine five aspects that are important in this approach. First, a crucial consideration is context and in considering FA discourse, a number of aspects of context need to be specified. For the purposes of this chapter, context includes extra-linguistic features such as who is speaking, to whom are utterances addressed, and purpose for utterances (cf. Hymes 1986). Context also includes (and is not limited to) the history of commercial aviation and FAs; advertising and concomitant expectations on FA behaviour; institutional constraints on participants' behaviour and interaction; power dynamics of participants; occupational training; economic factors, e.g., airlines' financial state, air travel cost; and culture, e.g., the national, folk, business, social, and geopolitical situation in which discourse is situated.

Second, is the idea of "practice". In the commercial aviation context, there are four broad types of routinized, repeated actions (or practices) in which FAs engage: institutional, occupational, practical, and linguistic. Institutional practices include tasks and expectations stemming from institutional regulations, rules, and laws (e.g., compliance with and enforcement of US Federal Aviation Regulations). Occupational practices relate to the FA job and include service duties, inflight emergencies, and emotional labour practices (e.g., external displays of caring, smiling at passengers; cf. Hochschild 2003; Williams 2003). Practical practices develop after working in the FA job and gaining familiarity with institutional and occupational practices, as well as daily contingent realities of commercial aviation, working with passengers, turbulence disruptions, and other real-life situations in which training does not necessarily provide hands-on experience. Linguistic practices develop or exist as a result of institutional, occupational, or practical practices and include the use of technical commercial aviation jargon and occupationally salient terms including slang terms for objects and concepts which have institutionally sanctioned normative names.

Third, is the idea of "indexicality" (cf. Ochs 1992). Ochs (1992) argues that certain linguistic and discourse features take on sociocultural meaning, owing in large part to the speakers who become associated with these features. These meanings create direct and indirect indexical stances (see also Eckert 2008; McElhinny 2005; Mullany 2007). As an example Ochs (1992) cites the use of certain sentence-final particles in Japanese which directly index a stance of deference. Because women are the primary users of these particles, an indirect indexical stance of "female" is created.

A fourth concept utilized by Bucholtz and Hall (2004, 2005) is "ideology". Ideology relates to the "conceptual boundaries of interpretation of group and individual beliefs, values, and intentions and how they are marked discursively" (Cotter and Marschall 2006, 3). Ideology is produced by and reflected in indexical stances (Bucholtz and Hall 2004, 379–380); thus ideologies are evident in and emerge from discourse itself (cf. Gal and Irvine 1995; Irvine and Gal 2009). For example, sentence-final particles in Japanese used primarily by women (i.e., linguistic practice) directly index deference, and indirectly index gender. These indexical stances produce ideologies of gender: women should be deferential in societal interactions, particularly to men. In this sense, ideology is theorized as "rooted in or responsive to the experience of a particular social position" (Woolard and Schieffelin 1994, 58).

Finally, "performance" is "highly deliberate and self-aware social display... an aesthetic component that is available for evaluation by an audience" (Bucholtz and Hall 2004, 380). Barrett (1999) offers a robust demonstration of discursive performance contrasting with mundane interaction in his work on African American drag queens, arguing that the use of polyvocalic speech calls attention to the performance of heteronormative femininity, with queens using the stage, clothing, makeup, and other concomitant accoutrements as accessories to heighten and call attention to their performative acts (see also Daems 2014). Various FA activities have been theorized as performances, including the balancing of safety and service tasks through a distinctive inflight announcement prosody (Banks 1994) and the reproduction of mundane cultural acts (e.g., eating, small talk) in order to mitigate the abnormality of air travel (Murphy 2002).

A number of features of the Bucholtz and Hall (2004) framework make it useful for the purposes of professional identity research. The framework provides a tangible, accessible conceptualization of the situated construction of identity in discourse, incorporating social, cultural, and other contextual factors. The framework can be adapted to local situations, and used to analyse a range of speech events, data sources, and research areas. The framework also recognizes that identity does not happen in a vacuum (see Clark 2013 for further discussion).

Two further issues of relevance to professional identity construction which Bucholtz and Hall (2004, 382) highlight and on which I focus in this chapter are "authentication and denaturalization" (see also Bucholtz and Hall 2005, 601–603). I am concerned here with notions of authenticity, realness, and artifice. Authentication focuses on how an identity is constructed as credible or genuine; denaturalization focuses on how an often-essentialized or taken-for-granted identity can be shown to be artificial. This chapter seeks to explore professional FA identity beyond socio-historical idealized FA images portrayed in advertising and other media, to understand what aspects of such essentialized "polished" FA identity portrayals is present in authentic FA discourse.

Flight Attendants and Commercial Aviation

FAs work in the global aviation industry, and are employed by companies to work in aircraft before, during, and after passenger-carrying flights for the purposes of providing safety and service to passengers and crew. FA training and oversight is regulated and mandated by national and other aviation authorities (e.g., Federal Aviation Administration (FAA); European Aviation Safety Agency; Civil Aviation Safety Authority [Australia]). While FAs were initially male, in order to entice nervous fliers onto aircraft, airlines decided to hire females, trained as nurses, to demonstrate that flying was so safe, even women were not afraid to fly (cf. Barry 2007; Tiemeyer 2013). As nurses, FAs could also provide more complete care and service-related duties to passengers and crew.

The FA profession has gone through four broad "eras", the first being "nurse/caretaker" in the early days of commercial aviation, outlined above. The 1950s and 1960s brought the "perfect wife and hostess"; indeed, the job of "stewardess" was sometimes known as Bride School, where women trained for the "ultimate female 'profession' of homemaking" (Barry 2007, 51). As many countries regulated airfares, airline competition came primarily via inflight service and female FA bodies; hence the "sexy stewardess" of the 1970s. The 9/11 US terrorist attacks and concomitant changes in commercial aviation safety- and security-related practices resulted in the "safety professional/hero" in the post-9/11 era (cf. Barry 2007; O'Keeffe 2007; Whitelegg 2007), where FAs now are considered by some trade unions and airlines to be "first responders".

FAs comprise half of the inflight crew, the other being pilots who work in the flight deck (i.e., cockpit) section of aircraft. Much occupationally-related FA/pilot interaction is motivated and constrained by two concepts fundamental to aviation operations: Crew Resource Management and the Chain of Command. Briefly, Crew Resource Management is a communication and interaction strategy which attempts to unite FAs and pilots into one "team" in order to maximize effective response to emergencies and non-routine events (FAA 2004; Helmreich, Merritt, and Wilhelm 1999; Kanki, Helmreich, and Anca 2010; see Clark 2013 for further discussion).

Chain of Command is a hierarchical concept placing captains at the top, giving them responsibility and institutional authority over the aircraft, passengers, and crew. First officers (or "co-pilots") are second in the Chain of Command. Below pilots is the position of Lead Flight Attendant (i.e., Purser or #1), responsible for coordinating communication between captain and FAs, among other duties. FAs come below pilots in the Chain of Command, and thus have less inflight institutional authority, power, and responsibility than pilots, by virtue of the Chain of Command structure. Note also that pilots ostensibly have institutional authority and power over activities in the aircraft cabin, and may not undergo training in cabin-related tasks.

Data and Approach

Data for the present chapter come from two sources. The first is a randomly selected corpus of 150 incident reports drawn from a larger public database of reports written by FAs and voluntarily submitted to the ASRS (Aviation Safety Reporting System), a subsidiary of NASA.[1] The reports document inflight incidents—non-routine events not resulting in human death or substantial airworthiness-related damage to the aircraft.

The report audience are ASRS analysts, none of whom have worked as FAs and therefore likely have no lived experience of the FA job. Instead, ASRS analysts are "highly experienced pilots, air traffic controllers and mechanics, as well as a management team that possess aviation and human factors experience" (ASRS 2016). The primary audience for the reports, therefore, can be seen to have greater institutional authority than the FAs submitting reports. The reports are also an institutionally sanctioned speech event, being created, maintained, and promoted by both the ASRS and airline employers as an institutionally-appropriate space to report inflight incidents.

There are two sections to the reports: the first are quantitative questions, e.g., aircraft type, departure airport. The second is a qualitative "narrative" section,[2] where FAs provide their experiences during the incident being reported, opinions of how the incident happened, and how the incident could be avoided in the future. The narratives are published on the ASRS website in their entirety after anonymization. The reporting scheme is non-punitive, existing solely to improve aviation safety.

The second data source is a website with several publicly-accessible discussion forums, aimed primarily at US FAs working for commercial airlines. There are several airline-specific sub-forums and a handful of non-FA sub-forums (e.g., for pilots, mechanics, and passengers). Broadly speaking, threads discuss the FA job, colleagues (especially other FAs and pilots), passengers, and specific airline employer issues. Data for the present chapter were selected based on applicability to the analytic focus, e.g., discussions about the FA job, co-workers, and passengers.

Because the forums are publicly available, the audience ostensibly is anyone who happens to stumble across the website. In reality, however, the primary audience are fellow FAs. The public nature of the forums is salient for many participants; over-hearers and secondary audiences are taken into consideration in some posts, particularly posts discussing information some participants consider to be confidential. Participants often hint that airline management "spies" read the forums, in order to catch out FAs who may violate contractual obligations of confidentiality.

The analytic approach used to examine the data draws on Interactional Sociolinguistics (see Gordon and Kraut this volume) and Ethnography of Communication methods (see Hymes 1986). Analysis is informed by the concepts of "footing", and "framing". "Footing" (Goffman 1981) refers to the discursive, relational, and social positions a speaker assumes with respect to other speakers within a given speech event. These positions emerge in discourse (cf. Kiesling 2001; Nevile 2004; Trester 2009). Footing can be indicated by, among other things, the code, key, or register (Hymes 2009, 163; cf. Tannen and Wallat 1993) a speaker uses in discourse, and if the speaker switches code depending on interlocutor or speech event (Goffman 1981, 126).

Footing is closely linked to the concept of "framing" (Goffman 1974; Tannen 1993), the discursive display of how participants understand, make sense of, and demonstrate their awareness of what is happening during a speech event. Schiffrin (1993, 233) defines "frame" as "what people think they are doing when they talk to each other." This definition is expanded to include written discourse. Footing is a key concept in understanding the relationships speakers assume and how they implicitly align with other participants in discourse.

Safety Reports and Authentication

Although the safety reports are asynchronous and FA reporters are anonymized, the reports share several features. For example, safety reports conform to aviation hierarchies, as seen in Example 30.1.[3]

Example 30.1

1 AT APPROX XA30, CAPT NOTIFIED #1 FLT ATTENDANT OF A HYD LEAK ON ACFT L SIDE.
2 ALL INDICATORS SHOWED A TOTAL LOSS OF FLUID.
3 HE DECLARED AN EMER AND GAVE THE #1 FLT ATTENDANT THE INFO VIA INTERPHONE.
4 WHEN IT WAS CLR TO ME WHAT SHE WAS DOING, I WENT TO THE BACK OF THE ACFT TO GET THE OTHER FLT ATTENDANTS.
5 #1 FLT ATTENDANT THEN ADVISED US OF OUR SIT AND TO IMMEDIATELY START OUR 'CHKLIST' THAT WE HAD 20 MINS BEFORE LNDG IN ORD.
6 **THE CAPT SAID THAT WE WOULD PROBABLY SMELL SOMETHING BURNING UPON LNDG AND TO BE VERY AWARE OF FIRE.**
7 WE WERE NOT TO USE ANY L-HAND SIDE EXITS.
8 WE BEGAN THE CHKLIST AND GOT AS FAR AS THE BRIEFING TO ASSIST.
9 SINCE I WAS THE #3 FLT ATTENDANT, I WAS ABLE TO CONTINUE WHILE ON THE JUMPSEAT.
   THE FLT LANDED WITHOUT INCIDENT.

Example 30.1 constructs the captain as the ultimate authority on the aircraft, positioning the captain as providing information and taking charge of the incident.

The reports also show FAs to be taking action when it is situationally appropriate, and displaying and demonstrating institutional knowledge appropriate to their position, demonstrated in Example 30.2.

> **Example 30.2**
>
> 1   I'D LIKE TO **BRING TO YOUR ATTN A SAFETY CONCERN** THAT I HAVE NOTICED ON THE B757 WHERE THE SAFETY BARRIER-GATE IS INSTALLED.
> 2   MY ACR USES DOOR L1 FOR BOARDING AND DEPLANING AT MOST GATES.
> 3   I HAVE NOTICED THAT WHILE BOARDING, PEOPLE GET STUCK ON THE GATE WHICH IS NOT POSSIBLE TO LOCK IN PLACE FIRMLY.
> 4   (IT HAS A LATCH AT THE TOP BUT THE BOTTOM CAN BE EASILY PULLED OUT IF CAUGHT ON SOMETHING AND THEN THE WHOLE GATE CAN COME UNDONE).
> 5   ROLL ABOARDS, FEET, COATS, ARMS, ETC, ALL SEEM TO CATCH ON THE GATE ON EVERY FLT.
> 6   I CAN ONLY SPEAK FOR WHAT I SEE ON THE B757 ACFT WHICH IS THE ACFT WE MOSTLY USE OUT OF THESE ARPTS.
> 7   I SINCERELY BELIEVE THAT **IN AN EVAC THE GATE WOULD BECOME** A SERIOUS OBSTACLE AND FOR THIS REASON I AM RPTING IT.

Example 30.2 constructs the FA reporter as taking action to report what they consider to be a potential safety hazard. Note that no actual incident is being reported. Instead, the reporter demonstrates practical knowledge gained working as cabin crew, inferring what could happen based on past experience.

Safety reports contain discourse which reflects situational awareness and knowledge of occupational expectations, while also reflecting the tension between emotional labour expectation (e.g., passenger care) and safety awareness. In addition to the features discussed and highlighted in Examples 30.1 and 30.2, safety reports share a number of similar concerns, linguistic features, and tacit understanding of communicative norms appropriate for the speech event.

Certain discursive features emerge from the safety reports, contributing to an authenticated identity. Safety report discourse is similar in key, tone, and footing, despite being written by different FAs. For example, reports focus on safety-related subjects, not service issues or inter-crew conflict. Reports use industry-sanctioned terms for co-workers, e.g., "Capt" (Example 30.1) instead of his first name (a standard address form while working). Reports portray captains as the ultimate authority both on the aircraft and in the Chain of Command, even when there is inter-crew conflict (unfortunately outside of the scope of this chapter; see Clark 2013).

Reports are concerned with broadly similar topics relating to various aspects of the FA job, e.g., being alert to potential safety issues, passenger care, and interaction with pilots. The safety reports draw on occupationally and institutionally relevant topics and resources, tactically used by FA reporters to portray FAs as knowledgeable, capable, and professional. The unique combination of discursive keys, tones, and topics reflecting knowledge and familiarity about occupational, institutional, and personal concerns of FAs mark the reports as discourse from professional, working flight attendants.

Discussion Forums and Denaturalization

As mentioned above, the discussion forum posts have a different primary audience to the safety reports; as we will shortly see, there are also differences in register, key, tone, and genre. Forum posts share occupational and institutional norms as in the safety reports, but forum discourse also reflects the lived experience of how FAs talk about these norms in a situationally appropriate manner with their peers.

Many forum posts provide personal opinions, normative assessments, and other emotive comments which would violate (tacit) interactional and communicative norms of the safety reports, as seen in Example 30.3.

Example 30.3

1 **We had a jackass** who wouldn't turn off his phone recently,
2 and after repeated requests by me and the #1, the #1 got on the PA and announced exactly what was going on—
3 this man won't turn off his cell phone and we may have to go back to the gate.
4 The jeers at this guy from the passengers in f/c were overwhelming.
5 It was depressing though, that it took THAT, and not respecting our instructions or the law, to make him turn it off.

Discussing disruptive passengers, Example 30.3 refers to a passenger by a taboo term while using occupationally relevant terms (e.g., *#1* [Purser]; *f/c* [First Class]) and practical practices that may not be part of "official" training but nonetheless occur while engaged in on-the-job work, most notable in lines 2 and 3, stating that the *#1* made a public announcement through the cabin to in effect shame the deviant passenger into complying with a US federal regulation that FAs are charged with enforcing. It is worth noting that several subsequent posts in the thread agreed with the opinion expressed in Example 30.3.

Forum discourse contains less downplaying of differences between FAs than in the safety reports, which report virtually no intra-FA disagreements or incidents. For example, opinions about pilots vary, as seen in Examples 30.4 and 30.5.

Example 30.4

1 Come on people give them a break we should be very proud of our pilots!
2 Strength in numbers
3 last I looked **we are on the same team**.

Example 30.4 constructs pilots and FAs as peers *on the same team*, in keeping with Crew Resource Management training. In contrast, Example 30.5 works to mitigate the power and institutional authority pilots have over FAs, as we can see in lines 11, 16, and 19. Notably,

> **Example 30.5**
>
> 1   Correct me if I am wrong but it is not listed in our job responsibility to wait on the pit. [. . .]
> 5   When one of the flight attendants went up to the pit while the f/o was in the bathroom the Captain scolded her for not checking on them enough.
> 6   He told her he was going to tell her but he would also explain to the rest of the crew that it was in our job description to take care of them and to check on them every 30 minutes during our flights. [. . .]
> 8   Now, of course I always take care of the guys but they come second I believe my job is taking care of the cabin and pax.
> 9   Of course I know that we are responsible for making sure they get their bathroom breaks but I am not going to interrupt service so I can check on them every 30 minutes.
> 10 He said the rule is every 30 minutes but he would be okay with every hour, never more than an hour.
> 11 When he came out to use the lav he **started to scold me like he is the big bad captain and I should worship him.**
> 12 I do respect he is the captain so I would never tell him off but I am going to politely disagree with him and he is not going to intimidate me. [. . .]
> 14 I explained how much more of service there is on a transcon first class and we honestly had not stopped moving and had not had a chance to call them yet.
> 15 He said you need to check on us every 30 minutes, taking care of us is your JOB and part of your job description and told me to calm down (I was totally calm).
> 16 **He could not stand the fact [that] I spoke up to him like he was a God Captain.**
> 17 Am I wrong?
> 18 I never ever heard of this.
> 19 **The F/O later apologized and said he [thought] the captain was wrong and some captains are just a**w*oles!**
> 20 Thoughts?

safety reports including reported confrontation between pilots and FAs nevertheless use institutionally sanctioned terms for pilots, which was not the case in discussion forum discourse.

In discussion forum posts containing non-institutionally sanctioned terms to describe pilots (as seen in Example 30.5), subsequent posts affirm the original poster's assertion and description of pilots. This solidarity work authenticates the identity being co-constructed in the forum—in the case of Example 30.5, that of a professional FA forced to work with childish captains. Solidarity work also denaturalizes the polished images airlines would seek to portray in advertising literature and campaigns, which still remain in some historic images and nostalgic attitudes, e.g., "the good old days of flying" (cf. Barry 2007; Omelia and Waldock 2003; Stein 2006).

Solidarity and similarity among FAs is portrayed in the discussion forum discourse as weaker than suggested in the safety reports, as seen in Examples 30.6 and 30.7, posts from the same thread discussing passenger service standards and practices.

Example 30.6

1. I am sorry but this is my biggest friggin [pet peeve].
2. After about the third row of coach I am over it on asking how you take your coffee.
3. When you go to starbucks do they know what you want?
4. Neither do I!!!
5. I am not a friggin mindreader, tell me [what's] in it.
6. Gotta love coming out of [Newark] heading south, when you ask Gina from Jersey City how she wants it, she looks at you and says in question form, cream and suga?
7. with the attitude to go along with it.
8. **Like [don't] you know you dip#$&t?**
9. sorry Gina, I guess I [didn't] get my coffee with cream and suga yet.
10. Sugar, s-u-g-a, sugar, [that's] the Jersey City schools for ya lol.

Example 30.7

1. It literally takes 0.5 seconds to say "cream sugar?".
2. Multiply that by 100 and you have 50 seconds out of your 4 hour flight bothering with asking people how they like their coffee.
3. When I get coffee at Mac Donald's, I always forget to say how I like it so it must be normal human nature not [to] think of it.
4. Even worse are FA's who make instructional PA's that sound belittling and snarky:
5. "if you're having coffee tell us how you take it",
6. "if you're eating, lower your tray table", [. . .]
9. It's tacky and kind of lazy.
10. **Just ask, yes each one if necessary, the same question over and over.**
11. **That's what we get paid for, it's not hard and that's what individual service is all about.** [. . .]

Example 30.6 foregrounds an "us" versus "them" relationship between FAs and passengers, especially in line 8. Example 30.7 disagrees with the assertions in Example 30.6, constructing an FA who is patient and understanding with passengers, contrasting with the misanthropic and impatient FA constructed in Example 30.6. The opinions expressed in Examples 30.6 and 30.7 work to authenticate the FAs who wrote and posted them as working FAs whose opinions, although contrasting, are shared by subsequent FAs in the ensuing discussion. FAs are constructed as capable of being both impatient and respectful, misanthropic and caring, depending on who the FA is, what time of day it is, and how long their work day has been, for example.

Identity constructed in the forum discourse denaturalizes the FA identity constructed in the safety reports which is unilateral, working together as a team, and undivided in attitude or opinion. Discussion forum discourse constructs FA identity as multifaceted and multidimensional, offering a perhaps more realistic construction of professional working FAs.

Speaking "Like a Flight Attendant"

There is more than one way to speak (and write) like a FA, and there is not just one "authentic" FA identity. FAs draw on situationally appropriate knowledge to signal to audiences that they are professional FAs. Authenticated ways of speaking like a FA are contingent on myriad contextual factors such as primary audience; (often tacit) situational norms of communication and interaction; communicative goals for report writers and forum posters; and speech event settings.

In both speech events, FAs demonstrate awareness of and conform to institutional authority. Incident reports and forum discourse portray captains as heads of the Chain of Command, irrespective of incident or inter-crew conflict (e.g., Examples 30.1 and 30.4). Even in Example 30.5, the FA does not her/himself refer to the captain by a taboo term; instead it is the first officer—who has greater institutional authority and status than a FA—who is constructed as doing so. Moreover, both speech events show FAs demonstrating knowledge and awareness of occupational roles, tasks, and duties, although discussed and discursively constructed in different ways.

Finally, FAs in both speech events display awareness of the institutional authority and hierarchy of the Chain of Command. The FA at the centre of Example 30.5 does not state that the captain in question should not be captain, or that the role of captain should not exist or be head of the Chain of Command. Instead Example 30.5 argues that the captain violates institutional and occupational behavioural expectations, which, due to his institutionally mandated and appointed role as the ultimate inflight authority, is worthy of comment and discussion.

Safety reports draw on institutional practices, and display knowledge of institutionally sanctioned norms, values, and expectation. These characteristics are present in discussion forum discourse as well; however, discussion forum discourse mitigates power and institutional authority differences between FAs and pilots as well as mitigating institutionally aligned footing in talk about passenger service duties, none of which is found in the safety reports.

Conclusion and Further Directions

This chapter shows that the idealized FA images portrayed in advertising and media are denaturalized by real-world passengers, pilots, and fellow FAs. Additionally, safety report and discussion forum FA identity is authenticated by their respective audiences: ASRS analysts by virtue of publication, and fellow forum participants, in that no forum participants presenting themselves as FAs are challenged in their identity work.

Speaking "like a FA" includes conveying the authority and knowledge commensurate with the position, which does not come overnight, nor solely via training. It comes from being in the job, gaining experience, and learning norms of communication, interaction, and interpretation appropriate with different occupationally and institutionally related situations.

This analysis is not merely academic in interest; professional identity can impact aviation safety. FA discourse reflecting their professional training and status can inspire passenger confidence in the ability of FAs to enact their safety training in the event of an emergency. Passengers may be more likely to follow the orders of someone who sounds like a FA (e.g., shouting emergency evacuation commands with authority and confidence) than one who does not (e.g., mumbling and looking at the floor, uncertain of their expected actions).

Given the paucity of linguistic research on FA discourse and professional identity, there is ample scope for future research in these areas. One area in particular that would be of both academic and applied interest is research on gender and professional FA identity. Despite the aviation industry becoming more diverse, the professions of pilot and FA are still, broadly speaking, gender stereotyped (e.g., pilot = male; FA = female). Research in this area could draw on the substantial body of work done in gender and (professional) identity (e.g., Bergvall, Bing, and Freed 1996; Bucholtz, Liang, and Sutton 1999; Holmes 2006; Mills and Mullany 2011; Mullany 2007). Intersectional research focusing on gender and FA professional identity can enhance our knowledge and understanding of the myriad social, cultural, historical, institutional, and other influences on discursive identity construction in professional settings, and how these influences impact aviation safety practices and emergency outcomes.

Further Reading

On professional identity and discourse see Holmes (2006) and Mullany (2007). On aviation and discourse see Hansen-Schirra and Maksymski (2013) and Nevile (2004).

Related Topics

Interactional sociolinguistics; Linguistic ethnography; Communities of practice; Service encounters; Miscommunication

Acknowledgements

The author is indebted to Colleen Cotter, Ren Reynolds, two anonymous reviewers, and myriad aviation professionals and linguistic anthropology colleagues encountered throughout the years. All errors are the author's own.

Notes

1 National Aeronautics and Space Administration; available at http://asrs.arc.nasa.gov/.
2 While the report refers to the second portion as a "narrative", this article does not approach or analyse it drawing from the significant body of work on sociolinguistic narratives; see Ladegaard (this volume). See Clark (2013) for further discussion.
3 Throughout the chapter, **bold text** indicates data salient to the analysis and discussion. More examples can be found in Clark (2013), along with more detailed discussions of examples. Numbers refer to lines in a narrative and are for ease of discussion and analysis.

References

Ashcraft, Karen Lee. 2007. "Appreciating the "Work" of Discourse: Occupational Identity and Difference as Organizing Mechanisms in the Case of Commercial Airline Pilots." *Discourse and Communication* 1: 9–36.

ASRS (Aviation Safety Reporting System). 2016. "About Our Staff." http://asrs.arc.nasa.gov/overview/staff.html (accessed 30 January 2016).

Banks, Stephen P. 1994. "Performing Public Announcements: The Case of Flight Attendants' Work Discourse." *Text and Performance Quarterly* 14: 253–267.

Barrett, Rusty. 1999. "Indexing Polyphonous Identity in the Speech of African American Drag Queens." In *Reinventing Identities: The Gendered Self in Discourse*, edited by Mary Bucholtz, A. C. Liang, and Laurel A. Sutton, 313–331. Oxford: Oxford University Press.

Barry, Kathleen M. 2007. *Femininity in Flight: A History of Flight Attendants*. Durham: Duke University Press.

Baxter, Judith, and Kieran Wallace. 2009. "Outside In-Group and Out-Group Identities? Constructing Male Solidarity and Female Exclusion in UK Builders' Talk." *Discourse & Society* 20: 411–429.

Bergvall, Victoria L., Janet M. Bing, and Alice F. Freed. 1996. *Rethinking Language and Gender Research: Theory and Practice*. London: Longman.

Bucholtz, Mary, and Kira Hall. 2004. "Language and Identity." In *A Companion to Linguistic Anthropology*, edited by Alessandro Duranti, 369–394. Oxford: Blackwell.

Bucholtz, Mary, and Kira Hall. 2005. "Identity and Interaction: A Sociocultural Approach." *Discourse Studies* 7: 585–614.

Bucholtz, Mary, A. C. Liang, and Laurel A. Sutton, Eds. 1999. *Reinventing Identities: The Gendered Self in Discourse*. New York: Oxford University Press.

Clark, Barbara L. 2013. "Safety Talk and Service Culture: Flight Attendant Discourse in Commercial Aviation." PhD diss., Queen Mary University of London.

Cotter, Colleen, and Daniel Marschall. 2006. "The Persistence of Workplace Ideology and Identity across Communicative Contexts." *Journal of Applied Linguistics* 3: 1–24.

Daems, Jim, Ed. 2014. *The Makeup of RuPaul's Drag Race: Essays on the Queen of Reality Shows*. Jefferson, NC: McFarland & Company.

Dyer, Judy, and Deborah Keller-Cohen. 2000. "The Discursive Construction of Professional Self through Narratives of Personal Experience." *Discourse Studies* 2: 283–304.

Eckert, Penelope. 2008. "Variation and the Indexical Field." *Journal of Sociolinguistics* 12: 453–476.

FAA (Federal Aviation Administration). 2004. "Crew Resource Management Training." Advisory Circular 120–51E (effective 22 January 2004).

Gal, Susan, and Judith T. Irvine. 1995. "The Boundaries of Languages and Disciplines: How Ideologies Construct Difference." *Social Research* 62: 967–1001.

Goffman, Erving. 1974. *Frame Analysis*. New York: Harper and Row.

Goffman, Erving. 1981. *Forms of Talk*. Philadelphia, PA: University of Pennsylvania Press.

Hansen-Schirra, Silvia, and Karin Maksymski, Eds. 2013. *Aviation Communication: Between Theory and Practice*. Frankfurt am Main: Peter Lang.

Helmreich, Robert L., Ashleigh C. Merritt, and John A. Wilhelm. 1999. "The Evolution of Crew Resource Management Training in Commercial Aviation." *International Journal of Aviation Psychology* 9: 19–32.

Hochschild, Arlie Russell. 2003. *The Managed Heart: Commercialization of Human Feeling*. 20th Anniversary edn. Berkeley, CA: University of California Press.

Holmes, Janet. 2006. *Gendered Talk at Work*. Oxford: Blackwell.

Holmes, Janet, Meredith Marra, and Bernadette Vine. 2011. *Leadership, Discourse and Ethnicity*. Oxford: Oxford University Press.

Hymes, Dell. 1986. "Models of the Interaction of Language and Social Life." In *Directions in Sociolinguistics: The Ethnography of Communication*, edited by John Gumperz, and Dell Hymes, 35–71. Oxford: Basil Blackwell.

Hymes, Dell. 2009. "Ways of Speaking." In *Linguistic Anthropology: A Reader*, edited by Alessandro Duranti, 158–171. Oxford: Wiley-Blackwell.

Irvine, Judith T. and Susan Gal. 2009. "Language Ideology and Linguistic Differentiation." In *Linguistic Anthropology: A Reader*, edited by Alessandro Duranti, 402–434. Oxford: Wiley-Blackwell.

Kanki, Barbara, Robert Helmreich, and José Anca, Eds. 2010. *Crew Resource Management*. San Diego, CA: Academic Press.

Kiesling, Scott F. 2001. "'Now I Gotta Watch What I Say': Shifting Constructions of Masculinity in Discourse." *Journal of Linguistic Anthropology* 11: 250–273.

McElhinny, Bonnie. 1995. "Challenging Hegemonic Masculinities: Female and Male Police Officers Handling Domestic Violence." In *Gender Articulated: Language and the Socially Constructed Self*, edited by Kira Hall, and Mary Bucholtz, 217–243. New York: Routledge.

McElhinny, Bonnie. 2005. "Theorizing Gender in Sociolinguistics and Linguistic Anthropology." In *The Handbook of Language and Gender*, edited by Janet Holmes, and Miriam Meyerhoff, 21–42. Oxford: Blackwell.

Mills, Sara, and Louise Mullany. 2011. *Language, Gender and Feminism: Theory, Methodology and Practice*. London: Routledge.

Mullany, Louise. 2007. *Gendered Discourse in the Professional Workplace*. Basingstoke, UK: Palgrave Macmillan.

Murphy, Alexandra G. 2002. "Organizational Politics of Place and Space: The Perpetual Liminoid Performance of Commercial Flight." *Text and Performance Quarterly* 22: 297–316.

Nevile, Maurice. 2004. *Beyond the Black Box: Talk-in-Interaction in the Airline Cockpit*. Aldershot, UK: Ashgate.

Ochs, Elinor. 1992. "Indexing Gender." In *Rethinking Context*, edited by Alessandro Duranti, and Charles Goodwin, 335–358. Cambridge: Cambridge University Press.

O'Keeffe, Douglas. 2007. *Jeff's Way*. Lincoln, NE: iUniverse.

Omelia, Johanna, and Michael Waldock. 2003. *Come Fly with Us! A Global History of the Airline Hostess*. Portland, OR: Collectors Press.

Schiffrin, Deborah. 1993. "'Speaking for Another' in Sociolinguistic Interviews: Alignments, Identities, and Frames." In *Framing in Discourse*, edited by Deborah Tannen, 231–263. Oxford: Oxford University Press.

Schnurr, Stephanie. 2009. "Constructing Leader Identities through Teasing at Work." *Journal of Pragmatics* 41: 1125–1138.

Stein, Elissa. 2006. *Stewardess: Come Fly With Me!* San Francisco, CA: Chronicle Books.

Tannen, Deborah, Ed. 1993. *Framing in Discourse*. New York: Oxford University Press.

Tannen, Deborah, and Cynthia Wallat. 1993. "Interactive Frames and Knowledge Schemas in Interaction: Examples from a Medical Examination/Interview." In *Framing in Discourse*, edited by Deborah Tannen, 57–76. Oxford: Oxford University Press.

Tiemeyer, Phil. 2013. *Plane Queer: Labor, Sexuality, and AIDS in the History of Male Flight Attendants*. Berkeley, CA: University of California Press.

Trester, Anna Marie. 2009. "Discourse Marker 'Oh' as a Means for Realizing the Identity Potential of Constructed Dialogue in Interaction." *Journal of Sociolinguistics* 13: 147–168.

Whitelegg, Drew. 2007. *Working the Skies: The Fast-Paced, Disorienting World of the Flight Attendant*. New York: New York University Press.

Williams, Claire. 2003. "Sky Service: The Demands of Emotional Labour in the Airline Industry." *Gender, Work and Organization* 10: 513–550.

Woolard, Kathryn A. and Bambi B. Schieffelin. 1994. "Language Ideology." *Annual Review of Anthropology* 23: 55–82.

Part V
Applications

31
Vocational Education
Stefano A. Losa

Language and Interaction Issues in Vocational Education

In recent years, issues of language, communication, and interaction in general have become topics of major interest in various areas of educational research. Concerning professional training and vocational education and training in particular, such a focus on language, communication and interaction is empirically founded in the socio-historical transformation of work itself. Indeed, in a context of globalization, two main aspects at least are consistently generating substantial changes in workplaces: the increasing movement of people, practices and ideas across different professions and disciplines (Tsui and Law 2007), and the increasing tertiarization of employment associated with the rise of the so-called "new economy" (see Van De Mieroop and Clifton this volume). This has resulted in a significant increase in the need for language and communication skills within and across work tasks (Heller and Boutet 2006).

Within this context, language use and communication skills become central aspects for all trades and professions. As such, they have significant implications for vocational education and professional training. As suggested by Filliettaz (2014, 228), three implications in particular should be mentioned. First, language and communication skills are no longer to be considered simple "soft" or general work skills, but rather as "key instruments for professional practice and as integral components of professional competences". Second, according to their professional centrality, language use and communication skills are expected to be learned and taught in order to "prepare and adapt the workforce to the multilingual, globalized and discourse mediated professional practices dominating the 'new work order'". In relation to this, vocational education turns out to be a major tool through which to equip people with contemporary requirements and to meet expectations. Third, according to socio-cultural researchers in vocational and adult education, language is increasingly considered not only a functional tool but "a means through which workers experience learning at work." In particular, language conveys meanings that are necessarily situated and emerging from the ongoing interaction process.

Historical Perspectives

Viewing Language as a Mediating Tool

In education research, linguists have been primarily interested in school and classroom settings and it is only at a second stage that applied linguists have started to deal with work practices. Despite this, the field of vocational training research is still young as workplaces are not yet systematically regarded as sites of learning or training (Filliettaz 2010b). Similarly, within research in education and vocational training, language and interactional dimensions are left in the background; the majority of research being empirically oriented to interviews and to ethnographic observation (Filliettaz 2010a).

The importance of language and discursive practices in learning situations becomes more explicit when taking socio-cultural theories of learning into consideration. By transposing these theories of learning to work situations (Boud and Garrick 1999; Candlin 2002; Sarangi and Candlin 2003; Billet 2001) and specifically to situations of vocational education (Lave 1988; Lave and Wenger 1991; Billett 2011; Filliettaz, de Saint-Georges, and Duc 2008), researchers have been able to show how much learning how to work and becoming a member of communities of practice relies on professional discourse and social interaction. Indeed, by drawing from a Vygotskian conception of psychological development and learning (Vygotsky 1978), such theories show that learning occurs when more experienced people afford assistance and interactional guidance to learners, allowing them to reach the needed level of understanding to accomplish tasks and solve problems. Learning is thus not an individual procedure of personal acquisition but rather a collective process in which "others" play a central role.

Similarly, the importance of language in interaction in orienting learners in their learning process is in strong affinity with Bruner's concept of "scaffolding" between adult and child (Bruner 1983). Transposed to the context of schooling in general and vocational or professional learning in particular, such concepts allow one to perceive how teaching and learning processes are mediated by discourse and language practices (e.g., explication of practices, verbalization of perspectives, experiences, judgments or emerging issues related to an activity). Ideas of guidance and direct interaction between learners and experienced workers are repeatedly advanced as key ingredients of vocational learning. In relation to this, the social dimension of learning is also made visible using anthropological concepts such as Lave and Wenger's "community of practice" and "legitimate peripheral participation" (Lave and Wenger 1991; see King this volume). Such concepts demonstrate how learning is far from being just about knowledge acquisition; rather apprentices gain access to knowledge and develop practical skills by adequately participating in social practices and becoming members of communities of practice (Losa, Duc, and Filliettaz 2014).

In more general terms, researchers interested in vocational education and training who adopt discursive and interactional frameworks have demonstrated the importance of language as a "mediating tool" between actors, activities, cultural practices and knowledge when learning and teaching processes occur: "language use is seen as a major mediating tool by which individuals engage in social practices and encounter local, cultural and psychological transformations" (Filliettaz 2014, 230). Such statements about the role of language in learning development go against current commonsense ideas according to which "language" is reduced to a secondary role and is limited to the classroom context, external to the workplace.

Critical Issues and Topics

Identity Transitions from School to Work

If vocational training is generally regarded as the period of apprenticeship in a trade, it is also associated with the transition from school to work. If, on the individual level, such a period coincides with the transition from adolescence to adulthood, on the professional level, it represents a period of research and construction of a professional identity. Such a process of identity construction is not necessarily linear nor automatic. It appears to be rather complex and occurs over a significant period of time (Cohen-Scali 2000; Duc 2012).

Apprentices performing vocational learning transitions tend to face numerous challenges and often contradictory expectations. In the case of Switzerland, for instance, recent studies have shown that between 20 per cent and 40 per cent of apprentices who enter the dual vocational education and training system do not complete their apprenticeship within the stated terms of their contracts (Stalder and Nägele 2011). Dropout rates are largely attributable to the quality of interpersonal relationships in workplaces and to the level of support provided by trainers to apprentices in the learning context (Lamamra and Masdonati 2009). In particular, the nature of the participation in a vocational relationship and participation in social interactions with various stakeholders appear to play a decisive role in the learning process as well as in terms of identity construction for apprentices (Filliettaz, de Saint-Georges, and Duc 2008; Duc and Lamamra 2014). In such a context, vocational training is far from limited to knowledge transfer activities and theoretical content. Rather, it seems to be characterized by a social activity of constructing and maintaining relations with others. Therefore, being involved in the training relationship means not only contributing to training activities in the narrow sense, but also implies fitting into the dynamics of interpersonal relationships based on positions locally endorsed by actors in interaction.

Faced with this problem, adopting a linguistic and interactional perspective on vocational education allows the fine analysis of interactional dynamics and communication as they occur between trainers and learners or colleague learners. How do learners address their trainers and vice versa? How does the learner participate in training activities? How does one participate in exchanges and discussions with the various stakeholders? Such a perspective can therefore significantly contribute to understanding interactional and interpersonal mechanisms that promote or prevent learning processes and which impact on vocational learning paths.

Current Contributions and Research

Becoming a Professional

In research on vocational training, the issue of professional socialization proves itself to be a significant subject of study in that it allows researchers to query not only the process of knowledge transfer but also the identity transformations learners are required to undertake and the effective interactional modalities through which learners gain expertise. Such a research perspective highlights not only the importance of language in the process of socialization but more comprehensively the role of language and discursive exchanges in the acquisition of professional expertise.

According to this, the adoption of a linguistic and interactional perspective is helpful for analysing and understanding the process of becoming a professional. It enables an analysis of the ways in which actors within a certain social structure linguistically and discursively enact institutional roles, identities, and cultural practices. Regarding the way professional expertise is acquired through language, it is worth mentioning the work of Gravengaard and Rimestad (2014). The authors analyse how trainee journalists leaving university and starting an internship in a newspaper newsroom are socialized into the professional journalistic culture to become members of a specific community of practice. The authors point to the way the socialization process occurs, namely when trainees also acquire tacit knowledge about cultural and professional norms. In particular, they show how through language and discursive practices in the newsroom, trainees develop a "professional vision" (Goodwin 1994) about what could be considered as a "good news story". Indeed, "newcomers learn in practice and from practice—from what is said and what is not said by their superiors, thus becoming an even more competent member of the social group" (Gravengaard and Rimestad 2014, 82).

Groups or communities that are organized around these different practices, whether in training situations or in work contexts, tend to share a repertoire of resources for learning such as language, particular sensitivities, specific tools and skills (Lave and Wenger 1991). However, collective training contexts not only share professional specific contents but a whole system (most often tacit and implicit) of normative and behavioural expectations reflecting standards, beliefs, values and attitudes peculiar to the community (Lave and Wenger 1991; Wenger 2000). In a study by Delbos and Jorion (1990) on fishing, salt production, and shellfish farming in coastal communities in France, any form of participation in work activities (even training situations) are seen as socialization spaces in which language and communication are both the means of knowledge transfer and the content itself of what is transmitted. In this sense, the transmission and learning of a trade involves empirical, operative, and practical knowledge whose nature is not limited to objective and/or procedural knowledge. As expressed by the workers themselves, *ce qui se transmet, ce n'est pas du savoir, c'est du travail* ("what it is transmitted is not knowledge but work") (Delbos and Jorion 1990, 46). Such a "transmission of work" becomes possible through language use and interactional practices, which provide novices with normative landmarks through which they can compose their activity. In other words, the transmission of knowledge and skills involves putting things into words, forms of verbalization such as scolding, prohibitions, and other forms of regulation. In these terms, the training relationship is less a matter of content to transfer than socialization to a "world order" or an ethos mediated by language.

Therefore, despite the fact that vocational training contexts do not cover stable and unified realities (Dubar 2000), each community of practice can be considered as a socializing space within which trade practices are transmitted but also where social relations between trainers, learners, and colleagues are shaped according to the normative expectations in force. One of the goals of a linguistic and interactional perspective is indeed to finely capture the linguistic and discursive practices through which social influences bring novices to adopt not only explicit contents and practices, but the local culture as well.

Vocational Guidance Practices

In the last decade, another important research area that has produced a number of studies is that of vocational education practices. Linguistic and interactional perspectives have been increasingly applied to investigate how apprentices are guided and assisted by their trainers and/or mentors in their vocational learning process. How do trainers afford or shape the manners through which learners increase their expertise or become professionals? How do they interactionally and discursively behave to make learning situations as insightful as possible to learners? What kind of guidance and assistance do trainers mobilize and how do they exploit them over time as meaningful learning practices?

When considering guidance practices within vocational relationships, scholars have investigated trainers' methods and strategies of supervision of trainees in particular. Indeed, some authors such as Kunégel (2005) have shown the manner in which the training relationship, as a form of social mediation, can be translated into typical forms of accompaniment and support (i.e., instruction, demonstration, guidance, and valuation). Moreover, these forms of accompaniment dynamically fit a more or less long period of monitoring, giving rise to forms of gradual familiarization until the novice reaches autonomous self-employment. In relation to this, in the context of air traffic control training, Koskela and Palukka (2011) analyse the ways in which trainers and trainees act and interact in training situations. They apply conversation analysis and ethnomethodology tools to video recordings of instructional interactions and to ethnographic material collected in a vocational institute of aviation, as well as to two aerodrome control tower units. First, they identify different instructional strategies that trainers adopt to guide trainees' practices. Second, they also reveal the ways these strategies are fine-tuned by trainers according to the training phase in which the trainee is positioned. The study shows that the guidance interactions evolve from being trainer-driven to trainer-guided, in line with the trainee's progression from the simulator-training phase to that of on-the-job training.

Such a progressive form of learner scaffolding and assistance has also been investigated in a research program on dual apprenticeship training in Switzerland, conducted by the Interaction and Training team of the University of Geneva (Filliettaz, de Saint-Georges, and Duc 2009). Naturally occurring training interactions in three different trades (car mechanics, automation, and electric assembly) were collected with ethnographic observations as well as video recording and analysed through an interactional and multimodal approach. The study highlighted two main models of training which were implemented by trainers. Within the first model, referred to as "assisted participation", apprentices do not work on their own but are closely assisted by experienced workers who give them local opportunities to gain access to practice. Within the second model, apprentices are instead given full access to engage in production work tasks in a relatively autonomous way; guidance is thus much more distant and more oriented towards productivity than training.

Still in the context of the Swiss Interaction and Training team, Filliettaz, Rémery and Trebert (2014) explored guidance practices in an early childhood education training programme. By adopting an interactional and multimodal perspective on guidance, the study investigated the ways in which training opportunities are provided by vocational trainers during internships. In particular, the study empirically identified three distinct interactional participatory configurations referred to as i) observation, ii) joint-action, and iii) display. Such configurations stress both the complexity and the dynamic nature of training practices. The authors draw on Billett's (2001) idea that workers do not learn just by performing specific tasks on their own. Instead, discursively and interactionally adequate resources need to be afforded, such as when more experienced workers share their knowledge and skills, and assist interns in their work.

Closely related to training supervision strategies, a number of studies have also revealed how language use and discourse practices are involved in vocational guidance work. These constitute key resources for both trainers and trainees to formulate, reformulate and resemiotize instructions (Filliettaz, de Saint-Georges, and Duc 2010) in order to turn local practice-based activities into meaningful learning situations. Zemel and Koschmann (2014), for instance, analyse interaction occurring during a surgery at a teaching hospital involving medical students and a surgeon included in a residency programme. They explore the ways in which the instructor surgeon uses demonstrations as instruction and the ways in which trainees respond by enacting their own versions of the instructor's demonstration in a particular accountable, displayable and evaluable way while the surgeon observes. By applying a conversation analysis lens to fragments of interaction, the study contributes to showing how through language, discursive practices, and embodied action, instructional work becomes meaningful and produces "learnables". Learnables are thus interactionally and collectively achieved according to how trainers and trainees enact instructions. In relation to this, the authors explicitly draw on Macbeth (2011), concluding that "for instruction to occur properly participants must be sufficiently competent in the practices of instruction to participate in instruction" (Zemel and Koschmann 2014, 180). Similarly, Lindwall and Ekström (2012) consider interactional and sequential accomplishment of instructions and instructed actions in the context of manual skills. They apply a conversation analysis perspective to a video recorded interaction involving a teacher demonstrating how to crochet chain-stitches, the teacher's request to students to reproduce the demonstrated action, and the teacher's ongoing corrections to students needing further guidance. Interestingly, the study shows how language and embodied action are central resources for both parties in performing the entire activity in a meaningful way. In other words, within these situations of "instruction-in interaction", "the student needs to turn what the teacher is saying and doing into practical courses of action" (Lindwall and Ekström 2012, 46) and the teacher produces on-activity assessments, corrections and instructed actions specifically designed and adjusted to the student's actual needs.

Language and interactional-based research on vocational guidance practices therefore, clearly points to the centrality of language use and discursive practices as key resources for both trainers and trainees to meaningfully endorse learning and training positions and roles. The fine-grained observation of guidance and supervision practices highlights the fact that learning experiences are far from being shaped solely by the kinds of knowledge locally available. Rather, it is also the verbal and non-verbal ways by which forms of knowledge are made available and visible to apprentices that strongly matter. In other words, linguistic and interactional approaches demonstrate to what extent the type of learning is clearly affected by the ways instruction and guidance are interactionally enacted and accomplished.

Participation as an Interactional Learning Process

In the field of vocational education and training, the issue of participation has mainly been approached in terms of identity positioning and belonging to a professional community of practice. For apprentices, this requires participation in joint activities and being able to "position themselves in a complex network of relations involving other apprentices, teachers, trainers and co-workers" (Filliettaz 2010a, 30). Thus, individuals involved in a learning process need to interactively align to what is normatively expected according to the social role they take on.

In relation to this, Billett (2001, 2004) shows how individual engagement and agency are key components of participation and learning within communities and professional environments. In particular, he pays attention to contextual and social conditions that may have an impact on learning opportunities by focusing on the forms and qualities of guidance processes through which experts provide support to newcomers in work and learning tasks. Learning is thus considered as the consequence of "participatory practices" enacted by learners and by means of which they may get access to learning opportunities. According to Billett, participatory practices consist of both social factors and individual factors. Social factors are characterized by the range of resources afforded by work environments (i.e., forms of guidance and expertise, material resources). Individual factors are associated with the ways novices elect to engage in work activities in relation to the resources afforded to them. By transposing such a perspective on a vocational education context, it becomes relevant to investigate how trainees and trainers involved in interaction participate and position themselves in relation to each other in a more or less expansive or restrictive way (Fuller and Unwin 2003). In other words, participation in communities of practices has to be considered as a reciprocal process or joint action (Clark 1996; Goffman 1959) in which participants permanently and mutually negotiate their roles, expressions, faces and ultimately their legitimacy. Participation is thus viewed as interactional participatory practices and defined as "a mutual orientation the interactants manifest to each other and the reciprocal engagement they display toward a joint activity" (Filliettaz, de Saint-Georges, and Duc 2009, 99).

In relation to this topic, the work of Nguyen (2006) demonstrates the importance for a learner to be able to handle "interactional competences" in order to convey expertise. By using a conversation analysis framework, the author investigates the ways in which a pharmacy intern performed his professional knowledge in the practice of patient consultation over time. By theoretically assuming that knowledge ability does not exist *per se* outside social interactions, the analysis shows how far novice professionals need to develop the interactional competence to construct themselves as experts in interaction. Thus, performing knowledge and skills effectively in social practices is a key factor for being an expert. Similarly, Losa, Duc, and Filliettaz (2014) explored the relationship between trainers and apprentices within training centres in the Geneva area (Switzerland). The authors highlighted how interactional processes can lead to a legitimate, recognized, and valued social position. Therefore, being involved in a valued and recognized way may have strong implications in terms of access to knowledge and membership within learning communities of practice.

As such examples show, participation in vocational learning contexts strongly relies on discourse and interaction practices. Only a language and interactional perspective fully reveals how far language use and discursive practices are involved in training and learning processes.

Main Research Methods

Interaction and Discourse Analytic Perspective: The Theoretical Framework

There is a variety of possible ways to characterize an interaction and discourse analytic perspective. A widely used definition is the one that considers this perspective as "the study of language use in relation to specific institutional and cultural contexts and with regards to its cognitive and social implications" (Filliettaz 2014, 231; see also Wodak and Meyer 2009). This perspective does not constitute a unified theoretical frame but must be understood as a multidisciplinary perspective whereby a range of approaches are involved such as interactional sociolinguistics (see Gordon and Kraut this volume), conversation analysis (see Toerien this volume) and critical discourse analysis (see Koller this volume). Such a framework combines several analytic approaches that are sometimes competing or contradictory for analysing discourse and interaction. Nevertheless, these approaches tend to simultaneously share common assumptions about language and social action. In particular, they consider language not only as an information transmission channel between parties but also as a means to take part in interactional dynamics such as participating in group activities, negotiating identities, collectively interpreting and understanding social situations, taking on roles, cooperating. In particular, these approaches provide valuable tools to "identify patterns of practice that make visible what members need to know, produce, and interpret to participate in socially appropriate ways" (Filliettaz 2014, 231).

In more detail, it is worth highlighting four key concepts which are widely mobilized in the different disciplines involved in the interactional analysis perspective and applied to research in education. A first concept is that of "situated identity". This refers to the way in which participants in social interactions are positioned in a reciprocal manner according to the local cultural and institutional expectations. In general, the situated identity is conceived not only with reference to general or pre-existing social categories, but also to more locally salient positions and roles that sequentially unfold in talk-in-interaction (Goffman 1961). Several authors propose typological distinctions between various forms of situated identities that are related to the ongoing activity (Filliettaz 2006) and to the role played during an exchange.

In connection with situated identity, a second concept, that of "contextual indexicality", provides understandings about how language and language practices are linked to contextual conditions. For if, on the one hand, discourses result from social, cultural or institutional contingencies, on the other hand, it is also important to consider the fact that language practices also do shape and produce contexts according to the way participants interpret and make sense of the ongoing situation of interaction (Duranti and Goodwin 1992). Especially in socio-linguistics, such a constructivist conception of contexts is particularly well illustrated by Goffman's framing theory (1974), where perception of reality is neither a direct nor univocal activity but needs to be filtered according to social frames. These frames are representations and images that participants convene to shape their own understanding of what is happening in front of their eyes, and enable them to define the contextual situation as a situation of a certain type. In addition to Goffman's analysis, contributions from interactional sociolinguistics account for the complex relations linking contextual information with participants' interactional behaviour in general, and the production of speech in particular.

In order to understand the ways contextual dispositions and emerging identities are interactionally achieved, interactional and discourse analysts also refer to the concept of "sequential organization". Initially the concern of conversation analysts and ethnomethod-ologists, such a concept allows the exploration of the dynamic order through which interactions unfold step-by-step (Sacks, Schegloff, and Jefferson 1978; Schegloff 2007; Mondada 2007). Indeed, it is empirically argued that participants position themselves towards one another during the interaction, in order to sequentially coordinate their action (e.g., turn taking). Such a fine-grained dynamic process rests on the fact that participants make their actions interactionally visible and publicly accountable.

Finally, participation in interaction and the related contextual endorsement of situated identities is far from being just a matter of linguistic or verbal outflow. On the contrary, communication deeply relies on a broad range of semiotic resources. These are used by participants as a complement to verbal resources in order to coordinate their participation in interactions and in accomplishing joint actions. Interaction and discourse analysts refer to the concept of "multimodality" (i.e., Kress and Van Leeuwen 2001; Norris 2004) when considering non verbal resources such as gestures, gaze, body position, interactions with objects and the material environment, that participants mobilize to contextually produce and interpret meaning and achieve communication.

Interaction and Discourse Analytic Perspective: The Methodological Toolbox

In keeping with the conceptual framework presented above, specific methodological principles have to be considered. First, educational researchers adopting an interactional perspective tend to assume an "ethnographic perspective" allowing them to focus on empirical data in order to document naturally occurring training and real learning practices as they occur in ordinary contexts (see Wilson this volume). Empirical data consists of oral, multimodal as well as written texts emerging from verbal and non-verbal interactions between, for example, apprentices and trainers. In addition, such a research stance implies taking into account the relational process in which, on the one hand, the observer progressively gains understanding of the observed practices and social relations and, on the other hand, his presence becomes more meaningful and acceptable to the observed participants.

A second methodological requirement related to the analytic perspective presented here is to capture as extensively as possible the indexical, dynamic, and multimodal nature of the targeted interactions in context. To do so, researchers increasingly make use of audio-video recordings to finely capture details of interaction unfolding. And finally, to render the audio-video recording operative and analysable, researchers commonly agree on the necessity to go through the transcription of the collected data. Transcripts "give a written and synthetic form of verbal and non-verbal behaviour as they unfold on audio-video recordings" (Filliettaz 2014, 234). If transcripts do not exhaustively capture all perceptible aspects of the recordings, they are able to make visible details relevant to the analysis (see Ochs 1979; Jefferson 2004). The increasing use of video technologies for data collection has an important impact on transcription practices whereby the dynamic as well as multimodal nature of talk-in-interaction is accounted for.

Future Directions

According to current research in vocational education involving interactional and discourse analytic perspectives, future directions point to the complex links between interaction, learning, and social relations. In particular, three main challenges have to be considered. First, the analytical focus on micro-interactional mechanisms needs to widen the scope of the vocational issues examined. As suggested by Erickson (2004) and Filliettaz, Losa, and Duc (2013), such a lens repositioning is possible by varying and contrasting contexts of study and situations of interaction as well as by integrating a dynamic perspective that considers various contexts and/or actors over time. This will contribute to linking microscopic qualitative analysis to macroscopic social realities and, thus, enhance the understanding of vocational education issues such as "situated trajectories of learning" (de Saint-Georges and Filliettaz 2008) and identity development. Second, by applying discourse analytic methodologies to vocational education practices it will be possible to significantly enhance the understanding and the visibility of processes, mechanisms, difficulties, and challenges faced by apprentices when crossing vocational context boundaries as well as transiting into working lives. Third, as currently explored by the Interaction and Training team at the University of Geneva, a particularly interesting challenge is to use collected empirical material to nurture training programmes for vocational trainers and educators in order to increase awareness of formal and informal guidance issues.

Further Reading

Billett (2011) is a foundational book about what constitutes the rich and diverse sector of vocational education.

Filliettaz and de Saint-Georges (2009) provides an introduction to the main questions and approaches available in the Francophone research area on "language and work". Some issues addressed are coordination, identity, power relations, professional discourse genres as well as methodological frameworks.

Zemel and Koschmann (2014) provides exemplification of the way language and instructional activity are interactionally linked and coextensive to participants' experiential learning.

Related Topics

Interactional sociolinguistics; Conversation analysis; Linguistic ethnography; Social constructionism; Communities of practice; Directives; Narratives; Intercultural communication; Multilingualism; Men's talk in women's work; Professional identity construction

References

Billett, Stephen. 2001. "Learning through Work: Workplace Affordances and Individual Engagement." *Journal of Workplace Learning* 13: 209–214.

Billett, Stephen. 2004. "Workplace Participatory Practices: Conceptualising Workplaces as Learning Environments." *Journal of Workplace Learning* 16: 312–324.

Billett, Stephen. 2011. *Vocational Education: Purposes, Traditions and Prospects*. Netherlands: Springer.

Boud, David, and John Garrick. 1999. *Understanding Learning at Work*. London: Routledge.

Bruner, Jérôme S. 1983. *Le développement de l'enfant: Savoir faire savoir dire*. Paris: Presses Universitares de France.

Candlin, Chris. 2002. *Research and Practice in Professional Discourse*. Hong Kong: City University of Hong Kong Press.

Clark, Herbert H. 1996. *Using Language*. Cambridge: Cambridge University Press.

Cohen-Scali, Valérie. 2000. *Alternance et identité professionnelle*. Paris: Presses Universitaires de France.

de Saint-Georges, Ingrid, and Laurent Filliettaz. 2008. "Situated Trajectories of Learning in Vocational Training Interactions." *European Journal of Psychology of Education* 23: 213–233.

Delbos, Geneviève, and Paul Jorion. 1990. *La transmission des savoirs*. Paris: MSH.

Dubar, Claude. 2000. *La socialisation*. 3rd ed. Paris: Armand Colin.

Duc, Barbara. 2012. "La transition de l'école au monde du travail: Une analyse interactionnelle et longitudinale des phénomènes de participation et de construction identitaire en formation professionnelle initiale." PhD diss., University of Geneva.

Duc, Barbara, and Nadia Lamamra. 2014. "Young People's Progress After Dropout from Vocational Education and Training: Transitions and Occupational Integration at Stake. A Longitudinal Qualitative Perspective." In *Psychological, Educational, and Sociological Perspectives on Success and Well-Being in Career Development*, edited by Anita C. Keller, Robin Samuel, Manfred Max Bergman, and Norbert K. Semmer, 45–68. Dordrecht: Springer.

Duranti, Alessandro, and Charles Goodwin. 1992. *Rethinking Context: Language as an Interactive Phenomenon*. Cambridge: Cambridge University Press.

Erickson, Frederick. 2004. *Talk and Social Theory: Ecologies of Speaking and Listening in Everyday Life*. Cambridge: Polity.

Filliettaz, Laurent. 2006. "Asymétrie et prise de rôle. Le cas des réclamations dans les interactions de service." In *Les interactions asymétriques*, edited by Marty Laforest, and Diane Vincent, 89–112. Québec: Nota Bene.

Filliettaz, Laurent. 2010a. "Dropping Out of Apprenticeship Programs: Evidence from the Swiss Vocational Education System and Methodological Perspectives for Research." *International Journal of Training Research* 8: 141–153.

Filliettaz, Laurent. 2010b. "Interaction and Miscommunication in the Swiss Vocational Education Context: Researching Vocational Learning from a Linguistic Perspective." *Journal of Applied Linguistics and Professional Practice* 7: 27–50.

Filliettaz, Laurent. 2014. "Understanding Learning for Work: Interaction and Discourse Analysis." In *International Handbook of Research in Professional and Practice-Based Learning*, edited by Stephen Billett, Christian Harteis, and Hans Gruber, 225–255. Dordrecht: Springer.

Filliettaz, Laurent, and Ingrid de Saint-Georges. 2009. "Francophone Research on Language and Work." In *The Handbook of Business Discourse*, edited by Francesca Bargiela, 423–435. Edinburgh: Edinburgh University Press.

Filliettaz, Laurent, Ingrid de Saint-Georges, and Barbara Duc. 2008. *"Vos mains sont intelligentes!": Interactions en formation professionnelle initiale*. Université de Genève: Cahiers de la Section des Sciences de l'Education.

Filliettaz, Laurent, Ingrid de Saint-Georges, and Barbara Duc. 2009. "Interactions verbales et dynamiques de participation en formation professionnelle initiale." *Formation et pratiques professionnelles*, 95–124.

Filliettaz, Laurent, Ingrid de Saint-Georges, and Barbara Duc. 2010. "Reformuation, resémiotisation et trajectoires d'apprentissage en formation professionnelle initiale: l'enseignement du giclage du mortier en maçonnerie." In *Reformulations pluri-sémiotiques en contexte de formation*, edited by Alain Rabatel, 283–305. Besançon: Presses universitaires de Franche-Comté.

Filliettaz, Laurent, Stefano A. Losa, and Barbara Duc. 2013. "Power, Miscommunication and Cultural Diversity." In *Multilingualism and Multimodality*, edited by Ingrid de Saint-Georges, and Jean-Jacques Weber, 153–181. Netherlands: SensePublishers.

Filliettaz, Laurent, Vanessa Rémery, and Dominique Trebert. 2014. "Relation tutorale et configurations de participation à l'interaction: Analyse de l'accompagnement des stagiaires dans le champ de la petite enfance." *Activités* 11: 22–46.

Fuller, Alison, and Lorna Unwin. 2003. "Learning as Apprentices in the Contemporary UK Workplace: Creating and Managing Expansive and Restrictive Participation." *Journal of Education and Work* 16: 407–426.

Goffman, Erving. 1959. *The Presentation of Self in Everyday Life*. New York: Doubleday.

Goffman, Erving. 1961. *Encounters: Two Studies in the Sociology of Interaction*. Indianapolis, IN: Bobbs-Merrill.

Goffman, Erving. 1974. *Frame Analysis*. New York: Harper & Row.

Goodwin, Charles. 1994. "Professional Vision." *American Anthropologist* 96: 606–633.

Gravengaard, Gitte, and Lene Rimestad. 2014. "Socialising Journalist Trainees in the Newsroom: On How to Capture the Intangible Parts of the Socialising Process." *Nordicom Review* 35: 81–97.

Heller, Monica, and Josiane Boutet. 2006. "Vers de nouvelles formes de pouvoir langagier? Langue(s) et économie dans la nouvelle économie." *Langage et Société* 118: 5–16.

Jefferson, Gail. 2004. "Glossary of Transcript Symbols with an Introduction." In *Conversation Analysis*, edited by Gene H. Lerner, 13–34. Amsterdam: John Benjamins.

Koskela, Inka, and Hannele Palukka. 2011. "Trainer Interventions as Instructional Strategies in Air Traffic Control Training." *Journal of Workplace Learning* 23: 293–314.

Kress, Gunther, and Theo Van Leeuwen. 2001. *Multimodal Discourse: The Modes and Media of Contemporary Communication*. London: Arnold.

Kunégel, Patrick. 2005. "Analyses du travail et formation: L'apprentissage en entreprise: L'activité de médiation des tuteurs." *Education permanente* 165: 127–138.

Lamamra, Nadia, and Jonas Masdonati. 2009. *Arrêter une formation professionnelle: Mots et maux d'apprenti-es*. Lausanne: Antipodes.

Lave, Jean. 1988. *Cognition in Practice: Mind, Mathematics and Culture in Everyday Life*. Cambridge: Cambridge University Press.

Lave, Jean, and Etienne Wenger. 1991. *Situated Learning: Legitimate Peripheral Participation*. Cambridge: Cambridge University Press.

Lindwall, Oskar, and Anna Ekström. 2012. "Instruction-in-Interaction: The Teaching and Learning of a Manual Skill." *Human Studies* 35: 27–49.

Losa, Stefano A., Barbara Duc, and Laurent Filliettaz. 2014. "Success, Well-Being and Social Recognition: An Interactional Perspective on Vocational Training Practices." In *Psychological, Educational, and Sociological Perspectives on Success and Well-Being in Career Development*, edited by Anita C. Keller, Robin Samuel, Manfred Max Bergman, and Norbert K. Semmer, 69–98. Dordrecht: Springer.

Macbeth, Douglas. 2011. "Understanding Understanding as an Instructional Matter." *Journal of Pragmatics* 43: 438–451.

Mondada, Lorenza. 2007. "Multimodal Resources for Turn-Taking Pointing and the Emergence of Possible Next Speakers." *Discourse Studies* 9: 194–225.

Nguyen, Hanh Thi. 2006. "Constructing 'Expertness': A Novice Pharmacist's Development of Interactional Competence in Patient Consultations." *Communication & Medicine* 3: 147–160.

Norris, Sigrid. 2004. *Analyzing Multimodal Interaction: A Methodological Framework*. New York: Routledge.
Ochs, Elinor. 1979. "Transcription as Theory." *Developmental Pragmatics* 10: 43–72.
Sacks, Harvey, Emanuel A. Schegloff, and Gail Jefferson. 1978. "A Simplest Systematics for the Organization of Turn-Taking for Conversation." In *Studies in the Organization of Conversational Interaction*, edited by Jim Schenkein, 7–55. New York: Academic Press.
Sarangi, Srikant, and Chris Candlin. 2003. "Categorization and Explanation of Risk: A Discourse Analytical Perspective." *Health, Risk & Society* 5: 115–124.
Schegloff, Emanuel. A. 2007. *Sequence Organization in Interaction: A Primer in Conversation Analysis*. Vol. 1. Cambridge: Cambridge University Press.
Stalder, Barbara E., and Christof Nägele. 2011. "Vocational Education and Training in Switzerland: Organisation, Development and Challenges for the Future." In *Youth Transitions in Switzerland: Results from the Tree Panel Study*, edited by Manfred Max Bergman, Sandra Hupka-Brunner, Anita Keller, Thomas Meyer, and Barbara Elisabeth Stalder, 18–39. Zürich: SEISMO.
Tsui, Amy B. M., and Doris Y. K. Law. 2007. "Learning as Boundary-Crossing in School-University Partnership." *Teaching and Teacher Education* 23: 1289–1301.
Vygotsky, Lev Semenovich. 1978. *Mind in Society: The Development of Higher Psychological Processes*. Cambridge, MA: Harvard University Press.
Wenger, Etienne. 2000. "Communities of Practice and Social Learning Systems." *Organization* 7: 225–246.
Wodak, Ruth, and Michael Meyer, Eds. 2009. *Methods for Critical Discourse Analysis*. London: Sage.
Zemel, Alan, and Timothy Koschmann. 2014. "'Put Your Fingers Right in Here': Learnability and Instructed Experience." *Discourse Studies* 16: 163–183.

32
Gender, Language, and Leadership
Enabling Women Leaders
Judith Baxter

Introduction/Definitions

Women leaders in the workplace are a comparatively recent historical phenomenon, and because of their minority position, there has been a growing interest from various social science disciplines in the often innovative ways in which women perform leadership, and the ways in which they challenge continuing barriers to their career progression (e.g., Anderson and Vinnicombe 2015; Eagly and Carli 2007; Wilson and Boxer 2015). While there are numerous studies investigating women's leadership from various organization, political, sociological, and psychological perspectives, there is relatively little research exploring the subject from a sociolinguistic viewpoint. Of the research that has emerged, most of this has been conducted in US or British European contexts. This chapter will review some of the adventurous work that is being carried out by scholars in the emerging field of gender, language, and leadership, and consider directions in which such work might develop in the future.

There are two central themes in current sociolinguistic research on women's leadership, which will be reviewed in this chapter. The first is largely descriptive, comprising studies that assess the language that women use to enact their authority and to accomplish leadership "effectively" when they occupy positions of power previously held by men. The second theme is more explicitly critical, comprising feminist studies that examine the sociolinguistic reasons why women encounter significant barriers to their career progress in workplaces that continue to be male-dominated at senior levels.

Statistics compiled by the United Nations (UN Women 2015) show that women are now entering traditionally male-dominated occupations in greater numbers. However, they are still rarely employed in jobs with status, power, and authority, and relative to their overall share of total employment, women are significantly underrepresented among managers, legislators and senior officials. Only one in four managers or senior officials are women; worldwide, women are paid 17 per cent less than men; and only 24 Heads of State or Government are women. Decades after women have achieved equal rights and opportunities in the western world at least, they are still struggling to become leaders within organizations even though many have put into place hiring, parental leave, recruitment, and mentoring policies to help women apply for promotion and sustain busy careers. Among these new policies and practices, it remains rare to find any initiatives addressing "linguistic" barriers within organizations. As I will explore, research shows that women leaders have a harder job than men to be effective through their talk: that is, to be listened to, be included in key decisions, be taken seriously, and to influence the views of others (Baxter 2014; Holmes 2006). Alongside this, the use of "gendered language" and the way women are often represented by others in the workplace can be prejudicial to both women and men as they go about their daily business, such as referring to grown women as "girls" in work contexts, or calling a female leader "scary" because she speaks as directly and assertively as her male peers. As long as significant gender inequalities in language use remain in workplaces around the world, it is surely crucial that leadership language is further investigated in gender and language scholarship.

As Mullany (2011) points out, leadership has proved a difficult concept to define, but from a sociolinguistic perspective, researchers have focused on how leadership is constructed through the linguistic choices that are made. Accordingly, leadership is defined in this chapter as the linguistic choices that leaders make as they go about their daily business of maintaining good working relationships with colleagues in order to make effective decisions and get essential work done. Aligned to this is the way in which the use of a leader's language is always bound up with power and with colleagues' perceptions of how well leaders exercise their authority. Women have a particularly challenging task in negotiating power relations with their colleagues as there are often entrenched, gendered expectations of leadership, enforcing women to invest extra linguistic work in demonstrating themselves to be as effective as their male peers (Baxter 2010; Kanter 1993).

This chapter will review the range of theories that explain the role of language as the principal medium through which women's leadership identities are performed, as well as the means of constructing barriers for women who aspire to leadership in the workplace. I will then present applied examples from the work of gender, language, and leadership scholars to show how we can intervene to raise women's awareness of the sociolinguistic strategies they can use, and the effects such strategies can produce in the workplace. Throughout this chapter, a distinction is made between individuals who self-identify as "women" and "men" (often but not always because of biological characteristics), and the notion that gender is a cultural construct which assigns conventional and stereotyped meanings to the performance of "masculinity" and "femininity".

Historical Perspectives

There are broadly three theoretical perspectives to research in the field of gender, language, and leadership, which in turn are strongly influenced by theories from both sociolinguistics and organization studies. The first two, dominance and difference, are reviewed in this section, while the third—the most generally adopted by scholars today—is reviewed in the next section.

The dominance perspective views leadership as primarily a masculine construct because historically, men have dominated most professions and have taken the majority of leadership roles (e.g., Kanter 1993; Koller 2004; Spender 1980). Following the "male as norm" rule, women in leadership positions are marked as "the other", the exception to the male norm, and therefore judged to be less "fit" or competent for the role. The prevailing stereotype is one which assumes that an effective leader uses language that is authoritative, assertive, adversarial, competitive, task-focused, goal-orientated, and single-minded (Holmes 2006; Sinclair 1998). According to this view, women often have to work twice as hard as men to gain the same respect as leaders, and in an attempt to do so, often have to adopt a masculine style of language to appear tough, calculating, and in control (Muhr 2011). More typically, they are trapped by the "double bind" by which, if they appear too "masculine" they are characterized by colleagues as aggressive, and if they appear overly "feminine", they are characterized as tentative or weak (Holmes 2006).

The difference perspective considers that women and men have grown up in differently gendered subcultures with men gravitating towards more "transactional" or goal-orientated styles of leadership, and women preferring more "transformational" or "change-orientated" leadership styles (e.g., Coates 1995; Tannen 1994; Vinnicombe and Singh 2002). These styles are reflected in the use of differently gendered leadership language. Masculine styles of language serve to produce leadership in a hierarchical, competitive way with individuals positioned either as potential leaders or subordinates. In contrast, feminine styles of language serve to produce leadership in a more distributed, co-constructed way with individual speakers positioned more equally so that everyone potentially has a voice. In a similar vein, the organization theorist, Helgesen (1990) demonstrated that women are more proficient than men in the use of "relational" styles of leadership, based on personal respect, openness, mutual trust, and social responsibility. All theorists argued that different leadership styles are a positive feature in the workplace because they enable women and men to contribute complementary leadership skill sets (see organization theorists, Rosener 1990; Sinclair 1998). Thus, difference theory was viewed as a breakthrough by theorists because the relational style appeared to give women "a female advantage" at a time of rapid technological change in the workplace (Helgesen 1990). However, Fletcher (1999) counter-argued that this association of women with purportedly "soft" qualities merely confirmed women's status as supporters of men within the masculinist workplace, which caused them, effectively, to "disappear". According to Eagly and Carli (2007, 810), the view that women actually have a "female advantage" because "effective leadership is congruent with the ways in which women lead" has often not benefited senior women in male-dominated environments, as men and women tend to be evaluated differently and unequally for using the relational leadership skillset. Whereas men are celebrated for being "emotionally intelligent", women are seen simply as delivering what is expected of them.

Regardless of theory, both dominance and difference perspectives assume that women's socialized speech styles are regulated by static and uncontestable, cultural norms. Social constructionist and discursive perspectives offer an alternative to the notion that either women's linguistic practices are governed by a deterministic, masculine universe, or that their speech styles are developed by gendered upbringing and cultural predispositions.

Current Contributions and Research

Sociocultural, social constructionist, and discursive theories are generally viewed as the current state of play in studies of gender, language, and leadership (Mullany 2011). This set of perspectives challenge the essentialist notion of differently gendered leadership styles of speaking that *belong* to individual men and women. Feminist sociocultural theory (e.g., Bucholtz and Hall 1995; Cameron 2006) works from two feminist types of approach that critique wider cultural practices. The first approach could be called "economic" or "material" and foregrounds issues to do with the availability and social distribution of linguistic resources or "capital" (Bourdieu 1991). This considers factors that might prevent women leaders from accessing the same range of linguistic resources as men such as familiarity with formal registers like public debating, or lack of access to old-boy networks such as the gentleman's club or golf course, where allegedly, so many business deals are done. The second type of approach places more emphasis on "symbolic" or ideological resources such as the "cultural attitudes, representations and practices that underpin women's exclusion or marginalization as speakers and writers in social contexts" (Cameron 2006, 9).

Specifically relevant to language use in leadership contexts are social constructionist and discursive theories. These contest the notion of a dichotomous binary relation between men and women, suggesting that actions are gendered not people. Marra, Schnurr, and Holmes (2006) have shown that "effective" women or men leaders are able to draw expertly on a repertoire of linguistic "strategies" stereotypically coded both "feminine" and "masculine". However this is not a free choice; leaders are also positioned by whether they work in a masculine or feminine "community of practice" (Holmes 2006). In other words, leaders work in gendered workplaces which can be viewed as a continuum from feminine to masculine and thus, workplace interactions take place in gendered social spaces. Most authors from this perspective emphasize the dominance of masculinist norms that operate to limit and constrain their women leaders far more than men.

Feminist poststructuralist theory (e.g., Baxter 2003; Weedon 1997), posits that individuals have multiple and competing identities that are only partially defined by gender, and that they move between a variety of discursively constructed identities as they speak and interact with colleagues. Applying the theory to leadership, individuals shift between a variety of "subject positions" as they speak and interact with colleagues, some of which are relatively powerful and others relatively powerless (Baxter 2003, 32). These subject positions are partly governed by gendered and other discourses such as "masculinization", "expertise" or "competing specialisms". Women leaders may therefore find themselves to be powerful within certain contexts but powerless within others depending upon how they are positioned by different discourses. In a study of a female leader who was the IT director, the participant was positioned powerfully in a senior meeting as the high status IT expert (by discourses of expertise and competing specialisms), but powerlessly by a discourse of "masculinization", when she was excluded from a golf club get-together involving her male director colleagues (Baxter 2003). Within this reframed perspective, gender is viewed as just one of many factors, albeit a powerful one, that may shape the ongoing construction of leadership identities.

Critical Issues and Topics

Drawing upon these different theoretical perspectives, discussions on gender, language and leadership have revolved around at least four critical issues and/or topics.

The Female Voice in Public Contexts

The idea of "voice" has always been important to gender and language scholarship, but it is particularly pertinent to women's leadership. Theorists tend to view the notion of "having a voice" both literally (as the barriers women experience when attempting to speak out and be heard in work contexts such as meetings), and metaphorically (as the historical phenomenon that women continue to be systematically marginalized and excluded from public spheres). The literal silencing of women in the workplace can take many forms. From the sociocultural perspective of language as a resource, women have traditionally lacked the educational training to gain access to professional domains such as engineering and construction, or to prestigious areas of work within any institutional domain such as sales, operations or finance. Whereas women may progress to senior roles within clerical and administrative functions, they are less likely to achieve senior management roles where there is greater influence over institutional policies and practices (Sealy, Doldor and Vinnicombe 2016).

More specifically, even if a woman does gain a senior position, her voice may not *count* in decision-making forums such as management meetings. My own research (e.g., Baxter 2010; 2014) has shown that women are often ignored, interrupted, mocked, criticized or not given a space to speak in management meeting settings. They learn a technique I have named "double-voicing" as a defence mechanism against this type of silencing, which means pre-empting possible criticism from others by stating that criticism themselves ("I realize I'm no expert at marketing, but . . ."). The metaphorical silencing of women in leadership roles is reflected in symbolic representations of women leaders as narrow and ineffective stereotypes, especially in the media (see below). More broadly, gendered discourses or ideologies (Sunderland 2004) continue to position and reconstruct women according to gender stereotypes so that women who break out of these narrow roles are viewed with suspicion by male and female colleagues alike.

Challenges Facing Women in a Masculine Working World

While there is relatively little research on the linguistic challenges facing women leaders, there is considerably more research on the linguistic and discursive pressures women experience in the masculinised space of many professions. McElhinny (2003) analysed the language of women police officers in Pittsburgh, USA, and found that they felt obliged to adopt particular masculine ways of speaking simply to appear to be doing their job in a professional way. Shaw (2006, 81) argued that the historically masculine setting of the UK Parliament is governed by rules of speaking and listening that promote "an adversarial 'bear pit'", where oppositional parties face each other and fight out issues in a confrontational manner. While this has changed in a number of European countries such as Norway, Sweden, and Spain, the UK Parliament remains hostile to the growing presence of women reflected in the "sexist barracking" by male Members of Parliament, and negative media representations they experience. Shaw also examined the styles of interaction used by parliamentarians and found that women face coercive forces that construct them as "interlopers", which may prevent them from taking risks (such as rule-breaking, filibustering) in the way that male politicians regularly do. In her view, this fear of risk-taking restricts the range of ways in which women MPs are prepared to engage in active parliamentary debates, and hence adversely affects their perceived effectiveness for senior cabinet posts.

Angouri (2011) conducted her research within the masculine world of the engineering industry and discovered that while women engineers draw on both normatively masculine and feminine interactional styles according to the context of the interaction and the co-constructed norms of their community (Holmes 2006), the industry is still perceived and constructed as a "masculine" domain. This potentially inhibits women's career progress within such professions as these are part of a broader social world where cultural norms penalise women who speak and act in consistently masculine ways (see also Mullany 2007). Similarly, Walker and Aritz (2015) studied how leadership emerges as it is negotiated through discourse among male and female participants in decision-making groups in a US masculine organizational culture (an MBA programme). While women participants were identified as "doing leadership", they were not recognized as leaders overall. From a masculine organizational perspective, they did not live up to the cultural stereotype of "being a leader".

In a contrasting setting, Litosseliti and Leadbetter (2013, 307–309) explored the gendered discourses that construct speech and language therapy (SLT) as a feminine profession or as "women's work". Their findings show that the lack of men in this profession is shored up by a range of gendered discourses and their associated social practices: discourses of SLT as a gendered profession; "gender difference" discourses; discourses of women as "carers/nurturers" and as "superior communicators"; and discourses of "gender and career progression". In this study, the research showed how gendered discourses could inhibit the progress of men just as much as women, and concluded that "extreme sex-segregated professions" may not be good for aspiring individuals of any gender.

Positive Ways in Which Women Have Negotiated Leadership and Enabled Their Position in the Workplace

In contrast to the feminist vein of the studies above, theorists have explored how women have succeeded in carving out public discursive space for themselves, and bringing something distinctive and valuable to leadership and the world of work. Holmes and her colleagues from the New Zealand Language in the Workplace Project (LWP) adopted an "appreciative inquiry" approach to studying women's leadership language. While acknowledging that women do suffer from "gender ideologies" in the workplace (Holmes 2006, 257), their focus is upon the ways in which women leaders skilfully balance the demands of "doing leadership" with "doing femininity". In this tradition, Schnurr and Mak (2011) contributed to the significantly under-researched area of gender, language, and leadership in Asian workplaces. They found that Sabitha skilfully adopted a range of normatively masculine and feminine linguistic strategies according to the speech context. In formal meetings, she tended to use strategies coded masculine, while in more informal settings, she used strategies normatively coded feminine. However admirable her performance, this was not viewed as entirely a free choice; Sabitha was compelled to negotiate her linguistic choices very carefully in order to fit into the masculinist culture of her company. Within all these studies, there is a strong recognition that women are advancing the cause of other women who aspire to be leaders. The appreciative inquiry approach has led the LWP team towards more consultancy and practitioner-based research in recent years (e.g., Vine 2016; see below).

Negative Representations of Women Leaders

A clear thread in feminist discussions of women's voice in workplace contexts is that of cultural representations of women leaders in the media and elsewhere. Cameron (2006) argues that people learn what is considered normal and desirable femininity or masculinity from representations as well as from first-hand experience. Thus, if women leaders are consistently constructed in negative and unflattering ways, such texts and images will promote the cultural norm that leadership is not for women. Kanter (1993, 211) proposed that women leaders are targeted because they are highly visible as people who are different, and yet they are not permitted the individuality of "their own unique, non-stereotypical characteristics." They are often women in a masculine domain, who are perceived to aspire inappropriately to the privileges of the dominant order. In line with Kanter, I argue that tokenistic, media constructions such as the seductress, the iron maiden, and the mother, seek to "contain" women leaders by limiting their range of behaviour and inappropriately sexualizing them (Baxter 2010). While I suggest that women business leaders can actively exploit such stereotypes as linguistic resources in the workplace, such representations do little in the longer term to enable women to fulfil their career aspirations.

(Media) representations of women leaders are often theorized within the gender, language, and leadership field as "gendered discourses" (Sunderland 2004). Scholars have identified a range of discourses that appear to shape and influence perceptions of women at work. For example, a "gender differences discourse" may reinforce or contest the distinction of "masculine" and "feminine" professions, or the idea that certain skills (e.g., caring, communication, people skills) are more "natural" to women. Mullany (2007) showed that collectively, gendered discourses serve to constitute women as limited by their assumed feminine identities. Bengoechea (2011) looked at the representation of the gendered identity construction of Minister of Defence, Carme Chacón in Spain's government through discursive representations of her by journalists in publications across the political spectrum, and found that there were many sexist discourses at play, especially from male journalists, who foregrounded her gender and portrayed her role as limited and tokenistic.

Main Research Methods

As scholars have become interested in the ways in which leadership identities are constructed by, or contest gendered norms and discourses, the use of intensive investigation of individual cases of female and male leaders at work has proved the most common way forward. This has led to an interest in the use of ethnographic, qualitative case study, and discursive methods of data gathering and analysis.

Ethnographic approaches to study often involve the researcher in visiting an institution or workplace such as parliament, businesses or courtrooms for an extended period of time to observe and/or participate within the work context. While "complete immersion" as a full participant within a work context is out of the question for most researchers, "partial immersion" is a common feature of many gender, language, and leadership studies. In order to gather data, researchers typically use methods such as observation of routine, daily events, field notes, interviews with participants, case studies of individual leaders, and documentary evidence (e.g., meeting agendas, policy documents). The workplace is a prime example of "a restricted research site" as access to senior management meetings, for example, is often viewed as sensitive. Ford (2008) was able to use her personal networks to gain access to a variety of work settings in science, engineering, and medicine companies in order to observe and video-record how women and men interacted within senior business meetings. Mullany (2007), in attempting to gain access to both a retail and to a manufacturing company, adopted a number of strategies such as approaching women at middle/senior levels of management in personnel departments who might be more sympathetic to the aims of her project on gender, while making it clear that the aims and outcomes of the project would be collaboratively achieved. Holmes and her team (e.g., Holmes and Stubbe 2003; Holmes and Vine forthcoming) provided their leaders with their own digital voice recorders so that they could control when they chose to record particular interactions. This had the disadvantage that researchers were not able to observe speech events first-hand, but the advantage that leaders could record a range of formal and informal events while minimizing "the observer's paradox".

In terms of data analysis, research on gender, language, and leadership adopts a diversity of largely qualitative approaches including critical discourse analysis (CDA), conversation analysis (CA), interactional sociolinguistic analysis (IS), feminist poststructuralist discourse analysis (FPDA), and corpus linguistic analysis. This array of approaches is in contrast to methods used by organization studies on women's leadership where non-sociolinguistic methods of analysis are mainly used such as content analysis, thematic analysis, or computer-assisted, survey techniques. Sociolinguists such as Ford (2008, 27) utilized CA to analyse women's talk in senior meetings as "social organization". Her analysis reflects CA's view of interaction as ordered, orderly, predictable, and accountable with no level of vocal or linguistic detail too trivial for comment. Ford fed back her observations to her participants on how women and men construct their work and leadership identities through talk, so that they could capitalize on these insights in future meetings. For example, "Florence" learnt to attract more attention to her contributions by the subtle act of taking more audible in-takes of breath.

Other researchers have preferred using IS when analysing women leaders' interactions. Like CA, IS is a micro-linguistic approach to discourse analysis, but rather than focusing primarily on turn-taking order as constituting a wider social order, it attends to the "contextualization cues" in speech, which index wider, interconnected cultural patterns such as gendered speech and/or ethnic variations in speech (Gordon and Kraut this volume). Holmes and Marra (2011) used IS to conduct a close, micro-analysis of the ways in which Maori leaders in a New Zealand workplace negotiate the competing aspects of their various identities in relation to gender, ethnicity and their professional status. The authors show that IS is a sufficiently nuanced method to index how different aspects of identity manifest themselves through the course of an event such as a business meeting. In my own research, I have used FPDA as a means of harmonizing the micro-analysis of single data extracts with macro-analysis of larger discursive patterns. The close textual analysis of a series of senior meetings provides evidence for identifying pervasive discourses such as "gender differentiation" or "masculinization", and "competing specialisms" that often combine to position women leaders at work, often in powerless ways (Baxter 2003, 2010).

Overall, the analysis of interactional data using one or more of these methods has tended to show that either women leaders can skilfully manoeuvre their way through many challenging leadership contexts (e.g., Holmes 2006; Schnurr and Mak 2011), or that women continue to face certain linguistic and discursive barriers in their working lives and to their career progression (e.g., Angouri 2011; Baxter 2014; Ford 2008; Litosseliti and Leadbetter 2013).

Recommendations for Practice

Until recently, the pattern of research in gender, language, and leadership has largely been researcher-driven: that is, scholars have identified the area of interest or problem that they wish to address theoretically and their studies are based on "real data" from empirical studies. However a growing trend in (socio)linguistic studies is to construct partnerships between scholars and practitioners in order to meet mutually important goals such as an interest in improving workplace communication or leadership competences (e.g., Vine 2016). Of the latter, two types of research partnerships have arisen: first, partnership-driven, collaborative or consultative research where researchers and practitioners have separate yet mutual goals that they wish to achieve from the study, and second, practitioner-driven or consultancy research where the researcher is effectively commissioned to conduct research and provide recommendations for practice.

While such partnership research is certainly happening in related disciplines such as professional discourse (e.g., Litosseliti and Leadbetter 2013), there is altogether less evidence of this within the field of gender, language, and leadership. One possible reason for the lack of practitioner-based research is that the feminist mission fits uncomfortably with the agendas of practitioners who are principally concerned to improve service, productivity, profit margins, accountability rather than to contribute to the cause of social justice *per se*. Gendered issues in the workplace may either be intensely personal, such as the case of a leader who experiences linguistic discrimination on gender grounds, or alternatively, deeply structural, requiring substantive cultural changes in the way an organization thinks and works. Today there is greater pressure upon western workplaces and specifically, Human Resources departments within organizations, to implement equality and diversity policies that actively tackle issues of gender inequality and discrimination (Sealy, Doldor and Vinnicombe 2016). However, in my experience, the ways in which language used in workplaces may discriminate against aspiring women leaders and, on occasions, men, still remains a low priority for many companies.

Given this, what can scholars in our field *do* to raise awareness of the importance of language in the workplace, which will enable women to be more effective at work and enhance opportunities for their future career progression? Below are some examples of partnership research and consultancy I have conducted over the years, which aim to transform the practices of women leaders (Baxter 2010, 2014, 2015). These include:

- A practitioner-commissioned case study of a woman leader who was experiencing difficulties with both her line manager and her own team. I used transcripts of her interactions in meetings so that she could identify "what went well" and "what went less well" with her colleagues. I discussed different linguistic strategies with her for the future.
- Case studies of whole teams of senior managers in which both women and men were present. Afterwards, I delivered both oral and written feedback reports to the teams that described some of the linguistic features of the interactions, identifying "helpful" and less "helpful" moments for women's participation and engagement in the meetings. The feedback enabled these teams to develop strategies to encourage women to participate more actively in future meetings.
- Training workshops for women on "the power of language" in formal and professional settings. These included identifying typical contexts and scenarios where language might act as a barrier to effective working relationships (such as a male colleague who keeps interrupting a woman as she speaks) and what might be done about this. The workshops also looked at how language could be turned into a resource for enhancing working relationships and effective leadership (such as training women to use visionary or transformational language to help colleagues to think strategically). The workshops provided participants with a forum to discuss difficult colleagues and contexts they were experiencing and to develop techniques to overcome these challenges.
- A series of online, gender, leadership and language booklets ("Women in Business Toolkits"), giving guidance on gendered scenarios in the workplace, for organizations such as the UK Chambers of Commerce, which members of the public could access. These were the digital, broadcast equivalent of the workshops above (Baxter 2014).
- Mentorship of women in my own organization in order to equip them with the linguistic strategies to overcome negative events and difficult colleagues. For example I mentored an associate professor who felt overcome by her job of chairing a meeting comprising male professors, all of whom were more senior than her. This enabled her to feel confident to challenge these colleagues in meetings as well as to develop her own voice as an expert in her field.

While each of the above examples of participant consultancy was specific to its own context, the common element has been that "aha" moment, when women leaders have suddenly grasped the contribution of language to their own leadership issues. Rather than the received wisdom that they need to understand psychology to enhance their effectiveness as leaders (e.g., Kotter 2001), women learn to understand that actions and outcomes are achieved through finely judged linguistic and discursive interactions.

Future Directions

I propose three ways in which the nascent field of gender, language and leadership might evolve in the future in order to continue to enable women leaders. First, there is a continuing need for research to move away from the ivory tower of academia, and towards engaging proactively with practitioner partners. While researchers can undoubtedly define a credible, critical agenda on equality and diversity issues, their mission is hugely strengthened by close collaboration with practitioners to explore the nature of a problem within specific leadership contexts. Collaborating with practitioners may be time-consuming, frustrating, and divisive on occasions, but the outcomes are far more likely to serve the needs of "real" women leaders. Second, research needs to retain a commitment to feminism as a political movement, which has always foregrounded the value of action-orientated research. While postmodernist feminism has challenged the universality of the female experience, the issue of gender inequality at leadership level remains a prominent international cause that feminist research should aim to address. Third, much research in gender, language, and leadership remains Eurocentric or North American. The voice of second and third world women is effectively silenced: women are struggling to be leaders in many countries around the world but are often denied that opportunity. Even if they have succeeded, there is little or no research giving their voice expression about the ongoing challenges of their roles. Where possible, such research can be enabled by supporting students around the world to carry out PhD studies on this topic, as Al A'ali (2013) achieved in Bahrain, very much against the odds. However, the quest to support more women internationally to take up leadership positions, and to conduct research on the few women who have, has only just started.

Further Reading

Baxter (2010) includes a final chapter on "how to achieve an effective language of leadership".

Baxter and A A'Ali (2016) examine the ways in which women leaders conduct leadership in Middle Eastern and Western business management meetings.

Lockhart and Mollick (2013) examine the ways in which women have used political rhetoric and political discourse to provide leadership, or assert their right to leadership.

Wilson and Boxer (2015) provide studies of women in positions of political leadership across the globe and reflecting a variety of cultures.

The 2011 issue of the journal *Gender and Language* includes a number of papers on gender, language and leadership from authors around the world.

Related Topics

Interactional sociolinguistics; Conversation analysis; Social constructionism; Communities of practice; Corporate settings; Relational talk; Gender; Leadership

References

Al A'ali, Haleema. 2013. "An Exploration of Female Leadership Language: Case Studies of Senior Women in Bahrain." PhD diss., Aston University, UK.

Anderson, Deirdre A., and Susan Vinnicombe. 2015. "Senior Women, Work-Life Balance and the Decision to Quit: A Generational Perspective." In *Handbook of Gendered Careers in Management: Getting In, Getting On, Getting Out*, edited by Adelina M. Broadbridge, and Sandra L. Fielden, 445–459. Cheltenham, UK: Edward Elgar.

Angouri, Jo. 2011. "'We are in a Masculine Profession ...': Constructing Gender Identities in a Consortium of Two Multinational Engineering Companies." *Gender and Language* 5: 343–371.
Baxter, Judith. 2003. *Positioning Gender in Discourse: A Feminist Methodology*. Basingstoke, UK: Palgrave Macmillan.
Baxter, Judith. 2006. *Speaking Out: The Female Voice in Public Contexts*. Basingstoke, UK: Palgrave Macmillan.
Baxter, Judith. 2010. *The Language of Female Leadership*. Basingstoke, UK: Palgrave Macmillan.
Baxter, Judith. 2014. *Double-Voicing at Work: Power, Gender and Linguistic Expertise*. Basingstoke, UK: Palgrave Macmillan.
Baxter, Judith. 2015. *Using Language Effectively Series*. www.birmingham-chamber.com/Policy-and-Media/Policy-and-Advocacy/Women-in-Business/Using-Language-Effectively-Toolkit.aspx. Accessed 5.11.15.
Bengoechea, Mercedes. 2011. "How Effective is 'Femininity'? Identities and Performances of the First Spanish Woman Defence Minister as Portrayed in the Media." *Gender and Language* 5: 405–429.
Bourdieu, Pierre. 1991. *Language and Symbolic Power*. Cambridge: Polity Press.
Bucholtz, Mary, and Kira Hall. 1995. *Gender Articulated: Language and the Socially Constructed Self*. New York: Routledge.
Cameron, Deborah. 2006. "Theorising the Female Voice in Public Contexts." In *Speaking Out: The Female Voice in Public Contexts*, edited by Judith Baxter, 3–20. Basingstoke, UK: Palgrave.
Coates, Jennifer. 1995. "Language, Gender and Career". In *Language and Gender: Interdisciplinary Perspectives*, edited by Sara Mills, 135–148. London: Longman.
Eagly, Alice H., and Linda L. Carli. 2007. *Through the Labyrinth: The Truth about how Women Become Leaders*. Boston, MA: Harvard Business School Press.
Fletcher, Joyce K. 1999. *Disappearing Acts: Gender, Power and Relational Practice*. Massachusetts, MA: MIT.
Ford, Cecilia. 2008. *Women Speaking Up*. Basingstoke, UK: Palgrave Macmillan.
Helgesen, Sally. 1990. *The Female Advantage: Women's Ways of Leadership*. New York: Doubleday.
Holmes, Janet. 2006. *Gendered Talk at Work*. Oxford: Blackwell.
Holmes, Janet, and Meredith Marra. 2011. "Leadership Discourse in a Maori Workplace: Negotiating Gender, Ethnicity and Leadership at Work." *Gender and Language* 5: 317–342.
Holmes, Janet, and Maria Stubbe. 2003. *Power and Politeness in the Workplace*. London: Longman.
Holmes, Janet, and Bernadette Vine. Forthcoming. "'That's Just How We Do Things Round Here': Researching Workplace Discourse for the Benefit of Employees." In *Crossing Boundaries: Interdisciplinarity in Language Studies*, edited by Vander Viana. Amsterdam: John Benjamins.
Kanter, Rosabeth Moss. 1993. *Men and Women of the Corporation*. 2nd edn. New York: BasicBooks.
Koller, Veronika. 2004. *Metaphor and Gender in Business Media Discourse*. Basingstoke, UK: Palgrave.
Kotter, John P. 2001. "What Leaders Really Do." *Harvard Business Review* 79: 85–96.
Litosseliti, Lia, and Claire Leadbeater. 2013. "Gendered Discourses in Speech and Language Therapy." *Journal of Applied Linguistics and Professional Practice* 8: 295–314.
Lockhart, Michele, and Kathleen Mollick, Eds. 2013. *Political Women: Language and Leadership*. New York: Lexington.
Marra, Meredith, Stephanie Schnurr, and Janet Holmes. 2006. "Effective Leadership in New Zealand Workplaces." In *Speaking Out: The Female Voice in Public Contexts*, edited by Judith Baxter, 240–260. Basingstoke, UK: Palgrave Macmillan.
McElhinny, Bonnie. 2003. "Fearful, Forceful Agents of the Law: Ideologies about Language and Gender in Police Officers' Narratives about the Use of Physical Force." *Pragmatics* 13: 253–284.
Muhr, Sara. 2011. "Caught in the Gendered Machine: On the Masculine and Feminine in Cyborg Leadership." *Gender, Work and Organization* 18: 337–357.
Mullany, Louise. 2007. *Gendered Discourse in the Professional Workplace*. Basingstoke, UK: Palgrave.
Mullany, Louise. 2011. "Gender, Language and Leadership in the Workplace." *Gender and Language* 5: 303–316.
Rosener, Judy B. 1990. "Ways Women Lead." *Harvard Business Review* 68: 119–125.
Schnurr, Stephanie, and Bernie Mak. 2011. "Leadership in Hong Kong: Is Gender Really Not an Issue?" *Gender and Language* 5: 343–371.
Sealy, Ruth, Elena Doldor, and Susan Vinnicombe. 2016. *The Female FTSE Board Report*. Cranford: Cranford University.

Shaw, Sylvia. 2006. "Governed by Rules?: The Female Voice in Parliamentary Debates." In *Speaking Out: The Female Voice in Public Contexts*, edited by Judith Baxter, 81–102. Basingstoke, UK: Palgrave.

Sinclair, Amanda. 1998. *Doing Leadership Differently: Gender, Power and Sexuality in a Changing Business Culture*. Melbourne: Melbourne University Press.

Spender, Dale. 1980. *Man-Made Language*. London: Pandora.

Sunderland, Jane. 2004. *Gendered Discourses*. Basingstoke, UK: Palgrave.

Tannen, Deborah. 1994. *Talking from 9 to 5: Women and Men in the Workplace*. New York: Avon.

UN Women 2015. *Women's Participation: Facts and Figures*. www.unwomen.org/en/what-we-do/leadership-and-political-participation. Accessed 4.8.16.

Vine, Bernadette. 2016. "The Wellington Language in the Workplace Project: Engaging with the Research and Wider Communities." In *Creating and Digitizing Language Corpora Volume 3: Databases for Public Engagement*, edited by Karen P. Corrigan, and Adam Mearns, 321–346. Basingstoke, UK: Palgrave.

Vinnicombe, Susan, and Val Singh. 2002. "Sex Role Stereotyping and Requisites of Successful Top Managers." *Women in Management Review* 17: 120–130.

Walker, Robyn C., and Jolanta Aritz. 2015. "Women Doing Leadership: Leadership Styles and Organisational Culture." *International Journal of Business Communication* 52: 452–478.

Weedon, Chris. 1997. *Feminist Practice and Poststructuralist Theory*. 2nd edn. Oxford: Blackwell.

Wilson, John, and Diana Boxer, Eds. 2015. *Discourse, Politics and Women as Global Leaders*. Amsterdam: John Benjamins.

33
Language Preparation for Internationally Educated Professionals
Julie Kerekes

Introduction

In the midst of increasing linguistic and cultural diversity of cities around the world, effective intercultural communication in the workplace has become vital (Lockwood and Forey 2010). In such multicultural and progressive cities as Toronto, Los Angeles, and Sydney, nearly half of whose inhabitants speak a home language other than English (the regions' official language), it is alarmingly difficult for even highly proficient speakers of ESL to obtain suitable employment (Kerekes *et al.* 2013). While a variety of reasons have been cited for the disproportionate un- and under-employment of internationally educated professionals (IEPs), including some institutional and prejudicial barriers over which job-seekers have no control, language ability, or lack thereof, is overused as an institutional justification for immigrants' failure to find suitable work (FC2I 2003; Kerekes *et al.* 2013).[1] Local settlement organizations and language programmes are increasingly sensitive to the value prospective employers place not merely on second language ability, but, more broadly, on the communication skills of their (prospective) employees: their abilities to interact successfully with clients/customers/patients as well as to work efficiently and amicably with co-workers, particularly where "teamwork" plays a role in workplace culture (Girard and Bauder 2007; Houghton and Proscio 2001). There is a push, therefore, to cultivate pragmatic competence in language programmes geared toward employment preparation for immigrants.

Pragmatic Competence

Beyond an expansive vocabulary, accurate grammar, and clear pronunciation, what does it take for people to communicate effectively with one another? The answer is the stuff of pragmatic competence, which refers to how people use language in such a way as to achieve what they want: the ability to convey a message successfully, and for its meaning—whether direct or indirect, blatant or subtle—to be interpreted by the hearer(s) as intended by the speaker(s). This entails, of course, not merely effective word choice and prosodic features, but also a mutual understanding of the contexts in which the communication takes place, and of its purposes. Such features as the relative status of the interlocutors, their institutional roles, and their sociolinguistic backgrounds—to name just a few—influence choices made in order to effect successful communication.

While pragmatic competence refers to interlocutors' ability to convey their messages effectively in a variety of contexts, "soft skills" is the preferred term in the employment sector. It is sometimes used interchangeably with "interpersonal skills", "social skills", or "people skills" (Bartel 2013). Bartel (2013, 110) defines soft skills as "self-awareness and cultural awareness as well as interpersonal skills, including verbal and non-verbal communication, that follow or reflect expected polite behaviour, especially in the business or workplace context." Politeness thus plays a key role in soft skills, but the vast variability of politeness rules across cultures and contexts (Bargiela-Chiappini and Harris 2006) makes the mastering of soft skills extraordinarily challenging; the goal is seemingly a moving target, as each new workplace setting, not to mention varying workplace tasks and people involved in the communications (Crystal 1997), requires different approaches and politeness strategies. In spite of this, ESL instructors, instructional materials, and curriculum developers are tasked with creating meaningful, useful ways to improve the communication skills—specifically, the pragmatic competence or soft skills—of ESL-speaking, employment-seeking individuals.

Pragmatics for the Intercultural Workplace

Pragmatic competence is the focus of much research on ESL instruction for workplace communication (Koester 2010). Applied linguists have been called upon to define language and instruction relevant to the needs of specific companies, resulting in research which has analysed discourse from workplace settings ranging from beauty salons and fast food restaurants to hospitals, physics laboratories, call centres, and other customer service organizations. Under the premise that workplaces in a changing world have, correspondingly, changed communicative needs and practices, Newton and Kusmierczyk (2011) review research describing the nature of language in the workplace. Among other conclusions, they note that informal modes of interpersonal communication play an important role in a variety of workplaces; that there is a great amount of overlap between employability skills and soft skills, including literacy, numeracy, use of technology, problem-solving skills, and interpersonal skills; and that awareness-raising can be used as a pedagogical tool to analyse, understand, and reflect critically on workplace communication in the process of acquiring pragmatic competence. They applaud the benefits of workplace language programmes that couple work with education in such a way that language instruction can be customized to specific workplaces and situations, and note the benefits of "experiential learning as a way of tapping into the language and practices of particular workplaces and communities of practice" (84). In other words, making lessons dependent on context is an important component of individualized or customized instruction. Newton and Kusmierczyk emphasize that instructors must also facilitate the empowerment of learners through the acquisition of observational and analytical skills that will enable them to judge power, distance, and formality factors in given workplace interactions.

Pedagogical approaches and materials addressing the pragmatic development of ESL learners for the workplace are challenged, however, by the reality of infinitely nuanced varieties of institutional speech act realizations and management of verbal interactions. Creating training materials and even, at times, partial scripts for prospective employees to follow, entails predetermining the ways workplace interactions are expressed; this necessitates oversimplifying hypothetical interactions in order to be able to offer generalizations about how they can best be carried out, which, in turn, makes them rather unrealistic. In their research on communications skills training in call centres, for example, Hultgren and Cameron (2010) critique the tendency to decontextualize lessons and to disregard "the complexities of spoken interaction" (43) in order to be able to define effective communication in quantifiable, measurable ways.

Within the field of workplace pragmatics, small talk, management of workplace relationships (also called "social talk"), and expressing appropriate levels of (in)formality and directness have been identified as critical areas in which nonnative speakers differ from their native speaker counterparts. Dahm and Yates's (2013) study of role-played medical interactions between native speaker doctors and nonnative speaker international medical graduates, for example, reveals that native speakers are more successful in their strategies for using small talk, directness, empathy/reassurance, softeners, colloquialisms, idioms, and lay terms. Holmes's (2000) analysis of naturally occurring workplace interactions also identifies small talk and social talk as problematic areas for many employees and employers.

While we associate small talk with helping to support, reinforce, and construct positive relationships with co-workers, it can also be used manipulatively. In a power asymmetrical interaction, for example, the higher-status person may be the one to introduce small talk as well as end it by changing the focus of the interaction to task-oriented talk (Holmes 2000). Holmes explains that, while small talk in New Zealand typically covers noncontroversial topics such as the weather, superficial inquiries about one's health, social activities outside of work, sports, the state of the economy, and compliments about one's interlocutor's appearance, there exist enormous cross-cultural differences in what counts as uncontroversial, what counts as a compliment, etc., increasing the potential for intercultural miscommunication.

Closely related to small talk is the concept of rapport. Establishing positive relationships with interviewers, (potential) employers, or co-workers requires a sensitive calibration of how friendly and personal one can get with one's interlocutor, without going overboard. In institutional/gatekeeping settings, one way of developing rapport is through the establishment of common ground, or co-membership with one's interlocutor (Johnston 2008; Kerekes 2006, 2007). This can be as concrete as discovering a shared interest outside of work (e.g., baseball, or travel, or a mutual friend), to a vaguer, covert recognition that one's interlocutor shares some values or circumstances such as having young children, which makes it difficult to work late at night, or having similar socioeconomic characteristics such as a shared religion or ethnicity. Hultgren and Cameron (2010) have pointed out that sometimes conversations, rapport-building, and empathizing in workplaces can resemble friendships more than business relations. But what counts as friendship or rapport varies tremendously from one culture to another, and is, therefore, particularly challenging for an IEP (potential) employee learning to navigate the twists, turns, and boundaries between friendships and collegial relationships in hierarchical settings in which the ultimate focus is not on friendship, but on getting the work done.

Finally, as mentioned above, our changing world leads to new communicative needs in the workplace and, consequently, new communication practices. These are reflected in new, web-based, instructional tools and tasks that teach, for example, the pragmatics of specific speech acts and intercultural communication (Waugh 2013), and podcasts and smart phones that are used to teach business soft skills (Viswanathan 2009). These technologies provide students with opportunities for self-assessment, reflection, and practice of various pragmatic concepts in line with recommendations from other scholars researching workplace pragmatics.

Soft Skills Research and the Vocational Language Classroom

While some vocational ESL (teacher training) programmes have been described and researched, less attention has been devoted to applying empirical evidence of successful workplace communication to the curriculum and instruction of such language and training programmes. One publication which not only describes vocational language programmes, but also, on their basis, makes recommendations for how soft skills should be taught to students in these classes, is Houghton and Proscio's (2001) report describing four American "workforce development programs" that focus on preparing future employees for workplace culture. The authors make the following recommendations for vocational ESL curricula:

1. Integrate soft skills training into every element of the curriculum
2. Create work or work-like tasks and establish teams to complete them
3. Put trainees in the employer's role from time to time, so that by managing they can learn to be managed
4. Establish the discipline of the workplace in all aspects of the programme
5. Recreate the physical environment of work to the fullest extent possible
6. Give participants lots of opportunities to get to know successful people
7. Support services and soft skills are not the same, but they go hand in hand.

It is evident from these recommendations that, in the classroom, simulated workplace activities are to be as authentic as possible, and great emphasis is placed on cultivating and maintaining positive interactions with people at work.

Overgeneralizing, Oversimplifying, and an Obsolete Native Speaker Model

Many pedagogical tools for vocational ESL involve teaching scripts for generic workplace situations,[2] but prescribing communicative practices in such general ways is increasingly criticized for being, at best, only marginally helpful, and, at worst, counterproductive (Hultgren and Cameron 2010). Intercultural trainers, whose direct task is to "impart . . . contrastive cultural information" to professionals working abroad (Hayman 2010, 149), are at risk of essentializing cultures and, thereby, cultivating cross-cultural misunderstanding—the exact opposite of their aim. Elias's (2010) survey of intercultural awareness training programmes in Filipino call centres, for example, exposes a frequent assumption "that culture is [seen as] a fixed set of learnings which, when mastered, give cultural understanding" (163). The prescriptive training programs in these centres feed students facts about American culture (clothing, sports and recreation, holidays). Because intercultural trainers often lack insider knowledge about the cultures about which they teach, they make generalizations, focusing on solutions and on squeezing an entire intercultural training programme into a few hours. "The task for the conscientious trainer then is to balance on the one hand the client's desire for hard facts with on the other hand the responsibility to convey the ambiguity and complexity at the heart of intercultural analysis" (Hayman 2010, 151).

Unfortunately, this balancing act results most commonly in an oversimplification of the pragmatic rules of workplace English, primarily because there really is no such singular thing as "workplace English"; rather, the language (and its rules) varies from context to context, situation to situation. Lu and Corbett (2012), in their description of American standards for the "multicultural citizenship" approach, bemoan the "reductive element to the specification of cross-cultural or intercultural communicative competence as an inventory of knowledge, attitudes and skills" (31). This approach is based on "5 Cs": communication, cultures, connections, comparisons, and communities. Cultural learning is manifested in attitudes, values, ideas, patterns of social interaction, and cultural products such as books, food, music, and laws. The Common European Framework (CEFR), a widely used framework for second language teaching across Europe and beyond, has similar goals, but also promotes "methods of modern language teaching which will strengthen independence of thought, judgment and action, combined with social skills and responsibility" (Council of Europe 2001, 4; cited in Lu and Corbett 2012, 24). In their textbook on the use of English in intercultural medical interactions, Lu and Corbett (2012, 130) caution that, while "knowledge of an individual's 'possible' culturally-influenced attitudes, values, beliefs and behaviour" can be useful, only through direct observation can a practitioner (a physician, in their discussion, but equally applicable to employees/employers in other institutional settings) understand how the "complex 'fluidity' of cultural influences in a globalised and multicultural world" are enacted in the individual's dispositions and interactions (131).

In an effort to achieve clear understanding between interlocutors of different cultural backgrounds, the goal of attaining intercultural "competence" is criticized by Lu and Corbett (2012) because it is about understanding and respecting difference which, common to both the CEFR and American Standards, is defined according to a native speaker ideal. In today's diverse workplaces, the native speaker model is obsolete: co-workers need to be able to communicate effectively with one another, not with an idealized native speaker. Workplaces are becoming increasingly culturally diverse (Waugh 2013); where English is the main language of the workplace it is often spoken as a lingua franca. Koester (2010) recommends, instead of using a native speaker model, comparing experts to non-experts. The experts are those who achieve successful communication in accordance with their professional goals and workplace culture.[3]

Research-Informed Pedagogy

To date, however, research-informed workplace communication pedagogy still relies, for the most part, on native speaker models. The "Workplace Communication Programme for Skilled Migrants" at Victoria University of Wellington, New Zealand, for example, includes instructional modules based on authentic workplace interactions between native speakers of English (Riddiford and Joe 2010). This ESL curriculum, focusing on sociopragmatics for skilled migrants (de Bres 2009), addresses both transactional and relational talk (e.g., small talk, social talk, humour). Its effectiveness was evaluated at the beginning, in the middle, and at the end of the course, as well as through participants' reflections on their classroom learning, and through collaborations with mentors in the workplaces in which these migrants were temporarily placed. Results indicate that both classroom learning and work placements are instructional in improving participants' sociopragmatic competence, and point favourably toward the use of "explicit instruction using authentic input" (Riddiford and Joe 2010, 523). Awareness raising and analytical skills were identified as the most important ways to empower prospective employees to make their own choices regarding the use of softeners, preparators, and other mitigators conventionally used when making requests. Significantly, de Bres also points out that newcomers and New Zealanders should share the responsibility equally for achieving positive experiences for the migrants.

Also with native speaker model data, Yates and Springall (2010) use data from two different role-plays performed by native Australian English speakers and second language learners, to examine how the two groups compared in making complex workplace requests. Findings show that the native speakers were more likely to speak with their (hypothetical) boss (to whom the request was made) as a colleague with whom they want to negotiate a solution, necessitating the use of various types of softeners. The learners, in contrast, were more likely to approach their boss with a problem they want the boss to fix. On this basis, Yates and Springall developed a curriculum involving a series of activities that enable language learners to listen, observe, reflect on, and then practice using softeners and informal vocabulary such as what was used in the interactions involving native speakers.

Much of the current research calls for authentic data on which to base workplace communication curricula. The early findings of Williams (1988), who showed large discrepancies between speech acts used in real workplace meetings versus what was taught in textbooks (Koester 2010), ring true in more recent studies as well (e.g., Cheng and Warren 2005, 2006). Louw, Derwing, and Abbott (2010) came closer to approximating authentic workplace communication by using simulated job interviews between native speakers and nonnative speakers in instructional materials to help ESL learners improve their job interviewing skills. Instructional tasks around observing the simulated interviews resulted in the language learners' improved ability to establish rapport and identify instances of cross-cultural misunderstanding.

Recommendation: Cultural Awareness and Analysis in the Classroom

An oft-proposed solution to the conundrum of how to teach pragmatic skills without essentialising cultures or disregarding context is to cultivate awareness among learners and teachers about how workplace discourse is characterized, by incorporating analytical and reflective activities and training into the intercultural communication curriculum (Hayman 2010; Koester 2010; Newton and Kusmierczyk 2011; Riddiford and Joe 2010). Including cultural awareness and analysis is resisted, however, by many language teachers, whose sensitivity to the inequities between second language learners and native speakers of English makes them reluctant to address such topics head-on. Intercultural trainers, in contrast, are "explicit about imparting contrastive cultural information" to their clients/students, and thus are in danger of oversimplifying differences by making generalizations about whole groups of people and cultures (Hayman 2010, 149).

Researchers' key points of language awareness applicable to workplace ESL education are:

- Workplace interactions differ from everyday interactions, in that the former are more hierarchical and goal oriented than the latter
- Language from the workplace uses different vocabulary from that used in everyday interactions
- In addition to transactional talk, relational talk in the workplace is important, including small talk, expressions of empathy, and establishing co-membership, rapport, and shared knowledge.

Furthermore, they make the following recommendations regarding the teaching of soft skills (de Bres 2009; Houghton and Proscio 2001; Louw, Derwing, and Abbott 2010; Riddiford and Joe 2010; Waugh 2013):

1 Use authentic materials such as audio or video recordings and/or transcripts from workplaces

2   Activities should aim to raise learners' awareness of and ability to reflect on what characterizes successful workplace communication
3   Activities should develop learners' observational and analytical skills
4   Contextualize discussions of appropriate workplace language
5   Instruction should offer flexible rather than rigid rules, and a number of possible strategies for communicating the same or similar intent
6   Promote empowerment through agency of the learners.

The question remains: do current vocational ESL textbooks reflect these empirical findings and recommendations?

Pragmatics in ESL Textbooks

Most current ESL textbooks, while including more materials on pragmatics than in the past, lack a methodical way of sequencing topics within pragmatics, and attend to only a few speech acts, while neglecting many others. Furthermore, those speech acts which are addressed are usually oversimplified and not adequately contextualized but, instead, presented in isolation (Diepenbroek and Derwing 2013). Canada's existing ESL programmes for adult immigrants are similarly criticized for superficial treatment of cultural facts and behaviours (Thomson and Derwing 2004). Guo (2013) addresses such programmes' disturbing and ongoing presumption of one ideal type of Canadian workplace, one ideal type of Canadian employee, and one White, Anglo-Saxon, middle-class, Christian set of values that correspond to these ideals.

Reviews of popular ESL textbooks are in agreement about the limitations of their coverage of pragmatics and oral fluency. Thomson and Derwing (2004) analysed 67 textbooks used for Canada's Language Instruction for Newcomers to Canada programme (LINC), which is mandated with teaching "Canadian values", and concluded that most of the books contain little Canadian content. Diepenbroek and Derwing's (2013) review of 12 integrated skills textbooks (totalling 48 books) found that the pragmatic contents of the texts inadequately address speech acts, conversation strategies (e.g., interpreting conversation cues and illocutionary force), and idioms.

Exceptionally, Tatsuki and Houck's (2010) edited volume, *Pragmatics: Teaching Speech Acts*, addresses the complexities of pragmatic competence more effectively. Its chapter on requests in the workplace, for example, informed by empirical research, offers carefully sequenced exercises based on authentic materials, and promotes the consideration of context and agency in selecting an appropriate form of a speech act. The authors of this book, as well as the other researchers mentioned above, concur in their assessment of the critical importance of observation, awareness, and reflection on the part of the ESL learner. It is the responsibility of instructors to cultivate these skills in their students.

One other review, carried out by my graduate assistant, Ivan Lasan, analyses the contents of 18 workplace ESL textbooks used in the Greater Toronto Area's workplace ESL training programmes, for their coverage of employment-applicable pragmatic skills (Lasan 2014). Like Diepenbroek and Derwing (2013), Lasan finds that the pragmatics contents of all 18 of the textbooks take the form of speech act lessons and/or conversation strategies. Of the speech acts covered, advice is most common, followed by requests, directions, (dis)agreement, refusals/acceptances, apologies, offers, and thanks. The most frequent conversation strategy addressed is management (e.g., initiating, maintaining, and closing conversations; turn-taking, rapport-building, changing the topic, showing understanding, and interrupting), followed by explaining/paraphrasing, illocutionary force,[4] small talk, and social expressions.

Lasan notes that slightly more than half (10 out of 18) of the books integrate pragmatics content into other types of lessons, while slightly fewer than half (eight out of 18) provide pragmatics content in isolation. Interestingly, while all 18 of the textbooks use examples and activities to practice the examples, only one also includes explanations of the rules and their examples. Furthermore, fourteen of the eighteen books present the pragmatics lessons without contextual information, and only four specify hypothetical participants, settings, and other contextual descriptions. Corroborating the lack of contextualization, the vast majority (16 out of 18) present rules of pragmatics as a rigid list of dos and don'ts and formulas, while only two present flexibility according to context, and only four present activities for awareness raising and cross-cultural reflection as additional components of the pragmatics lessons.

Some of the textbooks are to be applauded for conveying a tone of respect for language learners as pragmatically competent speakers of their L1s, which they can use to make reflective comparisons to conventional practices in English. In an exercise in McCullagh and Wright's (2008) *Good Practice: Communication Skills in English for the Medical Practitioner*, for example, students are prompted: "Indirect instructions can help put the patient at ease at the beginning of a consultation and can reduce embarrassment and anxiety. Do you use instructions in the same way in your language?" (57). The majority of the textbooks, however, fail to promote agency of the students in speech act and conversation strategy choices. Textbooks evidently have a way to go before they reflect empirical findings regarding effective teaching and learning of employment-related communication skills.

Internationally Educated Professionals' Employment Barriers, and Implications for Practitioners

The attitudes many IEPs face when seeking employment are not dissimilar to what they experience in most vocational ESL classes and textbooks: their identities as immigrants, learners of ESL, and members of cultures outside of the dominant culture are seen as a deficit (Guo 2013; Haque 2014). In Canada, for example, IEPs receive the message in their ESL classes and in encounters with (prospective) employers that the onus is on them to change and "become Canadian" (Kerekes 2017; Kerekes and Sinclair 2016; Laroche and Yang 2014); and not just any Canadian, but, significantly, the White-Anglo-Christian-Middle-Class prototype that represents the hegemony of their new home country (Kerekes et al. 2013). (Prospective) employees are told they must be able to "fit in" to a generic Canadian workplace culture, which is often falsely assumed to be a monolingual, White, Anglo culture (Guo 2013; Kerekes and Sinclair 2016; Ontario Society of Professional Engineers 2014). Yet it is futile for the majority of IEPs to attempt to "conform . . . to a presentation of the 'ideal Canadian employee'" (Guo 2013, 36); while they may have control over some factors in their identities, those whose skin colour is not white, whose English accents do not approach Standard North American, and whose other characteristics do not match the dominant prototype mentioned above, will remain marginalized and at a distinct disadvantage when it comes to employment opportunities, unless perceptions change.

There are, among others, two angles from which to consider diminishing the inequities—in North America and beyond. On the one hand, we can examine which factors IEPs do have control over, in order for them to successfully assimilate (Guo 2013; Haque 2014; Laroche and Yang 2014) to the expectations of prospective employers. Kerekes's (2003, 2006) gatekeeping encounter research, for example, demonstrates that a positive rapport with one's job interviewer, attained through the establishment of co-membership, results in successful gatekeeping encounters as frequently for second language speakers as for dominant English speakers. Her research shows that job candidates can also use concrete compensatory strategies to impress their interviewers as flexible, reliable job candidates worthy of being hired (Kerekes 2004).

On the other hand, we can consider the role practitioners may and should play in ameliorating IEPs' professional opportunities. Instructors, (prospective) employers, co-workers, and general workplace policies and practices need to take into consideration their own potential deficit, when blocking a diverse workforce from participating in their institutions. What are these stakeholders missing out on in overlooking the potential value IEPs can add to their workplace culture?

Applied linguists can and should, in turn, make their research findings useful for practitioners and other stakeholders (students, teachers, employers, and policy makers). That is, their research on pragmatics in the workplace and effective ways of teaching soft skills to ESL learners must be useful *and* accessible to the relevant parties. This can be achieved by a) sharing research findings with the stakeholders in an understandable format; b) knowing the goals and values of the stakeholders; and c) collaborating with the stakeholders to carry out directly applicable research (Grujicic-Alatriste 2015).

It is not only the IEPs who need training; adapting to a new culture and environment should be the responsibility of employers and co-workers as well, and it should entail cultivating mutual respect and understanding (Guo 2013; Tomalin 2010). As long as immigrants continue to be compared to their native-born counterparts as their model for success, however, the responsibility is not shared: the onus of adaptation remains largely on the newcomers (Laroche and Yang 2014).

Conclusion

The complexities of empowering IEPs who seek employment or employment preparation require coordinated, collaborative adaptation on the parts of employers and their institutions, vocational ESL instructors, and IEPs themselves. Pragmatics content of employment-related ESL classes should be situated within a specific context, alerting students to the fact that communicative interactions are defined by their settings and the relationships between interlocutors, among other factors. In addition, textbooks must make explicit that pragmatic norms vary across workplaces, social groups, countries and regions where the target language is spoken. Rather than treat ESL learners as lacking pragmatic ability, workplace communication courses should approach the learners as resources who are linguistically and pragmatically competent in their L1s. Learners can use this L1 knowledge as a basis of comparison and reflection on the similarities and differences between the pragmatic norms of their first language and culture and those of the target language and culture, and they can share the expertise they already possess in their dominant language. In this way, through awareness raising, learners can also become empowered to understand the possible consequences of making or ignoring choices available to them. This is far preferable to imposing a uniform, decontextualized standard for oversimplified, generic pragmatics in the workplace.

Further Reading

Newton and Kusmierczyk (2011) is a thorough literature review of workplace communication research and its applications to vocational language programmes.

Forey and Lockwood (2010) present a variety of empirical studies of communication skills in customer service encounters involving English as a lingua franca or ESL, and effectively combines research findings with applications. Of particular relevance are Hultgren and Cameron's chapter and Elias's chapter.

Koester (2010) reviews research on workplace communication, with particular focus on genre analysis and corpus-driven approaches as appropriate methodologies.

Related Topics

Rapport management; Relational talk; Intercultural communication; Vocational education; Language learning on-the-job

Acknowledgement

I am grateful to Ivan Lasan, whose excellent work as my Graduate Assistant aided me in reviewing literature for this paper.

Notes

1. See Munro (2003) for a discussion of accent discrimination.
2. See, for example, literature on call center training, such as Elias (2010) and Hultgren and Cameron (2010).
3. We must bear in mind, however, that such success is often achieved within a hegemonic environment in which a dominant culture prevails.
4. Lasan used Diepenbroek and Derwing's (2013, 7) definition of illocutionary force: "Making an utterance stronger or softer—extent of directness (*really, just*)".

References

Bargiela-Chiappini, Francesca, and Sandra Harris. 2006. "Politeness at Work: Issues and Challenges." *Journal of Politeness Research* 2: 7–33.
Bartel, Joan. 2013. "Pragmatics in the Post-TESL Certificate Course 'Language Teaching for Employment'." *TESL Canada Journal* 30: 108–124.
Cheng, Winnie, and Martin Warren. 2005. "//→well I have a DIFferent//↗THINking you know//: A Corpus-Driven Study of Disagreement in Hong Kong Business Discourse." In *Asian Business Discourses(s)*, edited by Francesca Bargiela-Chiappini, and Maurizio Gotti, 241–270. Frankfurt am Main: Peter Lang.
Cheng, Winnie, and Martin Warren. 2006. "'I would say be very careful of . . .': Opine Markers in an Intercultural Business Corpus of Spoken English." In *Managing Interaction in Professional Discourse. Intercultural and Interdiscoursal Perspectives*, edited by Julia Bamford, and Marina Bondi, 46–58. Rome: Officina Edizioni.
Council of Europe. 2001. *Common European Framework of Reference for Languages: Learning, Teaching, Assessment*. Cambridge: Cambridge University Press.
Crystal, David. 1997. *English as a Global Language*. Cambridge: Cambridge University Press.
Dahm, Maria R., and Lynda Yates. 2013. "English for the Workplace: Doing Patient-Centred Care in Medical Communication." *TESL Canada Journal* 30: 21–44.
de Bres, Julia. 2009. "Language in the Workplace Project and Workplace Communication for Skilled Migrants Course at Victoria University of Wellington, New Zealand." *Language Teaching* 42: 519–524.
Diepenbroek, Lori, and Tracey Derwing. 2013. "To What Extent Do Popular ESL Textbooks Incorporate Oral Fluency and Pragmatic Development?" *TESL Canada Journal* 30: 1–20.
Elias, Neil. 2010. "Reconceptualizing Culture for Workplace Communication." In *Globalization, Communication and the Workplace: Talking Across the World*, edited by Gail Forey, and Jane Lockwood, 159–171. London: Continuum.
FC2I (From Consideration to Integration Steering Committee). 2003. *From Consideration to Integration: An Environmental Scan of the International Engineering Graduate Experience Before Immi-*

gration and Once in Canada, Final Report from Phase I. Ottawa: Canadian Council of Professional Engineers.
Forey, Gail, and Jane Lockwood, Eds. 2010. *Globalization, Communication and the Workplace: Talking Across the World*. London: Continuum.
Girard, Erik, and Harald Bauder. 2007. "Assimilation and Exclusion of Foreign Trained Engineers in Canada: Inside a Professional Regulatory Organization." *Antipode* 39: 35–53.
Grujicic-Alatriste, Lubie. 2015. "Framework for Application of Research Findings: An Introduction." In *Linking Discourse Studies to Professional Practice*, edited by Lubie Grujicic-Alatriste, 1–18. Clevedon: Multilingual Matters.
Guo, Yan. 2013. "Language Policies and Programs for Adult Immigrants in Canada: A Critical Analysis." *Canadian Ethnic Studies* 45: 23–41.
Haque, Eve. 2014. "Neoliberal Governmentality and Canadian Migrant Language Training Policies." *Globalisation, Societies and Education* 1–18. Published Online DOI: 10.1080/14767724.2014.937403.
Hayman, Jane. 2010. "Talking about Talking: Comparing the Approaches of Intercultural Trainers and Language Teachers." In *Globalization, Communication and the Workplace: Talking Across the World*, edited by Gail Forey, and Jane Lockwood, 147–158. London: Continuum.
Holmes, Janet. 2000. "Talking English from 9 to 5: Challenges for ESL Learners at Work." *International Journal of Applied Linguistics* 10: 125–140.
Houghton, Ted, and Tony Proscio. 2001. *Hard Work on Soft Skills: Creating a "Culture of Work" in Workforce Development*. Philadelphia, PA: Public/Private Ventures.
Hultgren, Anna Kristina, and Deborah Cameron. 2010. "Communication Skills in Contemporary Service Workplaces: Some Problems." In *Globalization, Communication and the Workplace: Talking Across the World*, edited by Gail Forey, and Jane Lockwood, 41–56. London: Continuum.
Johnston, Alexandra. 2008. "Co-Membership in Immigration Gatekeeping Interviews: Construction, Ratification and Refutation." *Discourse & Society* 19: 21–41.
Kerekes, Julie. 2003. "Distrust: A Determining Factor in the Outcomes of Gatekeeping Encounters." In *Misunderstanding in Social Life*, edited by Julianne House, Gabriele Kasper, and Stephen Ross, 227–257. London: Pearson.
Kerekes, Julie. 2004. "Preparing ESL Learners for Self-Presentation Outside the Classroom." *Prospect: An Australian Journal of TESOL* 19: 22–46.
Kerekes, Julie. 2006. "Winning an Interviewer's Trust in a Gatekeeping Encounter." *Language in Society* 35: 27–57.
Kerekes, Julie. 2007. "The Co-Construction of a Gatekeeping Encounter: An Inventory of Verbal Actions." *Journal of Pragmatics* 39: 1942–1973.
Kerekes, Julie. 2017. "Language Mentoring and Employment Ideology: Internationally Educated Professionals in Search of Work." In *Negotiating Boundaries at Work*, edited by Jo Angouri, Janet Holmes, and Meredith Marra, 11–28. Edinburgh: Edinburgh University Press.
Kerekes, Julie, Joanne Chow, Alina Lemak, and Zhanna Perhan. 2013. "Trust or Betrayal: Immigrant Engineers' Employment-Seeking Experiences in Canada." In *Discourses of Trust*, edited by Christopher Candlin, and Jonathan Crichton, 297–313. Basingstoke, UK: Palgrave Macmillan.
Kerekes, Julie, and Jeanne Sinclair. 2016. "The (Hidden) Agenda in the Teaching of Soft Skills in Vocational ESL." Unpublished Manuscript.
Koester, Almut. 2010. *Workplace Discourse*. London: Continuum.
Laroche, Lionel, and Caroline Yang. 2014. *Danger and Opportunity: Bridging Cultural Diversity for Competitive Advantage*. New York: Routledge.
Lasan, Ivan. 2014. "Review of Research Focused on Pragmatics or Soft Skills in Workplace ESL and Employment Preparation Classes." Unpublished Manuscript.
Lockwood, Jane, and Gail Forey. 2010. "Introduction." In *Globalization, Communication and the Workplace: Talking Across the World*, edited by Gail Forey, and Jane Lockwood, 3–7. London: Continuum.
Louw, Kerry, Tracey Derwing, and Marilyn Abbott. 2010. "Teaching Pragmatics to L2 Learners for the Workplace: The Job Interview." *Canadian Modern Language Review/La Revue canadienne des langues vivantes* 66: 739–758.
Lu, Peih-ying, and John Corbett. 2012. *English in Medical Education: An Intercultural Approach to Teaching Language and Values*. Bristol, UK: Multilingual Matters.
McCullagh, Marie, and Ros Wright. 2008. *Good Practice: Communication Skills in English for the Medical Practitioner*. Cambridge: Cambridge University Press.

Munro, Murray J. 2003. A Primer on Accent Discrimination in the Canadian Context. *TESL Canada Journal* 20: 38–51.

Newton, Jonathan, and Ewa Kusmierczyk. 2011. "Teaching Second Languages for the Workplace." *Annual Review of Applied Linguistics* 31: 74–92.

Ontario Society of Professional Engineers. 2014. *From the World to the Workforce: Hiring and Recruitment Perceptions of Engineering Employers and Internationally Trained Engineers in Ontario.* Toronto: Prism Economics and Analysis. https://c.ymcdn.com/sites/ospe.site-ym.com/resource/collection/E88C7AF3-7300-4B51-B591-48F87116255B/OSPE-Research-Report-From-the-World-to-the-Workforce-Aug19.pdf (last accessed 20 October 2014).

Riddiford, Nicky, and Angela Joe. 2010. "Tracking the Development of Sociopragmatic Skills." *TESOL Quarterly* 44: 195–205.

Tatsuki, Donna, and Noël Houck, Eds. 2010. *Pragmatics: Teaching Speech Acts*. Alexandria, VA: TESOL.

Thomson, Ron, and Tracey Derwing. 2004. "Presenting Canadian Values in LINC: The Roles of Textbooks and Teachers." *TESL Canada Journal* 2: 17–33.

Tomalin, Barry. 2010. "India Rising: The Need for Two Way Training." In *Globalization, Communication and the Workplace: Talking Across the World*, edited by Gail Forey, and Jane Lockwood, 172–187. London: Continuum.

Viswanathan, Revathi. 2009. "Using Mobile Technology and Podcasts to Teach Soft Skills." In *Handbook of Research on Web 2.0 and Second Language Learning*, edited by Michael Thomas, 223–236. New York: IGI Global.

Waugh, Erin. 2013. "Teaching Pragmatics and Intercultural Communication Online." *TESL Canada Journal* 30: 98–107.

Williams, Marion. 1988. "Language Taught for Meetings and Language Used in Meetings: Is there Anything in Common?" *Applied Linguistics* 9: 45–58.

Yates, Lynda, and Jacky Springall. 2010. "'Soften up!': Successful Requests in the Workplace." In *Pragmatics: Teaching Speech Acts*, edited by Donna Tatsuki, and Noël Houck, 67–86. Alexandria, VA: TESOL.

34
Language Learning On-the-Job
Lynda Yates

Introduction

Learning to live and work in another language as an adult is a challenging and long-term undertaking. Yet this is the reality for many migrants who can find their employment opportunities limited if they do not acquire proficiency in the dominant language, leading to frustration and a loss of cultural capital on a personal level, and a serious underuse of human resources nationally (Colic-Peisker and Tilbury 2006; Green, Kler, and Leeves 2007). However, while language programmes for learners with beginner or near-basic proficiency in the language are often provided for new arrivals in many countries, classes at more advanced levels are often thin on the ground. This means that once they have basic mastery of the language, it can be difficult for migrants to develop the more sophisticated language and cultural skills needed for effective communication in the workplace. Even where language programmes are available, many drop out of formal classes prematurely in order to earn money to provide for their families (Yates 2010; Yates *et al.* 2015). Thus it is often the workplace itself that is the most significant site for migrant language learning.

In this chapter I explore on-the-job language learning. In considering the nature of workplace language and how it can vary across different roles, industries, and individual workplace cultures, I take a brief look at some of the trends and issues in workplace language and language learning. Drawing on data from a national, longitudinal study conducted in Australia, I then explore the language demands and language learning opportunities experienced by one group of migrants from a wide range of educational and language backgrounds as they take up employment in a variety of roles and settings. In the final section I suggest some implications for practice and future research.

Some Definitions

In its broadest sense, "workplace language" is simply the language used at work, and since we use language in all kinds of ways at work, this covers an enormous range of communicative purposes: explaining, describing, instructing, asking people to do things, arranging meetings, and so on. It includes both the language we need to achieve our goals and get things done (often referred to as "transactional language"), and the interpersonal language we need to do the relational work, that is, to manage relationships, encourage, soften onerous requests, make small talk, etc. Thus communication at work, as elsewhere, involves both types of language and, indeed, they cannot readily be separated. While historically pedagogical approaches to workplace language have tended to focus primarily on the former, often through a needs analysis of the specific sets of items and skills required at work (for example, Li So-mui and Mead 2000), recent research on how language is used at work tends to take a broader view. In this chapter I understand workplace language to include the whole range of linguistic, cultural and communicative resources needed for effective transactional and interpersonal communication at work.

At its most basic, the term "workplace" refers to the place in which we are employed to work. However, recent increases in global and job mobility and changes in technology and labour practices have challenged traditional notions of the separation between home and work. This means that the workplace is not always one particular, clearly defined location, and also that traditional distinctions between formal education preparing for the workplace, and informal education in the workplace, are no longer so clear (Duff 2008; Roberts 2010). New work patterns have also created a "new work order" where flatter hierarchical structures and new modes of communication have created demand for a "new word order" (Roberts 2010, 211), that is, a need for increasingly sophisticated workplace communication skills. Thus developing appropriate language skills is a crucial part of success at work. This can, however, also be a very challenging undertaking for migrants who, while keen to join the workforce and to acquire the relevant communication skills, often lack the support to do so effectively.

It hardly needs to be said, however, that workplaces, and thus the language learning opportunities and support available within them, vary enormously. Different industries, different working situations, contexts and locations, and the very many different roles that can be taken at work all demand and allow different language behaviours and therefore different conditions for on-the-job language learning. My focus in this chapter is on the factors impacting how immigrants learn this "part of the story" in different workplaces outside the home, and the role of these affordances—or lack of them—in their language development.

What Does Language at Work Look Like and What do Learners Need?

Communication in workplaces is typically multimodal and involves both written and spoken language as well as skills in newer hybrid forms such as email, that combine features of formal written genres with those of more casual spoken genres. While in formal language learning curricula, spoken and written skills are often timetabled and taught separately, in everyday communications at work they are often integrated in complex ways (see, for example, Kleifgen 2013, chap. 5; Schnurr 2013, chap. 1). However, while they share a core of features, spoken and written forms of a language also differ in many ways, leading to calls that their grammars are different (McCarthy and Carter 1995). From a pedagogical perspective, they not only demand very different skill sets (consider, for example the two very different challenges of mastering the spelling and the pronunciation of English) and different generic patterning, but also require different kinds of exposure and practice if they are to be learned successfully. Certainly, strong literacy skills do not always translate readily into oracy skills or vice versa, so that an ideal learning situation would provide opportunity for practice in both.

Workplaces and the different roles within them, however, offer very different opportunities for the development of these skills. While most jobs require some form of spoken communication, in lower level factory and service roles, opportunities may be very limited or repetitive (McAll 2003), and opportunities for the development of literacy skills may be even more restricted. Some, largely white-collar, roles demand the more sophisticated levels of written language required for reports, letters, and other public communications, but others may require only basic literacy skills for form completion or note-taking. Whatever the occupation or setting, however, opportunities to observe accurate and relevant models used by others, together with appropriate feedback on their own outputs, are important if migrants are to develop and extend their language rather than simply reproduce their own "best guesses".

The nature of the industry or profession can significantly influence how language is used at work and therefore both the quantity and quality of the language demands and learning opportunities found there. In addition to the more obvious differences relating to technical terminology, specialized vocabulary, and so on, there will be differences not only in the types of genres and language functions required, but also in expectations of social and professional interactions at work. In some occupational settings, a considerable amount of time will be spent on "frontstage" interactions, that is, representing the company and interacting with members of the public or clients, while in others, routine interactions will largely be private, "backstage" interactions between colleagues (Goffman 1969). Many, of course, include both. Thus in the hospitality industry, employees such as receptionists, waiters or hotel managers will spend a considerable amount of time interacting with customers, while others, such as laundry workers or kitchen hands, will scarcely see them at all.

Moreover, it is not only the transactional nature of daily exchanges that will vary across industries and settings—so, too, will the tenor of those interactions, and here the nature of joint tasks, employee background, gender, and the cultural traditions in an industry are likely to play a role. However, immigrants experienced in a particular domain in their home country cannot necessarily rely on their first language (L1) experiences as a reliable guide to industry-appropriate communicative practices in their host countries. Although professions share similar ways of working across cultures, they can also vary. Thus, while some aspects of interaction on a building site, hospital or kindergarten may look familiar, there may also be significant differences. Professionals trained in one setting may not therefore always be able to transfer their interactive style from one culture to another, even if their language is quite proficient. To take an example from the medical field, there are cultural differences in the way in which a consultation may be conducted, the contributions that doctor and patient are expected to make to the interaction and the kinds of topics that may be discussed. Even practitioners with many years of experience in their home country can find it challenging to understand the differences in expectations about how doctors talk to patients and to colleagues in their new work environments (Dahm and Yates 2013; Lu and Corbett 2012; Yates et al. 2016). While this makes it particularly important that migrants have the opportunity to observe and learn in the kinds of workplaces they intend to work in, some explicit language teaching intervention may also be useful since some of the cross-cultural differences are quite subtle in nature (Yates 2015).

Power differentials also influence the way people speak to each other at work, and it can be difficult for a worker trained in a different environment to recognize the sometimes rather different ways in which power is acknowledged and enacted. While in some workplaces different modes of address are expected according to rank (for example, in formal legal and medical settings), in many others, particularly in countries like Australia where overt hierarchical reference is often dispreferred (see Goddard 2006), power differentials are more subtly communicated through the degree of deference offered, an unequal distribution of rights to speak or the length of turns, and so on. Thus while business meetings or consultations may appear informal, contributions are nevertheless shaped and constrained in ways that may appear baffling to learners because of "the secret rules of language" (Bardovi-Harlig 2001), that is, the pragmatic expectations that guide how we use and interpret language in a context. Migrants used to different pragmatic "rules" in their home countries, where, for example, it might be routine for supervisors to give feedback to employees in a direct manner or for employees to pay overt respect to their superiors, can find this particularly mystifying. Thus in Yates and Major (2015), Mika from Japan was shocked at the informal and personal nature of compliments that her fellow employees paid to their boss, and Charles from Colombia came to realize that he should not be too direct in giving negative feedback to colleagues; he had to learn to "say without saying" (147).

In addition, there will be aspects of workplace language that relate to the specific culture of a particular workplace. While some of these may result from and therefore be accessible through top-down measures such as corporate style guides or communications training, communicative conventions that are generated bottom-up by colleagues working together will need to be learned on the job. The concept of a Community of Practice (CofP) (Lave and Wenger 1991; and see King this volume for a full exploration) has been influential in studies of how groups of people come to share ways of interacting around shared activities. Eckert and McConnell-Ginet (1992, 464) see a CofP as "an aggregate of people who come together around mutual engagement in an endeavour." However, as King (this volume) notes, mutual engagement does not characterize all ways of working within a group, and Schnurr distinguishes between a CofP and a workplace culture, defining the latter as "a system of shared meanings and values as reflected in the discursive and behavioural norms typically displayed by members that distinguish their workplace from others" (Schnurr 2013, 61).

The concept of a workplace culture is important when considering language learning and use in the workplace because of its role in influencing how behaviour is understood within a group. It becomes a prism through which behaviour is interpreted and evaluated, so that language that is entirely appropriate in one workplace may be seen as totally inappropriate in another. Daly *et al.*'s (2004) account of the communicative practices shared in a very effective work team in a New Zealand factory illustrates this very clearly. Members of the team they call "The Power Rangers" regularly swore at and used abusive language with each other as part of a bonding interactive style that was not only accepted, but expected and seen as solidarity. It is not difficult to see how this kind of behaviour might be perceived as offensive in other workplaces, and yet in the culture of this particular workplace, it was not only tolerated but an important part of how they communicated, contributing significantly to their success as a team. Joining the team would presumably involve learning to talk like a team member, something that would have to be learned on the job.

What Makes a Workplace a Good Site for Learning?

As noted above, it is likely that opportunities to use and learn language at work will be constrained in different ways by the industry, setting and particular workplace context. Since the right to speak can be highly constrained by power differentials at work, status can have an important impact on how much language an individual can use at work, and therefore also how much they can learn. Low-level workers are frequently particularly limited in the kinds of interactions they can have with others in their workplace. House cleaner Beatriz in Yates *et al.* (2015, 56), for example, like the fictional Sahila in Norton (2000), found that interactions with the boss were essentially restricted to routine social exchanges and brief task-oriented exchanges. While both were keen to speak more at work as a means to learn more language, both were constrained by their lowly roles as cleaners which neither demanded nor allowed extended interaction.

Another obvious factor impacting on how successfully the dominant language can be learned at work is the extent to which it is actually used in the workplace. In our era of "superdiversity" (Vertovec 2007), the monolingual workplace is increasingly unusual, even in English-dominant nations like the USA and Australia (Gunnarsson 2013), and this is particularly the case in the low-paid, blue-collar work settings where many migrants are typically employed. Moreover, the lingua franca of businesses owned by first- and second-generation migrants, where many newcomers find their first jobs post migration, is often their L1 rather than the dominant language of the host country. As Goldstein (1997) illustrates in her study of a factory in Canada, different community languages can have important and very different social meanings in the workplace, and mastery of other languages may take precedence over developing proficiency in the official dominant language. Even if English is the lingua franca, some workplace teams may communicate primarily in their L1, or they may find that opportunities to develop and extend their English are limited by the English language skills of fellow workers.

As we have seen, in order to facilitate language learning on the job, the workplace needs to provide the opportunity for regular use of both spoken and written forms of the dominant language in ways that both allow workers to contribute successfully, and offer them the potential to extend their language. Suitable models need to be available so that migrants gain the input they need to learn how language is used and how to modify their output to move closer to those models. Since learning from mistakes is an important part of language learning, feedback on language performance is crucial in order to understand what works well and what does not. However, this may not always be forthcoming. Colleagues and even supervisors can be reluctant to comment on language matters for a variety of reasons: they may lack the abstract knowledge they need to identify exactly where a problem lies or what can be done to fix it, or they may be wary of causing embarrassment or offence (Yates 2011).

However, whether or not the workplace is an ideal site, this is where many migrants, of necessity or by choice, find themselves learning the language of their new country, and yet we currently know very little about how this "informal" language learning unfolds. Below I look briefly at some experiences of language learning reported in a study of recent migrants to Australia.

Some Insights from a Longitudinal Study: Working and Learning English

In this section I look at the relationship between work and language learning among a group of immigrants to Australia who participated in a national, longitudinal study.[1] This was conducted in two phases. In the first (2008–2009), qualitative data on the language learning and settlement experiences of 152 new arrivals were collected, and in the second (2011–2014), 60 of the first phase cohort and 85 additional newly-arrived immigrants were followed. They came from a wide range of social, economic, and language backgrounds, and when they started in the study all were attending classes in the national on-arrival programme, the Adult Migrant English Program (AMEP), following an assessment that they did not have basic, functional English. A range of techniques was used to elicit their experiences through interview, observation and self-assessment. Details of the methodology and a full account of findings can be found in Yates (2010), Yates et al. (2015). Here I consider what they found helpful as they struggled to improve their proficiency in English in the workplace, and what hampered their efforts.

Applications

Factors that Facilitated Language Learning at Work

Some of our overall findings lend support to the idea that the workplace is an important ingredient in English language learning post migration. The first concerns the very strong motivation we found among most participants in both phases of the project to enter the workforce. Indeed, they were sometimes too keen, leaving their English language classes prematurely in order to start paid employment. This suggests that the drive to become financially viable may override concerns to perfect their English, that is, they did not necessarily see the need to learn English first and then find work in that order. For many, as Roberts (2010) argues, the boundaries between formal and informal learning were blurred. While this rush to informal learning is by no means always positive, and in several cases participants soon realized that they needed more English before they could work in the kind of job that they really wanted, it does suggest a level of motivation that can be usefully harnessed in both work-preparation and workplace language support classes.

In addition, particularly in the early days of their settlement, many migrants found very few opportunities to engage with the English-speaking community outside the classroom (see Yates 2010). In the second phase of the study we were able to track participants' use of English more closely, asking them to estimate at each interview the amount of time that they used all their languages, including English. We found that those who were employed reported using more English than those who were not. We also found that those who reported using more English, were more likely to assess their English at a higher level (for details see Yates *et al.* 2015, chap. 2 and 3). These findings suggest that, for some migrants at least, work offers the opportunity to make more use of, and thus, potentially make greater improvements in their language skills.

However, work situations varied enormously in both the quantity and quality of the opportunities for language development they offered. In general, higher-level jobs demanded more and thus offered more scope for learning. Not surprisingly, it was those who already had a higher level of English on arrival, that is, who had already studied some English before migration, who were able to secure such jobs more quickly. These largely professional participants who were able to find jobs commensurate with their pre-migration experience and qualifications often reported using considerable amounts of English across a range of skills. Abrar, for example, who had worked as a doctor in Iraq, found her role as a workforce development manager with a disease prevention programme obliged her to use English all day as she talked to colleagues, read material in English, and prepared presentations. She also had to write emails and draft reports. By her fifth interview, she reported a considerable improvement in her English after five years in Australia. Charles from Colombia reported similar success. His position as a furniture designer obliged him to negotiate contracts and salaries, discuss designs, make presentations to clients, and use English in emails and on the phone in ways that allowed him to extend his skills.

Some also found lower-level employment useful in developing their language learning. While interactions in basic customer service roles in stores, beauty salons and fast food outlets were repetitive, they helped participants gain in confidence, and where there were opportunities for extension and feedback, some were able to develop other aspects of their language. For example, unlike Merilinka, whose rather negative experiences are reported in Sandwall (2010), Cherry from China found that she gained enormously from working at an English-speaking childcare centre. Daily interactions with children, including telling them stories, making arrangements with parents, and chatting with Australian colleagues both at work and on social outings helped her grow in confidence and develop her language skills. She reported an enormous improvement not only in her spoken English, but also in her written skills as a result of feedback from her colleagues, who checked the grammar of the brief report she had to write daily in her capacity as room leader. Participants told us of the important role that co-workers played in their language development, teaching essential vocabulary items, speaking slowly to aid comprehension, repeating where necessary and accommodating to their level of English as they interacted during work time and breaks.

Some participants deliberately used lower-level jobs and job placements strategically as a way of acquiring the local experience and references that employers demanded, and thus as stepping stones to their ultimate goal of securing professional employment. Marimar, for example, a software engineer from Venezuela who arrived in Australia with good literacy but poor oracy skills in English, initially took a short-term casual job transcribing audio recordings. Although it was not demanding in the sense that it did not draw on her professional skills in IT, the job gave her considerable practice listening to English which she initially found challenging. She found this activity so useful, however, that even after the job ended she continued to practise transcription at home. Eventually she gained the confidence to undertake some retail and volunteer work, where interactions with co-workers and customers stretched her use of English. By her final interview she had found employment in her field. Svetlana, too, a graphic designer from Kazakhstan, found her work placement as a shop assistant in an office supplies store invaluable for improving both her language and her willingness to communicate and therefore a useful starting point on her journey towards a job in her field. Similarly, although the very brief and repetitive nature of her interactions as a waitress made Lucia feel "like a robot", she soon moved on to other more linguistically demanding roles (see Yates *et al.* 2015).

Factors that Interfered with Language Learning at Work

While low-level service jobs gave some the confidence to start interacting in English and forced them to try to understand unfamiliar accents, others found their English stagnating into a restricted range of routine, repetitive phrases. As in McAll (2003), some jobs offered little scope for language development. Irene, for example, found that she only needed to memorize a few technical words in order to undertake her responsibilities in a laundry. Similarly, at the baker's where she worked, Lily was only required to use very simple, formulaic phrases like "Which bread?" and "Here's your change", and while Dan's job as a security guard improved his confidence, he told us that "it didn't add anything to my language".

Opportunities to develop English at work were also limited by the language used in the workplace. Because many employers were reluctant to take on migrants with low levels of English and no local references, many participants found their first jobs through L1 community contacts in L1 environments such as community newspapers, shops, restaurants, and factories. Thus while Karen was able to move on from her first job with a Chinese newspaper, Charles remained working in a Vietnamese restaurant where there was little need to use English, and relied on his L1 network for all his needs. Yuan's initial job as a cleaner offered some limited opportunity to interact in English, but after moving to a job in a Chinese gift shop, she found that she used almost no English at all in her daily life.

Even where English was used at work as a lingua franca, participants reported great difficulty understanding the accents and varieties spoken by their colleagues. Some, like Gilberto, found it difficult to talk or understand colleagues because of the background noise in the kitchen where he worked. Others, like Anna and Beatriz, found that it was their bosses who limited opportunities for using English. Thus Beatriz was told not to disturb customers by talking in the massage parlour where she worked, and Anna and her colleagues were discouraged from talking as they worked in a factory producing spectacles.

Moreover, even if other conditions are ideal, it can be difficult to engage English-speaking colleagues in conversation, as the case of Karen exemplifies (Yates 2011). Although she found work in her area of expertise (landscaping) with a sympathetic boss, Karen felt that she was not included in office activities and talk and therefore missed out on opportunities to develop not only her English but also her English-speaking social network. It was not that her colleagues were rude or unfriendly to her; they simply did not include her in the social aspects of their lives. She felt like an outsider. Although she wanted to join in, she felt that she lacked some of the "insider information" she needed in order to do this, and that her colleagues did not help by explaining what was going on or what she needed to do. Rather than helping her understand more about her environment in the way that Cherry's colleagues did, Karen's co-workers avoided engaging with her, leaving her feeling isolated and a little lonely.

Any newcomer to a workplace can find it difficult to join an already established group, but this is especially challenging for someone who is still learning the language, and small talk can pose a particular problem (Mak and Chui 2013; Yates and Major 2015). Far from being an irrelevance, these apparently casual exchanges can play an important role, not only in fostering mutual understanding and team bonding, but also in transferring important information (Holmes 1999). They are also important for individuals from a social as well as from a language learning perspective, helping them to understand what is happening at work and reinforcing a sense of belonging. However, participating in casual talk at work can be very challenging, as our participants told us. They often found it difficult to find a way into, sustain, and understand a conversation, especially if they realized that it was supposed to be funny.

Recommendations for Practice and Future Directions

Thus while the workplace can potentially offer useful opportunities for language learning, its effectiveness depends heavily on the specific circumstances of the employment context and an individual's ability to make the most of them. An ideal job can provide the motivation, setting, and opportunity to develop language skills, but the prospect of financial security can also seduce migrants prematurely into the workforce where they can become stuck in routine jobs that do very little for their language development and drain their energy and self-confidence. What can start as a temporary job while they "find their feet" can turn into a trap from which they find it difficult to escape. It is therefore important that migrants have appropriate guidance to help them understand both the work and study possibilities in their new environment, and also the potential traps (Kozar, Yates, and Pryor 2016).

Since migrants anxious to establish themselves in a new country are likely to continue to find the lure of paid employment difficult to resist, language instruction programmes that include work placements potentially offer a way of offering some of the advantages of both worlds (see, for example, Yates et al. 2015 for a description of relevant programmes in Australia; and Riddiford and Holmes 2015 and Riddiford and Joe 2010 for accounts of a programme in New Zealand). Appropriately organized and offered in conjunction with instruction that opens up rather than limits horizons, work placements can give learners experience of the workplace and insight into how different jobs might contribute or otherwise to their language learning. It is important, however, as Warriner (2010) warns, that such programmes be construed and funded as a pathway to a range of career options, including further study, and not merely as the preparation of factory fodder.

Moreover, since it is not realistic to expect that formal instruction can cover everything a learner needs to know, language classes need to include a focus on helping migrants to develop their agency and skills so that they can take charge of their own learning. Whatever the work or study context they find themselves in, learners need to be able to make the most of the language learning opportunities that come their way, to become "language detectives" able to understand, analyse and acquire the language they need (Yates 2014). More studies focusing on these kinds of autonomous approaches to learning language would be useful in supporting the practical efforts of teachers and policy-makers towards increasing the effectiveness of on-the-job language learning.

Further Reading

Marra (2013) is an accessible review of issues related to English in the workplace and provides useful references.

Yates (2008) provides an accessible introduction to communication issues facing migrants at work together with four chapters of sample materials.

Yates and Springall (2010) provides a brief account of a study into an area of workplace communication and the teaching materials based on the findings.

Related Topics

Rapport management; Communities of practice; Corporate settings; Blue-collar workplaces; Intercultural communication; Vocational education; Language preparation

Note

1 I gratefully acknowledge support 2008–2009, 2011–2013 from the Department of Immigration and Citizenship, and 2013–2014 from the Department of Industry. Many thanks, also, to the many researchers who worked on these projects and to the participants who gave us their time and their experiences.

References

Bardovi-Harlig, Kathleen. 2001. "Evaluating the Empirical Evidence: Grounds for Instruction in Pragmatics?" In *Pragmatics in Language Teaching*, edited by Kenneth R. Rose, and Gabriele Kasper, 13–32. Cambridge: Cambridge University Press.
Colic-Peisker, Val, and Farida Tilbury. 2006. "Employment Niches for Recent Refugees: Segmented Labour Market in Twenty-First Century Australia." *Journal of Refugee Studies* 19: 203–229.
Dahm, Maria R., and Lynda Yates. 2013. "English for the Workplace: Doing Patient-Centred Care in Medical Communication." *TESL Canada* 30: 1–24.
Daly, Nicola, Janet Holmes, Jonathan Newton, and Maria Stubbe. 2004. "Expletives as Solidarity Signals in FTAs on the Factory Floor." *Journal of Pragmatics* 36: 945–64.
Duff, Patricia. 2008. Language Socialization, Higher Education, and Work. In *Language Socialization. Vol. 8 of Encyclopedia of Language and Education*. 2nd edn., edited by Patricia A. Duff and Nancy H. Hornberger, 257–270. New York: Springer.
Eckert, Penelope, and Sally McConell-Ginet. 1992. "Communities of Practice: Where Language, Gender and Power All Live." In *Locating Power. Proceedings of the Second Berkely Women and Language Conference*, edited by Kira Hall, Mary Bucholz, and Birch Moonwomon, 89–99. California: Berkely Women and Language Group, University of California.
Goffman, Erving. 1969. *The Presentation of Self in Everyday Life*. London: Penguin.
Goldstein, Tara. 1997. *Two Languages at Work: Bilingual Life on the Production Floor*. Berlin: Mouton de Gruyter.

Goddard, Cliff. 2006. "'Lift Your Game Martina': Deadpan Jocular Irony and the Ethnopragmatics of Australian English." In *Ethnopragmatics*, edited by Cliff Goddard, 65–97. Berlin: Mouton de Gruyter.

Green, Colin, Parvinder Kler, and Gareth Leeves. 2007. "Immigrant Overeducation: Evidence from Recent Arrivals to Australia." *Economics of Education Review* 26: 420–432.

Gunnarsson, Britt-Louise. 2013. "Multilingualism in the Workplace." *Annual Review of Applied Linguistics* 33: 162–189.

Holmes, Janet. 1999. "Managing Social Talk at Work: What Does the NESB Worker Need to Know?" *TESOLANZ Journal: The Journal of the TESOL Association of Aotearoa New Zealand* 7: 7–19.

Kleifgen, Jo Anne. 2013. *Communicative Practices at Work: Multimodality and Learning in a High-Tech Firm*. Bristol, UK: Multilingual Matters.

Kozar, Olga, Lynda Yates, and Liz Pryor. 2016. "Introduction of compulsory counselling: Insights from a nationally-funded ESL program." *TESOL Quarterly* 50: 507–517.

Lave, Jean, and Etienne Wenger. 1991. *Situated Learning: Legitimate Peripheral Participation*. Cambridge: Cambridge University Press.

Li So-mui, Florence, and Kate Mead. 2000. "An analysis of English in the Workplace: The Communication Needs of Textile and Clothing Merchandisers." *English for Specific Purposes* 19: 351–368.

Lu, Peih-ying, and John Corbett. 2012. *English in Medical Education: An Intercultural Approach to Teaching Language and Values*. Bristol, UK: Multilingual Matters.

Mak, Bernie Chun Nam, and Hin Leung Chui. 2013. "A Cultural Approach to Small Talk: A Double-Edged Sword of Sociocultural Reality During Socialization into the Workplace." *Journal of Multicultural Discourses* 8: 118–33.

Marra, Meredith. 2013. "English in the Workplace." In *Handbook of English for Specific Purposes*, edited by Brian Paltridge, and Sue Starfield, 175–192. Chichester, UK: John Wiley & Sons.

McAll, Christopher. 2003. "Language Dynamics in the Bi-and Multilingual Workplace." In *Language Socialization in Bilingual and Multilingual Societies*, edited by Robert Bayley, and Sandra R. Schecter, 235–250. Clevedon, UK: Multilingual Matters.

McCarthy, Michael, and Ronald Carter. 1995. "Spoken Grammar: What Is It and How Can We Teach It?" *ELT Journal* 49: 207–219.

Norton, Bonny. 2000. *Identity and Language Learning: Gender, Ethnicity and Educational Change*. Harlow, UK: Pearson.

Riddiford, Nicky, and Janet Holmes. 2015. "Assisting the Development of Sociopragmatic Skills: Negotiating Refusals at Work." *System* 48: 129–140.

Riddiford, Nicky, and Angela Joe. 2010. "Tracking the Development of Sociopragmatic Skills." *TESOL Quarterly* 44: 195–205.

Roberts, Celia. 2010. "Language Socialization in the Workplace." *Annual Review of Applied Linguistics* 30: 211–227.

Sandwall, Karin. 2010. "'I Learn More at School': A Critical Perspective on Workplace-Related Second Language Learning in and out of School." *TESOL Quarterly* 44: 542–574.

Schnurr, Stephanie. 2013. *Exploring Professional Communication: Language in Action*. Abingdon, UK: Routledge.

Vertovec, Steven. 2007. "Superdiversity and its Implications." *Ethnic and Racial Studies* 30: 1024–1054.

Warriner, Doris S. 2010. "Competent Performances of Situated Identities: Adult Learners of English." *Teaching and Teacher Education* 26: 22–30.

Yates, Lynda. 2008. *The Not-So Generic Skills: Teaching Employability Communication Skills to Adult Migrants*. Materials by Terry Griffin and Jenny Guilfoyle. Sydney: NCELTR. (www.ameprc.mq.edu.au/docs/research_reports/teaching_in_action/Teaching_in_action_navigable_lowres.pdf)

Yates, Lynda. 2010. *Language Training and Settlement Success: Are They Related?* Sydney: AMEP Research Centre, Macquarie University. Retrieved from: www.ameprc.mq.edu.au/docs/LanguageTrainingSettlement_.pdf.

Yates, Lynda. 2011. "Language, Interaction and Social Inclusion in Early Settlement." *International Journal of Bilingual Education and Bilingualism* 14: 457–471.

Yates, Lynda. 2014. "Learning How to Speak: Pronunciation, Pragmatics and Practicalities in the Classroom and Beyond." *Language Teaching*. doi:10.1017/S0261444814000238.

Yates, Lynda. 2015. "Intercultural Communication and the Transnational: Managing Impressions at Work." *Multilingua* 34: 773–795.

Yates, Lynda, Maria R. Dahm, Peter Roger, and John Cartmill. 2016. "Rapport and Teamwork in Australia: Insights for International Medical Graduates." *English for Specific Purposes* 42: 104–116.

Yates, Lynda, and George Major. 2015. "'Quick-Chatting', 'Smart Dogs', and How to 'Say Without Saying': Small Talk and Pragmatic Learning in the Community." *System* 48: 141–152.

Yates, Lynda, and Jacky Springall. 2010. "'Soften up!': Successful Requests in the Workplace." In *Pragmatics: Teaching Speech Acts*, edited by Donna H. Tatsuki, and Noël R. Houck, 67–86. Alexandria, VA: TESOL.

Yates, Lynda, Agnes Terraschke, Beth Zielinski, Elizabeth Pryor, Jihong Wang, George Major, Mahesh Radhakrishnan, Heather Middleton, Maria Chisari, and Vera Williams Tetteh. 2015. *Adult Migrant English Program (AMEP) Longitudinal Study 2011–2014. Final Report*. Linguistics Department Macquarie University, Sydney. (http://espace.library.uq.edu.au/view/UQ:364744/UQ364744_OA.pdf)

Index

access to workplaces *see* data collection
action, freedom of 275 *see also* politeness theory
activity types 29, 113
advice: in genetic-counselling 189, 190; legal 151
advice for practice 330
advice-giving 204, 221–222
alignment: cultural 90; display of 8; group 93; interpreters 299; participant 5, 377; with audience 36, 289; with expectations 394; with superiors 131; with workplace 369 *see also* footing *see also* framing
allowable contributions 29, 78, 130
anecdotes 244, 246–248 *see also* narrative
apologies 6, 7, 266
appreciative enquiry 79, 342, 406
argumentation 284–291 *see also* legal discourse/settings
asymmetry/asymmetrical: conceal 337; contest 259, 260; of knowledge 299; power 36, 272, 415; relationship 275, 279; skills 352 *see also* leadership *see also* power
authentication, of identity 375, 377–378, 382
authentic interactional data 44, 46, 114–115, 183, 304, 341, 417–418, 419
authoritarian style *see* leadership
authoritative stance 207
authority: and gender 9; and leadership 325–326, 330; institutional 6, 290, 375–379, 382; legal 153, 155; managerial 267 *see also* leadership
avoidance of interpersonal conflict/confrontation 8, 66, 94, 272, 324
awareness of: cultural norms 78, 341, 414; gender expectations 369; institutional authority 382; linguistic norms 121, 330; occupational expectations 378; performative nature of language 134; problems 264, 265
awareness raising: cultural 180, 418–419, 420, 421; linguistic 121; of negative effects 330, 402, 409; of performative nature of language 134; of stereotypes 318

backstage 45, 260, 427
back-to-work support 20–21

Baxter, Judith 10–11, 37, 313–314, 330, 405, 409
Berger and Luckman 89, 90–91
big D Discourse *see* discourse (big-D)
Billig, Michael 21
blue-collar workers/settings 105, 138–147, 208, 276, 338, 426, 428, 429
boundary-monitoring *see* gatekeeping
Brown and Levinson 68–70, 72, 73, 78, 205, 210, 211–212, 275
Bruner 243, 244, 390
Bucholtz and Hall 373–375

CA *see* conversation analysis
call centre discourse 47–48, 80, 175–184, 279, 280, 415, 416
CDS *see* critical discourse studies
Chain of Command 375–376, 378, 382
chair/chairing 120–121, 122, 328, 340, 409
challenges to identity 362–364
challenging: dominant stories 245; someone's point of view 244; power 33, 272, 350, 401, 409; rapport 79, 81, 84; social relations 77; superiors 129, 228
children in workplaces 156, 297, 303, 304
code-mixing 354
code-switching 157, 164–165, 192–196, 351, 357
co-leadership *see* leadership
collaboration with workplaces 407, 408, 417, 421
collaborative: agreement 366; decision-making 191, 192, 194; discourse 84, 90, 352; floor 368; humor 233; leadership 328; perspective 177
collegial: collegiality 85, 216, 218, 368; relations 79, 81–82, 366, 415; strategies 84
communities of practice: and directives 208–209; and gender research 317; and linguistic ethnography 46; blue-collar settings 140; concept of 101–109, 428; gendered 404; gender norms 364; humor 235; impoliteness 275–276; interactional sociolinguistics 9–10, 11; social constructionism 89; vocational education 390, 392, 394, 395; workplace 312, 316 363, 414

437

Index

competitive discourse 140
complaints/complaining: blue-collar setting 140; call centre discourse 180; corporate setting 132; group membership 93–94, 366–367; narrative 248; miscommunication 266; misunderstanding 6, 8 *see also* criticism
complexity theory 268
compliments/complimenting 8, 133, 217, 219–220, 234, 338, 415, 428
conflict avoidance 94
conflict talk 272–281
contextualization conventions 4, 6, 7
contextualization cues 4, 5, 7, 169, 408
control: and directives 206; call centre discourse 178; gender 314; gender and leadership 402; humor 236; in corporate settings 128, 131; intercultural communication 335; leadership 324; legal discourse 151, 152–153, 154, 156; narrative 252; relational talk 219; *see also* power
conversation analysis (CA) call centre research 182; courtroom language 152–153; dispreferred responses 277; genetic counselling 192; greeting 218; method and approach 15–23; service encounters 164, 165, 167, 168
co-participation 190–191
corporate settings 127–135
corporate values, establishment 348–350
corpus: definition 51
corpus analysis of workplace discourse (CAWD) 51–62
corpus linguistics 51–62, 182
corpus linguistics tools 53–61
Coupland, Wiemann and Giles 261, 264
courtroom language *see* legal discourse
credibility 35, 157, 290, 298
critical discourse analysis (CDA) 41–42, 47, 182, 260 *see also* critical discourse studies
critical discourse studies (CDS) 27–37
critical feedback 10
criticism: and complimenting 220, 229; and rapport management theory 84; implicit 266; in a corporate setting 133; intercultural communication 365; leadership 324, 343; narrative 249; pre-empted 405
cross-cultural: definition in relation to intercultural 335
cross-cultural communication 3–7, 78, 82
cross-cultural competence 416
cross-cultural differences 163–164, 180, 210–211, 213, 415, 427
cross-cultural miscommunication/misunderstanding 416
cross-cultural reflection 420
cultural assumptions, differing 7, 97, 213
cultural expectations: interactional sociolinguistics 4, 6, 8; intercultural communication 340;

social constructionism 95, 97; gender 315; genre theory 112; narrative 251–252 *see also* norms
cultural knowledge 4, 90, 181, 298–299
cultural stereotypes/stereotyping 8, 316, 405
cultural training 178, 181, 416, 418
culture, workplace *see* workplace culture

damage control 133
data collection 4, 40–48, 106–107, 114–115, 268, 317, 340–341
decision-making: and women 405; argumentation 285, 288–289; conflict talk 274, 279; in corporate settings 131; in genetic counselling 187–197; rapport management 80; leadership 326
denaturalization 375, 379–382
difference theory/perspective 403
digital contexts 11, 231–237, 318 *see also* email
directives 9, 70, 72, 203–213; procedural and non-procedural 209–210
directives NOW and LATER, 209, 213
directness 7, 167, 204, 415 *see also* indirectness
disadvantage 150–151, 156–157, 420
disagreement: and argumentation 284–291 and leadership 328; and power 275; distinguished from conflict 274, 279; in discourse 272–281; negotiation 106; sequence 274, 276; tolerance of 80, 274
disclosing *see* relational talk
Discourse, big D 31, 130
discourse, gender style *see* gender
discourse, little/small d 31, 130
discursive leadership 327–328
doctor-patient interaction (physicians) 5, 17–19, 20, 80, 211, 219, 427 *see also* health communication research
doing identity *see* identity
dominance theory 402–403, 404
double bind, gender 7–8, 9, 318, 402–403
downplaying status 8
Drew and Heritage 16
DYLAN-project 349–358

education settings/educational contexts: educator professional identity 108; empowering non-native speakers 114; humor 231; intercultural communication 337; leadership 328; linguistic ethnography 46; rapport management 81, 82; relational work 218, 219, 220, 221, 222 *see also* vocational education
Eelen 65, 66–67, 77
effective practice 2, 19, 20,
egalitarian systems/egalitarianism 128, 129, 133, 210
email 11, 47, 144, 211 *see also* digital contexts *see also* written workplace language

Index

emic perspective/emically-grounded 43, 73, 289 *see also* first order understandings
emotional labour 19–20, 378
employment interviews 79–80, 85 *see also* gatekeeping
employment preparation for migrants 413–422
empowered employees 128, 129, 131, 133, 134, 179
empowerment: of learners 113, 114, 179, 414, 417, 419, 421; of women 206, 316
empowerment value of research 44, 317, 318
enacting authority *see* authority
enacting identity *see* identity
enact politeness *see* politeness
encouraging 34, 217, 221–222, 342
enculturating 73
English for Specific Purposes (ESP) 113–114, 184
enhancement of language status 349, 350 *see also* reduction of language status
ethics and research 22, 46, 85–86, 317
ethnographic research: blue-collar contexts 140, 141, 146; call centre discourse 183; communities of practice 102–108; conflict talk 279; critical discourse studies 33–34; genetic counselling 192; gender and leadership 407; gender research 313, 315, 317; genre theory 114–115; (im)politeness theory 70, 72; interactional linguistics 4, 9; intercultural communication 341; interpreting 304; linguistic ethnography 40–48; miscommunication 262, 264, 268; multilingualism 349; vocational education 393, 397
ethnography of communication 40, 352 *see also* Hymes, Dell
etic understanding (analyst) 43
exclusion 29, 143–146, 196, 254, 260, 349, 350, 403–404 *see also* marginalization
expectations *see* cultural expectations *see* gender expectations *see* institutional/occupational expectations *see* leadership expectations
expert audience 96
expert knowledge 9, 104, 190, 235, 290, 394–395, 409, 417
exploitation 34, 36, 81, 178

face-protecting/saving 57, 68, 262, 266 *see also* Brown and Levinson
face sensitivities 78, 81, 84, 85, 86
face threat 32, 72, 140, 275
face work 131
factory contexts/settings *see* blue-collar
Fairclough 28–30, 129, 349
Fairhurst 327 *see also* discursive leadership
feminine norms 205, 213, 364, 406 *see also* gender *see also* stereotypes
feminine styles 205, 208, 312–315, 327, 364, 368, 405

feminist poststructuralist discourse analysis (FPDA) 37, 404, 407, 408
fieldnotes 44, 45–46, 48, 144–145, 147, 407
Filliettaz, Laurent 164, 289–290
first order understanding 66, 69 *see also* emic perspective/emically-grounded
Fletcher, Joyce K. 84, 86
footing 5, 10, 166, 168, 376–377, 382 *see also* alignment
Foucault 66–67, 91, 245, 312, 313, 349
frame 5, 11, 168, 235
framing 5, 8–9, 194, 376–377, 396 *see also* frame
frontstage 45, 427

gatekeeping 4, 6, 11, 79–80, 130–131, 415, 420–421 *see also* employment interviews
gender 311–319, 361–370, 401–410 *see also* gender expectations *see also* identity
gendered styles 7, 9, 205
Gendered Talk at Work (Holmes) 10
gender expectations 10, 312, 363, 402 *see also* norms
gender identity *see* identity
gender and leadership 10, 311–319, 330, 401–410
genetic counselling 187–197
genre knowledge 112–123
genre knowledge, development 114, 120–122
genre theory 112–123
gestures *see* non-verbal communication
glass ceiling 8, 311, 314, 327
globalization 74, 128, 178–179, 213, 389
Goffman: face 78; footing 166, 168; framing 5, 168; linguistic ethnography 41; management viewpoints 35–36; participatory practices 352, 396; sex-class-linked 8 *see also* frontstage *see also* backstage
Gricean pragmatics 66
group membership *see* ingroup *see* outgroup
Gumperz, John 3–7, 40, 338, 341

Haugh's interactional approach to politeness 65–74
health communication research: call centre discourse 177; doctor-patient 5; interpreting 295–305; miscommunication 259; nursing 361–370; patient choice 20; rapport management 80; social constructionism 89–98 *see also* doctor-patient interaction *see also* genetic counselling *see also* nurses/nursing contexts *see also* nursing handover meetings
Heritage, John 19, 22
high stakes encounter/contexts 113, 117, 258 *see also* employment interviews
hinting 72–73 *see also* Brown and Levinson
Holmes, Janet 9–10, 102, 106, 140, 228 *see also* Wellington Language in the Workplace Project

Index

humor: and critical feedback 10; and leadership 325–326; blue-collar workplaces 140; collegiality 45; digital communication 231–237; face-to-face 229–231; gender differences 7; in communities of practice 106; in narratives 246–247; intercultural communication 336–337, 342–343; rapport management 84; self-deprecating 7, 229, 235; subversive 11; teasing 5, 7, 229–230, 234, 325, 342
hybridity 314
Hymes, Dell 40–41, 113 *see also* SPEAKING framework *see also* ethnography of communication

identity: blue-collar workplaces 139–140; collective/group 78, 244, 248; construction 9, 34, 36, 80, 91–94, 108, 205, 207, 236, 244, 245, 407; enactment 95; ethnic 246; foreigner 11; individual 78, 244; interpreters 296, 298; lawyer 153; negotiation 5, 29, 92, 93, 95; normative 139; nurse 121; orientation 93; performance 105; plural 355, 357, 358; powerless 128; professional 131–134, 179, 208, 267, 285; shared 45; social 78, 92; spatial 47; teacher 108; transitions 391–392 *see also* gender *see also* identity *see also* leadership *see also* situated identity
impoliteness 33, 65–74, 273, 275–276, 278–280
impoliteness, mock 234
impoliteness theory 65–74 *see also* politeness theory
imposition 73; and directives 209–210, 211; freedom from 72; mitigating 177; of languages by management 349, 350
improve inequality and discrimination
inclusion 143, 349, 350
Incongruity theory 228
indexicality 312–313, 374, 396, 397
indigenous 10, 156, 230, 338
indirectness 6, 7, 10, 167 *see also* directness
indirectness, inherent 229
indirect participation 190, 191, 192
inequalities 3, 41–42, 311, 315, 402
ingroup 83, 91, 94, 140, 165, 336, 364–367, 369
ingroup cohesion, reinforcing 247–248
injustice 28, 84, 140, 151
in situ 96, 97, 98, 263, 324
institutional/occupational expectations: and genre 121; and miscommunication 266; blue-collar contexts 145; cabin crew discourse 374, 378, 382; clashes 11; communities of practice 108; corporate settings 130; language preparation 420; rapport management 78, 79–80; socially constructed 95; understanding differences 427; vocational education 391, 392, 396 *see also* norms

interactional sociolinguistics 1–12, 182, 192, 264, 338–339, 376, 396
intercultural: definition in relation to cross-cultural 335
intercultural miscommunication 4, 11, 415
interdependence 8
intergroup relations/relationships 4, 250, 263
interpersonal relations/relationships: and directives 207; and humor 235; and interactional sociolinguistics 8; and leadership 323; and miscommunication 259; and relational talk 216–224; call centre discourse 177, 179, 182; in (im)politeness theory 66, 67; in service encounters 162; rapport management 77–87
interpersonal skills *see* soft skills
interpreters/interpreting 46, 157, 191, 295–305
interpreting, conduit model 295–296
intersectionality 314
interview, post-recording 4, 46
interviews with participants 9, 45–48, 54, 341

Jefferson 16
journalistic training/workplaces/writing 47, 392, 407 *see also* media discourse

Kendall, Shari 9, 11
knowledge, shared 53, 336, 366–368
knowledge-based economy 128
Kotthoff, Helga 277

Labov, William 242–243, 245, 272
language barriers 82
language choice 164, 348, 349–353, 357–358
language competence 11, 143–144, 145, 181
Language in the Workplace Project *see* Wellington Language in the Workplace Project
Lave, Jean *see* communities of practice
leader-member relations 84–85
leadership: and ethnicity 10, 32, 314; authoritative identity 32; authority 290; co-leadership 328; construction 11, 92; credibility 290; distributed 104, 403; egalitarian/good mate identity 32; enactment 316, 323–332, 357, 369, 401–410; expectations 314, 402; feminine identity 314; hero 10, 32; identities 32, 267; masculine identity 32; mother identity 314, 406; paternalistic/father identity 32; stereotypes 10, 313–315
Leadership, Discourse, and Ethnicity (Holmes, Marra and Vine 2011) 10
leadership language, gendered 312–313, 316
learnables 394
Leech, Geoffrey 66, 67, 339
legal discourse/settings 150–158, 273, 288, 296–297
legal written language 150, 151, 152
legitimate peripheral participation 101, 390

life stories *see* narrative
lingua franca: English 81–82, 85, 417, 431; competent use 107; blue-collar contexts 146, 429; service encounters 170; genetic counselling 191; multilingualism 349, 357
linguistic ethnography (LE) 40–48
linguistic profile 113–117, 122
listening skills 84, 181, 217, 222–223
localization 74
localized practices 102, 106, 108, 260
Locher and Watts 275, 278
LWP *see* Wellington Language in the Workplace Project

macro-level: corporate settings 128; critical discourse studies 28, 29, 30–31, 33, 34; genetic counselling 188; genre theory 113, 119; rapport management 85; miscommunication 260, 262; multilingualism 353
majority groups 314, 335, 336, 337, 341
management of meetings 324, 325 *see also* topic management/control
marginalization 101, 107, 251, 254, 403–404, 420
masculine: bias 327; norms 7, 205, 213, 361, 364, 404, 405, 406; styles 315, 361, 364, 402, 405 *see also* gender *see also* stereotypes
maxims-based approach *see* Leech, Geoffrey
media discourse 81, 273, 316, 317 *see also* journalistic training/workplaces/writing
media portrayals 382, 405, 406 *see also* stereotypes
meeting talk 8, 274
meso-level 28–33, 105
Methods of Critical Discourse Analysis (Wodak and Meyer) 30
Methods of Critical Discourse Studies (Wodak and Meyer) 30
micro-communities of knowledge 104
micro-level: critical discourse studies 28–34; genre theory 119–120; call centre discourse 183; gender 317; genetic counselling 188, 189; interpreting 296, 304; leadership 328; multilingualism 349, 353, 358; rapport management 85; social constructionism 97
military workplaces 212, 273, 276, 279
minority group norms 337
minority groups 4, 6, 10, 336, 337, 350, 401
Mirivel's model of positive communication 216–224
misalignments 259, 280
miscommunication: interactional sociolinguistics 4, 11; intercultural 106, 415; interpreting 298; linguistic ethnography 44; legal settings 156, 157; overview and model 258–268; rapport management 79 *see also* misunderstanding
mission statements 34–36

misunderstanding: call centre discourse 180, 183; communities of practice 106; genetic counselling 194; implications for women 7; intercultural 338, 339; legal settings 153, 154; migrants 416, 418; rapport management 79, 81–82, 83 *see also* miscommunication
mitigating: directives 205, 208–212; refusals 211; miscommunication 11; power 85; strategies 9, 33, 133, 177, 229
mitigation 57, 81, 133, 220
mobility 28, 107, 138, 144, 348, 426
mock-hostility 7
modesty, overt 10, 219
multicultural workplaces 97, 122, 196, 337
multilingualism 107–108, 140–146, 164–165, 348–358
multimodality 17, 260, 287, 289, 393, 396, 397, 426
mutual engagement 82, 101–109, 428

narrative: and legal discourse 151, 153, 154, 155; argumentative 244, 248, 250; as indirect disagreement 249; cabin crew discourse 376; construction of identity 244; distancing 244; influence on genre theory 113; interpreting 297; leader 10; overview 242–255; barrier for migrants 141; self-deprecating 10
necessary evils 84
negative face 72, 73, 211 *see also* Brown and Levinson
negotiating: disagreement 106; problematic talk 267; relationships 218, 221, 367, 369
negotiation: in handover meetings 120; of damage control 133; of group membership 140, 244; of identities 5, 90, 92–93, 95, 260, 314–315, 336, 358, 369, 395, 408; of knowledge 89; of leadership 405, 406; of power 3, 236, 259, 260, 275, 402; of practice 45, 102, 327; of rapport 81; of role 45, 260, 395; of service 162–170, 177; strategies 80
negotiations 6, 85, 259, 272, 273, 299, 340
new capitalism 128, 132, 133, 135
newcomers: communities of practice 101, 104, 105, 106; directives 208; humor 228, 229–230; language learning on-the-job 429, 432; language preparation 417, 419, 421; rapport management 82; vocational education 392, 394 *see also* vocational education
new economy 128, 389
new work order 128–134, 389, 426
non-traditional jobs 361–370
non-verbal/non-vocal features of interaction: 54, 67, 169, 192, 340, 394, 396, 397 *see also* multimodality
normative gendered language 315, 363, 364, 405, 406 *see also* gender
normative gendered styles of directives 205–208, 213

norms: and conflict talk 276, 278; and humor 232, 235, 236; and miscommunication 259; argumentation 286, 289; blue-collar work settings 139; cultural 45, 85, 112, 223, 248, 335, 337, 338, 340–344, 392, 405; differing 97; gender 7, 8, 312, 314, 318, 364, 369, 404, 405, 407; leadership 327; negotiation of 344; newcomers 106; value laden 78; workplace 47, 74, 90, 132 *see also* expectations

nurses/nursing contexts 89–98, 112–123, 187–197, 298, 361–370, 375

nursing handover meetings 113, 116–121

obligations 35, 57, 60, 72, 77–87, 152, 340 *see also* rapport management theory

observation (ethnographic): blue-collar workplaces 146; call centre discourse 182–183; communities of practice 107; gender and leadership 407; interactional sociolinguistics 4, 9; linguistic ethnography 43, 47; vocational education 393

observation skills for learners 414, 419

observer's paradox 107, 317, 407

observer understanding/perspectives (second order) 66, 69, 73 *see also* politeness theory

Ochs, Elinor 312–313, 374

off-record 72, 73, 220, 249 *see also* Brown and Levinson

old economy 128, 132, 133

on-the-job language learning 425–433

opposition format 277–280

organizational socialization *see* socialization

outgroup 91, 94, 139, 247, 250, 252

overhearer 351 *see also* ratified overhearer/listeners

participant observer 46

patient choice 20

people skills *see* soft skills

performance appraisal interviews 131–133, 219

persuasion 29, 36, 57, 153, 284–291

phatic communion 40–41, 85, 168

Piller, Ingrid 335–336

pink collar settings 138

plurilingual identity 348–358

police officers/station/setting: conflict talk 273, 279; directives 211; interactional sociolinguistics 10; interpreting 298; legal discourse 150–152, 156; linguistic ethnography 45

politeness: and directives 204, 205, 206, 208–212; and impoliteness 33, 65–74, 275; call centre discourse 177–178; differing norms 414; service encounters 164, 165, 167

politeness theory 65–74, 339–340 *see also* impoliteness theory *see also* rapport management theory

political discourse/settings 34, 287, 288, 316, 405

positive politeness 140

positivism 51

power: and language choice 349–352; assymetry 36, 151, 337; call centre discourse 178–179; critical discourse studies 28–29, 33; differing norms 82, 427; display 179; interactional sociolinguistics 8; intercultural communication 337; linguistic ethnography 44; mitigation 85, 379, 382; multilingualism 349; negotiation 3; relationships 343, 402 *see also* authority *see also* leadership *see also* empowerment

Power and Politeness in the Workplace (Holmes and Stubbe) 10, 102

powerlessness 41, 128, 153, 206, 208, 212, 404, 408

practices, shared 276

preference reversal 278

problematic communication 79, 342, 415, 258–268, 272–281

problem-solving 272, 274, 278, 280, 414

professional development 46 *see also* situated learning *see also* vocational education

professional identity *see* identity, professional

professional socialization *see* socialization

qualitative methods 3, 51, 53, 60, 182, 407, 429

quantitative methods 22, 51–62, 140, 182, 317

quantitative tools and statistics 51–62

question-answer sequences 150

questionnaires 46, 47, 134, 212

rapport management framework/theory 67, 77–87, 181, 340

ratified by-standing 190

ratified overhearers/listeners 150, 351

ratified participants 190, 191, 192, 196

reduction of language status 349, 350 *see also* enhancement of language status

reflective practice 46, 134

refusals 33, 133, 211, 230, 277 *see also* right of refusal

register 5, 52, 151, 403

relational harmony 93

relational talk 216–224

relational work 19, 82, 211, 254, 275, 276, 278, 425–426 *see also* relational talk *see also* Locher and Watts

repertoire: plurilingual 348, 354–358; professional 363; shared 104–105, 106, 107, 235, 236, 275, 369, 392; skilful adaption 355, 404; wide 10, 312

requests: call centre discourse 175–184; directives 203–213; genre theory 120, 121; (im)politeness theory 72–73; interactional sociolinguistics 6; language preparation 417–418, 419; service encounters 162–170;

social constructionism 91–92, 94; vocational education 394
resistance, to style 178
restorative justice 156
right of refusal 204 *see also* directives
role, institutional 72, 206, 218, 301, 392, 413
role-based entitlement 70
role of chair *see* chair
roles, conflicting 263
routine practices 19

Sacks, Harvey 16, 218, 219
Schegloff, Emanuel 15, 21 *see* conversation analysis
schema 5, 6, 228
schematic structure 115, 116, 117, 119, 273
script, predetermined 48, 178
second order understanding *see* observer understanding/perspective
sequence organization 18
service encounters 4–5, 162–170, 279, 337 *see also* call centre discourse
sign language interpreters (SLIs) 46
silence, cultural value 8, 156
silence, multiple functions 180
silencing 133, 153, 155
silencing of women 404–405, 410
Silverstein 42
sisu 139
situated identity 396
situated learning 104, 106–107 *see also* vocational education
small talk: interactional sociolinguistics 8, 9; intercultural communication 342; language learning on-the-job 432; language preparation 415, 418; narratives 245–246, 254; rapport management 80, 82, 85; relational talk 218, 221; service encounters 165
social constructionism: communities of practice 102; conflict talk 275, 279; corporate settings 130, 132–134; discussion of as a theoretical paradigm 89–98; gender 312; gender and leadership 403–404; intercultural communication 335–336; narratives 245; nursing 363
socialization 11, 82, 90, 105–106, 140, 141, 229–230, 391–392
social justice 4, 408
social reality 28, 66, 69, 94, 95, 97, 98 *see also* social constructionism
social relations/relationships 29, 203
social skills *see* soft skills
socio-pragmatic interactional principles (SIPs) 78, 82 *see also* rapport management framework/theory
soft skills 180, 414, 415, 416, 418, 421
solidarity: blue-collar workplaces 139, 140, 428; cabin crew discourse 380–381; call centre discourse 179; conflict talk 275, 276; in interactional sociolinguistics research 8, 11; intercultural communication 336; leadership 324, 326; legal settings 153; narratives 244; nursing 367, 369; rapport management 80–83; service encounters 164, 168
spaces for learning 45
spatial identity 47
speaker-based mis(re)presentations 261
SPEAKING framework 113, 265
Spencer-Oatey, Helen *see* rapport management framework/theory
stance 89, 91–94, 207, 277, 278, 312, 314, 374
stereotypes: about men in non-traditional jobs 362, 369; about men/men's language/interaction 312–314, 315, 316, 402; about women/women's language/interaction 140, 205, 246, 279, 312–314, 361, 362, 369, 405; about workplace interaction 57; cultural 8, 141, 245, 246, 248, 327, 336; leadership 313, 402, 404, 405; outgroup 250, 252; raising awareness 318; reinforcing 363
Stivers, Tanya 17–18
stories/storytelling *see* narrative
style flexibility 10, 236, 297, 312, 364, 419
super-diversity 28, 429
Systemic Functional Linguistics (SFL) 113, 114, 163, 182

Talking from 9 to 5 (Tannen) 7
Talk at Work (Drew and Heritage) 16
Tannen, Deborah 5, 7–9, 11
teasing *see* humor
tension, defusing of 84, 177, 229, 369
thick description 73, 262, 317
Toolan, Michael 243
top-down: hierarchies 128, 131; humor 230; power 178; processes 128, 229, 428; research approach 29, 163, 164
topic, constrained 162
topic management/control 8, 155, 168
topic organization: circular 8; linear 8, 112
Toulmin 285–286
training, of CSRs 180–181 *see also* cultural training
training, vocational *see* vocational education
transcription 4, 16, 397
turn design 18
turn-taking 10, 78, 121, 155, 168, 273

unequal power *see* power

vagueness, strategic 58
veterinary medicine 86
vocational education 389–398, 416–419
Vygotski 390

443

Wellington Language in the Workplace Project (LWP): directives 208; gender and leadership 406; humor 338; interactional sociolinguistics 9–10; linguistic ethnography 47; miscommunication 260; narrative 342; relational talk 218; wide-ranging nature 32
Wenger, Etienne *see* communities of practice
Wodak, Ruth 30, 33–34
Work and Family Project at Georgetown University 11
workplace culture: blue-collar workplaces 140; gender 312, 313; importance in workplace language learning 428; language preparation 416, 417, 420–421; linguistic ethnography 44–45; narrative 247, 248–250; nursing 369
workplace practices, communication of/transmission 45
written workplace language 52, 55–56, 145, 289, 317–318, 376–383, 426–427, 431 *see also* email *see also* digital contexts *see also* legal written language *see also* mission statements

Yamada, Haru 8, 10
You Just Don't Understand (Tannen) 7